THE SOVEREIGN, SUBJECT, AND COLONIAL JUSTICE

This volume analyzes the trial of Bahadur Shah, a watershed moment in the 19th-century colonial history of India. The trial of Bahadur Shah raises the contentious issue of sovereignty – trial of Emperor Bahadur Shah, *de jure* power by *de facto* claimant to power, the English East India Company. There has been a lot of confusion and controversy over the trial ever since the proceedings began – its main architects could not define if it really was a juristic trial, a court of enquiry, a court-martial, or a general enquiry? This book sheds light on this event through the original, unprinted manuscript of the *Trial* at the end of the uprising of the 1857. It critically investigates the trial, mainly its architecture, grammar, functioning, and findings from historical, political, and juridical perspectives to determine, as far as possible, the actual position of Emperor Bahadur Shah, his strengths, and his weaknesses. Further, it examines the Rebellion of 1857, particularly in Delhi, and Bahadur Shah's role therein.

A key reading on justice in colonial history, this volume will be of interest to researchers and scholars of colonial and imperial history, modern history, political theory, and South Asia studies. It will also be of great interest to general readers interested in learning about the colonization of India by the British and its commercial arm East India Company.

K.C. Yadav was former Professor of History and Dean Academic Affairs, Kurukshetra University, Haryana, India. He has authored/edited over a dozen research books published from India and abroad, and has contributed about 40 research papers and chapters to research journals and books.

THE SOVEREIGN, SUBJECT, AND COLONIAL JUSTICE

Revisiting the Trial of Bahadur Shah, 1858

Edited by K.C. Yadav

Routledge
Taylor & Francis Group
LONDON AND NEW YORK

First published 2023
by Routledge
4 Park Square, Milton Park, Abingdon, Oxon OX14 4RN

and by Routledge
605 Third Avenue, New York, NY 10158

Routledge is an imprint of the Taylor & Francis Group, an informa business

British Library Cataloguing-in-Publication Data
A catalogue record for this book is available from the British Library

Library of Congress Cataloging-in-Publication Data
A catalog record has been requested for this book

ISBN: 978-0-367-72378-1 (hbk)
ISBN: 978-1-032-34088-3 (pbk)
ISBN: 978-1-003-32050-0 (ebk)

DOI: 10.4324/9781003320500

Typeset in Sabon
by Deanta Global Publishing Services, Chennai, India

FOR
DR F.W. BUCKLER AND SIR PERCIVAL SPEAR
– MY TRAILBLAZERS

Fig 0.1 Emperor Muhammad Bahadur Shah II (1775–1862; r. 1837–1858). *Source:* R. Montgomery Martin, *The Indian Empire*, London, 1859 (?).

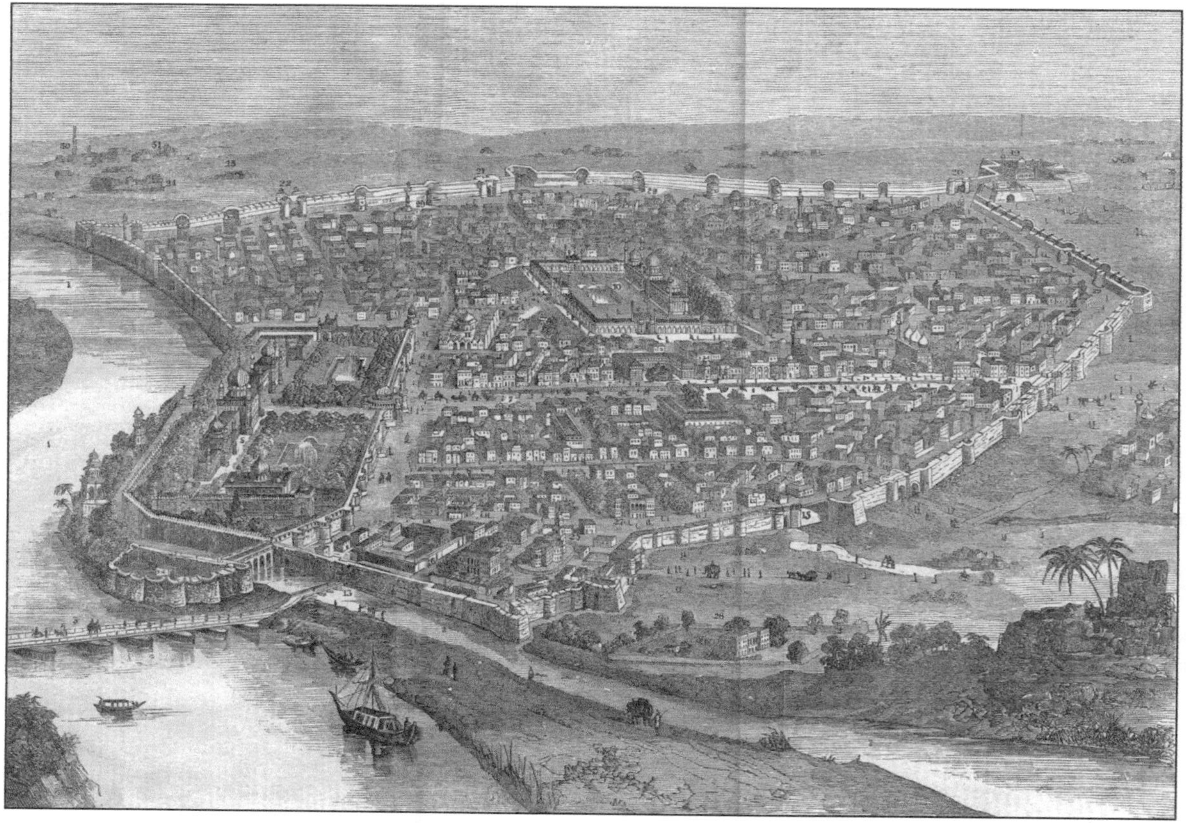

Map 0.1 Map of Delhi before the Revolt. *Source: The illustrated London News*, 16 Jan. 1858.

CONTENTS

ILLUSTRATIONS AND MAPS

Figures

Pictures

Maps

ABBREVIATIONS

ADJ.	Adjutant
BRIG.	Brigadier
BRIG. GEN.	Brigadier-General
CAPT.	Captain
C-IN-C.	Commander-in-Chief
COL.	Colonel
DA	Delhi Archives, New Delhi
DY	Deputy
IBID.	same (source) as quoted above (*Ibidem*)
LIEUT.	Lieutenant
LIEUT. COL.	Lieutenant-Colonel
LIEUT. GEN.	Lieutenant-General
MAJ.	Major
MAJ. GEN.	Major-General
NAI	National Archives of India, New Delhi
NI	Native Infantry
NAM	National Army Museum, London
OFFG.	officiating
OP. CIT.	book/journal already cited in the text
P./PP.	page/pages

ACKNOWLEDGEMENTS

It took me over three years to do this work. I had initially thought that it was just a year's job at the most. But when I got into it, I began to feel as if I had entered a *cul-de-sac*. Honestly, it would have been very difficult to manage to move out of it effectually had I not been fortunate enough to get help, support, and encouragement from a large number of scholars, friends, well-wishers, and institutions. I am particularly grateful to military historian, Sqn. Ldr. (Retd.) Rana T.S. Chhina, MBE, CAFHR, USI, Delhi; my grandniece, Rishika Yadav, LSE, London; Dr Ashutosh Kumar, NMML, Delhi; Prof. Udayvir Singh, Ambala; and Dr Rajesh Kumar, Director, ICHR, Delhi, for giving scholarly suggestions and tips relating to their specialties which have gone a long way in improving the quality of the timber of the work. In the matter of collection of archival material from their repositories, especially in tracing the handwritten copies of the trial and other rare relevant material, I am beholden to Sanjay Garg, Officer-in-Charge, Delhi Archives, Ratnesh Mathur, Director, Prarang, Noida (U.P), and Dr Sanjay Garg, Deputy Director, National Archives of India, Delhi. My thanks are also due to Dr Jogender Singh, Librarian, HIPA, Gurgaon, and Vijya Jain, Prabhu Books, Gurgaon, who helped me in laying my hands on some rare pictures, illustrations, maps, and other material. The scholarly studies of Prof. K.N. Panikkar, Prof. Amar Farooqui, and Dr Aslam Parvez have been helpful in doing the 'Historical Perspective', and of L.D. Bell (the University of Melbourne) in clearing many an issue from the British and international law perspectives. Mufti A.R. Qasmi, Naseem Ahmad, and W.A. Saed provided copies of rare books and other material in Urdu and Virjanand in Hindi. Comdr. (Retd.) Vivek Yadav, Dr Surender Kumar, Bhupender Panghal, and Puneet Kumar were helpful in a number of ways in completing the project. I am thankful to all of them.

I also owe special thanks to the following institutions and libraries for helping me in locating relevant material in their holdings: The National Archives of India (NAI), Delhi Archives (DA), the Nehru Memorial Museum and

Library (NMML), Indian Council of Historical Research (ICHR) Library, and the United Service Institution of India (USI) Library, all in Delhi, the Raza Library, Rampur (UP), Punjab State Archives, Chandigarh, Haryana Academy of History and Culture Library, Gurgaon, the Brown University Library, USA, the National University of Singapore Library, the Melbourne University Library, Australia, and Army National Museum, London.

Finally, my thanks go to my family, my wife Shashipriya, sons Neeraj and Nitin, and daughter Nalini, daughters-in-law Rita and Shraddha, and lovely granddaughters, Vidushi and Medha, for their love, care, and support, which kept me going steadily towards the bourn.

K.C. Yadav

PREFACE

The trial of Bahadur Shah, the last Mughal Emperor, by the East India Company after cessation of the Rebellion 1857, in Delhi, is, plainly put, no simple trial. It is a tangled web of confusion, clutter, and controversy. Even its main architects could not define – even to each other's satisfaction – as to what it really was – a juristic trial, a court of enquiry, a court-martial, or a general inquiry? The legitimacy of the prosecutors' authority, power, and prerogative to try the Emperor, and the bona fides of the instruments, i.e., the court, the juratas, the jurisprudence, and all else they put to use there, were, and are even now, over a century and a half after the event, not consummately out of the cloud of dubiety and disingenuousness.

Unfortunately, the contemporary sources which should have been helpful in clearing this fog and showing the reality are, in most of the cases, if not all, problematic. They betray the colonialists' universal policy of showing 'the naked truth' in their colonies, in Jean Paul Sartre's words, 'with clothes on'.[1] They hide many a thing in the interest of the state or the concerned state actors,[2] and orchestrate many myths, a number of which still rule the roost as authentic stuff of history, and distort and disorient to an extent even our present discourse.

Aware of this complication, I have critically examined here every turn and twist, shade and glint, line and crease, of the trial proceedings from historical, political, and juridical perspectives to set the record straight, and determine, as far as possible, the actual position of Emperor Bahadur Shah, his strengths, and his weaknesses; the rise of the East India Company as a political power and its relation with the Mughal rulers, especially Bahadur Shah; the question of sovereignty, whether it was vested in the Emperor or

1 Jean-Paul Sartre, 'Preface' to Frantz Fanon's magnum opus, *The Wretched of the Earth*, Eng. tr. C. Farrington, New York, 1963, p. 7.
2 *Ibid.*

the Company; the Rebellion of 1857, particularly in Delhi and Bahadur Shah's role therein; and finally, the trial itself, mainly its architecture, grammar, functioning, and findings.

There are, as already indicated, many versions of the 'Proceedings' – handwritten, printed, and published.[3] I have used Delhi Archives' handwritten version of the *Trial*, duly authenticated with their signatures by Maj. F.J. Harriott, Deputy Judge Advocate-General, and Lieut. Col. M. Dawes, President of the Court[4] (see Illustration 1.1). Since it has been found in the Delhi Archives (earlier Commissioner/Chief Commissioner Office), it can be circumspectly presumed that this is the Officiating Commissioner of Delhi, C.B. Saunders's office copy. The printed version of the *Trial* tabled in the British Parliament for its members (1859) is perhaps its copy. Another handwritten copy, but neither signed nor written as steadily as the first copy, is there in the National Archives of India, in the Foreign Department Collection, Miscellaneous, vol. 376/376 A, 1858. A handwritten copy is, I have learnt, in the Punjab Archives, Lahore (perhaps John Lawrence's office copy), though I have not seen it. An Urdu translation of the chargesheet (official), a copy of which was supplied to the Emperor 20 days before the commencement of the trial,[5] is also found in the Delhi Archives (see Illustration 1.2). No Urdu version of the rest of the *Trial* is, however, traceable.

In the introduction, a detailed critique of the trial proceedings is provided which will be helpful, I think, in negotiating the complexities and ambiguities in the proceedings.

For the convenience of the readers unfamiliar with the Urdu/Persian languages, a glossary of Urdu and Persian words and technical terms is given in the glossary. Along with it, a detailed bibliography, comprising relevant books, monographs, dissertations, research papers, documents/records, etc., has also been provided for those who want to delve still deeper into the subject.

K.C. Yadav

3 See *Bibliography*.

4 The copy is preserved, as indicated above, in the Delhi Archives (DA), New Delhi, in the Residency Records, Trial of Bahadur Shah Series, File no. 30 A, 1858.

5 The document is there in the DA, Residency Records, Trial of Bahadur Shah Series, File no. 37, 8 January 1858 (see Illustration 1.2).

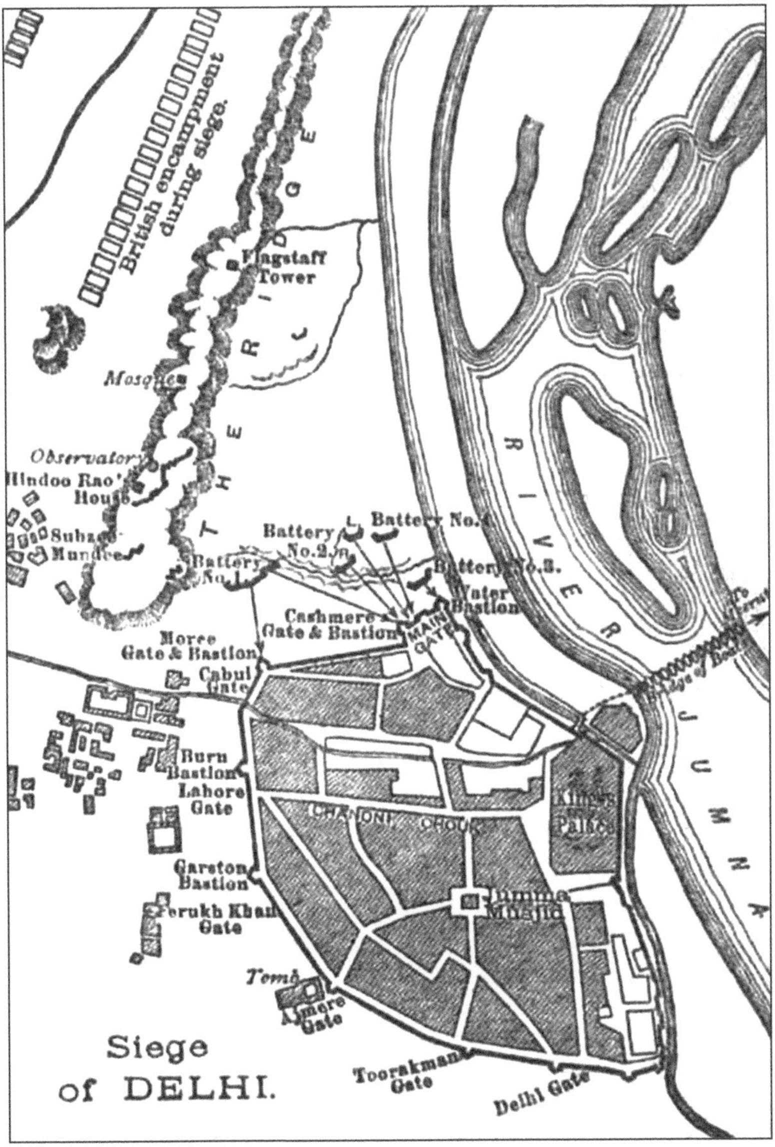

Map 0.2 Map of Delhi in 1857. Source: Evelyn Wood, *Our Fighting Services and How They Made the Empire*, London, 1916.

1

INTRODUCTION

> Next to battlefields, it is in the courtrooms that some of the greatest acts of injustice in the history of the world have taken place.
>
> – Maulana Abul Kalam Azad[1]

On 11 May 1857, fortune smiled on the Timurid House after about 157 years.[2] At midnight, 21 salvos were fired from the ramparts of the historic Red Fort, Delhi, announcing the restoration of power, authority, and imperium to Bahadur Shah II, the 17th successor of Babur, the founder of the House, which the British had surreptitiously blotted out over the years. But, as ill luck would have it, the 'smile' did not last, as discussed below, for long. The British reoccupied the historic city after a bloody struggle, the like of which they had hardly seen before, for over four-and-a-half months – 133 days, to be exact – on 20 September 1857. A day later, Bahadur Shah was in the British custody.

1 From the written statement of Maulana Abul Kalam Azad (1888–1958), one of the tallest leaders of the Indian national movement for freedom, submitted before a British court trying him for 'sedition'. See A.G. Noorani, *Indian Political Trials*, Delhi, 2005, pp. 216–22.

2 The unworthies who occupied the throne of Akbar and Aurangzeb for about 150 years after the latter had closed his eyes in death (3 March 1707), namely, Bahadur Shah I (1707–1712), Jahandar Shah (1712–1713), Farrukhsiyar (1713–1719), Rafiuddarajat (1719), Shah Jahan II (1719), Muhammad Shah (1719–1748), Ahmad Shah Bahadur (1748–1754), Alamgir II (1754–1759), Shah Alam II (1760–1806), Akbar II (1806–1837), and Bahadur Shah II (1837–1857), not only proved unequal to the task of checking the decline and downfall of their great empire, but also made substantial contribution to its dissolution. See W. Irwin, *The Later Mughals*, 2 vols., rep. Delhi, 2006; H.G. Keene, *The Fall of the Mughal Empire*, London, 1876; Jadunath Sarkar, *The Fall of the Mughal Empire*, 4 vols., Delhi, rep. 1991–97, Percival Spear, *The Twilight of the Mughal Empire*, Delhi, rep. 1991.

DOI: 10.4324/9781003320500-1

A can of controversies

There are three antipodal views on how the Emperor reached the British custody. Lieut. W.S.R. Hodson, commandant, Hodson's Horse, and head of the Intelligence Department (at Delhi), says that he had 'captured the King' on 21 September 1857 from the Humayun's Tomb, where he was then temporarily stationed. The task was difficult, and also dangerous, he says, but, thanks to his Indian deputy in the Intelligence Department, the one-eyed Maulavi Rajab Ali, and the Emperor's confidants – Hakim Ahsanullah Khan and his physician and prime minister, Mirza Ilahi Bakhsh, his close relative – he accomplished it after assuring the Emperor that his life and honour would be absolutely safe, and 'a dish of *pillau* alone was in store for him'.[3]

An equally informed person on the scene, Capt. F.C. Massey, the then Deputy Judge Advocate-General, however, gives a different version:

> All the stories that have appeared about the capture of the king (by Hodson), he says, are so much bosh. It was all an arranged thing under the advice of the Hakeem (Ahsanullah). One of the Royal family (Mirza Ilahi Bakhsh) came to our Meer Moonshi or native head of the Intelligence Department, named Rujjub Ali, a precious scoundrel, but clever and useful, as an emissary, at the instigation of the Hakeem and the Begum Zeenat Mahal and said that the King wanted to surrender himself and he was at Durgah or shrine.

On getting the message, Massey adds, Rajab Ali went with 100 cavalry men to the *Durgah*, met the Emperor, and assured him on behalf of his boss, Lieut. Hodson, of his safety and other things, and brought him to Delhi. About that time, Massey further adds, Hodson, who was on some expedition with some cavalry contingent, heard what had happened, rushed back, and 'met Emperor's cavalcade in the immediate vicinity of the city'. On Emperor's asking, after Hodson was introduced to him, he wanted Hodson to repeat the 'assurance' that his deputy and others had given on his behalf,[4] which he

3 W.S.R. Hodson, *Twelve Years of a Soldier's Life in India*, ed. by his brother, London, 1859, pp. 297, 304–8. Hodson's pledge was as follows: 'The King of Delhi gave himself up to me on a distinct pledge given to him that his life should be spared and that he should be subjected to no personal indignity (*be-izzat at the hands of the goral logue nahin hone pqaoge*). This promise was made in the first instance to Begum Zinat Mahal and her father through Mirza Ilahee Bakhsh and again on the day of King's arrest by Moulvee Rujjab Alee in my name. It was subsequently repeated by myself personally to the King at his request'. See Delhi Archives (DA), Residency Records, Bahadur Shah Trial Series, File no. 10, 30 October 1857. For 'a dish of *pillau*', see C.T. Metcalf, ed., *Two Native Narratives of the Mutiny in Delhi* (hereafter *Two Narratives*), Westminister, 1898, p. 71.

4 The account is based on a write-up titled 'Account by an eye-witness (Capt. F.C. Massey) of taking of Delhi Palace', in the *Journal of the USI*, vol. 60, 1930, pp. 169–81. Massey seems

did. Hodson took charge of the Cavalcade and went to the Fort. On reaching the destination, he told the world that he had 'captured the King'.[5]

Standing here, one may be curious to know as to what the official dispatches say in this regard. Maj. Gen. Wilson, commanding the Delhi Field Force, says in his dispatch of 22 September that 'the king, who accompanied the troops some short distance last night, gave himself up to a party of Irregular Cavalry whom I sent out in the direction of the fugitives and he is now prisoner under a guard of European soldiers'.[6]

On 23 September, Hodson went to Humayun's Tomb and arrested three princes – Mirza Mughal, Mirza Khair Sultan, Emperor's sons, and Mirza Abu Bakr, son of the late Prince Fakhruddin (commonly called Fakhru) and grandson of the Emperor. About a kilometre away from the Red Fort, he shot them most brutally in cold blood after stripping them naked near Delhi Gate.[7] To the civilized world, it seemed as if he had stripped the British justice and committed a murder most foul.

A question, arises here: why did Hodson tell a lie that he had 'captured' the King when he himself had surrendered on his own? And why did he murder the princes so savagely? The a*nswer* lie in Hodson's persona: a vainglorious swagger, he was obsessed with the 'I-have-done-it' complex, and would do and say anything, true or false, to gain name and fame. Well versed in the art of selling his false timber as genuine, he played the same trick here and became famous overnight. Everybody had nothing but a word of praise for the daredevil. Robert Montgomery, Judicial Commissioner, Punjab, for instance, wrote to him:

> My dear Hodson: All honours to you (and to your horse) for catching the King and slaying his sons. I hope you will bag many more! – In haste, ever yours: R. Montgomery.

---

to have confused Humayun's Tomb with the *Durgah*. The Emperor's stay at the *Durgah* was very short and secret, and no armed troops went there with him.

5 P.J.O. Taylor says, on the authority of a handwritten note of Capt. Massey, that Hodson's boast that he had captured the Emperor from Humayun's Tomb is a lie. See Taylor, *Chronicle of the Mutiny*, Delhi, 1992, pp. 67–71.

6 See Hodson, *Twelve Years*, p. 308 (f.n.).

7 Hodson had two blackest spots in his otherwise daring soldierly career: one, corruption, and the other, cold-blood murder of the princes. The nature and history punished him for the crimes squarely. Says Richard Collier, 'Six months would pass (the murder of princes) before he died as violently as the princes, a rebel bullet smashing through him (at Lucknow) as he charged sword in hand. 'Oh, my mother', he cried, then blood choked all further speech. Later his trunk (box) would be opened and the loot came to light, and the file (proof of his corruption in Punjab) of which he had sworn ignorance and the whole tarnished story became one to be whispered. But only the simulacrum of Hodson died that day. All that was redeemable died near the walls of Delhi, on the spot where the princes died'. See Collier, *The Great Indian Mutiny*, New York, 1964, p. 264.

Montgomery's boss, Chief Commissioner John Lawrence, called him 'grand captor'. Delhi Commissioner C.B. Saunders's reaction was laughable: '*By Jove! Hodson*', he bruited, '*they ought to make you the Commander-in-Chief for this*'.[8] Maj. Gen. Wilson's reaction was, however, not so enthusiastic. When Hodson went to report his 'great deed' to him, he simply said, says Hodson, 'Well, I'm glad you have got him (King): but I never expected either him or you again!' while other officers in the room were loud in their congratulations and applause.[9]

C.J. Grifffths, Hodson's Ridge-fellow, excels all of them. In his book, the *Siege of Delhi*, which is rated as an 'authoritative' eyewitness account, he does not mind using false colours and a bit of fiction to the story to give a larger-than-life image to his hero:

> On the afternoon of the 21st, he says, a most important capture was affected by Hodson. Shah Bahadur Shah, the old King of Delhi, was taken by the officer near the city while endeavouring of escape down country. Hodson with his accustomed daring and accompanied by 100 only of his own troopers, seized the person of the King from amongst thousands of armed dependents and rabble, who awed by his stern demeanour, did not raise a hand in resisting the capture.[10]

That's what is called a pinchbeck praise!

Anyway with two 'feathers' (capture of the king and murder of the princes) in his cap, Hodson was, understandably, on cloud nine. His hopes of getting something great –Queen's medal (Victoria Cross) or something else – rose still higher. But everything – his hopes, and his castle in Spain – dashed to ground soon after the conditions on which the King had elected to choose to surrender became known. He was accused of having 'played foul' and flouted, with impulse and impetuosity, as seen below, the orders of the Governor-General in Council.

This was not, let me clarify, the first incident of its kind, i.e., making overtures to the Emperor to surrender on the condition of 'protection of

8 R. Montgomery Martin, *The Indian Empire*, London, n.d., vol. 3, p. 449; for Saunders' remark, see Hodson, *op. cit.*, p. 307.

9 Hodson, *op. cit.*, pp. 307–8. What else he received from there, in Hodson's own words was this: 'I, and most other people, considered that I and my party had a right to all we found on the king and princes; but the General to whom I referred the question, thought otherwise, so I gave up all except some of the personal possessions of the princes (those of the King were taken by the General). The swords which I secured … are historically most valuable. One was worn by, and bears the name of Jahangire, and the other is stamped with the seal of Nadir Shah! They are singular and interesting trophies, or rather relics, of the house of Timur the Tartar'. *Ibid.*, p. 326. The weapons are now with the Imperial War Museum, London.

10 C.J. Grifffths, *A Narrative of the Siege of Delhi* …., Delhi, rep. 2015, p. 201.

his life and honour without authority to do so'. It was Hodson's old game, which he had begun to play in the beginning of June, through his one-eyed deputy, Rajab Ali, and the Emperor's 'kitchen cabinet', also called a bunch of traitors – his Prime Minister, his relatives, and his Queen. On getting some positive signals from these persons, not directly from the Emperor, Hodson approached Sir Charles Reid, the then Officer Commanding, Delhi Field Force, to permit him to do the job. But instead of coming back to Hodson, Reid went to John Lawrence, Chief Commissioner, Punjab, who was the *de facto* Governor-General in North India insofar as the Rebellion matters were concerned. Sir John, realizing the seriousness of the matter, took prompt action, telling Reid telegraphically that the King's life and pension could be guaranteed, if he had no European blood on his hands, and he (King) 'placed the British in possession of the city in which he could not be suffered'.[11]

However, when the issue reached the Governor-General's ears, he laid the whole thing to rest once and for all: he issued clear instructions to the Lieutenant-Governor of the North-Western Provinces (the then overall in charge of Delhi civil administration) on 20 June to tell everybody to desist from making '*any promises to the King of Delhi and the royal family ... as might be seized. They should be kept in close confinement and report to the Governor-General for further orders*' (emphasis added). A little later (9 July), another notification was issued by his office expressly declaring that

> *no authority whatever, other than the Governor-General in Council, should exercise the power of pardoning any State stipendiary or Native Chief who had joined in anyway whatever, or assisted mutineers or rebels, or any person belonging to the family of any such State stipendiary or Native chief.* (emphasis added)[12]

But even before the ink could get dry of the notifications, rumours reached Calcutta 'that overtures have been made by the King of Delhi to the officer commanding the troops' for surrender on some terms, and some people were inclined to oblige him. The Governor-General's office immediately wrote to the Lieutenant-Governor, NWP, and the Offg. Commissioner, Delhi, that

> *Should any negotiation of the sort be contemplated, a full report of all the circumstances must be submitted to the Governor-General in Council before the Government is committed to anything*' (emphasis added).[13]

11 Martin, *op. cit.*, vol. 3, pp. 434–35.

12 See G.F. Edmonstone, Secretary to the Government of India, Foreign Department, to H. Tucker, Secretary to the Lieutenant-Governor, NWP, DA, Residency Records, Mutiny Papers Series, File no. 1, 25 June 1857.

13 Edmonstone to C.B. Saunders, Offg. Commissioner, Delhi, 9 July 1857, *PMR*, *Correspondence*, pt. 2, pp. 301–2, 326.

Although all the instructions mentioned above were, according to the Secretary to the Governor-General, delivered to the concerned officials, those were, however, followed more in breach than in adherence, the most serious being the one committed by Hodson in netting the King by guaranteeing not only his life and honour, but also of his wife, son, his relatives, and others as well.[14]

Being a serious matter, especially when viewed in the light of the Governor-General's repeated warnings to one and all not to do any such thing without taking him into confidence, Hodson was asked to explain his conduct. To prove his innocence, Hodson, as was his wont, told a long story, the crux of which was that whatever he did was with the permission of Maj. Gen. Wilson, the then officer commanding the (Delhi) Field Force.[15] The higher authorities, who had little trust in Hodson, turned to Gen. Wilson for his views in the matter. The General played smart, and shifting the responsibility of the 'guarantee' upon the Delhi Commissioners, he stated that

> the late Mr. Greathed, Commissioner (Delhi) previous to the assault of the city, having reason to believe that the King had a wish to give himself up recommended to me to guarantee his life. On his doing so, Mr. Saunders, successor to Mr. Greathed, also made a similar recommendation to me after the city fell. To both these recommendations, I gave my consent. I also gave the same guarantee to Zeenat Mahal, but to none other.[16]

Now Greathed having died (16 September 1857), the ball went to the court of Saunders, who, in a frank communication to the Secretary to the Governor-General, said in a terse tone: '*I refuse to bear any responsibility with regard to my participation in the guarantee*' (emphasis added).[17] Thus cornered, the General retreated: 'I had Mr. Greathed's recommendation to guarantee the King's life', he wrote to Saunders. 'I have been mistaken in supposing I had yours also'.[18] The controversy, however, went on for some time, but after the death of Lieut. (then Capt.) Hodson (at Lucknow), and departure of Maj. Gen. Wilson from India, the case was literally closed.[19]

14 Queen Zinat Mahal and her son, Mirza Jawan Bakht, Mirz Ilahi Bakhsh, father-in-law of Prince Fakhru, and the Emperor's physician, Ahsanullah.

15 Hodson to Saunders, 28 November 1857, *PMR, Correspondence*, pt. 2, p. 323.

16 Maj. Gen. Wilson to Edmonstone, 23 October 1857, *ibid.*, pp. 334–35.

17 Saunders to Edmonstone, 31 December 1857, *ibid.*, pp. 335–36.

18 Wilson to Saunders, 28 December 1857, *ibid.*, p. 342.

19 Edmonstone to Saunders, 4 December 1858, *ibid.*, pp. 355–56. Though the case was closed, a small stricture was passed against Capt. Hodson. 'He had', the Governor-General recorded, 'no authority from Sir A. Wilson for guaranteeing the life of Zeenat Mahal and of her son Jawan Bakht, her father Ahmad Kooli Khan'.

No matter how it happened, the saving grace for the victors was that the Emperor was in their custody. It resolved, contextually, most of their problems, except one, that is, how to handle the prisoner-Emperor and his dominions? There were, simply put, two courses available to them: one, to treat him as a hostile, vanquished ruler and secure his person and his dominions on the principle of *juris gladii* (the right of the sword); and two, to claim his person and his dominions on the grounds of legality.[20] The first course was simple, the second problematic. Yet the victors chose the second. The reason behind their unusual decision, we are told, was 'image-building' – just to show to the world that they were civilized people who believed in justice, fair play, and rule of law.

For effective implementation of the above decision, again two measures were expedient: one, safe custody of the Emperor, and two, the mode of his trial. His presence in Delhi, they believed, could incite 'the dangerous classes' to rescue him. For ruling out this possibility, the man at the immediate helm in Delhi, C.B. Sunders, the Officiating Commissioner, tipped off Sir John Lawrence 'to deport the Emperor to Govindgarh (dist. Amritsar, Punjab) where he would be more safe'. He also sought his views on the nature of trial.[21] Agreeing with Saunders on the question of station, Maj. Gen. Wilson wanted the Chief Commissioner to clarify whether he would 'wish the Emperor to be tried previously to his departure from Delhi'.[22] Cecil Beadon, Secretary, Government of India, suggested his banishment to Hong Kong.[23] Surprisingly, when these suggestions were flying around, the Governor-General was not even aware of the terms on which the King had surrendered. It was for this reason that he gave vague instructions to the Punjab Chief Commissioner to send the King to Allahabad,

> if he had received from any British officer a promise that his life will be spared, to be tried under Act XIV of 1857. In case, there was no promise, then he should be tried in Delhi itself, under the same Act by a special commission consisting of Robert Montgomery, Judicial Commissioner, Punjab, G. C. Barnes, Commissioner, Cis-Sutlej States, and Lake, Commissioner, Trans-Sutlej States. C. B. Saunders was to act as the Prosecutor and collect the evidence and frame the charges.[24]

20 See Spear, *op. cit.*, p. 226.

21 Saunders to the Chief Commissioner, Punjab, DA, Residency Records, Trial of Bahadur Shah Series, File no. 4, 29 September 1857.

22 Telegram from Maj. Gen. Wilson to Chief Commissioner Punjab, 29 September 1857, *PMR*, *Correspondence*, pt. 2, p. 358.

23 S.N. Sen, *Eighteen Fifty-Seven*, Delhi, 1957, p. 108.

24 DA, Residency Records, Trial of Bahadur Shah Series, File no. 7, 17 October 1857.

Like his juniors, the Governor-General was also not playing a fair game with his subordinates here. Almost at the same time when he was issuing the above instructions on the subject to the Punjab Chief Commissioner, he was actually working, most secretly, without taking anybody into confidence, on a most sinister plot to 'banish' the King to the Cape Colony. On 11 October 1857, he wrote to George Grey, the Governor there:

> There is no place in India where his (Bahadur Shah's) presence, however well he might be guarded, would not produce excitement and constant uneasiness amongst large and dangerous classes. ... This mischief which lies in the mere name of the dynasty of Timour had been thoroughly established during the late events. *The people would infallibly cling to the wreck of the House, so long as a fragment of it remained in sight or in mind.* (emphasis added)[25]

'In that circumstance, the solution of the problem lay', he added, 'in the banishment of the "dangerous state-prisoner" to the Cape, a safe place'. Grey agreed 'to help him'.[26]

Thus assured, Canning sent the proposal to the Board of Control for necessary action. But the proposal, to his surprise and dismay, got jettisoned by no less a person than Lord Ellenborough, President of the Board of Control and a former Governor-General of India. 'Lord Canning had no power to transport the King of Delhi to the Cape', he said, and sharing his views with Ross Mangles, Chairman, Board of Directors, he cited his own example as to how his proposal 'to exile the King of Oude to the Cape was turned down'.[27] Canning was 'privately' informed to keep away from getting into 'a scrape'.[28] A wise man as he was, Canning at once gave up the Cape Plan and returned to his old plan – Allahabad/Delhi.

In those typically strange days, however, nobody seemed to have been listening to the Governor-General or caring for, as they ought to have, his orders. The Punjab Chief Commissioner, for instance, ignored his instructions 'to send the King to Allahabad if his life was guaranteed'. Maj. Gen. Penny, commanding of the Meerut Division, who also held the command of the Delhi Field Force, brought in a Military Commission in the place of a civilian one recommended by him. The Officiating Commissioner of Delhi asked

25 The account relative to the plot to banish Bahadur Shah to the Cape Colony is based, for the most part, on an informative article on the subject by Donovan Williams of the University of Calgary, entitled 'An echo of the Indian Mutiny: The proposed banishment of Bahadur Shah II to the Cape Colony, 1857', *Historia*, vol. 17, no. 4, 1972, pp. 265–68.

26 *Ibid.*

27 The Government of India could transport people to 'certain Crown Colonies' only. The Cape Colony could therefore 'invite action if they took the Indian King'. See *ibid.*, p. 267.

28 *Ibid.*

on his own the General to appoint a Deputy Judge Advocate-General who would frame charges against the King and place them 'before a court especially selected by you'.[29] The Punjab supremo, however, negated his proposal: 'I do not think it would be expedient', he told the Officiating Commissioner:

> to prepare any specific charges against the King of Delhi on which to try him, I would propose that the Commission be at liberty to hear and place on record all evidence bearing against the King and connected with the late insurrection. This is simply for record. He is not being tried for his life.[30]

Thus directed, Saunders tipped off the General to cancel the move to frame charges against the King. The Selected Military Commission should sit, he added, as a Court of Inquiry, which should hear and place on record all evidence 'bearing against the King and connected with the late insurrection'.[31] The military authorities were, however, not convinced with either his or the Chief Commissioner's logic.[32] The investigation can only be conducted satisfactorily, said the Deputy Judge Advocate-General, if the proceedings 'assume the form of a direct trial, *viz*. that charges should be framed and the ex-King be called upon to plead to them'.[33]

Gen. Penny concurred in the 'opinion expressed by the Deputy Judge Advocate-General'.[34]

A crisis of serious magnitude had thus arrived at a delicate moment. The military authorities had challenged their civilian counterpart – our way or no way. The Delhi Commissioner, however, rose to the occasion to save the situation. Half standing and half bent, he pleaded with Maj. Gen. Penny:

> I do not feel prepared to offer any opposition to the views expressed by the authorities so much better qualified to decide on questions relating to the forms of procedure which it is advisable to adopt in investigations or trials held before a Military Commission. ... I do not, however, consider it advisable to delay any further postponing of the trial, as the members of the Court are now assembled at Delhi and considerable inconvenience would be entailed by having to refer the matter to the Chief Commissioner at Mooltan or to the Supreme Government at Calcutta; and I am, therefore, prepared to take the responsibility of requesting you to issue such orders as

29 Saunders to Maj. Gen. Penny, 26 November 1857, *PMR*, *Correspondence*, pt. 2, p. 2.
30 John Lawrence to Maj. Gen. Penny and Saunders, 1 December 1857, *ibid*., p. 364.
31 Saunders to Maj. Gen. Penny, 1 December 1857, *ibid*., p. 365.
32 Maj. F.J. Harriott to Maj. Gen. Penny, 5 January 1858, *ibid*., pp. 366–67.
33 *Ibid*.
34 *Ibid*.

> you may deem advisable to the Deputy Judge Advocate with reference to the framing of charges against the *ex*-King and the mode of conducting the trial, being confident that Sir John Lawrence will readily acquiesce in the views taken by the military authorities.[35]

The Delhi Commissioner was right, but in part – Sir John did acquiesce in the views taken by the military authorities as regards framing of charges, but he still clung to his old views, and again trumpeted their expediency and worthiness. His Secretary wrote to the Delhi Commissioner, for being conveyed to the military authorities that

> the object of the enquiry is really rather with the view of elucidating important facts connected with the rebellion than to determine the precise nature and extent of the *ex*-King's complicity. *From the moment that his life was guaranteed there ceased, in the Chief Commissioner's judgment, to be any advantage in bringing him individually to trial. His complicity in the rebellion was open and notorious and under no circumstances could he ever obtain his liberty or be resorted to his former status.* (emphasis added)[36]

'Sir John', his Secretary added,

> *can only hope that you will lay before the Court every document of importance connected in anyway with the ex-King's conduct during the rebellion. All weighty circumstances explanatory of the origin and progress of the rebellion should also be placed on record.* (emphasis added)[37]

The military authorities knew their limits, and as such effected a climb down in an unmilitary manner, in order to accommodate the views of the Chief Commissioner as the following statement that the Deputy Judge Advocate-General made before the Commission would show:

> Evidence will be submitted to you which may not bear strictly on the charges (against the king). It is desired that all the circumstances connected with the late rebellion, even though not in direct relation to the indictment may be appropriately recorded.[38]

The Chief Commissioner approved the chargesheet and the trial procedure. Soon after, the Governor-General also affixed his seal of approval on both.

35 Saunders to Maj. Gen. Penny, 5 January 1858, *ibid.*, pp. 367–68.
36 Secretary to Chief Commissioner, Punjab, to Saunders, 15 January1858, *ibid.*, p. 369.
37 *Ibid.*
38 *Ibid.*, pp. 374–75.

Thus, the over four-month-old squabble came to an end. The substantive trial began in Delhi on 27 January 1858. The following middle-rung army officers constituted the Court:

President
Lieunt-Col. Dawes,[39] Artillery
Members
Maj. Palmer, HM's 60th Regiment
Maj. Redmond, HM's 61st Regiment
Maj. Sawyers, HM's 6th Carabineers
Capt. Rothney, 4th Sikh Infantry
Interpreter
James Murphy

Prosecutor for Government
Maj. F. J. Harriott,[40]
Deputy Judge Advocate-General

The Court (Military) tried the Emperor under Act XIV of 1857.[41] He was criminated on 5 January 1858 of the following charges:

(i) Being a Pensioner of the British Government in India, encouraged, aided and abetted, Muhammad Bakht Khan, and soldiers of the East India Company's Army in the crimes of mutiny and rebellion against the State;
(ii) encouraged, aided and abetted Mirza Mughul and others to rebel and wage war against the State;
(iii) being a subject of the British Government in India, became a false traitor against the State, proclaiming and declaring himself the reigning King and Sovereign of India; and
(iv) encouraged and abetted soldiers and others in murdering 49 persons of European descent on 16 May, and thus committed a heinous offence under Act XIV of 1857.

Ever since its effection, the trial has been, as seen above, a subject of considerable debate, discussion, and controversy, mainly around such questions as:

39 It was a flawed appointment. See constitution of the Court discussed below in detail.
40 His appointment was also not in order. This has also been discussed at length below.
41 A full version of the chargesheet is given below. Despite my best efforts, I could not find the original version (English) of the chargesheet. Fortunately, I could lay my hands on, as stated above, a copy of the Urdu translation (original) of the chargesheet (see Figure 1.2) which was supplied to the Emperor about 20 days before the trial started, in the DA, Delhi Residency Records, Trial of Bahadur Shah Series, File no. 37, 8 January 1858.

(i) Was Bahadur Shah a 'sovereign ruler' or an 'ex-titular King' or a 'protected vassal', or a 'pensioner', a 'subject' of the British?

(ii) Where did both, Bahadur Shah and the East India Company, stand in the eyes of the *jus gentium* (the law of the nations), the British law, the Islamic (Mughal) law, and the local law (the so-called 'Mutiny law') of the times?

(iii) Was Bahadur Shah not, on a higher plane, ethically, politically, and licitly well within his rights to wage war, or, in the words of the great Chartist leader, Charles Ernest Jones, 'rise in the holy right of insurrection', along with his countrymen, against a foreign power that had unlawfully and amorally usurped their country?

(iv) Was the East India Company legitimately competent to try Bahadur Shah?

The discussants have, no doubt, provided answers to these questions in their own ways, but still many a complexity remains to be simplified for a clearer understanding of things. An effort is being made here to look at the quandary from historical, political, and juridical perspectives through a wider aperture.

Historical perspective

In the calendar of the present problem, 3 March 1707 is an important date when the last of the great Mughals, Aurangzeb, as indicated above, closed his eyes in death, marking the beginning of the end of the biggest and the greatest Empire of its time in the world. Aurangzeb was succeeded by his son Bahadur Shah I. Unlike his predecessors, 'rivalling the magnificence and the power of the mighty Alexander, before whom nations were bowed as reeds bow before the tempest',[42] the new ruler was a pigmy, unworthy to manage the affairs of his great bequest. And, as ill luck would have it, his 16 successors[43] were no different. As a result of their misrule, mismanagement, and moral bankruptcy, the Empire broke like a rotten reed into pieces – literally. To take advantage of the situation, many political powers rushed in to try their luck.[44] An English trading company, popularly called the East India Company,[45] which had received a charter by Queen Elizabeth I of England on 31 December 1600 'to trade with all parts of Asia not in possession of a

42 Martin, *op. cit.*, vol. 3, p. 155.

43 For their names and other details, see f.n. 2 above.

44 They were Marathas, Afghans, Rohillas, Sikhs, Jats, and so forth.

45 There are many stories on the Company's origins, progress, and fall. For a critical study, however, see Nick Robins, *The Corporation that Changed the World: How the East India Company Shaped the Modern Multinational*, Delhi, 2006.

Christian Prince',[46] also begun to mark, through small gestures, its presence in the arena. But for about a century and a half, its chief concern remained by and large trading.[47] But not after that. Taking a serious stock of happenings around them, they jumped into the whirlpool of politics. Although the Pitt's India Act, 1784, Article 39, had clearly instructed that 'to pursue schemes of conquest and extension of dominion in India are measures repugnant to the wish, the honour, and the policy of the nation (England)',[48] they increased their armies manifold,[49] and went on doing what they were asked not to do.

On 11 September 1803, they knocked at the door of the Mughal capital, the historic city of Delhi.[50] The Maratha chief Daulatrao Sindhia, the *Vakil-i-Mutaliq* (Imperial Regent) who looked after the person and dominions of Emperor Shah Alam (r. 1760–1806), the blind old man,[51] sitting on the throne of Akbar and Aurangzeb, tried to defend it, but failed. The Governor-General, Lord Wellesley (1798–1805), rushed to have the Emperor under the Company's aegis, for he knew well enough that

> notwithstanding his Majesty's total deprivation of real power, dominion and authority, almost every state and every class of people in India continue to acknowledge his nominal sovereignty. The current coin of every established power is struck in the name of Shah Aulum. Princes and persons of the highest rank and family

46 See Jon Wilson, *Britain's Raj and the Chaos of Empire: India Conquered*, London, 2006, p. 33.

47 Robins, *op. cit.*, p. 143.

48 *Ibid.*

49 In 1763, the Company armies were estimated to be 18,000 strong, but in 1880s, their numbers increased about tenfold – 154,500, to be precise. See *ibid.*

50 During the last days of the Second Anglo-Maratha War.

51 Shah Alam was blinded by Ghulam Qadir Rohilla, son of Zabita Khan, Chief of Rohilkhand in 1788. There was a special reason why he perpetrated this crassest cruelty. During the course of the Maratha–Rohilla War (1773–74), the Marathas captured the wife and children of Zabita Khan, and handed them over to Shah Alam. Ghulam Qadir, son of Zabita, was one of them. Aged about 9–10 years, Ghulam was exceptionally handsome. Shah Alam liked him very much and got him castrated. Not only that, he was even asked to don female attires whenever he came to him. Qadir avenged his humiliation and loss by gouging out Shah Alam's eyes. See Aslam Parvez, *Bahadur Shah*, Delhi, 1986, p. 31.

The role of British in his blinding is also not unsubstantial. Historian F.W. Buckler says that 'the blinding of Shah Alam by Ghulam Qadir need never have taken place but for the betrayal of Sindhia's plans by Cornwallis. Sindhia had ordered his troops to remain in the Doab and Maj. Palmer was sent to meet Sindhia. When Ghulam Qadir had reached the ghats of Bareilly, three regiments were sent to watch him', but Lord Cornwallis, in his anxiety to be doubtlessly friendly with Rohillas, 'apprised Ghulam Qadir of intended march of the Detachment. Ghulam Qadir thanked Cornwallis and blinded Shah Alam'. 'F. W. Buckler's reply' to D. Dewar and H.L. Garret's rejoinder to his essay, 'Theory of Indian Mutiny', *Transactions of the Royal Historical Society*, vol. 7, 1924, p. 164.

> still bear the titles, and display the insignia of rank which they or their ancestors derived from the throne of Delhi, under the acknowledged authority of Shah Aulum, and his majesty is still considered to be the only legitimate fountain of similar honours.[52]

If left alone, the Governor-General feared, the Emperor 'could form a dangerous instrument in the hands of anyone possessing sufficient power, energy and judgment to employ it in prosecuting views of aggrandizement and ambition'.[53]

To ward off such an eventuality, the Governor-General kept sending tall promises and guarantees to the Emperor through his agent even before the war came to end. The crux of these promises was that should the Emperor accept the British protection,

> every demonstration of respect and every degree of attention which can contribute to the ease and comfort of your Majesty and the Royal family, will be manifested on the part of the British government, and adequate provision will be made for the support of your Majesty and your family and household.[54]

After the war had resulted in their favour, the Governor-General made, through General Lake, the following offer to His Majesty, which he, after a little vacillation, accepted:

> Rs. 90,000 per month as *peshkash* (present or tribute) plus a territory, called Assigned Territory, with the river Yamuna in the east, Najafgarh in the west, Bawana in the north and Faridabad in the south. In addition to that, the Emperor, was promised an increase to the extent of one lakh rupees per month for the Private expenses if the produce of assigned territory hereafter permits of.[55]

As was their wont, the Company authorities did not make any increase in the *peshkash*, even after much water had flowed under the bridges, despite being told several times to fulfil the promise. Wellesley responded with all kinds of excuses to justify his dereliction. He even went to the extent of interpreting the monthly payment of Rs. 90,000, the *peshkash*, as His

52 See NAI, Governor-General in Council to the Secret Committee of the Court of Directors, 13 July 1804.

53 NAI, Governor-General in Council to the Court of Directors, 13 July 1804.

54 Quoted in S.M. Burke and Salamuddin Quraishi, *Bahadur Shah, the Last Mughal Emperor of India*, Lahore, 1995, p. 22.

55 See Amar Farooqui, *Zafar and the Raj: Anglo-Mughal Delhi, c. 1800–1850*, Delhi, n.d., pp. 37–38.

Majesty's 'pension'/'stipend' to show himself, as Sir Percival Spear says, 'not his Majesty's 'minister but his protector; not as his agent but as his overlord'.[56] But what he proposed, his Commander-in-Chief innocently disposed. While forwarding the Governor-General's communication to the Emperor, General Lake wrote in his accompanying note just the opposite of what Wellesley wished him to convey.[57] He had spoiled Wellesley's game by assuming *'the tone of a subject instead of that of a friendly protector'* (emphasis added).[58]

Small wonder then, the Emperor came to believe that 'the status-quo between him and the British had been restored and that the Company had returned to its vassalage'[59] – i.e., the 1765 status as his *Diwan*, authorized by him to collect the revenues of the richest province of the Empire, Bengal, on the condition of making a yearly payment of Rs. 26 lakhs to him from out of the revenue they collected 'regularly'. The Company had paid the amount (revenue) till 1772, but stopped after that on the excuse that the Emperor had gone to the side of the Marathas. This had no sense, for servant had no right to ask his master to go according to his wishes. The non-payment of the agreed amount was thus a breach of agreement. The Emperor, however, thought that since the British 'had again come back to him', they will pay the due amount which was huge – as huge as £ 14.5 million, which Buckler says, 'greatly exceeded the Company's moveable capital'. According to Elphinston, Buckler further adds, the ravages of Nadir Shah cost the Mughal Emperor only 'eight or nine million sterling'.[60]

Thus, taking things at their face value, the Emperor came into his old self. He began to address the Governor-General, in all his correspondence, as 'his favoured son and devoted servant'. He called the Company officials as 'faithful servants'.[61] Though detestable, the Governor-General accepted the bitter pill. But he neither swallowed it nor threw it away, but followed instead the colonial strategy – always create confusion in such situations. As a result of their befuddled action, Company's historian, John W. Kaye, found Shah Alam in a typical position – he was 'a king, and yet not a king – something, and yet nothing – a reality and a sham at the same time'. Their

56 See Spear, *op. cit.*, p. 58.
57 *Ibid.*, p. 35.
58 *Ibid.* The old General was perhaps charmed by Emperor's humility, mannerism, and above all, the honour – *Khilat* – and the grand titles *Samas-ud-Daula*, *Asgar-al-Mulk*, *Khan Duran Khan Bahadur*, *Sipahsalar Fateh Jung* (the Sword of the Sate, the Hero of the Land, the Lord of the Age, the Victorious in War), bestowed upon him.
59 See Burke and Quraishi, *op. cit.*, pp. 25–26.
60 See F.W. Buckler, 'The political theory of the Indian Mutiny', *Transactions of Royal Historical Society* (4th Series), vol. 5, 1922, pp. 93–94; and his reply to his critics, in *ibid.*, vol. 7, 1924, p. 163.
61 Surprisingly, there is no evidence to the effect that the British ever expressed the displeasure over this development.

only 'solace' in the ball game here could be, Kaye adds, 'that we held the king'. But even that, he says in the next breath, was not adequate enough, because it was a 'puzzle to us how to play the card'.[62]

Surprisingly, in that confusing situation, there was only one man – the old, blind Emperor – who 'saw' things clearly, cracked the puzzle, and saved the situation for himself and his descendants, as Spear tells us:

> Mughal policy was to retain the nominal sovereignty of India by the utmost complaisance to the actual possessors of power. Behind this apparent pusillanimity lay the hope that the wheel of fortune might yet turn to make possible the reunion of actual to nominal authority.[63]

Spear is absolutely right. Even in his worst days, Shah Alam never gave up hope of regaining, one day, his lost world:

Aftab aj falak imroz tabahi didi
Bajfarda dehad ejan sar-o-sardari maa.[64]

[O Aftab (his pen name), unfortunately, what we see today is ruination. But tomorrow God would again give us our imperium.]

Hoping against hope, Shah Alam, surprisingly, kept the old baggage of sovereignty, rights, and privileges, however tardy, intact as long as he lived. The Governor-General wanted to pluck the cherry, but the home authorities would not agree.[65]

Leavening things in the womb of confusion and uncertainty, Shah Alam passed away on 19 November 1806. He was succeeded by his son Akbar II (earlier Akbar Shah). During his long reign – 1806–1837 – Akbar was mostly busy fighting three cases: one, to stop the nasty game of nibbling at his sovereignty; two, enhancement of his *peshkash*; and the third, the question of appointment of his heir-apparent. Going by chronological order, I would take up the third issue first. The Emperor wanted to appoint, under petticoat influence, his third son, Mirza Jahangir from his favourite wife Begum Mumtaz Mahal in place of the eldest one – Mirza Abu Zafar. According to the Islamic law, and the Mughal tradition, the Emperor had a right to choose his successor. But in British practice, the law of (male) primogeniture prevailed. The Emperor used every trick, to have his way. But to no avail. In desperation, he did not hesitate to be so mean as to blame

62 See John W. Kaye and George Malleson, *History of the Indian Mutiny*, London, 1889, vol. 2, p. 4; Spear, *op. cit.*, p. 34.

63 Spear, *op. cit.*, p. 34.

64 See Mahadi Husain, *Bahadur Shah II and the War of 1857 in Delhi with Its Unforgettable Scenes*, Delhi, 1958, p. 84.

65 Wellesley spoke in two voices: aggression here and passivity there (home).

Abu Zafar of having seduced his Begam (stepmother).[66] After a long tug of war, the Emperor agreed to have Mirza Abu Zafar as his heir-apparent (10 January 1810).

The second matter, i.e., nibbling at the sovereignty, which had actually started in Wellesley's time itself, took a harsher turn in the time of his successor, Minto (1807–1813). For instance, Minto told the Emperor in so many words that his Government's relation with him was 'only a complimentary recognition of a nominal sovereignty'.[67] He took several measures to prove the point. In June 1808, for instance, he refused to accept *Khilat*, robe of honour, which was conferred on their vassals/servants by the Mughal Emperors for centuries as a special favour.[68] Soon after, he hurled another blow by asking the Emperor not to bestow any title on any Company subject to avoid facing 'disappointment, degradation, and expense'.[69] The Emperor swallowed the bitter pills, but he did not sit idle on bended knees, crushing his fate: he took desperate measures to get his *peshkash* enhanced as per their promise made in the time of his father, Shah Alam, and royal prerogatives, sovereign authority, 'tribute', etc. He sent two missions, one of Raja Prem Krishan and the other of Raja Ram Mohan Roy, for presenting his case, first to the Governor-General in Calcutta and later to the King of England in London. The former failed almost completely, but the latter secured some success – not substantial, though.[70] Neither the *peshkash* was enhanced nor was the nibbling stopped – rather, it was continued with greater zeal.

Governor-General Minto's successor, Hastings (the Earl of Moira) (1813–1823), who derided the Emperor as 'mock majesty', was still more keen 'to make the British assertion of suzerainty perfect' in all respects. He gave a title to Nawab Faiz Mohammad Khan of Kanod (1813), *Khilats* to Nawab Samsuddin Khan of Feroze-Jhirka and Loharu (1815), and Raja of Bikaner (1828) much to the chagrin of the Emperor. Not only that, he even dissuaded the princess of Travancore to receive from the Emperor a *Khilat* for her son.[71] In 1818, he abolished the Imperial Mint at Delhi; and broke the bond of loyalty that existed between the Emperor and the rulers of Lucknow, prompting Nawab-Vazir Ghaziuddin Hyder to declare himself an 'independent' ruler – a *Badshah*. Three years later, he brought round the Raja of Jalor not to accept the Mughal Emperor as his sovereign, and enjoy the British patronage instead. The Raja presented *Nazar*

66 See NAI, Foreign secret consultation, no. 25, 26 February 1807.

67 Husain, *op. cit.*, p. 86.

68 It was later accepted by the Governor-General's Persian Secretary. But an indirect message was thus sent to the Emperor that the British were not his vassal/servant.

69 K.N. Panikkar, *British Diplomacy in North India*, Delhi, 1968, p. 121.

70 For details relating to the two missions, see *ibid.*, pp. 119–32; Farooqui, *op. cit.*, pp. 60–67.

71 See Panikkar, *op. cit.*, pp. 19–32.

to the Governor-General, ignoring the Emperor, which his ancestors took pride in doing. He removed the words *Fidwi Khas* (special servant) from the Governor-General's seal, and asked Indian ruling houses to do the same. In short, he made every effort to chop off as many branches of the tree of Mughal sovereignty as possible.[72]

Hasting's successor, Amherst (1823–1828), also followed his policy. But it seems that constant strikes had, by then, demoralized the old Emperor, and we find him agreeing to meet Amherst (1827) without any ceremonials, without which he had refused to meet his predecessor (Hastings). They met as equals. He also began to entertain 'letters from the Governor-General, bearing no signs of his (Emperor's) superiority in addresses'.[73] He also repeated Minto's statement that 'Your Kingship is but nominal; it is merely out of courtesy that you are addressed as King'.[74]

Bentinck (1828–1835), Amherst's successor, also followed his path. He replaced the Mughal coinage, which was in circulation till his time, by Company's own rupee, 'bearing the image of their own sovereign, the King of England in place of the Mughals'. Another equally damaging measure, if not more, was his insertion of the phrase *Hukam Company Bahadur* in public announcements.[75] The Emperor opposed these, and almost every other move that curtailed his Royal prerogatives and impaired his sovereignty as best as he could, till he reached his earthly extremity on 28 September 1837.

The Emperor's eldest son and heir-apparent, Mirza Abu Zafar, succeeded him at the ripe age of 62, with the title '*Abul Muzaffar Sirajuddin Muhammad Bahadur Shah Badsha Ghazi*', conveniently called Bahadur Shah II or simply Bahadur Shah Zafar[76] (1837–1857). The new Emperor as a prince was a favourite of the British who had, as seen before, made him heir-apparent in the teeth of stout opposition from his father and others. It was, thus, hoped that he would, unlike his predecessors who were always on quarrel, if not on war path, with them, pull on well. But no sooner had he touched the throne, winds began to blow in a different direction. The reason of friction between him and the Company was the appointment of Mirza Dara Bakht as heir-apparent. Though his eldest son, the Emperor did not like him to be his successor; his choice was his second son, Mirza

72 Gauri Shankar Mukherjee, 'Controversy over the question of sovereignty: A study of Mughal–British political relations', *The Quarterly Review of Historical Studies*, vol. 18, no. 1, 1978–79, pp. 178–79.

73 Panikkar, *op. cit.*, pp. 142–48.

74 Husain, *op. cit.*, p. 86.

75 Mukherjee, *op. cit.*, pp. 179–80. Earlier the mode of public announcement was *Khalq Khuda Ki/Mulk Badshah Ka*. See Husain, *op. cit.*, p. 86 f.n.

76 Bahadur Shah was also a well-known Urdu poet. He wrote his poetry as Zafar. Some critics find his poetry very ordinary. Ghalib, however, rates it pretty high. See Husain, *op. cit.*, p. 50.

Shah Rukh. This, and Company's arrogant behaviour in arranging the heir-apparent's investiture ceremony, without even informing the Emperor, on the day of his own accession against the Mughal tradition, made him bitter against the British.[77]

Unlike Bentinck's tenure, the Governor-Generalship of Auckland (1836–1842) was free of any tension; not because there was any change in the British policy vis-à-vis the Emperor, but because the Governor-General was awfully busy with the Afghan affairs. However, when his successor, Ellenborough (1842–1844), 'an enthusiast for the direct Government of India by the crown',[78] came, the situation began to boil again. To reach his set bourne, the Governor-General ordered his men to stop offering *Nazar* to the Emperor and other practices that enhanced his sovereign image. He had the peacock throne (replica) removed from the *Diwan-i-Khas* to an underground cell. *Diwan-i-Am* was also closed (1844) and the practice of holding durbars there was discontinued. Worse, the Governor-General wanted the Emperor to leave his royal title and palace before long.[79]

When the truth reached the Emperor, he protested and charged the Company authorities of violating the *Iqrarnama* (Agreement) between Emperor Shah Alam and General Lake at the behest of the then Governor-General, Wellesley. He sent his Royal *Vakeel* to the Governor-General (1843) to change his new policy and stick to the *Iqrarnama.*[80] But to no avail. Anguished and enraged, he engaged as his 'ambassador' an Englishman, George Thompson,[81] a social activist and founder of the 'Edinburgh Society for the Abolition of Slavery throughout the World' and the 'British India Society', to present his case to Queen Victoria. Thompson left for London on 7 November 1843, carrying the official 'letter from His Imperial Majesty, the Emperor of Delhi to her Most Gracious Majesty Victoria, the Queen of Great Britain and Ireland and all their Dependencies'. The letter contained three salient points:

(i) From the times of Akbar and Elizabeth to the present times (1840s) the two ruling Houses of India and England stood on *friendly footings* – never ever as master and servant;

77 Farooqui, *op. cit.*, p. 95.

78 Ellenborough, says historian of the 'British dominions', H.H. Dodwell, 'wanted the Emperor to resign the title ..., to be offered to the Queen (of England) despite the oddity – had his ideas been carried into effect – of her figuring as *Patshah Ghazi*, the Imperial Champion of Islam, which would have made a queer pedant to the *fider defensor*'. See H.H. Dodwell, ed., *The Cambridge History of India*, vol. 6, Delhi, rep. 1963, p. 606.

79 For details, see *ibid.*; Husain, *op. cit.*, pp. 84–90; Panikkar, *op. cit.*, pp. 162–64.

80 Mukherjee, *op. cit.*, p. 179.

81 For more details on the life and work of this distinguished Englishman, and the letter, see A. Parel, 'A letter of Bahadur Shah to Queen Victoria', *Journal of India History*, vol. 47, pt. 1, no. 139, April 1969, pp. 283–84.

(ii) The servants of the ruling House of England who came to govern their possessions here (except those at the helms now) always showed 'loyalty and respect' to the Indian (Mughal) ruling House; and
(iii) The relation between the Company and the Mughal ruling House was determined by the *Iqrarnama* (Agreement), 1803, between Emperor Shah Alam and General Lake (on behalf of the Governor-General Wellesley) where the former stood, as a sovereign, and the latter had the status of more or less a vassal.

In the end, the Emperor asked the British sovereign 'to command your servants (Company) ... to give prompt and just consideration to the representations and claims I have laid before them'.[82]

The Board of Control and the Court of Directors in London thwarted Thompson's every move to meet the Queen, deliver the 'letter, and seek justice from her'. In fact, 'the labyrinth of procedural technicalities, built into the administrative system in India' failed his mission. The saving grace, however, was that perhaps in the weather created by Thompson's public debate,[83] newspaper reports, etc., the proposals of Ellenborough were also not considered favourably by the Court of Directors. He was asked to wait till Bahadur Shah's death, which was, according to their estimate, not long in coming.[84]

Meantime, Ellenborough was succeeded by Dalhousie (1848–1856). Dalhousie shared Ellenborough's views, but not his philosophy. According to him, imperial interest was more sacrosanct than any law, convention, or tradition. It is appropriate, he used to declare every now and then, 'that we should appear before India ... as being paramount in name as also in authority and right'. He wanted to put 'an end to the Royal privileges of the House of Timur' on the passing away of Bahadur Shah, and deny the use of the Royal title (*Badshah*) and the Royal Palace (Red Fort) to his successor. He would be addressed simply as Prince and reside at Qutb, he explained.[85]

When Dalhousie sent his proposal to London for approval, it generated a serious controversy. The Court of Directors opposed the proposal by a huge majority (19 to 4). Its Chairman, Gelloway, told Dalhousie that no good would come out of his move. The Prince, he added, 'if he has one drop of

82 *Ibid.*, p. 300; Mukherjee, *op. cit.*, pp. 177–83. The full text of the letter is given in Parel, 'A letter of Bahadur Shah to Queen Victoria', *Journal of Indian History*, vol. 47, pt. 1, no. 139, April 1969, pp. 299–301.

83 The debate was held in the India Office on 18 December 1844 before the Proprietors of the East India Company. Though Thompson put up his case stoutly, the motion was, for obvious reason, negated. The content of the debate was reported in the British press. Parel, *op. cit.*, p. 294.

84 Panikkar, *op. cit.*, pp. 165–66.

85 *Ibid.*, pp. 168–71.

the blood of Timur rather sacrifice his life than quit the palace of his ancestors by compulsion'.[86] There was disagreement in Dalhousie's Council also. Only the Board of Control supported him. In that confused situation, he avoided taking any action for some time.

Meantime, the question of appointment of heir-apparent came to the fore. Mirza Fakhru being the eldest surviving son of the Emperor was Dalhousie's choice. But the Emperor, under the influence of his favourite Queen Zinat Mahal, favoured Mirza Jawan Bakht. Mirza Fakhru was not eligible to be his successor, the Emperor said, 'on grounds of illegitimacy and mutilation'.[87] The Company overruled both the objections, and he remained their choice. The Prince felt obliged to Dalhousie.

Dalhousie put his old scheme in a slightly modified manner before the grateful Prince. He offered 'an addition of Rs 25,000 to his income' should he agree to live at Qutb. He would be called-Emperor, he added, and have equal standing in dealings with the Governor-General. He employed Mirza Ilahi Bakhsh,[88] the self-serving 'traitor' who played a vital role in destroying the name, fame, and whatever standing was left of the Mughals during their last days, to make his son-in-law agreeable to the proposal. Fakhru proved to be devoid of any 'drop of Timur's blood': he agreed to shift to Qutb.[89] The grateful Governor-General 'appointed' him heir-apparent in an impressive investiture ceremony on 24 September 1852. The Prince was, however, not destined to enjoy his new assignment for long – he died soon (10 July 1856).[90] The Emperor, under the influence of Begum Zinat Mahal, again pressed the case of their son Mirza Jawan Bakht for heir-apprenticeship. However, before any action could be taken, Dalhousie's tenure came to end.

Dalhousie's successor, Canning (1856–1862) was more keen and determined not to give any 'solemn sanction to a sham'. But before he could give

86 *Ibid.* It may, however, be added here that Gelloway perhaps did not know that there was so much admixing of blood in the Royal dynasty over the years that not only in the Prince under reference, but even in most of others, there was hardly any trace of Timur's blood.

87 According to Bahadur Shah, none of the Mughal princes was circumcised since Humayun's times. Mirza Fakhru was an exception, which rendered him unfit to be a King. *Ibid.*, pp. 172–73.

88 Ilahi Bakhsh was, as indicated above, father-in-law of Mirza Fakhru. He was instrumental in making Fakhru to change his mind, as indicated above, and oblige the Governor-General. Later, he played the same game again to make his grandson, Fakhru's son, Prince Abu Bakr to surrender with his two uncles before Hodson in September 1857. Hodson killed all the three Princes in cold blood, and threw their dead bodies to rot for the whole day and night. Prince Abu Bakr was his daughter's son. Ilahi Baksh did not care to collect even his dead body and give him at least a proper burial.

89 A formal agreement to this effect was executed by the Prince on 23 January 1852. The Board of Directors and the Governor-General in Council had approved the modified proposal that the Prince would be called Emperor and will not be forced to quit Red Fort.

90 For details, see Panikkar, *op. cit.*, pp. 171–75; Farooqui, *op. cit.*, pp. 98–101.

effect to his intent, the Rebellion broke out, 10 May 1857, effecting, as Shah Alam and his successors had hoped,[91] 'reunion of actual and nominal authority'. Now Bahadur Shah was both *de jure* and *de facto* sovereign ruler of Hindustan.[92]

The above account shows that Delhi had, from 1803 through 1857, technically, two governments: one, of the Mughals, who had sovereignty but not power; the other, of the East India Company that had power but not sovereignty. As things stood then, the Company could have easily possessed both the things in 1803, either on the *de facto* ground of the right of conquest by deposing Shah Alam or through a treaty with him according to local/international law. They did neither, but tried to acquire, like a sneak-thief, the prized thing through indirect means. However, the Mughal Emperors, it must be said to their credit, though weak and effete, came out to oppose their every move in that direction as best they could in their worst days. As a result, despite their great efforts, the traders-turned-rulers could only divest the Emperors of the external trappings of sovereignty but not the soul, the sovereignty itself. It remained vested in the Emperors till the Rebellion 1857.

The Company's rule during this period was, as such, legitimate only till such time that it worked on behalf of the Emperors, but not after they discarded the practice. Some critics (like Dewer and Garret mentioned above), however, believed that such was not the case. Sovereignty without power to enforce its dictates was no sovereignty. The Company was sovereign because it had such power. Maybe so elsewhere, but in the East, especially India, sovereignty without power was also recognized as sovereignty. There are many such examples that prove the point. In Maharashtra, the Peshwas, for instance, ruled from Poona as a great power, but always looked towards almost 'a vanishing Kingdom of Satara', where the weak and effete descendant of Shivaji ruled, as their master: 'Each Peshwa solemnly sought investure from the King, although the King could only do as he was directed'. In Mysore, Hyder Ali and his son Tipu Sultan carved out a big *Raj*, but they preserved the 'old Hindu kingly family and showed its representative periodically to the people to draw legitimacy from him'. At Nagpur, the Bhonsles 'did not take the title of *Raja*, they gave it to a Gond Prince, the hereditary ruler of the region, and issued their orders in his name'.[93] Before 1857, the case of Bahadur Shah also belonged, as seen above, to this category. But after 10 May 1857, his position changed; he was sovereign even according to the Company's definition of the term. Besides *de jure* status, he had an army and power to enforce his orders, and was, thanks to the great

91 Even Shah Alam who was in most wretched condition cultivated hope that their better days would come someday. See Husain, *op. cit.*, p. 84.

92 Spear, *op. cit.*, p. 34.

93 See Dodwell, *op. cit.*, vol. 5, p. 608.

Rebellion, no more what the British called him '*a sham*', '*a shadow*', '*a puppet king*', and so forth.

En passant, a question arises here: Who brought about this situation in 1857? Let us look for the answer, in the mirror of history, i.e., the Rebellion in Delhi and Bahadur Shah's role therein.

The rebellion: role of Bahadur Shah

The Rebellion 1857 is perhaps the most written about event in the history of modern India.[94] A careful perusal of this voluminous literature shows, however, that many questions relating to Bahadur Shah's role which are, as indicated above, central to our understanding of the charges against him have not been answered satisfactorily. Take, for instance, his assumption of the leadership of the Rebellion on 11 May 1857. With a little difference in inconsequential details here and there, almost all the writers, who have touched Delhi, both British and Indians, tell us that on 11 May 1857, a few rebel sepoys from Meerut came to Delhi, perpetrated violence, along with local rabble, and installed Bahadur Shah on his paternal throne as the Emperor of Hindustan, which changed instantaneously a local mutiny of the sepoys into a pan- Indian political movement of great scope and significance.[95] The developments, they say, took the Emperor and others by surprise which goes to show that there was no prior contact with, and understanding (conspiracy) between the Meerut Sepoys and others in Delhi.

The oft-repeated above tale is straight and simple. But it provokes some complex questions like, for instance, how a few sepoys from Meerut – one at 7 a.m., 5–6 at 8 a.m., 30–40 a little later, some more at 11 a.m.,[96] 300 in all – could dare to think of 'storming' an unknown, well-fortified city, well-guarded Red Fort,[97] and approach the Emperor with such a high degree of confidence, if they had no earlier understanding with their counterparts and others in Delhi? Secondly, how could the sepoys, who had no political ingenuity to understand the complexities of high-level politics, take

94 *The Rough Bibliography of Indian Mutiny, 1857–1859* by H.E. Rough, Solihull, 2015, a most comprehensive and authoritative work on the subject, lists over 7,700 contemporary and current English and foreign language books, journals, and articles. There are about 300 books, articles, etc. in Indian languages also which have not been listed there.

95 Especially, S.N. Sen, *Eighteen Fifty-Seven*, Delhi, 1957, p. 411.

96 See the statement of the Emperor's counsel, Ghulam Abbas, who was almost all the while with the Emperor on 11 May. Martin, *op. cit.*, pp. 161–62.

97 The Red Fort was surrounded by 'walls a mile and a half in circumference and 100 feet high' with a moat 75 feet wide and 30 feet deep on the three sides and the Yamuna River on the other. The walls had loop holes on the top. 'No known engine of war could cross this great moat', says James Leasor *The Red Fort: An Account of Siege of Delhi in 1857*, London, 1956, pp. 48–49.

such a statesman-like decision of installing Bahadur Shah on the throne, and transforming their local mutiny into a political movement of all-India standing? And thirdly, it has remained unexplained so far as to how those sepoys – strangers – could make the people of Delhi – sepoys and civilians from the city, its suburbs, and villages[98] – in large numbers, eat out of their hands in no time and take them along to demolish the steely, awesome administrative structure so assiduously built by the British in over half a century (1803-1857), and destroy every vestige of their existence in about half a day?

These are no doubt complex and difficult-to-answer questions. But fortunately there are some meaningful clues in the contemporary literature that can be helpful in tackling them. Take, for instance, the following excerpt from the evidence of a most knowledgeable person then at the scene, Ahasanullah Khan, physician and prime minister of Bahadur Shah, and, at the same time, a well-wisher of the British:

> The Volunteer Regiment (38 NI) of Delhi had said that before the break out of mutiny, they had leagued with troops at Meerut, and that the latter had corresponded with the troops in all other places, so that from every cantonment troops would come to Delhi.[99]

Another equally knowledgeable person, the Emperor's Secretary, Mukand Lal, gives some more information. Deposing before the Court, he said:

> Some twenty days before the commencement of the late rebellion intelligence was received here (the Palace) that the troops at Meerut were about breaking out in open mutiny. ... I do not know whether any direct proposals came to the prisoner, but the King's personal attendants, sitting about the entrance to his private apartments, used to converse among themselves, and say that very soon, almost immediately, the army would revolt and come to the palace, when the Government of the King would be re-established and all the old servants would greatly promoted and advanced in position and emoluments.[100]

In view of this, it would not be wide of the mark to guess that during the 20 days, i.e., 21 April to 11 May, some understanding had developed between the Palace and the Meerut troops/leaders which made them enter into the Palace without any hesitation (on 11 May). There is also a direct hint of

98 Most of the writers, old as well as recent, call them without any evidence 'rabble', 'ruffians', 'badmashes', and so forth.

99 See Hakim Ahsanullah's evidence, supplement to the proceedings.

100 Mukand Lal's evidence, *The Trial*, 12 February 1858.

this in the following statement of Zakaullah, a trustworthy contemporary historian,[101] as far as Delhi affairs to which he was an eyewitness went:

> On the same Sunday (10 May) when the British blood was spilled (at Meerut), a carriage (*gaari*) full of Hindustanis had come to Delhi cantonment in the afternoon. What did they discuss among themselves and what did they do is not known in precise terms, but a guess can be made in the light of the fact that the next morning every regiment was ready for revolt.[102]

Not only the Delhi soldiery, but even the civil populace of Delhi knew well before the mutiny broke out as to what was going to happen in Meerut and Delhi soon. Zakaullah is again our source. He says that about 10 May, Mr F. Taylor, Principal, Delhi College, asked the senior Arabic teacher, Maulavi Sayed Muhammad, what is the news about the city ? He replied:

> This city is abuzz with the news that mutiny has happened in Meerut and the entire Bengal Army is opposed to the British. ... This shows that the delinquent *badmashs* in the city are waiting for the Rebellion, and they are cock sure that it would come.[103]

As in Meerut, so in Delhi, the people from the city, its suburbs and villages, as indicated above, joined the sepoys in large numbers, and two together killed all 'the enemies of the State' – Europeans,[104] Christians,[105] and their supporters, and pulled down, as indicated above, the entire (British) administrative structure that they had built over the years.

Lamentably, the narrative again lands into no tip-off zone, and we are hard put to answer the questions like, for instance, if there was a conspiracy between the Delhi and Meerut rebels, then who were its thread-holders?

101 For his qualities and qualifications as a historian, see C.F. Andrews, *Zakaullah of Delhi*, Cambridge, 1924, pp. 19–21.

102 Zakaullah, *Tarikh-i-uruj-i-saltanat-i-Englishia*, Delhi, 1904, vol. 2, p. 416. Its English translation from Urdu used here is done by the present Editor throughout.

103 *Ibid.*, vol. 2, p. 407.

104 The number of Europeans killed in Delhi in the first week of the Rebellion was about 154. For their names, etc., see Martin, *op. cit.*, vol. 3, pp. 158–59, 171–73.

105 There were about 330 Christians in Delhi in 1857. Not all of them were killed as several contemporary writers tell us, and even recent historians, otherwise eminent, like S.N. Sen, accept their versions (Sen, *op. cit.*, p. 7). In fact, those killed were active supporters of the British. We have references in the 'Mutiny Papers' that some Christians were given *parwanahs* by the Commander-in-Chief to the effect that nobody would interfere with them (Collection 103, no. 40, 24 June 1857); in another case, the C-in-C orders Kotwal to release four Christians detained in the Kotwali (Collection 103, 386, n.d.); in another case, the Kotwal releases two ladies (Christians ?) (Collection 101, no. 1, 21 May). There is no evidence that workaday people were ever touched.

Who brought countless civilians – like 'swamps of locusts and ants' (*Sirajul Akhbar*, vol. 13, no. 8, pp. 2–4) – from cities, suburbs, and villages to the city streets so soon, and inspired them to fight the British? The latter tried their best to find answers to these questions, but could not succeed. In fact, the local leaders, both sepoys and civilians, who worked at the grassroots level in those days, did their job through their small elite groups – *panchayats*[106] – with such finesse that none other than the concerned persons could know their identity. Take, for instance, the case of Musketry Depot at Ambala. As a protest against the use of the greased cartridge, the sepoys there burnt military houses, offices, stables, stores, etc. almost regularly from the last week of March to the first week of May (1857). The Deputy Commissioner (Ambala) was at work, the military authorities did their utmost, and 'there was an inducement of Rs. 1000 to anyone who would give any clue of the incendiaries, yet there was no progress'. They posted vigilant guards at every important point, so much so that English soldiers hardly got two nights a week in bed, but still there was no improvement. The Commander-in-Chief openly confessed that 'what was passing at Ambala sorely puzzled him'. 'Strange', he wrote to Canning (G.G.), 'that the incendiaries should never be detected. ... Everyone is on the alert, but still no clue to trace the offenders'.[107] The same thing happened at Meerut and several others stations. That is why Capt. Martinue, Senior Musketry Instructor at Ambala, remarked that 'a wide-spread conspiracy was there'.[108] This is corroborated by the evidence tendered by Hakim Ahsanullah, etc. during the trial.

A word about the general belief that the Rebellion was initiated and carried out, in the main, by sepoys alone, the civil society followed them later. Far from it, the civil society's role, even in sepoy mutinies, was much more important than what is generally made out. In fact, there is strong circumstantial evidence that no widespread, full-fledged sepoy mutiny had any chance of success, if the sepoys had no support of the civil society. There was, for instance, an outbreak at Berhampur on 26 February 1857;[109] a month later, on 29 March, there were serious developments at Barrackpur, which had the potential to burst into a big putsch;[110] and on 10 May, about

106 The *panchayats* were found in several local armies, but the institution was the strongest in the Punjab (Sikh) army. After the two Sikh wars, sepoys who had betrayed their King and were taken into the Company army, brought *Panchayats* to their regiments. The members of the *panchayats* were rated as gods (*panchprameshvara*). Nobody could defy or betray them easily.

107 NAI, Foreign, Secret, Consultations no. 100–3, 25 September 1857; also see K.C. Yadav, *The Revolt of 1857 in Haryana* (hereafter *Revolt*), Delhi, 1977, pp. 46–47.

108 Capt. Martinue informed the Assistant Adjutant General that 'Sepoys have placed in my hands letters from various regiments which convinced me that a wide-spread, conspiracy was there'. Quoted by J. Cave-Browne, in *The Punjab and Delhi in 1857*, Edinburgh, 1861, vol. 1, pp. 41–48.

109 See Martin, *op. cit.*, vol. 3, pp. 128–33.

110 *Ibid.*

nine hours before the outbreak at Meerut, the Indian regiments took their officers into their custody, and rose up in open revolt at Ambala,[111] but, for want of civil support, all the three efforts failed to take round to success. The same thing happened at a number of other places also where the situation was similar. But where the civil society came out in support of the sepoys, the uprising was a success. Look at Meerut. A day before the actual outbreak (9 May 1857), the entire city, we are told, was overcrowded with people, mostly armed, from the suburbs and the villages. Next day, they joined hands with the sepoys, and the two together, fired the first shot of the Rebellion that shook the very foundations of the British Empire.[112]

The story of Meerut was repeated, almost blow-by-blow, at Delhi too. The sepoys and civilians worked together to obliterate every vestige of the British rule from the city. Their unidentifiable leaders[113] chose the Emperor to lead the movement. The Emperor accepted the popular wish, it is alleged, under force. One can take a horse to water, but cannot make it drink by force, and especially so, when the horse happens to be a royal horse. The following developments and the Emperor's role therein tell a different story than what we are made to believe.

With the exit of the British (11 May), most of the writers, old and new, who have discussed Delhi of the Rebellion days, say that peace, tranquillity, and law and order that the British had established here with great effort were gone too. Anarchy, chaos, confusion, murder, mayhem, loot, plunder, arson, and destruction became the order of the day. The sepoys once known for their discipline, dutifulness, and dedication turned into monsters soon after entering Delhi, and became more interested in antisocial activities than the fight against their enemy. As a result, the shops were closed, and bazaars deserted. The people and sepoys were starved because of non-availability of the necessities of daily life on account of lawlessness in the countryside where they came from. The Emperor being old, infirm, and inexperienced could not rise to the occasion to set things right. Badly persecuted, the Delhiwallahs prayed day in and day out for an early return of the British rule.[114]

A critical scrutiny of the evidence on which these views are based takes us, however, to a different conclusion. Initially, soon after the collapse of

111 K.C. Yadav, 'Ambala and the Revolt of 1857', *Journal of Haryana Studies*, vol. 1, no. 1, 1969, pp. 31–41.

112 Commissioner Williams in his official report on the Meerut rising says that 'the towns people had armed themselves and were ready for the onslaught before the Sepoys had commenced the carnage, ... and the residents of the wretched hamlets which had been allowed to spring up ... were seen similarly armed, pouring out to share in what they evidently knew was going to happen'. See Kaye, *op. cit.*, vol. 2, p. 60.

113 The problem of identification of the leadership has been discussed above in detail.

114 The above referred writers do not restrict these tragic happenings to the initial few days only, but give the impression as if such conditions prevailed till September.

the Company's administrative edifice, the situation was really very bad, as bad, even worse, than what the British writers of the day and even the recent ones tell us.[115] But, amazingly, the old Emperor rose to the occasion sooner than expected, and set things right as far as possible in those highly troubled times. Let us count his steps in that direction.

To begin with, the Emperor rode out in a procession through the *bazaars* and main streets, appealing to the people to halt the violence and maintain peace and order, and to the shopkeepers to open their shops and carry on their business as usual without any fear.[116] His next step was the re-creation of all the departments of administration. There was, however, dearth of competent persons to man those departments. But fortunately, the police department was an exception.[117]

An admix of the old (Mughal) and the new (Company) organization, the police administrative structure was, broadly, as follows:

Kotwal[118]
I
Naib Kotwals[119]
I
Thanedars[120]
I
Policemen[121]
I
Chowkidars[122]

115 Even the insiders agree here. See, for instance, Zakaullah, *op. cit.*, vol. 2, p. 661.

116 Zakaullah has given an interesting account of the Royal procession (see his above cited book, pp. 61–62). But Montgomery Martin's account of the same is more graphic. After his formal installation on the 'Silver Throne' (which the British had taken forcibly and kept in the treasury since 1843) in the *Diwan-i-khas*, the King, he says, 'surrounded by the paraphernalia of Orient pomp, amidst the salutes of artillery ..., issued from the gates of the palace in Royal procession through the streets of Delhi, to announce by his presence the assumption of imperial power. The cavalcade upon this occasion was led by the Prince Mirza Mughul, one of his sons, whom he had appointed the chief commander of the army. Another Prince, Abu Bakr, rode at the head of the body-guards of the aged stimulator of imperial power, who presented himself to the gaze of the excited populace in open chariot .... The King slowly proceeded through the principal streets of the city to the Jumma Masjid where ... Empire of Hindustan was reclaimed'. Martin, *op. cit.*, vol. 3, pp. 157.

117 See Zakaullah, *op. cit.*, vol. 2, pp. 687–88.

118 Muinuddin was the first *kotwal* of the city. He was actually a British spy. The Emperor had taken him, on the recommendation of Hakim Ahsadullah, into service. But soon he showed his true colours and harassed people. He was, therefore, dismissed. For some time, Mohammad Faizullah served as *Kotwal*. Later Mubarak Shah held the post. See *ibid.*

119 The *Naib Kotwals* were Khuda Bakhsh, Bhao Singh, and Bhan Singh. *Ibid.*

120 See Appendix 3.

121 They were appointed by the *Kotwal* or *Naib Kotwals*.

122 They were appointed by *Thanedars* for their respective *ilaqas*.

The *Kotwal* was directly appointed by the Emperor. His responsibilities/duties were, as seen below at length, very heavy.[123] He was assisted by 2/3 *Naib Katwals* in discharging his multifarious jobs.

In the Company days, there were 13 *thanas* (police stations) to maintain law and order in the city and its suburbs; now *thanas* were as many as 23. Each *thana* was in the charge of a middle-rung police officer, called *Thanedar*, who functioned with the help of about 25–50 policemen, called *Burqindazs*, depending on its size. For night duty, there were 400 *chowkidars* (watchmen), who guarded the seven city gates and other strategic locations during the night.[124]

Besides restoring order and enforcing law, the police department also did the following jobs: to trace missing persons, especially women and children; to investigate each unnatural death; to appoint *chaudharis*, for supplying professional/servicemen, necessary commodities, and beasts of burden for army; to provide space to different army regiments for camping and to set up ration shops, etc. installed in their vicinity; to take necessary measures for disposal of corpses of humans and animals, and removal of garbage, etc.; to appoint suppliers of necessities of life, and to regulate and monitor their prices on daily basis; to help the courts in their work of dispensing justice; and to maintain communal harmony by enforcing, strictly, the government orders (for instance, ban on cow slaughter, interdict on use of bullocks for carrying garbage, quelling of communal clashes, etc.), and a number of other sundry jobs.[125]

The task was really formidable and the number of the police personnel was very low. The Emperor placed the services of an army regiment at the disposal of the *Kotwal* to use them as policemen to stop plundering and lawlessness.[126] Simultaneously, measures were taken to enlist policemen. On 15 May, Jiwan Lal tells us, 100 policemen were appointed.[127] Some old Company hands, who volunteered to serve their own regime, were also taken. The police and army men worked together. As a result, the law and order in the city, suburbs, and the countryside began to improve slowly but steadily. After some time, an air of near, if not total, normality blew all over. But the 'State (Company) Papers', Spies' Reports', contemporary loyalist writers' works',[128] etc. still painted an ugly picture without any basis. Let me elaborate:

123 The *Kotwal* was in fact the pillar on which the entire administrative edifice stood.

124 For details, see K.C. Yadav, 'Introduction', Delhi in 1857: A Documentary Study of Policing during the Rebellion (hereafter Policing forthcoming).

125 See *ibid.*

126 *Ibid.*

127 Metcalfe, *Two Native Narratives*, p. 91.

128 The State Papers did not report, according to their policy, what could have gone against the State. The spies painted the 'enemy' with tar brush and showed their weaknesses, even

Take their allegations of widespread looting and plundering of *bazaars* and *mohallas* by the rebels, both sepoys and civilians, and consequent closure of shops. There is hardly any grain of truth in their chaff. According to one of the most informed persons in the city, Zakullah,[129] who, though a British loyalist, was also, as indicated above, a historian who would not twist or distort anything that happened before his own eyes, no matter whether it related to the British whom he liked or the Emperor whom he didn't. The reality on the law and order front in his views was this:

> The shops in Khari Baoli, Chandni Chowk, Dariba were closed, although only a few shops were looted. In Dariba, for instance, only one shop was pillaged, but all the jewellers sent their ornaments and cash home, and, standing before their empty shops, cried loudly that they have been robbed of everything.
>
> (In the *mohallas*) when one house was plundered, it was reported that the entire *mohalla* has been plundered. If something worth Rs. 10 was looted, it was declared that things worth thousands of rupees have been depredated. The news of loot and plunder were actually highly exaggerated. In fact, not even 1/100th part of these (stories) was correct. There were hundreds of (small) *mohallas (shadah mohalle)* where even a thing worth a *cowrie* was not looted.[130]

Another misrepresentation proffered by a recent well-known historian:

> The chaos and anarchy that erupted in the countryside proved far more effective at blockading Delhi than the efforts at besieging the city attempted by the British from their perch on the Ridge. The price of food items escalated and supplies rapidly dwindled. Soon both the people of Delhi and the sepoys were on the verge of starvation.[131]

---

if those were not there. The writings of most of the Indian writers (who wrote just after the Rebellion) are mostly marred with fear and greed. They wrote flattering things. This is not to suggest, however, that these sources are wholly useless. They also contain some useful details. The case is that they should be used very critically and carefully.

129 For Zakaullah's life, achievements, and, contextually, historian's temperament, see Andrews, *op. cit.*, Cambridge, 1929.

130 Zakaullah, *op. cit.*, pp. 661–66.

131 William Dalrymple, *The Last Mughal: The Fall of a Dynasty, Delhi 1857*, Delhi, 2006, pp. 3–4. Initially there was anarchy no doubt. But local princes – Raja Nahar Singh, Nawab Akbar Ali, Nawab Ahmed Ali, Rao Tula Ram, Nawab Abdur Rehman Khan, Nawab Noor Samad Khan – and local leaders – Sadruddin, Gafur Ali, Dhanna Singh, Qalandar Panipati, Visarat Ali, Sabar Khan – brought situation under control and established order.

There was 'no blockading' and the supplies continued to come into the city constantly, unhindered, unchecked, says Zakaullah, whose own and his family's existence depended on those supplies:

> British could not check the supply of (necessary) things which came (in the city) every morning and evening regularly in as much measures as required. *Tattoos*, mules, carts, *chhakras* (laden with supplies) continued to come in succession (*tanta laga rahta tha*). The supplies were sold at several places in the *bazaars* and nobody could dare to lay their hands on them. Telangas also knew the rules of obtaining them, and used to gladly pay for whatever they purchased, knowing that if they did not, then supplies would cease to come and they would die of starvation.[132]

According to another source, the Mutiny Papers, the people faced hardly any difficulty in obtaining their necessities, which they could purchase direct from the markets near their homes. The *Thanedars* supplied the provisions to the troops stationed in their vicinity.[133] In case the troops were deployed away from the markets, shops were opened near their camps.[134] When the troop went to the 'front', they were mostly supplied things of their choice,[135] like sweetmeats and other things.[136] Barring some few hard cases, provisions were, says the *Kotwal*, regularly supplied to the troops.[137] Despite their best efforts, however, some troops did not get their provisions. They approached

There was no blocked either. The princes and leaders kept open major roads like Delhi–Faridabad–Hodal–Mathura, Delhi–Pataudi–Rewari, Delhi–Farrukhnagar–Jhajjar–Najafgarh–Rohatak, etc. See K.C. Yadav, *Revolt*, pp. 88–107, 170.

132 Zakaullah, *op. cit.*, vol. 2, p. 679.

133 Such references/hints are found in the Mutiny Papers, Collection 61, no. 233, 27 July 1857; Collection 100, no. 59, 28 May; Collection 110, no. 108, n.d.; Collection 110, no. 195, n.d.; Collection 110, no. 214–15, n.d.; Collection 110, no. 225, n.d.; Collection 110, no. 244, n.d.; Collection 110, no. 263, n.d.; Collection 110, nos. 264–65, n.d., Collection 110, no. 284, n.d.; Collection 111(a), no. 26, n.d.; Collection; 111(a), no. 28, n.d.; Collection 111(a), no. 36, n.d.; Collection 111(a), no. 56, n.d.; Collection 111(c), no. 26, n.d.; Collection 111(c), no. 102, n.d; Collection 111(c), no. 73, n.d.; Collection 111(c) no. 92, n.d.; Collection 111(c), no. 105, n.d.; and so forth.

134 Such references/hints are found in the Mutiny Papers, Collection 103, no. 320, n.d.; Collection 106, no. 15, `12 June 1857; Collection 110, no. 231, n.d.; Collection 110, no. 233, n.d.; Collection 110, no. 244, n.d., Collection 111(a), no. 26, n.d.; Collection 111(d), no. 126, n.d.; Collection 111(d), no. 174, n.d.; Collection 121, no. 78, n.d.

135 There was a demand from the sepoys at the 'front' to supply parched pulse, *sattu*, molasses, and brown sugar (*sakkar*). The *Kotwal* did the needful. See Collection 110, no. 241, n.d. Some other troops pleaded for opening sweet and milk shops in their vicinity. See Collection 121, no. 78, n.d.

136 Mutiny Papers, Collection 110, no. 108, n.d., Collection 121, no. 78, n.d.

137 See Mutiny Papers, Collection 111(c), no. 33, n.d.

the higher authorities for redressal of their problem.[138] Perhaps the authorities had resolved their problem, because we do not find them complain this time the police came to keep strict watch on the markets, and made sure that neither scarcity of provisions occurred[139] nor the prices went up.[140] Owing to their hard efforts, the situation soon became much better than what the vested interest has portrayed. Except for two occasions, as indicated above, no dearth of provisions was experienced by the civil society and the troops; the prices were by and large within fair limits.

The portrayal of violence, killing, etc. by the rebels is also a little overdrawn in the so-called 'mutiny annals'. At the initial stage, some people, no doubt, resorted to, as indicated above, bloodshed and bestiality. But there was even then, as Zakaullah tells us, a sort of method in the madness. There was selective killing of those who were or could potentially be the enemy of the state.[141] Later, as seen above, things changed considerably. Killings became the thing of the past. The ordinary citizens led a near normal life. Their existence was valued, and its loss – even caused accidently – was enquired into and reported to the higher authorities.[142] The poor among the citizenry were exempted from paying any contribution to the war fund.[143]

138 There are some references showing this in the Mutiny Papers, Collection 128, no. 39, 12 Jun 1857, Collection 57, no. 185–86, 28 Jul 1857, Collection 61, no. 296, 4 Aug 1857, Collection 110, no. 225, n.d., Collection 110, no. 214–15, n.d., Collection 111(a), no. 36, n.d.

139 There is a reference that *Chaudharis* were appointed for different markets who supplied commodities in demand. Tenders were floated for procuring necessary things. Mutiny Papers, Collection 128, no. 44, n.d.

140 There are some references that show that the prices were fixed daily by the *panchs* appointed by the Police (Metcalfe, *Two Narratives*, p. 222), and the price lists were handed over to the *Thanedars* of the local *thanas* under whose jurisdiction the markets were located, and to the higher authorities. See Mutiny Papers, Collection 130, no. 9, n.d., 24 July 1857; *ibid.*, no. 10, n.d.

141 Zakaullah says that the rebels killed only (i) the British citizens, (ii) Christians who were close to them, (iii) *Delhiwallas* who sheltered them in their houses; (iv) those who passed on intelligence to the enemy; and (v) supplied provisions to the British troops at the ridge. Zakaullah, *op. cit.*, pp. 662–66.

142 See the following examples: (i) *Thanedar* of P.S. Bhojla Pahari reported death of one Rajan, a female cobbler, to the C-in-C, who ordered investigation, Mutiny Papers, Collection 122, no. 20, n.d. (ii) Same *Thanedar* made a report of the death of one Lachhu, a blind beggar, (Collection; 122, no. 17, 28 July) duly signed by witnesses, to the C-in-C (Collection *ibid.*, no. 18., n.d.) to the *Kotwal.* (iii) *Thanedar* P.S. Chandni Chauk made enquiries about 'the death of a woman caused by fall in a well' (Mutiny Papers, Collection 61, no. 461, 28 August 1857). (iv) One Dalu (resident of P.S. Chandni Chauk) killed himself accidently. The *Kotwal* made a report verified by the *Thanedar*, the deceased's father and others to the Emperor (Collection 111(b), no. 17, n.d.). (v) *Thanedar* of P.S. Rajghat reported to the *Kotwal* death of a man, due to a house collapse. Collection 111(c), no. 121, n.d.

143 Mutiny Papers, collection 130, no. 79, n.d.

The rich and 'the wealthy were, however, asked to contribute liberally'. But, being the creatures of the 50-year rule of the Company, for whom they still carried good feelings in their hearts, they offered lame excuses for exemption. But as money was desperately needed to make the war mare go, they were forced to pay – a common practice in war days throughout the world – and in some such cases, the angry mobs even went as far as looting their houses and properties 'to punish the traitors'.[144] Such instances are mostly reported as plundering of innocent people.

This is not to suggest, however, that no undesirable and unwanted happenings took place anywhere. Taking advantage of the abnormal circumstances, some antisocial elements, no doubt, did indulge in such activities. Other crimes also happened. But the police took strict action against the lawbreakers the moment the cases were reported to them. Beside this, to prevent the occurrence of the crimes, the authorities prescribed harsh punishments for the culprits – not arbitrarily, but, strictly by the rule book. There are many instances in the Mutiny Papers that prove the point. At one place, the *Thanedar* of Chandni Chowk Police Station sought permission from higher authorities to search the house of a prostitute suspected of having kept stolen goods in her house.[145] On search, some material was found. In another similar case, the *Thanedar* begged permission to search the house of one Gulab Khan suspected of having kept stolen property in his house.[146] In yet author case, the *Thanedar* asks for orders to arrest a man who was reported to have stolen Rs. 3 from a confectioner's shop.[147] Sarfaraz Khan, Army man (?), gave shelter to one Dalu weaver, who had assaulted his (own) wife and absconded. The *Kotwal* approached the C-in-C for necessary action.[148] In another case, a *sawar*, Amir Ali, cheated some shopkeepers. The *Kotwal* wrote to the *Risaldar*, commanding the Gwalior Contingent to which the offender belonged, for strict action.[149] There is an interesting case of a sepoy having been robbed of his articles by a woman. The *Kotwal* gave the case to area *Thanedar* to trace the culprit.[150] On a complaint from some carts men of non-payment of their dues by their hirers, the *Naib Kotwal* asked the *Thanedar* of the concerned police station to arrest

144 This class was made of heterogeneous elements, Hindu bankers, Mahajans, usurers, old Company contractors, employees, Anglophile Mughal aristocrats, bureaucrats, etc., who were mostly creation of the Company rule. They were forced to pay to the war fund, when they refused to give anything voluntarily. See Metcalfe, *Two Narratives*, pp. 94, 134, 136, 139, 151.

145 Mutiny Papers, Collection 61, no. 550, n.d.

146 Some incriminating articles were found in her house. See Collection 61, no. 551, n.d.

147 Mutiny Papers, Collection 61, no. 215, 24 July 1857.

148 Mutiny Papers, Collection 103, no. 66, n.d.

149 Mutiny Papers, Collection 116 (b), no. 22, n.d.

150 Mutiny Papers, Collection 120, no. 171, n.d.

the offenders.[151] There are several cases where the police is seen making efforts to take care of the property and trace the heirs of the persons who had died without their known successors.[152] If the police failed to trace the heirs or none came forward on their own within 15 days, then the properties became state properties.[153] On their owners being not available/traceable, the unclaimed articles and animals were disposed of with the permission of higher authorities.[154] A case of honest dealings: the *Thanedar* of Bhojla Pahari sent four annas saved out of the money paid for preparing seal of the *Thana* to the C-in-C.[155]

There are many instances where the police does its job without favouring or fearing the high and mighty. We see them checking, for instance, a powerful prince[156] causing public nuisance, and arresting sepoys who indulged in undesirable activities at his behest.[157] Although everything required by the army – rations, carts, beasts, ammunition, and so forth – was supplied, as seen above, as promptly as possible without any hesitation, their unreasonable demands were curtly declined. For instance, on the eve of the arrival of the Nimach Brigade, Khuda Bakhsh, their representative, asked the *Kotwal* to find 'a big house' for the dancing women coming with the Brigade. The *Kotwal* refused to oblige.[158]

The above measures were, *sine dubio*, no small achievement of the Emperor in those climacteric conditions. And that was not all. He showed almost the same faculty and *savoir-faire* in tackling another crucial crisis – the acute shortage of finances. In the beginning, the troops from Meerut and Delhi came empty-handed. Though the Emperor had told them at the very outset that he had no money, he managed their affairs. He 'ordered his

151 Mutiny Papers, Collection 120, no. 128, n.d.

152 Mutiny Papers, Collection 111, no. 126, n.d.; Collection 120, no. 165, n.d.

153 *Ibid.*

154 There are many such cases mentioned in the Mutiny Papers. In one case, a *Thanedar* seeks permission of *Kotwal* to dispose of a sword belonging to a dead man to defray his funeral expenses (Collection 61, no. 509, n.d.). In another case, an unclaimed sword was disposed of and Rs 2-10-0 and the sale proceed were given in charity to a beggar, Hidayat Shah (Collection 61, no. 497, n.d.) A stray horse was found and sent by the *Thanedar* to higher authority for necessary action (see Collection, no. 61, 555, n.d.).

155 Mutiny Papers, Collection 122, no. 19, 29 July 1857.

156 Take the case of Prince Abu Bakr, grandson of the Emperor. He was young, handsome, and likeable. His licentious character and drunkenness, however, made him unpopular. One day, he created huge ruckus, in an inebriated state, in a *mohalla*. On police report, the Emperor not only scolded him, but also removed him from his army command (charge of cavalry).

157 Mutiny Papers, Collection 111b, no. 22, n.d. Some sepoys were arrested on the request of the Army officers. Two sepoys of the Nimach force fled way after cheating a jeweller. *The Naib Kotwal* asked their *Subedar* to arrest and realize payment from them. See Mutiny Papers, Collection 111c, no. 217, n.d.

158 Mutiny Papers, Collection 172, no. 4, n.d.

grocers Ram Sahai and Diwani Mal to provide (at his expense) for them 500 rupees worth of meal, pulse and gram daily' till such time that some proper arrangement was in place for them'.[159] Perhaps aware of the situation, most of the regiments that came after them brought funds wrenched from the government treasuries at their stations, and deposited a major part of them in the Royal Treasury. The Emperor, says Kashi Prasad, a well-informed British spy stationed in Delhi, kept that money 'separate and devoted it solely to their use and the purchase of ammunition. The King touched none of this for his own use; he borrowed himself from the City Bankers'. The practice, though congenial, could, however, continue only for about two months. After Bakht Khan's Bareilly's regiments came, no money, says the spy, reached the Royal coffers: 'The Bareilly men paid themselves for six months and kept the rest for themselves'. Their example was 'followed by the subsequent arrivals'.[160] As a result, the Royal Treasury again went dry.

Soon after, the situation got worse when some more troops came from far and near without any money, and the war became intensely fervid. The sepoys could not get their pay. The manufactures of war material were severely hurt. And unfortunately, almost all the potential funding sources – the local chiefs,[161] bankers, traders, well-heeled people in the city – evaded all appeals, and even Royal Orders to come forward and contribute to the cause, because most of them, if not all, were the creations and the sustainees of the Company and still had soft corner in their hearts for them. Worse, the Princes who were sent to collect funds, of course with tact, indulged instead in violence, extortion, and corruption to satiate their own hunger for pelf and power. It was for all this that the August–September air had got rife with remonstrations and protests of the sepoys and complaints and accusations of the civilians.[162]

To cut to the crux, the situation was really dangerous, but before it could burst forth into a storm that could have harmed the war efforts, the Emperor, it should be said to his credit, rose to the occasion and resolved the problems as best as he could in those climacteric conditions: he dealt with the plunderers and lawbreakers with a heavy hand,[163] reprimanded and punished the

159 For details, see Husain, *op. cit.*, pp. 180–81.

160 See *Records of the Intelligence Department of the Government of the North-West Provinces of India during the Mutiny of 1857*, William Muir, ed. W. Coldstream, Edinburgh, 1902, vol. 2, p. 39.

161 There were seven states under the Delhi Agency: Jhajjar, Dadri (Bahadurgarh), Dojana, Pataudi, Farrukhnagar, Ballabhgarh, and Loharu. Though all their chiefs paid lip allegiance to Bahadur Shah, their hearts lay elsewhere.

162 See the Diary of Jiwan Lal in C.T. Metcalfe, ed., *Two Narratives* for August and September.

163 This has been already discussed above in the 'Law and order' section.

Royal Princes for their wrongdoings,[164] and tackled the reasonable grouses of the soldiers with sincerity and utter openness. An example: on 25 August, a deputation of officers from different regiments went to the Emperor and, seething with anger, demanded money to be paid to their men who were literally starving. The Emperor listened to their grievances patiently and went into his residence, brought Crown jewels, and handed them over to the officers, saying 'Take this, and forget your hunger'. The officers, moved immensely, refused to take the jewels, saying, 'We cannot accept of your crown jewels, but we are satisfied that you are willing to give your life and property to sustain us'.[165]

And sustain he did the complainants and all others to the last by employing, records showed, no other means, but his bona fides, seriousness, and sincerity.

Another important phenomenon which has gone unnoticed so far is what type of government the Emperor wanted to set up – the old Mughal type of absolute monarchy or some sort of a responsible monarchy with a modern touch? From the day one, the Emperor is seen going to the latter: soon after resuming the reins of the Government, he wanted the administration to be run by a council of wise people. First, he appointed, as indicated above, a three-member Council of Nobles. But it failed to take off.[166] Then he wrote 'autograph letters' to rajas of Jaipur, Jodhpur, Bikaner, Alwar, etc. to come and run the administration. He was, he wrote,

> *desirous of annihilating the English, but inasmuch as he had no reliable person to organise and administer the very important affairs at this juncture, he wished to form a Confederacy of States: and if the States he now addressed with these letters would combine for the purpose, he would willingly resign the imperial power into their hands.*[167]

There was no response. After some time, he constituted a Court of some representatives from the army and his own nobility. That stayed but did not work effectively.[168] Different officials pulled in different directions. It was reorganized sometime towards mid-August. The Emperor then, says Jiwan Lal,

> issued order to all the officers to obey neither the orders of Mirza Mughal or any other General, inasmuch as His Majesty has

164 See Metcalfe, *Two Narratives*, pp. 197–99. Prince Mirza Abu Bakr and Mirza Khizr Sultan were reprimanded and punished. They were divested of Army Command.

165 *Ibid.*, p. 207.

166 Not only these particular 'Mughal nobles', but almost the entire nobility of the day was rotten, incapable of rising to such occasions.

167 Metcalfe, *Two Narratives*, p. 226.

168 See Husain, *op. cit.*, pp. 190–91.

> appointed a Court of twelve members, six to be appointed by the King and six by army for the future conduct of the administration.[169]

The army and civil society were to obey all orders issued by the Court.[170] The Constitution of the Court[171] being very interesting and ahead of its time, it deserves to be seen in full:

(I) A Court should be established and named Administration Court, that is, a Court to administer military and civil affairs.
(II) This Court should consist of ten members – 6 military and 4 civil. Of the military members two should be selected from the infantry platoons, two from the cavalry and two from the artillery.
(III) Out of these ten men, one should be appointed President *(Sadr-i-Jalsa)* and another Vice-President *(NaibSadr-i-Jalsa)* by a majority of votes. In every department there should be appointed secretaries according to need. The quorum for the Court meeting should be five whereby work should be done satisfactorily.
(IV) At the time of the appointment of these men, they should take an oath that they would do Court work with honesty, sincerity, great industry and with deep thought and care; and that they will not neglect even the slightest detail in matters administrative and that they would not covertly or overtly resort to taking and seizing, or do partiality of any kind and in any manner or at the time of dealing with matters of administration in the court. On the contrary, they will always keep themselves engaged in and apply themselves attentively and diligently to executing the State matters whereby the State should obtain security and people should enjoy peace and repose; and that they would not divulge any item of the Court work under consideration before its enforcement plainly or by allusion without the permission of the Court and *Sahib-Alam*.[172]
(V) Election of the Court members should be in this manner: by the majority of votes two men should be elected from the infantry platoons, two from the cavalry troops and two from the artillery; such men must possess a long record of service and must be clever and well-versed, able and intelligent. Should any person be highly clever,

169 Metcalfe, *Two Narratives*, p. 205.
170 *Ibid.*
171 In the present state of our knowledge, it is difficult to say who were the authors of the historic document. Some writers believe that it was the work of Maulavi Fazalul Haq (Khairabadi) in consultation with the King. Its content, however, does not support the view. It was, in all probability, the work of a team of enlightened citizens and soldiers, in association with the Emperor and Mirza Mughal.
172 Mirza Mughal.

intelligent, and learned and as adept in the administration of the Court work but lacking long service, this latter disqualification in that case will not obstruct the appointment of such a person. And in the same way will be appointed four civil members.

(VI) After ten members have been appointed, if any member gave his vote before the full Court regarding any matter in such a manner as to be against honesty and sincerity or calculated as partial to anyone, then that member will be removed from the Court by the definite majority of votes; and another person will be elected in his place according to regulation five. All the items of the administration to be considered should be first treated in the Court and after the approval of *Sahib-i-Alam* the decision of the Court should be communicated to His Majesty *(Hazur-i-wala)*.[173]

(VII) After the programme has been drawn by the majority of votes, it will be submitted for approval to *Sahib-i-Alam Bahadur* and the Court will remain under the control of the alluded *Sahib-i-Alam Bahadur*. And no matter of administration whether military or civil will be executed without the sanction of the Court and the approval of the *Sahib-i-Alam* and without the information of the same being given to His Majesty *(Hazur-i-wala)*. In the event of a difference of opinions and after being re-considered by the Court, the same matter – the difference still continuing – will be sent up through the *Sahib-i-Alam* to His Majesty the Shadow of God (*Hazur Zille Subhani*). The order given thereupon by His Majesty (*Hazur*) will be final.

(VIII) In the Court none, barring the *Sahib-i-Alam Bahadur* and His Majesty, the shadow of God *(Hazur Zille Subhani*) who will be entitled to be present, no non-member will be present, nor will he join the meeting. When out of the specified number of the Court members, anyone for some valid and acceptable reason be unable to attend the Court meeting, then the votes of the remaining members of the Court will be tantamount to the vote of the Court in full strength.

(IX) Should a member of the Court desire to express his opinion regarding any matter, he would first secure the consent of another member; then he may make the proposal of the same as a matter already agreed upon by two members.

(X) When an item is to be considered in the Court according to Regulation *nine*, then the proposer should first speak in the Court meeting. No one will interrupt his speech until he has finished it. If a member of the Court has any objection to make regarding it, he should explain it and no one will interrupt him either, until he has finished speaking. Should a third man make a speech amending or adding or

173 Emperor Bahadur Shah.

subtracting from the objection, and if the remaining members of the Court observe silence regarding it, then every member of the Court should write out his opinion separately. After consulting Regulation *eight*, decision will be arrived at by the majority.

(XI) Those who from every section of the military are elected according to Regulation *two*, should be appointed managers and administrators of that section. Under their control should work a committee of 4 men according to Regulation *four:* in that committee secretaries should be appointed according to need. And whichever proposal is formally put up in that committee by the majority of votes that proposal will be presented to the Court by those very officers of that committee. It should be executed by the Court according to Regulation *seven*. The same process should be adopted in every military and civil section.

(XII) At any time according to the demand of the occasion right should be vested in the Court to make amendments by majority of votes in this Constitution.[174]

It was indeed a visionary measure to have created such a representative institution in those difficult times. And, interestingly, it did not exist in theory alone; it was functional as the following statement of the Emperor shows:

> The mutinous soldiery had established a Court in which all matters were deliberated on and such measures as, after deliberation, were sanctioned by this Council, they adopted.[175]

Charles Ball throws some more light on the subject:

> Upon examining the apartments occupied by the King and his chief officers in the Palace many papers were found that threw a light upon the intended proceedings of the rebel monarch; and from them it appeared that the kind of government to be permanently established for the city and immediately surrounding country was more of the nature of a military than of a Mohammedan government. It seems to have been a sort of constitutional monarchical milocracy. The King was king and honoured as such like a constitutional monarch; but instead of a Parliament, he had a council of soldiers in whom power rested and of whom he was in no degree a military commander. No Arabic or Persian names, forms or terms appear to have been introduced; but on the contrary, the English

174 For the full text, see Mutiny Papers, Collection 57, no. 539–41, n.d. (Eng. tr. Mahdi Husain).

175 See The Emperor's Statement of Defence (?), *The Trial*, 9 March 1858.

> terms and modes of business were generally adopted. All petitions seem to have been presented to the king; but the great authority to which almost all of them on all matters, both civil and military, were referred (by order endorsed on petition), was the court – a body composed of a number of Colonels, a Brigade-Major and a *Seketur* (secretary). The latter functionary seems to have been the most important personage in Delhi. All the colonels etc. were sepoys who made their mark or at best signed in rough Hindoo characters[176] (read *Devanagari*).

In those days of serious crisis, this was by all means another enviable achievement of the leaders of the movement, whom our learned historians have chosen to call backward-looking reactionaries.[177]

Besides these measures, the Emperor chose to make an extraordinary decision to ensure that both the major communities, Hindus and Muslims, lived in peace and harmony.[178] How successful was he there can be guessed in the light of the fact that despite their best efforts, the British could not sow the seeds of disunity and disharmony among them.[179] The civil society cooperated with their ruler. Both the *pandits* and *maulavis*[180] came forward to inspire and encourage their faith-fellows to join the war. They specially raised the morale of the sepoys. To what extent some people got inspired by their exhortations can be seen from the example of Mohammad Sharif, a famous painter of Delhi, who, having donated his house and the entire property, except his wife's ornaments, went to fight the British. He never came back.[181]

In sum, Bahadur Shah, as the above account shows, had, despite Himalayan handicaps, risen to the occasion and created, to a large extent, order out of chaos, peace out of violence, and subsistence out of dearth. It is no small deal that the old, infirm monarch elicited praise for his performance even from his avowed enemy, Sir John Lawrence, who wanted 'the

176 See Charles Ball, *History of the Indian Mutiny*, London, 1858–9, vol. 1, p. 524.

177 See Sen, *op. cit.*, pp. 412–13; R. C. Majumdar, *The Sepoy Mutiny and the Revolt of 1857*, Calcutta, 1957, p. 241.

178 See, for details, the Mutiny Papers, Collection 103, no. 134, 11 July 1857; Collection 110, no. 18, n.d.; Collection 61, no. 245, 28 July; Collection 61, no. 254, 29 July; Collection 111c, no. 31, n.d.; Collection 111c, no. 43, 44, n.d.; Collection 120, no. 143, 144, n.d. Also see Zakaullah, *op. cit.*, pp. 660, 688.

179 See *Delhi Urdu Akhbar*, 5 July 1857, p. 1.

180 The *Pandits* (Hindu religious guides) told the sepoys the auspicious hours, after consulting their *patras* (almanacs), when they should go out to fight the enemy and secure success. The *maulavis* (Muslim religious guides) issued *fatwas* (religious diktats) and mobilized their followers to fight the enemy without any fear. No harm would come to them, they assured them, and success would be theirs. Zakaullah, *op. cit.*, p. 676.

181 *Ibid.*

rascal to be shot dead at the first opportunity'. After seeing the 'papers' that fell into the hands of his men in the palace, the Chief Commissioner observed:

> The papers referring to the system of the King's government exhibit in a remarkable manner the active personal share which the King himself took in the conduct of affairs. However wrongly he has assumed his position, it must be admitted that his orders were not unworthy of the situation. He did make an effort to preserve order in the city, to repress rapine and murder in the villages, to check malversation and to restrain the excesses of the soldiery.[182]

Richard Temple, whom John Lawrence had sent after the fall of Delhi, to help manage the affairs of the city, collected material for the trial which led him to the conclusion similar to his boss's. 'His (Emperor's) own signatures, annotations and orders after the outbreak showed him to have possessed more capacity than would have been expected from a man who had been immured all his life as a titular king in his ancestral palace'.[183]

A word about Army's role, which has not been touched so far. In the beginning, the strength of the Army in the city was as follows: *Delhi Force*: 38th, 54th, 74th Bengal Infantry Regiments; and 5th Light Field Artillery Battery, 3rd Company of the 7th Battalion Artillery.[184] *Meerut Force*: 3rd Bengal Light Cavalry Regiment; 11th and 20th Bengal Infantry Regiments.[185] They numbered, according to Muinuddin, 2,530 in all.[186] The Emperor was their Supreme Commander and Mirza Mughal served as Commander-in-Chief. Earlier the senior most officers commanded their respective regiments. But after some time – on 18 May, to be precise – the Emperor appointed, at the instance of the sepoys, his sons and grandsons to the following positions in the army:

Sons

Mirza Khizr Sultan General
Mirza Kochak Sultan Colonel of the Delhi Regiments

182 For John Lawrence's views, see R. Temple, Secretary, Chief Commissioner Punjab to the secretary to the Government of India with the Governor-General, no. 50, dated 29 April, 1858, vide *PMR, Correspondence*, pt. 2, p. 592.
183 Richard Temple, *Men and Events of My Times in India*, London, 1882, p. 135.
184 Zakaullah, *op. cit.*, p. 674.
185 Metcalfe, ed., *Two Native Narratives*, p. 61.
186 The strength of each Infantry Regiment was about 400 (5 Regiments × 400 = 2,000 men), each Cavalry Regiment was made of 350 sawars, and the Artillery Battery of 18 gunners, counting, 2,530 in all. *Ibid.*

Grandsons

Mirza Abu Bakr Colonel of the Cavalry Regiments
Mirza Medhu Colonel of the Meerut Regiments[187]

Except for Mirza Mughal, none of the princes proved worthy of the job they were given. Rather they proved a disaster. The former, on the other hand, not only managed the assigned job to the best of his knowledge and ability, but also helped the Emperor, as the Mutiny Papers show, in conducting the overall business of the state.

At the initial stages, when the restoration of law and order was the prime job of the new state, the Army played an important role there till such time that the policemen were not recruited in adequate numbers. Chuni Lal, the news writer, has given in his *Diary*, a day-to-day account of their activities in their new role: On 12 May, he writes, 'The King placed (under the city *Kotwal*), a Regiment of the sepoys and directed him ... to stop the plunder'.[188] The *Kotwal*, Muinuddin, being a British lackey, did precious little in the matter. The Emperor, says Chuni Lal,

> sent for all the *Subedars* of the rebel troops, and ordered them to place for service one Regiment of Infantry at the Delhi Gate and all the lattice of the palace, and one company at each of the Ajmeri, Lahore, Cashmere and Furrash Khana gate. The King further said that 'he did not wish to see the inhabitants plundered, and therefore ordered them to station one company of sepoys at Dureba for the protection of shops there'.[189]

Despite these precautions, the situation still remained somewhat disturbed. The incidents of plundering still reached the Emperor's ears. Even some irresponsible sepoys also indulged in such activities. As a result, the shopkeepers closed their shops. The Emperor ordered Mirza Mughal, the C-in-C, to take a company of Infantry and check the rot. Mirza Mughal at once went to the *Kotwali*, the Police Headquarters, on an elephant and had it

> notified in the city by tom-tom that should any sepoy be caught plundering any inhabitant, his nose and ears should be cut off; and

187 The sepoys had actually thought that the issue of appointment of their officers to the top posts could create bad blood among them. Hence the request. The Emperor obliged them. See *Memoirs of Hakim Ahsanullah* (hereafter *Memoirs*), ed., Moin-ul-Haq, Karachi, 1958, p. 7.

188 Spy Chuni Lal's Diary, presented at the trial to prove the different charges levelled against the Emperor. See *The Trial*, 23 February 1858.

189 *Ibid.*

> that if any shopkeeper would not open his shop, or declined to provide the sepoys with food (on payment, of course), he would be imprisoned and fined.[190]

To make it doubly sure that the shops were opened and normal business went on as usual, the Emperor himself moved out with two regiments on an elephant (13 May) and asked the shopkeepers to open their shops and provide the troops with supplies. This had solitary impact.[191]

The troops also did many other jobs, for instance, bringing treasures from a number of places like Gurgaon, Rohtak, Garhi Harsaru, etc. and dealing with the lawless elements in the countryside.[192] By mid-May, they had begun to receive reliable news that the British were preparing for an assault on the city, the Army authorities got the city walls repaired wherever necessary and placed guns on all the seven gates and at other strategic spots.[193] In short, the leaders of the movement utilized this period (12 May–8 June) not in doing nothing, as historian Sen says, but quite profitably – in 'setting their house in order' and 'preparing for the inevitable attack'.[194] As a result, the fortified city of Delhi became an impregnable fortress.

Like the noted historian S.N. Sen, the British high echelon also did not see the above reality. The Punjab supremo, John Lawrence, for instance, pressed the generals assigned with the task of retaking Delhi very hard – almost to the breaking point[195] – to knock at the city gate and wonder how it opened at a rate of knots. The Governor-General, Canning, also thought likewise. Their bosses sitting in London, Westminster, and Whitehall went

190 *Ibid.*

191 *Ibid.*

192 *Ibid.*

193 How effectively they had done this work has been explained, albeit briefly, by Gen. Wilson to the Governor-General, *vide* his letter, 15 August 1857, reproduced in Kaye and Malleson, *op. cit.*, vol. 4, pp. 2–3 (f.n.).

194 Historian S.N. Sen, relying on the spy reports and other such accounts, says that between 12 May and 8 June (1857) 'the leaders of the revolt had ample time to set their house in order and prepare themselves for the inevitable attack. But they wasted their opportunity'. Sen, *op. cit.*, p. 76.

195 John Lawrence's constant goading to attack Delhi right at once was, believed by many a person, one of the causes, if not the main, that hastened the end of two generals, General Anson and General Barnard, and invalidated the third (General Reid). See the following statement of Lieut. Col. Turnbull, who served with the Delhi Field Force from May to September 1857, and was observing all developments, at different ends with wide open eyes: 'The terrible anxiety of our generals, receiving constant entreaties (if not more) from Lahor (e) (i.e., John Lawrence) to do something; to take active measures to push on etc; when it would have been ruinous, if not practically impossible to do so; the fearful prostration of mind and body by such strain in a climate reaching sometimes 133 degrees in a headquarters tent ... all this seems to have pushed them into the jaws of cholera, nervous breakdown, etc.' See Kaye and Malleson, *op. cit.*, Appendix A, vol. 4, pp. 405–6.

ahead of each one of them – 'Cut off the enemy's water supply', said Lord Ellanborough, President Board of Directors; and 'surround Delhi and starve the mutineers into submission', counselled Vernon Smith, President of the Board of Control. Both 'wise' men did not know that the rebels had full command of the Yamuna River;[196] and the fact that they (British forces) were not 'besiegers' but 'besieged' (Wilson). The critics were, one could argue, civilians, but no, even military officers (read military bureaucrats) were no better. For instance, the military officers sitting in Calcutta seriously believed that *'the mutineers had played the British game by rushing into the walled city where they would be as rats in a trap'* (emphasis added).[197] These fanciful ideas seem to have emanated from the misreading of the past history of Delhi. Even military historian Col. G.B. Malleson suffered from the malady. Look at his views:

> In September 1803, the troops of Scindia had not offered the semblance of a resistance to the small army of General Lake. In the wards of the earlier Mughals with the representatives of the dynasties which they supplanted, Delhi had never offered any but the slightest resistance to the army which had been victorious in the field.[198]

The historian forgot to take note of the fact that 1857 was not 1803. Now the 'rebel sepoys' and the civil society had made the defence of Delhi so formidable that pushed hard by their civilian bosses almost on the daily basis, to attack the city at once, the British generals took about a month to muster courage to enter Delhi suburbs (7–8 June). And despite their success (courtesy Indian treachery) in occupying a strategic place – the Ridge – about six miles from the city, they could not take a decision[199] to attack the city itself

196 See James Leasor, *Red Fort: The Story of the Indian Mutiny, 1857*, London, 1956, p. 218.

197 G.B. Malleson, *The Indian Mutiny*, London, n.d., pp. 87–88.

198 *Ibid.*

199 The Ridge was not reached only on account of their superiority in arms, valour, and fighting spirit, treachery of the Indians also played a part there. One Risaldar Ahemad Khan of the 4th Bengal Cavalry went to the Emperor three days before the battle of Alipur and 'stated that the day the forces would meet, he would lead his men away to the right and join the mutineers. Ahmad Khan was received and treated with great courtesy. On third day, he took leave of the King and returned to the English forces. This man 'proved to be no rebel but loyal to the English'. On the day of the battle, the traitor positioned his regiment on the right flank and when they came towards the Indian side, Indians took them to be their new friends and welcomed them. But they proved to be wolves in sheeps' clothes and took the field by surprise; and thus paved the way to the Ridge. See Muinuddin in Metcalfe, ed., *Two Native Narratives*, pp. 62–63.

After about a week of occupying the Ridge, some young hawks and greybeards pressed the leadership at the Ridge to launch an attack on the city. A War Council meeting was

for over three months (8 June–14 September). The 'rats', on the other hand, moved out of their 'trap' and 'scarcely allowed them', says General Reid, the then Commanding Officer of the Delhi Field Force, 'a day to pass without attack or demonstration upon some parts of the British positions'.[200] And these sorties were not, as some people believe, whimsical moves of a 'crowd' of sepoys gathered in the city, but were a part of a well-designed 'policy', says J.W. Rotton, an eyewitness of the going-on at the Ridge, for 'harassing and wearing our men by daily attacks and constant exposure to the sun'.[201] Seeing the reality, Maj. Gen. Wilson (earlier Brigadier), the successor of Gen. Reid, who had broken down under the weight of stress and strain of the job, said: '*The force under my command is, and has been since the day we took over the position (8 June), actually besieged by the mutineers* (emphasis added)'.[202] And they attacked the British forces 24 times from 8 June to 31 July.[203] Their *modus operandi* was simple: they would come out of the city (as detailed), attack the British position, fight for some time, and then run back, and halt at a safe place near the city walls bringing their pursuers within the firing range of the guns at the ramparts and musket shots of the sepoys standing near them, leaving no other course with their pursuers but to flee for life, leaving their dead behind.[204] A representative example of such sorties is provided, very graphically, by James Leasor on the authority of Lieut. (later Field Marshal) Fred Roberts: 'There was a sudden attack', he says, on the Hindu Rao's one night. The British defended themselves,

> but suddenly, and quite unexpectedly, the mutineers began to retreat – and at once the whole British force were after them with such speed that within minutes they were actually within the sight

---

called, 14 June, to discuss the matter. There was no consensus. The meeting was again held on 15 June. Again there was no result. On the 16th, the idea was dropped. Brig. Wilson had played a big role in the matter. He told one and all frankly that no matter whether we win or lose the fight, we will remain losers – big losers. The rebels have 'shown', he observed, 'how well they can and will fight from behind cover, such as they will have (even when they entered Delhi as victors), in street fighting'. Gen. Reid, the then commanding officer, Delhi Field Force, agreed with him. See Kaye, *op. cit.* vol. 2, pp. 531–34; also see Collier, *op. cit.* p. 187. There was another decision to attack the city on 3 July. Everything was ready, but 'the General's resolution had failed him at the last moment. There was no assault'. Leasor, *op. cit.*, pp. 166–67.

200 Ball, *op. cit.*, vol. 1, p. 486.

201 J.W. Rotton, *Chaplain's Narrative of the Siege of Delhi*, quoted in James Hewitt, ed., *Eye-Witness to the Indian Mutiny*, London, 1972, p. 28.

202 Wilson to Canning, 20 August 1857, *vide*, Kaye and Mallsson, *op. cit.*, vol. 4, pp. 2–3, f.n.

203 *Ibid.*; Metcalfe, ed., *Two Narratives*, p. 120; Cave Browne, *Punjab and Delhi in 1857*, London, 1861, vol. 2, p. 31; Husain, *op. cit.*, p. 223.

204 Care-Browne, *op. cit.*, vol. 2, p. 31.

> of the city walls. The enemy's heavy guns and howitzers had a range of at least 1000 yards and the sepoys withdrew until they were almost beneath the ramparts, which were lined with mutineers excitedly firing canons and muskets and pouring down fearful shower of grape and shot on their pursuers at virtually point-blank range. Men (British soldiers) fell like leaves, for the enthusiasm of the pursuit had led them into a trap.[205]

In view of the fatal policy, General Wilson issued orders that 'in future our position should be, as far as possible, purely defensive, ... no attempt was to be made to follow' the rebels. Gen. Wilson also explained this terrible phenomenon to the Governor-General in these words perhaps to give him some idea as to what dangerous state of affairs he was facing:

> *The force under my command is, he said, and has been since the day we took our position, actually besieged by the mutineers, who, from the immense extent of suburbs and gardens extending nearly to the walls of the town, have such cover for their attacks that it has been very difficult to repel them and at the same time to inflict such a loss as would deter a repetition of them* (emphasis added). They have frequently been driven back with loss, but they immediately take refuge under the grape of their heavy guns on the city walls, and on our retirement, reoccupied their former positions; every such attack upon them has entailed a heavy loss upon our troops, which we can ill spare and has done as little good.[206]

Attacking Delhi and taking it was, he further added, not a child's play as he (the Governor-General) thought. 'The city is seven miles in circumference', he said,

> ... garrisoned by full 40,000 soldiers, armed and disciplined by ourselves, with 114 pieces of heavy artillery mounted on the walls, with the largest magazine of shot, shell, and ammunition at their disposal, besides some 60 pieces of field artillery, all of our manufacture, and manned by artillery men drilled and taught by ourselves; that the fort itself has been made so strong by perfect flanking defences erected by our own engineers, and a glacis which prevents our guns breaking the walls lower than eight feet from the top, without the labour of a regular siege and sap – for which the

205 Leasor, *op. cit.*, pp. 192–93.
206 Wilson to Canning, 20 August 1857, cited in Kaye and Malleson, *op. cit.*, vol. 4, pp. 2–3 (f.n.).

> force and artillery sent against it has been quite inadequate; that an attempt to blow in the gates and escalade the walls was twice contemplated, but that it was considered from the state of preparation against such attacks on the part of the rebels, such an attempt invariably had failed and have caused the most irreparable disaster to our cause; and their disposable for the attack would have been most certainly lost in the numerous streets of so large a city and have been cut to pieces.[207]

He would not move, the General told the Governor-General in no uncertain terms, till such time that reinforcements, guns, ammunition, etc. reached in good numbers. He would rather stay put at the Ridge. The sepoys, however, continued their business 'a war of guerrilla ambush fought under blinding sun, from behind clumps of spear grass and old stone walls'.[208]

This situation remained by and large in vogue, with some small aberrations here and there, till mid-August. But after that it started changing at a fast pace, especially after the siege trains and troops from Punjab arrived, which made substantial addition to their strength in terms of numbers,[209] arms, and ammunition.[210] Their most 'exiting and inspiring asset' was, however, a 34-year old man, newly promoted Brig.-Gen. John Nicholson,[211] head of the Punjab Moveable Column (1857), although, as facts stood, he hardly had any sparkling military credentials. In fact, he had, says Richard Collier 'seen little soldiering. Primarily a political officer, his promotion over the heads of his seniors had earned him the nickname '*Mr.* Nicholson; wise men levelled such gibes behind his back'.[212] But men in the camp, who were

207 *Ibid.*

208 Collier, *op. cit.*, p. 194.

209 Their strength, as on 2 September 1857, was as follows: Europeans: 3,890, and Indians: 4,895. The former were also aided by Kashmir State force: 2,200. For details, see S.A.A. Rizvi, *1857: Swatantra Dilli*, Lucknow, 1957, p. 189.

210 The siege trains carried the following 'heaviest metal' from Ferozepur and Philour magazines: 24-pounder guns: 6, 18-pounders: 8, 8-inch howitzers: 4, with 10,000 rounds of ammunition per piece for the former, and 10-inch mortars: 4 and 1,000 rounds to each, in addition to what was supplied earlier for the latter. The total amount of metal and ammunition supplied from the Philour magazine was '50 pieces of ordinance of various sizes, with 80,000 rounds of shot and shell, and nearly 500,000 pounds of powder; 5,000 muskets, and nearly 300,000 rounds of balled cartridges,' etc. From Ferozepur; the entire supply passed down to the camp exceeded 2,000 cartloads. The length of the siege train carrying the metal exceeded 13 miles of road'. See Cave-Browne, *op. cit.*, vol. 2, pp. 125–26.

211 Nicholson's Punjab colleague, Brigadier Neville Chamberlain, thought, for instance, that Nicholson 'ought to be worth a thousand to us', for 'with our present chief I see no chance of taking Delhi'. See Leasor, *op. cit.*, p. 170.

212 Collier, *op. cit.*, pp. 198–99. The author is right: Nicholson's army career was just ordinary: his first experience of army life in the field during the First Afghan War had landed

constantly losing their officers and other ranks to the sorties of the enemy, burning sun, deadly cholera, and so forth[213] because of the 'no-offence-but-defence' policy of Gen. Wilson, saw a ray of hope in Nicholson, who, they knew, was uncalculating, rash, aggressive, racist, and wanted to take Delhi without any delay whatever the costs or consequences.

Unsurprisingly, the demand for taking the city by *coup de main* became shriller after Nicholson's coming. Serious preparations began to be made on almost every front for the final assault. Breathing the new inspiring air, most people were convinced that 'another week would see them inside the city and the mutiny at an end'.[214] Perhaps Gen. Wilson was the only odd man out in the crowd who thought differently: he became a nervous wreck. 'Within his tent', says Collier,

> he trembled on the brink of tears. Beset by a growing fear that his brain was giving way, he had in the ten days before the final siege train arrived, bombarded Baird Smith (at the ridge, just very near him) with fully sixty letters.[215]

But on 4 September, his nerves were calmed – only a bit when the much awaited reinforcement came from Punjab ('the last succours' – John Lawrence), followed by a force from Meerut on the 6th, a contingent from Kashmir on the 8th, raising the total strength of the Field Force to 12,588 (3,766 Europeans and the rest Indians).[216]

The pro-attack party asked the General: what now? Baird-Smith, the Chief Engineer, put a plan of action before him, and urged him to act at once. Brig. Chamberlain, the Adjut. Gen. advised him to accept the proposal. Brig. Gen. Nicholson, who held the General in very poor light – 'I have seen lots of useless generals in my day; but such an ignorant croaking

him in jail (1842). In the Sutlej Campaign, he served with commissary. He only saw active field service for some months during the Second Sikh War, which was less of a military affair and more a game of treachery, deceit, and deception. As head of the Punjab Moveable Column during the Rebellion, his only 'remarkable contribution' was disarming of regiments, neutralization of their unarmed 'captive', ill-armed associates at some places, and killing, most ruthlessly, hundreds of civilians on the way to Delhi. Yet the bloodthirst of the 'Saint Nikkul Syne', called 'Strong, Silent God's Englishman', was not quenched. He wanted more. In every Indian he met on the way, he saw a murderer of women and children, and said, 'If I had them in my power today, and knew that I were to die tomorrow, I would inflict the most excruciating tortures I could think of on them with a perfectly easy conscience'. Kaye's quote, cited in Thompson, *op. cit.*, p. 44.

213 The forces at the Ridge lost to sun, stress, and cholera, according to Chief Engineer Baird-Smith, 'about 30/40 men every day'.

214 Leasor, *op. cit.*, pp. 171–72.

215 Collier, *op. cit.*, p. 248.

216 The figures are from Griffiths, *op. cit.*, p. 85.

obstructive as he is, I have hitherto never met' – was now determined to see him off his way if he still dug his heels.[217] However, the ugly situation did not arise – the General bent down under the pressure.[218]

Wilson, no doubt, gave consent to the Chief Engineer's proposal, as Nicholson says, but it was a 'qualified consent': he threw upon the Chief Engineer's shoulders 'the responsibility for the assault whose outcome, in his views, was doubtful', in the following words:

> It is evident to me that the results of the proposed operations will be thrown on the hazard of a dice, but under the circumstances in which I am placed, I am willing to try this hazard – the more so as I cannot suggest any other plan to meet our difficulties. I cannot, however, help being of opinion that the chances of success under such a heavy fire as the working parties will be opposed to, are anything but favourable. I yield, however, to the judgment of the Chief Engineer – A.W.[219]

Now the assault being a certainty, great preparations began to be made. According to Baird-Smith's plan, the city was to be attacked at its northern front formed by the Mori Gate, Kashmiri Gate, and the Water Bastions, with their 'connecting curtains' which was, relatively, less strong than the other gates. Four batteries were constructed to give safe cover to the heavy guns and gunners:

> The first, having 10 heavy guns and mortars, was set up at about 700 yards from the Mori Gate, the second, near Ludlow Castle, having 19 pieces of artillery, stood at a distance of 600 yards from the walls; the third, having six guns, was located at 180 yards from the water Bastion; and the fourth, having 10 heavy mortars, was located near the Kashmiri Gate.[220]

The entire assaulting force was divided into five columns: the First Column being led by Brig. Gen. Nicholson, the Second Column by Brig. Jones, the Third Column by Col. Campbell, the Fourth Column by Maj. Reid., and

217 Cited in Saul David, *The Indian Mutiny*, London, 2002, p. 293.

218 Pleased with the development, Nicholson, wrote to John Lawrence on 11 September: 'Fortunately, after making all kinds of objections and obstructions, and even threatening more than once to withdraw the guns and abandon the attempt, Wilson has made everything over to the Engineers.' Had the General carried out his threat of withdrawing the guns,' Nicholson added, 'he was quite prepared to appeal to the Army to set him aside and elect a successor'. Kaye, *op. cit.*, vol. 3, p. 550.

219 *Ibid.*, p. 553.

220 For details, see Kaye and Malleson, *op. cit.*, vol. 4, pp. 19–21.

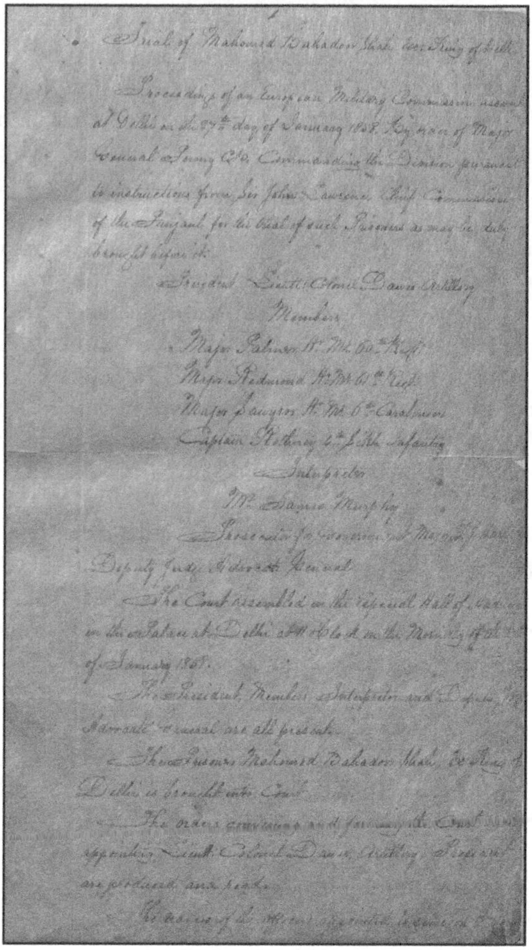
Trial of Mahomed Bahadur Shah Ex-King of Delhi

Proceedings of an European Military Commission assembled at Delhi on the 27th day of January 1858. By order of Major General Penny C.B., Commanding the Division pursuant to instructions from Sir John Lawrence Chief Commissioner of the Punjaub for the trial of such Prisoners as may be duly brought before it.

President Lieutt. Colonel Dawes Artillery

Members

Major Palmer H.M. 60th Rifles

Major Redmond H.M. 61st Regt.

Major Sawyer H.M. 6th Carabiniers

Captain Rothney 4th Sikh Infantry

Interpreter

Mr. James Murphy

Prosecutor for Government Major [illegible] Deputy Judge Advocate General

The Court assembled in the [illegible] Hall of [illegible] in the Palace at Delhi at 11 O'clock on the Morning of the 27th of January 1858.

The President, Members, Interpreter and Deputy Judge Advocate General are all present.

The Prisoner Mohomed Bahadur Shah, Ex-King of Delhi is brought into Court.

The orders convening and [illegible] the Court appointing Lieutt. Colonel Dawes, Artillery, President are produced and read.

[illegible]

Illustration 1.1a Facsimile copy of the handwritten proceedings of the trial. ©DA, Delhi, pp. 1–3 and last page, with permission.

the Fifth (Reserve) Column by Brig. Longfield.[221] The columns were to work under overall command of Brig.-Gen. Nicholson. Thus, everything was finally ready for the D Day – to be announced later.

What about the other side? They were also not sitting idle. Fortunately, they had a Chief Engineer, who was as good as the best on the other side, named Muhammad Ali Khan.[222] He got trenches dug at the strategic points

221 Griffiths, *op. cit.*, pp. 92–93.

222 Muhammad Ali Khan was a scion of a *talukdar* family of Rampur. Having passed out from the Roorki Engineering College, he joined the East India Company service as an Engineer.

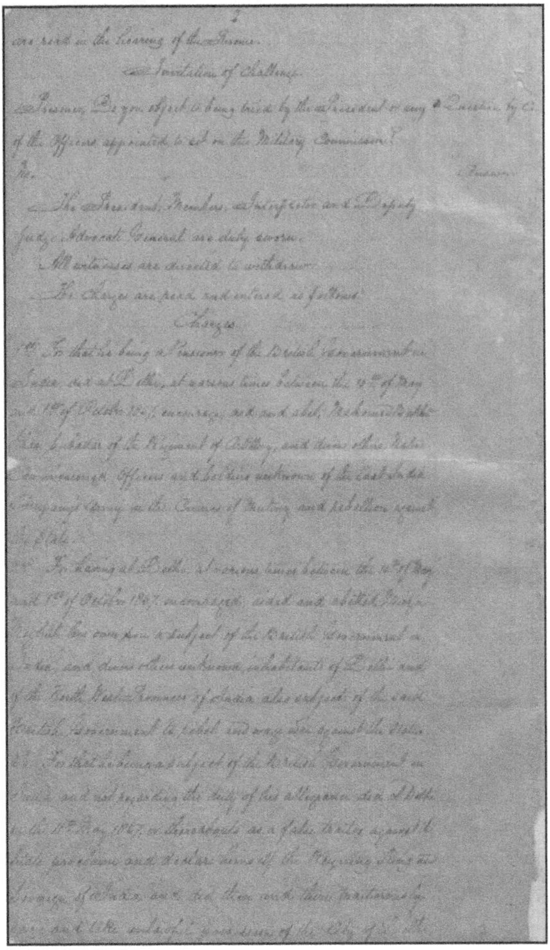
are read in the hearing of the Prisoner.

Invitation of Challenge.

Prisoner, Do you object to being tried by the President or any of the Officers appointed to sit on the Military Commission? — Question by C.

No. — Answer.

The President, Members, Interpreter and Deputy Judge Advocate General are duly sworn.

All witnesses are directed to withdraw.

The Charges are read and entered as follows

Charges

1st. For that he being a Pensioner of the British Government in India, did at Delhi, at various times between the 11th of May and 1st of October 1857, encourage, aid and abet, Mahomed Bukht Khan, Subadar of the Regiment of Artillery, and divers other Native Commissioned Officers and soldiers unknown of the East India Company's Army in the Crimes of Mutiny and Rebellion against the State.

2nd. For having at Delhi at various times between the 11th of May and 1st of October 1857, encouraged, aided and abetted Mirza Moghul, his own son, a subject of the British Government in India, and divers others unknown inhabitants of Delhi and of the North West Provinces of India also subjects of the said British Government to rebel and wage war against the State.

3rd. For that he being a subject of the British Government in India and not regarding the duty of his allegiance did at Delhi on the 11th May 1857, or thereabouts as a false traitor against the State proclaim and declare himself the Reigning King and Sovereign of India and did then and there traitorously [illegible] and take unlawful possession of the City of Delhi

Illustration 1.1b Facsimile copy of the handwritten proceedings of the trial. ©DA, Delhi, pp. 1–3 and last page, with permission.

Experiencing racial maltreatment at the hands of the British officers – even his juniors – he resigned. He went to England, first as Secretary to Maharaja Jung Bahadur of Nepal, and later to plead Nana Saheb's case with Azimullah Khan, visited the Crimean war fields where he saw the British troops receiving beating at the hands of Russians. He decided then and there to see that the story is repeated in India as well. He joined the rebel forces at Bareilly as Chief Engineer and came to Delhi with Bakht Khan. Here he held the same post. The arrangements, given below, were made by him to check the British onslaught. But for these, the British would have experienced an easy walk over as they did in 1803. After the fall of Delhi, he went to Lucknow and served as Chief Engineer there also. But for his defensive arrangements, Lucknow would have also fallen soon. For his life, achievements, and tragic end at the gallows, see K.C. Yadav, ed., *1857: Mohammad Ali Khan*, Gurgaon, 2008.

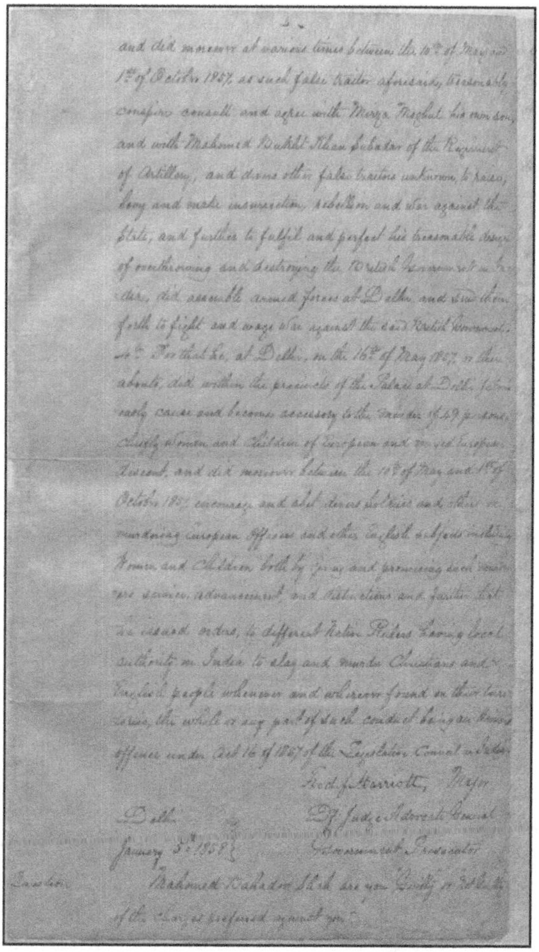

and did moreover at various times between the 10th of May and 1st of October 1857, as such false traitor aforesaid, treasonably conspire consult and agree with Mirza Moghul his own son, and with Mahomed Bukht Khan Subadar of the Regiment of Artillery, and divers other false traitors unknown, to raise, levy and make insurrection, rebellion and war against the State, and further to fulfil and perfect his treasonable design of overthrowing and destroying the British Government in India, did assemble armed forces at Delhi and send them forth to fight and wage war against the said British Government.

4th For that he, at Delhi, on the 16th of May 1857, or thereabouts, did within the precincts of the Palace at Delhi, feloniously cause and become accessory to the murder of 49 persons, chiefly women and children of European and mixed European descent, and did moreover between the 10th of May and 1st of October 1857, encourage and abet divers soldiers and others in murdering European officers and other English subjects including women and children both by [illegible] and promising such murderers service, advancement and distinctions and further that he issued orders, to different Native Rulers having local authority in India to slay and murder Christians and English people whenever and wherever found on their territories, the whole or any part of such conduct being an heinous offence under Act 16 of 1857 of the Legislative Council in India.

Fredk. J. Harriott, Major
Dy. Judge Advocate General
Government Prosecutor

Delhi
January 5th 1858

Translation
Mahomed Bahadur Shah are you Guilty or Not Guilty of the charges preferred against you?

Illustration 1.1c Facsimile copy of the handwritten proceedings of the trial. ©DA, Delhi, pp. 1–3 and last page, with permission.

outside the walls for the musket men, and posted a large number of them on the ramparts, walls, and breach tops on which over 50 heavy guns were also mounted. The batteries were constructed at several places, breast works were erected at important strategic points, and troops were laid, to make the enemy enter them to die at their hands.

The Emperor was apprised of the latest position of the enemy, and the action being taken by his troops to fight them by Gen. Bakht Khan.[223]

223 See Husain, *op. cit.*, pp. 269–71.

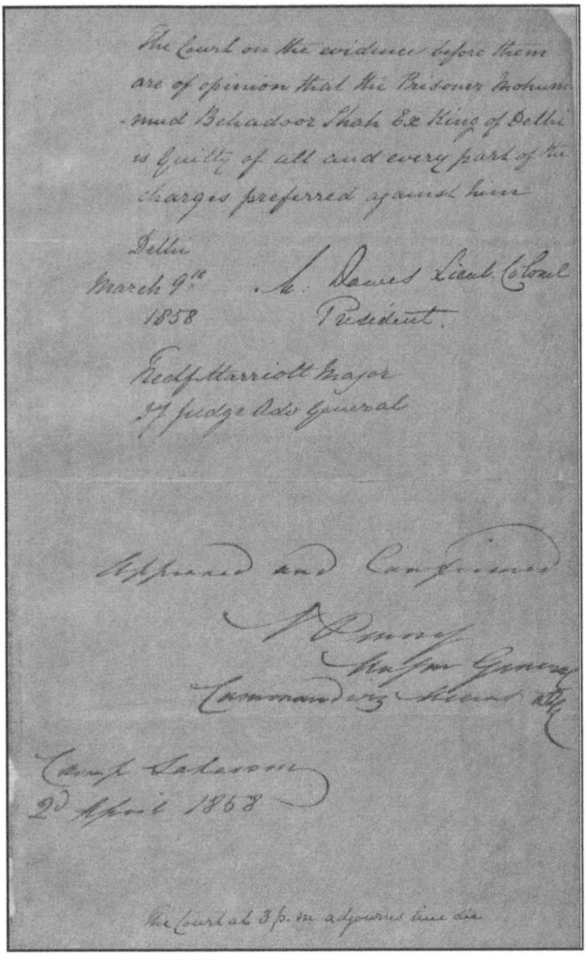

The Court on the evidence before them
are of opinion that the Prisoner Mohum-
-mud Behadoor Shah Ex King of Delhi
is Guilty of all and every part of the
charges preferred against him

Delhi
March 9th
1858

M. Dawes Lieut. Colonel
President.

Fredk Harriott Major
Dy Judge Adv General

Approved and Confirmed

Major General
Commanding

2d April 1858

The Court at 3 p.m. adjourns sine die

Illustration 1.1a–d Facsimile copy of the handwritten proceedings of the trial. ©DA, Delhi, pp. 1–3 and last page, with permission.

The Emperor found his statement long on rhetoric and less in substance and instead of taking him in, he asked all the regiments directly to 'show their mettle and die fighting at their posts'.[224] After two days, realizing the seriousness of the situation, the Emperor ordered that

> every adult whether Hindu or Musalman in the King's service or out of his service, a resident of the city or visitor, should go out and attack the English. All plunder after the victory, except arms and

224 *Delhi News*, 6 September 1857.

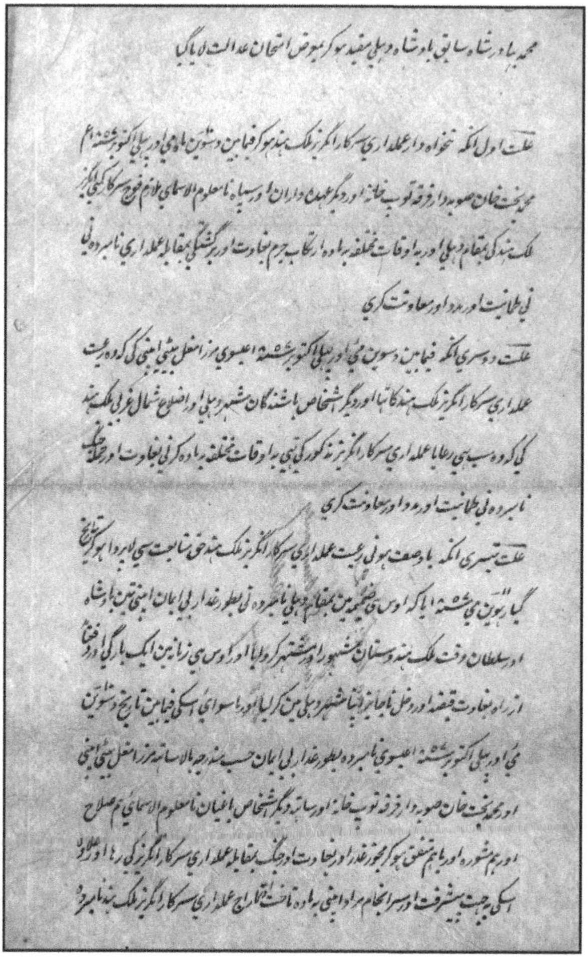
محمد بہادر شاہ سابق بادشاہ دہلی مقید ہو کر بعوض امتحان عدالت لایا گیا

Illustration 1.2a Facsimile copy of the Urdu translation of the 'Chargesheet' which was given to the Emperor 20 days before the trial commenced. *Source:* ©DA, with permission.

> ammunition, is to belong to the captors. Let everyone strive his best, as his eternal and temporal interests depend upon his exertions.

He who 'wilfully neglects his duty', the Emperor warned, 'will be considered an enemy of the Government'.[225] Thus, both Army and the civil society were readied to fight the enemy assault when it came.

225 *Ibid.*, 9 September 1857.

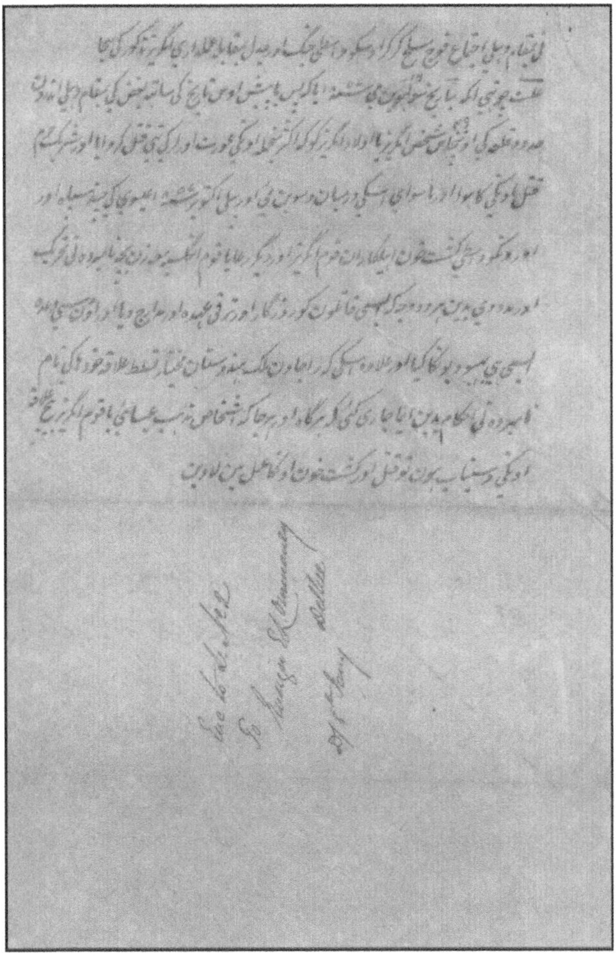

Illustration 1.2b Facsimile copy of the Urdu translation of the 'Chargesheet' which was given to the Emperor 20 days before the trial commenced. *Source:* ©DA, with permission.

After their batteries were complete in all respect (6 September), the British Artillery came into action: 'Fifty guns and mortars were now pouring shot and shell on the city bastions and walls'.[226] The Indians gave befitting reply:[227] they killed and wounded their 350 men, and caused great loss to their Battery No. 2; other batteries received minor hurts. Next day, they adopted their old

226 Griffiths, *op. cit.*, p. 89.

227 Jiwan Lal says, 'Throughout the day and night the artillery fire was constant, canon answering canon'. Metcalfe, ed., *Two Native Narratives*, p. 48.

Picture 1 Emperor Muhammad Bahadur Shah II (1775–1862), the last Mughal Emperor.

Picture 2 Begum Zeenat Mahal (1823–1886), favourite wife of the Emperor. Both the miniatures, by an unknown Indian artist, were originally attached to a bracelet which was presented to Lady Henry Lawrence by Maharaja Ranjit Singh. *Source:* © NAM, London, ooc.

Picture 3 Prince Mirza Mughal (1828–1857) – Governor-General, Delhi, 1857. *Source:* Courtesy D.A., Delhi.

Picture 4 Prince Jawan Bakht (1841–1884), whose blind love led his mother, Begum Zeenat Mahal, astray in 1857. *Source:* https:// commons.wikiindia.org, wiki/File:Prince Mirza Bakht.

Picture 5 Sir John Lawrence (1811–1879) – Chief Commissioner, Punjab. *Source:* Bosworth Smith, *Life of Lord Lawrence*, London, 1883.

Picture 6 Maj. Gen. Archadale Wilson (1803–1874) – Commanding, Delhi Field Force, 1857. *Source:* E.H. Nolan, *The Illustrated History of British Empire and the East*, London, 1878(?).

Picture 7 Brig. Gen. John Nicholson (1821–1857), later killed by rebels in Delhi. *Source:* F.M. Fredrick Roberts, *Forty-one Years in India*, London, 1897.

Picture 8 Capt. W.S.R. Hodson (1821–1857), who 'captured' (read 'abducted') the Emperor. *Source:* ©NAM, London, ooc.

Picture 9 'Capture of the Emperor of Delhi'. 'Capture' of the King of Delhi by Hodson. The depiction is wrong on several counts. Firstly, the Emperor was not captured, but he had surrendered on his own volition. Secondly, even if we accept Hodson's version, the Emperor came out in a palanquin and not on foot. Here a man has caught the king by hand and two princes standing behind him are held tight by someone. The Emperor did not dismount the palanquin and no prince accompanied him or was arrested that day. The Emperor was closely followed by Begum Zeenat Mahal in another palanquin which is nowhere around here. Coloured litho by William Sampson et al. after G.F. Atkinson. *Source:* ©Anne SK. Brown Military Collection, Brown University Library, used with their permission.

technique: emerging from the Lahori and Ajmeri Gates, they reached the rear of the enemy camp, hit hard, and ran away, suffering 30 casualties. How much loss the enemy suffered is not mentioned.[228]

In the evening, Wilson held a War Council meeting, discussed the modalities of the attack, and assigned their tasks to the assaulting columns: the first was to attack the breach at the Kashmiri Gate; the second, the beach near the Water Bastion; the third, the Kashmiri Gate after it was blown by engineers; and the fourth was to cover the advance of the First Column and form the reserve.[229]

On the night of the 13–14 September, Gen. Wilson gave the much awaited order to the troops to attack the city with a prodigious force at 3 a.m. Almost all the officers and men received the order with great joy, but as the actual meaning of entering the 'valley of death' sank in after some time, enthusiasm of most of them, if not all, began to water down by a strange

228 *Ibid.*
229 *Ibid.*, p. 49.

Picture 10 Murder of princes by Hodson. Cold-blooded murder of Princes Mirza Mughal, Khizr Sultan (Emperor's sons), and Abu Bakr (grandson), Delhi, 22 September 1857, by Capt. Hodson. Coloured litho by William Sampson et al. after G.F. Atkinson. The depiction is absolutely wrong. Hodson had not shot the princes from horseback but at point-blank range standing close to them. They were not wearing clothes at the time of murder. Hodson had stripped them naked, taking their ornaments and swords, and threw them to rot. *Source:* ©NAM, London, ooc.

mix of anxiety, panic, and confusion. And it was perhaps the reason that they could fall in for the task only after the day break.[230] Nicholson, the Chief Commander, gave signal to the columns 'to advance to cross the ditch at different points by the aid of scaling ladders, to clear the outer defences of the city, taking possession of all bastions, guns, and gateways, and establishing defensible posts'. After this, the columns were advised

> to clear the streets of the city. ... The roads to the Palace and Salimghur (Salimgarh) having been rendered practicable, a vigorous bombardment of those places was to be undertaken with the least possible delay, every available mortar being conveyed into the city and placed in the magazine or other suitable position.[231]

230 Though some other reasons are given by some writers for the delay, the above seems to be more plausible.

231 Kaye, *op. cit.*, vol. 3, pp. 589–90.

Picture 11 Perhaps the last photograph, taken by an unknown photographer, of the Emperor Bahadur Shah in prison in Rangoon (Burma). *Source:* ©NAM, London, ooc.

Though they found it difficult to calculate, in exact terms, how much time would it take to accomplish the above tasks, many of them strongly believed that

> much might be done on the first day; as the enemy, panic-struck and confused, dreading the terrible retribution which could descend upon them, might betake themselves to sudden flight and clear the way for the advance of the English.[232]

232 *Ibid.* The young Fred. Roberts, now Quarter Master-General, believed that 'on the morning of the 12th (September) *at the latest* (emphasis his), Delhi will, with God's help, be ours. The city was taken by us for the first time on the 11th September, 1803, we may perhaps manage to come to time in '57'. Roberts to his mother, Delhi, 7 September, in his *Letters Written during the Mutiny*, Delhi, rep. 1979, p. 54.

To the disappointment and shock of the forecasters, however, this did not happen. Delhi proved a far harder nut to crack than they had anticipated. As the columns advanced and reached near their targets, they began to meet aggressively stiff opposition from the defenders.

The first taste of the coming catastrophe was experienced by the First Column led by Nicholson himself when, with the Second Column, he led the left attack. As they reached near the moat, a hail storm of fire from the defenders let the hell lose on them. The men fell like weathered leaves from an autumn tree – 100 were dead within ten minutes.[233] It must, however, be said to their credit that after sacrificing many other lives, they got some success in crossing the moat and sealing the wall. But the entire affair affected the nerves of the men to such an extent that they lost the 'sense of time and direction'. Even Nicholson, and several other men in command took wrong turns and instead of going north moved south.

About this moment, Nicholson saw terrific firing coming from the Lahori Gate. Having collected a force, rather 'a mere rabble', as Kaye says, made of 'officers without their men and men without their officers',[234] he advanced to take the Gate. Nichloson, it should be remembered, was no Anson, Barnard, or Wilson. He was essentially, as indicated above, a 'political officer', who had acquired, for no professional reasons, a larger-than-life stature somehow as a General,[235] and surprisingly, had overshadowed everyone, even Gen. Wilson, after landing in the camp. The present offensive proves the point to the hilt.

Without taking proper stock of the ground realities, existence of barricades, masked batteries, and the skilled marksmen (sepoys) and civilian fighters positioned in long narrow lanes, Nicholson pushed the troops forward.[236] After reaching Kabuli Gate, he moved towards his target. He had by now, says Leasor, 'his eight officers and 60 men either killed or wounded'.[237] Yet he marched on. When he had gone only a small distance, there came 'the terrible barrage from an unseen enemy behind wall turrets, window shutters and roof parapets'. To save themselves from sure death, the troops inched

233 Collier, *op. cit.*, p. 253.

234 Kaye, *op. cit.*, vol. 3, p. 597. Fred Roberts says that 'The first day all was confusion. Soldiers lost their Regiments in the streets'. See his *Letters*, p. 59.

235 Nicholson had no war experience as the other Generals had. He had simply hunted the fugitive sepoys, mostly unarmed or ill-armed, during the Rebellion in Punjab, as seen above, but had no experience of leading his men to battles. What about Najafgarh soon after coming to Delhi? Didn't he fight a pitched battle there? No, says Mahdi Husain, 'since it was mere a surprise and no pitched fighting, it would be perhaps better to call it action instead of battle'. Husain, *op. cit.*, p. 251 (f.n.). But in the contemporary accounts, and even in later ones, he has been shown as a great General.

236 Kaye has stated these facts, but not with a historian's straightforwardness. See Kaye, *op. cit.*, vol. 3, p. 597.

237 Leasor, *op. cit.*, p. 311.

into a lane. But this was like falling from a frying pan into the fire. As a result, says Collier, 'panic animated uncontrollable, swept every man. Eyes dilated, breath sobbing from their lungs, they surged like frightened cattle in head long retreat'.[238] Nicholson, who was at the trail of the formation, stopped them, and pushing some at the right and others at the left, he, mad with rage, rushed forward waving his naked sword over his head, yelling on them, as was his wont, a racist taunt – '*Come on, men! Come on, you fools. I never should have thought that Europeans would quail before heathens. Come on you ...*' (emphasis added),[239] but before he could complete the sentence, a marksman, Kale Khan, shot him down, breaking his ribs and puncturing one of his lungs badly. It was a fatal blow.[240] The Fusiliers had many officers and others killed in the course of a few minutes. To avoid complete rout, the only course left with them was to flee for their life.

There is a generally accepted view that it was the great quality of a death-defying bravery that cost Nicholson his life. Nicholson was, no doubt, a brave man, but the cause of his death was not his bravery, but bare rashness. Worse, his men did not obey his orders to march to what they knew was a death 'trap'. A good General would have seen it before his men saw it. Perhaps he had thought that if he entered the trap, his men would follow him. But none came forward, and left him alone to face the music. He was also weak at reading his people's mind.

This was not a single example of the British soldiers disobeying their officers in Delhi. There were many other such instances which made Hodson to react: '*I grieve to say (that) for the first time in my life, I have had to see English soldiers refuse repeatedly to follow their officers. Grenville, Jacob, Nicholson, and Speke were all sacrificed to this* (emphasis added)'.[241]

To resume the story: the Fourth Column, led by Maj. Reid, did rather worse. Following the order 'to clear the suburbs of Kishanganj (and) enter the city through Lahori Gate, he started well'. Being an experienced soldier, 'his strategy, his tactics worked wonders'. But only for a short while. When

238 Collier, *op. cit.*, p. 258.

239 *Ibid.*

240 An aside: there was a stark weakness in Nicholson's character. He was a loner, and not a team man. Though a very popular man in general estimation (and in writers' accounts), he was, because of this trait, not liked by his immediate seniors (e.g., John Lawrence whom he called, out of hatred, 'an old woman', and Wilson a most 'useless general'). Worse, because of his haughty disposition, he had alienated his juniors (soldiers and subaltern officers) to such an extent that on 14 September, they did not obey his orders to advance, but left him to go alone to die. There was no change in his attitude even after being fatally wounded. To the soldiers who rushed to take him to a safer corner, he announced that 'the men who would not follow me, shall not lift me', he said, 'from the ground' (Collier, *op. cit.*, p. 258). They left him to the care of two doly-bearers who also ran away after a while. Lieut. Roberts sent him to hospital where he died a slow death on 23 September. *Ibid.*

241 See Hodson, *op. cit.*, p. 296.

he had hardly measured a small distance, the enemy checked him. 'The native officers rode in among the ranks of the mutineers', says Chamberlain, the Adj. General who was watching the scene from a distance, 'urging them and leading them on to the battle against the British'. The civilians stood by them. There was torrential rain of bullets from all sides, and Reid's strong force began to crack. The Kashmir Contingent was the first to run away. The Sirmor Contingent (mostly Gurkhas) followed the suit, leaving 40 of their dead men behind. Reid was hit on the head and collapsed (but not dead). Many others met the same fate. The entire force retreated. Kaye, reading the military reports and other accounts of the day before him, could not help saying, 'The enemy (Indians) fought well – never better than on this occasion'.[242]

On the other side, the Kashmiri Gate affair was equally perilous. The heavy bombardment from ten heavy guns breached the Gate, but not fully – only a small part of it was gone. Reaching near it, however, proved to be a costly job. Many lives were lost on the way. Further on, in blowing the massive timber gate, two men died but the third daredevil succeeded. Almost every writer has said that mad with joy, the Third Column and reserve men rushed to enter into the city. Truth, however, is a little different: the very thought of entering into the city seems to have unnerved the British soldiers. Sergeant John Smith, before whose very eyes everything happened, says that 'the bugler had sounded at least fifty times' to make them move.[243]

Their onward journey was almost uneventful as long as they did not reach about 100 yards short of the great Jama Masjid. But that was the dead end. The Emperor had asked the citizens of Delhi, both Hindus and Muslims, a day before the attack, to come out in numbers to fight their enemy. As a result, thousands turned up. There was a hand-to-hand fight between the British troops and the sepoys and the civilians, wielding *lathi* (stick), *danda* (short stick, not *broken lathi* as some writers have translated it), sword, etc. The British suffered considerable losses. Not getting support from any other side, especially the First and the Second Columns, that were detailed for the task, Brig. Compbell decided, much against his wishes, to retreat. But even that was no easy thing: the enemy was constantly firing upon them from all sides. Dodging them somehow, the column sustaining losses on the way, here and there, managed to reach Begum Bagh. The Bagh was considered a better place for the camp. But that was not to be: the moment they touched the Bagh, they 'faced an even hotter fire from houses directly opposite. Suffering some losses here too, they left the place and ran fast to reach the Church, half a mile away'.[244]

242 See, for details, Kaye, *op. cit.*, vol. 3, pp. 604–11.
243 Sergeant John Smith's note on the 'Explosion of the Cashmere Gate', cited in Kaye, *op. cit.*, vol. 3, p. 675.
244 For details, see Kaye, *op. cit.*, vol. 3, pp. 603–4; Leasor, *op. cit.*, pp. 308–10.

It should have been, on the whole, a day of disappointment to the English, especially so, when they were hearing from their leadership, both civilian and military, barring some loners (read realists) like Gen. Wilson, every now and then that Delhi would fall at their first knock. But after suffering huge losses they were, by the evening, again back to square one. The word of their 'set back, retreat and failure went round from unit to unit; and it seemed clear (to one and all) that the attackers could press no further forward that day'.[245]

After the fighting ceased and the columns returned to their resting places, a hurried calculation of the gains and losses was made. By a rough estimate: they had been able to gain 'a portion of the walls of Delhi' (Forrest) at the following cost – 'Europeans: 8 officers killed, 52 wounded. Rank and file: 162 killed and 510 wounded. Natives: 103 killed and 310 wounded' Roughly, about 'two men in nine were killed or wounded'.[246] A careful reading of the day's proceedings, sometimes even between the lines, shows however, that the figures are underdrawn. The losses were more. Compared to them, loss of their enemy was, owing to their better location, much less.

The worst thing was that soldiers were, says Kaye, 'much exhausted by fatigue and much depressed by the mortality that surrounded them. They saw the dead gathered up and the dying carried of ... to hospitals in the camp'.[247] Where there were no rooms for such a large number, they were laid on the floor

> on the heaps of the straw on the ground. The straw was running with blood. On verandahs, on rough wooden tables, other soldiers lay with uniform torn, sodden with blood, and crawling with flies, all waiting their turn to go to the operating table. Surgeons, and even their apothecaries were pressed into service for the many amputations. Bearers ran in and out carrying away arms and legs. ... All round the hospital the earth was trodden into a mud reddened with blood that stank and steamed as the sun warmed it. Vultures and other carrion birds wheeled round the sky in wide, cautious sweeps, settling on the roof of the hospital ... greedy for its fruits.[248]

The horror of the scene depressed the soldiers beyond imagination. On the other side, Gen. Wilson was in a 'wretched state'. His nerves failed him. He

245 Leasor, *op. cit.*, p. 311.

246 Kaye, *op. cit.*, vol. 3, p. 616 (f.n.); also see G.W. Forrest, *History of Indian Mutiny*, London, 1903, vol. 1, pp. 146–47.

247 *Ibid.*

248 Leasor, *op. cit.*, p. 319.

was not able to stand up or concentrate on anything and in that hopeless state of mind, the only way he could think of to escape complete rout was to go back to the Ridge. Wilson's plan, it is said, somehow reached the dying Nicholson. His immediate reaction, they say, was 'Thank God, I have strength yet to shoot him, if necessary'.[249] With ruptured lung and serious injuries which led to profuse inner bleeding, I doubt he was left with any strength by then to do the daring deed.

Surprisingly, Gen. Wilson, who had 'made arrangements to cover the retreat of the assaulting columns', again yielded, not to Nicholson's threat, but to 'adverse councils' in his war room: he decided to go by Clive's wisdom – 'to stand still is danger; to recede is ruin' – and asked his commanders to finish the unfinished job at any cost.[250] The commanders, on their part, took full one day to collect their men, and ready them for action. To their surprise, however, they were still tired, exhausted, and somewhat frightened. But on the 16th, a relieving tiding reached them – on the 15th night, 'the enemy had evacuated Kishanganj', which was, a day before, a theatre of one of their most unsuccessful operations in their annals of the Rebellion. Next day, they found the field waiting for them. They could capture the magazine, containing 'immense supply of ordinance stores very cheaply' – only three persons wounded. Surprisingly, Gen. Wilson was still not out of depression, or say the fear of the street fighting. Writing on 16 September (2 p.m.), he said:

> This advances us a little, but it is dreadful slow work. Our force is too weak for the street fighting, when we have to gain our way inch by inch. ... We have a long and hard struggle before us.[251]

The developments of the very next day (17 September) proved that the General was right: the British forces launched a forceful attack to clear the streets leading to the Fort – the Palace, to be precise. But 'in almost every instance', says Kaye,

> they had been repulsed. ... The Magazine and bank had been captured and occupied. But the Lahore Bastion was still in the enemy's hands. And his men were in no mood to risk their lives that had been saved in the last bloody fight by a whisker, to take it.[252]

The same story was repeated, to every commander's dismay, the next day – 18 September. The fighting of the whole day resulted in almost in a naught.

249 Collier, *op. cit.*, p. 260.
250 Kaye, *op. cit.*, vol. 3, p. 620.
251 *Ibid.*, pp. 621–22. The sepoys had, perhaps for strategic reasons, left the Kishanganj area to take position on the second line of defence, the Chandni Chowk–Lahori Gate, region.
252 *Ibid.*, pp. 625–26.

A little early in the day, they had succeeded in capturing the Lahori Bastion, but so great was the fear of the enemy attack to recover it that they left it to them without an opposition.[253] At another hour, another assault was made after serious planning by Col. Edward Greathed and the engineers, on the Lahori Gate itself, which still stood intact teasing them. Greathed proceeded smoothly up to a good distance. But the moment he reached the outer Gate of Chandni Chowk, the defenders flung it open, and rained torrential fire from a six-pounder and other weapons on them, causing a substantial loss. Greathed ordered the men of the 75th to 'charge under the cover of the smoke, when the gun should be fired'. But to no avail – 'the 75th did not charge'. The 8th Regiment was then ordered to the front. But 'they also refused to charge'. Thus, 'the Artillery (English) were left to be fired at by the insurgents who', says Kaye, 'exhibited more gallantry than our own people'. Greathed ordered the force to make a retreat. But, surprisingly, his men refused to retreat either. Nothing doing, they said, unless provided with safe cover. Greathed called a new contingent for the purpose, and then they agreed to move back.[254]

Having read the bad news, Gen. Wilson again developed cold feet. Writing on the 18th (afternoon), he poured out his confusion, anguish, and fear of the failure thus:

> We are still in the same position in which we were yesterday. An attempt was made this morning to take the Lahore Gate, but failed from the refusal of the European soldiers to follow their officers: One rush and it would have been done easily, but they refused to make it. The fact is our men have great dislike to street fighting ... and get a panic and will not advance. This is very sad ... disheartening. I cannot see any way out at all. If I work to attempt to push on in the city, they would be lost in such innumerable streets and masses of houses and would be annihilated or driven back. ... It has been a hard task imposed upon me, almost too hard; both (my) mind and body are giving way.[255]

On the 19th, the General was, however, a changed man – cheerful, bright, and inspirited, and wrote: 'The king evacuated the Palace yesterday afternoon with most of his followers, finding too hot to hold him; report says, very few are left in it'.[256]

253 *Ibid.*, p. 627.
254 *Ibid.*, pp. 628–29.
255 Reproduced in *ibid.*, p. 630.
256 Reproduced in *ibid.*

The General is not right: the King had not 'evacuated the palace' because the British had made it 'too hot' to hold. His own man, a 'shrewd observer', refuted him in the columns of *The Times* of 2 December 1857, thus:

> I do not think that the enemy were actually forced out by our shells. I was surprised to find that how little damage was done by them. The walls of the Palace are almost intact; so are by far the greater portions of the buildings inside; and it is quite clear that the chances were yet very much in favour of such as chose quietly to sit in them.[257]

Also his own statement, given above, when read carefully betrays the truth that his soldiers had no stomach left for the final fight. The very word 'street fighting' gave them panic and 'will not advance' to attack the palace. If still they are pushed hard, the General believed, result would be, for sure, their annihilation or retreat. In view of this, there seemed hardy any possibility of any further attack on the Emperor. If so, then a couple of questions come up: why did the sepoys, their associates, and the Emperor, suddenly left the field of action? Was it the sepoys' own decision? Or the Emperor's? Technically speaking, of neither of them. But of the 'Gang of Four' in the Royal Palace, namely Mirza Ilahi Bakhsh, Hakim Ahsanullah Khan, Mirza Ali Quli Khan, and the Emperor's favourite Queen, Zinat Mahal, who had, as seen above, long mortgaged their souls to the British for *dal–chapati*. They fed the Emperor with 'fake news' and used every instrument they could muster to break his morale. When the nut did not show any sign of cracking, they worked on his weaknesses – old age, ailments, loneliness, insecurity, etc. They, the betrayers of the salt of their master (*namakharam*), falsely, treacherously, and shamefully assured him his life, his status, his honour, and 'a dish of *pillau*', safe life, should he surrender to 'their' masters. The old man bent under the pressure.[258] Acknowledging the debt of this gang, Kaye says about its leader, Mirza Ilahi Bakhsh:

> We owed much also to a traitorous or as it was the fashion to say, a 'loyal' member of the house of Delhi, the Meerza Elahee Bukhs, who was the father-in-law of the late heir-apparent, Mirza Fakhru. This man who was said to be more 'respectable' than the majority of his kinsmen, was also more sagacious. ... Believing that the British would triumph in the end, he saw clearly that his own

257 Quoted in Martin, *op. cit.*, vol. 3, p. 444.

258 They had been playing this game for months – since mid-June, to be precise – but to no avail. Their this, last bid, however, succeeded.

> interests would be best served by covertly aiding the infidels, while assuming the part of a friendly adviser of the Mogul.[259]

When the army came to know of the Emperor's 'decision', they saw no reason to stay put there. But before leaving, Gen. Bakht Khan went to the Emperor with some other officers. The Emperor told them that when Delhi was gone what was the sense in staying here. Well then, Bakht intervened, you accompany us:

> What if Delhi is lost, still the entire country is in your hands. We will fight and win because the blessings and benedictions (*barkat*) of your name and status still inspire the people.[260]

The Emperor kept quiet, and dismissed Bakht Khan asking him to come to the Humayun's Tomb the following day for the *Answer*.

Mirza Ilahi Bakhsh, the 'traitorous', took the Emperor, after much persuasion, to his house where

> they spent the night ... (and) used all his efforts to keep the king from joining the insurgents. ... So with great effort and extreme endeavour when Bakht Khan and other chiefs of the Imperial Army met Bahadur Shah and princes at the Hoomayoon's Tomb, the Meerza (had) made so many good arrangements that neither the king nor his sons did ever listen to them, and none of them have ever gone with the officers of the ungrateful regiments.[261]

Bakht Khan and other officers were disappointed, if not shocked, and walked away.

Soon after Hodson appeared on the scene, as discussed in detail above, and made the Emperor, who was going to surrender on his own, prisoner on

259 Kaye, *op. cit.*, vol. 3, p. 644. The British rewarded Illahi Bakhsh handsomely for his treachery: see, DA, Delhi Residency Records, Mutiny Papers, File no. 692, Pol., 6 June 1860, no. 624, Pol., 11 June, 25 July, no. 219, Pol., 29 July, no. 171, Pol., 4 October, no. 70, Pol., 15 April, 1861, no. 263, Revenue, 3 October 1861; King of Delhi Series, no. 204, Revenue, 31 August 1860 (76 members of Illhai Bakhsh's family got pension.)

260 Zakaullah, *op. cit.*, vol. 2, p. 647. There are many differing accounts of this visit. But there is a sort of consensus that the Emperor wanted some time to think over the suggestion, and asked Bakht Khan to come the following day to the Humayun's Tomb to hear the *Answer*.

261 Kaye, *op. cit.*, vol. 3, p. 644. The British rewarded Ilahi Baksh handsomely for his treachery, DA, Delhi Residency Records, Mutiny Papers, File no. 692, Pol., 6 June 1860, no. 624, Pol., 11 June, no. 866, Pol. 12 July, no. 231, Pol., 17 July., no. 168, Pol., 25 July, no. 219, Pol., 29 July, no. 171, Pol. 4 Oct., no. 70, Pol 15., April 1861, no. m 1, 17 September 1861, no. 263, Revenue, 3 October 1861; King of Delhi Series, no. 204, Revenue, 31 August 1860, as many as 76 members of Ilahi Baksh's family got pension.

the outskirts of the city. Despite the promise by Hodson only a few moments before, that his honour, status, and privileges would be restored, he threatened 'to kill' the Emperor 'like a dog, if he tried to ignore his commands'. The Emperor lost no time in understanding the game, and repented over his wrong decision: 'If *I had gone with the sepoys*', he lamented brashly, '*I would have still remained a king*' (emphasis added). 'But that was not the time', says Zakaullah, 'to brood when he had already turned Bakht Khan away'.[262]

The above account shows that Bahadur Shah had provided, keeping in view the prevailing circumstances, by and large a good government to the citizens of Delhi from 12 May to 20 September 1857. The whole world saw with wide open eyes his grand stand. But, as ill luck would have it, he fell from that height on 19 September when he was about to win the war. Thanks to his nobles, relatives, and the favourite Queen, he walked into a trap where defeat, humiliation, pain, agony, disappointment, untold miseries, and sufferings received him with open arms. The misstep turned him from a hero into a non-hero and deprived him of an exalted place as a victor or a martyr in history.

The old man got the first taste of the new life after his entry into his Fort as a prisoner. There he 'was made to stand', says Mahdi Husain,

> in the midst of his blood-thirsty enemies, one of whom (a soldier), gnashing his teeth, stepped forward and struck him on thigh a blow. Seeing this an Abyssinian slave of the Emperor rushed at the assailant, and gripping him fast threw him on the ground. The faithful slave was immediately set upon and killed by other English soldiers.[263]

The Emperor was 'lodged' (read imprisoned) for some time in the *haveli* of Begam Zinat Mahal (Lal Kuan *Mohalla*) and then shifted to a humble house belonging to a *salatin*, Mirza Nazir Husain,[264] where he died a hundred deaths daily as long as he lived there. The following excerpts given below from the accounts of some of the visitors, both biased and neutral, who visited him in prison prove the point.

The first person to have visited the prisoner-Emperor (22 September) was C.J. Griffiths, whose regiment was guarding him. He found the Emperor

> sitting cross-legged on a *charpoy* in the verandah of a courtyard. ... There was nothing imposing in the appearance save long white

262 '*Is waqt Bahadur Shah ko sujhi ki agar main sepah ke sath chala jata to Badshahi karta. Magar jab woh Bakht Khan ko rukhshat kar chuka tha to ab is sochne ka waqt nahin raha tha!*' Zakaullah, *op. cit.*, p. 469.

263 Husain, *op. cit.*, p. 428.

264 *Nusratnama Government*, p. 43, cited in Parvez, *op. cit.*, p. 122.

> beard which reached to his girdle. … Not a word came from his lips; in silence he sat day and night, with his eyes cast on the ground. … On another bed, three feet from the king, sat the officer on guard, while two stalwart European sentries, with fixed bayonets, stood on either side. The orders given were that on any attempt to rescue, the officer was immediately to shoot the king with his own hands.[265]

Sometime later, another visitor, named Richard Temple, John Lawrence's representative at Delhi, saw a glimpse of 'kingliness' still there in the wretchedness of the prisoner which could 'move' anybody:

> It was a strange sight, he says, to see the aged man seated in a darkened chamber of his palace. The finely chiselled features, arched eye brows, equiline profile, … nervous twitching of the face, delicate fingers counting beads … altogether made up a curious picture upon which no spectator could look unmoved who was acquainted with Asiatic history. … He whose very shoe the faithful had been long forced to lick was now himself grovelling in dust.[266]

As time passed, living in dark, dingy, dirty room, fed on an unnourishing diet – less than two annas a day – with dishonour and disgrace, the man whose health, the doctors (English) reported, was better than anybody of his age in Europe, was reduced to a physical wreck.[267] Even the 'Kingliness' which Richard Temple saw in him the other day was gone. A widow of a Bishop, Mrs. Coupland, who visited him around X-mas with some friends, found him in a most pitiable condition.

> We drove down corridor into a dirty street … and entered a dirty-looking house. Pushing aside the purdah, we entered a small, dirty, low room … and there, on a low charpoy, cowered a thin, small old man dressed in a dirty white suit of cotton, and rolled in shabby wraps and rezais, on account of the cold. At our entrance he laid aside the hookah he had been smoking, and he, who formerly thought it an insult for anyone to sit in his presence, began salaaming to us in the most abject manner, and saying 'burra kooshee' (very glad) to see us.

From there, they, out of ladies' curiosity, removed a chick in the room to see what lay on the other side:

265 Griffiths, *op. cit.*, pp. 120–21.
266 Temple, *op. cit.*, pp. 136–37.
267 The Emperor was not given the food that he was used to. As a result, he fell sick, vomiting every now and then.

> They found a small bare shabby room where seated on a charpoy we beheld a large bold-looking woman (Zinat Mahal) ... she seemed about forty ... wore a cotton dress of black print and but a few ornaments. ... Looking at my black dress, she sneeringly asked me what had become of my 'sahib'. I was angry, that I said 'Chupero' (silence), and walked out of her presence.[268]

After some time, in the month of January (1858), the Emperor was pushed into another affliction – trial. It was, as already indicated, a highly complex and shaded thing. To make some head and tail of it, let us place it in a juridical perspective.

Juridical perspective

For proper dispensation of justice, three things are considered exigent: a competent court, word-perfect chargesheet, and bi-sided evidence. The Delhi helmsmen, however, thought differently, at least in the present case, if not always. For them, the dispensation of justice was penalization of the Emperor (*even ex parte*); and made everything that mattered there subservient to that end. Take the Court. It consisted of, as stated above, a President, four Members, a Prosecutor for the Government, and an Interpreter. The contemporary evidence (mostly unused so far) tells us, albeit implicitly, that the composition of the Court was biased more on the principles of pliability and commitment than qualifications and capabilities of its members. Take, for instance, the appointment of the President of the Court and the Judge Advocate, the two main pillars of the edifice. Maj. Gen. Wilson, Commanding, Delhi Field Force, had appointed Brig. Longfield as the President of the Court. But soon after he went on leave, Maj. Gen. Penny, who took over the command, appointed, without cancelling his appointment, or informing him, first Brig. Gen. Showers, and then, on Showers's being assigned some other job, brought in Lieut. Col. Daves one and a half hour (12.30 a.m.) after the commencement of the trial at 11 a.m. on the first day.[269] A question arises here: why did the General play such a game? There is, and can be, unlike the two officers,[270] only one answer: Brig. Longfield's pliability was untested.

268 R.M. Coupland, *Lady's Escape from Gwalior*, London, 1859, pp. 274–77.

269 Brig. Longfield came to know about the change and the commencement of the trial very late – on 29 January 1858 – when he wrote to seek information as to when should he come to attend the proceedings. By this time, two sittings of the Court had already taken place under the presidency of Lieut. Col. Daves. What an embarrassment for the old man! For fuller details, see Martin, *op. cit.*, vol. 3, p. 163.

270 They had worked with him, and he knew of their suitability for the purpose. Brig. Longfield, on the other hand, was an upright officer. Maj. Gen. Wilson had even recommended

The case of the Judge Advocate, Maj. Harriott, was even more intriguing. He lacked sense of balance and objectivity, two basic qualities of a judge. While heading the 'cruel court martial' of the 85 sepoys at Meerut, he did not allow the ones among them who tried to plead their case 'with little skill but considerable truth' and gave harshest punishment to them for doing, in Montgomery Martin's words, 'their religious duty' and defending their 'social rights' – injustice! And yet boasted to a friend officer – 'The court is over and these select few fellows had ten year a-piece. You will hear of no more mutinies'.[271] But a lot of people, including the highest executive authority in India, Governor-General Canning, believed that '*the first great act of rebellion was the immediate result of a severe sentence carried out, with very degrading accessory, at Meerut*' (emphasis added).[272]

Maj. Gen. Penny knew of all these developments, yet he chose Harriott for handling such a high-profile trial! Why? Capt. F.C. Massey, also of the Judge Advocate-General Branch, and very much concerned with the affairs in question, has given a revelatory explanation:

> On the 10th (October) ... I had a great fight with him (Maj. Gen. Penny), Brig. Chamberlain and Mr. Saunders about the King's trial. They wanted me to undertake that (at once) and that General was very nearly ordering to do it. *I represented that the evidence was as yet far from complete ..., and moreover, if the King was to be tried at once the proper officer to conduct the trial was Gen. Penny's own Judge Advocate, Maj. Harriott.* (emphasis added)[273]

And it was on that 'far from complete evidence' that the Emperor was tried by Maj. Harriott, 'Gen. Penny's own Judge Advocate'. Not much is known about the four other members of the Court: Maj. Palmer, Maj. Redmond, Maj. Sawyers, and Capt. Rothney. None of them has shown his individuality as a judge throughout the proceedings of the Court dominated by the President and the Judge Advocate. Perhaps being good soldiers, they had left everything to their senior officers. The seventh and the last member of the Court was the Interpreter. Because of the nature of his job – translation of the material from English into Urdu/Persian, and vice versa – he had no role in decision-making.

The Court's other inadequacies were that barring the interpreter, none of the members knew Urdu/Persian, the chief source of evidence, well enough

him to be his successor – Commanding Delhi Field Force – while in a hurry to go on sick leave after the fall of Delhi.

271 See Martin, *op. cit.*, vol. 2, pp. 144–46.

272 The quote is from Henry Cunningham, *Earl Canning*, cited in Thompson, *op. cit.*, p. 35.

273 See 'Account of an eye-witness (Capt. F.C. Massey) of the taking of the Delhi Palace on the 20th September 1857', *Journal of the USI of India*, vol. 60, 1930, p. 180.

to be of some use in the trial.[274] Also there is nothing on record that could have shown that they knew the Islamic (Mughal) juridical practices and international law. Their knowledge of the Indian history, tradition, and psyche, if at all it was there, was too superfluous to be of any use in understanding the complexities and intricacies involved in the trial.

Now, let us also see how the Court manned by these persons, despite these debilities, accomplished the tasks assigned to it, namely collection of evidence, framing of the charge sheet, and conducting of the trial. The first task, i.e., collection of evidence, was by far the most important matter, but it was the weakest of all. The authorities at the helm seemed to be more keen to lay their hands on the evidence relating to the 'conduct' of the Rebellion than anything else; even the conduct of the Emperor was of somewhat secondary nature, as C.B. Saunders, the man who collected (?) the evidence, says:

> The whole of the records, found in the palace, or in the camp of the rebel army, and all numerous vernacular documents fell into many hands after the final occupation of the city by our troops, have been carefully collated and examined, and those which directly or indirectly bore upon the conduct of the rebellion, whether implicating the King or not, as well as those which bore his autograph order or his signatures have been recorded among the proceedings, and will be found to disclose many points of interest and importance.[275]

It has already been mentioned at some length that in October (1857), Capt. Massey, the then Judge Advocate, Delhi, had frankly told Gen. Penny that the evidence was 'insufficient' for the trial of the King; and on the basis of that evidence, his *own man*, Harriott, would be ready to try the Emperor. The General ignored the first part of Massey's sane statement, and acted on the second part. Three days later, 13 October, Maj. Harriott was there in Delhi. Capt. Massey made over all the evidence to him and left for his new place of posting.[276] There is no reference to any new evidence being added to it by Maj. Harriott.

They were in utter haste to begin the trial at the earliest and punish the Emperor. Unfortunately, in those days, he was on the deathbed as the following excerpts from a letter of C.B. Saunders, Offg. Commissioner Delhi to Sir John Lawrence, shows:

274 Charles Ball says that the President knew Urdu. Some others add knowledge of Persian also to his qualifications. But even if it were so, his knowledge was too inadequate to be of any use here in reading and understanding the old court Persian and Urdu.

275 Saunders to R. Temple, Secretary to the Chief Commissioner, Punjab, No. 632, Delhi, 12 April 1858, vide *PMR*, *Correspondence*, pt. 2, p. 380.

276 Massey, *op. cit.*, p. 180.

> The king has been more or less ill, suffering from fever and other diseases attendant on extreme old age. The Civil Surgeon and his professional advisor, Hakeem Ashanullah have been in daily attendance on him, the latter prescribing for him. The Civil Surgeon has certified that the Ex-King is totally unfit to be moved or to stand his Trial, during the last two or three days his disability and other symptoms have so far increased to make it probable that he will not rally again from his bed of sickness.[277]

Harriott framed the chargesheet in great haste based on the 'insufficient evidence' which is, as seen below, a good example of how not to draw such an important legal document. Look at it charge-wise:

1st. For that he, being a pensioner of the British Government in India, did, at Delhi, at various times between the 10th of May and 1st of October 1857, encourage, aid and abet Muhammad Bakht Khan, subadar of the regiments of the artillery, and divers others, native commissioned officers and soldiers unknown, of the East India Company's army, in the crimes of mutiny and rebellion against the State.

2nd. For having at Delhi, at various times between the 10th of May and 1st of October 1857, encouraged, aided and abetted Mirza Mughal, his own son, a subject of the British Government in India, and others unknown, inhabitants of Delhi, and of the North-West Provinces of India, also subjects of the British Government, to rebel and wage war against the State.

3rd. For that he, being a subject of the British Government in India, and not regarding the duty of his allegiance, did, at Delhi, on the 11th of May 1857, or thereabouts, as a false traitor against the State, proclaim and declare himself the reigning king and sovereign of India, and did then and there traitorously seize and take unlawful possession of the city of Delhi, and did moreover, at various times between the 10th of May and 1st of October 1857, as such false traitor aforesaid, reasonably conspire, consult, and agree with Mirza Mughal, his own son, and with Muhammad Bakht Khan, subadar of the regiment of Artillery, and diverse other false traitors unknown, to raise levy, and make insurrection, rebellion and war against the State, and further to fulfil and perfect his reasonable design of overthrowing and destroying the British Government in India, did assemble armed forces at Delhi, and sent them forth to fight and wage war against the said British Government.

277 C.B. Saunders to Lt. E.H. Paske, Offg. Secretary to the Chief Commissioner, Punjab, no. 21, dated Delhi, 19 January 1858, *PMR, Correspondence*, pt. 2, p. 373.

4th. That he, at Delhi, on the 16th of May 1857, or thereabouts, did, within the precincts of the palace at Delhi, feloniously cause, and become accessory to the murder of 49 persons, chiefly women and children of European and mixed European descent; and did moreover, between 10th of May and 1st of October 1857, encourage and abet divers soldiers and others in murdering European officers, and other English subjects, including women and children, both by giving and promising such murderers service, advancement, and distinctions; and further, that he issued orders to different native rulers having local authority in India, to slay and murder Christians and English people, whenever and wherever found on their territories; the whole or any part of such conduct being a heinous offence under Act XIV or 1857 of the Legislative Council in India.[278]

There is hardly any legal exactness, brevity, and unambiguity in the charge sheet. Besides that, it also has several legal dissonances, the important ones being the following: (i) In almost every charge, the dates on which alleged offences were committed by the Emperor fell between 10 May and 1 October (1857), whereas he had participated in the Rebellion only from 12 May to 20 September. (ii) The first three charges (of the four charges) (Charge I to III) do not mention as to which law the Emperor had actually violated there.[279] (iii) Only one charge, Charge IV, mentions that the Emperor is held guilty under Act XIV of 1857 of having complicity in the murder of 49 persons of 'European descent' on 16 May, and in encouraging others citizens and native princes to do the same.[280] (iv) Surprisingly, neither the scope of the trial nor its nature – whether formal and regular or something else – were defined, as the following statement of the Judge Advocate shows: '*The scope of the investigation is not in any way confined by the observance of technicalities such as belong to a more formal and to a regular trial*' (emphasis added).[281]

It was, to say the least, a vague, arbitrary exercise, leaving the juridical field open to the vested interest to play the game the way it liked. *En passant*, it was not here alone, we notice the element of arbitrariness almost everywhere, as discussed below, in recording the proceedings. Nor did they care to answer any of the following fundamental legal questions (based on evidence) that the Judge Advocate promised to do in the beginning 'to the satisfaction of one and all':

278 See *The Trial*, 27 January 1858.

279 The lapse has rendered the charges legally vague, leaving no scope for pinpointing the offence/offences.

280 Here also the charge is, as seen below, not supported by any direct evidence.

281 See *The Trial*, opening statement of the Deputy Judge Advocate-General, 27 January 1858.

- Was the sovereignty vested in Bahadur Shah or the East India Company?
- Did the Company Government recognize him as the King of Delhi?
- Did he enjoy sovereign immunity from British courts?
- Was he a 'British subject' or 'national'?

Let me elaborate: beginning with the first question relating to sovereignty. The British say that the sovereignty was vested in them. They were, as discussed above, the sovereign rulers of Delhi. There is not even a tiny shred of evidence in the history of British presence in Delhi, from 1803 to 1857, that they had taken the sovereignty, which was vested in the Mughal Emperors, from them through the two means that were legally and morally available to them to do so, i.e., one, the *de facto* right of conquest by deposing Shah Alam (1803) and, two, through a treaty with him according to local or international law. They, fearing strong popular reaction, did neither, but tried to take possession of the prized thing, like a sneak-thief, through indirect and deceptive means. It must, however, be said to the credit of the Mughal Emperors that, though weak and effete, they came out to oppose their every move in that direction as best as they could in their worst days. As a result, despite their great efforts, they could only divest them of the external trappings like *Nazar, khilat*, etc. of sovereignty, but not the soul of it, i.e., the sovereignty itself.[282] It remained, in fact, with the Emperors till the Rebellion.

Thus beaten, the Company authorities put forth another thesis: sovereignty without power to enforce its dictates was no sovereignty. The Company was sovereign because it had such power. I have, through the examples of some very powerful states in India, like the Peshawas of Poona, Hyder Ali and Tipu Sultan of Mysore, and the Bhonsles of Nagpur, who always looked towards the 'vanishing kingdoms' of Satara (of Shivaji's descendants), the old Hindu kingly families of Mysore and the Gond Prince, the old hereditary ruler of the Nagpur region, respectively, for legitimacy, show that in India the sovereignty without power was also sovereignty in every sense of the term. It was also the case in the eyes of the Mughal jurisprudence and Indian history (1757–1857), as F.W. Buckler, Allen Scholar in the University of Cambridge, says in a powerful critique of the trial (1922):

> The continuity of the Mughal Empire down to the deposition of Bahadur Shah II in 1858 ... (was) an effective source of political

282 C.S. Hardinge, ADC to his father, Lord Hardinge, has aptly described this phenomenon in his book, *Reflections on India* (1847): 'King, who is a miserable old man, stripped of all authority, and, in fact, a mere puppet in our hands ... still considers himself, "every inch a king", addresses the political agent in the terms as "slave", and talks of "My Royal Sister of England"'. Quoted by D. Dewer and H.L.O Garret, in 'Reply to Mr. F. W. Buckler', *Transactions of the Royal Historical Society* (4th Series), vol. 5, pp. 71–100.

> authority and as the *suzerain de jure* of the East India Company in the capacity of *Diwan* of Bengal, arrogating the title of the British Government in India. ... The source of the Company's authority in India lay, not in the Charters of the King of England, nor in the Acts of the British Parliament, nor in the sword, but in the *farmans* of the Mughal Emperor. That all honour claimed by the Company against the Emperor, belonged to the Emperor, its suzerain. That all censure and opprobrium levelled against him recoil on the Company, his disloyal vassal. ... The army turned to its sovereign's allegiance against its rebel officer. Hence if in 1857 there were any mutineer it was the East India Company.[283]

Like their master, Buckler says, the Trial Court, their creation,

> was also ignorant of the real status of Bahadur Shah.[284] Its questions ... were unintelligent and its answers were recorded with that fidelity found only in unintelligent witnesses. ... Indeed, the use of the term 'Mutiny' – unless wilful, to obscure the issue – is conclusive evidence of that ignorance. Kaye alone of the historians of the outbreak seems to have understood its meaning, which he labours, painfully, but vainly, to suppress.[285]

Buckler considered the Company's claim that the Emperor, being their subject, had failed in carrying out his 'duty of allegiance' to them and playing a false traitor against the State by proclaiming and declaring himself the reigning King and sovereign in India (Charge 3)[286] was, thus, absolutely baseless. Buckler is right.

The Prosecution submitted 158 documents to support its case. Surprisingly, there was not even a single document which could prove that the Emperor was, by any means, a 'subject of the British Government' and had 'a duty of allegiance' to them. Nor is there anything on the basis of which it would be established that by declaring himself the 'reigning king and sovereign', he became 'a false traitor against the State'. There is only an oral testimony from a middle-rung serving Company employee in Delhi, the

283 Buckler, *op. cit.*, pp. 74–75.

284 This ignorance of the Court, says Buckler, 'constitutes the main value of the document (Proceedings of the Trial)'. To support his contention, he appends the following footnote: 'Eg. The charges, especially the first and third (*The Trial*, p. 2); the question of Mr. Saunders (*ibid.*, p. 94), the speech for the prosecution (pp. 136f, 141); the attempt to find a day of proclamation of the King, as if his reign only began in May 1857 (pp. 28, 87, 88)'. (The citations, page numbers, etc. are from Buckler's copy of the trial.)

285 Kaye, *op. cit.*, vol. 2, pp. 1–2; Buckler's quote, p. 75, f.n. 3.

286 Buckler, *op. cit.*, pp. 77–78.

Officiating Commissioner and Agent of the Lieutenant-Governor of Agra, C.B. Saunders, that touches upon the subjects. Saunders avers that it was on the 14th of September 1803, when General Lake entered Delhi after defeating the Marathas, its defenders, the Emperor Shah Alam became, a 'pensioned subject of the British Government'. After some time, he says 'the prisoner (Bahadur Shah) succeeded to the titular sovereignty of Delhi' in 1837.[287] Both the words, 'pensioned subject' and the 'titular sovereignty' are his creation. He cited no authority or made no reference to or produced copy of any treaty/treaties or official documents to substantiate his coinage or statements. It is strange that the Court accepted the charge of such great historical nature and great legal importance on the strength of such a hollow oral deposition.[288]

Bahadur Shah was not a 'pensioned subject of the British Government', or a king with 'titular sovereignty, as Saunders says, or 'a deposed king', or 'ex-king of Delhi', as is interchangeably referred to in the trial proceedings, as Buckler has proved on the basis of contemporary records and Mughal law. Recently, L.D. Bell, a scholar from Melbourne University (Australia) who has thoroughly examined all the issues from the perspectives of International and British law, has also reached almost the same conclusion. Citing the Privy Council (London) rulings, Bell says that the Government of India had recognized that Bahadur Shah was a sovereign and that the Kingdom of Delhi was a foreign 'state' in British law and did not form a part of British territory. It had every feature of statehood 'a definite territory, a permanent population and a system of Government'.[289] He was a full-fledged king, and a sovereign for that matter, with his own kingdom,[290] where, legally, no British Court, civil or military, by any law, International to British to local, could interfere. His trial by the Military Court was, thus, a blatant breach of law.

287 For his full deposition, see *The Trial*, 12 February 1858.

288 It was not even a written signed statement. It was an oral reply to a loose question by the Court – 'Can you give the Court any information as to the circumstances under which the King of Delhi became subject and pensioner of the British Government'? As was the question, so was the reply – a statement supported by no verifiable fact whatsoever.

289 See L.D. Bell, The 1858 Trial of Mughal Emperor Bahadur Shah II 'Zafar' for Crimes against the State', PhD thesis, Faculty of Law, The Melbourne University, 2004, pp. 91, 121.

290 In a well-known case, *Raja Saligram versus the Secretary of State for India*, the Privy Council, London, notes Bell, 'ruled clearly that Bahadur Shah was an independent king. He was the grandson of Shah Alam, and neither he nor any of his ancestors had ever been deposed by his own subjects, or by the British Government or by any other power'. Further the court also clarified the issue of annual payment to the Emperor, which the Government called 'pension'. It ruled that 'the annual sum of revenue paid to the kings of Delhi from 1803 onwards was essentially a term of a treaty between the Emperor Shah Alam II and the EIC concluded in 1805 which was still on foot in 1857'. In view of this, no British Court could try Bahadur Shah, a sovereign ruler. Bell, *op. cit.*, p. 91.

If this was the position, a question arises: why did the Emperor agree to be tried by the Court? Why didn't he boycott it? The question is, no doubt, devious. But fortunately, the proceedings of the last three days clear the brume and help us in getting an answer. On the 3rd March, according to the official version, the proceedings ended with the following sentence: 'The court at 2 P.M. adjourns till 11 A.M. tomorrow morning, to enable the prisoner to complete his defence'. But contemporary historian Montgomery Martin has given a differing account: 'On the 3rd March, the court assembled for the nineteenth time', he says, 'for further evidence, and again adjourned until the 9th of that month (March)' – not 4th March.[291] Also, he has not recorded anything happening on that day, suggesting, albeit implicitly, that court did not assemble on that day, ... or if at all it did, it should have, unlike other days, transacted the business secretly in camera. How could otherwise a historian who has meticulously recorded the day-to-day developments in the court, albeit briefly, without leaving out substantial details, many of which even the official version has left out, as a policy, have missed only this sitting of the court and its deliberations?

Leaving it here at the moment, let us look at the other side. According to the official version, the court assembled at 11 a.m. on 4 March. Soon after, the 'prisoner', delivered 'to the court his defence in Hindustani' (emphasis added). The interpreter read it in original.[292] The proceedings were over in one and a half hour – shortest time, but left behind a serious doubt on the authenticity of the Emperor's undated statement of defence. The court language in those days was Persian and not Hindustani/Urdu. The Emperor would always write official letters/documents, etc. in Persian. Then, the question arises: how come he wrote this important document, as alleged, in Hindustani? The only reasonable answer is, and can be, that the document is forged. For a proof, we need not go anywhere, 'the post-script' added to the document proves the point to the hilt. There, reaching to an order alleged to have been written by him to Mirza Mughal, the Emperor is shown to have said:

> I have no recollection of such an order having been issued (by me). The order in question is in the Urdu tongue, contrary to the rule in my secretariat office where all such papers were written in Persian, and I accordingly do not know how and where it was prepared.[293]

Had the statement of defence been shown to the Emperor, the guess is, his reaction might have not been different from what it was on seeing the above

291 Martin, *op. cit.*, vol. 3, p. 184.
292 See *The Trial*, 4 March 1858.
293 *Ibid.*

document – that it is not his work; he did not know how and where it was prepared.

Besides this, a critical examination of the content and style of the document also supports the contention. The statement does not contain a word of what the Emperor used to say almost every day for the past 20 years, and his ancestors had been saying since 1803 – they are sovereign rulers of their kingdom.[294]

Though the original copy of the statement is not traceable, even a cursory look at its translation shows that style-wise, it is not the Emperor's composition. He always wrote briefly, clearly, and matter-of-factly. The statement is by and large devoid of all these things. And lastly the question of morality is also there. In that old Mughal, who had been rotting in the British jail and suffering the worst of inhuman treatment for the last 164 days, there should have been left some drops of the blood of his great ancestors in his veins to check him from stooping so low as to holding (in his so-called 'Defence') his two sons and a grandson, who were beastly butchered and humiliated by the enemy, responsible for what he knew he had himself done, to save a few days of wretched life left with him. All these reasons together whisper dubiety on the Emperor's authorship of the 'Defence'.

Leaving this matter here, let us proceed to 9th March. According to the official version, the court assembled at 11 a.m. First, the Judge Advocate presented an English translation of the Emperor's fake 'Statement of defence' and his own address painting the Emperor with the blackest tar. And then 'the court, on the evidence before them' adjudged that 'the prisoner Mohammad Bahadur Shah, ex-king of Delhi, is guilty of all and every part of the charges preferred against him'. But the unofficial version (Martin's) gives a hugely different account:

After the court assembled,

> the Vakeel of the prisoner, says Martin, declared in the name of his royal Master, that he did not recognise the authority of the tribunal before which he had been brought, and therefore declined to make answer to any charge brought against him.

After this, Martin adds, 'the Judge Advocate made a speech proving his allegations', and the court, after a short deliberation,

294 Right from Shah Alam to Akbar Shah to Bahadur Shah, each ruler protested openly through different means and raised voice so that the helmsmen from Delhi to Calcutta to London could hear that what the Company was doing to them was wrong and illegal. Even in their worst situation, says Percival Spear, 'The Mughal policy was to retain the nominal sovereignty of India by the utmost complaisance to the actual possessors of power. Behind this pusillanimity lay the hope that the wheel of fortune might yet turn to make possible the reunion of actual to nominal authority', Spear, *op. cit.*, p. 34.

> by the virtue of the authority vested in it by Act XIV., of 1857, sentenced him (Bahadur Shah) to be transported for life to the Andaman Islands, or to such place as should be selected by the Governor-General in council for his place of banishment.[295]

To say which of these two versions is right is a vexed question, but not quite. A critical examination, especially in terms of objectivity and freedom from executive or any other influence, can be helpful in solving it. Take the official version. It falters on both the counts, because the court was, as discussed above in detail, made of members who were selected more on the principles of pliability and commitment than qualifications as capabilities.[296] And on the top of it, the Punjab Supremo Sir John Lawrence, who had received 'full authority' to carry out any measures to deal with such matters from the Governor-General in those critical days,[297] hardly left any elbow room for them to move about in any matter whatever:

He tied their hands thus:

> The prisoner's complicity in the mutiny was open and notorious, and under no circumstances could he ever obtain his liberty or be restored to his former station.[298]

But being a wise man, Sir John knew that the evidence at hand was not enough to serve their purpose – hold the Emperor guilty. He, therefore, took this safe, albeit a legal stand – the case being open and well known, needed no investigation. The Deputy Judge Advocate-General played to his tune and changed the scope and form of the trial on its very first day:

> It must be clearly understood, he observed, that the scope of investigation is not in any way confined by the observance of technicalities such as belong to a more formal Trial.[299]

295 Martin, *op. cit.*, p. 184. Surprisingly, no recent writer has taken note of this important statement except L.D. Bell (referred to above). But he has also not taken it as a reliable thing for two reasons: one, no record is available to corroborate the statement. and two, statement is not recorded in the proceedings (Bell, *op. cit.*, p. 46). The developments that took place on 4 and 9 March, which I have discussed at length, prove that though the court did not record the Emperor's version, it could not, despite playing tricks, hide the truth that Martin has recorded.

296 See 'Juridical perspective' above.

297 See Governor-General's message for Punjab Chief Commissioner, dated Calcutta, 3 July,1857, *PMR*, *Correspondence*, pt. 1,pp. 182–83.

298 From Lieut. E.H. Paske, Offg. Secretary to the Chief Commissioner, Punjab, C.V. Saunders, Offg. Commissioner, Delhi, 15 January 1858, *PMR*, *Correspondence*, pt. 2, p. 369.

299 *The Trial*, 27 January 1858.

Almost the same approach is so often reflected here and there, if not everywhere, in the official proceedings. Hence many a lack and left out.[300] Compared to this, Martin's version is more reliable. And why shouldn't it be? He is after all, in the words of the fair-minded writer Edward Thompson, 'on the whole much the best historian ... who wrote with detailed knowledge and fearlessness of judgement'.[301] He had, unlike the authors of the official version, no axe to grind.[302] He loved both his Empire and the historical principles.

Before closing the account, let me clarify some more points. A serious reading of Martin shows that what the Emperor did on the 9th March (through his counsel) was not a sudden development. He had actually started saying almost the same thing, albeit differently, from the beginning. For instance, on the very first day, 27 January 1858, he 'declared himself profoundly ignorant of the charges levelled against him'.[303] Again on being shown some documents to prove his complicity in the rebellion on the fourth day, 30 January 1858, he 'made some remarks on the conclusion of each' (which they did not comprehend) and concluded, albeit through signs, that 'he knew nothing whatever about them'.[304] On the 12th day, 10 February 1858, he declared, not once, but several times during the session, 'his innocence'![305]

After building the arsenal little by little, thus, he dropped, as discussed above, a deadly bomb through his counsel on the 21st day, 9 March 1858. The Deputy Advocate did not take, understandably, any note of it, for if he would have not done so, their whole case would have fallen flat to the ground and raised questions on the legitimacy of their rule. Wisely (or cunningly?) they ignored it and blew their own trumpet on 4 March and finally, as noted above, on 9 March 1858 and closed the case in their favour on the strength of the 'colonial justice'!

The finale

After the trial was over, the prisoner-Emperor received treatment that even the worst of criminals were not given in a civilized country. Mr Layard, an ex-member of the British Parliament for Aylesbury, who visited the prisoner-Emperor in those days found him in the most wretched condition. On

300 The lacks have been pointed out in the footnotes in the text of the proceedings.
301 See Thompson, *op. cit.*, p. 195.
302 The weaknesses of the official sources have been described in detail in the Preface, f. ns. 1 and 2.
303 Martin, *op. cit.*, vol. 3, p. 162.
304 *Ibid.*, p. 164.
305 *Ibid.*, p. 168.

going back to London, Layard shared, his pathetic story with a large audience at the St James Hall, London, on 11 May (1858):

> Many persons regret, he said, that the king of Delhi had not fallen in just punishment for his offence. I saw the King of Delhi; and I will leave the meeting to judge, when it has heard me, *whether or not he is punished*! I saw that broken down old man, not in a room but in a miserable hole of the palace, lying on a bedstead with nothing to cover him but a miserable tattered coverlet. As I beheld him, some remembrance of his former greatness seemed to rise in my mind. He rose with difficulty from his couch, showed me his arms, which were eaten into by disease and by flies, and partly from want of water; and he said, in a lamentable voice, that he had not enough to eat. I will not give any opinion as to the manner in which we are treating him is worthy of a great nation, but is this a way in which, as Christians, we ought to treat a king? I saw his women too, all huddled up in a corner, with their children, and I was told that all he was allowed for their support was 16 shillings-a-day! Is not that punishment enough for one that has occupied a throne?[306]

'The lecture', excited, as it was intended to do, huge sympathy (for the old man) among the audience, and 'opinion ran strongly against the alleged treatment to which the royal octogenarian captive was subjected'. Its echo soon reached Delhi, and a spokesman of the Government challenged the accuracy of Layard's statement:

> I hope, said the official spokesman, his (Layard's) speech is incorrect. ... For a man of his years the ex-king of Delhi is particularly active and intelligent and I have seldom seen so old a man in England with equal mental and bodily energy. He resides not in a hole but in a large room square, with windows. ... The old man has no deficiency either of clothes, pillows and cushions. There is no limit ... to the amount of water. ... The ordinary pay of an inferior workman at Delhi is 7 rupees per month that is sufficient to feed and clothe man, wife and children. Very few adults consume more than 3 penny a day. The Offg. Civil Surgeon, Delhi.[307]

What a logic! What a comparison!

Despite contraventions and explanations, the Government could not hide the truth: after about a month, William Russell, the *Times* correspondent

306 See Martin, *op. cit.*, vol. 3, p. 185.
307 *Ibid.*, pp. 185–86.

who visited the Emperor on 5 June, reiterated by and large what Layard had said. He found that the

> King was sick, with bent body he seemed nearly prostrate over a brass basin into which he was retching violently. ... The passage in which he sat contained nothing that I could see but a charpoy such as those used by the poorest Indians. .... As he sat before us, I was only reminded of the poorest form of the Israelitish type. ... His hands and feet were delicate and fine; his garments scanty and foul. And this is the descendant of him who on the 12th of August 1765, conferred on the East India Company the Dewanee (or lordship) of the Provinces of Bengal, Bihar and Orissa.[308]

This painful phase of the unspeakable suffering of the Emperor in a humble dwelling-turned-jail in his own grand Palace ended on 7 October 1858. At about 4 o'clock in the morning, the Emperor bid adieu, with heavy heart and weeping eyes, to his and his ancestors' capital. His new destination was Rangoon, Burma (now Yangon, Myanmar), where he was to spend, in no less misery and suffering, in a prison-house four long years.

On 7 November 1862, at about 5 a.m., the Emperor died. But he did not die alone. With him died each and every vestige of the 330-year-old great Empire of the Mughals as well. On its grave stood now a middle-aged woman, Queen Victoria of England. And it was from there that she and her successors structured another great Empire – the British Empire. But, as the law of nature is, its sun also set after 90 years in 1947, yielding space to the Indian Republic and Pakistan.

308 Russel, *op. cit.*, vol. 2, pp. 58–61.

2

PROCEEDINGS OF THE TRIAL, 1858

Trial of Muhammad Bahadur Shah,[1] Ex-King of Delhi

Day one: 27 January 1858

Proceedings of a European Military Commission assembled at Delhi on the 27th day of January 1858, by order of Major-General Penny, C.B., Commanding the (Meerut) Division[2] pursuant to instructions from Sir John Lawrence, Chief Commissioner of the Punjab, for the trial of such prisoners as may be duly brought before it.

President
Lieut. Colonel Dawes, Artillery
Members
Major Palmer, H.M.'s 60th Regt.
Major Redmond, H.M.'s 61st Regt.
Major Sawyers, H.M.'s 6th Carabineers
Captain Rothney, 4th Sikh Infantry
Interpreter
Mr. James Murphy
Prosecutor for Government
Major F.J. Harriott
Deputy Judge Advocate-General

The Court assembled in the Special Hall[3] of Audience in the Palace at Delhi, at 11 o'clock, on the morning of the 27th of January 1858.

1 The Emperor's name is spelt in the official handwritten copy of the proceedings (Delhi Archives), which I have mostly used, as 'Mahomed Bahadoor Shah'. I have, however, used the popularly current spelling here, i.e., 'Muhammad Bahadur Shah'. The spellings of some other names have also been changed for convenience of the present-day readers. The text has, however, not been touched in any way whatsoever. The footnotes/comments at the end of which Ed. is written, are by the Editor of the official copy (Delhi Archives' handwritten copy). Other footnotes/comments (at the end of which nothing is written) are mine.
2 He was also Commanding Officer of the Delhi Field Force.
3 In the official handwritten copy, the spelling is 'Especial Hall'. I have, however, followed the popular (translated) version 'Special Hall ...'

DOI: 10.4324/9781003320500-2

The President, Members, Interpreter, and Deputy Judge Advocate-General are all present.[4]

The Prisoner, Muhammad Bahadur Shah, Ex-King of Delhi, is brought into Court.

The orders convening and forming the Court, and appointing Lieut. Colonel Dawes, Artillery, President, are produced and read.

The names of the officers appointed to serve on the Court are read in the hearing of the prisoner.

Invitation of challenge

Question by Court: Prisoner, do you object to being tried by the President, or any of the Officers appointed to sit on this Military Commission?[5]

Answer: No.

The President, Members Interpreter, and Deputy Judge Advocate-General are duly sworn.

All witnesses are directed to withdraw.

The charges are read and entered as follows:

Charges

1st: For that he, being a Pensioner[6] of the British Government in India, did, at Delhi, at various times between the 10th of May and 1st of October

4 The fact is that the Court was not in order till 12.30 p.m. because the President of the Court Brig. Gen. Showers, was absent, for he was suddenly sent out of Delhi on some other assignment; and his substitute, Lieut. Col. Dawes was informed very late of his new job. He came to the Court at 12.30 p.m. The official version of the Trial does not mention this fact. The Emperor who had come at 11 a.m. sharp, was kept waiting before his *Diwan-i-khas* like an ordinary criminal till 12.30 p.m. under a strong guard of the 60th Rifles.

'When the clock struck half-past twelve', says H.L.O. Garret, the Keeper of the Records of the Government of Punjab, 'order was given to bring in the prisoner; and to those assembled in the grand audience chamber of the Mughals the appearance of the old man (critically ill) as he tottered into court, supported on one side by his only remaining son and on the other by one of his attendants *was an event of intense interest* (emphasis added). It became specially so when the proud antecedents of his race were compared with wretched position of their miserable descendant.' See Garret, ed., *The Trial of Bahadur Shah* (1932), Delhi, rep. 2007, p. 15 (Introduction). Perhaps Garrent has borrowed the details from Martin, *op. cit.*, vol. 3, p. 161; Charles Ball, *The History of the Indian Mutiny* (1859?), Lahore, rep. 2007, vol. 2, p. 261.

5 This was an unusual gesture not seen in trials in those days. Besides that, its non-mention by Martin raises some doubt on its authenticity, because he was given, albeit briefly, but candidly, day–to-day account of the trial without missing any important detail in the proceedings. See Martin, *op. cit.*, vol. 3, pp. 161–62.

6 Whether or not the Emperor was a 'pensioner' of the British Government has been discussed at length in the 'Introduction'.

1857, encourage, aid, and abet, Muhammad Bakht Khan, Subedar of the Regiment of Artillery, and diverse others, Native Commissioned officers and Soldiers unknown, of the East India Company's Army, in the crimes of Mutiny and Rebellion against the State.

2nd: For having at Delhi, at various times between the 10th of May and 1st of October 1857, encouraged, aided, and abetted Mirza Mughal, his own son, a subject of the British Government in India, and others unknown, inhabitants of Delhi, and the North-West Provinces of India also subjects of the said British Government, to rebel and wage war against the State.[7]

3rd: For that he, being a subject[8] of the British Government in India, and not regarding the duty of his allegiance, did, at Delhi, on the 11th of May 1857, or thereabouts, as a false traitor against the State, proclaim and declare himself reigning King and Sovereign of India, and did then and there traitorously seize and take unlawful possession of the City of Delhi, and did moreover, at various times between the 10th of May and 1st of October 1857, as such false traitor aforesaid, reasonably conspire, consult, and agree with Mirza Mughal, his own son, and with Muhammad Bakht Khan, Subedar of the Regiment of Artillery, and diverse other false traitors unknown, to raise levy and make insurrection, rebellion, and war, against the State, and further to fulfil and perfect his treasonable design of overthrowing and destroying the British Government in India, did assemble armed forces at Delhi, and send them forth to fight and wage war against the said British Government.

4th: For that he, at Delhi, on the 16th of May 1857, or thereabouts, did, within the precincts of the Palace at Delhi, feloniously cause, and become accessory to the murder of 49 persons, chiefly women and children of European and mixed European descent; and did moreover, between the 10th of May and 1st of October 1857, encourage and abet diverse soldiers and others in murdering European Officers, and other English subjects, including women and children, both by giving and promising such murderers service, advancement, and distinctions; and further, that he issued orders to different Native Rulers having local authority in India, to slay and murder Christians and English people, whenever and wherever found on their Territories; the whole or any part of such conduct being a heinous offence under Act XVI of 1857, of the Legislative Council in India.

7 In a judicial document, the dates have got to be exact. The Emperor's involvement in the Rebellion is dated 11 May to 1 October 1857. It should have been 12 May to 20 September 1857.

8 It is also highly controversial that the Emperor was a 'subject' of the British Government. See 'Introduction'.

Delhi
January 5th 1858[9] Sd./-

Fred J. Harriott, Major[10]
Dy Judge Advocate-General, &
Government Prosecutor

Question – Muhammad Bahadur Shah, are you 'guilty' or 'not guilty' of the charges preferred against you?
Answer – Not Guilty.[11]
All witnesses are directed to withdraw.

Prosecution

Judge Advocate's address to the Court:

Gentlemen,
Before proceeding further in this case, it may be necessary to mention, that evidence will be submitted to you, which may not bear strictly on the Charges that have just been perused. It is deemed that all the circumstances connected with the late rebellion, even though not in direct relation to the indictment, may be here appropriately recorded; indeed, up to a late date, it had been decided, that as the King's life had been guaranteed, this investigation should not be accompanied by Charges at all, or even assume the form of a trial, but should embrace all such matters as the discovered correspondence, and other reliable sources of information, might indicate.

I know not whether the Court would, under such circumstances, *viz.* the absence of specific accusation, have been called upon to record an opinion; but feeling that any investigation in reference to the Prisoner must be more satisfactory if he himself were a party to it, and had the opportunity of refuting by documentary or other testimony, such allegations as might appear to his detriment, I suggest that it would be better to have these in a specific and tangible shape, so that on such points guilt or innocence might be clearly

9 The date '5th' is not in the printed versions of the trial. Only Delhi Archives official copy has it in Harriott's hand in blue ink (see Illustration 1.2a, b).

10 There Harriott's signature is in blue ink (see Illustration 1.2a, b).

11 Again a fairly trustworthy account of the episode is given by Martin as follows: 'The prosecutor then put the question, through the interpreter, "guilty or not guilty?" ... There was some difficulty in explaining it to him. He then declared himself profoundly ignorant of the nature of the charges against him. ... After some more delay, the Prisoner pleaded 'not guilty'. See Martin, *op. cit.*, p. 162. Ball has also recorded these facts, surprisingly, in almost the same language (Ball, *op. cit.*, vol. 2, p. 261). Maybe their source was the same who did not want them to disclose his identity. By the way, Martin's work is slightly earlier than that of Ball.

established, this has been acceded to, and hence the Charges that I have just had the honour of perusing; but it must be clearly understood that the scope of the investigation is not in any way confined by the observance of technicalities, such as belong to a more formal and to a regular trial.

The official letter which I addressed to Major-General Penny, C.B., Commanding the Division, on the subject of investigating charges against the Prisoner, having met with his approval, is now laid before the Court for their information.

No. 59
Delhi, January 5th, 1858

Sir, I have the honour to report, for your information, that having finished the trial of Ballabhgarh,[12] I am now prepared to enter on such investigation as may be deemed requisite in reference to the complicity of the Ex-King of Delhi in the late rebellion, etc.

To render such investigation satisfactory, it is in my opinion necessary that it should assume the form of a direct trial, *viz.* that Charges should be framed, and the Ex-King be called upon to plead to them.

I do not perceive how, under other circumstances, any result can be arrived at as to the Ex-King's guilt or innocence, that will not be open to the objection of being one-sided and unjust.

If a verdict be sought on any points that may come under investigation, it is surely desirable that both sides of the case should be heard equally considered. Such a verdict, whether one of conviction or acquittal, will have the stamp of authority, and stand a final and decisive record, either in favour of or against the prisoner. I beg then to suggest that this course be adopted, as the only means of coming to a conclusion satisfactory to the Court, the prisoner, and the Public. Should I obtain your concurrence for so doing, I will at once draw up charges on which the Ex-King can be arraigned, and proceed on his trial with the forms usual in such cases. Awaiting your instructions.

I have the honour to be,
Sir,
Your obedient servant,
Sd./- Fred J. Harriott
Dy. Judge Advocate-General

To Major-General Penny, C.B.,
Commanding of Meerut Division,

12 That is, Nahar Singh, Raja of Ballabhgarh. The Raja was tried, found guilty, and was hanged.

Delhi.

I fully concur in the opinions expressed by the Deputy Judge Advocate-General.

Sd./- N. Penny,[13] Major-General
Commanding, Delhi Field Force

This letter having been forwarded to Mr. Saunders, Offg. Commissioner at Delhi, it was decided that the suggestions in it should be acted on; and the Charges have been framed and this trial commenced accordingly; but still, the part of the original intention to enter into a full and complete investigation of all points in reference to the Rebellion has not been abandoned, and I have mentioned these circumstances to account for the introduction of matter that otherwise appear extraneous, and to prepare the Court for the reception of it. Having finished this preliminary statement, I will say a few words on the nature of the pending trial, and the proof likely to be brought in support of the indictment.

The trial, whether it be considered in reference to the once exalted rank of the prisoner, to the position which his birth and descent still give him in a political point of view, to the magnitude of the crimes imputed to him, or to his connection with events which will for ever remain recorded in the pages of history must be of no ordinary interest. The trial, indeed, will be an unusual one, for, under all circumstances, it will close with the Verdict; but still that Verdict will be looked for by thousands with feeling such as are seldom awakened by the proceedings of a Court of Criminal jurisdiction.

The following extracts from a letter No. 19, of the 26th November 1857, addressed by C.B. Saunders, Esquire, Officiating Commissioner at Delhi, to the circumstances of the Court being restricted to a Verdict, and that it is owing to Major-General Wilson having guaranteed the prisoner his life, that sentence, even in case of conviction, has been barred.

The letter of Mr. Saunders is written under instructions from Sir John Lawrence, Chief Commissioner of the Punjab, and the extracts from it are as follows:

> I have at the same time to inform you that the life of the Ex-King having been guaranteed to him by Captain Hodson, acting under instructions from Major General Wilson, it will not be in the competency of the Military Commission to pass any sentence on him even should a conviction be the result of their enquiries.[14]

13 His signature is also in blue ink. See Illustration 1.2a, b.

14 Besides this, many commitments were made to the Emperor. But none was followed. Why, a question arises, were they so keen to honour this commitment (life-sparing)? It will be, I think, not wholly wrong to suppose that, as the Revolt was not yet over in many parts of the country, the execution of the Emperor whom a large multitude still accepted as their legitimate ruler would have set the country on fire.

I have the honour to forward such documentary evidence in reference to this case, as I have been able to obtain, and shall be at all times ready to give you any assistance in my power in furthering the object in view, by procuring the attendance of witnesses, & c.

I have had the vernacular documents very carefully translated by Mr. James Murphey, Deputy Collector of Customs at Delhi, who is an excellent linguist, and can, if you approve, place his services at your disposal for employment as an interpreter.

The documentary evidence is of great extent, and to render it as intelligible as possible, I have arranged it under 5 different heads, *viz., 1st.*-Miscellaneous papers; *2nd.*-Those which refer to a loan; *3rd.*-Those which refer to the pay of the Soldiery; *4th.*-Relating to all Military matters; and *5th*-Those which relate to murders committed, and which bear special reference to the 4th charge. A very great number of these documents are supposed to have orders on them written by the Prisoner himself, and evidence to this point will be called; the genuineness of the other papers will be established in such a manner, as under the circumstances of the case may be found possible; but some, I fear, will have to be presented to you without direct proof of having come from those to whom they are attributed. In such cases the Court will bear in mind that a full investigation is the great desideratum and that such cannot be perfected, if evidence, credible in itself, be rejected merely because some important formulas cannot be complied with. They will recollect the difficulties as to proof which must ever attached to documents not in the handwriting of those who are the authors of them, and who, at the present moment, have weighty reasons for declining to acknowledge anything that may connect them with the prisoner under trial. The oral testimony I need not dilate on. I shall endeavour to procure it from the most reliable sources; but it must still be borne in mind, that almost every Native that I can easily that I can possibly bring before this Court as an evidence, will have some interest in giving his narrative a colouring as favourable to himself and to the circumstances which he relates, as may be consistent with those broad and acknowledged facts of the Mutiny and Rebellion, which are already known to us all. I shall now commence with the documentary evidence, and bring forward my first witness in proof of the handwriting of the prisoner and of others who may have taken in it.

Fred S. Harriott, Major,
Dy. Judge Advocate-General &
Government Prosecutor

1st evidence – Ahsanullah Khan, late physician to the Ex-King, is called into Court, and duly affirmed.

Examined by the Judge Advocate

Papers under the head Miscellaneous, numbered 2, 3, 4, 13, 14, 19, 20, 21, 22, 24, 27, 30, 33, 39, 40, 41, 43, 44, 48, 50, 52, 53, 54, are shown to the Witness, who declares that the orders written at the head of each are in the handwriting of the prisoner. Also the following are shown to the witness, Nos. 6, 15, 18, 25, 26, 31, 32, 35, 36, and 45, who recognizes the special cypher as being affixed by the Prisoner's own hand. Paper Nos. 5, 16, 29, 34, and 38 are shown to the witness, and he declares that the writing in all of them is that of Mukund Lal, who was special Secretary to the prisoner, and that the seals on three of them, *viz.* Nos. 4, 16, and 34, are impressions from the King's State Seals. Paper Nos. 12, 23, 28, 37, 42, 46, 51, and 55 are shown to Witness, who does not recognize the handwriting in any of them, but says the seal on No. 23 is that of Mirza Mughal, the Commander-in-Chief; on No. 37, the impressions of the seals of the Chief Police Officer, and of the Chief Court of Justice of Delhi; on No. 42 there are impressions of the Office Seal of the Police Station of Budderpore, and of the King's own Secretariat; on No. 46, the seal is an impression of that of Mirza Mughal. He does not recognize anything in reference to the other numbers. Paper Nos. 1, 7, 8, 9, 10, 11, 17, and 49 are shown to the witness. He recognizes the seals on all these eight papers as impressions from the special seal engraved with the King's cypher, and with the exception of the writing in paper No. 10, he recognizes that on all the others as that of Mukund Lal, the Prisoner's special Secretary. No. 56 is shown to Witness; he recognizes it as the handwriting of Mukund Lal, and as bearing the King's own State Seal.

The Judge Advocate now peruses the translations of the above papers down to No. 36 which are entered as follows:

Papers arranged under the Head of Miscellaneous

No. 1

Order under the seal engraved in the King's special cypher

Dated 14th May 1857

To – The Special Slave Muhammad Ali Beg, Subordinate Collector of Land Revenue of the Southern Division of the District.

Be it known to you. You are directed immediately on receipt of this order to proceed to the Royal presence, and to bring with you the Revenue you have collected. You are directed further, to make complete arrangements for the preservation of order throughout the limits of your jurisdiction. You will consider these orders imperative.

No. 2

Petition from Maulavy Muhammed Zahir Ali,[15] Police Officer of Najafgarh

Dated 18th May 1857

To – The King! Shelter of the World!

Respectfully sheweth, That the orders of the Royal missive have been fully explained to all the Thakurs, Chaudharis, Kanungoes and Patwaris of this township of Najafgarh, and the best arrangements have been established. Further, that, agreeably to Your Majesty's injunctions, steps are being taken to collect horsemen and footmen, and it is explained to them, that their allowances will be paid from the Revenue of this Division of the District. Your Slave's assurances on this point, however, will not be believed, till some Ghazees, recently engaged, shall have arrived. As regards Nagli Kakrowla, Dachaoo-Kallan, and other adjacent Villages, your Slave has to represent, that, unrestrained by the dread of consequences, and bent on all sorts of excesses, the inhabitants have commenced plundering travellers. Two petitions regarding the conduct of these lawless disturbers of the peace have already been submitted, and I am now in hopes that some Royal Prince of reputation and capacity, may be deputed, with a sufficient force of Cavalry, Infantry and Ghazees, to settle the portion of the Country constituting your petitioner's jurisdiction, your Slave will then point out these lawless Villagers, and will be able for the future to preserve order, and prevent crime. If delay or indecision is allowed to occur, many lives, it is to be feared, will be sacrificed. Some of the Establishment at this Station were very much straightened in pecuniary means, and had no choice but to go away. If with king's consideration, therefore, some funds are granted, a portion will be given to the men here referred to, and horsemen and footmen will be entertained to preserve order. But Your Majesty is the Lord and Master.[16] This petition is forwarded to Your Majesty by the hands of the cartmen who were recently subjected to lawless treatment. I would beg that Your Majesty's orders may be sent by these men. Signed and Sealed, the Slave Muhammad Zahir Ali, Police Officer of Najafgarh.

Autograph order by the King, in pencil

Mirza Mughal will quickly send a Regiment of Infantry, with its Officers, to Najafgarh.

No. 3

Petition of Captain Dildar Ali Khan

Dated 23rd May 1857

15 In almost every published version, the name is wrongly written as Zohur Ali. The name, as per the Delhi Archives version, is Zahir Allah which is correct.

16 A formal petition to close a petition, showing that the writer has done his/her duty and now the Master should take care of the situation. Ed.

To – The King! Shelter of the World!

Respectfully sheweth, That the Guard which had been stationed for the protection of your Slave's house, having been withdrawn within the last four or five days, ill-conducted characters of the City have been going, in mobs, to plunder it. It is in this house that your Slave's wife and children reside, and he therefore prays that a Guard may be stationed to protect it. Petition of the home-born slave, Captain Dildar Ali Khan.

Autograph order by the King, in pencil

Mirza Mughal will station a Guard, from the 20th Regiment Native Infantry, at the petitioner's house.

No. 4

Petition of Rajab AliJamadar of the Delhi Magazine

Dated 24th May 1857

To – The King! Shelter of the World!

Respectfully sheweth, That we, Slaves, who are nurtured by your salt, leave our families at our homes, and are, agreeably to Your Majesty's orders, daily engaged in the Magazine from morning till night. The disorders and disturbances prevailing in the city, being beyond all limits, we present ourselves at the Royal threshold, and pray that orders, under Your Majesty's Seal, may be issued to all the Police Officers, that they maintain efficient arrangements, in the several jurisdictions, for the protection of the houses of the Magazine servants; moreover, your Slaves, residing in the Khalassy lines which are situated in the Nigambodh Police Station, as well as the rest of the inhabitants, wearied of their lives, by the excessive oppression they are suffering, pray that the present Police Officer may be transferred to some Station outside the City, so that your petitioner may obtain rest and quiet. Petition of the Slave, Rajab Ali, Jamadar of the Delhi Magazine.

Autograph order by the King, in pencil[17]

Mirza Mughal will station all the men who brought treasure from Bulandshahr at the Magazine, and the Soldiers of the Royal Levies are not to be allowed to carry away anything from the Magazine, without special permission.

No. 5

Order under the State Seal of the King

Dated 25th May 1857

To – The Shelter of Syuds, Syud Abdul Hasan.

17 This order has no connection with the petition and was written on it evidently by mistake. Ed.

Learn. That from the day you left Rohtak, no account has been received from you of the state of affairs there. You are, therefore directed, immediately on the receipt of this special mandate, to communicate detailed particulars of the state of that district, as to whether or not you have succeeded in bringing it under entire subjection. Submit your petition in this matter without delay. Consider this order extremely imperative.

Note on the Reverse – 'Copy taken'.

No. 6

Order under the autograph cypher of the King, in pencil

Dated 27th May 1857

To – Mirza Mughal.

Son, the illustrious and valiant Mirza Zahur-ud-Din, otherwise Mirza Mughal Bahadur. Learn, that the articles, which are detailed below, and which are forthcoming in the Magazine, are required to strengthen the Bridge over the Jumna. You are, therefore, directed to have them made over, by the Superintendent of the Magazine, ChuniLal, the Superintendent of the Bridge.

Cables,[18] large, as many as may be required.

Planks, large, as many as may be required.

String, as much as may be required.

Iron hatchets	2
Iron axes	2
Iron saws	2
Iron chisels	2
Iron nails, large	100

No. 7

Order under the seal engraved in the King's special cypher

Dated 29th May 1857

To – The Emblem of Dignity, Jang Baz Khan, Police Officer of Alipur.

Learn, That your Slave, have been nominated and posted to the situation of Police Officer of Alipur. You will take heed to conduct the duties of this appointment with all integrity, honesty, and care, and you will, moreover, under all circumstances, maintain such efficient arrangements throughout your jurisdiction, that pillage, highway robberies, and murders may not occur.

Note on the Reverse – 'Copy taken'.

18 The word *Langar* in the original means either a cable or an anchor. Ed.

No. 8

Order under the special seal engraved in the King's cypher

Dated 29th May 1857

To – The Slave, Emblem of Resolution, Muhammad Ali Beg.

Consider yourself favoured, and know that you are directed, agreeably to our Royal orders, to establish the Office of the private Revenue of the King,[19] and the principal subordinate Office of the District for the collection of the Land Revenue,[20] in the house of James Skinner Bahadur, and in that recently purchased by the wife of the said James Bahadur. Be assured of our favour.

No. 9

Order under the seal engraved in the King's special cypher

Dated 31st May 1857

To – Het Ram, Landholder of the village of Goramra.

Make efficient and effectual arrangements for the supply of Commissariat necessaries, and you shall be fully rewarded by our Royal Government.

No. 10

Order attested with the seal engraved in the King's special cypher

Dated 5th June 1857

To – The Men of the Royal Levies, and One Company of the British Native Infantry, Constituting the Guard at the Lahori Gate.

To the effect, that some pipes of spirits, offensive to the sight, and forbidden by the Mahommedan religion, were taken in plunder. That three of these, of the large size, were left in the Magazine for the manufacture of Powder: that one was sent to the Hospital to the Doctor, and that the rest are now bestowed, according to the detail below, on the Writers of the Kayash caste, old servants of the King. It is therefore incumbent that no hindrance to the conveyance of the pipes to the houses of the Writers may be offered at the Gate. They will be removed according to these orders, of our Royal presence, and no man accordingly is to question or hinder their removal.

Munshi MukundLal	1 pipe
Sheo, late Clerk in the private Office of the King	1 pipe
Samman, late Inspector of the Farash Khana	1 pipe
Sukhan Lal and Juwalla Prashad	1 pipe

19 *Khalsa Sharifa*. Ed.

20 *Hazur Tahsil*. Ed.

Sant Lal, Lakshman Das, Officers of the Pay Department	1 pipe
Jowlea Nath	1 pipe
To the Doctor at the Hospital	1 pipe

No. 11

Order attested with the seal engraved in the King's special cypher

Dated 6th June 1857

To – The Emblem of Dignity! The honoured of the Sovereign, Muhammad Takki Khan.

Learn. That whereas you, our special Slave, were formerly appointed Superintendent of our Hall of special Audience, you are now, in consideration of your high literary attainments, and your honesty and dignity, nominated to the Office of Sudder Amin of Shahjahanabad[21] (Delhi), the seat of the Imperial Government, in room of the *Kerany*[22] dismissed. You will conduct the duties of this appointment, in subjection to the authority of the highly distinguished paragon of accomplishments, the Moulvi Sudder-ud-din Bahadur.

No. 12

Petition of Zabtay Khan, attached to the Police Station of Basant

Dated 16th June 1857

To – The King! Adoration of the World!

Previous to this, Your Majesty's orders were received to the effect, that 40 footmen, from the force here, should be detached to the Police Station of Paharganj, but delay occurred in carrying out these orders, in consequence of diverse necessaries not having been ready. Today, your Slave has been honoured with a second order, reiterating the first: your Highness, agreeably to Your Majesty's orders, your Slave will attend the Royal presence tomorrow, bringing 40 footmen of his Station, and will afterwards, install them at the Paharganj Station. These men have been paraded and mustered, in the presence of Nathia Khan, Trooper. (Prayers for the King's prosperity.) Petition of the Slave, Zabtay Khan, attached, to the Police Station of Basant.

Note on the Reverse – 'The contents have been learned 16th June 1857'.

No. 13

Order under the autograph cypher of the King, in pencil

Dated 18th June 1857

21 Old Delhi.

22 *Kerany*, a corrupt, as also contemptuous form of the word Christian (*Kristann – Kerany*)

To – Mirza Mughal.

Son, The illustrious and valiant Mirza Zahaur-ud-din, otherwise Mirza Mughal Bahadur! Learn, that yesterday, an order was passed, under our own special signature, on a petition from the inhabitants of the old Fort, prohibiting acts of devastation against the petitioners, and that this petition was then sent to you. It is surprising that, up to the present time, no arrangement should have been made, and that you should not have given effect to the prohibition, by sending out some Cavalry. It is the business of the Army to protect, and not to desolate and plunder. The Officers of the Army will, therefore, immediately restrain their men from the commission of these improprieties, and further, as the intelligence of the approach of the Enemies' Troops was false, these lawless Soldiery should not now be kept in the old Fort, but, on the contrary, entrenchments should be constructed for them, at the distance of five or six miles, and they should be stationed there, so that our subjects may obtain immunity from the hardships complained of; and that, at the same time, a barrier may be raised against the approach of the Enemies' Troops. You will immediately take steps to arrange this matter, and will allow no neglect to occur, in reference to it. Be assured of our kindness. In pencil, in the King's handwriting, to give the order greater force, no doubt.

'Make arrangements quickly'.

No. 14

Joint Petition of Chand Khan and Ghulab Khan, on behalf of themselves and other Residents of Jysinghpur and Shahganj, otherwise known as Paharganj

Dated 19th June 1857

To – The King! Shelter of the World!

Respectfully sheweth, That whereas in these days of auspicious prospects, we poor residents of Jysinghpur and Shahganj,[23] otherwise known as Paharganj, and of other places, forming a community, pass our time, under your Royal and light-dispensing prestige, in freedom from all grievances. Whereas this township of Paharganj has always borne the Royal name and whereas frequently the Troops of the State, emerging from the Ajmiri Gate, visit Paharganj, and oppressing the shopkeepers, forcibly take away their wares, without the payment of privies, and also, entering the dwelling houses of the destitute and indigent, forcibly carry away all such articles, as beds, woods, vessels, etc., that they can lay hands on, and wound with firearms and swords, those who may supplicate their forbearance: wearied by this oppression from the Army, we are reduced to the necessity

23 *Shah Ganj, the King's Ganj.* Ed.

of petitioning our august presence, that, from regard to justice, as well as from kind consideration for our condition, the Officers of the Army may be ordered to explain to, and enjoin on their men, that they desist from oppressing us, and the other poor residents of Paharganj. Petition of the lowest Servants, Chand Khan and Ghulab Khan.

Autograph order by the King, in pencil

Mirza Mughal will adopt such measures against these devastators as will compel them to desist from plundering, so that our subjects may not be aggrieved or oppressed.

No. 15

Order under the autograph cypher of the King, in pencil

Dated 20th June 1857

To – Mirza Mughal.

Son, The illustrious and valiant Mirza Zahur-ud-din, otherwise Mirza Mughal Bahadur. Learn, that Abdul Hasan, alias Mir Nawab, son of the lawyer, Mir Taffazul Hasan, is a suspicious character, and it is our Royal pleasure that he be not allowed to come into the Palace. We have recently heard that this man is with you. You are therefore directed to have him ejected immediately, and to have orders conveyed to both Gates, that on no account is he to be allowed admission into the Palace, for the future. Consider these orders imperative. Moreover, listen to no intercessions that may be made by others, in this man's favour. Be assured of our favour.

No. 16

Order under the King's State Seal

Dated 24th June 1857

To – The Slave Emblem of Power, Jumma-ud-Din Khan.

Learn. That your petition soliciting permission to open a Newspaper press has been received and read, and that your request is granted. You are, accordingly, authorized hereby to start the Newspaper in full confidence. You are, however, directed to observe great care, that false intelligence, or that statements by which the characters of respectable individuals, or of the residents of the City, may be aspersed, directly or by implication, be not inserted.

No. 17

Order under the seal engraved in the King's special cypher

Dated 25th June 1857

To – Mirza Mughal.

Son, The illustrious and valiant Mirza Zahur-ud-din, otherwise Mirza Mughal Bahadur. Learn, that orders have, day after day, been issued to the Officers of the Cavalry to vacate the Garden, and they have, till now done nothing, but make excuses and promises. Definite orders are therefore now issued, to the intent that you, our Son, will summon the Officers, and will tell them that if they consider themselves the servants of the State, they will not go to the batteries tomorrow, but will leave the Garden and remove their quarters to Keetur's[24] house, situated under the Palace, where there is abundance of accommodation, and ample shelter of trees. What they urge in reply, you will submit for our consideration.

No. 18

Order under the autograph cypher of the King, in pencil

Dated 27th June 1857

To – Mirza Moghul and Mirza Khair Sultan.

Sons, The illustrious and valiant Mirza Zahur-ud-din, otherwise Mirza Mughal Bahadur and Mirza Kabir Sultan Bahadur. Learn, that your petition, regarding the proceedings of four or five ill-conducted men, who assuming, as a disguise, the appearance and dress of soldiers of the Native Infantry of the Company, have gone about plundering the inhabitants of the City, and have now left for the country, and representing the detriment to the Government which must ensue, in consequence, and further requesting permission to take measures for suppressing such practices, and for capturing the men alluded to, has been perused. It is a matter of some surprise, that from the lawless doing of but four or five men, so much plunder and devastation in the City, and so much ruination of the people generally, should result; and that, on their capture alone, the establishment of order should be expected to depend; for not a day has elapsed, since the arrival of the Army, and its taking up quarters in the City, that petitions from the townspeople have not been submitted, representing the excesses committed by numerous Infantry Sepoys, about whom there could no suspicion of disguise, and that orders have not been issued, day after day, to you, our Sons, to take measures with the aid of a Military force, to suppress these disorders. Considering all this, it seems now altogether unlikely that order can be secured while the Army remains in the City. However, you, our Sons, are nevertheless directed to send to our glorious presence, someone able to recognize the vagabonds alluded to, that he may be sent, accompanied by horsemen and footmen of our own Royal Levies, with a mandate, to the Chief Police Officer of the City, and his subordinates, to arrest and forward without delay to our presence, those whom he may point out, and if any

24 A corruption perhaps of some English name. Ed.

villainy or instigation to plunder shall be proved against those who may be thus apprehended, they will revive punishments adequate to their guilt. But you, our Sons, are directed to take all proper steps, to prevent the men of the Army from plundering and desolating the City. In every case of an offence of these kings being proved, or where a man may be found in the private residence of any of the inhabitants, the Officers will award punishments to the offender so that these evils may be suppressed. Be assured of our kindness.

No. 19

Petition of Muhammad Khair Sultan

Dated 27th June 1857

To – The King! Shelter of the World!

Respectfully sheweth, That 162 Sheep and Goats, which were being taken to the English, have been captured, and brought in by Sheo Das Pathak and Narayan Singh, Sepoys of the 46th Regiment Native Infantry, serving in the Batteries, and that 5 European Soldiers have been killed on this occasion. It is submitted for information. Petition to the humble Khair Sultan.

Autography note by the King, in pencil

162 Sheep and Goats have been received.

Note on the top – 'Index No. 290'.

No. 20

Petition of Boldeo, farmer of Ferozabad

Dated 28th June 1857

To – The King! Shelter of the World!

Respectfully sheweth, That owing to the unsettled state of the times, and in consequence of the City gates being kept closed, your Slave has stored the produce of his Winter crop of Grain of the Agricultural year 1264, on the premises; of a relation in the old Fort. The Officers of the Regiment stationed there now oppose; its removal, and your Slave is pressed for payment of his rent for the year referred to, by his landlord Syad Abdulla, Mafeedar.[25] Your Slave therefore trust that an order, under your Royal signature, may be sent to the Officers stationed in the old Fort, directing them not to oppose the removal of the Grain to the City, so that your Slave may sell it and pay his rent. The petition of the Slave Baldeo, Cultivator of the Village of Ferozabad Khadir endowment to the Shrine of Sharif Hazrat Muhammad Chisti.

Autograph order by the King, in pencil

Note on the Reverse – Ahsanullah Khan, have an order written.

25 Rent-free tenant.

No. 21

Petition of Syad Abdulla, Priest at the Shrine of Hazrat Sheikh Muhammad Chisti

Dated 29th June 1857

To – The King! Shelter of the World!

Previous to this, your petitioner submitted a petition, representing that some of the Cultivators of the rent-free Village of Ferozabad Khadir had not paid their rents on account of the Winter crop of the Agricultural year 1264, and he requested that aid might be granted to enforce payment. Up to that time no damage had been sustained by the crops which the Cultivators could urge as a reason for delay. Now, however, the whole of the Autumnal crop of Sugarcane, Churree, etc., of the Agricultural year 1265, has been totally devastated, and more than this, the very implements of Agriculture, such as ploughs, the wood-work on wells, have been all carried away, in plunder by the Soldiers, under these circumstances, certainly the rents cannot be realized and as the Revenue of this Village has been assigned, as an endowment to support the expenses of the Alms-house under your petitioner's management, he depends on your Royal kindness and consideration, and trusts such arrangements will be adopted, as will ensure that no Soldier shall cause loss to the Agriculturists of the said Village. A petition from the Cultivators, also, is being submitted. Petition of the Anchorite Syad Abdullah son of Syad Shah Sabur Ali Chisti. Official Seal of the Shrine.

Autograph order of the King, in pencil (illegible)

No. 22

Joint petition of Jogal Kishwar, and Sheoprashad, Merchants

No date[26]

To – The King! Shelter of the World!

Your Majesty, Paying, agreeably to Your Majesty's orders, Rupees 1,200 into the Royal Treasury, we obtained a document, under your special signature, assuring us that we should for the future have full immunity from all vexation and annoyance at the hands of the functionaries of the State, the Princes Royal of Illustrious descent, the Soldiers of the Army, and all others. Notwithstanding all this, however, some Troopers, bent upon plunder, still come daily to your Slave's house, in the name of the Princes, and wish to take our lives or carry us prisoners. Left without other choice, we have been sitting concealed for the last three or four days, and our servants and retainers being subjected to every grievance and hardship, have not known

26 Date of final order is 1st July 1857. Ed.

what to do. Denied ingress and egress to and from our house, we have been rendered houseless as it were, and the privacy of our families has been completely ruined. If the Prince Royal, delegated to protect the subjects of the State and the poor, begin themselves to plunder and oppress, where then can there be any safety for the subject? From Your Majesty's goodness, clemency, and justice, equal to now Sherwan's, we expect that a written order will be addressed to each of the Royal Princes of illustrious ancestry, namely his Highness the Lord of the World, Mirza Muhammad Mughal Bahadur, Mirza Khair Muhammad Abdulla Bahadur, and others, to the effect that for the future, no soldier of the Cavalry or Infantry be permitted to go to your Slave's house and commit acts of aggression there, and that the Military Guard at present stationed there, be removed, because lawless characters of the City take advantage of the Guard being changed to plunder your Slave's property. We further expect from Your Majesty's kindness and consideration that a Guard of Militia from the Chief Police Station of the City may be placed at our house, that we and our servants may not be hindered in going in and out, and may be protected from the ill-conducted characters of the City, and we pray, moreover, that a written order may be sent to the Chief Police Officer, that none of the ill-conducted characters above alluded to, may be permitted to get up disturbances with your Petitioners. (Prayers for the prosperity of the reign.) Petition of the Slaves, Jogal Kishwar and Sheoprashad, Merchants.

Autograph order by the King, in pencil

Mirza Mughal Bahadur Will station a Guard at the house of the Petitioners.

No date. Index No. 218

Note on the Reverse – Agreeably to His Majesty's Commands written order has been issued, dated 1st July 1857

No. 23

Petition of Mirza Mughal

Dated 2nd July 1857

To – The King! Shelter of the World!

Respectfully sheweth, That a petition has this day been received from the inhabitants of the City, to the effect that they have been directed by the Chief Police Officer to wait armed and in a body, on the Officers of the Troops arrived from Bareilly. It does not appear what the object of this order is. Your petitioner therefore suggests that such orders as may be necessary in this case may be issued, so that they may be complied with. Petition of the Slave, Mirza Muhammad Zohaur-ud-din Bahadur. Official Seal of the Commander-in-Chief Bahadur.

No Order.

No. 24
Petition of Syad Muhammad, Ascetic

Dated 4th July 1857

To – The King! Shelter of the World!

Respectfully sheweth, That the Soldiers of the 9th Regiment Native Infantry quartered near Skinner's house, which is close to the Cashmere Gate, are destroying the houses adjoining the Ailkhnad Khan Police Station, and situated in the rear of Skinner's house. Several tenements, forming a square, some of brick or stone, and some of mud or unbaked bricks and belonging to Ascetics, are situated in the locality. The aforesaid Soldiery had before dug out and taken away the doors and door-frames. They are now destroying the roofs. As Your Majesty dispenses justice to all, your Petitioner depends on Your Majesty's goodness and favour, and prays that the entire demolition of these houses by the Soldiers may be prevented, so that what remains of them may be saved from their aggressive hands. It was necessary, and has therefore been submitted. (Prayers for the King's prosperity.) Petition of the Ascetic, the lowly Syad Muhammad.

Autograph order by the King, in pencil

Mirza Mughal Bahadur will lay strict injunctions on the Officers of the 9th Regiment, Native Infantry, to refrain from the spoliation complained of.

Note on the Reverse – The order has been written.

Number on the face (Index number probably) '204'.

No. 25
Petition of Ahsan-ul-hak

Dated 4th July 1857

To – The King! Shelter of the World!

Respectfully sheweth, That Mirza Abu Bakr Sahib has lately been in the habit, with unrestrained licence and recklessness, of visiting for evil purposes the house of Princess Farkhnunda Zamani, situated in Bahram Khan's Teraha (your petitioner's houses being in the same division of the City), and of indulging in the practice of all those acts which may be expected to result from drunkenness. According to his custom, he came yesterday before noon to the said Princess's house, and remained, drinking spirituous liquors, and hearing singing for the rest of the day. About an hour and a half after sunset, he prepared to leave; but the key of the street gate, accidentally being with the watchman, and he not coming immediately, the Mirza was delayed. Upon this, the Mirza being in a hurry, drew his pistol and fired it at your Slave, who happened at the time to be sitting at his door with some friends. Your Slave kept silent, although no pretext had been afforded for this violence; but the Mirza nevertheless gave unlimited hand to his tongue, and thought to enter your Slave's house, and to plunder and to carry off all the property it contained. Your Slave, however, shut the door, fixed on the chain, and got inside. The Mirza had intended to kill your Slave, and it was with this object he discharged his pistol at him; but as some little portion of your Slave's life remained uncompleted, the shot did not take effect. After the door had been closed, the Mirza drew his sword, and made several attacks upon it, and moreover directed his servants to throw stones at different places over the walls, and at the doors. He further gave orders that the Artillery, Infantry, and Cavalry, should plunder the house and slaughter the inmates. The watchman stationed at the Faiz Bazaar arriving, the Mirza forcibly threw him on the ground, and it was probable that he would have severed the watchman's head from his body. This did not occur; but the Mirza so bruised the watchman's back and head with blows, as to leave him half dead. Moreover, the Mirza kept striking with his drawn sword in all directions, and very much injured the door with successive shots from muskets, and so distributed the Infantry Soldiers in the Bazaar, at the same time ordering the Troopers to plunder and murder, that many of the people passing in the streets, were hit by the bullets. The Assistant to the Chief Police Officer of the City was hit by one....[27] Nothing remains of the property that belonged to the residents of this part of the City, or to the Police Officer.... All the goods and chattels likewise, which happened to be in the yard in front of the house, were carried off in plunder, and the Mirza, then destroying the door left a guard, and went away. If this disturbance, your Slave has had a foretaste of the day of judgement. Whatever has passed, now depending on Your Majesty's kindness, I trust that full punishment may be awarded. Otherwise, tomorrow is not far from today, and the said Lord of the World, Mirza Abu Bakr, bent on evil purposes, will certainly come with cannons, muskets, and swords, and will carry out his designs, and what we helpless subjects will have suffered will be something astounding.

List of property carried off.

Cotton carpet, 5 yards long, valued at 7 Rs.	1
Copper vessels (*Lotas)*	2
Copper saucers and covers, valued at 1 Re	2
Janumaz, valued at 2 Rs.	1
Benares scarf, valued 7 Rs.	1
A horse, colour, dun, valued 200 Rs.	1
A small portable hookah	1
A pair of bullocks, value 100 Rs.	1 pair
A sword, valued 15 Rs.	1

27 This portion of the original petition is torn out. Ed.

Petition of Muhammad Ahsan-ul-hak

Order under the Autograph Special Cypher of the King, in pencil, in reference to the circumstances represented in the above petition, 5th July 1857.

To – Mirza Mughal.

Son, the illustrious and valiant Mirza Zahur-ud-din, otherwise Mirza Mughal Bahadur. Learn, that you are directed to search out, and recover from the servants of Mirza Abu Bakr Bahadur, a sword and a pink turban, the property of Kamdar Khan, watchman of the Faiz Bazaar, who was wounded, and to forward them to the Royal presence; you are directed also to recover from the men of the said Mirza, the property of Muhammad Ahsan-ul-hak, son of the Mufti (Professor of the Mahommedan Law) Ikram-ud-din, whose petition is enclosed, as also to recover and forward to the Royal presence, the property of Khuda Baksh Khan, Assistant to the Chief Police Officer. Be assured of our kindness.

No. 26

Order under the autograph cypher of the King, in pencil

Dated 11th July 1857

To – Mirza Mughal.

Son, the illustrious and valiant Mirza Zahur-ud-din, otherwise Mirza Mughal Bahadur. Learn, that you were formerly directed, by a special mission, as well as by our verbal injunctions, to make search for a horse, a pistol, and other property belonging to the Assistant to the Chief Police officer of the City. We learn today, from the representations of the Chief Police Officer that Jugga Sais, has just come, after recognizing the Assistant's horse, in the Camp of the Cavalry at the Ellenborough Tank. You, our Son, are therefore directed to have the horse; pointed out tomorrow without fail, and recovering him from the Troopers, to restore him to the Police Officer. Be assured of our kindness.

Order on the Reverse, without signature or seal, but given by Mirza Mughal apparently. Let an order be issued to the Officers of the Cavalry, directing the institution of enquiries regarding the horse in Question – If the horse pointed out, is proved to be the property of the Assistant Police Officer, he must be sent here immediately. Dated 12th July 1857.

Note under the Order – 'This order should have been written on a separate paper. It has been written here by oversight'.

No. 27

Petition of Mirza Mughal

Dated 11th July 1857

To – The King! Shelter of the World!

Respectfully sheweth, That the pistol sent through Yusuf Beg, has been received. In regard to Your Majesty's orders communicated verbally through your petitioner's foster father your slave submits, that Your Majesty knows every particular of your slave's conduct, without his explaining it. Nothing is hidden from Your Majesty. Your slave affirms, with the solemnity of an oath, that no orders are ever issued, but such as Your Majesty has been previously made acquainted with, or if any are issued, the physician, at least, is always informed of them. Your slave issues no orders whatever without Your Majesty's knowledge. Father, as regards the distribution of money to the Troops your slave prays, that Bindi Banker may be summoned, and may be made to declare an oath, whether or not your slave has always regarded the smallest fraction, and a lac of rupees, as sums equally insignificant, and whether the embezzlement of the least trifle can have occurred. Petition of the slave, Zahur-ud-din. Attested with the Official seal of the 'Commander-in-Chief Bahadur'.

Autograph order by the King, in pencil

'Institute inquiries'.

'No. 401' (Apparently Index number)

No. 28

Petition of Jamuna Das, Landholder, Resident of Muttra

Dated 14th July 1857

To – The King! Shelter of the World!

Respectfully sheweth, That your exalted Highness. Your slave has for some years, been staying at his home without occupation, and has passed his time as best he was able. He has now come to Your Majesty's threshold in search of his subsistence, and prays that orders may be issued from your Royal presence, empowering him to make arrangements for settling the Country from Delhi to Muttra, and thence on to Agra. As your slave is a resident of Muttra, and is in consequence fully acquainted with the whole of that District, he will, through Your Majesty's auspices and the favour of God, be able to establish arrangement which will be thoroughly efficient. Your slave, moreover, knows near 2,000 men in that District, who are practised in the use of firearms. All he requires is Your Majesty's orders, and he will then establish Postal and Commissariat arrangements in every City and Town, from Delhi to Muttra, etc. Ten or 15 days after reaching Muttra, your slave will send ten Lacs of rupees to the Royal Treasury, for the expenses of the State. He prays, therefore, that the matter being taken into favourable consideration, one piece of ordnance, with shot and powder, and some Infantry, may be made over to him, to proceed in that direction.

Arriving in that District, your slave will, with the blessing of God, make thoroughly efficient arrangements, and Your Majesty's Government will be firmly established. Without your Royal authority, your slave is unable to do anything, and that which is accomplished, will hereafter be thoroughly manifest to Your Majesty. Beyond this, matters are in the dispensation of God. It was necessary, and has therefore been submitted. (Prayers for the prosperity of the reign.)

Piece of Ordnance with powder and shot	1
Regiment of Infantry with Cavalry	1
Seal, to certify King's authority for the petitioner's proceedings	1

Besides the above, whatever else it may please His Majesty to bestow. Petition of the slave Jamuna Das, Putail, of old nourished by His Majesty's salt, resident of Muttra, at present staying at Delhi.

Signature of the Petitioner in Hindi.

Note: No order on the petition; but there is a separate one in reference to it from the King, to Mirza Mughal, which has been translated as a separate paper.

No. 29

Petition from Rattan Chand, Superintendent of the Royal Gardens, and private Estates of the King attached to Sahibabad etc.

No date

To – The King! Shelter of the World!

Respectfully sheweth, That the Troopers quartered in the Chandni Chouk have picketed their horses immediately in the front of the shops. Many of the tenants have, in consequence, vacated their shops and gone away, and those that remain are ready to follow the same course, from dread of the Troopers. Much loss of rent, as well as damage to the shops, which having been plastered with mortar are yet in repair, is now occurring. Your petitioner prays, therefore, that orders according to the Royal salt, the slave Rattan Chand, Superintendent of the Gardens, and personal Estates of the King, at Sahibabad, etc.

Note in the Margin – 'Copy taken'.

Order by the King, in reference to the above petition, without signature, seal or cypher, dated 16th July 1857

To – Mirza Mughal.

Son, the illustrious and valiant Mirza Zahur-ud-din, otherwise Mirza Mughal Bahadur. Learn, that we are informed, by a petition from Rattan Chand, Superintendent of the Sahibabad Garden, which is herein enclosed in original, that the Troopers of the Cavalry come from Jodhpur have picketed their horses in front of the shops, and have taken possession of a number of them. That some of the shopkeepers have, in consequence, vacated their shops; and gone away, and that those of the tenants who remain are ready to do the same. Under these circumstances, loss to our personal Revenue must ensue. You, our son, are therefore directed to cause these Troopers to remove from their present location, and to assign them some other place to stay in, so that this cause of loss to our Revenue may be checked. Be assured of our kindness.

No. 30

Petition of Sheodial and Shadiram, Merchants

Dated 17th July 1857[28]

To – The King! Shelter of the World!

Respectfully sheweth, That great mobs of people go daily to the mercantile shops of your slaves, situated near the Cashmere Gate, and commit the most riotous proceedings there. Sometimes they bring the Chief Police Officer of the City, at others, the soldiery, accusing your slaves, as a plea for their conduct, of sending supplies to the Enemy. Be it manifest to Your Majesty, that we are the hereditary and home-born slaves of your illustrious house. From such proceedings, our total, ruin and impoverishment must ensue; we therefore pray that our shops may be placed under the lock and key of the State, so that it may be protected, and we may obtain safety from the grievance represented. (Prayers for the prosperity of the reign.)

Petition of the slave, Shadiram and Sheodial, Shopkeepers. No date.

Autograph order by the King, in pencil

Mirza Mughal will provide for the protection of the petitioners.

On the Reverse – 'No. 557'.

Order on the reverse, without signature or seal, apparently by Mirza Mughal, in furtherance of the King's order:

This petition, bearing an order in the Royal handwriting, directing arrangements, has reached this office today. The petitioners request that their shops may be placed under the lock and key of the State, and that it may be protected. It is therefore ordered, that a written order be sent to the Chief Police Officer of the City, to the intent that agreeably to the request for the petitioners, he place their shops under lock and key, and attend so to its protection that no damage may be allowed to occur to it. It is not necessary to send the liquors here.[29] Dated 17th July 1857.

Note under the Order – 'An order has been written'.

28 There is no date on the petition. This is the date of the final order on it. Ed.

29 This sentence appears to bear allusion to some verbal request of the petitioner. Ed.

No. 31

Order under the autograph special cypher of the king, in pencil

Dated 17th July 1857

To – Mirza Mughal.

Son, The illustrious and valiant Mirza Zahur-ud-din, otherwise Mirza Mughal Bahadur. Learn, that on perusal of the petition of Syad Husein Ali Khan, Police Officer of Paharganj, regarding the wounding of a Jamadar and some Policemen by the violent hands of the Goojurs of Aliganj, Mallanji, Hasangarh, and Alapur, a special order was sent to you, with the said petition in original. Today, on perusal of a representation from the Police Officer of Mahrowali, we learn that the same Goojurs are now engaged in highways robbery and in plundering the country. The suppression of such disorders is of the utmost moment, and you are directed therefore immediately to send out one Company of Infantry and 50 Troopers, to capture the Goojurs in question, with the Chief men of their villages. If they are captured, they shall receive the punishment due to their misdeeds, and complete order will ensue. Be assured of our favour.

Note on the Face – 'Received 27th July 1857, Number 849'.

No. 32

Order under the autograph cypher of the King, in pencil

To – Mirza Mughal.

Son, The illustrious and valiant Mirza Zahur-ud-din, otherwise Mirza Mughal Bahadur. Learn, that from the petition of Jamuna Das, landholder, resident of Muttra, now staying in Delhi, it is ascertained that he has 2,000 men at his command, experienced in the use of firearms, that he promises to bring ten lacs of rupees to the Royal Treasury, that he declares his ability to make efficient arrangements along the road from Delhi to Agra, and that he requires a Military force, comprised of Artillery, Infantry, and Cavalry, together with ammunition, and a seal of authority. As it is necessary to enquire – firstly, in what way this man will carry out all the above projects, and how he will proceed to prove what he says, you, our Son, are directed to assemble a Court of all the principal Officers of the Army, and to confer and consult with them about the matter, and to submit, for our consideration, distinctly noticing every particular, whether or not it is likely, that he can bring what he proposes to a successful issue, and, if he can, what course he will adopt. You will also state what the wishes of the Officers of the Army may be in this matter, and whether the man has the capacity for this business, or whether he will only pillage and plunder on his own account. All these points affecting the plan, the means, and the proceedings by which he can carry out all that is said in his petition, you will state distinctly for consideration, and definite orders will then be issued. The original is enclosed in this missive, make yourself thoroughly acquainted with its contents, and whatever may be clearly ascertained and proved in this matter, submit for our consideration. Be assured of our kindness. Secondly – Does this man propose to dig up a buried treasure of ten lacs of rupees, or does he know of any Treasury where this money is deposited, or does he intend to plunder any one for it? It is necessary he should be questioned on this point also.

No. 33
Petition of Imam-Baksh, Chowdary, and all the men of the ice-pits No date, Date of final order, 18th July 1858

To – The King! Shelter of the World!

Respectfully sheweth, That we, your slaves, have from time immemorial, been cherished and nurtured by the salt of Your Majesty's house. The Troops which have now arrived have encamped near your slaves' houses, which are contiguous to the ice-pits opposite the Turkoman Gate, and your slaves are, in consequence, exposed to great annoyances and ruination; the very timbers of the roofs of their houses the ice used by Your Majesty's butler[30] is supplied from his ice-pits. Your Majesty desires the fostering care and protection of all God's creatures. Your petitioner therefore prays that Madhuganj, the property of the Rajah of Jypur, adjoining Rajah Jysing's Observatory,[31] and near to the Turkoman Gate, its enclosing wall being still in preservation, may be graciously bestowed on him, and that an order may be issued to the force come from Bareilly, prohibiting opposition and hindrance, so that your slaves obtaining safety by night and say pray for Your Majesty's prosperity. We further beg that the order to the Officers may be issued under your special signature. Petition of the slave Imabakhsh, and all the men of the ice-pits.

Autograph order by the King, in pencil

Mirza Mughal Bahadur will give the petitioners place in the Observatory, and will have an order written.

Order on the reverse, without Signature or Seal, apparently my Mirza Mughal, in furtherance of the King's order:

Let orders in accordance with those of the Royal presence be issued, dated 18th July 1857.

Note below the Order – 'An order has been written'.

No. 34
Translation of a Firman from Delhi, addressed to Muhammad Khan, Nawab of Najibabad

30 *Abdarkhana*. Ed.

31 Jantar-Mantar (Observatory) near Connaught Place.

Seal

Abuzafar-Sirajud-din Muhammad
Bahadur Shah. Padsha-i-Ghazi
1253 A. Hijri, and 1st of Reign

Amir-ud-dowlah, Zia-ul-mulk, Muhammad Mahmud Khan Bahadur, Muzafar Jang, our own special servant, worthy of kindness and protection, the object of our favours.

Know! The petition of that special servant, containing full particulars respecting the disturbed state of all the Pergunnahs of that Zillah from the acts of plunderers and rascals, and the method adopted for putting a stop to the same by entertaining as many footmen and horsemen as possible, and calling to mind the hereditary services of that faithful one towards our Royal house, and requesting that our Royal attention may devolve upon that Zillah as of old, has been perused, and all has become known. Of a truth, the forefathers of that especial servant have ever been the objects of favours to former Emperors; but that special servant has always been looked upon by us with particular favour, inasmuch as you left me no service which was becoming unperformed for Mirza Shah-Rukh, deceased, the light of our Royal eyes.

Therefore you are entitled to our special kindness.

If you, in addition to your former good acts, render still more efficient service, then will the Royal favour be increased, and your request that the arrangement of the whole Zillah be made over to you shall be complied with. Until a perfect sunnud be issued, you are to keep in deposit the revenues of the District, after paying the Troops and the Revenue Officers, and you are to remit the balance to us.

With reference to the large amount of Treasure, chattels and horses, which came into your hands after the flight of the British officers, you must send them at once with account current by the hands of Mathura Das (N.B. this the name of the Royal Treasurer, father of the Bijnore Treasurer) and two of the Royal Sowars, in order that the real value of your professions may be at once tested, and that you may obtain promotion.

28th Zu'l Kadat, 21st year of our reign, corresponding with the 21st July 1857.

(True translation)
(Sd.) J.C. Wilson
Judge of Moradabad,
SB. Court, Meerut Division.

No. 35
Petition of Karim Bakhsh, Alias Natthua
No date, Date of King's Order, 22 July 1857

To – The King! Divine and Merciful!

Respectfully sheweth, That a week or ten days ago, Jawahar Bakhsh, Private of the 11th Regiment of Infantry, stole a black female mule, the property of your slave, from the street known as the Kazi-ka-Howz. Your slave, with much difficulty, found the mule after five day's search, when Jawahar Bakhsh restored it, after claiming 11 rupees for doing so. Three days subsequently to this, the said Private, accompanied by another, came to your slave's house, which is situated in the Turkoman Police jurisdiction, and seizing him as a delinquent, took him before Mirza Sultan Beg, Doctor of the 11th Regiment of Infantry. The Doctor placed your slave in arrest and said the mule was his, and that your slave should either bring the animal, or remain a prisoner. Fearing that his life was in jeopardy, your slave made the mule over, when the 11 rupees he had formerly given, were returned. The truth is, that about five months ago, your slave purchased the animal in question from Ramzan Khan, Risaldar, of the 5th Troops, 8th Regiment of Irregular Cavalry, who is a resident of Delhi. Your slave prays that with fostering concern for the protection of the poor, Your Majesty will enquire of the above-named Risaldar, and of four or five other Officers of his Regiment, so that your slave may obtain justice, and even pray for Your Majesty's prosperity. It was necessary, and has therefore been submitted. (Prayers for the prosperity of the reign.) Petition of the slave Karim Bakhsh, *alias* Natthua, claimant for justice, proprietor of the mule.

Autograph Order of the King, in ink, authenticated with Cypher. No. 631 dated 22nd July 1857.

Let an order be written to the officers of the 11th Regiment of Infantry.

Now in a corner on the Reverse. 'The written order' in this case, has not been issued.

No. 36
Order under the special autograph cypher of the King, in pencil, No. 643
Dated 22nd July 1857

To – Mirza Mughal.

Son, the illustrious and valiant Mirza Zahur-ud-din, otherwise Mirza Mughal Bahadur. Learn! Formerly some troopers took up quarters in the Hayat-Bakhsh and Mahtab Gardens, and owing to the injury these gardens suffered from the Troopers staying in them, they were made to remove, agreeably to our Royal orders. But now near 200 soldiers of the 54th

Regiment Native Infantry, and a doctor, with his family, have located themselves there, and thus, unless they remove, the causes of damage to the said Gardens will continue as before; moreover, our Royal Cortege frequently condescends to go in that direction, and much inconvenience is felt on such occasions. You, our Son, are therefore directed to speak to the officers of the Court on this matter, and to have these Soldiers and the native doctor removed from the gardens. In doing this, you will secure our extreme divine approbation. Be assured of our kindness.

It being half past two o'clock, and the Prisoner requiring an adjournment, the Court – adjourned accordingly until 11 a.m. tomorrow.

Day two: 28 January 1858

The Court reassembled this day, at 11 a.m., in the Hall of Special Audience, in the Palace at Delhi, pursuant to adjournment of yesterday.

The President, Members, Interpreter, and Dy. Judge Advocate-General are all present.

The Prisoner is brought into Court.

Ahssanullah Khan is called into Court, and reminded of his former affirmation.

The Prisoner now requests that a Lawyer of the name of Ghulam Abbas, may be allowed to attend and assist him in Court. To this Court accede, and Ghulam Abbas takes his seat in Court accordingly.

The Interpreter now peruses the originals of the papers, the translations of which were read by the Judge Advocate yesterday, and it is explained to the prisoner's assistant what evidence in respect to each paper was given by the Witness yesterday. The Interpreter having perused the Persian original down to No. 36, the Judge Advocate resumes reading the English translations down to No. 56 which are entered as follows:

No. 37

Order under the Seal of the Royal Court of Justice

Dated 22nd July 1857

To – The Emblem of Valour, the Chief Police Officer of Delhi.

The files of papers relating to the cases of two out of the five prisoners sent by you are present in this Office, as specified below; but those of the remaining three are not forthcoming. If you have in your possession any receipt of this Royal Court for the three missing files, you are directed to submit it, and for the future, it is necessary that all prisoners who are forwarded to this Court, should be accompanied by the usual form of committal, with all prisoners in the same way.

List cases
Files forthcoming

Case of Gumani, defendant
Case of Rahm Ulla, defendant
Files not forthcoming
Harsukh
Ghulam Ali
Khuda Bakhsh
Petition of Mubarak Shah, Chief Police Officer of the City, on the reverse of the above Order

Dated 24th July 1857

To – The King, & c.

The explanation called for by this order is submitted in a separate petition, which is enclosed.

Petition of the slave, Mubarak Shah, Chief Police Officer of the City of Delhi.

Enclosure referred to in the above.

To – The King! Shelter of the World!

Respectfully sheweth, That Your Majesty's order, to the effect that five prisoners dispatched from the Chief Police Officer of the City had reached, and that of these, the files of the cases of Gumani and Rahimullah are in the Office of the Royal Court of Justice, but that those of Harsukh, Ghulam Ali, and Khuda Bakhsh have not been found, and, therefore, directing that, if any receipt of the Royal Court is forthcoming in this Office, it be submitted; and further enjoining that in future cases, the usual form of committal, the plaintiff, and the proofs of guilt be sent with the prisoners, has been received. Your Exalted Highness, the particulars are these. Harsukh was apprehended by the subordinate Police officer of Allahabad, on suspicion of obtaining his livelihood by evil practices, and was sent to this Police Station as a character of this sort; but as there was no plaintiff, and no stolen property was found in his possession, no papers were prepared in his case. As regards Ghulam Alithe particulars are these. He was sent to me, from the case, against him, to witness, that the following stolen property had been found in his possession:

Brass Vessels, the property of Jammnaji Cashmiri. Sheep and Goatskin shoes, belonging to Muhammad Ali, seller of shoes, clothes and other things, the property of Ghulam Haidar Khan. In the investigation, at the Chief Police Stations, the charge having been conclusively proved by the written statement of the subordinate Police Officer, by the testimony of witnesses, and by Ghulam Ali's own confession, the property was made over to the claimants on their several receipts, their ownership being first fully ascertained, and a full statement of the case, together with the papers received from the subordinate Police Station, was forwarded to Your Majesty. In reference to the prisoner, in this case, it was specifically mentioned in my report, that he had formerly been a Watchman in the division of the City known as the Turkoman, but that the Clerk of the Chandni Chowk Police Office had, on his own authority, removed him to the front of the Ashrafi-ka-Katra. Perhaps, the Clerk approved of these services[32] of the Watchman! Accordingly, a copy of this report is present in the book of copies, amongst the petition from the Police Station, for the 15th July 1857. With advertence to the case of Khuda Bakhsh, on a reference to the Diary of this Police Station, it is ascertained from the entry for the 17th July 1857, that Khuda Bakhsh, Trooper, apprehended the prisoner, as one engaged in evil practices for a livelihood, and brought him to this Station, affirming that he, the Trooper, had lent a pistol to one Nanneh, son of Kaulia Khan, mendicant, that the prisoner had forcibly taken the pistol from Nanneh, and ran off with it, and that from that day he had been in hiding, and had only now been seized. This was the Trooper's charge, and it was confirmed by the testimony of Kaulia Khanm mendicant. The report in this case was forwarded to the presence of His Highness, the Commander-in-Chief, Sahib Mirza Mughal Bahadur, in view to orders being issued, but none have as yet been received. It is further submitted that search having been made in the Office of the Police Station, no receipt of the Royal Court on account of the papers in this case, could be found. The reason is that, frequently, when papers are forwarded, no receipts are given from the Royal Court, and it is accordingly a matter which cannot be helped. Such as the particulars were, they are submitted. For the future, great care will be observed, and when a prisoner is forwarded, the form of committal, the plaintiff and the proofs will be sent at the same time. All the subordinate Police Officers of the City have been made acquainted with the orders on this subject, and will carefully conform to them. (Prayers for the prosperity of the reign.) Petition of the slave, Syad Mubarak Shah, Chief police Officer of the City of Delhi, attested with the Seal of the Chief Police of the seat of Government, 'Shahjahanabad'.

Note in a corner at front – 'Copy taken'.

No. 38

Royal Manifesto or Proclamation, without signature, cypher or seal, probably an office copy, kept for record, dated 23rd July 1857

To – All the Inhabitants of the Town of Rohtak.

Proclamation is made, That one man is not to stretch out the hand of violence against another, and that all are to continue in full subjection to the Authority of the principal landholders, who are known to be the

32 The term services is used ironically and collusion with the Watchmen is hinted against the Chiefs. Ed.

well-wishers of the State. Civil Establishment and a sufficient Military force will very soon be sent to make all necessary arrangements. Anxious concern for the welfare and comfort of his subject is cherished by His Majesty; but all such as shall be guilty of acts of the turbulence or disobedience against lawful authority will be most severely punished. This Proclamation is therefore issued for public information.

No. 39

Petition of Mirza Mughal

Dated 24th July 1857

To – The King! Shelter of the World!

Respectfully sheweth, That 14 middle-sized horses, with some magazine cart drivers, have this day been seized and brought to your Slave, by some Infantry Soldiers. The Drivers assert that these horses are their own private property. The truth of this statement can (not?) be ascertained without an investigation. Your petitioner submits that, if he be so directed, he will, without entering into any enquiry, attach these horses to the Royal Artillery. Some of them are equal to the draft of Guns; but others being small and weak are totally unfit; or if such is the Royal pleasure, these horses can, for the present, be kept here, till all the forms of a regular investigation shall have been gone through, when they can be sent to the Royal presence. Let instructions, agreeably to Your Majesty's pleasure, be issued under the Royal signature, so that, in accordance with them, steps may be taken. It was necessary, and has been submitted. Petition of the slave, Zahur-ud-din.

Autograph order by the King, in pencil

No. 859

Institute an enquiry, and lay the result before the Royal presence.

Note below the Order – 'Received 27th July 1857'.

No. 40

Petition of Mubarak Shah, Chief Police Officer of the City

Dated 25th July 1857

To – The King! Shelter of the World!

Respectfully sheweth, That information was brought at noon today, that a great crowd of Infantry Soldiers had assembled, and broken into the house of Alopi Prashad and Rurmall, Khatries, on the pretext of searching the Europeans. I immediately dispatched my assistant to prevent excesses on the part of misconducted characters, and being still anxious, sent such other aid as appeared necessary. The Assistant returned and reported, that the Officer of the Regiment had sent him away, saying that he would preserve order, and that there was, accordingly, no necessity for the Assistant's presence. I have just now heard that no suspicious property or European was found in this search; but nevertheless, the owners of the house cannot but have suffered some loss, the extent of which it would be difficult to determine. I have further heard that the Soldiers have taken away the two owners of the house, and have placed them in arrest. The proceedings in this case were altogether at variance with the usage according to which search should be conducted, and by such proceedings the subjects are aggrieved and oppressed. In those cases in which the statements of the informers are deemed worthy of credit, no oppression or disgrace is inflicted on any person who is not guilty, if search is made after the established usage by four or five trustworthy men, in company with the Police establishment. I submit the petition for Your Majesty's prerogative, to settle this matter. It was necessary, and has therefore been submitted. (Prayers for the King's prosperity). Petition of the slave Syad Mubarak Shah Khan, Chief Police Officer. Seal of 'the Chief Police Officer of the Seat of the Imperial Government, Shahjahanabad'.

Autograph order by the King, in pencil

Mirza Mughal will quickly send the Officers of the Regiment, and will have these poor innocent men released from arrest.

No. 41

Petition of Imam Ulla Khan, trooper

Dated 26th July 1857

To – The King! Shelter of the World!

Respectfully sheweth, That our Slave's horse has become unserviceable, in consequence of a crack in one of his hoofs, and that depending on Your Majesty's fostering consideration for your home-born slaves he trusts he may be allowed one month's leave of absence, that he may search for and bring another. (Prayers for the prosperity of the reign.) Petition of the least of all home-born slaves the Bargir,[33] Iman Ulla Khan, Trooper, attached to the Pay Department.

Autograph order by the King, in pencil

The officers of the Pay Department will give one month's leave of absence.

No. 42

Petition of Saligram, proprietor of Bullock train

No date, Date of King's Order, 28th July 1857

To – The King! Shelter of the World!

Respectfully sheweth, That your slave's Bullock train, for passengers and parcels, had been long running between Delhi and Muttra. When the revolt

33 *Bargir* is a Trooper in a Corps of Irregular Cavalry.

of the troops occurred all his arrangements were deranged, and one of his wagons, which had been coming from Muttra, remained at the Arab Serai, in consequence of the disturbed state of the Country. The people in whose charge the wagon was left now decline being responsible for its safety, and importune your slave to have it brought away to Delhi. Your slave depends on Your Majesty's kindness and consideration, therefore, to allow him the aid of a peon to have the wagon brought in in safety from the Arab Serai, and your slave will ever pray for Your Majesty's life and prosperity. It was necessary, and has therefore been submitted. (Prayers for the prosperity of the reign.)

Petition of the slave Saligram, proprietor of Bullock train, subject of the King, resident of the Dariba. No date.

Order on the reverse, attested by the State Seal of the King

Ordered, that the Police Officer submit a statement

Dated 27th July 1857

Separate slip attached, being a short abstract of Saligram's petition, with amplification of the King's order. 'A wagon belonging to the petitioner is standing at the Arab Serai'.

Exposition of order

Mirza Mughal Bahadur will send a peon with Saligram, Bullock train proprietor, to have the wagon brought into the city in safety.

Police Officer's report of the order having been carried into effect.

To – The King! Nourisher of the Poor!

Your Majesty, Agreeably to the Royal orders, I have had the wagon made over to the claimant, by Tara, Brahman, and his receipt for the same is submitted, under cover of this report. Dated 29th July 1857. Petition of the slave, Khawaja Nazir-ud-din Khan, Police Officer of Bhadrapur, staying at the Arab Serai. Personal seal of the petitioner, and that of the Bahadrapur Police Officer.

Saligram's receipt enclosure to Police Officer's report.

I, Saligram, son of Moti Ram, by caste Brahman, resident of Delhi, having left a wagon at the Arab Serai, in the charge of Tara, Brahman, have now received the same through the Police Officer of Bhadrapur, who is staying at the Arab Serai, agreeably to the orders of His Majesty the King. I have therefore given this in writing, that it may remain as a testimony and be of use. Dated 28th July 1857. Witnesses' signatures in the Hindi character of Chajju and Maida. Shop papers of Arab Serai. Saligram's attestation by mark.

Order on the margin of the Police Officer's report repeated on Saligram's receipt, without signature or seal.

'File in the Office.'

Dated 30th July 1857

No. 43

Petition of Dundi Khan, farmer of the Old Fort

No date. Date of final order, 30th July 1857

To – The King! Shelter of the World!

Respectfully sheweth, That your petitioner is a poor farmer, and has of old been Your Majesty's subject. That he has claims against his tenants on account of the Autumnal crop, but cannot obtain payments from them; and that when he applies to them, they put him off with promises from day to day. He therefore depends on Your Majesty's favour and goodness and expects that an order will be issued to the Officers stationed in the Old Fort, to have the money which is due to your slave, realized for him, so that he may pay his instalment of the Government revenue. Your petitioner further submits that if he is authorized, he will collect the revenue of the hamlets connected with the Old Fort, agreeably to the papers of the Village Accountants, and will bring it to the Royal presence, for now, it is being uselessly lost. In its reaching the Royal Treasury, your slave will have obtained distinction, furthermore, your petitioner represents, that when he speaks to the farmers to carry on their sowings and the agricultural operations, in view to provide for future production, they do not heed his injunctions, and that, if some do take steps to cultivate their lands, the people of the army, camel-drivers, & c., destroy their cultivation. Seeing them, cow-herds, & c., let their cattle loose into the fields, and when your slave remonstrates, the said camel-drivers come forward to resist him forcibly. Your slave's preservation or ruin is in Your Majesty's hands, and he therefore prays that five Troopers, and a petty Officer of Cavalry, may be assigned to aid and protect him, so that his agricultural operations may be put in train of commencement, and when they have been sufficiently advanced, after a month or 15 days, if Your Majesty wishes, the Troopers may be re-called. Otherwise, how shall we, farmers, be able either to pay the Government Revenue for the present season, or support ourselves and our families, for we shall have been utterly ruined, and rendered houseless? However, Your Majesty is Master.

Petition of the slave, of old nourished by His Majesty's salt, Dundi Khan, farmer, resident of the Old Fort. No date.

Autograph order by the King, in pencil

Mirza Mughal will peremptorily enjoin on the Officers of the Infantry and 7th Cavalry that damage be not done to the cultivation of our subjects.

Note in a corner at the top, bearing the Royal Signature.

Order without Signature or Seal, apparently by Mirza Mughal. – Let the farmers of the Old Fort be summoned. Dated 28th July 1857.

The King's orders have been carried out. There is no need to summon the farmers. Dated 30th July 1857.

Note below the Order – 'Orders have been issued to the Officers of the Infantry, and the 7th Cavalry, stationed at the Old Fort'.

No. 44

Petition of Mirza Mughal, and Mirza Khair Sultan

Dated 6th August 1857

To – The King! Shelter of the World!

Respectfully sheweth, That owing to the suspension of remittances to and from the Country, there is at present a great scarcity of money, and unless a mint for coinage is set in operation, it will soon not be procurable. We, therefore pray that your Divine Majesty's order may be issued, that we slaves, making all necessary arrangements connected with the measure, may have the operations of coinage commenced. We therefore submit enclosed herein, a petition from a person offering to contract for the mint, and from Your Majesty's kindness and favour, we expect that this tender of contract will be accepted. It was necessary, and we have therefore submitted it. (Prayers for the prosperity of the reign.) Petition of the slaves, Mirza Muhammad Zahur-ud-din, and Mirza Muhammad Khair Sultan.

Autograph order by the King, in pencil

It is approved of.

No. 45

Order under the autograph special cypher of the King, in pencil

Dated 7th August 1857

To – Badr-ud-Din Ali Khan, Seal Engraver.

You are directed to prepare and present, executed in the best style of finish design and showing his titles, a Seal for the adviser of the State, the respected of the Country, our own special slave, Muhammad Bakht Khan, Lord Governor Bahadur, Controller of all matters Military and Civil. As is usual, insert the year of our reign 21 in the Seal.

Note in the Margin – 'Similar to the Royal cypher', meaning perhaps the same size as the special Seal of the King, engraved in the cypher.

Impression of a Seal in the margin illegible, with a note at its side. 'It is like'.

Note on the Reverse – 'Copy kept'.

No. 46

Address from Mirza Mughal, on the part of the King, attested with the Official Seal of the Commander-in-Chief, rambling and unconnected, and from the style, appearing to have been written from the King's dictation

Dated 9th August 1857

To – The Officers of the Bullumtair (Volunteer) Paltan, 36th[34] Regiment of Native Infantry.

The orders of the Royal presence are to the following effect.

34 This appears to be a mistake. The 38th Regt. Native Infantry was 'Bullumtair Paltan'. Ed.

In the first place, it is to be observed, that setting aside all regards for my own life even, I have done all in my power to satisfy and please the soldiery in every matter. The reason was, I had assured the Army that I should regard them as my own children. The petulance of one's own child has to be borne with, and so I have been with yours, indulging you in all your wishes. But it is to be deplored that you have, notwithstanding, shown no concern for my life, and have had no consideration for my old age. It is incumbent on you now to reflect on my infirmities, and the changes my health is momentarily undergoing. The care for my health was altogether in the hands of the Physician, Ahsanullah Khan, who kept himself constantly informed of the changes it underwent. Now, there is none to care for me, but God, while the changes in my health are such as may not be imagined. All the soldiers and Officers ought now, therefore, to gratify me in this matter, as I have even indulged them in every wish of theirs, and should remove the guard at present over the Physician, and release him from arrest, so that he may be at liberty to come and go, whenever he may think it necessary to examine my pulse, moreover, if my enemy is instigating you, you should not heed his insinuations. Should any one insinuate suspicions against Physician, you should tell him to intercept some letter attested with his Seal; and bring it to you, that you may have proof that he is an enemy; and that you will then yourselves punish him. Furthermore, the property that was plundered from the Physician's house belonged to the King. It is therefore proper that it should be traced and collected, and should be sent to our presence, and that the people, through whose instigation it was plundered, should be adequately punished, agreeably to the decision of the Court. If you are not disposed to comply with the requests let me be conveyed, in safety, to the Khwaja Sahib.[35] I shall there sit and employ myself in the occupation of a Mujawir[36] and, if this even is acceded not to, I shall relinquish every concern, and go away. Let those who think they can detain me, attempt to do so. Not having been killed by the hands of English, I shall be killed by yours. Further the oppression that is at present being inflicted on the people, is not inflicted on them, it is inflicted on me. It is incumbent on you all to take measures to prevent it. Or let me have my answer and I shall swallow a diamond and kill myself.[37] Moreover, on the plunder of the Physician's house, a small box containing our Seal was carried away. No paper, of a date subsequent to the 7th August 1857, bearing the impression of that Seal, will be valid.

No. 47

Order by the King without signature, cypher, or seal

Dated 11th August 1857

35 A shrine of the great Sufi saint *khwaja* Nizam-ud-din Chisti near Qutub.

36 One who cleans the mosque.

37 It is a popular belief that a diamond if swallowed can kill a person. Ed.

To – The ever faithful Muhammad Akbar Ali Khan Bahadur! Ruler of Putoodhi.[38]

Consider yourself receiving favour, and know! That, agreeably to the representation of Durga Prashad, Registrar of Landed Proprietary Rights of the District of Patandi, all the particulars of the outrageous conduct of Muhammad Khan Risaldar, against you, our special slave, and of your having gone away from Patandi, in consequence of the said Risaldar having been killed by the farmers of the Ranghur caste, of the Patandi District, as well as the devastation of your Territory, and the plunder of your property, by the peasantry of that part of the country, have fully come to our Royal knowledge. It has been clearly ascertained that the wounding and slaughter of the Risaldar and the Troopers who were with him cannot be ascribed to anything but the said Risaldar's own misconduct, and you, our special slave, are therefore directed to return to your residence, and restoring your ancient demesne, in all confidence and assurance, to its former order and tranquillity, to continue obedient to your Royal orders. Understand, that your doing this will lead to your benefit and advantage. Be assured of our kindness.

Note on the Reverse – 'Copy kept'.

No. 48

Petition of Mirza Mughal

No date. Date of an Office Note as below, 18th August 1857

To – The King! Shelter of the World!

Respectfully sheweth, That Your Majesty has directed me to pay 200 rupees to be expended on repairs to the bridge, whereas already the daily hire of the labourer is paid every evening. There is no necessity, accordingly, for the payment of this 200 rupees. There is no contract on account of the bridge, that the money should be given, the hire of the labourers is distributed to them daily, and now, too, it will be paid every evening. It was necessary, and I have therefore submitted it.

Petition of the slave Mirza Zahur-ud-din. No date.

Autograph order by the King, in pencil

Mirza Mughal will make the necessary arrangements.

Note on the face – Received 18th August 1857. 'This is to be kept with the receipts'.

No. 49

Royal Missive under the seal engraved in the King's special cypher

Dated 20th August 1857

38 Pataudi, small state in Haryana.

To – Our Sons, Wassih Ali Shah, Safi-Ud-Din Sultan, Muhammad, Mirza Bahadur, Bakhht Bahadur, son of Mirza Muzafffar Bakht Bahadur, Mirza Taimur Shah, Sultan Husein, Mirza Safari Sultan Zain-ul-ab-din, Mirza Safi Sultan, Safi-ud-din Wassih, Muhammad Mirza, Safi Sultan Hyder Mirza, Safi Tehmanseb Mirza, Mirza Zia-ud-din Bakht, and Mirza Khurshed Kadh Khan, son of Mirza Usman Kadir.[39]

Learn! That all the particulars of the ruinous hardships and distresses you, our Sons, have suffered in the province of Oudh, as embodied in your petition, have come fully to our Royal knowledge. In the wonderful changes now occurring, the will of God has come to pass. Nevertheless, hearing of these matters, fraught as they are with dangers, we have to some extent been grieved and concerned in mind. However, what the Great Almighty in His unbounded and universal mercy has willed, he has willed for the best, and that which may hereafter happen. Under all circumstances, preserve unanimity amongst yourselves, and stay in the quarter of Lucknow, called Aminabad; and pass your time in confidence of safety and protection from the present dangers. Please the ever-revered God! The present calamities and confusion will now, with His divine help, speedily come to an end. The appearances of order are already becoming manifest, and you will soon see reason for entire confidence reflected in the mirror of your own minds. Continue to cherish perfect assurance. Be assured of our kindness.

No. 50
Petition of Pir Bakhsh Beg, Tinke

No date

To – The King! Shelter of the World!

Respectfully sheweth, That your slave kept a tinker's shop in the precincts of the Palace, at which the culinary vessels and other articles of the Royal household were tinned and that the Infantry Soldiers, having destroyed the forge, have taken possession of the house, and will not now be prevailed on to vacate it. Your slave, therefore, depends on Your Majesty's gracious favour and consideration, for the issue of an order to Mirza Mughal, to the effect that he take your slave with him, and have the shop vacated, in order that your slave may resume his occupation of tinning the Royal vessels. It was necessary, and I have therefore submitted it. (Prayers for the prosperity of the reign.)

Petition of the slave Pirbakhsh Beg, tinker, servant of the State. No date.

Autograph order by the King, in pencil

Mirza Mughal will have the matter settled agreeably to this petition.

39 Princes of the ruling house of Oudh.

No. 51

Petition of Mirza Mughal

No date

To – The King! Shelter of the World!

Translations having been made by one able to read English, it is ascertained that the three English papers found on Khabru Sai, who was brought in by some Cavalry men, are testimonials of good and satisfactory service, which have been given to him by the English.

Two Certificates of good character, from Harriot (a part of illegible) year 1853.

One Certificate of good character, from (illegible) Lieutenant, in favour of the same Khabru, year 1856.

Petition of the home-born slave Zahur-ud-din.

No. 52

Petition of the shopkeepers of the Chatta

No date

To – The King! Shelter of the World!

Respectfully sheweth, That a body of Soldiery have established their residence immediately in the front of our shops, and we slaves are unable to open them in consequence. We pray, therefore, that in conformity with justice, orders may be issued to the Officers of the State, for the removal of these Soldiers from their present locality, or that, otherwise, the goods in the shops may be made over to us, in the presence of the servants of Your Majesty's Government. Petition of the slaves, the shopkeepers of the Chatta.

Autograph order by the King, in pencil

Mirza Mughal will have their shops given to these shopkeepers.

No. 53

The petition of Ahmad Khan and Muhammad Khan

No date

To – The King! Shelter of the World!

Respectfully sheweth, That we slaves having built a house, with one open hall and one room, at our own personal expense outside the Fort, on ground the property of the State near Ellenborough Tank, for which we have paid ground rent, to Your Majesty, for the last 10 or 12 years, and had our residence there. Since yesterday, the Troopers of the Regiment of Cavalry, which left the HayatBakhsh Garden, and has come out of the palace, have forcibly occupied your slave's dwelling above referred to. We have, from antiquity, been Your Majesty's home-born slaves and servants, and we accordingly depend on your fostering consideration, for the issue of a prohibition, against our being molested in the occupancy of our house. (Prayers for the prosperity of the reign.) Petition of the slaves, Ahmad Khan and Muhammad Khan, Mace-bearers, servants of the King.

Mirza Mughal will issue orders that the Troopers were directed to encamp outside the City. They will accordingly now go out. If they require Marquees or Tents, they will be supplied with them. They must not oppress old residents. Let them indent on the Government for Tents and Marquees.

Transcript of the King's Order on the reverse in ink.

Note on the Reverse: 'A written order has been issued'.

No. 54
Petition of Bhutia, landholder of Faridabad

No date

To – The King! The Shelter of the World!

Your Majesty, This slave is a landholder of Faridabad, and is a Silversmith by caste. The matter he has to submit is that 50,000 rupees, more or less, belonging to the Government of the East India Company, are now present in the subordinate Revenue Office at Palwal. Some of the Ballabhgarh Rajah's Officials went there, but the landholders of the place would not allow them to take the money. Your slave, therefore, prays that 100 Horsemen and 50 Infantry may be sent with him, that he may bring it away, and pay it into the Royal Treasury. Your zealous slave is exerting himself solely that he may obtain a subsistence. It was necessary, and is submitted. Further on perusal of this petition let orders be issued, and, with the Cavalry and Infantry, let a means of conveyance for your slave be also bestowed. Petition of Bhutia, landholder of Faridabad.

Autograph order by the King, in pencil

Mirza Mughal will speak to the Officers of the Army, and will immediately take steps to send for this Treasure.

No. 55
Petition of Nabi Bakhsh Khan

No date

To – The King! Shelter of the World!

Respectfully sheweth, That it is manifest to Your Majesty, that justice is approved of, and lawless cruelty condemned by the Creator of the Universe. I therefore pray, if in Your Majesty's estimation it is proper to do so, that you should tell the Officers of the Army, who request your permission to slay the ladies, children, and other prisoners, that agreeably to their prayers, you placed your hand on their heads, and joined them in the case of the faith; but that in killing the prisoners in question, you will abandon the tenets of your religion. That they must first obtain a Fatwa[40] and a Bywasta[41] and that, if these shall sanction the slaughter, they can slay the prisoners alluded to; but that Your Majesty will not give an order on the subject, contrary to the laws of the Prophet; and that if they do not approve of this, they may first wreak their rage on your own Royal person. I trust that Your Majesty's orders, agreeably to the suggestions above submitted, will be issued to the Officers of the Army in a tone of decision. Considering it necessary, I have laid the subject before your Royal presence.

Petition of the slave, Nabi Bakhsh Khan, agent of his Highness Arsh Aramgah.[42] No date.

No. 56

Order under the seal of the King different from that in the cypher

No date

Seal The Father of Victory! The Candle of Religion! Muhammad Bahadur Shah, King, Defender of the Faith!

To – The Special Slave, worthy of kindness and favours. The Lion of the State! The honoured of the Country! Muhammad Abdul Rahman Khan Bahadur.[43]

The Tiger in battle: Receive our kindness and know: that owing to the occurrence of many unpleasant circumstances, and being unable in consequences of our advanced age, and debility of body to attend to the affairs of the Government and Country, we have now no desire left but to engage in such good works as are approvable to God and mankind, and to spend the remainder of our life in the service and worship of God. It is therefore our fixed resolve in our present griefs and sorrows, shortly to go in the garb of an ascetic. *First,* with all the members of the exalted house of Taimur, to the shrine of his reverence Khawaja Kutb-ud-din, of eminent holiness, and arriving there, and making arrangements for all the necessaries of the journey, to proceed thence to the holy tabernacles (Mecca and Medina), may God increase the veneration and respect in which they are held! For this perishable world affords no certain dependence. You, our slave, are therefore written to, to come quickly to our Royal presence, with those of your retainers and

40 A deceased according to Islamic law.

41 A decree according to the Hindu *Shastras.*

42 Posthumous title of the late Emperor Akbar Shah, father of Bahadur Shah.

43 Nawab of Jhajjar, a state in Haryana.

attached followers in whom you may have the fullest confidence, in whatever way your doing so may be practicable, and accompanying us to the said shrine have all the property and chattels of the whole of the members of the Royal family conveyed thither in safety. Moreover, such cumbrous property as the Princes will not at the present time be able to take with them, they will leave in their several residences in the Palace, and for the protection of this, in concert with the Royal servants, you will station some of your soldiers, and leaving also and adequate force for a few days at the said shrine, to protect our divine person till our departure for the holy house of God (Mecca) you will return to your fief (of freehold). In acting thus you will secure our entire divine approval and pleasure, and your fame will likewise spread through mankind, that you, the selected from amongst all well-wishers, have at a time like the present, from regard for old relations (of Sovereign and Subject) rendered services such as none others of our oldest protégés had the grace (or virtue) to afford. Accordingly, whatever haste you are able to make in this matter will be extremely proper and necessary. Be assured of our kindness. *Secondly,* there is no carriage whatever (procurable) here. Be sure, therefore, to bring 400 or 500 Carts, and 500 or 600 Camels with you. No date.

The Prisoner complaining of faintness, the Court adjourns at 20 minutes to 2 p.m. till 11 a.m. tomorrow.

Day three: 29 January 1858

The court reassembled this day at 11 a.m. in the Hall of Special Audience in the Palace at Delhi. The President, Members, Interpreter, and Dy. Judge Advocate-General are all present.

The Prisoner is brought into Court, and Ghulam Abbas[44] attends as his assistant

The Interpreter now peruses in the original, Persian papers, the translation was read by the Judge Advocate yesterday, *viz.* down to No. 56.[45]

Ghulam Abbas is now duly affirmed as a Witness.

44 He was Emperor's Counsel.

45 Bahadur Shah was mentally, if not physically, alert till his last days. He knew what would be the outcome of the trial. He, therefore, took no interest in its proceedings. He would close his eyes and pretend as if he was sleeping. What the Judge Advocate reading was, says Martin, 'of little moment to him … and appeared lost in the land of dreams … Occasionally, however, when a particular passage was read from any of the documents the dull eyes might be seen to light up and bowed head would be raised', Martin, *op. cit.*, vol. 3, pp. 162–63. The Judge Advocate has not recorded his this state in the trial proceedings.

The Emperor's following verse is perhaps the most apt explanation of his above state during the trial:

Kaan se sabh ki sunta hun, Aur muhn se kuchh na kahta hun.
Hosh bhi hai, baihosh bhi hun, Kuchh sota hun, kuchh jagta hun.

(I am hearing everything with open ears, but do not speak. I am conscious, and unconscious too. I remain a little awake, but I am also asleep.)

Examined by the Judge Advocate

Question – Where were you on the morning of the 11th of May 1857, when the mutinous troops came from Meerut?

Answer – I was at the entrance of this very Hall of Special Audience.

Question – Relate all that you witnessed on that occasion.

Answer – At about 8 o'clock in the morning, I heard of the arrival of five or six Troopers of the Company's Cavalry, and of their being in front of the gilt dome over the King's special sitting-room. They cried out clamorously, upon which the King told his immediate attendants to ascertain who were making such noise. One of them went to the balcony, and had some conversation with the Troopers, and then returned with his report to the King. I don't know what report he made; but the King came out into the apartment adjoining the sitting-room above-mentioned, and called for me. The King then told me that these Troopers said they had revolted and come from Meerut, resolved on fighting for their faith, and killing the Europeans, and directed me to go immediately to Captain Douglas, tell him the matter, and request him to make suitable arrangements; the King at the same time directed one of the household attendants to close the gate under the sitting-room. I went to Captain Douglas as ordered, and explained my message. Captain Douglas immediately accompanied me, saying he would see what the matter was. He arrived at this Hall of Special Audience, and the King immediately came out and joined him; the King at this time was strong enough to walk about without other help than that of a stick, the King asked Captain Douglas if he knew what was the matter, and how it was that this force had come, and suggested that he should at once take steps to make any arrangements that might be necessary for the occasion. Ahsanullah Khan and I were both present at this time. Captain Douglas requested that the gate under the King's sitting-room might be opened, that he might go and speak to the Troopers. The King said that he would not allow him to do so, as they were murderers and might kill him also. Captain Douglas again tried to persuade the King to have the gate opened, but the King would not consent, and laid hold of Captain Douglas' hand, saying, 'I won't let you go'. Ahsanullah Khan at the same time took hold of Captain Douglas' other hand saying, 'if you want to see and speak to these men, you can do both one and the other from the balcony'. Upon this, Captain Douglas came up to the railing between the King's apartments and the Hall of Special audience, overlooking the spot where the Troopers were collected. I accompanied Captain Douglas to the railing, and there perceived about 30 or 40 of the Troopers below. Some had their swords drawn, others had pistols and carbines in their hands, more were coming from the direction of the Bridge, accompanied by men on foot, apparently Grooms with bundles on their heads. Captain Douglas said to the Troopers 'don't come here, these are the private apartments of the ladies of the Palace, your standing opposite them is a disrespect to the King'. On this, they gradually one by one went off in the direction of the Rajghat Gate, and when they had all gone Captain Douglas went again to the King, who said, 'have the gates of the Palace as well as those of the City closed immediately, lest these men should get in'. Captain Douglas assured the King that there was no cause to fear, that it was his duty to attend to the business, and that he would go and make arrangements immediately. On this, both the King and Captain Douglas went each to their own apartments, and I and Ahsanullah Khan, the Physician, came and sat down in this Hall of Special Audience. After remaining about half an hour, we both went to Ahsanullah Khan's room in the Palace. We had been there about an hour when a servant of Captain Douglas came running with a message requiring the attendance of Ahsanullah Khan. At the request of the latter, I went up with him. The man who had come for us said that Captain Douglas was in the key-room; but on nearing the place, we heard that he had gone back to his own quarters. It was at this time I noticed there was a good deal of smoke rising from the direction of the quarter of the City known as the Daryaganj, and heard from some of the passersby that it was caused by the Troopers having fired the bungalows. We thus went on the Captain Douglas' quarters over the Lahori Gate of the palace. On reaching his room I noticed that Captain Douglas was in the third apartment, and we met Mr. Simon Fraser in the intermediate one. Ahsanullah Khan went on to see Captain Douglas, and I returned with Mr. Fraser agreeably to his request, who directed me to go and ask the King for two guns and some of his Infantry to protect Captain Douglas' residence. I and Mr. Fraser came down the stairs accompanied by another gentleman, whose name I don't know, had a pistol in one hand and a gun in the other. Mr. Fraser desired me to go quickly; he was himself on his way to the King, but I preceded him. On my reaching the King's apartments I sent word to him, when he came out of his sitting-room, and I explained to him Mr. Fraser's request. The King immediately gave orders to the men in attendance to take two guns and all the Troops that were present, with such of the Officers as could be found, to Captain Douglas' quarters. At this time Ahsanullah Khan arrived and told the King that Captain Douglas had requested that two palanquins might be sent for the two ladies that were staying with him, and that they might be brought away and concealed in the apartments of the ladies of the Palace. The King told Ahsanullah Khan to make arrangements, and he instructed the servants in attendance to take two palanquins with the proper complement of bearers, and carry them, not by the direct way but round by the Garden, so as to avoid the crowd of mutinous Troops who had by this time got into the Palace. The King, while these orders were being given, stood inside urging their completion, Ahsanullah Khan standing by him. After a short time, one of the servants who had gone for the palkees returned and reported that they had been sent, and very soon after, the attendant who had been sent with the palkees returned, and said that Mr. Fraser had been killed. This was shortly before 10 o'clock. Ahsanullah Khan on this sent other men to see if the report was correct, and to get particulars of what was occurring, and to ascertain how and where Captain Douglas was. These men came back very soon after, and stated that not only Mr. Fraser, but Captain Douglas and the ladies and the other Europeans residing with them had all been killed. Hearing this, the King went inside, and Ahsanullah Khan and I came into the Hall of Special Audience in perfect bewilderment as to what should be done. Immediately after this, two Companies of Infantry which were on guard at the Palace Gates, followed by the mutinous Cavalry that had come from Meerut, marched into the courtyard of the Hall of Special Audience, and commenced firing their muskets, carbines, and pistols in the air, at the same time making a great clamour. The King hearing the noise came out, and standing at the door of the Hall of Special Audience, told his immediate attendants to direct the troops to discontinue the noise they were making, and to call the native Officers forward, that they might explain the object of such proceedings. On this, the noise was quelled, and the Officers of the Cavalry came forward mounted as they were, and explained that they had been required to bite cartridges, the use of which deprive both Hindus and Mahommedans of their religion, as the cartridges were greased with beef and pork fat, that they accordingly killed the Europeans at Meerut and had come to claim his protection. The King replied 'I did not call for you, you have acted very wickedly'. On this, about 100 or 200 of the mutinous Infantry, the Infantry from Meerut having also arrived by this time, ascended the steps and came into the hall, saying, 'that unless you the King join us, we are all dead men, and we must in that case just do what we can for ourselves'. The King did so, and each withdrew saying just what came into his mind. When the crowd became excessive I retired. The tumult and noise at this time was very great, all speaking loudly together. After a little while the King went to his own apartments, and the Troopers picketing their horses in the courtyard, the mutinous Troops took up their quarters and spread their bedding in the Hall of Special Audience and placed guards all about the Palace. After this I went after 4 o'clock, in the evening, I heard the report of a great explosion, and on going out, observed a great column of dust in the direction of Magazine. The people about at the time said that the Mutineers had attacked the magazine; but I afterwards learnt that the British officers in the place had blown it up. About 5 o'clock I heard that the Mutineers had seized some Europeans, men, women, and children, to the number of about seven or eight, and that they had applied to the King for permission to kill them; but that the King had asked the Sepoys to give their prisoners over to him and that he would have them kept in safe custody. They accordingly made them over on the condition that the guards should be furnished from among themselves. Upon this, the King had them confined in some apartment, and issued orders that their food should be regularly supplied at his expense. After sunset I was intending to go to my house in the City, when on reaching the courtyard of the Hall of Public Audience, I found a great concourse of Troops there also, and learnt that they were from the Delhi Regiments. After this, I mounted my house and went home. On coming to the palace next morning, I learnt that the guns, the reports of which I had heard at 10 or 11 o'clock the night before, had been fired by the Delhi Native Battery as a salute to the King. I can't say whether it was on his assuming the reins of Government or any other cause. I then came on the Hall of Special Audience, where I met Ahsanullah Khan, whom I asked if the King had decided on any measure to put down the disturbance. He told me that the King had dispatched a letter on the subject by camel express to the Lieutenant-Governor at Agra, and about 15 days after I again asked him if any answer had been received. He said that the camel-rider had returned without a receipt or reply, but said he had delivered the letter, and was told a reply would be sent afterwards. After the occurrence of the first day, I discontinued my regular attendance at the Palace, coming only occasionally once in three or four days, and even on those occasions I merely paid my respects to the King and then went away and accordingly can't speak of after events.

Question – Did you hear who had murdered Mr. Fraser? Was it done by servants of the King, or by whom?

Answer – At the time, it was said the Soldiers had risen, and Mr. Fraser had been killed in the riot; but subsequently I heard that he had been cut down by a man who was a lapidary by trade, and had a shop in the Bazaar immediately under Captain Douglas' residence. I am unable to say what the man's name was, or where he is now.

Question – When the King put his hand on the heads of the Native Officers and Soldiers, what was the meaning of his doing so? Was it in acceptance of other service?

Answer – It was equivalent to an acceptance of their allegiance and services; but I cannot say what the King's intentions were at the time.

Question – When was it that the King's authority was publicly proclaimed in Delhi, or when was it that it was generally known that he had assumed the reins of Government here?

Answer – I do not know of any regular proclamation having been made, though such may have been done without my hearing of it; but the very day of the outbreak the King's authority was established.

Question – Was it on this account that the guns were fired, as a salute to him?

Answer – I don't know, all I heard was that the Artillery men fired it, as a salute on the occasion of their coming under the King's rule.

Question – You know how many guns were fired on this occasion?

Answer – The usual Royal salute is I think about 21 guns.

Question – On what day did the King hold his first public Court?

Answer – He commenced holding his Court daily from the very day of the outbreak; the audience he gave the Troopers may be considered as the first Court he held.

Question – Prior to the outbreak, had you been a frequent inmate and associate of the King and his family?

Answer – I used to come to the Palace daily, and interchange of all communications between the Agent of the Lieutenant-Governor and the King was carried on by me. I was a servant of the King but had been appointed through the influence of the late Sir Theophilus Metcalfe.

Question – Had you any opportunities of knowing of what passed in the Palace or the general subjects of conversation that were indulged in prior to the outbreak?

Answer – I had such opportunities; but I never heard anything in particular.

Question – Were you so much in the confidence of the King, or of those about him, as to be likely to be entrusted with any secrets or measures that they might wish to conceal from the British Government?

Answer – I was not among those who would be likely to be consulted, or informed of such matters; but Ahsanullah Khan and Khwaja Mahbub Ali Khan were more likely to be entrusted.

The Court at 4 o'clock adjourns till 11 a.m. tomorrow.[46]

Day four: 30 January 1858

The Court reassembled this day at 11 a.m. in the Hall of Special Audience in the Palace at Delhi. The President, Members, Interpreter, and Dy. Judge Advocate-General are all present.

The Prisoner is brought into Court.

Ghulam Abbas the Witness is re-called, and examined on his former affirmation.

Examination by the Judge Advocate (continued)

Question – Had you before the outbreak any opportunities of becoming acquainted with the Prisoner's handwriting?

46 An interesting fact which Martin gives (and not Harriott) is that 'a request was made by Bahadur Shah during the proceedings to be allowed to smoke his hookah, and the permission was granted'. Martin, *op. cit.*, vol. 3, p. 163. In fact, the members of the Court also smoked cigarette, took beer, etc. and snacks during the session.

Answer – Yes, I used frequently to see his writing, and should be able to recognize it.

Question – In the papers submitted to the Court, and which purport to bear the Autograph writing of the prisoner, and his Seal, have you any reason to object on account of their not being genuine?

Answer – The generality of the papers bear the writing of the King; there may perhaps be a doubt about one or two.

Question – Were you present when any women and children of European descent were murdered in the Palace?

Answer – No. I was not in the palace; but I heard afterwards that some had been murdered.

Question – Do you know by whom they were so murdered? Was it by the soldiery or by the Prisoner's own servants?

Answer – I can't speak positively on the subject; but when I came into the Palace two or three days after, I asked Ahsanullah Khan why he did not use his influence to stop the slaughter. He said, he did all he could; but the Mutineers would not be restrained.

Question – Did Ahsanullah Khan give you to understand that he was present on the occasion?

Answer – No, he didn't distinctly mention whether he was present or not.

Question – How many Europeans were murdered on that occasion?

Answer – I did not know the number before, and it is just possible that I may have heard it, and may have forgotten; but I now learn, that is within the last 10 or 15 days, that the number was about 50, including women and children.

Question – Were these women and children murdered with the Prisoner's consent?

Answer – I have no further knowledge on the subject beyond what I heard from Ahsanullah Khan, who said that the King had prohibited the slaughter, but unavailingly.

Question – Do you know whether a diary of events was kept during the rebellion by any of the King's Servants, and if so, who wrote it?

Answer – I do not know whether one was kept or not; one was kept before the outbreak.

Question – Was Mirza Mughal, the King's son, appointed the Commander-in-Chief of the Rebel Army in Delhi, and if so by whom and when?

Answer – Mirza Mughal was certainly appointed Commander-in-Chief of the Army and it was generally said that he had been appointed by the King in compliance with the request of the Army.

Question – Previous to the outbreak, had you ever heard of any discontent in the native Army?

Answer – Yes, I did hear that in Calcutta two Regiments had mutinied in consequence of having to use greased cartridges, and that they had been disbanded.

Question – Before the outbreak at Delhi, did you hear that the Regiments at this Station were in any way dissatisfied?
Answer – No.

Examined by the Court

Question – Did you at any time after the murder of the Europeans, see either bodies, blood, or other traces of such murders having been committed?
Answer – I saw nothing of the kind.
Question – Do you know the spot where these women and children were murdered?
Answer – I heard they were murdered in the first courtyard, as you enter the Palace from the Lahori Gate, near the Cistern; people about the place mentioned this, but did not point out the exact spot.
Question – Do you know what became of the bodies?
Answer – I don't know how they were eventually disposed of; but I heard they were removed in carts.

Re-examined by the Judge Advocate

Question – Do you know whether these women and children were imprisoned before being murdered, and if so, where?
Answer – I heard they were imprisoned, and were kept confined in the King's kitchen or in an apartment adjoining.
Question – How many days were they confined?
Answer – About a week or ten days.
Question – Who kept the Prisoner's State Seals during the rebellion?
Answer – They used to remain in the Prisoner's private apartment.
Question – Was the use of them entirely under the control of the Prisoner?
Answer – The seals were never affixed, but with the King's authority.

The Prisoner declines to cross-examine.

The witness resumes his seat as assistant to the Prisoner.

The following papers in Persian, under the head Miscellaneous, from Nos. 57 to 77 having been fully established as genuine before the Court on the trial of the Rajah of Ballabhgarh, are now received without further evidence regarding them, and the translations are read as follows.

No. 57
Order from the King, under the State Seal

No date

To – The Special Slave, worthy of Favour and Kindness, Rajah Nahar Singh Bahadur.

Know! That we have heard that you have appointed a Police Officer of your own to Bahasrapur; one, however, by name Nazir-ud-din Khan, already stands appointed by the Government, and he is now present in Arab Serai. You, our slave, will therefore, according to the dictates of your own devotion, dismiss the man you have nominated.

No. 58
Petition of Rajah Nahar Singh, of Ballabhgarh

No date

To – The King, Shelter of the World! Dispenser of Justice! &c.

Respectfully sheweth, That, as the state of the road to Delhi was very unsettled your slave has, according to Your Majesty's orders, been engaged, night and day, in instituting the most efficient arrangements. Still, however, the lawless inhabitants of the Village of Pali, which adjoins the Ballabhgarh boundary, and which, during the Foujdaree[47] was attached to this State, have broken out into reckless and lawless violence; and have so taken to highway robbery and plunder, that the whole population is in great distress in consequence, notwithstanding that I, your slave, am bringing them into order little by little, yet still I cannot venture to act, to any full extent, without Your Majesty's orders. If your Royal permission is granted, such efficient arrangements will be adopted, that the miscreants and rebels of the said village, will not have the daring to continue in their present practices, and the arrangements along the road, from Ballabhgarh to Delhi, will be perfected. Further, I have heard from some persons who had requests to make to me, that it has been represented to Your Majesty, that the Chief of Ballabhgarh has secreted two Englishmen, with their wives and children. God is witness that this is entirely a false and unfounded calumny. How could your slave dare to commit an act of the kind, without Your Majesty's wishes and orders! A native, however, who was formerly a Christian, had been 12 years in my service; but I put even him away, fearing Your Majesty's displeasure. This man has now discarded Christianity and embraced the Mahommedan religion, and he is accordingly deserving of mercy and forgiveness. If Your Majesty permits it, I shall have him re-called. (Prayers for the prosperity of the reign.) Petition of the ancient slave and servant, Nahar Singh, Chief of Ballabhgarh. Seal of Rajah Nahar Singh Bahadur.

47 By this term is meant the time when the Rajah of Baharatpur held his principality under the Mahommedan Government, in consideration of certain sources which were assigned to him, and which were called the Foujdaree. Hence it is that the Jats of Bharatpur and the surrounding districts called themselves Foujdars, and even when asked their castes, replied that they were Foujdars. Ed.

No. 59
Petition for Nahar Singh, Chief of Ballabhgarh

No date

To – The King, Lord of Mankind, Shelter of the World, & c.!

Respectfully sheweth, That Your Majesty's order, directing my attendance at the Court as of old to superintend and direct the Police arrangements of the City of Delhi and its environs, accompanied by a second order to give my attention to the protection of the road, and to use measures for the safety of travellers, supplies, & c., has been received. I declare it solemnly as the truth, that considering myself exceedingly honoured and exalted in receiving these orders, I offered my thanksgivings, with humble prostrations, in the house of God. May He condescend to accept my midnight prayers and forever preserve Your Majesty in prosperity and good fortune.

My Lord! Although by the influence of your Royal auspices, the most complete tranquillity exists in this your slave's territory, for that I am night and day engaged making arrangements, and maintaining order, still some refractory and turbulent characters, inhabitants of the village of Pali, which adjoins the Ballabhgarh boundary and the rebels and reckless characters of the town of Palwal likewise, which also is near the boundary, have become so insurrectionary, and have so entirely adopted a course of highway robbery and plunder, that how shall I describe it? Although from certain prudential considerations of my own, as well as on the request of the Revenue and Police Officers, and registrars of landed proprietary rights of the said town, I have made arrangements to some extent, by affording them the aid of some Cavalry and Infantry; but, without Your Majesty's orders, I do not wish to interfere to the degree which is necessary and desirable. I have enlisted new horse and foot levies for the efficient protection of the high road from Ballabhgarh to Delhi, and am night and day occupied in arrangements to maintain order. I am your ancient and hereditary slave, and as I may be ordered, so will I act, God willing! I shall shortly realize the honour of presenting myself; before Your Majesty, after efficient arrangements and tranquillity shall have been established, for certainly, the existing state of things is disgraceful, and involves the dread of the Royal displeasure. It was necessary, and I have therefore submitted it. (Prayers for the prosperity of the reign.) Petition of the home-born slave, Nahar Singh, Chief of Ballabhgarh. Seal of Rajah Nahar Singh Bahadur.

No. 60
Petition of Ahmad Ali, confidential agent of the Rajah of Ballabhgarh

No date

To – The King! Shelter of the World!

Respectfully sheweth, That on his departure from this, some time ago, agreeably to Your Majesty's orders, to attend to the arrangements in his territory, the Rajah left certain necessary articles here, such as clothes, etc., which he has now sent for. I pray, therefore, that a passport may be granted, to the effect that the carts coming from Ballabhgarh are not to be molested by any one, and that when the things are being sent, the Soldiers at the Delhi Gate are not to pose any hindrance. (Prayers for the prosperity of the reign.) Petition of the menial slave, Ahmad Ali, confidential Agent of the Rajah of Ballabhgarh. Seal of Ahmad Ali.

Mirza Mughal will have the pass made over and given.

No. 61

Petition of the Rajah of Ballabhgarh

Dated 20th May 1857

To – The King! Shelter of the World!

Respectfully sheweth, That previously to this I have submitted several petitions, but have not been honoured with a reply to even one. I now again submit that the refractory inhabitants of the village of Pali, etc., have taken to committing highway robbery and plunder in all directions, and are grievously oppressing the populace and subjects. Although I have brought the said village, little by little, into some order, I cannot nevertheless, without Your Majesty's orders, presume to act with confidence in any matter. I am engaged, night and day, raising new Cavalry and Infantry levies. Besides this, my health is frequently affected by the adverse state of the weather. Setting this aside, however, I shall make efficient arrangements and provision against all the refractory and rebellious characters of this District; and will then present myself at Your Majesty's Court. I have sent Kalandar Khan Risaldar, to the Royal presence, with some Cavalry and Infantry, agreeably to Your Majesty' orders; as he is directed so he will act. Petition of the hereditary slave, Rajah Nahar Singh, Chief of Ballabhgarh. Seal of Rajah Nahar Singh Bahadur.

No. 62

Petition of the Rajah of Ballabhgarh

Dated 21st May 1857

To – The King! Shelter of the World!

Respectfully sheweth, That by Your Majesty's order, the protection of the high road to Delhi, and the arrangements of the Police Station of Bahadrapur, had been assigned to your devoted petitioner. Nevertheless, since another Police Officer has been appointed by Your Majesty, I have, agreeably to your orders, dismissed the whole of the Establishment of the said Police Station, and have installed Your Majesty's nominee. I had dispatched Kalandar

Bakhsh Khan, Risaldar, with some Cavalry and Infantry, agreeably to Your Majesty's orders, to assist in the arrangements; but when they arrived at the gates of Delhi, they were prevented from entering the City; and the Guards told them that they should first give up their arms. Your Majesty knows, that a Soldier's arms are his decorations and adornment, and his remaining in attendance without them would be improper, as inconsistent with the profession of soldiery. They therefore returned, and have temporarily taken up their residence in the Old Fort. Let an order, therefore, be issued, that these men may come before your Royal presence; and devoting their lives, may zealously engage in all necessary and becoming services. I, who am your ancient servant, consider that obeying your commands advances my dignity. I learn from the Clerk of the Bhadrapur Police Office, and submit the same for our information, that the Police Officer appointed by Your Majesty has arrived. (Prayers for the prosperity of the reign.) Petition of the slave and ancient servant, Nahar Singh Bahadur, Chief of Ballabhgarh. Seal of Raja Nahar Singh Bahadur.

No. 63
Petition of the Rajah of Ballabhgarh
Dated 22nd May 1857

To – The King! Shelter of the World!

Respectfully sheweth, That Your Majesty's orders, with which your slave has been honoured, whether as regards the arrangements for the protection of the high road from Ballabhgarh to Bhadrapur, and thence on to the Delhi Gate, or in the village of Pali, and towns of Palwal and Fattehpur, and other places, have, by the blessing of god, and Your Majesty's auspices, been effectually carried out, and Police and Revenue Officers have everywhere been established. The efficiency of your slave's measures and arrangements have become generally known, in so much that it must have come to Your Majesty's hearing also. Adoration of the World! Some thoughtless characters, enemies and rebels against this State, who have absconded after committing every injury in their power, and who are now amongst those who present themselves at the Royal Court, are not pleased at hearing of the success of the above arrangements, and desire that disrepute should be made to attach to my good name and exertions; and they ever instigate the regular Infantry Soldiers, stationed at the City Gates, against me and my servants. I fully believe it probable that, in their stupidity they may even to Your Majesty, utter sentiments prejudicial to your hereditary slaves, but let not their allegation ever be believed; for formerly too it was their practice, from feelings of enmity to speak disparagingly of your slave; and then too their calumnies used not to be heeded in the least. I pray, therefore, that from a regard for proper arrangements, Your Majesty will, with due consideration, peremptorily order the Regular Infantry Soldiers at the Gates not in any way to object to, disagree with, or hinder the servants of the Ballabhgarh State in any matter whatsoever, otherwise detriment to the arrangements will ensue – to arrangements which have been made for the protection of your subjects, solely in conformity with Your Majesty's orders. Further, Your Majesty is master, and I am your old servant. In carrying out Your Majesty's orders, I wish that nothing like the least deficiency should occur; and accordingly, the enlistment of Cavalry and Infantry to be employed in keeping order, is going on. In a short time hence, I shall send some more Cavalry and Infantry for the Police and other general arrangements. Your slave is under all circumstances devoted in heart and soul. (Prayers for the prosperity of the reign.) Petition of the ancient slave and servant, Nahar Singh Bahadur, Chief of Ballabhgarh. Seal of Rajah Nahar Singh Bahadur.

No. 64

Petition of the Rajah of Ballabhgarh

Dated 24th May 1857

To – The King! Shelter of the World!

Respectfully sheweth, That I have had the very great honour to receive Your Majesty's letter, intimating the issue of orders to the Guards at the Gates, prohibiting their interference with the servants of the Ballabhgarh State; granting my Cavalry and Infantry permission to encamp under the Palace window; and, at the same time, with your wonted kindness, directing my attendance at the Royal Court. For the very great honour conferred on me by this order, I made my offering of thanks in humble prostrations before God. May God ever preserve Your Majesty in the enjoyment of every blessing.

Adoration of the World! I, your devoted slave, consider obeying your orders, my happiness. But, owing to the necessity for arrangements, to put down the rebellious characters of the Village of Pali, & c., I have been helpless and unable to appear at the Royal presence. But, please God! I shall have much happiness in doing so, after the disturbers of the peace; of the surrounding Country shall have been effectually brought into subjection. My Lord! That is Sunday, and according to my usual custom, I went to take an airing in the Dilkhusha garden. While I was there, the new moon of the festival of the Eid appeared, and was about the same time distinctly seen by all residents of this place. From regard for my obligations, as your home-born slave, I offer my wishes that this good news, full of promise, namely the festival of the Eid, which is an occasion for rejoicing, may be the forerunner of good fortune and happiness to Your Majesty. (Prayers for the eternal prosperity of the reign.) Petition of the slave and servant, Nahar Singh, Chief of Ballabhgarh. Seal of Rajah Nahar Singh Bahadur.

No. 65
Petition of the Rajah of Ballabhgarh

Dated 25th May 1857

To – The King! Shelter of the World!

Respectfully sheweth, That I yesterday submitted a petition, connected with the state of affairs, from which every particular must have come to Your Majesty's knowledge. By God's blessing, and Your Majesty's good fortune, the arrangements, up to the Delhi Gate, and in the country around this District, are now perfect. It is necessary, in my opinion, however, to place one Police Officer of the lower grade, and ten soldiers, at the Hanuman Station, and one Police Officer and 25 soldiers, at Mahrowali. After that, through your Royal prestige, the arrangements will be thoroughly complete. If Your Majesty is pleased to issue orders to that effect, the proposed arrangements shall be made for both places. (Prayers for the eternal prosperity of the reign). Petition of the home-born slave Nahar Singh, Chief of Ballabhgarh. Seal or Rajah Nahar Singh Bahadur.

No. 66
Petition of the Rajah of Ballabhgarh

Dated 27th May 1857

To – The King! Shelter of the World!

Respectfully sheweth, That I have had the very great honour of receiving Your Majesty's order, directing the suppression and prevention of the crimes of murder and pillage; and my sending 20 horsemen to the Police station s of Mundka and Shahdari, to preserve order and arrangements there. Feeling myself highly honoured and distinguished, I have offered up my thanks in humble prostrations before god. Adoration of the World! I shall speedily make arrangements to dispatch the horsemen, as I am ordered by Your Majesty; but, in the meantime, some of my servants are being sent to look after the place, agreeably to Your Majesty's orders. I am unceasingly engaged in arrangements and plans for the prevention of crime; but now the ill-conducted; and refractory Goojurs, Mewattee, and other castes have discovered a more determined spirit of violence, and are daily resolved on making a sudden attack on the town of Faridabad and even on Ballabhgarh itself. But as the blessing of God, and the influence of Your Majesty's prestige, are both in my favour, I shall certainly make effectual arrangements, and will then shortly realize the honour of waiting on Your Majesty, for this is my earnest desire. (Prayers for the prosperity of the reign.) Petition of the home-born slave, Nahar Singh, Chief of Ballabhgarh. Seal of Rajah Nahar Singh Bahadur.

No. 67

Petition of the Rajah of Ballabhgarh

Dated 30th May 1857

To – The King! Shelter of the World!

Respectfully sheweth, That some days have now elapsed, that I have not been made acquainted with the continuance of Your Majesty's good health, and I have been anxious in consequence. May God preserve you in prosperity and happiness. From Your Majesty's order to the address of Moulvi Ahmad Ali, I have today learnt the circumstances of the plunder of the carts at Bhadrapur. I have accordingly, in conformity with Your Majesty's commands, issued stringent injunctions to the Police Officer at Bhadrapur to search for and trace out the property and the offenders. Please God the matter will be thoroughly investigated. I have just now sent off 20 more horsemen to Your Majesty, to be employed in maintaining order. I mention this for your information. (Prayers for the prosperity of the reign.) Petition of the home-born slave, Nahar Singh, Chief of Ballabhgarh. Seal of Rajah Nahar Singh Bahadur.

Autograph order by the King, in pencil

The contents of this petition have been learnt. This slave is our well-wisher.

No. 68

Petition of the Rajah of Ballabhgarh

Dated 28th May 1857

To – The King! Shelter of the World!

Respectfully sheweth, That I yesterday sent an answer to Your Majesty's missive, and it must have come under your perusal. Through God's blessing, and Your Majesty's auspices, there is complete tranquillity in every respect throughout this District today. I send 5 gold mohurs as a congratulatory offering on account of the festival of the Eid-ul-Fitr. As a mark of favour and regard for your home-born slave, let this offering be accepted. (Prayers for the prosperity of the reign.) Petition of the home-born slave Nahar Singh, Chief of Ballabhgarh. Seal of Rajah Nahar Singh Bahadur.

Autograph order by the King, in pencil (illegible)

No. 69

Petition of the Rajah of Ballabhgarh

Dated 31st May 1857

To – The King! Shelter of the World!

Respectfully sheweth, That Your Majesty is fully aware how entirely my former Officials had the most complete authority in every matter, and how unreservedly every business was confided to their care. These men, in their short-sighted cupidity, embezzled and made away with property worth lacs of rupees. When the secret of their misconduct became disclosed, and I took steps to compel them to render their accounts, and to make restitution for the deficiencies, they one and all, upon one plea or another, went off to Delhi, where they are now residing in their respective homes. So little do they dread being brought to account by Your Majesty's Officers, that they have prepared themselves or further acts of ingratitude, and use their worst endeavours to the prejudice and injury of all cases connected with this State, which happen to come before Your Majesty's Government. Thus, for instance, Your Majesty having been more than ever graciously disposed towards this slave, these men have succeeded, by their false and unfounded representations, in making me the object of your aversion and anger; for they have made you believe that, while I am professedly a servant of the State, in heart I am a friend to the English, that I am collecting stores of lead and powder with traitorous designs; and that I have closed the high road to all travellers and traffic. So completely have Your Majesty's feelings of gracious kindliness been changed for those of anger, displeasure and resentment, that Ahmad Ali, who was the trusted Agent of your distrusted slave, and who remained in attendance at your Royal Court, feeling himself in utter disgrace, has come away to this place, at the same time that Kalandar Bakhsh Khan, Risaldar, who had been in attendance according to Your Majesty's own orders, has received his dismissal. Your exalted highness, all that my enemies have alleged, adverse to my interests, which must in the end fail of their object. They trust by such conduct as they have been pursuing, to impress Your Majesty with a firm belief of their own zeal and devotion, hoping, by this means, to secure immunity from all question or enquiry on the part of the Officers of Your Majesty's Government, and the quiet and unmolested enjoyment of the immense riches they have amassed by their frauds against this State. My ancestors and I have ever been the ancient and hereditary devoted slaves and servants of this exalted dynasty, and have never entertained an idea of disloyalty against you, who dispense mandates to the six cardinal points.[48] And the seven kingdoms of the world for unalloyed gratitude and fidelity, I am as silver which has been thoroughly tried. If you test me a hundred times, I shall not fail in the test. The proof of this profession and statement is this. Before the present disturbances I was staying at Delhi on some business. If I did not cherish the most heartfelt devotion and fidelity for Your Majesty even then how was it that I made proposals through the Superintendent, Mir Fatteh Ali Sahib, that I might be allowed the honour of an interview? If the obligations of fidelity and loyalty were not impressed in their brightest colours on the tablet of my heart, how was it then that this secret and long-cherished wish should have been

48 The six cardinal points are the East, West, North, South, Zenith, and Nadir. Ed.

disclosed, and should have received expression in words? Let my enemies do what they please. I your ancient slave, shall still, under all circumstances, continue your devoted well-wisher.

My eyes will not take the impression of any face but yours,
My mirror will not reflect the countenance of a stranger.

Moreover, although I your ancient slave, profess the Hindoo religion, having observed the conduct and behaviour of those who say that God above is supreme, I have remained in subjection to the guidance of the leaders of the Mahommedan faith, in so much that, although from the first existence of the town, there had been no Mahommedan Mosque, either in the Fort or outside in the market, I have caused a lofty one, for congregational prayers, built of stone, to be erected within the Fort itself. I have, moreover, had an Eidgah, a place set apart exclusively for prayers at the festival of the Eid, built near my garden called the Dilkhusha, to encourage and conciliate the Mahommedans. I your ancient and eternal well-wisher, have ever desired that the Mahommedan faith should be extensively proclaimed. Your Majesty! Let your displeasure now be changed for feelings of graciousness, and let me, who am expectant of your kindness, be as before, regarded anew with eyes of favour and benevolence, and let not Your Majesty give credence to the false allegations and absurd statements of my enemies and adversaries – be watchful against your associate in position,

'For water, though pure by nature, is the rival of the mirror'.

Moreover, in your unbounded favour and graciousness, let orders be issued to the servants of Your Majesty's Government, to seize the above enemies and inimical characters, and to make them over to me, so that their villainies may come to an end, and the cloud of Your Majesty's displeasure and anger may be dispelled; and that I may bring them to an account for my losses, amounting to lacs of rupees, as regards the petition presented to the Lord Saheb Bahadur by Rustam Ali, a resident of Kuraoli, that Gaindah and others, 11 persons, were taking two carts laden with wheat and wheat-meal, as supplies to Delhi, and that the Rajah's Police Officer seized and sent them to Ballabhgarh, where the freight of the carts were confiscated, I urge that the statements of the petitioner are altogether false, and contrary to facts. The true features of this business, without reserve or exaggeration, are Gaindah, who is a leader of ill-conducted characters and highway robbers, had, in the first instance, accompanied by some desperados, residents of his own village, plundered the village of Nuglee, in the Bhadrapur jurisdiction, and conveyed the booty to his own and adjoining villages. Subsequently, bent on plunder, they made a raid on the village of Mugrowlee, in the Ballabhgarh jurisdiction. By the merest chance, the police and revenue officers of Faridabad happened in their patrolling excursion to come to the Magrowli boundary, and saw what was going on, when these plunderers and highway robbers immediately consulted their safety in flight; but the Revenue Officer acting with decision and promptitude, seized some of the miscreants, and having pinioned their arms forwarded them to the Criminal Court of this place. The file of papers compiled in this case is forthcoming. If, in proof of what is here stated, it be so ordered, the original, or a copy, as may be required, shall be submitted for Your Majesty's inspection, when you will be thoroughly informed of all facts. The case of the Buggy and Nabi Bakhsh Merchant is similar. The particulars of this matter are that my servants had purchased the Buggy, which has been attached from a Brahman Subedar of the 11th Regiment of Native Infantry, and Nabi Bakhsh, Merchant, was proceeding in it to Ballabhgarh. So pray Your Majesty! Certainly enquire into this case. As one or two English letters were found in the buggy, I solemnly swear by god, that I, or my servants, have no knowledge of them whatever, as to who is the writer, who the addressed, or what their purport. It accordingly appears evident that some enemy of this State has had these letters written surreptitiously, by someone acquainted with English, and has had them concealed in the Buggy. Let Your Majesty certify yourself of the truth of all that is here submitted, by the testimony of the priests, at the shrine of Muhammad Shah Nizam-ud-din. May he ever be blessed. I beg I may be honoured with a favourable reply to this petition. (Prayers for the prosperity of the reign.)_ Petition of the slave, Rajah Nahar Singh Bahadur, Chief of Ballabhgarh. Seal of Rajah Nahar Singh Bahadur.

No. 70

Petition of the Rajah of Ballabhgarh

Dated 5th May 1857

To – The King! & c., c.

Respectfully sheweth, That blessed and happy is the lot of those who enjoy the bliss of remaining in Your Majesty's presence. Although I have not been able to realize this happiness, and am still actually at a distance, but, with a hundred solemn assurances of my good intentions as of old, and with a thousand sincere professions of my fidelity as throughout time immemorial I ever had, I nevertheless feel as though I were amongst those who are immediately near your exalted throne. Humbly and respectfully presenting my congratulations, I send eight gold mohurs, as an offering of felicitation on account of the festival of the Eid, and trust they will be condescendingly accepted. Prayers (the most extravagant) for the prosperity of the King, and invectives and curses the most rancorous and bitter against his enemies.

For Your Majesty	5 gold mohurs
For the Queen[49]	2 ditto
For the Prince, Mirza Jawan Bakht	1 gold mohur

49 Begum Zeenat Mahal.

Petition of the slave Rajah Nahar Singh Bahadur, Chief of Ballabhgarh. Seal of Rajah Nahar Singh Bahadur.

No. 71

Order by the King, without signature cypher or seal

Dated 8th August 1857

To – Rajaj Nahar Singh.

Your petition with an offering of eight gold mohurs has been received; and has been the means of confirming our confidence on your good intentions. As you are a hereditary slave, it is incumbent on you not to neglect any one of the obligations of fidelity and devotion. Be assured of our kindness.

For myself	5 gold mohurs
For the Queen	2 ditto
For Mirza Jawan Bakht Bahadur	1 ditto

No. 72

Order by the King, without signature, cypher, or sea, dated 9th August 1857

To – The special Slave, worthy of kindness and favour! Rajah Nahar Singh Bahadur.

Consider yourself receiving the Royal favour, and know that your missive sending a present of eight gold mohurs as a present of congratulation on the occasion of Eid-i-Zuha has not removed my displeasure in the least. As it has not been the custom of this Court to return such presents, yours has been accepted. It is imperative on you to follow in the path of your father and your grandfather, and from your heart to engage in acts of devotion and zeal. Be assured of our kindness.

No. 73

Petition of the Rajah of Ballabhgarh

Dated 14th August 1857

To – The King! Vicar of God! & c.

Respectfully sheweth, That I have had the very great honour to receive Your Majesty's missive, acknowledging the receipt of my congratulatory present, on the occasion of the festival of the Eid. I have considered myself highly honoured and distinguished; but where is the tongue, or where the language with which I could appropriately express my praises and thanks for such eminent condescension and graciousness, and as regards the intimation that the cloud of Your Majesty's displeasure has not yet been entirely dispelled, do my Lord! Let me urge, that I am, as is already well known to you, an old and ancient, true and faithful servant of Your Majesty's house, that I am from my heart, every moment and every second, occupied in carrying out Your Majesty's orders. There is not a day that my heart forgets to think upon all your kindness, there is not a moment that my tongue does not speak of your great condescension. Pray do, under all circumstances, consider me your slave, as one of the lowliest of Your Majesty's servants, and condescend to regard me with the eyes of graciousness and favour, for Your Majesty's countenance and protection in every variety of way, were ever abundantly conferred on me personally also. Depending on all these former abounding and conspicuous kindnesses, mercies, and favours, I trust that the cloud of displeasure which, owing to the false and unavailing statement of my enemies, has dimmed the mirror of Your Majesty's mind naturally bright as the sun, will now be dispelled and dissipated, and the dust of anger and dissatisfaction, which has from the same cause settled on the edge of Your Majesty's disposition towards me, will be washed off and removed. Moreover, my trusted representative at Your Majesty's Court has, for some time, been denied the happiness of presenting himself, and I pray now that he may be directed to attend. I present the same request in reference to the Risaldar of my troop of Cavalry. I further pray that I may be favoured with kettle-drums and standards, as a means whereby Your Majesty's fame and greatness may be proclaimed to the four quarters, and the six cardinal points of the world, and at the same time, the credit and dignity of me, your faithful and devoted standard-bearer, may be advanced amongst all classes, an auspicious desire to wait on Your Majesty continues impressed on my heart; but as yet I have been so unfortunate, as not to have been able to realize this heartily cherished purpose, in consequence of the numerous ailment with which I have been afflicted since I came from Delhi, and from which I have not yet obtained complete relief. May Your Majesty's victorious and conquering standards always be elevated, and may defeat for ever attend on your enemies. Petition of the slave Rajah Nahar Singh Bahadur, Chief of Ballabhgarh. Seal of Rajah Nahar Singh Bahadur.

No. 74

Order without signature, cypher, or seal, apparently from Mirza Mughal

Dated 16th August 1857

To – The Especial Slave, Emblem of Good Intentions, Rajah Nahar Singh of Ballabhgarh.

Consider yourself honoured. Frequent occasions for verbal instructions occur, and a necessity so then felt for the presence of the trusted representatives of our faithful retainers. It is accordingly necessary and proper that an agent from you, our special slave, should remain in attendance. You are therefore directed to nominate two of your trusted servants as your agents, and to send them to the Royal Court, so that whenever verbal orders may be necessary, no difficulty may be experienced. Entertain every confidence, and in sending the agents allow no delay to occur, for with the blessing of God, it is not possible or probable that they can have anything to dread or fear from this Court. Consider yourself honoured.

No. 75
Petition of the Rajah of Ballabhgarh
Dated 22nd August 1857

To – The King! Vicar of Gold! & c., & c.

Respectfully sheweth, That it is well impressed on Your Majesty's mind, that your petitioner is, by ancestry, the home-born slave of your illustrious house; and that I your slave, and my ancestors, as I still continue to do, have ever remained in subjection to Your Majesty's orders, and have always been engaged in acts of obedience, devotion, and zeal; and I therefore cherish the most anxious desire to present myself at your Court. The proof of this statement and profession is, that if I did not consider myself as nurtured and reared by your hands, and if I did not in my heart cherish and preserve the most anxious desire to obtain an interview, knowing what unbounded benefits I should realize, how then was it that during the Government of the English, I repeated my petition through Mir Fateh Ali, for permission to wait on Your Majesty. When I did so, you were pleased to observe that my heartfelt fidelity and devotion were manifest, but that from prudential considerations, necessary at the time, my attendance in your presence would not be proper, lest some evil might ensue. That your slave now has the misfortune not to realize the happiness of presenting himself at your Court, is to be ascribed to two reasons. The first is, that since the day of my return from Delhi, I have been suffering from various bodily complaints and ailments, external and internal. The second reason is, that as my enemies have alienated Your Majesty's kindness and goodwill from me, by means of their false and calumnious statements, I have been afraid, lest on my going to Delhi, they might devise some plan for my being subjected to indignity and disgrace, and by feeding the fire of Your Majesty's wrath, with the oil of falsehood boldly and audaciously advanced, might raise its flames to twice their present fury. I have, moreover, learnt from several quarters that the Officers and servants of the State are just now very much straitened in pecuniary means, and that they have accordingly arranged for demanding a contribution and present in money from me, although my income is very limited. Your Majesty, who is thoroughly acquainted with the whole of the affairs and circumstances, public and private, of all your retainers, knows also that compared with the states of all the other Chieftains, your slave's territory is considerably the smallest, and that its revenue has never been equal to its necessary and unavoidable expenses; but that on the contrary, the State has always been thousands of rupees in debt. As regards that which had been accumulated by the ancestors of this least of the lowest of your servants, it is to be submitted that the former Officials of my Government, by embezzlement and fraud, plundered and carried away the whole of that, and emptying my treasure and store rooms, have abundantly filled their own houses with the money and property they had contained. Having absconded from this, they went off to Delhi, where they are now staying at their homes, concocting and propagating every variety of calumny and scandal against my government. Under these circumstances, then, how could I, your slave, whose means are so limited, arrange for a contribution, a present in money, and the expenses of the Army? Yes, certainly, if Your Majesty's advisers and the servants of your government will, according to the list below, apprehend and make over to me my former faithless and corrupt officials, who are now residing in Delhi, and who, by their embezzlements, have robbed me of about 1,125,000 rupees, half of whatever I may be able to recover from them of their plunder I shall pay into the Royal Treasury. If, on the other hand, it is not deemed advisable that they should be seized and made over to me, then let Your Majesty's servants themselves apprehend that may be thus recovered, let them pay such portion as they may think fit into the Royal Treasury, and let them return the rest to me. The emblem of nobility and greatness, Mir Fateh Ali, condescendingly took the trouble to come here, and by doing so has laid me under obligations as if he had conferred unlimited kindness. He evinced, moreover, a very kind and fatherly interest in my affairs. All the orders which were entrusted to Mir Fateh Ali for verbal communication I have been made acquainted with by him, word for word, as the answers were such as it was not expedient should be put into writing, I have explained them to the Mir Sahib, who will communicate them to Your Majesty verbally. A further petition is, that whatever he may urge on behalf of me, who am a slave deserving of your kindly graciousness and favour, may in every respect be accepted and approved of, with that wonted kindness, condescension, support, and benevolence from ancient times. All that was necessary I have submitted for Your Majesty's information. May Your Majesty's servants ever be cheered by victory and conquest, and; may your destitute enemies ever be dispirited and humbled by calamities and oppression.

The Physician Abdul Hak, Prime Minister of the State	Rs.10,00,000
Mukta Prashad, Lawyer	15,000
Rajah Lal, Chief Secretary	10,000
Nisar Ali, Deputy Prime Minister	10,000
Jowalla Nath Pandit, Treasurer	30,000
Sher Khanm the said Physician's	

personal friend	25,000
Hissar-ud-din, Jamadar and Superintendent	5,000
Amir Ali, Superintendent of Buildings and Store-rooms of my landed property in Delhi, who was also assistant to my Lawyer	10,000
Saadat Ali Khan, Police Officer	8,000
Ahmad Mirza, farmer of Ballabhgarh Villages and of my vineyard in Delhi	10,000
Mubarak Ali Khan	2,000

Petition of the slave, Rajah Nahar Singh Bahadur. Seal of Rajah Nahar Singh Bahadur.

No. 76
Petition of the Rajah of Ballabhgarh
Dated 1st September 1857

To – The King! Vicar of God! & c. & c.

Respectfully sheweth, That I have had the very great honour to receive Your Majesty's missive replying to my petition, intimating your acceptance of my present of a dun horse, and directing me to entertain no fears of oppression from the Army. The acceptance of my present has conferred on me the highest distinction. Let Your Majesty ever consider me your devoted and ancient slave and servant. If with your unlimited graciousness and favour, you will be pleased to bestow the Pali and Palwal sections of the District on me, I shall make the most complete Judicial and Revenue arrangements there. So complete shall these arrangements be, that everyone high or low, rich or poor, will be satisfied with them, and Your Majesty also will graciously view your slave's tact, exertions, and plans, approving favour and kindness. Prayers for the continuance of the King's victories and conquest. Petition of the slave, Rajah Nahar Singh Bahadur. Seal of Rajah Nahar Singh Bahadur.

No. 77
Petition of the Rajah of Ballabhgarh
Dated 2nd September 1857

To – The King! Vicar of God! & c., & c.

Respectfully sheweth, That I have had the very great honour to receive Your Majesty's missive, intimating your acceptance of my present of a dun horse, and directing me to be assured that no one of the Army shall commit any act of oppression or grievance against the Ballabhgarh State. I feel as though I were elevated to the very summit of distinction. The tongue and language are alike altogether at fault adequately to express thankfulness commensurate with such signal and abounding graciousness and condescension. May God preserve and protect Your Majesty, to the end of time, in the performance of similar acts of favour and support! Refuge of Royalty! It is a most extraordinary circumstance, that Your Majesty has ordered that no one connected with the Army shall commit any act of oppression against the Ballabhgarh State; and today, the 2nd of September 1857, I receive a letter from Muhammad Bakht Khan, Commander-in-Chief of the Army, saying that all the prisoners throughout the country had been set at large, but that Hardeo Bakhsh, Pran Sukh, and others, Dhusar, and Jamayat Khan, coach-man, were still in imprisonment, and directing me to forward them to the army, together with their bonds and engagements, in the custody of the ten Troopers he had sent. It is fully known to Your Majesty that the above-named prisoners are accountable to this State for frauds amounting to lacs of rupees, and have agreed to pay this money, for which they are so accountable. How then can men responsible for such claims and demands be released; for if they should be set free, the loss to me, your slave, would be excessive. The above prisoners are not like those incarcerated in Criminal Jails, from whose enlargement and release from prison no manner of loss could result. If such detenus as the above are released, endless evils, mischievous to my arrangements, will arise, and their suppression afterwards will be exceedingly difficult. Under these circumstances, then, I humbly supplicate that an order may be issued to the Commander-in-Chief to refrain from requiring that persons responsible to the Ballabhgarh State should be sent to him, and that he will on no account call for them, as from such proceedings on his part, it is in every point of view evident that damage to the very foundations of this State must accrue. I trust, therefore, that my request will receive the honour of approval, for I, your slave, am an old and devoted servant and well-wisher of your throne, which is the threshold of earth and heaven. I expect, moreover, that Your Majesty's servants will make over Hakim Abdul Hak, Pandit Jowala Prashad, and others, my Officials, as I have claims against them, amounting to about 1,125,000 rupees, so that I may realize this money from them. Prayers for the King's prosperity. Further, I forward the Commander-in-Chief's letter in original. After perusal, let it be kindly returned, with a favourable answer to this petition. Petition of the slave Rajah Nahar Singh Bahadur. Seal of Rajah Nahar Singh Bahadur.

Ahsanullah Khan, Physician, is re-called and examined on his former affirmation.

Paper Nos. 4, 5, 6, 7, 8, 9, and 13 arranged under the head of loan, are shown to witness, who declares that the seals on all are impressions from the special seal in the prisoner's cypher. The witness declares further that the papers with the exception of No. 6, are all in the handwriting of Mukund Lal, the Prisoner's secretary. Papers 1, 2, 3, 10, 11, 12, 14, 15, and 16 are now shown to witness, and with exception of 2, 3, and 12, of which he knows nothing, he gives the following statement of the others: No. 1 is in the handwriting of Mukund Lal, and attested as genuine by King's autograph cypher, and No. 11 is also attested with autograph cypher; but witness does not recognize the handwriting. The translations of the 16 papers under the head of Loan are now read and entered, as follows:

Papers arranged under the Head of Loan.

No. 1

Paper under the autograph cypher of the King, in pencil

Dated 8th July 1857

To – Mirza Mughal.

Son, the illustrious and valiant Mirza Zahur-ud-din, otherwise Mirza Mughal Bahadur! Learn! That you, the light of our eyes, already know, that a very small balance of cash remains in our Treasury. That there is no immediate prospect or revenue from any quarter, and that the little money which remains must of necessity be very soon expended. You are directed to call together, during the day or tonight, all the Officers of the Regiments which first arrived, in order that they may deliberate and decide on means to be adopted for raising funds to meet the daily necessary and emergent expenses. A meeting of this kind, in the language of the Soldiery, is called a 'Court'. You are to use stringent injunctions in this matter, and the result of the deliberations, in the shape of a feasible plan for replenishing the Treasury, whatever it may be, you will cause to be embodied in a petition from them, which you will lay before the Royal presence tomorrow. It is a necessary measure of prudence and precaution, to make arrangements in this matter before the Treasury is quite exhausted. Moreover, as no private Treasury was ever kept by us, and as the contributions to the State loan have not been realized, all our servants, old and new, are now in pecuniary difficulties. The money, amounting to 125,000 rupees, which was levied last month as a loan at interest from the merchants of the City for our private expenses, was not all received accordingly. Under these circumstances, how are the expenses of others to be provided for? You will explain all these points, particularly and clearly, to each Officer, and having their answer put into writing, will not fail to submit it tomorrow for our consideration.

Note on the Face – 'Received 14th July 1857'.

No. 2

Petition of the Members of the court

Dated 10th July 1857

To – The King! Nourisher of the Poor!

Respectfully sheweth, That we have had the honour to be favoured by Your Majesty's order, and besides other particulars, we learn that Your Majesty's commands are to the effect, that the treasure which was brought has been nearly all expended in meeting the requirements of the Army, and the little now remaining must shortly be paid away to the same end, and that we, the Officers of the Court, are therefore directed to devise some feasible expedient to replenish the Treasury. Your Majesty, in our judgement, as the first step in this matter, the Army should go out.

Proposition First – That money on loan at interest be obtained from some Merchants and that this loan, with interest, be paid off on the establishment of order.

Proposition Second – That a force consisting of 1,500 Infantry, 500 Cavalry, and two Horse Artillery Guns, be sent out into the Country to establish Police Stations, Revenue Offices, and Postal arrangements, so that it may become widely known that Your Majesty's rule has been established. Further, that this force be empowered to take charge of all money which may be found collected anywhere on account of the revenues of the State, and which may be voluntarily made over to it. But it should be thoroughly impressed on all its members, that such of them as shall commit any act of plunder, tyranny, or oppression, will be severely punished.

Our first prayer is, That both the above written suggestions for raising money, may be adopted.

Our second prayer is, That one of Your Majesty's nobles, in whose integrity Your Majesty may have the most complete confidence, may be sent with the force, to make arrangements for the Civil administration of the Country.

Our third prayer is, That the noble Your Majesty may depute should, however, be warned, as though by this Court, that if, on going out, he shall oppress any poor landholder or any subordinate Collector of Revenue, or if he shall take bribes or douceurs, he will be punished according to the decision of this Court. The settlement of the property rights of landholders may be effected after the following way.

In each case, it shall be ascertained that the name of the claimant is one record in the papers of the registrar of proprietary rights in land,[50] or in those of the Village Accountant[51] and the claimant shall be required to file receipts of his former payments of land rent, to show that he contributed to the finances of the State, and that the settlement of assessment had been made in his favour. If, on inspection of their documents, and on the testimony of witnesses, *viz.* of the Registrar of landed rights, the Village Accountant and other respectable men of the place, it shall be clearly proved that the

50 *Qanungo.*
51 *Patwari.*

claimant had really been the landholder, and the principal man or one of the Principal men, recognized by the Government, as answerable for the Revenue of the whole Village, or of a considerable section of it, the settlement will be made in his name. If a subsequent claimant shall come forward, his petition will be taken, and an order will be recorded on it, to the effect that a final award will be given after investigation. But in the first instance, the appointment to the position of Headman responsible for the Revenue of the Village will be given to those who had formerly held the situation.

Our fourth prayer is, That, if the noble deputed to settle the Country does not act in every particular according to these orders, the land holders will be at liberty to lay their complaints before this Court, and if, after due deliberations, it is found that the noble's orders have been such as should be reversed, they will be annulled, and the real owners will be installed in their just rights. The Petition of the slaves, the Officers of the Court, Jiwaram Subedar Major Bahadur, Sheoram Misr Subedar Major, Tahniyat Khan Subedar Major, Hetram Subedar Major, and Beniram Subedar Major.

No. 3
Petition of Mirza Mughal

Dated 12th July 1857

To – The King! Shelter of the World!

Respectfully sheweth, That Your Majesty's order, dated 10th July 1857, directing with reference to the small balance of Cash in the Treasury, that the members of the Court should deliberate on the matter, and that I should submit their petition on the subject, has been received. In conformity with Your Majesty's orders, the petition, prepared after due deliberation by the Members of the Court, is submitted to the Royal presence, enclosed herein. Such orders as may be issued in this business will be carried into effect. Petition of the slave and bondman Zahur-ud-din.

No. 4
Order under the seal engraved in the King's special cypher

Dated 15th July 1857

To – Mirza Mughal.

Son, The illustrious and valiant Mirza Muhammad Zahur-ud-din, otherwise Mirza Mughal Bahadur, Learn! That, just now, we are under the necessity of raising a temporary loan, at an interest of 1% per mensem, from the Merchants of the City, to defray the allowances of the Army. Many of the merchants paid up the amounts that were claimed from them. Others, however, on the ground of non-payment, were apprehended and brought to the Palace by the Soldiers of the Royal Levies, and are now detained as prisoners in the Captain's Guard, attached to the Office of the Court

Chamberlain. We have just heard that with the collusion of some Infantry Soldiers, the relations of these merchants have devised plans to liberate them from custody. Even just now a Private of the Infantry coming from the direction of the Guard at the Lahori Gate of the City, which is included in the Tamaku-ka-katra, entered the Captain's Guard; and on the instigation of one Lakshmiram, said he would take away Lakshmiram's son. The Officers and men of the Guard interposing, the Private in question used much violent language towards them, and even threatened to shoot them and liberate the lad. From the representations of the Officers, it is further ascertained that he will return in the afternoon, accompanied by 18 or 20 other soldiers, in order to raise a disturbance with the men of the Captain's Guard. You, our son, are therefore directed this instant to send a reinforcement to the Captain's Guard for the effectual custody of the prisoners confined there, and you will direct that no soldier be allowed to take away any prisoner. Do not allow the neglect or delay of a second to occur in this matter, for, if such things be permitted, our authority must be deranged. Be assured of our kindness.

Note on the Reverse by Mirza Mughal probably, but without Signature or Seal.

A guard has been stationed, agreeably to the orders of the Royal presence, at the Captain's Guard. Dated 15th July 1857.

No. 5

Order under the seal engraved in the King's special cypher

Dated 28th July 1857

To – Mirza Mughal.

Son, The illustrious and valiant Mirza Zahur-ud-din, otherwise Mirza Mughal, Commander-in-Chief Bahadur! Learn. That no money whatever remains in the Treasury for paying the daily and monthly allowances of the Troops, nor yet for defraying the daily urgent expense of the Magazine, the Artillery, and the manufacture of powder. Without powder the active operations against the infidels must be interrupted. It is necessary, therefore, quickly to devise some plan for raising funds through the means of a loan, without interest, from all the Punjabi and other merchants, and from the rich servants of the English, and forward it to the Royal treasury. You are further directed to forward drafts of notes of hand, specifying the amount of contribution in each, so that corresponding notes of hand, under our special Seal, promising payment on the realization of the revenue of the Country, and the capture of treasuries, may be granted. No fraction of any portion of this loan will be left unpaid. You will give full assurance to all parties on this point, as well as that, in the event of their arranging for the money required, besides being repaid the loan, as a mark of favour, they will be elevated to appointments and emoluments proportioned to their qualifications, but if, notwithstanding such assurances, and the hopes of advantages thus held out, any of the people mentioned do not exert themselves to arrange for the money, but advance unfounded excuses, you, our Son, are empowered to chastise them as may be proper, so that severity may bring them to the path of propriety, and obedience to our Royal orders may be result, and the expenses of the Magazine, the Artillery, and the manufacture of powder, may be no longer interrupted, and all necessary operations may be prosecuted daily. You will use such well advised steps in this matter as will result in your collecting and sending the money to the treasury within three days. You are directed to enjoin on your agents, however, to refrain from making any demand now on such of the merchants as assisted in the former loan, arranged through the late deceased Manir-ud-dowlat, or on such of them as have given written engagements to pay the balances of their several contributions within fixed periods. You will lay no further demand or claim on the whole of these men, so that nothing at variance with the terms of the agreements given under our special Seal may occur, and no cause for distrust to others may arise. Be assured of our kindness.

No. 6

Order under the seal engraved in the King's special cypher

Dated 29th July 1857

To – Brindaban alias Bindi Mali, Treasurer to the Artillery.

To the effect that a bond, under our special Seal, for 4,198 Rupees and 9½ Annas for the distribution of six months' pay to the Artillery, as being bestowed on you our slave, it is incumbent on you to arrange that this money be forthcoming. Be assured that the funds on loan promised by the City Merchants will now be very soon realized by Rai Mukand Lal, when the amount of this bond will be repaid with every fraction of interest. Entertain every confidence that most stringent orders will be issued for the speedy repayments to you of this loan, and that it will be very soon repaid. Consider this order imperative, and act as you are being written to.

No. 7

Order under the seal engraved in the King's special cypher

Dated 29th July 1857

To – The Special Slave! Rai Mukund Lal Bahadur.

Consider yourself receiving mercies and know. That the balance of a contribution to the State Loan, amounting to 5,300 Rupees, has been realized, through Gangaram peon, and a voucher under our special Seal has been granted for it; and know also that a special order has been addressed to you, our special slave, to repay this sum from the receipts on the account of the loan promised by the City Merchants. 4,198 Rupees and 9½ Annas have now been obtained from Rai Brindaban as a temporary loan, at an interest of 1% per mensem, in order that six months' pay may be given to the Artillery. You, our special slave, are therefore ordered, to realize quickly the money claimable from the City Merchants, and to repay this aggregate sum of 4,198 Rupees and 9½ Annas with interest, when you will recover and lay before our Royal presence the vouchers granted under our special Seal. Such sums as you will afterwards realize, you will pay into the Royal Treasury. You will consider the words in this matter imperative.

No. 8

Order under the seal engraved in the King's special cypher

Dated 29th July 1857

To – Mirza Mughal.

Son, The illustrious and valiant Mirza Muhammad Zahur-ud-din, otherwise Mirza Mughal Bahadur. Learnt! That as our servants of the Artillery branch are in pecuniary difficulties in consequence of the revenue from Rohat, Kakrol, and other Villages not having been received, and as we mercifully cherish a concern for the comfort of all our dependants, and most especially for the comforts of this branch of them, who are now to receive pay after six months, an order has been issued to Brindaban, *alias* Bindi Mall, Treasurer, to arrange for the payment of their allowances, and a bond, under our special Seal, has, at the same time, been granted to him, for 4,198 Rupees and 9½ Annas, it being definitely specified that the money on loan, promised by the City Merchants and to be realized through the agency of our special slave, Rai Mukand Lal shall be the source from which this sum will be repaid. Do you, our Son, therefore, also issue an order for the same Treasurer's greater satisfaction and confidence, so that, being fully assured, he may exert himself effectually to arrange for the money; and that this very day six months' pay may be distributed to the Artillery, after the usual manner, and they, having their difficulties removed, may in this respect be placed on the same footing as the rest of the Government servants. Be assured of our kindness.

No. 9

Bond or Promissory note for money borrowed under the seal engraved in the King's special cypher, dated 29th July 1857 to the effect, that the sum of 4,198 Rupees and 9½ Annas has been paid into the Royal Treasury, as a temporary loan, at an interest of 1% per mensem, by Brindaban Treasurer, for the payment of six months' allowances to the servants of the Artillery branch, and it has been definitely settled that this debt will be repaid from the receipts on account of the loan promised by the City Merchants. When, therefore, Rai Mukand Lal shall in a few days, according to the Royal orders, have realized, from the City Merchants the money promised on loan, the whole and entire sum of 4,198 Rupees and 9½ Annas will be repaid to the said Treasurer, together with the interest, and no balance to the extent of the smallest fraction will be left unpaid, and, moreover, before the liquidation of this debt, no portion of the money that will be realized on account of the State Loan will be paid to any other person, or be appropriated even to the Royal requirements. This document is therefore executed as a bond.

No. 10

Petition of Mirza Mughal

Dated 6th August 1857

To – The King! Shelter of the World!

Respectfully sheweth, That all the influential men of the City, as well as the inhabitants generally, urge that they have no objection to raise funds for the expenses of the Army, but that it would be more gratifying to them, if the contributions of all, rich or poor, Hindu or Mohammedans, were realized through the influential men of both religions, and that, at the same time, by this arrangement, a much larger sum in the aggregate would be obtained. I therefore pray that this proposal of the City inhabitants may be approved of, and that Your Majesty's orders may be issued to the influential men named in the accompanying separate list, to carry it into effect. (Prayers for the prosperity of the reign.) If the whole of the inhabitants contribute, a very considerable amount will be realized, and no one will entertain suspicion against this slave of embezzlement or appropriation. All being attested by the influential men of the City, a list of whom is enclosed, according to their several ability, no individual will have room for excuses or delay.

The Hindus will be assured that Your Majesty regards Hindus and Mussalmans with equal favour, and the Army will see, that the whole of the inhabitants, whether Hindus or Mussalmans, are sharers in the arrangement for raising funds to meet its expenses. Petition of the slave Zahur-ud-din.

Autograph order by the King, in pencil

The arrangement is a judicious one, and is approved of.

No. 11

Order under the King's autograph special cypher

Dated 19th August 1857

To – The Special Slaves, Worthy of Favours and Kindness, the members of the Court.

Consider yourselves receiving mercies and learn: That as agreeably to the request of you, devoted and zealous servants of the State, you are being empowered to arrange and work out all matters and affairs, general and particular, connected with the collecting of the Revenue from the Country, and the bringing to a satisfactory issue the project of a loan from the Merchants and influential men of the City, it is incumbent on you to act with zeal and integrity in the matter with which you have been entrusted, and that you should make efficient arrangements for carrying on the operations of war, and for obtaining final victory over the hostile host of infidels, as well as for protecting the City and its inhabitants. All your acts and arrangements will be approved of and sanctioned. In reference to you, no representations of any interested parties whatever will be heeded; and in all such orders as may emanate from your Court, none of the servants of the State, nor the Princes Royal, will in any way interfere. The money you may collect on account of the loan from the Merchants and the influential men of the City, will be deposited in your Court, and will be expended in paying the Army, and on account of the necessities of the Magazine, & c., and when the Revenue of the Country shall have been realized, first of all the loan from the City Merchants, together with its interest, shall be repaid. Be assured of our kindness.

No. 12
Petition of Mathura Das and Salig Ram (Saligram? – Ed.), Merchants of Delhi

Dated 23rd August 1857

Abstract of Petition on the face, Above the Address.

We slaves, selling our culinary vessels, and overcoming thousand difficulties, have already paid 7,500 Rupees in the first instance to Your Majesty, and in the second to Mirza Khair Sultan Bahadur. The Members of Court and the Officers of the Army, intent on our ruin, now demand a third payment. We therefore pray that Your Majesty's injunctions may be laid on the servants of the State and the Officers of the Army, to refrain from imposing any further demands on these faithful slaves.

To – The King! Shelter of the World!

Respectfully sheweth, That let it not be hidden from your divine Majesty's knowledge that, previous to this, Your Majesty's commands were laid on us, your faithful slaves, to pay 6,000 Rupees into the Treasury; and we were told that we should be subjected to no further demand. Your slave's house had been previously plundered of everything it contained, and of all we possessed, by the Soldiery and other people, on the day of the arrival of the troops from Meerut in Delhi, and all our banking and mercantile transactions were, in consequence, utterly ruined and suspended. Unable therefore though we were to meet Your Majesty's commands, nevertheless that Your Majesty's orders should be obeyed, we sold such articles of Jewellery, culinary vessels, & c., as still remained in our possession, and borrowing besides to make up the full sum, we paid the money into the Royal Treasury on the 3rd and 5th of June 1857. Recently again, the Commander-in-Chief Bahadur, and Mirza Khair Sultan Bahadur placed us under strict and pre-emptory injunctions to make a second money payment, to meet the expenses of the Army. Feeling our utter helplessness, after a thousand difficulties we succeeded in making up 1,500 Rupees, which we gave to the said Royal Princes, obtaining in return a receipt, together with an order, under the seal and signature of Mirza Muhammad Khair Sultan Bahadur (may his prestige last for ever) that no further demand was, on any account, to be made on us by the servants of the State, or by the Officers of the Army. Notwithstanding all this, the Members of the Court and the other Officers of the Army now a third time require money from your faithful slaves, and are determined on their ruin. Whereas we, Your Majesty's well-wisher, have no protection, but that of God, or Your Majesty; and whereas on two former occasions, despite the difficulties we had to overcome, we obeyed Your Majesty's orders and paid money into the Treasury, and whereas we are now with difficulty able to procure even the daily necessaries of life, we therefore present this petition, and pray that according to the claims of justice, and the dictates of Your Majesty's desire to foster the poor, Your Majesty will be pleased to issue orders to all the servants of the State and the Officers of the Army, to refrain from imposing this third demand on your slaves by these repeated demands, which they try to enforce by every means of coercion, so that thus obtaining justice, we may pray for the increase of Your Majesty's wealth and power. Otherwise, in consequence of the dread of degradation, and from their inability to raise the funds required, the lives of your slaves will be sacrificed. It was necessary, and has therefore been submitted. Petition of the slaves Mathura Das and Salig Ram, merchants of Delhi. Signatures of the firm of Mathura Das and Salig Ram in the Hindi mercantile character.[52]

No. 13

Order under the Seal engraved in the King's special cypher

Dated 27th August 1857

To – Mirza Mughal.

Son, The illustrious and valiant Mirza Zahur-ud-din, otherwise Mirza Mughal Bahadur. Learn! That the Merchant, Ramjidas Gurwalla, having twice paid money into the Royal Treasury, and having, moreover, in conformity with our orders, made arrangements for the loan of the State, it is incumbent that you, our Son, should make no further demand on him. You

52 Called *Modi/Munda* script.

will consider our injunctions stringent in this matter, and will act in accordance with these orders.

No. 14
Petition of Nabi Bakhsh and others

No date

To – The King! Shelter of the World!

Respectfully sheweth! That in the present anarchy, your slaves have suffered heavy and ruinous losses inasmuch as whatever commerce we carried on, whether at Calcutta, or Benares, or Cawnpore, or Delhi, or Amballah, or Lahore, has been ruined, and all our mercantile stores have been plundered and devastated, while the burden of our former debts still lies on our shoulders, and we are now without even the means of meeting the daily expenses necessary for the subsistence of ourselves and our families. Let Your Majesty ascertain the truth of this statement from trustworthy parties, and by an inspection of our mercantile books. Mirza Mughal Sahib now demands 50,000 Rupees from us. Whence can we produce the same? At present, we should find it extremely difficult to raise even 5,000 Rupees. We, your slaves, have now been three days prisoners in the arrest of Captain Mir Haidar Husein Khan, and the said Captain would not allow us out of custody, even to join in the prayers on the Eid-i-Azha. Left without other resource, we petition Your Majesty (at the same time praying to God to protect and preserve you over the heads of us, your Slaves) that Your Majesty will issue an order for our release from arrest. We have now for 20 days been administering to the wants of 1,200 Mujahids, and shall continue to do so. But more than this is impossible, is out of our power to perform, and cannot be done. We depend on Your Majesty's consideration, equalling that of Cyrus, that, with a fostering concern to nourish and cherish the poor, Your Majesty's orders will, with condescending goodness, be issued for our release. It was necessary, and we have submitted it. (Prayers for the prosperity of the reign.) The petition of the slaves Nabi Baksh, Hajii Mullah Baksh, Karim Baksh, Jawan Bakht, Pir Baksh, Fateh Muhammad, Muhammad Husain, Muhammad Baksh, Taimur Ahmad, Karim Bakhsh, Kutb-ud-din, Saifulla, Haji Rahim Bakhsh, Karim Bakhsh Ahmad, Karamdin, Haji Ahmad, and others.

Autograph order by the King, in pencil

Mirza Mughal will take recognisance for future good behaviour so that they may not again, in infringement of positive orders, send Commissariat necessaries or other supplies to the infidels, and provided the advice of the Lord Governor coincides, have will then release them all.

No. 15
Petition of Mirza Mughal

No date

To – The King! Shelter of the World!

It is known to Your Majesty, that the Army having been reduced to starvation in consequence of not being paid their daily allowances, your slave, as well as they, were constrained to petition Your Majesty on the subject, when, having condescended to view the distress, you were pleased to issue orders that some plan for raising a loan, to carry on the expenses of the Army, should be devised, and accordingly, a Royal missive was bestowed on your slave in this matter. In accordance there with, your slave summoned the Merchants and Punjabis of the City, and conferred with them on the subject, and some gave written engagements to pay in a day or two, and then went away. I have just learnt, that Muhammad Bakht Khan has received a written order also, to summon the Merchants and obtain money from them. A circumstance like this is calculated to cause disunion and dissension in the Army. Let Your Majesty consider this, and recall the order given to Muhammad Bakht Khan, and let Your Majesty also prohibit his taking steps in this business, because arrangements for the money have already been made by me. Considering it necessary, I have submitted this petition.

Petition of the slave Zahur-ud-din. No date.

No. 16

Petition of Muhammad Khair Sultan

No date

To – The King! Shelter of the World!

Respectfully sheweth, That aided by 200 Troopers and a Brigade Major, placed at his disposal by the Lord Sahib, your slave has been assiduously engaged, since morning, in collecting the money required by Your Majesty's Government. Just now, however, the Merchants of the City have put forward the objection, that Gouri Shankar has ordered them, on no account, to give the money to any of the Royal Princes, but to pay it into the Court only. Your Majesty! Under such circumstances, extreme conclusion and derangement of plans is to be expected, and mischief-makers shall have been severely punished, till then arrangements which will result in success cannot be made. It is submitted for information. (Prayers for the prosperity of the reign.)

Petition of the lowly Muhammad Khair Sultan. No date.

Autograph order by the King, in pencil

Besides the shopkeepers, you will realize money tomorrow morning, as may be advisable, from Merchants also, and will forward it to the Royal presence. Let no one be put to inconvenience, nor yet let the business of the State be interrupted (a couple of words here are illegible, but the sense is not affected or left incomplete). This, which is here written, is the only prohibition, and there is none other.

The court adjourns till 11 a.m. on Monday, the 1st February 1858.

Day five: 1 February 1858

The Court reassembled this day at 11 a.m. in the Hall of Special Audience in the Palace at Delhi. The President, Members, Interpreter, and Deputy Judge Advocate-General are all present.

The Prisoner is brought into Court.

The Interpreter reads in Persian the original papers under the head of Loan, the translations of which were perused on 30th ultimo.

Ahsanullah Khan is re-called on his former affirmation, and the 8 papers arranged under the head of Pay are shown to him.

Examined by the Judge Advocate

Question – What do you know of the handwriting or seal on these papers?

Answer – The orders on six of the papers, *viz.* No. 1, 4, 5, 6, 7, and 8 are in the handwriting of the prisoner. The writing of No. 2 is that of Mukund Lal, the prisoner's secretary. And the seal is an impression from the special one engraved in his cypher. The writing, in paper No. 3, which is petition from the prisoner's son Mirza Mughal and is attested by his official seal as Commander-in-Chief, appears to be in the handwriting of Jowalla Nath, one of his clerks.

The translation of these papers is now read and entered as follows:

The papers in original Persian are also now read to the Prisoner.

No. 1
Petition of Mirza Mughal, Dated 1st June 1857

To – The King! Shelter of World!

The Army has been two days at the Shahdari Battery, and did not come to receive their daily allowances. Three days' accumulated arrears are due today, and the Army is going in to demand payment. Tomorrow a fourth day's allowances will be payable, and a second application will be necessary. To prevent this I pray I may at once be favoured with 15,000 rupees as the aggregate allowances of four days. Petition of the slave Zahur-ud-din.

Autograph order by the King, in pencil

Bussunt will give 15,000 Rupees out of the Treasury. Further, Mirza Mughal, enjoining all diligence on Mirza Fazil Beg Khan,[53] will have an account prepared of all the money he has caused to be paid out of the treasury up to this date, and will lay it before us.

53 Accountant with Mirza Mughal. Ed.

No. 2

Order attested with the seal engraved in the King's special cypher, Dated 22nd June 1857

To – Mirza Mughal.

Son, The Illustrious and Valiant Mirza Zohar-ud-din, otherwise Mirza Mughal Bahadur. Learn! That by the representations of Samman Lal, we are informed, that in the first instance, sweetmeats were given as daily rations to the Artillery men serving the guns in the Cashmere and Baddarraw Gate Main Guard, and other Bastions through the agency of the Mu'awzzaz-dowlat Bahadur,[54] and that, subsequently, from 11th June 1857, daily-money payments have been made instead, as per separate list. That although the supply of rations, or the daily allowance of money instead, is a matter appertaining to the Military Department, in the above instances, the expense was defrayed from the Royal Treasury, and that under these circumstances he prays for an order under our Royal treasury, and that under these circumstances he prays for an order under our Royal signature, to our illustrious Son, Mirza Mughal Bahadur, to the effect that he should cause reimbursement to be made. You are directed to remit to Samman Lal the sum of 110 Rupees, agreeably to the statement furnished by him, the details of which are subjoined. You are further directed to make arrangements for the future payments of the daily allowance to the Artillery men the same as those, according to which, they are paid to the whole of the Infantry Regiments. Be assured of our kindness.

	Rs.	A.P.	Rs.	A.P.[55]
11th June 1857 to Kanlai Khan, Artillery man	8	0 0		
12th June 1857 to Kanlai Khan, Artillery man	4	0 0		
13th June 1857 to Kanlai Khan, Artillery man			12	0 0
14th June 1857 to Kanlai Khan, Artillery man	4	0 0		
15th June 1857 to Kanlai Khan, Artillery man	4	0 0		
15th June 1857 to Artillery man at the Lahori Gate	3	0 0		
15th June 1857 to Artillery man at the Main Guard	3	0 0		
			10	0 0
16th June 1857 to Kanlai Khan	5	0 0		

54 Title of Gen. Bakht Khan.

55 Rupees, Annas, Paise – 12 *Paise* made an *Anna* and 16 *Annas* made a Rupee.

16th June 1857 to Artillery man at the Main Guard	3	0 0	
16th June 1857 to Artillery men at the Lahori Gate	3	0 0	
			11 0 0
17th June 1857 to Kanlai Khan	5	0 0	
17th June 1857 to Artillery man at the Lahori Gate	3	0 0	
17th June 1857 to Artillery man at the main Guard	3	0 0	
			11 0 0
18th June 1857 to Kanlai Khan	5	0 0	
18th June 1857 to Artillery man at the Lahori Gate	3	0 0	
18th June 1857 to Artillery man at the main Guard	3	0 0	
			11 0 0
19th June 1857 to Kanlai Khan	5	0 0	
19th June 1857 to Artillery man at the Lahori Gate	3	0 0	
19th June 1857 to Artillery man at the main Guard	3	0 0	
			11 0 0
20th June 1857 to Kanlai Khan	5	0 0	
20th June 1857 to Artillery man at the Lahori Gate	3	0 0	
20th June 1857 to Artillery man at the main Guard	3	0 0	
20th June 1857 to Blue Bastion	3	0 0	
			14 0 0
21st June 1857 to Kanlai Khan	5	0 0	
21st June 1857 to Artillery man at the Lahori Gate	3	0 0	
21st June 1857 to Artillery man at the main Guard	3	0 0	
21st June 1857 to Blue Bastion	3	0 0	
			14 0 0
	Total		1100 0

No. 3
Petition of Mirza Mughal

Dated 9th July 1857

To – The King! Shelter of the World!

Respectfully Sheweth, That your slave having adopted means to assure the whole of the Army, Infantry, and Cavalry, of their being paid and promoted, as soon as the Country shall have been settled, the Revenue realized, and the Enemy finally and fully defeated, encloses a copy of an outline of these measures, and trust that agreeably to it, an order will be graciously issued by Your Majesty, so that the Army may be made acquainted with Your Majesty's feelings of favour and kindness on their behalf, and being thus inspired with hopes of advancement and distinction, each and all may fight in Your Majesty's cause even to the sacrifice of their lives. (Prayers for the prosperity of the reign.) Petition of the slave Zahur-ud-din, attested with the Official Seal of the Commander-in-Chief Bahadur. No order.

No. 4
Petition of Mirza Mughal

Dated 10th July 1857

To – The King! Shelter of the World!

Respectfully sheweth, That a petition, with a nominal list, has this day been received from Muhammad Jahangir Khan, Captain of the Gwalior Rajah's Artillery, praying that some pecuniary provisions may be made, to enable him to meet the expenses of the daily exigencies of existence. Your Majesty's orders are to the effect, that all newly arrived troops are to be referred to the Bareilly General.

The aforesaid petition and list are therefore submitted herewith in original. Such orders as may be issued in this case will be acted upon. Petition of the slave, Zahur-ud-din.

Note at the Foot of the Petition – This petition is without the enclosures. Signed Kalyan Narayan, 8th August 1857.

My life! Inform the General so that they may learn that the Treasury has been quite exhausted.

Number in a corner at the top (Index number apparently) '778' and note immediately below 'Received 26th July 1857'.

No. 5
Petition of Mirza Mughal

Dated 12th July 1857

To – The King! Shelter of the World!

Respectfully sheweth, That the sum of 37,000 Rupees, with the additional 2,000 Rupees from the Commissariat funds, with which your slave was favoured on the 12th of July 1857, has been all expended, and not a fraction now remains in hand, and while such is the case, Your Majesty has passed and order on the petition of the Cavalrymen recently arrived, that your slave will make arrangements for paying their daily allowances. The Cavalrymen shown in the subjoined list claim arrears for 16 or 20 days each, that is to 12th July 1857. Your petition therefore prays that 10,000 Rupees may now be granted in order that these arrears may be paid off; and be further prays that in future he may be placed in funds each day, to pay the allowances for that day.

	Rs. A. P.
Muouz-ud-din Khan, Risladar, 15 days	3,696 40
Mardan Khan, 10 Men, to 12th July 1857	428 20
Turradar Khan, and Faiz-ud-din Khan, 10 days	1,594 20
Syad Dulzar Ali, 22 Men, 28 days, to 12th July	140 00
Ghazi-ud-din Khan, Risaldar, 125 men, 13 days	1,950 00
Abdul Majid Khan 2 Men, 19 days of the month Zeekhan	133 00
Ahmad Khan and Madari Khan, Risaldars, 9th Regiment Cavalry, number of men and days not ascertained	
Karim Baksh Risaldar, who has been paid to the end of the month and more, now claims allowances for 20 days of the month Zu'l Kaadat	

Petition of the slave, Zahur-ud-din, attested with the Official Seal of the Commander-in Chief Bahadur.

Autograph order by the King, in pencil

In consequence of the scarcity of funds in the Treasury, so large an amount cannot be given. Those who are willing to be satisfied with a trifle, may be paid something as pecuniary assistance.

No. 6

Petition of Mirza Mughal

Dated 13th July 1857

To – The King! Shelter of the World!

Hitherto, Karim Bakhsh, Risaldar of the 1st Lucknow Irregular Cavalry, and the Men of his Corps, have been paid monthly. He has now presented a petition, dated the 12th July 1857, soliciting payment of daily allowances, in the same way that they are paid to others, and demanding arrears for 19 days. The real state of the matter is that these people have learnt that there is very little money in the Treasury, and it is on this account they now apply for daily allowances. Such orders, as may be issued, will be complied with. Petition of the slave Zahur-ud-din.

Autograph order by the King, in pencil

Those who are paid monthly will not get daily allowances.

Note at the Top – 'Received 26th July 1857', 'No 798' (Index number probably).

No. 7

Petition of Mirza Muhammad Azim[56]

No date

56 Asst. Patrol (Customs) at Bhattu (Hisar); connected with Royal family; played prominent part in the Revolt.

To – The King! Shelter of the World!

Respectfully sheweth! That the servants of Your Majesty who came from Hansi and Hissar, and who have been placed under your slave, have not received their pay for 2 months and 20 days. As the treasuries of Sirsa, Hissar, Hansi, and other places, were, with great care and zeal, brought by them, and lodged in the Royal Treasury, and here too, accompanying your slave in every engagement, three or four of these servants daily certify their fidelity with their lives, they therefore now demand their pay. Your slave, actuated by zeal, has arranged that Your Majesty will now grant one month's pay out of the two months and 20 days' arrears which are due, he will satisfy the men. If, on the other hand, no pay whatever is now granted, the force will have cause to be disheartened. It is strange that all the rest of the Army should have been paid. I transmit enclosed in this petition, an abstract for one month's pay for all the men of the force, in expectation that orders may be issued. It was necessary and has been represented. Petition of the special slave, Muhammad Azim, doorkeeper (may his sins be forgiven)!

Autograph signature. Note below the signature – 'The Seal was not at hand just now'.

Autograph order by the King, in pencil

Mirza Mughal will give one month's pay.

No. 8

Petition of Mirza Mughal

No date

To – The King! Shelter of the World!

Agreeably to Your Majesty's orders, 10,000 Rupees, part of the Revenue received from Garhi Harsaru, were drawn from the Treasury and distributed to the Troops in payment of four days' allowances. Two days' allowances more are now due; and of the Revenue received from Garhi Harsaru, a balance of 7,010 Rupees and 13 Annas remains in the Treasury. It is expected, from Your Majesty's condescending kindness, that orders will be issued to draw this money, and distribute it in payment of daily allowances to the Cavalry and Infantry. It was necessary and I have submitted it. (Prayers for the prosperity of the reign.) Petition of the slave Mirza Zahur-ud-din.

Autograph order by the King, in pencil

The sum of 5,000 Rupees was on each of two former occasions granted as the allowance for two days, and is now again sent. Do you distribute it? No date.

Papers arranged under the head of Military.

No. 1

Joint petition of Shekh Bansu, Corporal, and 60 Privates of the 44th Regiment Native Infantry

Dated 24th May 1857

To – The King! Shelter of the World!

Respectfully sheweth, That your slaves started from Agra for Meerut, in charge of 90 Arab horses; brought their charge in safety to Aligarh, and came on thence to Bulandshahr. On arriving at Bulandshahr, they found that disturbances had commenced, and saw hundreds of the country people riotously plundering the Treasury. Feeling it a duty to their faith, and assured of God's sanction, they attacked these rioters, and secured what remained of the treasure, and brought it and the horses to Delhi, intending to make them over to our Majesty, as the property of the State. On our arrival at the bridge of boats, there remained in our possession 83 horses and the treasure, *minus* 45,000 Rupees, which were laden on two wagons and were plundered from us on the road. When we crossed the bridge, we were met by numbers of the townspeople who beat the grooms, and forcibly took away several of the horses. Had your slaves not been under the impression that these men had been sent by Your Majesty for our protection, your slaves would have used resistance. The treasure and the 22 horses which remained with us have been made over to the Government. The missing horses are, however, still with the Cavalrymen and others who took them from us, and can be recognized by the grooms. We therefore pray that orders may be issued to Mirza Mughal, to recover them, as they are pointed out by the grooms, from the men, in whose possession they are, and to restore them to the State.

Autograph order by the King, in pencil

Mirza Moghul will institute enquiries, and tracing the horses, upon the clues the petitioners may give, will settle this matter in the way that may be proper.

Note on the Reverse – 'Remained in abeyance'.

No. 2

Petition of Mirza Mughal

Dated 29th May 1857

To – The King! Shelter of the World!

As Your Majesty's Army is about marching to Meerut, in view to efficient arrangements being made for collecting and protecting Commissariat supplies, it is urged that 20 horsemen and 50 footmen of the new levies, may be assigned to your slave for this purpose. Petition of the slave Zahur-ud-din.

Autograph order by the King, in pencil

Mir Haidar Husein Khan will depute 20 horsemen, and Shah-Rukh Beg 50 footmen (*illegible*[4]).

No. 3

Petition of Gauri Shankar Sukal, of the Hurrianah Light Infantry Battalion

To – The King! Shelter of the World!

The state of affairs here is, That by the blessing of God, and through Your Majesty's auspices, Your Majesty's rule was established at 10 a.m. today. The District of Hissar and Sirsa are both in the possession of this Regiment, and be assured the corps will shortly come to Your Majesty's presence, bringing treasure with them. We urge for your consideration that our strength is that of only one Regiment, and some men are absent on general and special leave. Moreover, we have hitherto furnished detachments which were relieved monthly, for the command duties at Sirsa and Hissar. The distance from Hansi to Sirsa is 90 miles, and that from Hansi to Delhi is 90 miles more. It will be difficult for us, being only one Regiment, to travel over this 180 miles with the Treasuries of two Districts. It is on this account urged for Your Majesty's consideration, that a reinforcement of Artillery and Cavalry may be sent to our aid, as also a relief to take our place here. An order is also required specifying whether we shall come by the way of Rohtak, or by that of Jhajjar. A further petition is, that the British Troops from Karnal will certainly come to cut us up. It is necessary, therefore, that Your Majesty should reflect on this, and issue your commands accordingly. Petition of the slave Gouri Shankar Sukal, Harrianah Light Infantry Battalion.

Autograph order by the King, in pencil

Mirza Mughal will make all necessary arrangements.

No. 4

Order attested with the seal engraved in the King's special cypher

Dated 30th May 1857

To – The Officers and all the Troopers of the 4th Regiment Irregular Cavalry. To the Men of two Companies of the 5th Regiment of Native Infantry, and of one Company of the 29th Regiment Native Infantry, and to all other Cavalry and Infantry, besides Chuni Lal and Ramcharan, Troopers of the 5th Troop, 4th Regiment of Irregular Cavalry have come into our Royal presence, and affirmed, that the whole Army, Cavalry and Infantry, entertain the resolve to tender their allegiance at our Royal Court, and that they can bring with them treasure and the various munitions of war. In acceptance of their prayers it is ordered, provided that murder and the pillage of villages on the way, and in the vicinity of the seat of the Imperial

Government, shall not be perpetrated, and provided also that after reaching the Royal presence you will observe full obedience in all matters – then without hesitation or delay present yourselves at our Court, bringing the treasure alluded to. The Royal favour will in every way be bestowed on you slaves.

No. 5

Petition of Mirza Mughal

Dated 9th June 1857

To – The King! Shelter of the World!

Your Majesty has been pleased to direct that your slave should proceed in to the Batteries, and your slave accordingly sent for and consulted General Abdul Samad Khan Bahadur,[57] telling him that he should also go. He, however, replied that, as no further confidence could be placed on the Infantry, and the Cavalry only could be depended on, his advice was not in favour of my going, nor would he go himself. He added that when the forces of the Chief's (Jhajjar Nawab) Government, however, shall have arrived, the soldiers composing them being experienced and tried veterans, his and my going into the Batteries them, will be proper. Your Majesty's orders directed that I should not act in any matter without the said General's concurrence; and he not giving his consent in this business, your slave refrained from going with some Troopers, who came and clamoured for his accompanying them. Other particulars relating to this matter is shall submit verbally, and as regard Your Majesty's commands, that Mir Haidar Husain, should not be allowed to have anything to do with the Artillery, or I should be visited with Your Majesty's displeasure and reprehension, your slave had prohibited his interference: but the Troopers themselves seized Haidar Husain, and carried him away. (Prayers for the King's prosperity). Petition of the slave Mirza Zahur-ud-Din.

Autograph order by the King, in pencil

The contents of the petition have been understood. Act according to Abdul Sammad Khan Bahadur's suggestions.

No. 6

Order under the autograph special cypher of the King, in pencil

Dated 10th June 1857

To – The Mirza Mughal.

Son, The illustrious and valiant Mirza Mughal Bahadur! Learn! That Gula and Jowalla Singh, residing in Pahari Dharang (Dhiraj) convey supplies

57 Father-in-law of the Nawab of Jhajjar.

to the enemy, and intelligence has just arrived that they are now there. You are imperatively directed immediately to dispatch one company of Regular Infantry and 50 Troops of the Regular Cavalry to arrest them and their associates. Do not allow any delay in this business.

Note on the Reverse – 'Orders issued'.

No. 7

Petition of Zabita Khan attached to the Police Station of Basant

Dated 16th June 1857

To – The King! Adoration of the World!

I have this day received certain information that near 2,000 Troops, who have revolted from the British, and are now coming from Nasirabad, are encamped at Garhi Harsaru today, and will be here tomorrow. There are no means for arranging for the usual supplies at this place. I hope, therefore, that some Officer or Troopers will be deputed by Your Majesty on this duty. (Prayers for the King's property.) A further petition is, that your petitioner had no previous knowledge of the approach of these Troops, or he might have made arrangements in anticipation. The information brought today was quite unexpected. May it be suggested that such orders should now be issued as can be carried out. Petition of the slave Zabita Khan, attached to the Police Station of Basant. No order on the petition.

Note on the Reverse – 'Orders have been issued, 16th June 1857'.

No. 8

Order under the autograph special cypher of the King, in pencil

Dated 20th June 1857

To – Mirza Mughal.

Son, The illustrious and valiant Mirza Muhammad Zahur-ud-din, otherwise Mirza Mughal Bahadur! Learn! That six carts have been prepared to bring in Saltpetre, which is stored outside the City, as it is required for the manufacture of powder. You will, therefore, assign 25 men of the Regular Infantry to protect it on the road, so that the quantity required may be carefully conveyed to the Magazine, and you will also issue a written order to the Military Guard at the Lahori Gate not in any way to hinder the passage in and out of the carts employed in its conveyance.

No. 9

Order under the special cypher of the King, in pencil

Dated 18th June 1857

To – Mirza Mughal.

Son, The illustrious and valiant Mirza Zahur-ud-din, otherwise Mirza Mughal Bahadur! Learn! That we have received a petition from the Officers of the two regiments of Infantry, and of the Artillery and Cavalry come from Nasirabad, submitting, that if permission is granted, they will raise Batteries on three sides and attack the enemy, and urging that it is necessary for the Regiment of Sappers and Miners to construct the Batteries, and for the whole of the Cavalry present to protect every part of the rear of the attacking Force, so that the petitioners may make the attack the day after tomorrow. This petition has been laid before us, in order that measures may be adopted to carry out its suggestions, and you are accordingly directed to issue written orders to the Sappers and Miners, and to the whole of the Cavalry, to accompany the Nasirabad Force, the first to construct the Batteries, and the second to cooperate in the attack, the day after tomorrow.

No. 10

Order under the autograph cypher of the King, in pencil

Dated 20th June 1857

To – Mirza Mughal.

Son, The illustrious and valiant Mirza Zahur-ud-din, otherwise Mirza Mughal Bahadur ! Learn! That owing to the large daily expenditure of powder, none is now left in the Magazine, and orders have in consequence been issued that materials required in its manufacture should be purchased: and though large numbers of power-makers are employed, it cannot be produced as expeditiously as is necessary, the whole daily demand for it is very emergent. You are directed to collect it from the men named in the subjoined list, as well as all that you may find after search in places where barrels of it are likely to be forthcoming, and to have all you may thus collect conveyed to the Magazine by tomorrow. Consider this business as taking precedence in importance above all others, and see that every necessary precaution is observed in conveying the powder to the Magazine, so that when it is required, there may be no interruption to the operations, and a cause of complaint as well as of danger to the men when fighting, may be removed. Be assured of our kindness.

From our Son, the illustrious Mirza

Khair Sultan Bahadur 350 Barrels From the 74th Regiment Native Infantry at the Lahori Gate 232 Barrels From the men of the 38th Regiment Native Infantry stationed At the Delhi Gate of the palace 80 Barrels From the Cashmere Gate 70 Barrels From all the Regiments, all that may be found with them ...

No. 11

Order under the seal engraved in the King's special cypher

Dated 21st June 1857

To – Mirza Mughal.

Son, The illustrious and valiant Mirza Zahur-ud-din, otherwise Mirza Mughal Bahadur! Learn! That you are directed to take ten Marquees and ten Sepoys' tents from the 20th, 74th, 38th, and 11th Regiments of Native Infantry, and to have them given over to the 30th and 15th Regiments of Native Infantry, and to the Artillery going into the Batteries to oppose the enemy. Be assured of our kindness.

No. 12

Order under the seal engraved in the King's special cypher, in pencil

Dated 24th June 1857

To – Mirza Mughal.

Son, The illustrious and valiant Mirza Zahur-ud-din, otherwise Mirza Mughal Bahadur! Learn! That you are directed to see that the rations for the men of the Cavalry and Infantry be sent to the Batteries with the same regularity as the ammunition, and that no one be permitted to take or make away with these rations on the road. The supplying of rations to the Army is a matter of pre-eminent importance. You are, moreover, directed to apply by petition for all articles which may be required for the rations, and they will be dispatched immediately.

Note on a corner at top – 'No. 26'.

No. 13

Order under the King's State Seal

Dated 27th June 1857

To – The Emblem of Honour, Khawaja Nazir-ud-Din, Police Officer of Bhadrapur.

Be it known to you! That information is derived from your petition of the arrival, in Arab Serai, of some men of the Cavalry and Infantry of the Neemuch Force, and of their demanding large quantities of Commissariat necessaries and confectionaries from the Bazaar people, which, in consequence of the paucity of the population, are not procurable. It is observed also that you request that the Chief Police Officer of the City may be directed to send out the supplies required, and, accordingly, orders in this particular were immediately issued to him. But, owing to the unsettled state of affairs in the City, the presence of the soldiery of the Regular Infantry, and to the circumstances of most of the shops being closed, it will be difficult to supply confectionary in the quantity needed: meal, & c., may be procured. Moreover, agreeably to the request of you, emblem of honour, 20 men of the Infantry and 10 of the Cavalry, servants of the King, are sent that you may make use of their services on this occasion, on the departure of the Force you will allow these men to return. A special order to the Officers of the Force in question is enclosed. You will have this delivered immediately, so that no excesses or ill-usage may be committed against the Bazaar people, or other residents of the place.

Note on the Reverse – 'Received 26th July 1857'.

Police Officer's answer on the reverse

Dated 27th July 1857

To – The King! Nourisher of the Poor!

Your Majesty! The 20 foot soldiers and 10 Troopers who were sent to your slave, in view to his using their services, were sent back to your Royal presence after the departure of the Force which came from Neemuch. Wazir Ali, Jamadar and the Infantry Sepoys afforded the services required from them in full accordance with your slave's wishes. Your slave has further to submit that the supplies sent by the Chief Police Officer of Delhi arrived at 3 o'clock in the afternoon after effectual arrangements had been made here, and were returned. Petition of the slave, Khwaja Muhammad Nazir-ud-din Khan, Police Officer of Bahadrapur, staying at Arab Serai.

Seal of the Bahadrapur Police Officer, engraved in the year of the King's reign 21st. Also seal of Khwaja Muhammad Nazir-ud-din Khan.

Order without signature or seal.

Ordered that this be filed in the office.

No. 14

Order under the King's special autograph cypher, in pencil

Dated 29th June 1857

To – Mirza Mughal.

Son, The illustrious Mirza Zahur-ud-din, otherwise Mirza Mughal Bahadur. Learn! That the river has today risen very considerably, whole intelligence has been received that the Bareilly Troops will arrive tomorrow; stringent orders have accordingly been issued to the Superintendent of the Bridge to get together all the boats he can collect, and to have this Force ferried across the river. Using boats, it will have to cross in portions, and the whole of the Force will not be able to get over at once; and as a measure of precaution therefore, you, our Son, are now directed to issue an order to the Officers under your seal that no one, neither Officer nor Private, of these crossing in the boats, subject the Superintendent or boatmen to any ill-usage or violence, as stringent orders to repair the Bridge have also been issued. The inconvenience of day or two therefore, they ought to put up with cheerfully.

No. 15

Petition of Mirza Mughal

Dated 30th June 1857

To – The King! Shelter of the World!

Respectfully sheweth, That an Elephant taken from the batteries of the enemy, has this day been brought in, escorted by some troopers and some Jahadis; and is now forwarded with this petition, to your Royal presence. Your slave trusts, he will be favoured with a receipt. (Prayers for the King's prosperity.)

Petition of the slave Mirza Zahur-ud-din.

Autograph note by the King, in pencil

The Elephant has reached the Royal presence.

Note in Ink – 'Received 16th July 1857'. '499'

No. 16

Joint petition of Mirza Mughal and Mirza Abdulla

Dated 1st July 1857

To – The King! Shelter of the World!

Respectfully sheweth, That the Bridge has now been thoroughly completed, and that the petitioners trust, therefore, that the Troops arrived from Bareilly, & c., and now encamped on the opposite side of the river, may be allowed to cross over during the night, as during the day the shot and shell of the English continue to fall. It is so ordered, these Troops will be made to encamp outside the Ajmir Gate. On the other hand, whatever orders are issued will be complied with. The petition of Mirza Zahur-ud-din and Mirza Abdulla Sahib.

Autograph order by the King, in pencil

Direct this Force to encamp outside the Turkoman Gate.

Note in the Margin – 'Index No. 242'.

Order on the Reverse, without Signature, but authenticated by an Official seal impression just sufficiently legible to show that it is the seal of the Commander-in-Chief Mirza Mughal.

Ordered that the orders in this case having been carried out, his petition be filed in the Office. Dated 2 July 1857.

No. 17

An autograph order of the king, in pencil

No date

To – The Especial Slave, the Lord Governor, Muhammad Bakht Khan Bahadur.

Receive our favour and understand that whilst the Neemuch Force has reached Alapur, its baggage is still here, and that you are, therefore, directed to take 200 Troopers and 5 or 7 Companies of Infantry, and to have all the baggage alluded to, such as tents & c., together with Commissariat Supplies, conveyed by these Ghazis to Alapur. You are further directed not to allow the infidels staying near the Eidgah to advance. Be it known to you further that if the Army returns without victory, and divested of its appliances of war, the consequences must be disastrous. You have been premonished, and you are to consider these orders stringent.

No. 18
Petition of Mirza Mughal

Dated 9th July 1857

To – The King! Shelter of the World!

Respectfully sheweth, That Sarfaraz Khan, Duffadar, and Muhammad Khan, artilleryman, coming over with their horses from the batteries of the enemy, report the capture of the hostile battery at Sabzi Mandi and of two of the enemy's guns by the Ghaziz of Your Majesty's victorious Army. May this auspicious event be a subject of grandulation to all well-wishers of the State. These two men who have now come to Royal presence were the servants of the enemy. They have now girded their loins in Your Majesty's cause. (Prayers for the prosperity of the reign.) Petition of the slave Zahur-ud-din, attested with the official Seal of the Commander-in-Chief Bahadur.

Autograph order by the King, in pencil

The contents of this petition have come to our knowledge. May the event be auspicious for you – the light of our eyes also.[58]

No. 19
Petition of Mirza Mughal

Dated 12th July 1857

To – The King! Shelter of the World!

Respectfully sheweth, That Your slave, agreeably to Your Majesty's orders, explained your wishes to the Chiefs of the Army, and that yesterday, Muhammad Bakht Khan General Bahadur came to your slave. Hearing your wishes from him, I again explained them to all the Officers of the Army, to the best of my ability, but they would not assent to them. Your slave therefore encloses the petition of the Officers for Your Majesty's consideration. Further whatever orders. It was necessary, and has therefore been submitted. Petition of the slave Mirza Zahur-ud-din, attested with the Official Seal of the Commander-in-Chief Bahadur.

No. 20
Petition of Mirza Mughal

Dated 12th July 1857

58 *Ankhon ka noor*, i.e., dear son.

To – The King! Shelter of the World!

The musket locks and other Magazine property, which have been found in the house of Hulasi Lascar, are forwarded to Your Majesty's presence, with a separate detained list. Petition of the slave Zahur-ud-din.

Separate list

List of Magazine property found in the house of Hulasi Lascar in the presence of Siddhai, Jamadar of Lascars, Kalka Tewari, sepoy – the Company of – Regiment Native Infantry, and Karim Baksh, Trooper of the 4th Irregular Cavalry, on 12th July 1857, on information lodged by Raghunath Rao, Sepoy of the Regiment Native Infantry:

Pistol barrel with ramrod	1
Brass mountings of a stock	1
Pistol ramrod (iron)	1
Musket bayonets	6
Musket and pistol locks, large 9, small 20	29
Pieces of the work of a lock	3
Nails and hooks	14

Have reached the Royal presence.

Autograph note, authenticated by King's cypher, in pencil

No. 21

Petition of all the Officers of the 11th Regiment, Native Infantry

Dated 16th July 1857

To – The Nourisher of the Poor! His Highness the General Sahib Bahadur!

Yesterday about noon, Kalyan Singh, Corporal, having eaten his dinner, went to the ramparts, where he found Mahabal Singh, Sepoy of the 2nd Company 11th Regiment Native Infantry, who was on duty at the time, as sentry over the guns, asleep at his post. Seeing this neglect, the Corporal took away the sentry's musket, and then awakening him, asked him what had become of it. The sentry replied that he did not know who had taken it away. The Corporal immediately reported the circumstance to Somair Singh, Subedar Bahadur, and agreeably to his orders, the Sepoy was placed in arrest. Today all the officers of the Regiment assembled as a Court, and the prisoner, Mahabal Singh, appearing before them, acknowledged having been asleep while on duty as a sentry. The offence of the prisoner being thus established by his own confession, he is forwarded to Your Highness with this petition. The punishment which may be awarded by Your Highness will be approved of by all of us. The petition of all the Commissioned and Non-Commissioned Officers of the 11th Regiment Native Infantry, stationed at the Ajmir Gate.

Order by the King

Ordered. That your petition, reporting the offence of Mahabal Singh, Sepoy, in going to sleep while on duty as a sentry, as established by his own confession before the Court and forwarding him to the Court of the Commander-in-Chief Bahadur, with the view that the punishment necessary in the case might be awarded, has been considered. Your Court are therefore directed yourselves to determine what punishment may be adequate, and to carry it out at once. Your decision will be approved of.

Authenticated by the King's Autograph cypher in ink

Dated 17th July 1857

Note below the Order – 'An order has been written'.

No. 22
Petition of Mirza Mughal

Dated 17th July 1857

To – The King! Shelter of the World!

Respectfully sheweth, That Your Majesty is cognizant that before Muhammad Bakht Khan came, active operations of war were carried on daily, and without intermission and Your Majesty knows likewise that since the arrival of the Bareilly General, several engagements have taken place. It so occurred today that your slave, purposing to make an attack, had formed the Army and taken it outside the City, when the above-named General interposed, and for a long time kept the whole Force standing inactive, wanting to know by whose orders it had gone out; and saying that it was not to proceed without his permission, caused it to return. A proceeding like this, even an open enemy would not attempt, namely, that the Army should be proceeding to an attack, and one should interfere and cause it to return. Your slave therefore supplicates, that if the entire control and management of the Army have, from the Royal presence, been bestowed on the said General, and are to yield obedience to him. Having his orders reversed cannot but cause vexation and chagrin to any Officer, high or low. If, on the other hand, the control of the Army is supposed to be vested in your slave, the said General should not interfere. He has entire authority over his own Regiments. Such demand as are made for the service of his Regiments from this, he should invariably comply with. Petition of the slave Zahur-ud-din. No order.

No. 23
Petition of Mirza Mughal

Dated 19th July 1857

To – The King! Shelter of the World!

Your petitioner's prayer is that through Your Majesty's propitious auspices arrangements have now been completed for carrying on active offensive operations daily, night and day, and that, since yesterday, this has been done. If aid could be afforded now from the direction of Alapur, with the Divine blessing, and through the influence of Your Majesty's ever-enduring prestige, a final and decisive victory, it is to be expected, would soon be obtained. I therefore pray that positive orders may be issued from the throne to the Bareilly General, to afford the aid in question, that is, that he be directed to proceed with his Troops to Alapur, and to make an attack on the infidels from that directions, while your slave, with his Division of the Army, makes another on this side, so that the two Forces cooperating in the fight, may, in one or two days, consign all the damnable hell-doomed infidels to hell. Moreover, it is to be expected that the Force going to Alapur will cut off the enemy's supplies. It was necessary and has been therefore submitted. Petition of the slave Zahur-ud-din.

Autograph order by the King, in pencil, authenticated with cypher

Mirza Mughal will make whatever arrangements may be proper.

Order on the Reverse without Signature or Seal. Ordered that an order be written to the Bareilly General. No Date.

Note below the above order – 'It has been written'. On the face – 'no. 1024', add immediately below it – 'Received 30th July 1857'.

No. 24

Petition of Mirza Mughal

Dated 30th July 1857

To – The King! Shelter of the World!

Respectfully sheweth, That a petition has this day been presented by Amir Khan, Risaldar of the 4th Troop, requesting that the horse gear, detailed in the subjoined list, might be supplied to him. Your Majesty is therefore petitioned for permission to have the things in question made over. Petition of the slave Mirza Zahur-ud-din.

Autograph order by the King, in pencil

Mirza Mughal will have the horse gear given as demanded. No. 200

Order on the reverse, without signature or seal. Ordered that when the gear of all the horses is given, these will also be supplied. Dated 30th July 1857.

No. 25

Petition of Khwaja Khairat Ali, Clerk in the General's Office

Dated 1st August 1857

To – The King! Shelter of the World!

It is fully manifest to Your Majesty, that since yesterday, 20,000 Troops have been suffering the greatest inconvenience and discomfort, exposed to rain, and unsupplied with food. I therefore trust that an order may be issued to the Chief Police Officer of the City to dispatch, for the present, 100 maunds of parched Gram to the Camp on the other side of the Bussye Bridge. Otherwise, this will be the second day of starvation to the Troops. It has been submitted for information. Petition of the slave Khwaja Khairat Ali, Clerk in the General's Office.

Autograph note by the King, in pencil

The purport has been learnt.

Note on the face – '3rd August 1857, index No. 1165'.

No. 26

Petition of Khairat Ali, Clerk in the General's Office

Dated 1st August 1857

To – The King! Lord of the World!

Respectfully sheweth, That one Company of the 18th Regiment Native Infantry has since yesterday been present in the battery at the Eidgah, while the said Regiment has gone with the Lord Saheb to Alipur. This Company also is now ordered to proceed thither. Your petition begs that a relief may be sent from the Regiments in the City, to take its place in the battery. Beyond this, it is for Your Majesty to determine. Petition of the slave Khwaja Khairat Ali, Clerk in the General's Office.

Autograph order by the King, in pencil

Mirza Mughal will arrange this immediately.

Note in the margin – 'Received 3rd August 1857'.

No. 27

Petition of Ghulam Mu'id-ud-din Khan, Principal Risaldar

No date to the petition, date of final orders 2nd August 1857

To – The King! Shelter of the World!

Respectfully sheweth, That your slave has come to this City from Tonk, accompanied by nearly 500 men, who are organized as a body, and by nearly 1,500 besides, who have come devoting their lives, to fight in the religious war against the infidels. That he and his followers joined in the attack yesterday, that 18 infidels were dispatched to hell by your slave's own hand, and that five of his followers were killed and five wounded.

Your Majesty! The rest of the Army gave us no help while we were engaged in combat with the infidels. Had they even stood by, only to make a show of support, it was to have been expected that with the help of Providence, a complete victory would yesterday have been obtained. But there is no remedy against the will of God. I trust that some arms, together with some trifling funds, may be bestowed on my followers, so that they may have the strength to fight against and slay the infidels, and in doing this, may realize their desire. (Prayers for the prosperity of the reign.)

Petition of the lowly slave Ghulam Mu'id-ud-din Khan, Chief Risaldar, came from Tonk. No date.

Order on the reverse, without signature, cypher, or seal. Probably by Mirza Mughal Order that at present there are no arms. When some shall have arrived, they will be given. Funds will also be arranged for and bestowed.

No. 28

Petition of Bakht Khan

Dated 4th August 1857

To – The King! Shelter of the World!

Respectfully sheweth, That I have on two or rather on three former occasions, petitioned Your Majesty for Artillery, and now again submit this petition, to be supplied with the following ordnance:

12-Pounder Guns, four. If four can be granted, well; otherwise, let two certainly be given.

18-Pounder Guns, also four. If four can be granted, it will be just what is desired; if not, the presence of two is certainly advisable.

24-Pounder Guns, let the same number be granted, and it will be extreme kindness to your slave; otherwise, the presence of two is extremely desirable. Also 32-Pounder guns, four or two. It will be a great favour.

Mortars 10 inch, four; 8 inch, four; and 5½ inch, four, and 24 Howitzers, eight.

And I also trust I may be favoured by Your Majesty with the full allowance of ammunition for these guns, such as shell, shrapnel, and common shells.

Petition of the special slave, attested with the seal of Muhammad Bakht Khan.

No. 1183

Autograph by the King, in pencil

Mirza Mughal will make arrangements.

Order on the reverse, without signature or seal apparently by Mirza Mughal, in furtherance of the King's order. Let an answer be written. It is known what number of guns there are (*?*). Dated 3rd August 1857.

No. 29

Order under the seal of Mirza Muhammad Khair Sultan Bahadur, son of Muhammad Bahadur Shah, King, Defender of the Faith

Dated 11th August 1857

To – The Officers, Subedars, Chiefs and others of the whole Military Force coming from the Bombay Presidency.

To the effect, that the statement which some person has made to you, of the defeat of the Royal Troops at Delhi, is altogether a false and lying fabrication, contrived by the contemptible infidels, namely the English. The true story is that nearly 80,000 or 90,000 regular organized Military Troops are now present here, and nearly 10,000 or 15,000 Regular and other Cavalry. These troops are constantly engaged, night and day, in attacks upon the infidels, and have driven back their batteries from the ridge. In three or four days hence, please God, the whole ridge will be taken when every one of the base unbelievers will be humbled and ruined, and will be sent to hell. You are therefore directed immediately on seeing this order, to use every endeavour speedily to reach the Royal presence, so that joining the army of the faithful, you may give proofs of your zeal, and may establish your claims to renown. Consider this imperative.

Order from Mirza Khair Sultan to the Bombay Army, Dated 11th August 1857.

Giving assurance that the report of the defeat of the Royal Army is a lying invention of the English, who will themselves be exterminated in three or four days.

No. 30

Order under the seal engraved in the King's special cypher

Dated 13th August 1857

To – The Slaves, the Emblems of Valour! Karimulla Khan, Risaldar, 1st Regiment. Lal Singh, Subedar, 1st Troop of Artillery. Sahib Lal, Subedar, 2nd Troop of Artillery. Sheikh Imam-Bakhsh, Subedar, 3rd Troop of Artillery. Lal Pandit, Subedar, 4th Troop of Artillery. Ram Singh, Subedar, 5th Troop of Artillery. Amanat Ali, Subedar, 1st Regiment of Infantry. Lalla Prashad, Subedar, 2nd Regiment of Infantry. Jiwa Singh, Subedar, 3rd Regiment of Infantry. Ram-Din, Subedar, 4th Regiment of Infantry. Basharat Ali, Subedar, 5th Regiment of Infantry – of the Gwalior Contingent Force, and the Officers of the Morar Infantry.

Learn! That the petition of your slaves has been perused, and the brave acts of your valiant Soldiers experienced in war have been ascertained. It is incumbent on you, that, accompanied by the Infantry of the Gwalior State and the Rajah, you should engage in steps to capture the Fort of Agra, or you may obtain treasure from the Rajah, and use means to capture the Fort with your own forces. From the officer down to the private, each and every individual will be deemed deserving of our highest favour and consideration, and will be honoured with favours and preferments beyond limit, and will in gradation be advanced to the ranks of Adjutant, General and Colonel.

No. 31

Petition of Muhammad Baksh Ali, formerly Jail Superintendent of Jhansi

Dated 18th August 1857

To – The King! Dispenser of Blessings on the World! Shelter of Mankind, etc.

Respectfully sheweth, That the order passed on your slave's petition, that besides the 500 Soldiers now present, he may entertain sufficient men to complete a Regiment of Infantry, shall be carried into effect. Your petitioner's request, however, was that orders might be issued, to change the designation of the force under your slave, from that of Ali-Ghol for any other which Your Majesty might be pleased to select, as the men composing it have been thoroughly drilled and disciplined.

Whatever designation Your Majesty may now assign them, they will always retain. Your Slave, therefore, prays that orders under Your Majesty's Seal and Signature may be issued in this matter. Petition of the lowly Muhammad Baksh Ali, Superintendent of the Jhansi Jail, officer of the Ali-Ghol.

Autograph order by the King, in pencil

Shamshir-ud-dowlat Bahadur will have an order written after the usual form of such orders. The name 'Faiz' is assigned to this regiment.

Note on the revers – 'An order has been written'.

Dated 18th August 1857

No. 32

Order from the King, without signature, cypher, or seal, apparently an office copy

Dated 21st August 1857

To – All the Officers of the Bombay Army, 25 Regiments of Infantry and the Artillery.

Giridhari Singh, Subedar of the Grenadier Company of the 16th Regiment, has come into our Royal presence, and given an account of your valour, bravery, and laudable aspirations, which we have been extremely gratified to hear. You are, from this day, to be reckoned our home-born slaves and servants. It is incumbent on you, therefore, immediately on seeing this order, to make double marches, and hasten to the Royal presence. On no account make any delay, for we are looking out for your arrival with anxious expectation. Use every activity, and come without making any halts on your march.

No. 33

Petition of Bhawani Singh, Private of the 30th Regiment Native Infantry

Dated 23rd August 1857[59]

59 The petition bears no date. 23 August 1857 is the date of the final order. Ed.

To – The King! Shelter of the World!

Respectfully sheweth, That before men are employed in the Magazine, it is necessary that each individual should be made to declare his place of residence; and the correctness of his statement on this point should be tested by a reference to the place itself, or he might be made to furnish security. And further, a descriptive roll of him should be prepared and should be placed in the office, and he should then be employed. If these precautions are observed, no fears for the safety of the Magazine need be entertained; but if, without enquiry, everyone is indiscriminately engaged, emissaries of the enemy may obtain admission, and cause much damage. Moreover, one officer with a clerk might be stationed in the Magazine, for the sole purpose of mustering and inspecting the labourers, morning and evening, to see that no strangers or agent of the enemy are admitted. Your slave presents this petition solely from feeling of zeal and relies on Your Majesty's kindness and consideration for the issue of orders, under Your Majesty's signature, that efficient arrangements for the protection of the Magazine may be observed. (prayers for the prosperity of the reign.) Petition of the slave Bhawani Singh, Private of the 30th Regiment Native Infantry.

Autograph orders by the King, in pencil

Mirza Mughal will quickly make the necessary arrangements. Precautions in this matter above all others are pre-eminently necessary.

Order without signature or seal, apparently by Mirza Mughal. Ordered that arrangements be made. Dated 23rd August 1857.

No. 34

Order by General Muhammad Bakht Khan attested with his official seal
Dated 23rd August 1857

To – The Officers of the Regiment of Sikhs.

His Majesty the King just now summoned our Highness to his presence and said he had every confidence that the Sikh Regiment will perform great achievements of valour, and with condescension spoke of you in terms of the greatest praise, you are therefore written to the intent that immediately on reading this order, five Companies will get under arms, and go to the Shamgir Battery.[60] You will on no account allow any delay to occur in this matter.

Signature at top illegible, office seal of the General Sahib.

Reply, on the Reverse, of the officers of the Sikh regiments without signature, seal or date.

60 This was the Battery which was constructed on the other side of the river, and annoyed the piquet at the Metcalfe house. Ed.

Your Highness, we have learnt the purport of your orders, we have to submit, however, that our Regiment went into the Teli-wars Battery at 4 p.m.

No. 35
Petition from Muhammad Bakht Khan
Dated 23rd August 1857

To – Mirza Mughal, The Lord of Gifts, & c., Mirza Muhammad Zahur-ud-din, Commander-in-Chief Sahib Bahadur!

The order directing me to send one officer from each corps of Infantry, Cavalry, & c., to meet as members of the Court arranged by Your Highness's wish has been received. I sent for the Commissioned Officers in question, and explained to them the necessity for their attendance at your Court at 10 a.m. tomorrow. They have all willingly and heartily agreed to attend, as they have been directed. They urge, however, that their baggage has just been laden; but that, after reaching Palum, they will return, and Will, with hearty pleasure, attend the Court in Question. This petition is submitted for your information. Petition of the slave Muhammad Bakht Khan, Lord Governor-General, attested with the seal of Muhammad Bakht Khan, Commander-in-Chief of the Army.

Note on the face– 'the purport of the petition has been learned'.

No. 36
Petition of Jewaram Ajodhya Chobe and others, Commissioned Officers of the 3rd Regiment, Native Infantry
Dated 26th August 1857

To – The King! Shelter of the World!

Your Majesty's orders in the first instance were to the effect that such men as were late in joining the Royal forces, should be kept on as supernumeraries, in the grades in which they had formerly served. This order gave entire satisfaction to all the Officers and Soldiery. Those men who have been late in arriving have now, however, given a petition, and have had a seniority list prepared. All the Private and Non-Commissioned Officers have in this matter accordingly represented to their Commissioned Officers the justice they will suffer, if, to the prejudice of the evident claims of those who, coming long before, have been daily in the batteries, and have on every occasion yielded obedience to all Your Majesty's commands, places are given to men who have joined after such great delay. We, all the Commissioned Officers of the 3rd Regiment of Infantry, therefore pray that Your Majesty's first order, which gave such entire satisfaction to the whole Army, may be allowed to continue undisturbed force. Considering it necessary, we have laid the matter before Your Majesty. (Prayers for the prosperity of the reign.) Petition of the slaves Jewaram, Ajodhya Chobe and others, all the Commissioned Officers of the 3rd Regiment of Infantry.

No order or note of any king.

No. 37

Petition of Nur Muhammad Khan, Risaldar, 10th Irregular Cavalry

Dated 29th August 1857

Abstract of petition in the margin above the address

The petitioner was of the 10th Regiment of Irregular Cavalry, which consisted of 600 Troopers; 50 of them are now here present, and have come to fight for their faith. The petitioner prays that he may be authorized to call in the whole of the Troopers, and re-enrol them.

To – The King! Shelter of the World! Nourisher of the Poor!

My Corps, the 10th Regiment of Irregular Cavalry, was stationed at Peshawar in the Cantonment of Nowshera. Five of the Officers, Keshri Singh, Kalandar Khan, & c., combining with the infidels, and practising deceptions on the men, had us called out to a parade, and had our arms, such as carbines, swords, & c., taken from us. Cheerfully enduring the greatest hardships and difficulties for two months, we slaves have now come to your Royal presence to defend the faith and to offer up our lives in protecting Your Majesty's throne. Moreover, the English having placed their Guns in position against us, we abandoned all our property, money, and here months' arrears of pay, and having accomplished the journey, have now presented ourselves at your Royal door to sacrifice our lives. Most of the Troopers of the 10th Irregular Cavalry have gone to their homes, but their residence is near. If I am authorized I shall immediately call them all in, and set up the Corps at once, when it will remain in attendance, and will employ itself, night and day, in giving effect to Your Majesty's orders. It will, besides, join in the attacks against the batteries, and its members will willingly sacrifice their lives, if necessary. This alone is your slave's ambition also. Let a written order be bestowed, that he may at once enrol the Troopers of the 10th Irregular Cavalry.

About 50 of them are now present with your slave. On obtaining Your Majesty's order, he will enrol the rest. It was necessary, and I have therefore submitted it. Secondly, if Your Majesty's orders are kindly bestowed on your slave, and some horses are given to him, he will remain in attendance. Petition of the slave Nur Muhammad Khan, Risaldar of the 10th Regiment of Irregular Cavalry, come from Peshawar from the Cantonments of Nowshera, expectant of the Royal favour.

Autograph order by the King, in pencil

Be assured that favourable provision will be made for you.

No. 38

Petition of Colonel Ahmad Khan, stationed at Ghazi-ud-din-Nagar

Dated 9th September 1857

To – The King! Nourisher of the Poor!

Respectfully sheweth, That leaving your imperial presence, your slave came to Ghaziabad, and here learnt that yesterday, the 8th of September, some Europeans, assisted by the Jats, burnt and sacked Pilkhowa, and three or four neighbouring villages. The force engaged in this destruction was comprised of about 30 Europeans, 300 Jats of the Duhia (Dahia) tribe and four Guns. They are still encamped there, and the farmers of the surrounding country, fearing similar devastation, and feeling their helplessness, are paying the revenue. Moreover, definite intelligence has been received today, that near 50 Europeans and Jats, with two or three Guns, have assembled at Begamabad with the intention of destroying the bridge over the Hindon, and of desolating Ghaziabad; and have cut off the supplies which used to be taken to Delhi from Pilkhowa, & c. it is therefore prayed that, with kind consideration, Your Majesty will send some Royal troops, accompanied by Guns, in this direction for the punishment of the infidels, so that full chastisement may be inflicted on them, and the collection of the revenue of the State may be commenced. If, however, delay shall occur, the bridge over the Hindon will be broken, and the Enemy will desolate Ghaziabad. Furthermore, there is a very strong fortress of masonry at the Village of Mukimpoor, near Pilkhowa, in which there are about 50 or 60 maunds of old gunpowder. Should the Europeans get into this fortress, their expulsion afterwards will be very difficult, and a second Dum Dumma will come into existence, and I shall then be utterly unable to counteract their operations. If my Regiment of Infantry accompanied by Guns could be thrown into the said fortress, by tomorrow the English might be well punished, and would certainly be routed with deserved chastisement. But Your Majesty being master, it is your prerogative to decide. Such orders as may be issued, will be carried out. Petition of the slave, attested with the seal of Ahmad Khan, stationed at Ghaziabad.

Autograph order by the King, in pencil

Mirza Mughal will adopt measures, agreeably to this petition.

On the reverse, an order, apparently autograph, attested by the King's cypher in ink. 'The Brigade Major Sahib will know that he is to act as may be proper'.

Another order, also on the reverse without signature or seal, probably by the Brigade Major. 'Ordered, that the 14th Regiment march on this duty. Dated 10th September 1857'.

No. 39

Petition of Kasim-ud-din, Private of the 7th Company, 59th Regiment Native Infantry

No date

To – The King! Shelter of the World!

Your Divine Majesty! Your slave was a Private in the 7th Company of the 59th Regiment of Native Infantry, which was stationed at Amritsar. The English disarmed the men and made them prisoners. Those of them, however, who get opportunities made their escape, and come away. Your slave has presented himself solely to fight for the faith. His arms, however, were taken from him by the English at Amritsar, and such personal property as he had been plundered from him by the Goojars. He is now without funds to meet his daily expenses of food, and he is also without arms. He therefore trusts that he may now be enrolled in the 53rd Regiment of Native Infantry, in which a brother of his, by name Kasiruddin, is serving. Your slave also trusts that as he has come solely to fight for the faith, pecuniary assistance and arms may be bestowed on him; and obtaining the means of subsistence he will ever pray for Your Majesty's prosperity.

Petition of the slave Kasim-ud-din, Private 7th Company, 59th Regiment Native Infantry, come from Amritsar. No date. No order.

No. 40

Petition of Ghulam Ali, Superintendent of the Magazine

No date

To – The King! Shelter of the World!

Respectfully sheweth, That there is a flat-roofed house, situated near the Court of Justice, and at present in the possession of Mirza Kochuk Sultan, the same in the front of which musket bullets are being moulded, and the Magazine Stores which are your slave's charge, and are kept in the Hall of Public Audience, are not sufficient. For instance, the wax and other things are lying outside and the men of the Army carry away what they please; your slave therefore trusts that the flat-roofed house aforesaid may be taken from the Mirza above respectfully alluded to, and made over to him, so that the wax and other things being all necessary articles may be deposited there and kept in safety.

Petition of the slave Ghulam Ali, Superintendent of the Magazine. No date.

No. 41

Joint Petition of Mirza Mughal, Mirza Abdul Hassan, Shah Bakhtawar, and Mirza Khair Sultan, Sons of the King

No date

To – The King! Shelter of the World!

Respectfully sheweth, That four Regiments of Infantry, 2 of Cavalry, and 12 Guns of Horse and Foot Artillery, according to the detail below, with a full supply of ammunition, other necessaries of war, and some treasure, may proceed to Paneeput, and may there, through Your Majesty's auspices and by God's blessing, obtain immediate and complete victory and at once return to the Royal presence. This day has been fixed for our departure.

74th Regiment of Native Infantry	1
38th dittoditto	1
54th dittoditto	1
38th dittoditto	1
Volunteers	400 men
Corps of Gwalior Cavalry1	
Corps of Regular Cavalry1	
24-Pounder Guns	4
Howitzer and Mortar	2
Companies of Militia	2
Jhajjar Cavalry	100 troopers

Petition attested with the seals of Mirza Sultan Zahur-ud-din, Commander-in-Chief Bahadur; Mirza Muhammad Abdul Hasan, Colonel of the 20th Regiment of Native Infantry; Shah Bakhtawar, son of the King, Abu Zafar, and Mirza Khair Sultan Bahadur.

Autograph order by the King, in pencil

The departure of you, our sons, is exceedingly right and proper; but first get a petition from the Officers of the Regiments expressing their willingness to accompany you, and lay it before us, that we may have assurance on this point.

No. 42

Order under the seal engraved in the King's special cypher

No date

To – Mirza Mughal.

Son, The illustrious and valiant Mirza Zahur-ud-din, otherwise Mirza Mughal Bahadur. Learn, that the numerous applications presented by men of valorous aspirations who have already done much service, in the hope of obtaining employment as foot soldiers and horsemen, which you have submitted, enclosed in your petition, have been received. Considering the want of funds in the State treasury, the absence of all present prospects of the realization of the land revenue from the different subdivisions of districts owing to the circumstances that no military force has as yet gone out to arrange this matter, and the prevalence of murder and pillage; in the immediate vicinity of the seat of Government, and further, in consideration of the collection in the city of large organized military forces from all parts of the country, and the insufficiency of the treasures brought by them for their own daily expenses, permission to employ these men cannot be accorded, for whence can they be aided with funds, or pay, to meet their expenses? Such being the case, it is injudicious to give hopes to people whose homes are far distant; it is therefore ordered that you will distinctly inform the men giving the petitions referred to, and all others who may hereafter present similar petitions, that such of them as can remain for one or two months without requiring pecuniary assistance, may stay. When order shall have been established, and the revenue of the country realized, they will be rewarded with appointments commensurate with their several qualifications; but this, even then, will only be done when the prior claims of the regular Military troops shall have been satisfied. It is inexpedient, therefore, retaining men who are in pecuniary destitution, on the indistinct hope of employment hereafter, based on the contingency of the establishment of order. Please God, when the present disturbed state of affairs shall have given place to tranquillity, when Officers to receive the revenue shall have been established throughout the country, and the revenue shall have begun to come in from all directions, thousands of men may then be employed. At present there is no option. Two of the petitions have been signed. The purport of all is the same, inform all the petitioners. Be assured of our kindness.

No. 43

Joint Petition of Jawahir Singh, Sepoy, stationed at Meerut, Roushan Singh, Landowner of Brajbihari, and Chandi Ram, Landowner

No date

To – The King! Shelter of the World!

Respectfully sheweth, That two days have now elapsed since your slaves submitted a petition, regarding arrangements in Babughar, Aligarh, & c.; but nothing appears to have been done by the Government as yet in the way of dispatching troops or adopting measures. It is to be apprehended that delay in the settlement of the said districts may lead to loss to the State, besides that involved in the loss of the Treasuries at present in safety at Babughar, Aligarh, Chataur, and other places. Cherisher of the Poor! At Babughar there are 20,000 Rupees under the safe custody of 24 Military men, and at Chataur there are 20 Lacs of Rupees in the charge of Mardan Khan, guarded by 600 Jats, while the Treasury at Aligarh is forthcoming, guarded by 3 Companies of Regular Infantry. Moreover, there are 15,000 horses at Babughar, together with the money for their necessary current expenses. If Your Majesty will take immediate steps for dispatching troops and for establishing arrangements in the above places, it is to be expected that the whole of the above said property will be secured and will come into Your Majesty's possession; but if a delay of one or two days is allowed to occur, there is undoubtedly room for apprehension that it will be all lost. There is not a man of the English Army in the whole of the space between the two rivers[61] from Saharunpur to Agra, who will offer to oppose one Regiment of Infantry sent by Your Majesty. There is only one Turnbull, who, with the Joint Magistrate at Bulandshahr, continues exciting disturbances, enlisting men, and communicating intelligence. In case of delay on Your Majesty's part, Your Majesty's loss is to be apprehended. The inhabitants of 60 villages, men of the Kshatriya caste, are ready to lay down their lives for Your Majesty. But the residents of the other side of the Ganges do not fully credit what your slave tells them. However, when these landholders shall have seen a small body of troops placed under your slave, together with Your Majesty's written order, and will have had the evidence of their own eyes, they will all engage to die in Your Majesty's cause. I trust, therefore, that an order under the state Seal will be bestowed on your slave, directing him to raise new horse and foot levies. Assured of the help of the Military Force, 84 villages in the holding of Kaihar Singh. Landholder of Mukimpur, in the District of Meerut, and, in the same way, 87 villages, with Devi Singh, farmer of Bhumrahi, who have already resolved to sacrifice their lives for Your Majesty's Seal openly engage with all their energies in Your Majesty's cause. They are, as one body, animated by one soul, all of one mind with Your slave. Your slave's only ambition is the welfare of Your Majesty's Government. If delay is allowed to occur, serious loss to the State will be the certain result. Beyond this Your Majesty has the power. It was necessary, and I have therefore submitted it, from zeal for Your Majesty. It is requested that one Regiment of Infantry with Artillery, may be placed at your slave's disposal. (Prayers for the prosperity of the reign.) Petition of the slaves Jawahir Singh, Sepoy, stationed at Meerut, Roushan Singh, Landholder of Brajhari, and Chandi Ram, Landholder. Seal of 'Roushan Singh, year 1253'.

Autograph order by the King, in pencil

Mirza Mughal will immediately issue orders to the Officers of the Infantry, and as regards the dispatch of troops, will act agreeably to Jowahir Singh's requisition.

No date to either petition or order.

No. 44

Petition of Mirza Mughal

No date

To – The King! Shelter of the world!

Respectfully sheweth, That numbers of men who have recently arrived, expecting employment and are now in attendance at the Royal threshold, have presented petitions, praying that daily allowances may be assigned to

61 *Doab.*

them. These petitions are enclosed herein, and I trust that such orders as are issued, may be written on the face of each petition, so that they be acted upon. (Prayers for the prosperity of the reign.) Petition of the slave Zahur-ud-din.

Autograph order by the King, in pencil

As regular Military Troops are now coming in great numbers, from all directions, and there is no money in the Treasury, under these circumstances what (a portion of the order here is illegible) is it to be done? You are accordingly directed to write in fuller detail.

In a corner at the top. 'No. 763'.

No. 45
Petition of Rajjab Ali

No date

To – The King! Shelter of the World!

Respectfully sheweth, That your slave has been sending for the Ordnance Stores from the Magazine, and having them placed for safety in certain cells in the place, ever since the day of the revolution. Nathu Khan, however, now objects to sending these stores and opposes your slave's requisitions for their being brought from the magazine to the palace. Your slave therefore depends on Your Majesty's kindly kindness and consideration and trusts that an order may be issued to the Lord of the World, Mirza Muhammad Mughal Bahadur, that whatever stores your slave may write for may, on his requisition, be immediately forwarded from the Magazine, that they may be placed in safety. (Prayers for the prosperity of the reign.) Petition of the home-born slave Rajab Ali.

Autograph order by the King, in pencil

Our son, Mirza Mughal, will imperatively direct Nathu Khan to forward to the Palace, without delay, all Magazine Stores that Rajab Ali may send for. Moreover, it is not proper that Nathu Khan should remain in the Magazine. You will, therefore, appoint some other trustworthy person in his stead.

Note on the reverse – 'Orders have been issued'.

No. 46
Petition of Rambaksh, Subedar of the 74th, and Kuli Yar Khan, Subedar Bahadur, of the 9th Regiment of Native Infantry

No date

To – The King! Shelter of the World!

Respectfully sheweth, That we entertain no manner of objection to go out and fight and to raise entrenchments in conformity with Your Majesty's orders, to the address of us home-born slaves; but this is a day of the week on which it is unpropitious to proceed towards the East. We shall accordingly leave at a propitious hour. However, we will commence with the entrenchments, & c., at 3 o'clock. We have submitted this for Your Majesty's information. The petition of Rambaksh, Subedar, 74th, and Kuli Yar Khan, Subedar Bahadur, 9th Regiment of Native Infantry.

Autograph order by the King, in pencil

Both Regiments taking the necessary ammunition, will start tonight or certainly tomorrow.

No. 47
Petition of Mirza Mughal

No date

To – The King! Shelter of the World!

Your Exalted Majesty may keep your mind free from every dread of the Enemy. Your slave has personally been staying in the batteries with the Troop for two days, and where the batteries of the infidels were, there they are still. They have made no advance. If their batteries had advanced very considerably, they must have come in to the City. The whole Army is prepared to slay the infidels, and an attack is about being made immediately. Through Your Majesty's prestige, the batteries will be speedily taken. And as some of the soldiers come in to Your Majesty's presence, and report what they have heard, and not what they have seen, pray do not believe their statements; but be fully assured that so long as there is life in the dispensation of God. Your slave is not neglectful. Let it be known to our Majesty that he stays personally in the batteries. Petition of the slave Zohour-ud-din.

Autograph order by the King, in pencil

The purport has been ascertained. Kadir Baksh[62] too is with you. Do whatever is proper. No date.

No. 48
Petition of Ghulam Mirza Hussain, Risaldar, 18th Regiment of lrregular Cavalry

No date

To – The King ! Shelter of the World!

Respectfully sheweth, That your slave's forefathers and ancestors were, from antiquity, the servants of Your Majesty, and all such dignities and distinctions as were conferred on them by Your Majesty's illustrious house,

62 Officer-in-charge, of Sappers and Miners.

are on record in the Royal archives. The day that the sun of Your Majesty's dominion and power suffered eclipse, that same day desolation and ruin came to your slave's prospects and fortunes. Left destitute of option, he consented to serve the infidels, and accordingly continued 55 years in the rank of a Risaldar. Hearing the fame of Your Majesty's auspicious accession at Peshawar, where my Regiment is still stationed, after a thousand difficulties, I obtained leave from the commanding Officer, and have now presented myself at Your Majesty's door having left all my property worth thousands of rupees with the Regiment, in consequence of the displeasure of the English. Besides the loss of the property thus abandoned, your slave has suffered the following to other losses. One house recently built by him at an outlay of 5,500 Rupees, and five old houses worth 3,000 Rupees were razed to the ground on account of the Railway, and a bill for 3,500 Rupees on the Gurgaon treasury, which your slave dispatched before leaving the Regiment, was never cashed, owing to the disturbances, the Treasury itself indeed having ceased to exist. Moreover, on the way, the Rajah of Patiala (doomed to banishment from God's sanctuary) had your slave plundered from hand to hand, of all the property, such as cattle, tents, and marquees, which he had with him. So completely did he do this, that your slave has not a horse left to ride. Having ten days ago, presented himself at Your Majesty's door, now submits this petition, and prays that he may receive the distinction of being attached to some Force, or of being appointed to some Districts that he may efficiently and carefully discharge the duties which may be conferred on him. In consequence of your slave's having camels, a travelling carriage drawn by bullocks, servants, & c., his daily expenses are 7 or 8 rupees. Considering it necessary, I have detailed every particular. (Prayers for the prosperity of the reign.) Petition of Ghulam Mirza Hussein, Risaldar of the 18th Regiment, resident of the District Gurgaon, Subdivision of District Palwal, village of Saadatnagar. Seal of 'Syed Ghulam Mirza Hussein, 1255'.

Autograph order by the King, in pencil

Mirza Mughal, I send the Petitioner to you, as he is an old Soldier.

No. 49

Petition of Mohan Pande, Subedar, and Ishwari Prashad Pathak, Jamadar

No date

To – The King! Nourisher of the Poor!

Your Majesty! The usual menial servants not having been procurable, were not entertained in your slave's company. They have, however, now been engaged, according to the list below, and we trust that their allowances from the date of their being entertained, may be granted. We have submitted this petition as being necessary.

Brahman to supply water	1
Barbers	2
Washermen	2
Tailor	1
Shoemaker	1
Scavenger	1
Total	8

Petition of the slaves Mohan Pande, Subedar, and Ishwari Prashad Pathak, Jamadar.

Autograph order by the King, in pencil

In consequence of there being no money in the Treasury, nothing can be done just now. No date. 'Index No. 776'.

No. 50

Joint petition of Kamdar Khan and others of the Constabulary Force

No date

To – The King! Shelter of the World!

We slaves, 50 men of the Constabulary Force, who were stationed over the Jail at Meerut, having come thence to your Royal presence, are now discharging all such duties as are assigned to us, by the orders of the Commander-in-Chief Bahadur. Your Army is now about to leave for Meerut, and 16 of our numbers are anxiously eager to go and fight in its company. We therefore trust that Mirza Mughal may be ordered to direct us to go also, that through Your Majesty's prestige, never to be overthrown, we may share in the victory. It was necessary and has been submitted. Petition of Kamdar Khan and others of the Constabulary Force.

Autograph order by the King, in pencil

The Officer of the Meerut Jail on duty under the Palace lattices, will know that he is to go whithersoever our son Mirza Mughal may send him, and to forward to him any number of men that he may call for. He is to be obedient to all orders of our said son.

No. 51

Order under the seal engraved in the King's special cypher

No date

To – Mirza Mughal.

Son, The illustrious and valiant Mirza Muhammad Zahur-ud-din, otherwise Mirza Mughal Bahadur. Learn! That agreeably to orders of yesterday, the articles detailed below are now sent to you. Have them placed in the custody of your servants, and as the Commissariat arrangements are under your direction, do you act in this matter also as you may think proper. The distribution of money to the troops is entrusted to you, and is satisfactorily managed, inasmuch as each individual receives the full amount of his claim. In the same way, with similar facility as regards these articles, you will be able to give different portions of the Army, Cavalry, and Infantry, such quantities as they may severally require, and they will receive them at once. Be assured of our kindness.

Gram	63 Maunds
Satu (meal of parched barley)	13 Maunds, 30 Srs
Sugar	13 Maunds, 29 Srs
Gur (jaggery)	61 Maunds
Sweetmeats	30 Maunds

Further, you, the light of our eyes, are at liberty either to appoint a contractor or to manage the matter yourself, by making your own purchases in the market. No date.

The Court adjourns till tomorrow at 11 a.m.

Day six: 2 February 1858

The Court reassembled this day at 11 a.m., in the Hall of Special Audience in the Palace at Delhi. The President, Members, Interpreter, and Dy. Judge Advocate-General are all present.

The Prisoner is brought into Court, and Ghulam Abbas, his assistant, is also in attendance.

The Interpreter reads in the original Persian the papers, the translations which were perused yesterday.

Ahsanullah Khan, the Physician, is re-called into Court, and examined on his former affirmation.

Examined by the Judge Advocate

Question – Look at these six papers, and see if you recognize the handwriting of any of them.

Six Persian papers arranged under the head of 'Murder' are now shown to the witness.

Answer – The Orders on Nos. 1 and 6 are in the handwriting of the prisoner, papers 2, 3, and 4 are in the handwriting of Khairat Ali, who was clerk in the Office of Bakht Khan, as Governor-General: this man was in the habit of bringing papers; of the king ready, prepared and having them attested with the King's seal, and so attested used, with the Prisoner's sanction, to dispatch them accordingly to their address.

Question – Was it usual to retain office copies of such papers?

Answer – Yes, he used frequently to bring two copies of each paper, on one the seal used to be impressed, frequently so by the King's own hand, and this copy used to be returned to him for dispatch, while the second copy unattested was retained for record in the Prisoner's office.

Question – Do you know anything about Paper No. 5?

Answer – No, I do not recognize the writing.

Question – Is it possible or likely that this may be an office copy in the handwriting of some newly employed clerk, whose hand you are acquainted with?

Answer – Yes, I believe it to be the handwriting of some clerk in Muhammad Bakht Khan's Office.

The translations of the six papers, arranged under the head of 'Murder' are now read by the Judge Advocate, and entered as follows:

The papers in the original Persian are now read by the Interpreter.

Papers arranged under the head of 'Murder'.

No. 1
Petition of Ghulam Abbas Daffedar, 1st Troop, 4th Regiment of Cavalry, Dated 29th July 1857

To – The King! Shelter of the World!

Respectfully sheweth, That your petitioner was a Duffadar[63] in the 4th Regiment of Cavalry. Having disposed of the English at Muzaffarnagar, he reached your Royal presence on the 23rd June 1857. He is now serving with devotion in Your Majesty's cause, and bears his share in the engagements. Your slave's ancestors have, from antiquity, been nourished by Your Majesty's salt. Your slave therefore expects that, on the capture of the ridge occupied by the British, he will now, through Your Majesty's favour and consideration, be elevated to some appointment of distinction, so that reaching his ambition, he may ever pray for Your Majesty's prosperity.

Petition of the slave, of old nourished by Your Majesty's salt, Ghulam Abbas, Duffadar of the 1st Troop 4th Regiment of Cavalry, come from Muzaffarnagar. Seal of 'Ghulam Abbas'.

Autograph order by the King, in pencil

Mirza Mughal will nominate the petitioner to some appointment, according to the usage of the Army.

63 Junior Commissioned Officer in Cavalry. Equivalent to Havildar in Infantry.

No. 2

Order from the King without signature, cypher, or seal, evidently an office copy retained for records

Dated 7th August 1857

To – The ever Faithful, Rao Bhara, the Ruler of Kutch Bhoj.

Consider yourself receiving the Royal favour, and know! That Girdhari Singh, Subedar of the Grenadier Company of the 16th Regiment of the Bombay Native Infantry, being introduced by the adviser of the State, the honoured of the country, the special slave, Muhammad Bakht Khan Governor-General Bahadur, has come into the Royal presence and affirmed, that you, ever faithful one, having put the whole of the infidels to the sword, have thoroughly cleansed and purified your domains of their unclean presence. We have been extremely gratified to hear of such conduct on your part, and you are therefore honoured with this address, to the intent, that you will institute such arrangements throughout your territory, as that none of the creatures of God may in any way be aggrieved or oppressed. Further, should any numbers of infidels reach your dominions by sea, you will have them slain. In doing this you will act entirely in accordance with our pleasure and wishes; and all such desires, as you will entertain, and all such requests, as you will make to our presence, will in every point be acceded to. Be assured of our kindness.

One copy, and extract transcript. To the ever faithful Rawal Ranjit Singh, Ruler of Jaisalmair. Dated 11th August 1857.

No. 3

Order from the King, without signature, cypher, or seal, an office copy apparently retained for record

Dated 11th August 1857

To – The ever Faithful, Ranjit Singh, Chief of Jaisalmair.

Consider yourself receiving the Royal favour and know! That the Chief, Chamman Singh, brother of the Ruler of Jaipur, having obtained the honour of admittance to our august presence, through the adviser of the State, the honoured of the country, the special slave, Muhammad Bakht Khan, Lord Governor-General Bahadur, Director of all matters Military and Civil, has declared and affirmed that you, emblem of fidelity cherish an anxious desire and wish to come to the Royal presence,[64] and only delay doing so, pending the issue of a special order; you are therefore honoured with this address. It is clear to our belief that throughout our dominions, the name or trace of those ill-omened infidels, the English, must not have remained; if, however,

64 In the original to kiss the Royal feet. Ed.

by any chance or possibility some have escaped till now, by keeping hidden and concealed, first slay them, and after that, having made arrangements for the administration of your territory present yourself at our Court, with your whole Military following. Considerations and friendliness a thousand-fold will be bestowed on your slave, and you will be distinguished by elevation to dignities and places which the compass of our qualifications will not have capacity to contain. Be assured of our kindness.

No. 4

Order of the King, without signature, cypher, or seal

Dated 11th August 1857

To – All Hindus and Muhammadans who wish the advancement of religion.

Be it known to you! That Falak-ud-din Shah, being one of those who have pledged themselves to fight for the Mahommedan faith, in the religious war against the infidels, and being Director of Finance and the Army, is sent to collect Ghaziz[65] as well as money for the expenses of the armies bestowed by God, which have come from all directions, and have assembled at the Royal threshold for the destruction of the Christians; and which have already sent thousands of the British Soldiery, and others of the English, to hell. It is incumbent on you to consider well your own advantage, and to forward to the Royal presence, such amounts of treasure as he may determine, at the same time sending your accredited agent also. You will, moreover, give the above-named Falak-ud-din Shah such aid, in Military forces, for arrangements on the way, and for the slaughter of Christians, as he may demand. Those who will join in the cause; of the faith and of religion; will receive distinctions; and those who will confederate with the Christian will be utterly despoiled of life and property.

List	Rs.
The Chief of Chhatari to contribute 7 guns and	50,000
The Chief of the Town of Parrawe	10,000
The Chief of the Town of Dharmpur	5,000
The Chief of the Dhanpur	5,000
The Chief of the Pahansu	5,000
The Chief of the Sadabad	5,000
The Chief of the Dattowli	2,000
The Chief of the Begampur	10,000
The Chief of the Badoun	10,000
The Chief of the Town of Jairu	5,000
The Merchants of the City of Muttra	50,000

65 Men voluntarily pledging their lives to fight in name of Islam. Ed.

The Rajah of Ballabhgarh	1,00,000
The Chief, Ghulam Hussein of Attrowli	20,000
The Rajah of Bharatpur	5,00,000
Total	12,45,000

No. 5

Petition of Muhammad Bakht Ali, formerly Jail Superintendent of the Jhansi District, now officer Commanding the Ali-Ghol

Dated 16th August 1857

To – The King! Dispenser of Blessings on the World! Shelter of Mankind, & c.

Respectfully sheweth, That, in a former petition, Your Majesty was made acquainted with the acts of devotion and resolution, which your slave performed in the Jhansi, Orai, Calpee, Etwah, Mynpoory, and other Districts, as regards the slaughter and ruination of the accursed sect, the Nazarenes[66] as also with the devotion your slave, and the soldiers accompanying him, have displayed from the date of their arrival in Your Majesty's presence, the 16th of July 1857, up to the present moment in the several attacks on and engagements with the Nazarenes; a list of these soldiers has been deposited in the archives of Your Majesty's Government; your slave, therefore, expects that when complete victory shall have been gained, rewards similar to those which may be bestowed on the rest of the Army, will be conferred on your slave and his family, and on his equally devoted follower. Moreover, as at present, only 500 soldiers, designated the Ali-Ghol, who, with your slave, are ready to sacrifice their lives in Your Majesty's service, are in attendance at the Royal door; if the Royal permission is granted, a complete regiment will be raised. But as several bodies, all bearing the same title Ali-Ghol, who, with your slave, are ready to sacrifice their lives in Your Majesty's service, are in attendance at the Royal door; if the Royal permission is granted, a complete regiment will be raised. But as several bodies, all bearing the same title Ali-Ghol, have arrived from different places, such distinctive appellation as Your Majesty may select for that under your slave, will be adopted, so that it may be generally known. Agreeably to our Majesty's commands, our slave is about proceeding to Malagarh, he therefore submits this petition, that orders may be issued. (Prayers for the prosperity of the reign.) Petition of the slave Muhmamad Bakht Ali, Superintendent of the Jail, Jhansi District, at present Officer Commanding Ali-Ghol. Countersigned 'Muhammad Bakht Khan' agreeably to the request of the petitioner.

66 Christians. Ed.

Autograph order by the King, in pencil (unintelligible)

Bakht Ali's request is accepted, but as yet no one has paid except from the receipts of some places. So long as all cannot be paid their regular allowances, no single individual will receive any thing.

Paper marked A is now produced enclosed in its original envelope, on which is the Delhi Post Office Stamp, proving that it was posted at Delhi on the 25th of March 1857, and another stamp of the Agra Post Office proves that it was duly received there on the 27th of March 1857. The Judge Advocate explains that this important document was found among the papers of the late Mr. Colvin, Lieutenant-Governor at Agra. The translation is now read, and entered as follows:

Translation of a Petition from Muhammad Darwesh, to His Honour the Lieutenant-Governor, North-Western Provinces, Dated 24th, posted at Delhi 25th and received at the Agra Post Office, 27th March 1857.

Nourisher of the Poor! May your prosperity continue! Your Highness! The arrangements for the dispatch of letters from the King of Delhi to the King of Persia, through the Pir-zada Hasan Askari, have been stated in a former petition, and must have come to your knowledge. I, who am a mendicant of itinerant habits, have since learnt, for a certainty, that two men, with letters from the King of Delhi through the said Hasan Askari, proceeded about three or four months ago towards Constantinople in company with a Caravan going to Mecca. Hasan Askari has now assured the King of Delhi that he has certain information that the Prince Royal of Persia has fully taken possession of and occupied Bushire, and that he has entirely expelled the Christians or rather has not left one alive there, and has taken many of them prisoners, and that very soon indeed, the Persian Army will advance by the way of Candahar and Cabul towards Delhi. He told the King also that His Majesty was altogether too careless about corresponding with the King of Persia. The King then gave Hasan Askari 20 gold mohurs, and requested him speedily to dispatch letters to Persia, and directed him to give the gold mohurs to the man who should take the letters, for the expenses of his journey. Hasan Askari accordingly took the money and returned to his house and has prepared four men to carry the letters, making them assume the coloured garments of religious mendicants, and it is reported that they will leave for Persia in a day or two. The petitioner has not been able to ascertain their names. In the palace, but more especially in the portion of it constituting the personal apartments of the King, the subject of conversation night and day, is the early arrival of the Persians. Hasan Askari has, moreover, impressed the King with the belief that he has learnt, through a divine revelation, that the dominion of the King of Persia will, to a certainty, extend to Delhi, or rather over the whole of Hindustan, and that the splendour of the sovereignty of Delhi will again revive, as the sovereign of Persia will bestow the crown on the King. Throughout the palace, but particularly to the King, this belief has been the cause of great rejoicing, so much so that prayers are offered and vows are made, while at the same time Hasan Askari has entered upon the daily performance, at an hour and a half before sunset, of a course of propitiatory ceremonies to expedite the arrival of the Persians and the expulsion of the Christians. It has been arranged that every Thursday, several trays of victuals, wheat-meal, oil, money in copper coin, and cloth should be sent by the King in aid of these ceremonies, and they are accordingly brought to Hasan Askari. Some of the higher functionaries of the Government, drawn into a faith in this man by his frauds and deceptions, are in the habit of visiting his house, and consider his words and actions entitled to the greatest reliance. Where would be the use in my naming these traitors? May the Almighty god confound the enemies of the Government! Our petitioner keeps learning these matters from certain of his friends who have admittance to the presence of this King of Delhi, and who are moreover in the habit of visiting Hasan Askari also. Actuated by goodwill, I have communicated the above particulars. It rests in the province of the ever-enduring government to make necessary and effectual arrangements. Petition of the well-wisher Muhammad Darwesh. Dated 24th March 1857. Seal of 'Fakir Muhammad Darwesh'.

Witness Examined by the Judge Advocate

Question – Did you know a man at Delhi of the name of Muhammad Hasan Askari, a priest by descent?

Answer – Yes, I did, he lived near the Delhi Gate, and used to visit the King very frequently.

Question – How long ago is it since you saw him?

Answer – I saw him last some 20 days before the English troops re-took Delhi.

Question – Do you know where he went to, or what became of him?

Answer – No, I do not.

Question – At what time were his visits so frequent to the King, and do you know about what time he was first introduced to the King's presence?

Answer – He was first introduced about four years ago. A daughter of the King became a disciple of his, and she spoke so highly of his sanctity that the King employed him during his illness to pray for him, and send him charms to effect his recovery, and within the last two or three years his visits to the King became very frequent. This daughter used to live at the Delhi Gate in a house adjoining Hasan Askari, and it was commonly reported that she was also his mistress.

Question – Did this man Hasan Askari pretend to possess miraculous powers, or to be able to foretell future events?

Answer – He used to interpret dreams, and also foretell coming events, and professed to be inspired.

Question – Do you know whether he ever predicted anything relative to the war which was then being waged between the English and the King of Persia?

Answer – Not while the war between the British and Persians was going on; but two years ago he got 400 rupees from the prisoner, which were given to a man who it was said was going to Mecca; but it afterwards transpired that he had not gone on the Mecca pilgrimage, but had proceeded to the King of Persia. The man's name was Sidi Kambar; he was an Abyssinian, and I suppose came from Abyssinia.

Question – Do you know why it was given out that this man was going to Mecca, when his real destination was to the King of Persia?

Answer – I cannot account for the deception. I was told by one of the Court spies, by Jattu of Jat Mall,[67] that Hasan Askari had sent this man to Persia instead of Mecca, and on making enquiries from some of the Court servants, I found this information was correct.

Question – Did you ever hear of what was the object of this man's mission to Persia?

Answer – No; but I heard from Kuli Khan and Basant, two of the King's body servants, that Hasan Askar had given Sidi Kambar some papers at nighttime, attested with the King's seal, and sent him off to Persia.

Question – Was the war between the Persians and British frequently the subject of conversation at the Delhi palace, and did the King appear much interested in the issue of it?

Answer – No, it was not particularly the subject of conversation; the native newspaper coming into the palace used to contain particulars of its progress, and the King never seemed to me to evince any marked interested either one way or the other.

Question – Did this war, among the Mussalman population of Delhi generally, excite much interest, and was it looked upon as a religious war?

Answer – No, the Mussalmans of Delhi are Sunnis, and those of Persia are Shias; the former did not consequently take much interest in the war.

Question – Are you aware whether in March last, *viz.* about ten months ago, the King gave Hasan Askari 20 gold mohurs for any particular purpose?

Answer – He used to give him money; but I don't know on what account, or on what particular occasion.

Question – Have you ever heard of any men being sent from here to Constantinople in company with a Caravan going to Mecca?

Answer – No, I never heard of any men being sent to Constantinople on any occasion.

67 A news writer, probably a double agent of both the Emperor and the English.

Question – Do you know any one at Delhi under the title of Muhammad Darwesh?

Answer – No, I do not.

Question – Was there any document purporting to bear the seal of the King of Persia pasted up on the Jama Masjid or other part of the City of Delhi a few months prior to the outbreak?

Answer – Yes, a few months before the outbreak, I heard that a paper purporting to be a proclamation from the King of Persia, was pasted on the Jama Masjid.

Question – Did you ever hear how the paper came there?

Answer – No, but I heard the contents were such as would have been written by the sect of Mahommedans called Shiahs.

Question – Was it generally supposed that the document was a genuine one?

Answer – People were not certain about its authenticity; they generally seemed to doubt it.

Question – What was the purport of the document?

Answer – I heard that it exhorted all classes of Mahommedans to set aside their sectarian differences, and to combine as one body of Mohammedans at the present time, and be ready to fight under the same banner, should there be any cause for so doing.

Question – Did not this document create a great discussion and sensation in the City?

Answer – No, not to any very great extent.

Question – Did you hear this document talked of in the Palace, or by the prisoner?

Answer – The Prisoner never spoke of it before me; but I heard it alluded to by a few other persons in the Palace.

Question – Did the annexation of Oudh by the Company cause much feeling of dissatisfaction among the Mussalman population of Delhi?

Answer – No, it caused no dissatisfaction whatever; on the contrary, the Mussalmans of Delhi were very much pleased with it, as the people of Lucknow being, Shiahs, had killed Maulavy Amir Ali, who was a Syed and a Sunni.

Question – Were any other notices or warnings pasted up on the Jama Masjid a short time before the outbreak, intimating dissatisfaction on the part of the Mussalmans?

Answer – I don't recollect any.

Question – Did the Native Newspapers at Delhi, any time before the rebellion, urge the necessity or propriety of a religious war against the English?

Answer – No, they never did; had such been done, the Government Officer would have noticed it.

The Prisoner declines to cross-examine.

The Court at 4 p.m. adjourns till 11 a.m. tomorrow.

Day seven: 3 February 1858

The Court reassembled this morning at 11 a.m., in the Hall of Special Audience in the Palace at Delhi, pursuant to adjournment of yesterday.

The President, Members, Interpreter, and Dy. Judge Advocate-General are all present.

The Prisoner is brought into Court attended by his assistant Ghulam Abbas.

Ahsanullah Khan, Physician, is re-called into Court, and examined on his former affirmation.

Examined by the Judge Advocate

Question – You have heard the petition of Muhammad Darwesh read. Do you know anything of the trays of food, wheat-meal, oil, money in copper coin and cloth said to have been sent by the King in aid of the ceremonies performed by Hasan Askari?

Answer – Yes, all these things were usually sent; but I do not know that they were sent for the special purpose mentioned in the petition.

Question – You have mentioned that Jat Mall was one of the Court spies, did the King pay him for news given?

Answer – No, he was not a servant of the King; he was news-writer on the part of the British Government.

Question – How was it then that you came to get secret information from him, and how, being known as Government news-writer, was it that this man was entrusted with such a secret?

Answer – Jat Mall used to go about the Palace collecting all sorts of news, and having heard the matter, asked me what I knew of it, at which time I was quite ignorant of the subject, and it was only subsequently that I heard it confirmed.

The witness withdraws.

Jat Mall, formerly news-writer to the Lieutenant-Governor at Agra, is called into Court, and duly affirmed.

Examined by the Judge Advocate

Question – Did you know a man of the name of Hasan Askari here?

Answer – Yes, I did.

Question – Was he frequently in attendance on the Prisoner?

Answer – Yes.

Question – Relate what you know of his transactions with the King?

Answer – He used to come and repeat incantations over the King, and after praying, breathe on him; he used also to profess to be possessed of miraculous gifts from heaven, the gift of prophecy, the power of interpreting dreams.[68] Hasan Askari used to declare that he was frequently audibly addressed from heaven; he used to come daily to the prisoner at various hours just as he was sent for and frequently used to come uninvited – especially in the evening, when he would have secret audiences with the King.

Question – Did you ever hear any particular dream which this man Hasan Askari interpreted to the King?

Answer – Yes, about the time that the Persian forces came to Herat, I heard that Hasan Askari communicated one of his own dreams to the King to the effect that he had seen a hurricane approaching from the West, which was followed by a great flood of water devastating the country; that it passed over, and that he noticed that the King suffered no inconvenience from it, but was borne up over the flood seated on his couch. The way in which Hasan Askari interpreted this dream was that the King of Persia with his army would annihilate the British power in the East, would restore the King to his ancient throne and reinstate him in his kingdom, and at the same time the infidels, meaning the British, would be all slaughtered.

Question – Do you know whether, through the means of this man Hasan Askari, letters were sent to the King of Persia or communications kept up with him?

Answer – Yes, I do know that letters used to be sent. About a year and a half or two years ago, a *kafilah* was going to Mecca. A man of the name of Sidi Kambar, who was chief of the Abyssinians in the Palace, asked permission to accompany it as a pilgrim. This was granted, and according to the custom on such occasions, he was given a year's pay in advance, and it was said at the time that according to a usage common to the Mahommedans, the Prisoner had sent a petition, addressed to God, to be posted up on his account on the walls of the shrine at Mecca. After some eight or nine days, I heard that Sidi Kambar's going to Mecca was only a pretence, and that in reality he had started direct for Persia with letters from the King of Delhi to the King of Persia. I heard this from Khwaja Bakhsh, a messenger of the King's, and from one of the Prisoner's armed personal attendants whose name I do not recollect. I acquainted Captain Douglas with this matter at the time, who said it was a very serious business, and directed me to make every possible enquiry about it, because such correspondence on the part of the King of Delhi with the King of Persia was interdicted. I accordingly asked Ahsanullah Khan, the physician, the particulars, as he was fully entrusted with the direction of all

68 The Prisoner here voluntarily declares his belief that Hasan Askari did really possess the powers attributed to him. Ed.

private matters that required to be written. Ahsanullah Khan denied having any information on this subject, and declared that if anything of the kind had happened, it was without his knowledge. I communicated this to Captain Douglas, and still continued my enquiries, and some 20 days afterwards learnt, I forget now from whom, that Haider Husain, Commandant of the Prisoners' Artillery, and Hasan Askari, had some letters written, and having them authenticated, in some way, had them dispatched to Persia by Sidi Kambar. I communicated this to Captain Douglas, and explained to him that as it was known that the circumstances had reached his ears, the people about the Prisoner were on their guard in speaking of it, and that therefore I could elicit nothing further. I also suggested to Captain Douglas that arrangements might be made for intercepting Sidi Kambar beyond Lahore. He, however, replied that there could be no certainty as to which route he had taken, and said it would be useless to take any steps about it.

Question – Was the subject of the war with Persia much talked of by the King and those about the Palace?

Answer – Yes, it was a frequent subject of conversation both in the palace and in the City.

Question – Do you know whether it was talked of and referred to in the light of a religious war or one through which the Mohammedans of this City were to be restored to power?

Answer – Yes, that was the general impression throughout the country, but some who were better informed knew and used to say, that the King of Persia was not by any means able to cope with the English.

Question – Do you know whether any communications were ever attempted or made from the Prisoner or others in his confidence to the Native Officers or Sepoys of the Company's Army?

Answer – No, I never heard of any communication originating with the Prisoner of his confidential Agents, except in one instance about three and a half years ago, when some 10 or 12 Mohammedans on one occasion, and four or five on another, came to the Prisoner, offering to become his disciples, a request which the Prisoner complied with. This had not gone far when the late Sir Theophilus Metcalfe heard of it, and immediately took measures to check the practice.

Question – Was the annexation of Oudh by the Company much discussed by the King or the inmates of the Palace, and if so, what was the light in which they viewed it?

Answer – No, I only heard the annexation spoken of twice, once when the Troops were going down towards Cawnpore, on which occasion the Prisoner asked Mr. Fraser and Captain Douglas if Oudh was to be annexed. They both stated that they had no information on the point; but about a month after it was reported generally that the annexation had taken place.

Question – Did Hasan Askari every predict anything as to the King's length of life, or his future success against the English?

Answer – Yes, he told the King that he had assigned 20 years of his own life to prolong that of the King but I never heard that he predicted such success against the English beyond what I have mentioned as the interpretation of his dream.

Question – Did you ever hear anything talked of in the Palace about the centenary of the Battle of Plassey, or was there any prophecy that the English rule would terminate at the end of 100 years from its commencement?

Answer – No, I never heard of it.

Question – Were you aware that the Regiments of the East India Company at Delhi were in any way dissatisfied before they broke out into mutiny?

Answer – There was an evident feeling of disaffection among them from the little I could observe myself passing in and out of the Palace. Some 20 or 25 days before the outbreak, the Sepoys used to talk among themselves about the burning of the houses at Ambala, coupling the circumstances with the greased cartridges and avowing their determination not to use them.

Question – Was this subject, *viz.* the disaffection of the Sepoys, discussed in the Palace?

Answer – Yes, the burning of the houses, and the general disaffection of the Troops, on account of the greased cartridges, used to be commonly spoken of in the Palace; but I never heard it referred to by or before the King. I heard a few days before the outbreak from some of the Sepoys of the Gate of the Palace, that it had been arranged in case greased cartridges were pressed upon them, that the Meerut Troops were to come here, where they would be joined by the Delhi Troops, and it was said that this compact had been arranged through some Native Officers, who went over on court-martial duty to Meerut.

Question – Did you mention or report this to any one?

Answer – No, it was a Military matter, and I did not like to speak about it; my reports were all confined to subjects immediately connected with the King.

Question – Were you here when the mutinous Troops came from Meerut?

Answer – I was at my own house in Delhi when I heard that some of the Cavalry from Meerut had killed the Toll Collector at the Salimpur Bridges, and burnt the Tollhouse. I, however, did not credit the report, and went on writing my newsletter. Having completed it, I came to the Palace, and I then learnt that Captain Douglas, Mr. Fraser, Mr. Hutchinson, the Magistrate, and Mr. Nixon, the Head Clerk of the Commissioner's Office, had gone in the direction of the Calcutta Gate, to make arrangements against the Mutineers. I consequently followed them, and there saw that they had the Calcutta Gate, *viz.* the one nearest to the Bridge of Boats, closed. While occupied there, someone happened to report that the Mutineers had entered the City by the Zinat-ul-Masjid Gate, and were then in Daryaganj, and had already fired the Staging Bungalow, and certainly the smoke was then visible. This was about 8 o'clock in the morning, and just afterwards I saw three of the Company's Cavalry coming from the direction of Daryaganj, pursuing at a gallop some European gentlemen, at whom one of them fired his pistol as they came up, but missed his aim. This gentleman rode on in the direction of the Magazine and escaped. Just then Mr. Fraser took a musket from one of the Constabulary Guard at the Gate, and shot one of the troopers; the other Troopers then shot the horse of the man who had been killed, and Mr. Fraser then got into his buggy, accompanied by Captain Douglas and Mr. Hutchinson, both on foot, proceeded in the direction of the palace. Mr. Hutchinson had by this time been wounded in the right arm just above the elbow, by a pistol shot from one of the Troopers, while Mr. Fraser was proceeding to the Palace some more Troopers had arrived, and one of these coming up behind fired his pistol, but missed Mr. Fraser. At this time, Bakhtawar, who was an Orderly Chaprassy of Captain Douglas, was seated behind the buggy of Mr. Fraser. Captain Douglas, seeing that he was surrounded by these Troopers, jumped into the Fort ditch, and in doing so fell upon some loose stones and was much hurt in consequence. The Troopers by this time began to disperse in pursuit of the Europeans in all directions, so getting an opportunity, Bakhtawar and other Native Government servants took Captain Douglas out of the Fort ditch in a state of insensibility, and carried him to his apartments over the Palace Gate. When he recovered his speech and senses a little, he issued instructions to people about him to bring in Mr. Hutchinson, who had also been wounded, which was done. Mr. Fraser, who was walking in the covered way below adjoining the Lahori Gate of the Palace, accompanied by some gentlemen who had only that morning arrived from Calcutta, directed Pran messenger to go and procure two cannons from the King. Pran had just left on this errand, and Mr. Fraser had just come under the centre opening of the covered way, when by this time a great crowd of men and boys of all ages having collected, began clapping their hands as a kind of insolent bravado at what was occurring. Mr. Fraser, seeing such marked feelings of hostility, began to return to Captain Douglas' quarters, and as he reached the foot of the stairs, Haji lapidary raised his sword to make a cut at him. Mr. Fraser who had a sheathed sword in his hand, turned sharply round, and thrust at him, with the sword in its sheath, saying to the Havildar of the Gate Guards 'What kind of behaviour is this?' upon which the Havildar made a show of driving off the crowd; but no sooner was Mr. Fraser's back turned, than the Havildar nodded with his head to the lapidary, to signify to him that now he should renew his attack. The lapidary, thus encouraged, rushed upon Mr. Fraser who at once fell, when three other men of the names of Khalak Dad, a Kabuli Pathan, Mughal Begh or Mughal Jan, and Sheikh Din Muhammad, who had been concealed in an out-house adjoining, rushed out and cut him with their swords, over the head, face, and chest till he was quite dead. Sheikh Din Muhammad was an armed orderly in the King's pay, and Kahlak Dad and Mughal Beg were also armed retainers of Mahboob Ali Khan the King's Prime Minister. These three men, after having dispatched Mr. Fraser, followed by a crowd of others, ran upstairs, to Captain Douglas' apartments over the Palace Gate. After they had arrived at the second landing place, a servant of the Government in attendance on Captain Douglas, by name Makhan, told him of the circumstances, and was ordered to close the staircase. While this was being done on the North side of the apartment numbers of the crowd rushed in by a corresponding staircase on the Southern side, and came down and forced open the door which Makhan had closed, and thus gave admission to the armed crowd, headed by the three men already mentioned as having cut Mr. Fraser when he had fallen. These people successively murdered Captain Douglas, Mr. Hutchinson the Collector, the Reverend Mr. Jennings, Miss Jennings, and Miss Clifford, all of whom were in Captain Douglas' apartments. The stranger who had arrived that morning from Calcutta contrived to get out on the ramparts of the palace wall, and had gone unobserved as far as Mirza Kochak's house near the Delhi Gate of the Palace, when he was fired at by somebody, and wounded in the shoulder. On this, he retraced his steps and was eventually cut down at the foot of the Southern staircase leading to Captain Douglas' apartments. All these murders were committed in about quarter of an hour. The details, as given here, I collected from Makhan, Bakhtawar, Pran, and Kishan, servants of the Government in attendance at the time on Captain Douglas; but of the circumstances up to the death of Mr. Fraser, I was myself an eyewitness.

It being 4 p.m., the Court adjourns till Friday, the 5th instant, at 11 a.m.

Day eight: 5 February 1858

The Court reassembled this morning in the Hall of Special Audience in the Palace at Delhi, pursuant to adjournment of Wednesday.

The President, Members, Interpreter, and Dy. Judge Advocate-General are all present.

The Prisoner, attended by his Counsel, is brought into Court.

The Witness Jat Mall is re-called into Court, and reminded of his former affirmation.

Examined by the Judge Advocate

Question – After the Europeans in Captain Douglas' apartments had been murdered, what did the populace or soldiery proceed to do?

Answer – Immediately after the murder of the Europeans, I went to my home in the City, and did not come to the Palace again for several days.

Question – When did the King assume the reins of Government? Was a Royal salute fired on the occasion?

Answer – He began to take possession of the Government stores, *viz.* the gunpowder outside the City, and all the ordnance arms, & c., in the Magazine on the second or third day after the arrival of the Meerut Troops, and in a week or so, began generally to issue Royal orders to the different Departments, and to receive petitions on Government business. A salute of 21 guns was certainly fired during the night of the 11th of May; but I am not certain what was the occasion of it. Some said it was the salute to the colours of the Regiments come from Meerut, and some said that the prisoner had gone into Salimgarh, and the guns had been fired as a salute to him.

Question – When was Mirza Mughal appointed Commander-in-Chief?

Answer – He was virtually Commander-in-Chief from seven or eight days after the outbreak, inasmuch as the native officers used to go to consult and confer with him, and receive their orders from him; but it was not till a month had elapsed, that he was publicly proclaimed and received his dress of honour. On the same occasion, the other sons of the King and the grandsons of the King were severally made Generals and Colonels, each receiving their dress of honour.

Question – What part did Hasan Askari act during the time of the rebellion; was he one of the King's chief counsellors?

Answer – He continued in the same position with reference to the King as formerly, and did not appear to take any such active part in the rebellion as to be particularly remarkable. A daughter of the Prisoner was avowedly a disciple of Hasan Askari; but people generally said that there was an improper intimacy between them.

Question – Do you know whether any ladders were taken from the Palace for the purpose of scaling the Magazine?

Answer – I heard that scaling ladders were used at the magazine; but I don't know where they were brought from.

Question – Did you ever hear of the circulation of Chapaties about the country some months before the outbreak and if so, what was supposed to be the meaning of this?

Answer – Yes, I did hear of the circumstances. Some people said, that it was a propitiatory observance to avert some impending calamity; others that they were circulated by the Government to signify that the population throughout the country would be compelled to use the same food as the Christians, and thus be deprived of their religion; while others again said, that the chapaties were circulated to make it known that Government was determined to force Christianity on the country by interfering with their food, and intimation of it was thus given, that they might be prepared to resist the attempt.

Question – Is sending such articles about the country a custom among the Hindus or Mussalmans; and would the meaning to be at once understood without any accompanying explanation?

Answer – No, it is not by any means a custom; I am 50 years old, and never heard of such a thing before.

Question – Did you ever hear that any message was sent with the chapaties?

Answer – No, I never heard of any.

Question – Were these chapaties chiefly circulated by Mahommedans or Hindus?

Answer – They were circulated indiscriminately, without reference to either religion, among the peasantry of the country.

Question – When did you first return to the Palace after the 11th of May?

Answer – I had heard a report in the city that the Europeans were to be slaughtered. I don't know the exact date, but it was some seven or eight days after the outbreak; and I got into the Palace among the crowd. This was about 8 o'clock in the morning. On my reaching the first courtyard of the Palace, I saw the Europeans seated in a row, with their hands tied behind their backs along the edge of the square reservoir, and also along the small canal leading to it; there were men, women and children. Shortly after I arrived, one of the Meerut Cavalry mutineers fired a pistol at them. He was standing at the same distance on horseback. The shot missed the Europeans and hit one of the King's sepoys, who was standing some way off behind them. This man died in consequence, and owing to this accident, the crowd decided on killing the Europeans with swords. The King's retainers as well as some of the mutineers drew their swords to carry out this resolve; but I had not the nerve to stay and witness the execution, so went home, and subsequently heard that they had all been slaughtered by the King's servants and the mutinous soldiery.

Question – Were any guns fired as a token of joy on the occasion?

Answer – No, I heard none.

Question – Did the prisoner give his consent to the murder of these Europeans?

Answer – On the first day of the soldiery making a request that the Europeans should be executed, the King refused his sanction; but it was said that on the day following, Basant Ali Khan, a personal attendant of the King and a man notorious for his savage disposition, went among the soldiers and instigated them to insist on the murder of the Europeans. They did so, and the King ordered the Europeans to be given up to them; at least this is what I subsequently heard at my own house. On the morning of the massacre, Basant Ali Khan is stated to have stood in the courtyard of the Hall of Special Audience, and to have called out loudly, that the King had sanctioned the slaughter of the Europeans, and that the personal armed retainers of the prisoner were directed to go and assist in carrying it into effect.

Question – In your opinion, could the King, had he been anxious to do so, have saved the Europeans, especially the women and children?

Answer – I heard in the city that the King did wish to save the Europeans, particularly the women and children, but that he was overruled by the violence of the soldiery, and had not the firmness to oppose them.

Question – Was there not ample room for the women and children in the apartments occupied by the females of the King's Establishments, and would not the European women and children have been safe there?

Answer – Certainly there was abundance of room, 500 people might have been concealed, and been safe there; there are also several secret recesses and crypts, which, had the rebels even dared to violate the sanctity of the women's apartments, would have escaped all search.

Question – Were you present in Delhi during the whole siege by the British?

Answer – I continued in Delhi for three months and a quarter after the outbreak, when the King's people began to search for servants of the British Government on suspicion of sending intelligence to the English. I then made my escape from the city, and did not return till some time after the city had been re-taken.

Question – Are you aware whether any other Europeans were murdered after the massacre of those in the Palace?

Answer – No, I don't know that there were any left to be murdered; but before the massacre above described, I heard that some 38 40 had defended themselves in some underground recess, and being starved out, were killed about two or three days after the outbreak.

Question – Did you ever hear the Sepoys allege any other ground of complaint besides that of the greased cartridges?

Answer – No, I never did.

Question – How did the Sepoys generally speak of the Company's Government during the siege?

Answer – The soldiery generally talked of the Government with bitter complaints of the attempt on their caste and religion, and always avowed their intention to kill Europeans whenever they met them. Those, however, who were wounded contrasted the neglect with which they were treated in Delhi, with the care they would have experienced under similar circumstances had they been fighting for the English.

Question – Do you think there was any difference between the Mahommedans and Hindus in regard to their feelings for or against the English Government?

Answer – Yes, certainly; the Mahommedans as a body were well pleased at the overthrow of the British Government, whole merchants and respectable tradesmen among the Hindus regretted it.

Question – Was there no difference of feeling on this point among the Mahommedans and Hindu soldiery; were both equally bitter against the English Government?

Answer – The general feeling throughout the Army was the same, both among the Hindus and Mahommedans.

Question – Do you think the arrival of the soldiery from Meerut was expected in the palace?

Answer – Yes, they were expected. Letters came in from Meerut on Sunday, bringing intelligence that 82 soldiers had been imprisoned, and that a serious disturbance was to take place in consequence. Owing to this, the guards at the gate of the Palace made no secret of their intentions, but spoke openly of what they expected to occur, which was that some of the troops after mutinying at Meerut would come over to Delhi.

Question – Have you any means of knowing whether this was communicated or made known to the Prisoner at this time?

Answer – No, I have not.

Question – Can you judge from any circumstances that occurred either at the time or afterwards, that the prisoner had any foreknowledge of the coming of the troops from Meerut?

Answer – Nothing came under my observation either before or afterwards from which I could draw such a conclusion.

Cross-examined by the Prisoner

Question – You stated in your evidence the day before yesterday, that a gentleman who tried to make his escape in the direction of Mirza Kochak's house, was wounded by a shot there, do you know whether Mirza Kochak was in his house at the time?

Answer – No, I can't speak to particulars of the kind.

Question – Do you know whether the people who murdered Mr. Fraser were encouraged to do so by me, or were they instigated to the act by the Army?

Answer – As far as I know the King had not had time to hear of the murder before it was committed; the rioters were sufficiently disposed to murder, and being encouraged by the Army perpetrated it at once.

Question – Did you hear that I expressed a wish to have the corpses of the murdered Europeans removed, and that the soldiery would not allow me?

Answer – No, I have no knowledge on the subject.

Question – Do you know whether I gave the order to my armed retainers to assist in slaying the Europeans, or did Basant Ali Khan falsely gave out that I had done so?

Answer – I can't say.

Examined by the Court

Question – At the time you saw the Europeans bound before being slaughtered, did you observe that any of the King's confidential servants or officers were present?

Answer – No, I saw none of these in the courtyard; but Mirza Mughal, one of the King's sons, was standing on the roof of his house overlooking the courtyard, and at the same time other sons and two grandsons of the King were standing on their houses, apparently for the purpose of witnessing the massacre.

Question – Did you observe that any of these made any attempt to save the women and children from being murdered, or otherwise?

Answer – No, they appeared to be spectators. It had been determined that the massacre was to take place, and there was no necessity for their urging execution of it.

The Witness withdraws.

Captain Forrest, Assistant Commissary of Ordnance, is called into Court and duly sworn.

Examined by the Judge Advocate

Question – Were you in Delhi on the 11th of last May?

Answer – I was.

Question – Did you on that occasion see any of the mutinous soldiery from Meerut?

Answer – I did. I first saw them, *viz.* some Cavalry in front (nearly a Regiment) followed by the 11th and 20th Regiments of Native Infantry crossing the Bridge on the road from Meerut. They were coming up in military formation. I would say in subdivisions of companies with fixed bayonets and sloped arms, at about 9 o'clock. I did not see any of them previous to this; but I was informed that a small portion of the Cavalry had arrived on the Delhi side of the Bridge much earlier, *viz.* about 7 o'clock. I was in the magazine at the time I saw the troops passing over the Bridge, having gone there a short time before in consequence of a communication with Sir Theophilus Metcalfe made to me, to the effect that the Mutineers were expected in from Meerut, and he wished me to get two guns out of the Magazine, so as to place them in position, to sweep the Bridge and prevent the mutineers from crossing; but there were no cattle to draw out the guns, neither were there any Artillery men to man them, so Lieutenant Willoughby concurred with me in thinking that the best plan would be to close the Magazine gates, and defend the place as long as we could; and we thought that if we could hold the Magazine till evening, the European Troops would be certain to arrive from Meerut and relieve us. Between the hours of 9 and 10, a Subedar of the 38th Native

Infantry, who was commanding the Magazine Guard outside, informed me through an aperture, that the King of Delhi had sent a guard to take possession of the Magazine, and to bring all the Europeans there up to his Palace, and that if they did not consent to this, none of them were to be allowed to leave the magazine. I did not see the guard at this time, but I saw the man who had brought this message. He was a well-dressed Mussalman. We told the Subedar of the Guard that he was to pay no attention to any orders he might receive from any one, unless it was Lieutenant Willoughby or myself; but we held no communication with, nor did we design any Answer to the man who had brought the above message. Shortly after the above, a native officer in the King's service arrived with a strong guard of the King's own soldiers in their uniform, and told the above-mentioned Subedar and the Non-Commissioned Officers, that he was sent down by the King to relieve them of duty. The same orders were given to the Subedar by myself to pay no attention to such authority. At this time the native officer who had come down with a strong detachment of the King's Soldiers, placed guards of about 12 men under a Non-Commissioned Officer, that he was sent down by the King to relieve them of duty. The same orders were given to the Subedar by myself to pay no attention to such authority. At this time, the Native Officer who had come down with a strong detachment of the King's Soldiers, placed guards of about 12 men under a Non-Commissioned Officer over each gate of the Magazine. These men took up their posts in regular military style, posted their arms, received their orders, and behaved altogether like regular soldiers. They were all in the full uniform of the King. This was some time between 10 and 11 in the morning, about an hour after which the doorkeeper on the outside of the gate called out that he wished to speak either to Lieutenant Willoughby or myself. We both approached the Gate together, when the man and sentry at the gate both informed us that the King of Delhi had sent people to carry away the whole of the Government stores there on the outside of the gate, and that they were unable to prevent them. To this, neither Lieutenant Willoughby or myself gave any *Answer*; but on looking through the gate we could distinctly see the stores being removed. The men who were employed in this work were common labourers, superintended and controlled by a guard of the King's soldiers in their own regular uniform. Shortly after this, the Subedar of our guard again expressed a wish to see either Lieutenant Willoughby or myself, we accordingly went to him. He told us that a messenger had come from the King to say that if we didn't immediately open the gates, that he would have scaling ladders sent down to scale the wall, and these ladders shortly afterwards arrived, and were placed against the south-eastern turret or corner of the Magazine. The native establishments of the Magazine observing this immediately ascended by a sloped shed on the inside of the wall, gained the ladders, and made their escape out of the magazine. This being done, the mutineers without delay ascended the ladders, and commenced attacking us inside the Magazine, which they continued to do till half past 3 in the evening. As they ascended the ladder, they gained admission into the small turret, and as soon as a sufficient number was collected, and were about descending into the Magazine, we opened on them with grape from four field pieces, using two at a time, and keeping two loaded in reserve. There was only Mr. Buckley and myself to man these guns. Two guns, however, were placed at the other gate of the Magazine double charged, under sub-contractor Crow and Sergeant Edwards; they remained with lighted matches in their hands, with orders from Lieutenant Willoughby not to fire till the gate was forced. Both these men were killed in the Magazine. Another gun was placed on the river face under the charge of Conductor Shaw who escaped to the main guard at the Cashmere Gate, after the Magazine was exploded, and was there shot by a sepoy of the 54th N.I. Lieutenants Willoughby and Raynor were active, going from post to post, giving such orders as were required, superintending the defence, and also personally assisting in it. During the time this was going on, Lieutenant Willoughby and myself frequently went to the gate which was close by, and asked who was leading or commanding the attack, and the same Answer was given us on every occasion, *viz.* a son and grandson of the King's were present organizing the attack on us; but the men who ascended the scaling ladders and entered the Magazine were all sepoys of the 11th and 20th Regiments N.I. Another message at about 1 o'clock came in the King's name to say, that if we did not surrender, he would mine and blow up a part of the wall, which was known to be weak, and so effect an entrance.

It being 4 o'clock, the Court adjourns till 11 a.m. tomorrow.

Day nine: 6 February 1858

The Court reassembled this day in the Hall of Special Audience in the Palace at Delhi.

The President, Members, Interpreter, and Dy. Judge Advocate-General are all present.

The Prisoner, attended by his attorney Ghulam Abbas, is brought into Court.

Captain Forrest, Assistant Commissary of Ordnance, is re-called and reminded of his former oath.

Examined by the Judge Advocate (continued)

Question – You narrated what occurred at the Magazine up to half past 3 o'clock. What ensued after that?

Answer – About that time we had expended the last rounds of ammunition for the field pieces, and the Magazine having been entered in two places, further defence was impossible. Conductor Bucklery had been shot in the arm, and I had been hit twice on the hand. Lieutenant Willoughby, who commanded in the Magazine, had, early in the morning made arrangements, to enable us to blow up the Magazine, should circumstances render such an extreme measure necessary, and now at half past 3 p.m., seeing the moment had arrived to do so, he ordered preconcerted signal to be made; which was done by Mr. Conductor Buckley turning to where Conductor Scully was standing, and lifting his hat. Conductor Scully, seeing this, at once fired the Train, and the Magazine was blown up that same second with a fearful explosion, killing hundreds of the natives about. Fragments of the building were said to have been thrown half a mile and upwards, and several European women and children who had fled to the Magazine were killed and severely injured. Conductor Scully was himself so dreadfully wounded that his final escape was impossible. I saw him after the explosion, but his face and head were so burnt and contused, that I don't think life could have long remained in him. I have only to add to this that not one man of the Native Establishments in the Magazine (the Bengalee writer excepted), remained true to us. They all took the first opportunity of escaping with the arms given to them for the purpose of aiding us in the defence of the Magazine. Lieutenant Willoughby and myself escaped to the main guard at the Cashmere Gate. Lieutenant Raynor and Mr. Buckley escaped in another direction, and finally reached Meerut; all the remainder were killed, either by the explosion or after quitting the Magazine. Lieutenant Willoughby was killed two or three days afterwards, on the road to Meerut.

Question – Did the ladder brought to scale the Magazine appear to be new, or made purposely for that object?

Answer – I could only see a foot of the ladder that reached above the walls, so am unable to *Answer* these points.

Question – Was there anything unusual in the dress or conduct of any of your Native Establishment at the Magazine before the outbreak, from which it may be informed that they were cognisant of what was going to occur?

Answer – I noticed nothing in the dress of the men; but their behaviour for several days previous to the outbreak was insolent and overbearing, especially that of those who were Mahommedans. Mr. Buckley and I had both remarked this, and spoken to each other about it. On the morning of 11th May, when I went to the Magazine, I remarked that the Sirdars and Durwans were well dressed, better than I had ever seen them before; also the magazine men did not appear in their usual working dress, but were much cleaner. This I remarked at the time to Lieutenant Willoughby, who coincided with me, and said the circumstances had struck him also.

Question – Have you any reason to suppose that any of your Native Establishment at the Magazine had been in correspondence on the subject of the cartridges with the Sepoys of the Army?

Answer – I had no suspicion of such a circumstance while I was at Delhi; but on reaching Meerut, and going into Hospital about the 19th of May on account of my wounds, I was asked by the Artillery Hospital Sergeant there whether there had been a clever native at the head of the Magazine Establishment at Delhi. I told him there was, and mentioned one in particular, *viz.* Karim Bakhsh, who was an intelligent man and also a good scholar capable of writing Persian well. The Sergeant then said to me that a native had been to him that morning and informed him, that someone in the Magazine at Delhi had been sending circulars to all the native Regiments, to the effect that the cartridges prepared in the magazine had been smeared with a composition of fat, and that they were not to believe their European officers, if they said anything in contradiction of it. This man, Karim Bakhsh, was very active during the time the natives were attacking the magazine, in communicating with them, and so suspicious did his whole conduct seem that Lieutenant Willoughby ordered me to remove him from the gate, adding that I was to shoot him if he attempted to return to it. This man has since been hung for his treacherous conduct on that occasion.

Cross-examined by the Prisoner

Question – What kind of uniform did the men wear whom you say were my soldiers, and went to claim possession of the Magazine on my account?

Answer – They wore a blue dress with a forge cap and a small design in brass, of a gun on it. the uniform was such as I have seen for the last 30 years worn by your Artillery soldiers, and these men, when asked who they were, with one voice exclaimed, that they were your soldiers.

Examined by the Court

Question – Have you ever ascertained where the scaling ladders were brought from?

Answer – No, I have not.

The witness withdraws.

Makhan, a mace-bearer of Captain Douglas, is called into Court, and duly affirmed.

Examined by the Judge Advocate

Question – Were you in attendance on Captain Douglas on the 11th of last May?

Answer – Yes, I was present on that morning at the entrance into Captain Douglas' apartments.

Question – What did you witness on that occasion?

Answer – About 7 o'clock a Cavalry soldier rode up to the Lahori Gate of the Palace, and demanded admittance to the interior, which the guard at the gate refused. He however persisted, and a report was immediately made to Captain Douglas, who at once went down to enquire into the matter. Captain Douglas asked the man what he wanted, when he replied that he had mutinied at Meerut, and arriving at Delhi had come to the guard for a drink of water and a pipe. Captain Douglas gave orders to seize him, when he immediately galloped off. Returning from the gate, Captain Douglas was yet in the covered way, when a messenger sent by the King met him and reported that a number of Troopers had arrived, and were collected under the lattices of the Palace. Hearing this, Captain Douglas came on at once to the Hall of Audience, and going to the balcony asked the Troopers what they wanted there. One of them replied, 'We have mutinied at Meerut, and have come here for justice'. Captain Douglas said, 'Go to the old Fort of Firozshah, and you shall have justice'. After this, Captain Douglas returned to the Lahori Gate of the Palace, where he heard that Mr. Fraser was engaged in making arrangements at the Calcutta Gate, accompanied by the principal Police Officers of the City, and the guard allowed for the protection of the Agency, and immediately went on to join Mr. Fraser. I and the chaprassy present went with him. At the Calcutta Gate were collected Mr. Fraser, Mr. Hutchinson, and two other gentlemen whose names I do not know. Mr. Fraser was directing the chief Native Police officer of the City to take two of his Sowars and see that there was no laxity in the arrangements at the Gates. While he was thus engaged, four or five Cavalry troopers were seen approaching at full speed with drawn swords from the direction of the Palace. One of them approached and fired his pistol at Mr. Fraser, who immediately jumped out of his buggy, while Bukhtawar Singh, chaprassy, took a musket from the Police Guard at the gate, and handed to his master. The musket was loaded, and Mr. Fraser shot the Trooper dead on the spot. This dispersed the man's comrades, who, however, before making off, wounded Mr. Hutchinson in the arm. An excessive crowd having by this time collected, Captain Douglas jumped into the Fort ditch, and was severely hurt in the feet and back by so doing. Mr. Fraser then came to the Lahori Gate of the Palace in his buggy, while Captain Douglas and Mr. Hutchinson walked along in the ditch of the Fort. On reaching the gate Captain Douglas had to be assisted out, and being considerably hurt, asked to be taken into the room called the Kuliyat Khana till he should recover a little from the shock he had received. In the meantime, the Reverend Mr. Jennings came down to him, and he and Mr. Hutchinson conveyed him to the apartments over the gate. At this time Mr. Fraser remained below, trying to suppress the disturbance, and while thus engaged, I noticed that Haji lapidary cut him down with a tulwar, and almost at the same instant some of the King's servants cut at him with swords till he was dead. I was at the head of the stairs, and this was perpetrated at the foot of them. One of Mr. Fraser's murderers was an Abyssinian. After this, they made a rush to the upper apartments, when I immediately ran round by another door, and closed the door at the top of the stairs. I was engaged in shutting all the doors when the crowd who had found entrance by the southern stair, having forced one of the doors on that side, came and gave admission to the men who had assisted in murdering Mr. Fraser. These immediately rushed into the apartments where the gentlemen, *viz.* Captain Douglas, Mr. Hutchinson and Mr. Jennings had retired, and attacking them with swords, at once murdered them and the two young ladies. On this, I ran down the staircase. As I got to the bottom, I was laid hold of by one Mamdoh, a bearer in the service of the King, who said, 'Tell me where Captain Douglas is, you have concealed him'. He forced me upstairs with him. I said, 'You have yourselves killed all the gentlemen already;' but on reaching the room where Captain Douglas was, I saw that he was not quite dead. Mamdoh perceiving this also, hit him with a bludgeon on the forehead and killed him immediately. I saw the other bodies including those of the two ladies. Mr. Hutchinson was lying in one room, and the bodies of Captain Douglas, Mr. Jennings and the two young ladies in another, on the floor, with the exception of that of Captain Douglas which was on a bed. A gentleman had arrived that morning travelling from Calcutta, and he was killed somewhere in the direction of the Delhi Gate of the Palace, he having tried to escape on that side. All the murders were perpetrated within a quarter of an hour after Mr. Fraser's death, and it was now between 9 and 10 a.m. After the death of the gentlemen, the crowd began plundering their property, and fearing for myself, I ran off to my own house in the city, and never returned to the Palace till after the recapture of Delhi.

Question – Did you accompany Captain Douglas when he went from the covered way in the Palace to the Hall of Special Audience, and, if so, did he at that time have any interviews or conversation with the Prisoner?

Answer – Yes, I accompanied Captain Douglas, following him at a distance of about two paces, and can aver that he had neither interview nor conversation with the King of any kind, and that he returned to his own apartments without having spoken to him at all.

Question – Can you positively affirm that, from the time Captain Douglas rose in the morning of the 11th of May to the hour of his death that same morning, he had neither interview nor conversation with the prisoner?

Answer – I can and do positively affirm that he had neither interview nor conversation with the King on the morning.

Question – Did any other servant of Captain Douglas accompany him to the Hall of Special Audience with yourself?

Answer – Yes, Bukhtawar Singh and Kishan Singh, messengers, were also with us.

Cross-examined by the Prisoner

Question – Did Captain Douglas in your hearing require that the gate under the prisoner's sitting-room should be opened, so that he might go and speak to the mutinous cavalry below?

Answer – Yes he did; he said to us: 'I shall go down to the Mutineers', and we dissuaded him from doing so.

Question – Was not the Prisoner in the Hall of Devotion when Captain Douglas passed on to the balcony, and in doing so did not the latter go through the usual form of salutation to the King?

Answer – Yes, the King was there, and Captain Douglas saluted him at a distance, and passed on, but did not speak to him.

Question – How far did Captain Douglas pass from the King?

Answer – About 15 paces.

Question – Did you hear the prisoner dissuading Captain Douglas from going down to the Troopers standing under the lattices?

Answer – No, I did not.

Question – Did anything pass between Ahsanullah Khan and Captain Douglas that morning?

Answer – Yes, when Captain Douglas returned hurt by his fall, Ahsanullah Khan went up to his room, I was not present at the interview, and don't know what passed between them.

Question – Do you know whether Ahsanullah Khan went to Captain Douglas of his own accord, or was he sent for?

Answer – I don't know.

Question – When Captain Douglas came to the palace did any conversation take place between him and Ahsanullah Khan or myself or any other of the King's servants?

Answer – I think not; but I did not observe closely.

The witness withdraws.

It being 4 o'clock, the Court adjourns till 11 a.m. on the 8th instant.

Day ten: 8 February 1858

The Court reassembled this morning at 11 a.m. in the Hall of Special Audience at the Palace at Delhi, pursuant to adjournment of Saturday.

The President, Members, Interpreter, and Dy. Judge Advocate-General are all present.

The Prisoner, attended by his attorney, Ghulam Abbas, is brought into Court.

Sir Theophilus Metcalfe is called into Court and duly sworn.

Examined by the Judge Advocate

Question – Some short time before the outbreak in May last was there any paper stuck up on the walls of the Jama Masjid, purporting to be a proclamation from the King of Persia?

Answer – Yes, it was a small dirty piece of paper with a naked sword and shield depicted one on the right and the other on the left of it, and the purport of it was that the King of Persia was about to visit this country, and he called upon all the faithful followers of the prophet Muhammad to join with him in extirpating the English infidels, and offering landed estates and other large rewards to all who would do so; it was further stated that there were 500 men in Delhi at the time of putting up the placard, who were devoted to his interest.

Question – Was there any allusion in it to the effect that the Shiah sect and Sunni sect of Mahommedans should forget their differences, and make common cause against the English?

Answer – No, I don't think there was.

Question – Was the document palpably a false one in purporting to come from the King of Persia?

Answer – Yes I think so.

Question – How long did it remain on the walls of the Jama Masjid?

Answer – About three hours. It was put up there at night. I don't know the exact date, but was about six weeks before the outbreak, and I supposed it may have remained up about three hours; in the morning a concourse of people was collected round it, and on hearing of this I had it taken down.

Question – Did it, as far as you are aware of, excite much discussion or interest among the natives of Delhi?

Answer – No.

Question – Was any effort made to trace where it came from?

Answer – None; it was considered altogether too contemptible. Any disaffected person in the city might have put such a paper, and to have made a fuss about it, would only have been investing with undue importance.

Question – From any other source or cause had you any reason to suppose that about this time there was any unusual amount of disloyalty to the English government among the population of Delhi?

Answer – No, not among the people of Delhi; but they were perfectly aware of the want of fidelity in the Sepoy Army, and the subject was frequently discussed. As an instance, it was currently reported, about 15 days before the outbreak, that an anonymous petition had been presented to the Magistrate stating that the Cashmere Gate of the City would be taken out of the possession of the English. This gate being our chief stronghold in the city, and main connection with the cantonments of Delhi, it would naturally be the first point seized in any attempt at insurrection in the city, and it was also the only gate at which there was any military guard, the importance of it, therefore, in a strategically point of view, must have been obvious to all. This petition was never received; but the current report about it was indicative of what was then occupying the thoughts of many of the Natives. As a further proof of the feeling then existing, a Sidi of the King, telling him, as an inducement to do so, that before the hot weather was over, the Russians would have come to India, and the Government of the English be at an end. The Risaldar communicated this to me: his name is Everett. He speaks English, and is partly of European extraction. He also informed me that about six months before the King had sent an emissary to Russia. This Risaldar is now at Belaspur.

Question – Can you give the Court any information about the chapaties which were circulated from village to village some months before the outbreak, and has it been ascertained how they originated, or what was the purport of their being circulated?

Answer – There is nothing but conjecture regarding them; but the first suggestion made by the natives in reference to them was, that they were thus sent about in connection with some sickness that prevailed; but this clearly an error, as I took the trouble of ascertaining that these chapaties were never sent into any Native States, but were confined always to government villages; they were spread through only five villages of the Delhi territory, when they were immediately stopped by authority, and they never proceeded further up-country. I sent for the men who had brought them from the District of Bulandshahr, and their apology for circulating them was that they believed it to be done by order of the English Government, that they had received them elsewhere, and had but forwarded them on. I believe the meaning of the chapaties was not understood in the Delhi District; but originally they were to be taken to all those who partook of one kind of food, connecting a body of men together in contradistinction to those who lived differently and had different customs. I think these chapaties originated at Lucknow, and were no doubt meant to sound a note of alarm and preparation, giving warning to the people to stand by one another on any danger menacing them.

Question – Did you ever hear that the subject of the advance of the Persian upon Herat was much discussed among the natives?

Answer – Yes, very much so; and frequently in connection with the idea of Russian aggression upon India. Every native newspaper had, at this time, its correspondent in Cabul, and there was a constant communication kept up with the North, every newspaper having its weekly quota of information from thence.

Question – So you know where the Sidi who tried to induce Mr. Everett to abandon Government service now is?

Answer – Yes; he was killed at Arab Serai.

Question – Can you give the Court any other information relative to any agitation that about this time prevailed among the sepoys or native population of Delhi?

Answer – Yes; I know that about five or six weeks before the outbreak it was currently reported in the lines of the sepoys, and much discussed among them, that 100,000 Russians were coming from the North, and that the Company's Government would be destroyed, in fact the idea of a Russian invasion was universally prevalent.

Question – Are you aware whether the king of Delhi, his relatives or other adherents had any secret or treasonable correspondence or communications with the Company's Native Army at any time before the outbreak?

Answer – No, I cannot speak to any such point.

Question – Do you know whether the king of Delhi, his relatives or other adherent had any secret or treasonable correspondence or communications with the Company's Native Army at any time before the outbreak?

Answer – No, I cannot speak to any such point.

Question – Do you know whether the King of Delhi, his relatives or other adherent had any secret or treasonable correspondence or communications with the Company's Native Army at any time before the outbreak?

Answer – I have heard that he did, but cannot speak positively.

The Prisoner declines to cross-examine.

The witness withdraws.

Hasan Askari, Pirzada, is called into Court and duly affirmed.

Examined by the Judge Advocate

Question – Were you in Delhi at the time of the outbreak, and, if so, what was your occupation?

Answer – Yes, I was at Delhi; my occupation was that of a priest, and on one occasion when the King was sick, and had other priests to pray for him, he eventually sent for me. I went through some prayers and afterwards breathed on him, and the King recovering, used afterwards frequently to send for me, but finding this inconvenient, I begged that I might not be called for in future, and the King then promised with an oath that he would send for me only when he should be seriously unwell.

Question – Did you know a man called Sidi Kambar, a servant of the King?

Answer – I knew several of the Abyssinians amongst the armed attendants of the King by sight; but I knew by name only two or three of the King's servants; Sidi Kambar was not one of them.

Question – It has been given in evidence before this Court that you entrusted an Abyssinian of the name of Sidi Kambar, a servant of the King, with letters from the King of Delhi to the King of Persia; what do you know about this?

Answer – I know nothing of the matter whatever.

Question – It has been given in evidence that you professed to have the power of prophecy, that you could interpret dreams, that you pretended to have been audibly addressed from heaven, and also that you claimed miraculous power: to the truth of this the Prisoner has himself assented; what have you to say in reference to these subjects?

Answer – I call god to witness that I never pretended to anything of the kind.

Question – What made you, as you say, breathe upon the king; did you suppose that your breath had any curative effect?

Answer – It is written in our book that when a man prays for another and then breathes on him, it is likely to have a beneficial effect.

Question – Did you ever tell the King that you had had a dream about a hurricane from the West, or any other quarter, coming upon India, devastating the land with a flood, which would bear up the King and annihilate the English?

Answer – God knows, I never had such a dream, nor did I ever say so; but people from the Palace used frequently to come to me, telling me that they had been having dreams of that kind. I told them it was all a fallacy, and that I had no faith in dreams myself.

Question – When did you leave the city of Delhi, and what has been the reason of your concealing yourself till discovered by the police?

Answer – When it became generally known that the city was to be carried by assault, it was understood that the inhabitants were required to leave the place, and they began to flock out in crowds. I went out too. I first went out and stayed at Shahr Mirza-ud-din, till told to go away from that also. I next went to the Kutb, and from that to Garhi Harsaru, where I fell sick. I also went to other places till I reached Laknowti, where I heard that a search was being made for me at Gangoh. I accordingly decided on going there of my own accord, and went. On intelligence reaching of my brethren there that I was coming, the Troopers hearing of my being in the vicinity came out and seized me while I was at my prayers in the shrine of the Imam Sahib.

The Prisoner declines to cross-examine.

The witness withdraws.

Bukhtawar Singh, Chaprassy, in the service of the Government, is called into Court and duly affirmed.

Examined by the Judge Advocate

Question – Were you in Delhi on the 11th of May last?

Answer – Yes, I was.

Question – Relate what you witnessed on that occasion.

Answer – I was the servant on duty supervising the repairs of the Fort ditch, and was going with the account book for Captain Douglas' inspection. I was on my way when a Trooper came galloping up from the direction of Calcutta Gate. The Trooper had not reached the Palace gate when I observed that Captain Douglas was standing there. I saw Captain Douglas speaking to the man; but before I reached the palace Gate myself the Trooper turned his horse and rode off. Captain Douglas told me to go up to his apartments and said that he was going to the interior of the Palace and should return immediately. Captain Douglas did so, and I stayed at the gate, Makhan, Kishan Singh and others accompanied him. Captain Douglas had hardly gone when Mr. Fraser arrived in his buggy and enquired for him. Mr. Fraser alighted and walked on through the covered way up to the opening. He then said to me he was going to the Calcutta Gate, and that I was to tell Captain Douglas so on his return. I then myself proceeded in the direction of the King's apartments and met Captain Douglas returning in a state of excitement. I gave him Mr. Fraser's message. Captain Douglas went to the Lahori Gate of the Palace, and told the native officer on guard there to close it, which was done. Captain Douglas at the same time gave orders that no crowd was to be allowed to assemble on the Bridge leading into the Palace. Just about this time an officer of the King's, styled a Captain, also came there from the direction of the main street of Delhi. The gate had been closed and Captain Douglas' buggy was inside, so he directed me to ask this native officer for his buggy that he might go in as far as the Calcutta Gate, whither Captain Douglas proceeded in it, I occupying the seat behind. At the Calcutta Gate, we found Mr. Fraser, Mr. Nixon, Head Clerk, and four or five other gentlemen. The gate was closed after a short time. Mr. Fraser and Captain Douglas got into the buggy together, and were returning to the Palace accompanied by the other gentlemen on horseback, but had not proceeded far when four or five Troopers came galloping up at full speed from the direction of the Ellenborough Tank. About this time, there was a general cry that the Troopers had come. On reaching the party of gentlemen, one of the Troopers wounded Mr. Hutchinson in the arm with a pistol shot; the others also fired, but without effect. On this, Mr. Fraser and Captain Douglas both got out of the buggy and went out of the way of the mutineers, and stood by the guard room of the Constabulary Force at the Gate; two more gentlemen joined them there. Mr. Fraser got a musket from the Constabulary Force, and shot one of the Troopers. This checked the others, and they turned and fled. A great crowd had by this time collected, and Captain Douglas and another gentlemen jumped into the Fort ditch, along which they came on to the Palace Gate, Mr. Fraser and others coming by the road; but there was such confusion at the time, I can't say how. Captain Douglas was in a fainting state from the injuries he had received from jumping into the ditch, and we accordingly laid him on a bed in the Kuliyat Khana. In a short time Mr. Jennings, the clergyman, came down, and at his suggestion Captain Douglas was taken up to the apartments above the gate, where he was placed on a bed, Mr. Jennings sending the servants away, and telling them not to crowd about the place. We then received an order to go for the King's physician, and Abdullah, Chaprassy, fetched him accordingly. The physician Ahsanullah Khan had just left, when we servants who were sitting there saw five Mahommedans, King's servants, coming along the covered way calling out 'Din'. Just at this time, Mr. Fraser happened to come down to the foot of the stairs, and these men immediately attacked him and killed him with their swords. While this was happening on the north side of the gate, a mixed crowd, armed with swords, bludgeons, & c., ran up the stairs on the south side, and gained the apartments above, those assembled on the north side joining them there. By this time everyone tried to make his own escape, and I did so with the rest. From that date, I never came to the palace till I returned to Delhi from Jabbu-ka-Katla. I should mention that at the commencement of the attack the crowd was headed and urged on by a Mussalman Havaldar of the 38th Native Infantry, who was one of the guard at the Lahori Gate of the palace. I know nothing more.

Kishan Singh, Chaprassy of the Government, is called into Court, and duly affirmed.

Examined by the Judge Advocate

Question – Were you present in Delhi on the morning of the 11th of May last?

Answer – Yes, I was in attendance on Captain Douglas.

Question – Were you present when Captain Douglas went in the direction of the King's apartments to speak to the mutinous Cavalry beneath the balcony; and, if so, can you state whether Captain Douglas spoke to the king or not on the occasion?

Answer – Yes, I was present, and there was some little conversation between Captain Douglas and the King the latter advised him to go down among the Mutineers, and as Captain Douglas was going away, the prisoner requested that his own servants, in reference to the gates having been closed, might not be denied admittance to the Palace.

Question – How far was Captain Douglas from the King when this was said?

Answer – He was passing by, and did not stop to speak; he may have been about four paces, as the King had come out of his Hall of Devotion, and was standing by the doorway.

Cross-examined by the Prisoner

Question – On returning, did Captain Douglas go by the passage nearest the Hall of Special Audience, or the other one?

Answer – He went by that next to the Hall of Devotion.

Question – Did not the Prisoner remark that he had been very comfortable under the English Government?

Answer – No, he did not speak in allusion to the Government, but to the attentions he had received personally from Captain Douglas, who he said had been kind to him.

Question – Did Captain Douglas make a request to the prisoner to be allowed to go down to the Cavalry beneath the balcony, and, if not, how did the Prisoner learn that he wished to do so?

Answer – I don't remember; it occurred nine months ago; but Captain Douglas expressed a wish to have the gate below opened.

It being 4 o'clock the Court adjourns till 11. a.m., tomorrow.

Day eleven: 9 February 1858

The Court reassembled this morning at 11 a.m., in the Hall of Special Audience in the Palace at Delhi, pursuant of adjournment of yesterday.

The President, Members, Interpreter, and Dy. Judge Advocate-General are all present.

The Prisoner, attended by his attorney Ghulam Abbas, is brought into Court.

Chuni, News-writer for the public, is brought into Court, and duly affirmed.

Examined by the Judge Advocate

Question – Were you present in Delhi on the morning of the 11th of May last?

Answer – Yes, I was at my house.

Question – Did you witness the soldiers coming from Meerut on that day; if so, state all that you know relative to it?

Answer – No, I did not see them coming; but hearing that the City gates were being closed, I went out to see what was happening; and on my coming into the Chandni Chowk street I saw the chief police officer of the city busy having the shops closed. I heard from him that Sir Theophilus Metcalfe was similarly engaged. I went with the crowd in the direction of the Calcutta Gate, and there saw Mr. Fraser and four or five other gentlemen. Mr. Fraser's personal guard of Jhajjar Troopers was with him. Mr. Fraser went to the top of the gate accompanied by another gentlemen and Sharif-ul-Hak, the chief police officer of the city, and at this moment the police officer of the second class at the Sabzi Mandi. After a while Mr. Fraser came down and dispersed the force present, by telling the Jhajjar Trooper, to fall in and form, and at the same time made the Constabulary Guard form and draw their swords, himself taking a position between them. This had just been done when about seven Troopers, and two men mounted on camels, galloped up by the road along the palace from the direction of Daryaganj, and immediately on coming within pistol shot distance, the whole party fired at the European gentlemen at the gate. On this, the crowd dispersed in all directions, and I also went home, I observed, however, before leaving, that the Jhajjar Sowars made no resistance but deserted Mr. Fraser, and fled immediately when the Troopers came down. After that I did not leave my house till evening, and know nothing of the further incidents of that day.

Question – When you went down to the Calcutta Gate was a large crowd already assembled there?

Answer – There were at least 400 or 500 people collected in the small space known as the grape-garden.

Question – At what hour was this?

Answer – It was near 9; but I can't speak with certainty as to the time.

Question – What was it, do you suppose, that made such a number of people collect there, the quarter not being one of traffic?

Answer – The unusual stir caused by the closing of the Gate led to the collecting of the rabble there, the crowd being increased by the bathers from the river hurrying to get in before the gates should be closed.

Question – You say you were a News-writer, you consequently ought to be well informed on what was passing; do you believe that no information had been given to many of the people a day or two before of what was likely to occur on the 11th?

Answer – I heard nothing of a preconcerted outbreak arranged particularly for the 11th of May; but there was considerable agitation and excitement in the City, consequent, first, on a paper purporting to be a proclamation from the King of Persia, and, secondly, on the reports which arrived of the burning of the Bungalows at Ambala, and of the reported disaffection of the Troops in consequence of their being required to use greased cartridges.

Question – Did you edit a paper of your own, and, if so, what was the title of it?

Answer – I did edit a paper, and headed in Delhi News; but it was not known by that title or any other; it was a mere explanation of the contents. I wrote it daily, and took the manuscript round and read it to my subscribers.

Question – Used you to file copies, and, if so, have you any in your possession now?

Answer – I did file the originals regularly, both before and after the outbreak. I succeeded in preserving all those issued since the 11th of May by building them up in a wall, and on the recapture of Delhi I made up any deficiencies with the assistance of Nandkishwar, and, putting them in a complete form I made them over to Colonel Burn, the Military Governor of Delhi, who had them translated.

Question – How many Jhajjar Sowars had Mr. Fraser with him on the 11th of May?

Answer – Including Officers, the Guard comprised 2 or 3 and 20 men, and the whole of them were apparently with Mr. Fraser when he was attacked.

Question – You have said that all these men, though in regular formation at the time, turned and fled on the approach of five or six Cavalry Troopers: to what do you attribute this; do you believe that these men had previous information of what was going to happen?

Answer – My opinion is that they had no previous knowledge on the subject; the Mutineers calling out 'Din Din'. The Jhajjar men acted on the impulse of the moment in deserting Mr. Fraser.

Question – You did not previously state that they had called out anything, how is it you forgot to do so?

Answer – It is 8 months ago since all this happened; as the different incidents come to my recollection I mention them. When I left, the Troopers were calling 'Din Din', and were assuring the crowd on both sides that they would not harm or molest any of the natives.

Question – What were the general points of information of news you used to give in your papers previous to the 11th of May; did any of the articles ever refer to the Native Army, or the disaffection supposed to exist in it?

Answer – My paper used to contain articles on all subjects of general interest, and all information that I could glean from printed papers. I remember on some few occasions having alluded to the cartridge Question, and the mutinous spirit evident by the Army in connection with them.

Question – Do you remember ever writing any articles on the advance of the Persians upon Herat?

Answer – I don't remember particularly having done so; but generally I used to insert such news concerning Persia as I was able to obtain from the journals of the city printed in Persian.

Question – As you read these articles yourself to your subscribers, you must know which generally excited the greatest interest. Was the disaffection supposed to exits among the sepoys much attended to?

Answer – It caused no excitement among the Hindus; but the Mahommedans took a marked interest in the news about Persia, and used to go about exulting and boasting that the Persians were coming, and would do this, that, and the other. As regards the general disaffection of the Troops, the Mahommedans only seemed affected by it, and certainly appeared to be very much excited and interested.

Question – At the time the Persians were said to be coming, was there much talk also regarding the Russians?

Answer – Yes, they were both spoken of; but the Persians more frequently so.

Question – Were there any native newspapers circulated at Delhi whose general tone and tenor were adverse to the British Government?

Answer – There was one such paper, a weekly, published by Jamal-ud-din, the article in which evinced decided enmity against the Government; it was called the *Sadikul-Akhbar*, or the *Authentic News*.

Question – Had this paper a great circulation, and was it a printed one?

Answer – It had a circulation of some 200 copies in and out of the City of Delhi, and lithographed.

Question – Did this paper confine itself to its weekly publication, or did it sometimes issue Extracts on particular news arriving?

Answer – Yes, on occasions of important intelligence arriving, Extracts were issued.

Question – Among whom or what class of men had this paper its chief circulation?

Answer – It had an equal circulation amongst all classes capable of reading, without distinction of caste.

Question – Two hundred appears a very small number of copies for so populous a place as Delhi; is it customary among the natives to read their papers among knots of friends if assembled to hear the news, and does one copy or a paper suffice for several families?

Answer – Yes, it has been the custom among the subscribers to circulate their copies amongst their relations and friends.

Question – Was the *Authentic News* considered the leading journal in Delhi, and what was its circulation as compared with others?

Answer – Yes, it was considered the leading journal; the articles in it were better written, and some being extracted from papers published in English, had more interest for the Mahommedans. I cannot speak what relative circulation it had with others; but the copies of it sold were certainly much more numerous than of any other native paper.

Question – You have mentioned it was very hostile in tone to the British Government, can you recollect the subject of any particular articles which evinced this feeling?

Answer – I cannot remember any particular article in which such feeling was more conspicuously evinced than in others; but in those relating to Persia and the Russians, the style and tone of composition was always hostile, and very bitterly so.

Question – Did you ever hear of any anonymous petition being sent to the Magistrate to the effect that an attack was to be made upon the Cashmere Gate, and that it was to be wrested from the possession of the English?

Answer – No, I never heard any report of the kind.

Question – Do you recollect the circumstances of the chapaties being circulated from village to village?

Answer – Yes, I remember hearing of it before the outbreak.

Question – Was this subject discussed in the native newspaper; and, if so, what was considered the meaning of it?

Answer – Yes, it was alluded to, and it was supposed to portend some coming disturbance, and was moreover understood as implying an invitation to the whole population of the country to unite for some secret object afterwards to be disclosed.

Question – Do you know whence these chapaties originated, or to what quarter general opinion among the natives attributed them?

Answer – I have no knowledge as to where they were first started; but it was generally supposed that they came from Karnal and Panipat.

Question – Do you know whether a copy of the *Authentic News* used to be sent to the inmates of the palace?

Answer – Yes, several copies used to be sent to the palace; but I do not know by whom they were taken.

Question – Was a Court Journal kept by order of the Prisoner during the rebellion?

Answer – Yes, one was kept, and it was published at the Royal Lithographic press in the palace; before the outbreak it contained chiefly items of intelligence connected with the palace, but other matters too were occasionally admitted to it. It was called the Suraj-ul-Akhbar or the Sun of Intelligence.

Question – Were you present in the palace on the occasion of any Europeans being massacred?

Answer – I was. One morning about five or six days after the outbreak on the 11th of May I heard at my house that there was a great disturbance going on in the palace. I accordingly proceeded there, and entering by way of the Delhi Gate, I had reached the new palace, when I saw the King's personal armed attendants, and some of the mutinous soldiery were slaying the Europeans. It was about half past 9 or 10 o'clock. At this time, one of the King's servants spoke to me saying, 'you collect news for the English; if you continue to do so, you shall be served in the same way as these have been.' This man's name was Bhika, and he was in the service of Mirza Abdulla, one of the sons of the prisoner.

Question – Where were the Europeans brought from?

Answer – I don't know; but I heard they were brought from the King's kitchen.

Question – Is this kitchen in the same square or courtyard with the King's apartments?

Answer – The King's apartments may be said to be on one side of the palace, and this place called the kitchen, in which the Europeans were imprisoned, was on the opposite side, the intermediate spaces being occupied by the courtyard, in which are the buildings of the Hall of Special Audience and that of Public Audience; the distance from the King's apartments may be 200 or 250 yards.

Question – What kind or rank of people generally occupied this place assigned to European ladies and children?

Answer – The building was used as an office by the King's professor of the Mohammedan Law.

Question – Do you mean to say that such buildings as these ladies and children were confined in were used in any way by persons of rank or importance?

Answer – No, they certainly were not.

Question – By whom then were they used?

Answer – They were partially used as sheds for lumber; and formerly culprits imprisoned by the King, used to be kept there.

Question – Was there any means of guarding the ladies and children there if such had been wished, or is the place open to the entrance of any rabble who might fancy to go in?

Answer – No, it was an open building, without protection or privacy.

Question – Would any native of ordinary respectability not consider it a great indignity to be put there?

Answer – Yes unmistakably; he would consider himself disgraced and dishonoured by being sent there.

Question – Was this the only vacant spot in the palace in which ladies or children could have been kept in confinement?

Answer – There was no scarcity of buildings in which they might have had every comfort.

Question – By whose orders were these Europeans murdered?

Answer – It was done by the King's orders; who else could have given such an order.

Question – Did you see any of the King's sons present on the occasion looking on at the slaughter?

Answer – There was a great crowd; I did not notice any of them. I observed, however, some people standing on the roof of Mirza Mughal's house, and heard that he himself was looking on through the lattices.

Question – Were the Europeans bound with cords before they were murdered?

Answer – I did not notice.

Question – Were they made to sit down in a row before the slaughter commenced?

Answer – I was not able to go up to the spot, and remained in the Trepolia. I could not see the crowd; but after the slaughter had been completed, and the crowd dispersed, when orders came from the King to remove the bodies, and they were being laden on carts, I went and asked the sweepers employed, and learnt from them that 52 people had been killed. The corpses on the ground then were lying in a circle.

Question – How many corpses of men were among the number?

Answer – Only five or six; the rest were women and children.

Question – Do you know what was subsequently done with these bodies?

Answer – Yes, they were taken in two carts in the direction of Salimgarh in order to be thrown into the river in conformity to the Prisoner's orders.

Question – When the massacre had been accomplished were any guns fired as a token or expression of joy on the occasion?

Answer – I heard no guns myself, nor did I hear from anyone else that any had been fired.

It being 4 o'clock, the Court adjourns till 11 a.m. tomorrow.

Day twelve: 10 February 1858

The Court reassembled this day in the Hall of Special Audience in the Palace at Delhi.

The President, Members, Interpreter, and Dy. Judge Advocate-General are all present.

The Prisoner is brought into Court attended by his attorney Ghulam Abbas.

Chuni, the witness of yesterday, is re-called into Court, and examined on his former affirmation.

Examined by the Judge Advocate

Question – Can you give the Court any information about any other persons murdered in other quarters of the City of Delhi?

Answer – I witnessed no other murders but those I have already spoken of; but I heard that some Europeans, about 25, so long as their ammunition lasted, defended themselves in the Kishangarh[69] Rajah's House. On their ammunition failing, they were brought out from an underground apartment, and killed by some of the Mahommedan inhabitants in concert with some of the mutinous troopers.,

Question – Was the King's authority ever proclaimed in Delhi, and if so, when?

Answer – On the 12th of May, the King's orders directing the reopening of the shops was proclaimed by beat of drum, and about two days after the King went out in state, mounted on an elephant, and accompanied by a regiment of Infantry, some guns, his own special armed retainers, and a band of musicians. This was done with the object of having the

69 A princely State in Rajasthan.

shops reopened; he went as far as that part of the main street, where the houses are built, so as to form a crescent on either side, and returned with the same pomp and ceremony as that with which he had set out. There was salute of 21 guns fired on his departure from the Palace, and a similar one on his return to it.

Cross-examined by the Prisoner

Question – Did you ever hear that the mutinous troops which came from Meerut did so at the King's suggestion, or on the impulse of their own wills?

Answer – I have no information on the subject either one way or the other.

Question – You stated yesterday that the building in which the ladies and children were confined was used by the King's Professor of the Mahommedan Law; you afterwards stated that any native of respectability sent there would unmistakably consider himself disgraced and dishonoured by it, how do you reconcile these statements?

Answer – All sorts of people, high and low, used to collect there owing to its being an office; and from this it is evident that it could not have been considered a fit place for the detention of people having any claims to respectability. It was not the residence of the Professor, it was merely where he used to discharge his office duties.

The witness withdraws.

Chuni Lal, Pedlar, is called into Court, and duly affirmed.

Examined by the Judge Advocate

Question – Were you in Delhi on the 11th and 12th of May last?

Answer – Yes, I was, on both dates.

Question – Did you on either of those dates hear the King's authority proclaimed by beat of drum?

Answer – On the 11th of May, about midnight, some 20 guns were fired in the palace. I heard the reports at my house, and next day at about noon a proclamation was made by beat of drum that the country had reverted to the possession of the King.

Question – Did you witness any procession made by the King on an elephant in state?

Answer – No, I left the Palace a few days after the outbreak. I never saw the King's procession; but on one occasion I witnessed the state procession of Mirza Mughal as Commander-in-Chief.

The Prisoner declines to cross-examine.

The witness withdraws.

Gulab, a messenger, is called into Court, and duly affirmed.

Examined by the Judge Advocate

Question – Were you in Delhi at the time the European ladies and children were massacred in the palace in May last, and, if so, did you see them on that occasion?

Answer – Yes, I was, and saw them murdered.

Question – When did you first hear that they were to be killed?

Answer – I heard of it two days before the occurrence; it was said the Europeans would be killed in two days, but I do not recollect what day it was. On the day fixed for the slaughter arriving, great crowds of people were flocking to the Palace at about 10 a.m. I entered with them. On reaching the first courtyard, I saw the prisoners all standing together, surrounded on all sides by the King's special armed retainers, or, what you may term, his bodyguard, and some of the Infantry mutineers. I did not observe any signal orders given; but on a sudden the men just mentioned drew their swords and all simultaneously attacked the prisoners, and continued cutting at them, till they had killed them all. There were at least 100 or 150 men employed in this work of slaughter.

Question – Did anyone make any attempt to save them, or did you ever hear that anyone had interceded for them with the King?

Answer – No, no one made any attempt whatever to save them, nor did I hear that anyone ever intercede with the King on their account.

Question – You have stated that the time for murdering these women was fixed two days previous; was it stated by whose orders they were to be murdered?

Answer – I did not hear whose orders had been issued in the matter; but without orders it could not have happened.

Question – Was it generally understood that the King sanctioned the murder of these women and children?

Answer – This was not known at the time; but people spoke about it, saying 'The prisoners are to be killed the day after tomorrow'.

Question – Was any authority in Delhi capable of giving an order for their murder beyond that of the King?

Answer – There were only two sources from which the order could have emanated, the King and his son Mirza Mughal. I don't know which of them gave the order.

Question – How many Europeans do you suppose were murdered on this occasion, and were they tied previous to being killed?

Answer – I can make no estimate; they were standing together in a line, surrounded by their murderers; but the great portion of the prisoners were children; they were not tied in any way.

Question – Do you know what was done with the bodies.

Answer – No, the Palace was cleared of the crowd by the soldiery immediately after the slaughter, and I never heard what became of the bodies.

Question – Did you witness the murder of any people at the bank?

Answer – Yes, I was witness to the murder of Mr. Beresford and his family. When the bank was attacked by the mutineers and the rabble, Mr. Beresford and his family retired to one of the out-offices for concealment, and when discovered were on the roof of the building. Mr. Beresford was armed with a sword and Mrs. Beresford had a spear. The mutineers being afraid to approach them by the staircase in front, two of the rabbles suggested that they should go round and scale the wall in the rear of the house. Mrs. Beresford struck one of the assailants with a spear and killed him, they were, however, overpowered and all killed. I do not know what number of persons were killed at the bank; but there were several. This occurred on the day of the outbreak at about 12 o'clock.

Question – Were any of the bodies taken away, or were they all killed at once?

Answer – They were all killed immediately; none were retained as prisoners.

Question – Were any of the King's armed retainers among the assailants at the bank?

Answer – No.

Question – Was the King proclaimed as the Reigning sovereign immediately after the outbreak?

Answer – Yes, the proclamation was made by beat of drum on the very day of the outbreak, about three in the afternoon, to the effect that it was now the King's Government.

The Prisoner declines to cross-examine.

Examined by the Court

Question – Do you know why the prisoners were kept so many days in confinement, and was there any reason for appointing any particular day for their murder?

Answer – No, I have no knowledge on either point.

Ahsanullah Khan, the Physician, is re-called and examined on his former affirmation.

Examined by the Judge Advocate

Question – Was a Court diary of occurrences at the Palace kept by the order of the King during the rebellion?

Answer – The Court diary was kept up as usual, according to the custom which had long preceded the outbreak.

Question – Look at this leaf, and see whether you can recognize the handwriting in it?

Answer – Yes, it is in the handwriting of the man who kept the Court diary, and this leaf is a portion of it.

Translation of an Extract from the Court diary for the 16th of May 1857

> 'The king held his Court in the Hall of Special Audience. 49 English were prisoners, and the army demanded that they should be given over to them for slaughter. The King delivered them up, saying "The army may do as they please", and the prisoners were consequently put to the sword. There was a large attendance, and all the Chiefs, Nobles, Officials and Writers presented themselves at the Court, and had the honour of paying their respect'.

Question – Were you present on the 11th of May at Delhi?
Answer – Yes, I was.
Question – Relate what you witnessed on that occasion.
Answer – On the morning of the 16th or Ramzan, alias the 11th of May, at about 3 a.m., a Hindu sepoy of the 38th Regiment of Native Infantry came up to the door of the Hall of Special Audience in the palace, and said to some of the doorkeepers that happened to be on the spot, that the native army at Meerut had mutinied against the State, and were now on the point of entering Delhi; that he and the rest of them would no longer serve the Company, but would fight for their faith. My house is near the palace and close by the Hall of Special Audience, and I was immediately informed by one of the Mahommedan doorkeepers of what the 38th sepoy had said. I had hardly received this information, when the King of Delhi sent for me. I attended on him immediately, and His Majesty said, 'Look, the Cavalry are coming by the road of the Zerjharokha'. I looked and saw about 15 or 20 of the Company's Regular Cavalry, then about 150 yards distant. They were dressed most of them in uniform, but a few had Hindustani clothes on. I immediately suggested to the King to have the gate fastened by which entrance to the palace from the Zerjharokha is obtained, and this had scarcely been done when five or six of the Sowars came up to the closed gate which leads directly under the Saman Burj palace, where the King has his own private residence in close contiguity with the apartments of the Queens and other secluded females of the establishment. The Sowars commenced calling out 'Dohai Badshah' or – 'Help O King! We pray for assistance in our fight for the faith'. The King hearing this, made no response, nor did he even show himself to the men beneath; but told Ghulam Abbas, Shamshir-ud-dowlat, who was also present, to go to Captain Douglas, Commandant of the palace guards, and apprise him of the arrival of the Sowars, and request him to do whatever might be necessary in the case. The King then retired to his

inner apartments, and I went to the Hall of Special Audience, and almost immediately Ghulam Abbas returned accompanied by Captain Douglas. The latter instantly went to the balcony overlooking the Zerjharokha, where the Cavalry still remained, and said to them 'Go away from this: this is the King's Palace, your presence here is an annoyance to the King'. On this, the Cavalry went off in the direction of the Rajghat Gate which gives an entrance to the city immediately to the south of the palace. The King on hearing that Captain Douglas had come, went out and met him in the open space between his private residence and the Hall of Special Audience, when Captain Douglas said to him 'Don't be alarmed, the disturbance shall be put down at once, I will have the men apprehended'. He was going off apparently for this purpose, and requested that the gate under the Saman Burj, which I had closed, might be opened to enable him to go and speak to the Cavalry for the purpose of reasoning with them. The King said: 'You have neither pistols, guns or soldiery with you, your going among these men would be indiscreet'. So Captain Douglas then went off to his own apartments. A very short time subsequently to this, Pran Jamadar, a servant of Captain Douglas, came and said that Captain Douglas wished that I and Ghulam Abbas would go to him. We accordingly went, and on seeing Captain Douglas he said to us I have sprained or hurt my foot. There was another gentleman with him whom I did not recognize; he was lying down on a couch and had a sabre wound on his right arm. Captain Douglas said: 'Send two palanquins with bearers immediately that the English ladies here may be taken to the Queen and placed under her protection'. And just at this time Mr. Simon Fraser, the Commissioner, came into the room and said: 'Get from the King two guns with Artillery and place them at the gateway underneath us'. On this, Mr. Fraser came down from Captain Douglas' apartment above the gateway accompanied by myself and Ghulam Abbas. I and Ghulam Abbas went straight to the King to deliver the above message, and Mr. Fraser stayed at the opening of the gateway. We, with the King's permission, immediately sent the palanquins for the ladies, and also gave instructions about the guns; but shortly after this, information reached us that the Cavalry had entered the palace enclosure by the Lahori Gate where Mr. Fraser wished the guns placed, and over which Captain Douglas had his residence: it was also told us that they had killed Fraser and had gone up to Captain Douglas to kill him. This was instantly confirmed by the return of the palkee bearers, who told us that they had witnessed Mr. Fraser's murder, that his body was in the gateway, and that the troopers had ascended to the upper building for the purpose of murdering those there. The King, on hearing this, gave orders for all the gates of the palace to be closed; but answer was given that the Infantry, *viz.* some of the 38th Native Infantry who were on guard at the palace, would not allow of such being done. After a lapse of some time the Cavalry, to the number of about 50, rode up to the Hall of Special Audience, dismounted and picketed their horses in the adjoining garden. The infantry, I am not sure of what regiments, but I think of all the three Delhi regiments, also came into the palace enclosures, and laid down their beddings in any of the palace buildings that they could make available. The Infantry from Meerut did not reach Delhi till about 2 p.m. of that day; they did not reach Delhi in a body, but came straggling in, and as they arrived joined the Infantry of the Delhi regiments in spreading their bedding over all parts of the palace enclosures. There was no regular Court that day; but the King came out some three or four times to the Hall of Special Audience, where the mutineers were lying about all over the palace: and the mutinous troopers came flocking into the palace the whole day and even after the night set in. The 54th came in the evening, and went off at once to occupy the Salimgarh Fort, where they the next day fixed guns which they brought out of the Magazine for the purpose of checking any advance of European troops from Meerut. For three days constant alarms, and especially at nights, were given that the Europeans were coming, when the bugles sounded and the mutineers got under arms. On the 12th of May, the Prisoner's three sons Mirza Mughal and Mirza Khair Sultan and his grandson Mirza Abu Bakr applied for the principal commands in the army. I represented to the King that they were not of sufficient age and experience for such appointments, nor would they understand any of the duties, and they were much displeased in consequence. The matter remained unending that day. The next day, however, they got Mirza Mendu, Mirza Bakhtawar Shah, and Mirza Abdulla, together with the officers of the army, to join them in their request, and accordingly two days after, they were severally nominated to commands and received dresses of honour.

Question – You have said that on a requisition being made the King sent palanquins for the two ladies in Captain Douglas' apartments; when he heard that they and Mr. Fraser had been all murdered, did he take any steps to secure or punish the murderers?

Answer – No, there was such confusion that nothing was done.

Question – It is in evidence that the King's own special servants murdered Mr. Fraser and different persons in the palace on that day: were these servants continued in pay and employment?

Answer – I never heard that any of the King's servants had joined in the murders; but certainly none of them were ever dismissed on this account.

Question – Do you mean to say that it was not generally known by whom the murders were committed?

Answer – No, it was not generally known, nor did I hear who committed the murders.

Question – Was the slightest investigation ever made on this point?

Answer – No, none whatever.

Question – How many armed retainers did the King possess before the outbreak?

Answer – About 1,200 of all descriptions.

Question – Were these men in different branches of the army, such as Artillery, Cavalry, and Infantry?

Answer – Yes, they were divided into Artillery, Cavalry and Infantry.

Question – How many cannons did the King possess?

Answer – There were six serviceable ones, and I don't know how many others were lying about which were not in use.

Question – How was this force employed on the 11th of May, the day of the outbreak?

Answer – They were distributed in guards at the different gates and other houses of the principal palace officials; some who held appointments in consideration of money advances, seldom attended, but received their monthly stipends and remained at home.

Question – How was it that so many English women and children were brought to the Palace and placed in confinement?

Answer – The mutineers took them in and about the city, and having established their own quarters in the palace, they brought their prisoners in with them too.

Question – Do you mean to say that each man who took an English person prisoner retained the custody of him, or of her, or of the children?

Answer – No, as they brought them in they reported the circumstance to the Prisoner, and in each successive case they were told to take the Europeans to the kitchen and keep them confined there.

Question – Who appointed this kitchen as the place of their confinement?

Answer – The King said that it was a large capacious building, and told the mutineers to keep the prisoners there.

Question – Who commanded the King's armed retainers before the outbreak?

Answer – Mahbub Ali Khan (The Chief Eunuch) virtually did so.

Question – Did any of them go and attack the Magazine on the 11th of May, and, if so, by whose order was it done?

Answer – No, none of them went according to any orders that I heard of; nor do I know of any having gone at all; but some or all of those living out in the city may have gone for all I can say.

Question – Do you know whether any emissary from the King, or any relative of his is at this moment or has been lately at the Court of the King of Persia?

Answer – No, I cannot speak as to the present time; but about two or three years ago, I remember reading in Muhammad Bakr's Gazette, the Mirza Najaf, one of the Prisoner's nephews, had gone to the Persian Court, and had been received by the King of Persia with much courtesy and kindness.

Question – Was this man sent by the King of Delhi?

Answer – I don't know; but this man's brother, two years before, was sent as an ambassador with a great number of papers to the Government at Calcutta.

Question – Cannot you give the Court any information relative to Hasan Askari sending Sidi Kambar to Persia? It is in evidence that you were trusted in all matters of importance, and such as required writing; and it is believed you know all about the matter now alluded to.

Answer – I solemnly, and feeling myself on oath, declare that I have not concealed or misrepresented a single particular. I might have been confided in but still I was a servant; many points of importance were not entrusted to me, for instance, when the King wished to repudiate his wife Taj Mahal, who was by caste a Mahommedan Domni, one of the lowest orders, and to whom he had been reunited in regular marriage, I was not at all consulted; nor was I acquainted with the intrigues going on to secure the succession of Jawan Bakht and other equally important matters. I know nothing of what may have been transacted between the prisoner, Hasan Askari and Sidi Kambar.

Question – Do you know whether the King through his adherents by correspondence, or in any manner whatever, kept up any communication with native officers or soldiers of the Company's Army, before the outbreak?

Answer – No, I don't know that he did; it is possible there may have been a correspondence; but I don't think it is likely there was.

It being 4 o'clock, the Court adjourns till 11 a.m. tomorrow.[70]

Day thirteen: 11 February 1858

The Court reassembled this day at 11 a.m., in the Hall of Special Audience in the Palace at Delhi pursuant of adjournment of yesterday.

The President, Members, Interpreter, and Dy. Judge Advocate-General are all present.

The Prisoner is brought into Court.

Ahsanullah Khan, Physician, is brought into Court, and reminded of his former affirmation.

Examined by the Judge Advocate

Question – Are you aware whether the paper called the *Sadik-ul-Akhbar or Authentic News* was generally perused by the Prisoner before the outbreak?

70 The Court worked normally from 11 a.m. to 4 p.m. Today, the Emperor, though in good mood, felt, on account of his age and sickness, physically exhausted and asked for a 'stimulant' (Martin, *op. cit.*, vol. 3, p. 168). What was the 'stimulant', one may ask here? Well, we do not know. But one thing is certain, it was not opium or any such drug or drink, because he never used them in his life. The guess is, it was some herbal concoction.

Answer – He used not to read it regularly, but occasionally some of the princes army have communicated a portion of its contents.

Question – Did any of the princes appear to take much interest in or attach importance to the articles about Persia, and was it generally represented that the English were being defeated by the Persians?

Answer – I never read the paper myself, but I heard it was generally represented that the English were being defeated by the Persians, and the princes moreover attached importance to this intelligence, and seemed to credit it.

Question – Before the outbreak did the Mahommedans generally believe that the reign of the English was coming to an end, did the princes join in propagating this idea?

Answer – No, I did not hear of any such belief.

Cross-examined by the Prisoner

Question – You said that there were 1,200 soldiers in the King's service; describe the uniform of the three branches of the King's army, and what were the appellations of the different regiments?

Answer – There were two regiments of infantry composed of 500 men each; the colour of their uniform was severally black and brown, the turbans and waistbands of both being red; there were no devices or ornaments about the uniform beyond what was necessary to distinguish the different grades. The artillery consisted of about 40 men; their uniform was dark blue, the turbans and waistbands red; they had no ornaments or devices about their dress; the special guard of the Prisoner was dressed in red coats, with dark blue turbans and waistbands.

The witness withdraws.

Mrs. Aldwell, wife of Alexander Aldwell, a Government pensioner, is called into Court, and duly sworn.

Examined by the Judge Advocate

Question – Were you in Delhi on the 11th of May 1857?

Answer – Yes.

Question – Where were you residing; and at what time did you first hear that the native troops from Meerut had come to Delhi?

Answer – I was residing in the part of the city known as Daryaganj, and I got intimation of the sepoys coming from Meerut between 8 and 9 a.m. on the 11th of May.

Question – Relate all you witnessed on that day.

Answer – One of my saises came and told me that the troops had mutinied and come from Meerut, and had murdered all the Europeans they met with on their way here, and recommended that our carriage should at once be got ready to take us away, as the soldiers had determined on murdering all the Europeans in Delhi also. While I was speaking to the man our next door neighbour Mr. Nowlan confirmed the report that the sais had just brought, and asked if he could speak to Mr. Aldwell. The two consulted together, and as our house was the largest and strongest, it was determined that all the Europeans in the neighbourhood should collect there and defend themselves as long as they could, or till such time as help should arrive. After that Mr. Aldwell and Mr. Nowlan went to the guard at a hospital close by. This guard was composed of Native Infantry sepoys, and Mr. Nowlan and Mr. Aldwell asked them whether they would assist in defending us, adding that the Europeans would, in return, render them all assistance that might be in their power. 'Go and mind your business, and we will mind ours', was the reply given by these sepoys. At this time, shortly after 8 o'clock, the Meerut sepoys had not even crossed the bridge, and could not therefore have communicated with this guard. After this, the Europeans who had by this time collected in our house began barricading the doors, and the women and children were sent upstairs. I think we must have numbered, inclusive of men, women and children, upwards of 30 people. We then saw the mutineers crossing the bridge at about 9 o'clock. A good number of them were cavalry and some infantry: this portion of the mutineers passed close under the walls or parapets of our house, which is immediately on the banks of the river, and some of them fired at one of the gentlemen who was then on the top of the house, this body then went off in the direction of the jail, with the intention, as we supposed, of setting the prisoners free. Shortly after that we heard they had entered the city and were murdering the Europeans wherever they met them. About this time one of the city people, a Mahommedan and a dyer by trade, rushed into our grounds with a drawn sword in his hand, reeking with blood, repeating the *Kalima*, and calling out to know where the Europeans were. Mr. Nowlan asked him who and what he was, and on his not replying, shot him dead. This man was the only one who had entered the grounds, but then 50 or 60 of his followers, city people, collected at our gate. About 11 o'clock, a Mrs. Foulon was brought into our house by a Mahommedan; she had been severely wounded in the head by some of the city people, who had entered and plundered her house. Nothing further of consequence happened till about 3 p.m., when the Magazine blew up. I then requested Mr. Aldwell to let me and my three children leave the house, as the servants told me that the mutineers had gone for the purpose of bringing guns to bear upon it, and I was anxious to obtain concealment elsewhere. Myself and three children then dressed ourselves as natives, and left the house in two native dollies, and were taken to the residence of one of the Kings grandsons, by name Mirza Abdulla. His wife and sister received us kindly, for Mr. Aldwell and myself had known the family before. We remained there till 8 that evening, when Mirza Abdulla came and said he would remove us to a house of greater security, *viz.* to one belonging to his mother-in-law. He removed us there, keeping some of our property with him, saying it would be dangerous for us to take it in the streets, and that I was to send my munshi for it the next morning. I accordingly sent my munshi for this property, *viz.* 200 rupees in money, and some silver plates; but Mirza Abdulla denied having received it, and sent word that if we didn't remove from his mother-in-law's house he would send people down to murder us, and accordingly that evening, at about 6 o'clock, he sent his uncle and some of his servants to see if we had left the house, and if no, to murder us there. I did not see the uncle, but I saw the servants, and they had drawn swords in their hands, when my munshi's mother upbraided, saying, 'Is this the Mirza's hospitality; if this had been his intention, why did he not refuse to receive us? Why promise shelter and safety merely for the purposes of murder'. She also added, 'If you are determined to kill anyone, kill me first; I have eaten the Christian's salt, and cannot now see them murdered'. She also added tauntingly, 'By killing me you will perform a very meritorious action, as I am a Syadni and a Shiah'. This was in allusion to the King's family being Sunnis, and the sect of Sunnis having originally murdered the sons of the prophet or the Syads. The men replied to her that if they were to do so they would be as bad as infidels; but that they were determined to killing all the Christians, and advised all who were not so either to leave the house and let them kill us there, or to turn us out of the house, and they would murder us in the street. It was finally permitted to us to remain till next morning, on condition of our then leaving. During the night, however, my munshi brought my tailor to me; and I asked if he knew of any place where he could take and conceal us. He said that he had heard that Nawab Ahmad Ali Khan was sheltering Europeans, and he would take us there. He went to get the Nawab's conveyance; but when he returned he said the mutineers had already got information of Europeans being concealed in the Nawab's residence, and had brought guns to bear on it; but that he would take us to his own house. He did so; and while we were there, he said that he had heard that several Christians had been taken to the Palace, and that the King had guaranteed their lives there, though he had put them into confinement, and he advised us as the safest place to go there. On Wednesday night, at between 7 and 8, this tailor and one of the cavalry mutineers, by name Kadirdad Khan, escorted us to the Palace. This trooper had formerly received some kindness from the tailor, and on this account agreed to escort us, saying at the time he would not prove ungrateful to him, although they had all taken an oath to murder every European. On reaching the Lahori Gate of the Palace, we were made prisoners by some of the King's police stationed there as a guard. These men took us to Mirza Mughal, who ordered us to be confined with the rest of the European prisoners then in confinement. We were accordingly taken there on Wednesday night, the 13th of May. As far as I can guess, I should say, men, women and children included, there were from 46 to 50 persons imprisoned. Their names, as far as I and my children have been able to recollect them, are according to the following list: Mrs. Scully and three children, Mrs. Glynn, Mrs. Edwards and two children, Mrs. Mollony and two children, Mrs. Sheehan and child, Mrs. Corbet and daughter, Mrs. Staines, Mrs, Cochrane, Miss Staines, Miss M. Hunt, Miss E. Beresford, Miss L. Ryley, Master Richard Shaw, Miss Alice Shaw, Miss Ann Shaw, Mr. Roberts and son, Mrs. Crow, and Mr. Smith. There was one other man whose name I don't know, nor can I recollect the names of the other women and children. We were all confined in one room, very dark, with only one door, and no window or other opening. It was not for the residence of any human being, much less for the number of us that were there. We were very much crowded together, and in consequence of the sepoys and everyone who took a fancy to do so, coming and frightening the children, we were obliged frequently to close the one door that we had, which then left us without light or air. The sepoy used to come with their muskets loaded and bayonets fixed, and ask as whether we would consent to become Mahommedans, and also slaves, if the King granted us our lives; but the King's special armed retainers from which the guard over us was always furnished, incited the sepoys to be content with nothing short of our lives, saying we should be cut up in small pieces, and given as food to the kites and crows. On Thursday, some of the sepoys came and told the ladies that they intended to kill us all by mining and blowing up the Palace. We were very indifferently fed; but on two occasions, the King sent us better food. Nothing further of consequence occurred till Friday afternoon, when one of the King's special servants asked one of the ladies (I think it was Mrs. Staines), if the English were ever restored to power, how they would treat them, and she replied, 'Just as you have treated our husbands and children'. The next morning, between 8 and 9 o'clock, *viz.* on Saturday, the 16th of May, the whole party of the Europeans, with exception of myself, three children, and an old native Mahommedan woman who had been confined with us for giving food and water to some Christians, were taken out and murdered.

Question – How do you know that these people were all murdered, and how was it that an exception was made in favour of yourself and children?

Answer – Before leaving my tailor's house I had a petition written addressed to the King, and was taking it myself in hopes of seeing the king, and being able to present it to him in person; but when I was taken prisoner by the guard at the Lahori Gate, the men composing it took the paper from me; in it I had stated that myself and children were from Cashmere and were Mussalmans. On this account, we had our food given to us separately, and the King's own servants evidently believed we were Mussalman is, as they ate and drank with us. Since the outbreak on Monday I had learnt and had taught my children the Mahommedan confession of faith, and we were all able to repeat it. It was from believing us Mussalmans that our lives were spared. On the morning of the 16th of May, some of the King's special servants, attended by a small number of Infantry sepoys, came and called out to our party, that the Christians were to come out of the building, and that the five Mahommedans were to remain. The women and children began crying, saying they knew they were going to be murdered; but the Mahommedans swore on the Kuran, and the Hindus on the Jumna that such was not the case, that they wanted to give them a better residence, and that the one they were then in would be converted into a Magazine. On this, they went out, were counted; but I do not know the number; a rope was thrown round to encircle the whole group, the same as prisoners are usually kept together with when on the move, and in this manner they were taken out of my sight, and, as I heard, brought under the pepal tree by small reservoir in the courtyard, and there murdered with swords by the King's private servants. None of the sepoys took part in killing them. The privilege, for it was so considered, of murdering them was particularly reserved for the King's own servants, as it was believed by them that killing an infidel would ensure them a place in paradise. I was told of this at the time by the wife of a sweeper, and afterwards when residing in Delhi during the whole time of the rebellion, frequently heard this circumstance confirmed. Two guns were fired immediately after the massacre had been completed, and I was then informed that this was intended as a token of joy. About an hour after the massacre an old man, who used to be known as the Mufti Sahib, came and said to the King's private servants who were guarding us, that he wanted to see the five prisoners who had been saved he told us that our lives had been spared, and told the King's servants to conduct us to some place of safety, but on no account to do it during the day, as the sepoys or city people might murder us. (I may mention that some of them had suspicion of our being Christians.) In the evening we were taken back to my tailor's house, and the following Tuesday we were again made prisoners by the police officer of the quarter where we were hiding. We were brought s prisoners before Mirza Mughal. The police officer informed him that we were Christians in disguise, and he gave orders that we should be executed; but the sepoys of the 38th prevented this being carried into effect, saying they would take us. We were then taken and confined in Captain Douglas' apartments, where we were kept in confinement till the day after the battle of the Hindan, when we were released by the

38th sepoys. When the sepoys, who returned defeated on that occasion, came back to the city, the man began talking despondingly, saying they would have no chance against the English. The Hindu sepoys especially upbraided the Mahommedans, saying: 'This is your first engagement with the English; is this the way you intended to fight for your faith?' They also already spoke in terms of much regret of the turn that affairs had taken, reproached the Mahommedans for having deceived them on pretences of their religion, and seemed to doubt greatly whether the English Government had really had any intention of interfering with their caste. Great numbers of the Hindu sepoys at this time declared that if they could be sure their lives would be spared, they would gladly go back to the service of the Government; but the Mahommedans, on the contrary used to assert that the King's service was much better than that of the English, that the Nawabs and Rajahs would supply the King with large forces, and they must eventually conquer.

Question – During your stay in the city of Delhi, had you any opportunity of observing that there was a marked difference between the bearing of the Mahommedans generally and that of the Hindus in reference to the rebellion?

Answer – Yes, the Mahommedans always seemed glad that the mutiny had taken place, and during the Muharram festival, I heard the Mahommedan women praying, and teaching their children to pray, for the success of their faith, and these prayers were generally accompanied by execrations against the English.

Question – Had the Mussalmans and Hindus quarrels or discussions among themselves on the score of religion when they were in Delhi together?

Answer – I think when the troops first came, the Hindus made the King promise that there should be no oxen killed in the city, and this promise was kept. I believe that not a single ox was killed in Delhi during the whole time of the rebellion. On the festival of the Bakr-Eid, when the Mahommedans usually slaughter an ox, a disturbance was expected; but the Mahommedans refrained from doing so on this occasion. On the morning of the 9th of September I effected my escape from Delhi in native disguise, and, accompanied by my three children and two servants, reached Meerut.

The Prisoner declines to cross-examine.

Examined by the Court

Question – From what has come to your knowledge, do you believe that any European females were treated with great insult and indignity, either by the native soldiery or populace of Delhi?

Answer – Yes.

The witness withdraws.

It being 4 o'clock, the Court adjourns till 11 a.m., tomorrow.

Day fourteen: 12 February 1858

The Court reassembled this morning at 11 a.m. in the Hall of Special Audience in the Palace at Delhi.

The President, Members, Interpreter, and Dy. Judge Advocate-General are all present.

The Prisoner is brought into Court.

Mr. C.B. Saunders, Officiating Commissioner and Agent to the Lieutenant-Governor, is called into Court and duly sworn.

Examined by the Judge Advocate

Question – Can you give the Court any information as to the circumstances under which the Kings of Delhi became subjects and pensioners of the British Government of India?

Answer – Shah Alam, Emperor of Delhi, after having his eyes put out and having suffered every indignity from the hands of Ghulam Kadir, fell into the hands of the Mahrattas in the year 1788. The Emperor, although vested with nominal authority over the city of Delhi, was kept in confinement, more or less rigorous, until the year 1803, when General Lake[71] having seized Aligarh, marched with the British troops against Delhi. The Mahratta Army drawn out at Patparganj 6 miles from Delhi, was attacked by General Kake and utterly routed. The city and fort having been evacuated by the Mahrattas, the Emperor Shah Alam sent a message to General Lake, applying for the protection of the British Authorities, and on 14th September, the date since rendered more memorable by the successful assault in 1857, the British troops entered Delhi: from that time the Kings of Delhi have become pensioned subjects of the British Government[72] and have exchanged the state of rigorous confinement in which they were held by the Mahrattas, to one of more lenient restraint under the British rule. The prisoner succeeded to the titular sovereignty of Delhi in 1837. He had no power whatever beyond the precincts of his own Palace; he had the power of conferring titles and dresses of honour upon his own immediate retainers, but was prohibited from exercising that power on any others. He and the heir-apparent alone were exempted from the jurisdiction of the Company's local courts; but were under the orders of the Supreme government.

Question – Was there any limit to the number of the Prisoner's armed retainers?

71 Gen. Lake (1744–1808) was the C-in-C of the British Army.

72 This is, as already discussed in the Introduction, false. He was never a pensioned subject of the British. See Introduction.

Answer – The Prisoner requested Lord Auckland[73] to be permitted to entertain as many men in his service as he thought proper. The Governor-General, in reply according to permission to his entertaining as many men as he could pay out of the income allotted to him.

Question – Can you state the amount of pension granted by the Government to the Prisoner at the time of the outbreak?

Answer – He was in receipt of a stipend of 1 lakh of rupees per mensem, of which 99,000 rupees were paid at Delhi, and 1,000 at Lucknow to the members of his family there. He also was in receipt of revenue to the amount of 1.5 lakh of rupees per annum from the crown lands, in the neighbourhood of Delhi. He also received a considerable sum from ground-rents of houses and tenements in the city of Delhi.

The Prisoner declines to cross-examine.

The witness withdraws.

Major Paterson, of the 54th Native Infantry, is called into Court and duly sworn.

Examined by the Judge Advocate

Question – Were you in Delhi on the 11th of last May?

Answer – Yes.

Question – Relate what you witnessed on that occasion.

Answer – There was a parade on the morning of the 11th for the purpose of hearing some order, and it passed off as usual without anything occurring to point suspicion of any outbreak being at hand; but about 9 o'clock the regiment was ordered to parade for the purpose of proceeding to the bridge of boats over the Jumna to prevent some mutineers of the 3rd Cavalry from crossing, it being then understood that these men were on their way from Meerut. Arriving on parade I was ordered by the late Colonel Ripley to take two companies, my own (the grenadiers) and No. 1, for the purpose of escorting a couple of guns down. The Colonel directed me to proceed in the first instance to Captain DeTeissier's house for orders, that being on the road down, and Captain DeTeissier told me to take my companies to the Sudder Bazzar, and wait till the guns came. I was there for about three-quarters of an hour, and the guns not coming, I sent my subaltern, Lieutenant Vibert, to ascertain the reason of the delay, and to save time I proceeded with my two companies in direction of the bridge, thinking the guns would overtake me. Lieutenant Vibert rejoined me halfway, saying that the native gunners were just turning out, but that the guns would now come up immediately. They joined me when I was 1½ miles from the

73 Governor-General, of India, 1836–42.

bridge. On our arriving within about 100 yards of the Cashmere Gate I was met by Captain Wallace, 74th Native Infantry, field officer of the week, who requested me to hasten in as fast as I could, as the Cavalry mutineers had arrived and had shot down all the officers of the 54th Native Infantry. I immediately ordered the two companies to load, and while this was being done Colonel Ripley came out of the Cashmere Gate wounded in several places, and supported by the File-Major. I then marched on expecting to meet the mutineers, but there was not one to be seen – not even a sepoy of the 8 companies of the 54th Native Infantry that had gone in advance with Colonel Ripley – but merely the usual main guard of 50 men of the Native Infantry under Lieutenant proctor. Captain Wallace told me that these men had seen Colonel Ripley cut down within a few yards of them by the cavalry troopers, and though he urged them to rescue him, not a man attempted to do so. The sepoys of the 54th must, of course, have behaved in an equally shameful manner. I saw the following officers lying dead in the open space to the west of the church, *viz.* Captain Smith, Captain Burrows, Lieutenant Edwards, and Lieutenant Waterfield, and also the Sergeant-Major, all of the 54th Native Infantry. Having placed the guns in position and sentries at the different points, I proposed to Lieutenant Vibert that we should go and bring in the bodies of the officers; the sepoys of the companies advised us not to do so just yet, as the troopers were about and looking out for officers. The sepoys said they would do it, as they would not be touched: they did not, however, do so at this time. Shortly after this, we were joined by the Adjutant, Lieutenant Osborn, and Lieutenant Butler, who had been wounded by the city people. Ensign Angelo also joined us, and everything at this time was perfectly quiet at Cashmere Gate; but at about 12 a sepoy of the light Company came to me and said that the Havildar Major had sent him to ask where the regiment was to go. I then enquired where it was, and he told me at Sabzi Mandi; that on the troopers shooting down the officers, the men had run away and assembled there. I directed him to go and order them up to the Cashmere Gate. They came up without any European officer, and the Havildar Major told me that they had been followed the whole way by some of the troopers who were inciting them to join in the mutiny. After this, the officers, assisted by some of the sepoys, went and brought in the bodies above-mentioned. We were now joined by the 74th under Major Abbot, and also a couple of guns of Captain DeTeissier's Battery. I think it was about this time, 2 p.m., that we heard heavy firing in the direction of the Magazine, which continued till about half past 3, when it was blown up. I forgot to mention that on my arrival at the Cashmere Gate, Mr. Galloway came and asked me to strengthen his guard at the treasury, which I did, Lieutenant Willoughby joined us, having made his escape from the Magazine, when he told us how he and the few Europeans with him had defended it, and of the King having in the morning sent down men to take possession of it, and that this being refused, scaling ladders had been sent down at 2 o'clock, according to a threat given by them. We remained at the Cashmere Gate till about 5 o'clock, when all of a sudden, as I was standing near the outer Cashmere Gate, a volley was fired, which passed close in front of me, killing Captain Gordon and Lieutenant Revely, of the 74th, and wounding Lieutenant Osborn, of the 54th. A sepoy of the Light Company then put his arm on my shoulder and told me I had better go or I should be shot down, and seeing it was useless to remain, the sepoys of the 54th being no longer under control, I went out and was joined by an Officer of the 74th. We were going down to the Flag Staff by the main road, but the sepoy of the Light Company (the only one who stood by me) recommended me going off the road through the several compounds, the main road not being safe. We did so, and on reaching the Flag Staff I reported to Brigadier Graves all that I had noticed. There were two guns and about 300 of the Native Infantry at this time with Brigadier Graves, who, as far as I could perceive, were still obeying orders; but I was not there more than 15 minutes when a retreat was determined on, the men saying they would retreat with us wherever we went. They fell in, marched down the hill, took the road through cantonments: but on getting near their lines went off by ones and twos to their huts, and on my asking them what they were going to do, said they were going to drink water. They took off their arms and accoutrements, and in fact went off together. On seeing this I went to my own Quarter Guard. This was about half past 7. I endeavoured to persuade the guard to come along with me, and remained talking to them for about half an hour, and at last the Havildar Major and two sepoys agreed to accompany me. We then started off, but lost our way during the night and found ourselves not more than 4 miles from Delhi in the morning. I remained three days in the vicinity of the ice-pits, about 3 miles from the city. The Havildar and one of the sepoys left me the first morning under the pretence of bringing me food, the other left me the next day, and I finally made my escape, assisted by a fakir, to Karnal.

Question – From what you observed of you own men on the 11th of May, or any time immediately preceding it, do you think the sepoys of the 54th Native Infantry had been apprised of the coming of the mutineers from Meerut, before they were generally known to be near?

Answer – Not from anything that I observed on the 11th or previous to it; but I now am convinced, from their whole conduct on that day, as well as from information I have since received, that they knew generally what was going to occur. Lieutenant Vibert in September last told me that the Subedar Major of the Regiment, Sheikh Imam-Bakhsh, had stated to the late Captain Russell that men had been in our lines two months before the 11th of May, coming and going away and instigating the sepoys to rebellion. Captain Russell was killed at Badli-ki-Serai on the 8th of June last; the Subedar Major is, I believe, still at Meerut, and it was there after the outbreak that I imagine Captain Russell got this information from him.

The Prisoner declines to cross-examine.

The witness withdraws.

Mukund Lal, Secretary to the Ex-King of Delhi, is called into Court and duly affirmed.[74]

Examined by the Judge Advocate

Question – Do you know anything concerning the origin of the late rebellion in the Native Army?

Answer – The King of Delhi has for some two years been disaffected against the Government, and was disposed not to respect his obligations to the English. The particulars are as follows: when Mirza Haidar Shikoh and Mirza Murid, sons of Mirza Khan Bakhsh, son of Mirza Sulaiman Shikoh, came here from Lucknow, they, in concert with Hasan Askar, arranged and suggested to the King that he should have a letter prepared and dispatched to the King of Persia. This letter, they suggested, should represent that the English had made the King a prisoner, and had suspended the appointment of an heir-apparent. It was further to represent that his wishes in reference to the appointment of any particular son as heir-apparent were not attended to. Under these circumstances the letter was to request that such an understanding might be established that mutual interchanges of visits and letters might be the result. Sidi Kambar, who was one of the King's special armed retainers, was presented with 100 rupees, through Mahbub Ali Khan, for the expenses of his journey, and was dispatched in the direction of Persia, with a letter that had been prepared in the King's private secretariat office. After this, Mirza Haidar and his brother returned to Lucknow, and having dispatched his brother

74 How Harriott treated defence witnesses about whom he had some doubt that they might not toe to his line, shabbily. He did that with Meerut witnesses (see Introduction), and repeated the same here. An example: When Mukand Lal, Secretary to the Emperor, came in, Harriott 'admonished him badly', says Martin, 'for displaying a want of respect to the court, in first neglecting to make his obeisance on entering, and then took his place without permission in the usual position for witnesses. He is a short and rather stout Hindu'. He trembled awfully, fearing severe punishment. After some moment, 'on recovering his equanimity, he assumed a very humble attitude and stood with clasped hands while his statement was read and translated to the court, the President inquiring at every dozen words or so whether he adhered to it on oath to which he generally replied in the affirmative'. Martin, *op. cit.*, vol. 3, p. 169.

Mirza Najaf, a distant relation of the King, with Mirza Bulaki, son of Mirza Musharraf-ud-din, son of Mirza Agha Jan, to Persia, reported the same to the King in writing. It is now about three years since some infantry soldiers stationed at Delhi became the disciples of the King through Mirza Ali, whose duty it was to receive and present all petitions, and also through Hamid Khan, Jamadar; and on that occasion the King gave each of them a document detailing the names and orders of those who had preceded him in the direct line, together with a napkin dyed pink as an emblem of his blessing. The Agent of the Lieutenant-Governor hearing of this occurrence, enquired regarding it, and for the future prohibited the King's making any more of the men of the army his disciples. It may be said that from that day a sort of understanding was established between the army and the King. Some 20 days before the commencement of the late rebellion intelligence was received here that the troops at Meerut were about breaking out in open mutiny but it has not been heard that they were to come here. When the troopers arrived, they first came under the Palace windows, and told the King that they had come to him after killing all the English at Meerut, and that they would slay immediately those that were here; and they further said that they would, for the future, consider the prisoner their King, and that now there was not an Englishman left in all India – all had been slain. They further said the whole army would obey the King's orders. The King said that if they had a disposition to come that they should prepare themselves for all consequence, and if they were so prepared, they were at liberty to come and take the management of matters into their hands. While this disturbance was going on, these traitors got into the city; the special armed retainers joined them, and Kaladad Khan, a resident of Cabul, slew the Resident, Mr. Fraser, while some of the infantry soldiers, with others of the King's retainers went to the apartments of the Commandant of the Palace Guards, and slew him there. After that the English were killed all about the city wherever they were met with. The same day proclamation was made by beat of drum throughout the city that God was the Ruler of the World, and that Bahadur Shah was Sovereign of the country, and had the supreme authority. The next day, the 12th when the troops from Meerut and those at Delhi had coalesced, the King took his seat on the throne, a salute of guns was fired, and Mahbub Ali Khan, the minister, was ordered to give the whole army a feast. Accordingly they were all supplied with confectionary, the native officers receiving in addition a present in money. Formerly a silver throne had been kept in the Hall of Special Audience, on which the King used to take his seat on special state occasions; but since the year 1842 the presentation of the usual offering by the Agent of the Lieutenant-Governor on occasion of interviews and salutes was disallowed. This throne was then removed and placed in a recess in the passage below the King's sitting-room, and since that time was in disuse till the 12th of May, when it was brought out again, and the King took his seat on it, as on a throne.

Question – Before the 11th of May were any proposals sent by the army to the King?

Answer – I don't know whether any direct proposals came to the Prisoner, but the King's personal attendants sitting about the entrance to his private apartments used to converse among themselves, and say that very soon, almost immediately, the army would revolt and come to the Palace, when the Government of the King would be re-established, and all the old servants would be greatly promoted and advanced in position and emoluments.

It being 4 o'clock the Court adjourns till 11 a.m. tomorrow.

Day fifteen: 13 February 1858

The Court reassembled this day at 11 a.m. in the Hall of Special Audience in the Palace at Delhi.

The President, Members, Interpreter, and Dy. Judge Advocate-General are all present.

The Prisoner is brought into Court, attended by his attorney, Ghulam Abbas.

Mukund Lal, the Ex-King's Secretary, is called into Court, and examined on his former affirmation.

Examined by the Judge Advocate (continued)

Question – Who were the personal attendants of the King who used to talk in this way?

Answer – Basant Ali Khan, and the whole body of them.

Question – How many days previous to the outbreak were they talking in this way?

Answer – Four days.

Question – According to your statement it appears that Mirza Haidar Shikoh took part in the consultation relative to the correspondence with Persia; but it is known that the King complained against Mirza Haidar Shikoh for having calumniated him at Lucknow, how do you explain this?

Answer – This was merely a deception adopted as a precaution against the chance of the true state of affairs coming to light, so that should such happen it might be brought forward as proof that there could be no combination, but on the contrary dissension between the two parties.

Question – By whose orders were the ladies and children that were prisoners in the Palace murdered?

Answer – These people were being collected for three days: on the fourth day the infantry and cavalry soldiers, accompanied by Mirza Mughal, came to the entrance of the King's private apartments, and requested the King's permission to kill them. The King was at this time in his own apartments: Mirza Mughal and Basant Ali Khan went inside while the soldiery remained without; they returned in about 20 minutes, when Basant Ali Khan publicly and in a loud voice proclaimed that the King had given his permission for the slaughter of the prisoners, and that they could take them away: accordingly, the King's armed retainers, in whose custody the prisoners had been, took them from the place of confinement, and, in conjunction with some of the mutinous soldiery, killed them.

Question – Do you know anything further?

Answer – After the fighting had commenced, whoever brought in the head of an European soldier, or officer, received a reward of two rupees.

Question – On any occasion was any soldier or officer taken prisoner and brought in alive?

Answer – No.

Question – Previous to this outbreak had the Mahommedans entered into any conspiracy or combination to bring about this insurrection?

Answer – When the mutineers arrived here the Mahommedans joined them at once: is it not to be inferred from this that some combination must have previously existed between them? – but it was only the lower and not the higher orders that joined them.

Question – Can you name any men among the higher classes of the Mahommedans that did not join in rebellion against the British Government? The King and all the princes most certainly did so.

Answer – My former answer was in allusion to the day of the outbreak, and not to anything which occurred subsequently.

Question – Who were the persons that were admitted to the private confidential conferences with the King?

Answer – Mahbub Ali Khan, a eunuch and Prime Minister, Hasan Askari, the priest, Zeenat Mahal, the favourite Queen, Nani Begam, the Prisoner's daughter, Agha Begam, another daughter of the Prisoner, and Ashraf-un-nissa, one of the King's wives, and when there was a necessity for anything being written, it was done by the Physician Ahsanullah Khan, and a person who was by caste a Kayastha, but had the same name as myself, *viz.* Mukand Lal.

Question – Persian papers Nos. 2, 3, and 4, arranged under the head of '*Murder*' are shown to witness, and he is asked if he recognizes the handwriting of them?

Answer – I do not. They may have been written in the new office set up by Subedar Bakht Khan: one of his writers, a Maulavy, used to prepare the papers and bring them to have the King's seal affixed.

Question – Were you never admitted to the private confidential conferences of the King?

Answer – No.

Question – How then did you become aware of what you have related, in reference to the mission to Persia.

Answer – I used to remain in attendance on Mahbub Ali Khan, the Minister. I was a servant of the King, but was attached especially to the service of Mahbub Ali Khan, and used to hear some subjects of confidence from him.

Question – Was it generally supposed in the Palace that Hasan Askari had great influence with the King?

Answer – Yes, not only in the Palace but throughout the city also, it was known that Hasan Askari, the priest, and Mahbub Ali Khan exercised the greatest influence over the King.

Question – Was not one of the daughters of the King a disciple of Hasan Askari, and was either of the two you have mentioned as admitted to the confidential conference the one alluded to?

Answer – A daughter of the King's named Nawab Begam, the wife of Mirza Zaman Shah, had become a disciple of Hasan Askari, but she died one and a half years ago; the other two I have named did not professedly become his disciples, but they always avowed great faith in his sanctity.

Question – Did the Prisoner on any occasion go out of the Palace for the Purpose of encouraging the troops to fight against the English?

Answer – Yes, two days after the assault, *viz.* on the 16th September, he went in an open litter in the direction of the Magazine, at the head of the army; but had scarcely proceeded 200 yards beyond the Palace when he halted for an hour, and then returned, the army in the meantime dispersing.

Question – Do you know what induced the Prisoner to halt after proceeding so short a distance, and to what was it generally attributed?

Answer – He had gone out with the army in order to dislodge the British from the city: when the troops became engaged, he stayed to encourage them.

Question – Did the King habitually peruse the paper called the *Sadik-ul-Akhbar*?

Answer – I can't say as to his always reading it; but this paper and others used to come to him.

Question – Was there more than usual agitation and excitement among the Mussalmans of Delhi against the British Rule some few months before the outbreak?

Answer – I don't know.

Question – Were you in the habit of reading the *Authentic News*, the *Sadik-ul-Akhbar*?

Answer – No, I never read it.

The Prisoner declines to cross-examine.

Examined by the Court

Question – Were any persons of the Hindu faith, admitted to the private confidential conferences of the Prisoner, except Mukand Lal Kayasth?

Answer – No, no other Hindu was so trusted.

Question – Are you aware whether any emissaries were dispatched from Delhi, after the outbreak, to induce the native regiments that had not at that time revolted, to come and join the mutineers in Delhi?

Answer – I don't know.

The witness withdraws.

Captain Tytler, of the 38th N I., is called into Court and duly sworn.

Examined by the Judge Advocate

Question – Were you in Delhi on the 10th of May last?

Answer – Yes.

Question – Did you on that day see or hear any carriage, such as is used for travelling post, go into the lines of your regiment; if so, state all the circumstances?

Answer – Yes, about 3 p.m. on Sunday, the 10th of May, I heard a bugle and the sound of carriage wheels pass my door. This being very unusual where I resided, I told a servant of mine to run out and see if anyone was coming to my house. He went and returned immediately, and said it was a carriage with natives going towards the lines. My house being a corner one, the carriage was obliged to pass three sides of the grounds; so before it passed a second side, I directed the same servant to run to the lines, and give my salaam to the Subedar Major of the regiment, and say I wanted to see him, for it occurred to me that he and the other native officers of my regiment who had been to Meerut on Court-martial duty must be returning in this carriage. The servant returned shortly afterwards and said, there are a great number of natives in the carriage from Meerut, but none belonging to our regiment, by which I distinctly understood he alluded to soldiers.

Question – What did you witness on the 11th of May?

Answer – On the morning of the 11th of May, I think about 9 o'clock, one of my servants rushed into the room and said Lieutenant Holland had sent over to say that troops were marching on Delhi. I put on my uniform and went over to him. He joined me and we then went together to Lieutenant Gambier, the Adjutant, where we met Colonel Knyvett, Commanding the regiment, Captain Gardner and the Brigade-Major, Captain Nicol; and I then learnt that mutineers were marching from Meerut on to Delhi; and I was ordered to proceed at once to the lines, and take my own company along with Captain Gardner's completing them to the strength of 200 men, with the usual allowance of ammunition in pouch, I was then ordered to proceed to a house on the ridge above the new powder magazine, outside the city, and to be very particular that no body of men crossed over from the opposite side of the river. Captain Gardner and I went immediately to the lines; we found the men of our companies rather excited, and it was with some slight difficulty that we succeeded in completing each of our companies to 100 strong. A slight delay now took place in serving out the ammunition, and after sending repeatedly to the Magazine to ascertain the cause, I went myself, and the Khalassies said: 'What can we do? The sepoys about here who have come for ammunition are quarrelling and squabbling with us about the cartridges and caps, and we cannot give either without counting them'. I hurried the work and returned to the company. When the cartridges and caps were being served out many of the men seized more bundles than they were entitled to, therefore to prevent further delay at the time, I had these men marked, that I might punish them afterwards. Captain Gardner also remarked to me that the men of his company showed the same anxiety to secure more ammunition than they were entitled to. The order was now given to the companies to march. Both Captain Gardner and myself remarked the excited manner in which the men left the lines, shouting vehemently every now and then, and which neither of us could prevent. I wish here to record a circumstance that occurred on the morning of the 11th, but which I have omitted mentioning. There was a Brigade parade that morning to hear the sentence of a General Court-martial read regarding a native officer, Ishwari Pande, at Barrackpore when I remarked a murmur of disapprobation throughout the whole regiment. Though it lasted but a few seconds, it struck me forcibly as something extraordinary, never having witnessed anything like it before. When we arrived at the house over the Magazine I placed sentries at different points which commanded the bend of the river. The rest of the men, after piling arms, I took into the house; it was a very hot day, and as some of our men had procured water melons and some sweetmeats, they brought them to us, and insisted on our partaking of them; both Captain Gardener and myself remarked the great attention our men were paying us. In the meantime we were called out to see fires that were every now and then appearing in the city. Shortly after this, we heard a roar of cannon. All this we could not account for. Captain Gardner remarked to me how lucky it was that our men seemed so well disposed, as we were convinced that there was something serious going on in the city, particularly as we remembered the fires that had broken out in Ambala and other places. We now remarked that our men were forming small groups in the heat of the sun. I ordered them to come in and not expose themselves thus. They said: 'We like being in the sun'. I ordered them in again. When I went into one of the rooms I remarked, for the first time, a native, from his appearance a soldier, haranguing the men of the companies, and saying that every power or government existed their allotted time, and that it was nothing extraordinary that of the English had come to an end, according to what had been predicted in their native books. Before I could make a prisoner of him the Magazine in the city exploded, and then the men of the two companies with a tremendous shout took up their arms and ran off to the city, exclaiming '*Prithvi Raj Ki Jai*' or 'Victory to the Sovereign of the World'.

Question – Did you notice anything before the 10th of May that led you to suppose that the sepoys of your regiment were disaffected?

Answer – No.

Question – Did any other circumstances come to your notice from which you might infer that a disturbance at Delhi had been expected before it broke out?

Answer – Yes, one of my old servants, a man who had been about 26 years in our family, was about this time going on leave, and when I urged him particularly to return, he on several occasions, with a sorrowful expression, said, 'Yes. Sir, provided your hearth,[75] is still in existence that is, provided you and your family are in a condition to give me service. He made use of these expressions about a week or ten days before the outbreak. He left me about this time, and I have not seen or heard from him since.

The Prisoner declines to cross-examine.

The witness withdraws.

Sergeant Fleming, late Bazzar Sergeant at Delhi, is called into Court and duly sworn.

Examined by the Judge Advocate

Question – Was your son sometime before the outbreak here in May last in the habit of riding and exercising the horses of the Prisoner's son, Jawan Bakht?

Answer – Yes, he had done so for five or six years.

Question – What was the age of your son?

Answer – He was about 19.

Question – A short time before the outbreak did he complain to you of any language used to him by the Prisoner's son, Jawan Bakht?

75 The words he spoke were: If your Choola still burnt bright. To clarify the meaning of this phrase, the Emperor 'was asked by the interpreter what was the meaning of the above remark by the bearer, and he laughingly replied that it meant nothing in particular that the man who made it must been some hungry fellow who was always thinking of eating', Martin, *op. cit.*, vol. 3, p. 170. Actually it meant 'if your condition is good enough to hire me'.

Answer – In the latter end of the month of April 1857, he came from Mr. Fraser's office, where he used to write, and told me that he had that day gone in the morning to the Prime Minister's house as usual, and had there seen the Prisoner's son, Jawan Bakht, who resided in that quarter, and that this Jawan Bakht had then told him that he was not to come again; that he did not like to see the face of an English infidel, and that before many days he would have them all killed and under his feet. Jawan Bakht then spat at him. My son told Mr. Fraser of it at the time, but Mr. Fraser replied that he was a fool, and was not to listen to such nonsense. After this – as far as I recollect about the 2nd of May – the Prime Minister sent for my son to pay him up, and on this occasion again, the Prisoner's son, Jawan Bakht, abused him still more, saying he would have his head off in a few days. This son of mine was killed in the palace here during the rebellion.

The Prisoner declines to cross-examine.

The witness withdraws.

The Court, at half past 3 p.m., adjourns till Tuesday, the 23rd of February, to allow of other witnesses being sent for, and enable the Interpreter to translate certain requisite papers.

Day sixteen: 23 February 1858

The Court reassembled this morning at 11 a.m. in the Hall of Special Audience in the Palace at Delhi.

The President, Members, Interpreter, and Dy. Judge Advocate – General are all present.[76]

The Prisoner is brought into Court attended by his attorney, Ghulam Abbas.

Captain Martineau,[77] of the 10th Native Infantry, is called into Court and duly sworn.

Examined by the Judge Advocate

Question – Were you at Ambala from January till May 1857 as Instructor of Musketry at the Depot there?

Answer – Yes, I was.

Question – Did a detachment of sepoys from every native regiment in India attended at this depot for the purpose of receiving instruction in musketry?

76 It is not correct – one of the members was not present in the court at 11 a.m. He came late by one hour. Hence the proceedings started at 12 o'clock. See Martin, *op. cit.*, p. 171.

77 Instructor at the Ambala Musketry Depot before and during the Revolt.

Answer – Not from every native regiment, but five men from 44 of the native regiments, attended.

Question – Had you any conversation with these men relative to some chapaties that were circulated to different villages in these districts before the outbreak?

Answer – Yes, I had frequent conversations with various sepoys on this subject. I asked them what they understood in reference to them, and by whom they supposed that they were circulated: they described them to me as being in size and shape like ship biscuits, and believed them to have been distributed by order of Government through the medium of their servants for the purpose of intimating to the people of Hindustan that they should be all compelled to eat the same food: and that was considered as a token, that they would likewise be compelled to embrace one faith, or as they termed it, 'One food and one faith'.

Question – As far as you could understand, was this idea generally prevalent among all the sepoys of the various detachments at the depot?

Answer – It was prevalent, as far as I could judge, among all the sepoys of every regiment that furnished a detachment to the depot at Ambala.

Question – Was there any report of the Government having mixed ground bones with flour for the purpose of having it distributed to the sepoys, and so destroying their caste?

Answer – Yes, I first heard of this in the month of March. It was told me that all the flour retailed from the Government depots for the supply of troops on the march was so adulterated.

Question – Do you think the sepoys generally firmly believed in this?

Answer – I have seen correspondence from various men which the sepoys of the depots voluntarily placed in my hands, the writers of which, themselves sepoys, evidently believed that such was the case.

Question – Did the sepoys ever speak to you about any other cause of complaint or points on which they sought information?

Answer – Their complaint or rather fear was this. They apprehended that Government was going forcibly to deprive them of their caste.

Question – Did any of them ever speak about Government interference regarding the remarriage of Hindu widows?

Answer – Yes, they alluded to that as an invasion of their social rights.

Question – Did any of them ever refer to the annexation of Oudh, as a measure indicating that Government wished to annihilate all the Native Independent States?

Answer – At Ambala the subject was occasionally alluded to, as if it were not agreeable to the them; but subsequently at Karnal some troopers of the 3rd Cavalry, about a week after the mutiny, on my speaking to them about the revolt of their comrades, said to me: 'You have conquered and absorbed everything in Hindustan, you have no more foreign countries to take, and now you have determined upon a crusade against our religion and our faith'. I was on duty as Commissariat Officer at Karnal at this time and the men of the 3rd Cavalry to whom I am alluding, were those that have remained faithful.

Question – Did you ever hear any of the sepoys speak complainingly of the efforts of English missionaries to convert Natives to Christianity?

Answer – No, never in my life; I don't think they cared one bit about it.

Question – Were the cartridges which the sepoys were called on to use at the depot at Ambala in any way greased?

Answer – No, not as issued from the magazines. They were not allowed to touch any that had been greased previous to distribution; they greased their own cartridges with a composition of *ghi*, that is, clarified butter and bee's wax; these materials they themselves purchased from natives, whenever they pleased to get them.

Question – Did you observe any difference in making complaints about forcible deprivation of their religion between the Hindus and Mussalmans?

Answer – Yes, as far as the cartridge question went the Mahommedan sepoys laughed at it; it was only the Hindus that made the complaints in reference to losing caste; but in regard to those who spoke of the annexation of Oudh as a grievance, I can't say whether they were Mahommedans or not.

The Prisoner declines to cross-examine.

Examined by the Court

Question – Did you observe anything peculiar in the conduct of the sepoys under your command previous to the outbreak, or any intimation of what was about to take place?

Answer – Yes, they told me in plain language that there would be an outbreak; and there was every evidence of it in nightly fires at Ambala. The first fire commenced on the very day we fired the first Enfield cartridge, and continued nearly nightly, up to the 10th of May. We commenced using the Enfield cartridges on the 17th of April, the men themselves remarked, that although Government offered large rewards to anyone who would give information of the incendiaries, yet no one was found to do so; and that this was a certain sign of general dissatisfaction and some impending outbreak. I made a public report to the above effect to Army Head-Quarters then present at Ambala, and I also made a private representation of the same kind to Captain Septimus Becher, Assistant Adjutant-General of the Army.

The witness withdraws.

Mrs. Fleming, wife of Sergent Fleming, is called into Court and duly sworn.

Examined by the Judge Advocate

Question – In the end of April last were you in the house of Zeenat Mahal, the Prisoner's wife, and did you there see his son, Jawan Bakht?

Answer – Yes.

Question – Relate what passed on that occasion?

Answer – I was sitting down with his sister-in-law, and Jawan Bakht was standing by his wife. My own daughter, Mrs. Scully, was also present. I was talking with Jawan Bakht's sister-in-law, when Mrs. Scully said to me: 'Mother, do you hear what this young rascal is saying; he is telling me that in a short time he will have all the infidel English under his feet, and after that he will kill the Hindus (the actual word was Kaffirs (Europeans)'. Hearing this, I turned round to Jawan Bakht and asked him: 'What is that you are saying?' He replied that he was only joking. I said if what you threaten were to be the case, your head would be taken off first. He told me that the Persians were coming to Delhi and that when they did so, we, that is, myself and daughter, should go to him, and he would save us. After this, he left us. I think this must have occurred about the middle of April 1857.

The Prisoner declines to cross-examine.

The witness withdraws.

Copies of Newspapers written by Chuni Lal, news-writer, from 11th to 20th of May (both dates inclusive), having been seized in his house, are here read in original, and the translation of them is also read and entered as follows:

Narrative of Occurrences in Delhi, from 11th to 20th May 1857, both dates inclusive, in the form of a Diary, by Chuni Lal, news-writer.

Sometime during the night of the 10th May 1857, Mr. Fraser received a letter from Meerut, intimating the mutinous conduct of the infantry and cavalry there; but he did not make any arrangements then. In the morning, intelligence arrived that the 3rd cavalry and two regiments of Native Infantry had a fight at Meerut on Account of the cartridges, and were coming to Delhi, when Mr. Fraser immediately directed the trooper in attendance as his orderly to call the Agent of Jhajjar Nawab. Sir Theophilus Metcalfe at the same time came into the city, and directed the chief police officer to place guards of the constabulary force at the gates and to have them closed; the police officer carried out these orders immediately. Mr. Fraser also came into the city in his buggy, accompanied by the troopers of the Jhajjarcavalry, constituting his personal guard. It was now ascertained that some cavalry men had arrived at the bridge, and had murdered the toll-collector, setting fire to his house. One of these troopers was very insolent to the Commandant of the Palace Guards, and fired a pistol at him, but without effect. The troopers above referred to collected under the Palace windows, and telling the king they had come to fight for the faith, requested him to have the gate at this point opened for them. The King immediately sent word to the Commandant of the Palace Guards that some troopers had come from Meerut, and were bent on causing a disturbance. On receiving this message Captain Douglas at once came to the King, and directed them to go away: they replied they would settle with him. Mr. Fraser in the meantime came to the Cashmere gate and reasoned with the guard there, telling them they had been nurtured in the service of the East India Company; that some mutinous troops had come from Meerut, and that he required them to assist him in making arrangements. They, however, refused, saying that had an enemy come against him, they would have had no objection to do as they were ordered. Mr. Fraser then, accompanied by some gentlemen, went to the Calcutta Gate, and made such arrangements there as were necessary. Jowala Singh, Mr. Fraser's personal Jamadar, now urged him to leave the city, telling him that all the Mahomedans were disposed for a revolt. Mr. Fraser replied that he would not do anything of the kind. About this time all the shops in the city were closed. The Reverend Mr. Jennings and another gentleman were watching the troopers coming from Meerut with a glass, from one of the turrets of the apartments occupied by the Commandant of the Palace Guards. Captain Douglas getting into his buggy joined Mr. Fraser at the Calcutta gate, and taking a letter out of his pocket gave it to him to read. Mr. Fraser then told the troopers of his personal guard to remain in a state of preparation. The Mahomedans of the Thanbi-Bazar went to the Rajghat, and having made a solemn compact with the mutineers, opened the gate and allowed them to come in, when they immediately commenced firing the houses and killing the Europeans. Having killed the Europeans who resided in Daryaganj, and set fire to their houses, they murdered Chaman Lal, the native doctor, as he was standing in front of the dispensary. The Mahomedans of the city now told the troopers that Mr. Fraser was at the Calcutta Gate. They immediately went thither, and fired their carbines and pistols at the gentlemen who had collected there, and killed two of them. Mr. Fraser's mounted guard, being Mussalmans, made no defence; but Mr. Fraser taking a carbine from one of the guard in question wounded one of the mutinous cavalry men. Mr. Fraser and Captain Douglas then retreated to the Palace in a buggy. The latter went up to his apartments over the gate, and the former was about ascending the stair when he was attacked by some of the mutinous cavalry, seconded by the armed retainers of the King, and killed on the second step. His murderers now rushed up to the apartments above, where they killed Captain Douglas, the Reverend Mr. Jennings and his daughter, and another gentleman. At this time, the Mahomedans of the Palace and city were going about, plundering the apartments of the Commandant of the palace Guards, and the houses of the Europeans residing in the city. Sir Theophilus Metcalfe mounted on a horse, and having a drawn sword in his hand, was pursued by the mutinous cavalry as far as the Chandni Bazar, and got away out of the city by the Ajmer Gate, notwithstanding that the saddlers living there turned out with bludgeons to prevent his escape. The three infantry regiments of Delhi joined the mutineers, and murdering a number of their officers came into the city. The whole mutineers then killed all the Europeans, male and female, whom they could find concealed in Daryaganj, about the Cashmere Gate, and in Major Skinner's house. After this, joined by the Mussalmans and some Hindus of the city, they destroyed the chief and the 12 subordinate police officer hid himself; but his assistant made his escape after being wounded. When the mutineers and rebels attacked the bank, two gentlemen and three ladies with two children took refuge on the roof; one of the mutineers climbed a tree, and was shot by one of the gentlemen. The mutineers then set fire to the bank. The cavalrymen after this rode away; but the Mussalmans remained and killed the gentlemen and ladies with bludgeons. The Mahomedans continued going about with the mutineers, shouting cheers for the success of their religion. The Rajah of Ballabhgarh had gone to visit one of the railway officers, and returned about 10 o'clock. The three infantry regiments of Delhi plundered the treasury, and shared the money amongst themselves, and having plundered also the civil and judicial courts and the college, set fire to the buildings. The cavalry went to the cantonments and fired all the houses there. Having accomplished all this, the regiment of cavalry and two regiments of infantry which had come from Meerut, together with the three that had been stationed at Delhi, waited on the King, and requested his support and countenance, promising to establish his rule throughout the whole country. The King replied that he cherished a hearty disposition to show them every favour and kindness, and directed them to take up their quarters in Salimgarh; remarking at the same time that all the streets and bazaars had been closed, and suggesting that plunder and robbery should be prevented. The cavalry and infantry hearing that some Europeans with their wives had gone into the Magazine, brought two guns from Daryaganj, and loading them with stones fired them at the gates, the Europeans within returning the fire from several pieces with grape. Subsequently the Magazine blew up, when several of the men of the city were killed, and many of the houses in the neighbourhood destroyed. The Europeans, men and women, who had been in the Magazine, fled in the direction of the river. They were, however, pursued by the cavalry and killed. Three sergeants and two women were brought prisoners to the king. One of the sergeants begged the King's protection for himself and fellow-prisoners, saying that otherwise they would be killed by the mutineers, and the King had them placed in the House of Devotion. At about an hour before sunset Rajah Nahar Singh[78] taking his wife, his brother, and his brother-in-law, and Mr. Munro in dis-

78 The Jat Raja of Ballabhgarh.

guise, left for Ballabhgarh. The infantry mutineers attacked the house of Salimgram, the treasurer, but were made an entrance, and in conjunction with the Mahomedans of the city, plundered the place of all the property it contained. Some sergeants were taking away two guns from the cantonments, but the cavalry came up with them and brought the guns back. There was a salute of 21 guns fired under the palace, and all night, throughout the city, the greatest uneasiness and tumult continued to prevail in consequence of the plunder, pillage, and burning of houses.

Tuesday, 12th March 1857 – The King came into the Hall of Special Audience, where the chiefs paid their respects. The Subedars of the 54th Regiment waited on the King, and begged that some person might be appointed to arrange for the daily supplies. Ramshay Mall and Dilwani Mall were accordingly to provide 500 rupees worth of meal, pulse and gram, &c., daily, and to have them conveyed to the regiments. Four European gentlemen were concealed in the house of Muhammad Ibrahim, son of Ali Muhammad, merchant. The troopers hearing this went there, and killing the Europeans, plundered the house. A European woman, dressed as a native, was going along near the Ellenborough Tank, and was killed by the troopers. The infantry soldiers forcibly entered and plundered the shops of the confectioners in all the streets of the city. On hearing this, the King appointed Mirza Munij-ud-din Khan, formerly police officer of Paharganj, to the governorship of the city, and sent him to the chief police office with a regiment of infantry, directing him to make arrangements to prevent plunder and pillage. The Mirza represented that the soldiery were then engaged plundering the Churi Bazar. On this, the King sent for the Subedars of all the infantry regiments, and directed them to place one regiment at the Delhi Gate of the city, and one under the palace windows, one company each at the Ajmir, Lahore, Farash Khana, Cashmere, and other gates, and one company in the Darya Bazar, saying that he did not approve of his subjects being plundered. After this, the infantry and cavalry made an attack on the Nagar-Seth Street, with the view of plundering it. The inhabitants closed the gates and attacked the soldiery with brick bats, and drove them off. Several clerks with their wives had taken refuge in the house known as that of Rajah Kalyan Singh, of Kishan Garh. The troopers went and attacked them with carbines and pistols. The Europeans defended themselves with their firearms. The troopers then brought two pieces of artillery with them, when the clerks, with their wives, retired to an apartment underground, and the troopers came away. The King directed Mirza Mughal to take a company of infantry, and adopt steps to prevent the plunder in the city. Mirza Mughal accordingly went to the principal police stations, seated on an elephant, and had proclamation made that every individual convicted of plunder would be punished with the loss of nose and ears, and all shopkeepers not opening their shops, and refusing to supply the soldiers, would be fined and imprisoned. Her Excellency the Queen Taj Mahal was released from confinement. Two European gentlemen going along in the disguise of natives were killed by the troopers in front of the chief police station. The King seated on an elephant, with Jawan Bakht in the hind seat, and accompanied by two regiments of infantry and some guns, went in state to have the shops of the principal streets of the city opened, directed the shopkeepers to resume their occupations and supply the army with necessaries, and then returned to the palace. Hasan Ali now obtained a presentation through Ahsan Ulla Khan. He submitted an offering of one gold mohur, and was directed to remain in attendance, the King remarking that he wished to have a conference with him. The King bestowed a dress of honour on Mirza Manir-ud-din Khan on his appointment to the governorship of Delhi. The Mirza presented 4 Rupees as earnest of his thankfulness.

Wednesday, 13th May 1857 – The King came to his House of Devotion: Nawab Mahbub Ali Khan, and other chief paid their respects. The chamberlain, Hasan Mirza, was ordered to bring Mirza Amir-ud-din Khan. The chamberlain returned and reported that the Mirza was unwell, and was in consequence unable to attend. Mirza Manin-ud-din Khan, chief police officer, was told that the necessaries of food were not supplied to the army, and was directed to make arrangements. Hasan Ali Khan[79] being in attendance, the King said to him: 'The army has collected in the palace, what is to be done?' The said Khan replied that these soldiers were murderers who had killed their masters, and that they could not with prudence be trusted. Shah Nizam-ud-din, a descendant of the priests, and Budhan Sahib, son of Nawab Muhammad Khan, deceased, were ordered to join in the deliberative conferences. Mirza Moghul, Mirza Khair Sultan, Mirza Abdulla, &c., were appointed Colonels of regiments of infantry, and were directed to proceed severally with two guns each to the Cashmere, Lahore, and Delhi Gates to preserve order. Shah Nizam-ud-din represented that the cavalry had seized Nawab Mir Hamid Ali Khan at his house, and had brought him on foot to the jewel room to the physician Ahsan Ulla Khan, on the plea that the said Mir affirmed that he was ready to acknowledge himself an offender if any Europeans should be discovered so concealed. On this, the King directed Shah Nizam-ud-din to go with the cavalry and infantry, and allow Mir Hamid Ali Khan's house to be searched. Shah Nizam-ud-din and Mirza Abulbakr accordingly went and made a search, and no Englishmen or Eurasians being found there they had the property restored which

79 Nawsab of Dojana, a small princely state in Haryana.

had been plundered by the cavalry and infantry, the said Mir being at the same time released. Mirza Abulbakr was appointed Colonel of the cavalry regiment. Intelligence was brought that 29 persons, clerks, women, and children, were concealed in the house of Raja Kalyan Singh of Kishangarh, and the cavalry and infantry going and making them prisoners, shot them with volleys of musketry. Some cavalry men went to the house of Colonel Skinner,[80] seized and brought away the son of Mr. Joseph Skinner, and killed him in front of the chief police station. Instigated by some person, the cavalry and infantry went to the houses of Narayan Das and Ram Charan Das, Deputy Collector, and alleging that Europeans were concealed there, plundered them of all their property. Kazi Pannu and his son were killed by some of the infantry soldiers. Two English gentlemen dressed as natives were going out by the Badarran Gate, and were killed by some cavalry men. The King presented all the regiments with 400 rupees each for their expenses. Mirza Manir-ud-din, chief police officer, had it publicly proclaimed that all such persons as wished to take service should come forward, bringing their own arms, and that all those in whose houses Europeans should be found, would be dealt with as offenders. Nawab Ahmad Ali Khan and Walidad Khan of Malagurh attended agreeably to summons, and paid their respects, and were ordered to attend Court daily. The King summoned the principal grain dealers, and ordered them to regulate the rates, and to open their granaries, and to commence selling the grain in the market. Mirza Mauin-ud-din Khan having entertained some 200 men has placed them in the Darya, the principal street, and other parts of the city for the preservation of the peace. Two water carriers who stole some butter from a shopkeeper in the street, called the Lal Kunwa, were taken up. Kuli Khan and Safaraz Khan, two notorious bad characters, as well as some men accused of having committed acts of plunder in Teliwara and Sabzi Mandi, were also apprehended.

Thursday, 14th May 1857 – The King came from his private apartments into the Hall of Devotion. The chamberlain Hasan Mirza, Captain Dildar Ali Khan, and Hasan Ali Khan, and according to summons, Mirza Amin-ud-din Khan, Mirza Zia-ud-din Khan,[81] and Maulavy Sadr-ud-din Khan,[82] were in attendance, and paid their respects. The Maulavy presented one gold mohur. The King told him to conduct the duties of the civil and judicial courts. The Maulavy, however, requested that he might be excused. After this, the treasurer Saligram attended according to orders and presented one gold mohur. The King enquired

80 A *jagirdar* of Hansi (Haryana), staunch British loyalist.

81 Two brothers (Nawabs) from the princely state of Loharu, Haryana.

82 A *maulavi* from Meerut.

> what amount of money there was in the principal treasury. He replied he did not know. The King then directed him to send an agent of his to the treasurer. The treasurer said he would do so. Rahmat Ali Khanwas introduced by Hasan Ali Khan, and presented one gold mohur. The King asked who he was, and was informed that he was the son of Nawab Faiz Muhammad Khan, and nephew of Hasan Ali Khan, who had presented him. Muhammad Ali Khan, son of Sar Jang Khan, presented one gold mohur. The King enquired who he was, and was informed he was the nephew of Bahadur Jang Khan, the Chief of Dadri.[83]

The confidential agent of the Chief of Sanowt presented himself and submitted that the chief was unwell, and had therefore been unable to come to Court, and intended going to Jaipur. An order was accordingly written to the address of Raja Ram Singh, Ruler of Jaipur, directing his early attendance at Court with his army, and the confidential agent above said declared he would leave for Jaipur immediately. After this, orders were respectively issued in writing to Nawab Abdul Rahman Khan of Jhajjar, Bahadur Jang Khan of Dadri, Akhbar Ali Khan of Pantaudih, Rajah Nahar Singh of Ballabhgarh, Hasan Ali Khan of Dojana, and Nawab Ahmad Ali Khan of Farrukhnagar, directing their attendance at Court. Orders were also issued to Mirza Amin-ud-din Khan and Mirza Zia-ud-din Khan to look after the management of the district of Jhirka-Firozpur, and that of Gurgaon, which was lying unoccupied. Intelligence was received that the Goojurs of Chand Rawal were every night plundering the shops in Sabzi Mandi, Teliwara, Rajpur, Mandersa, &c., and Mirza Mughal was ordered to suppress these evil practices of the said Goojurs. Mirza Abulbakr accordingly went to the village in question with his regiment of cavalry, and had it plundered and burnt. Bahadur Singh, superintendent of the landed property belonging to the Lucknow State, presented an offering of one gold mohur. A European soldier who came as a spy from Ambala was seized and brought before the King, and was likewise brought, and he also was sent to the jail. Some Subedars and infantry soldiers, having their shoes on, came and stood on the carpets, and the King reprehended their conduct with anger and displeasure. An order was issued to Muin-ud-din Khan, chief police officer, to take the 38th Regiment Native Infantry, and to proceed to the Delhi Cantonments, and to make arrangements to prevent the depredations being committed there, in Sabzi Mandi, Pahari Durrung, and other places. Four men coming from Meerut told the soldiery that Europeans troops were on their way from that station for their extermination. The soldiery were not pleased at this intelligence, and placed the four men in question in arrest. The police officer of the Nigambodh section was ordered to have the corpses of Mr. Fraser

83 A small princely state in Haryana.

and Captain Douglas buried in the graveyard, and those of the European men and women thrown into the river. This order was accordingly carried into effect. The Goojurs have plundered and carried away all the furniture of Mr. Fraser's house, and have torn up the whole of the records of the Commissionership and of the Agency to the Lieutenant-Governor.

Friday, 15th May 1857 – The king was in his private apartments, and Maulavy Abdul Kadir submitted a list he had prepared of the pay of the troops. His Majesty bestowed a pair of shawls on the Maulavy on account of his appointment to the situation of assistant to Nawab Mahbub Ali Khan. The Maulavy then went home seated on an elephant. The agent of the Chief Sheo Singh of Samnowt presented a bottle of the extract of the Pandonus Adoratissumus and a phial of essential oil, on the part of his client, and received a written order to the address of the Rajah of Jaipur directing his attendance. Ghulam Nabi Khan, superintendent of the Kaulah Mahal, accompanied by Mir Akbar Ali, trooper, who used to remain in attendance of Mr. Fraser, came into the Royal presence and stated that 50 horsemen who had been sent by the Nawab of Jhajjar were in attendance, but that the Nawab himself had not been able to come in consequence of the unsettled and disturbed state of his territory. Maulavy Ahmad Ali attended on the part of Rajah Nahar Singh of Ballabhgarh, and presented an offering of one rupee together with a petition in which the Rajah submitted that he was unable to present himself at Court in consequence of the plunder and violence the Goojurs were carrying on; but that he will attend the Royal presence after making provision for the suppression of these evils. Orders were issued for his early attendance. Intelligence was received that the Magistrate of Rohtak had run away, and that treasury, it was likely, would soon be plundered. It was reported that the Gurgaon treasury had been plundered. On hearing this, the King ordered that one regiment of infantry and some troopers should go and bring away the money in the Rohtak treasury. Orders were issued to Abdul Karim to enlist 400 foot soldiers and one Regiment of Cavalry, the pay of each foot soldier to be 5, and that of each trooper 20 rupees per mensem; about 200 men have accordingly been entertained. The printer Abdul Kadir presented some papers for the King's inspection, and said he would make every arrangement. An order was issued by the King to the officers of the cavalry, intimating that Mirza Abdulbakr had been dismissed from the command of their corps, and that they would remain under the orders of the King. Kazi Faiz Ulla came before the King and presented an offering of 5 rupees, and a petition requesting he might be appointed chief police officer of the city, and his request was granted. A goldsmith killed a man of the same trade against whom he had an enmity and was apprehended. The Mewatis of Jaisinghpura had plundered the house of the railway officer of 4,000 rupees in cash and other property. The cavalry and infantry were accordingly arranging to go and seize the Mewatis and to destroy Jaisinghpura, when the confidential agent of Lala Budh Singh, the agent of the Rajah of Jaipur presented a petition claiming the King's protection for the population of Jaisinghpura. An order was passed on this petition that no soldier of the cavalry or infantry was to be permitted to go to Jaisinghpura without the King's orders. Information was submitted that the soldiers of the cavalry and infantry, as a practice, patrolled the bazars, streets and lanes of the city with drawn swords, and that the shops in the bazars were not opened in consequence of the dread this inspired. Hearing this the King sent orders to the gates of the Palace, enjoining that no person should go about the city with a drawn sword. An order was issued to the Commandant of the Jhajjar Cavalry to take up his quarters in the Mahatab garden. It was reported that 14 boats laden with wheat and other grains, belonging to Ramjidas Gurwalla had arrived in the morning, and an order was thereupon issued to Dilwani Mall, appointed to arrange for supplies, to have the cargo of the said boats landed and to bring it away. Two infantry soldiers had secured 200 rupees and lodged the money with the firm of Ramjidas Gurwalla, arranging that they should receive it in Lucknow. The two soldiers, however, happened to have a disagreement when the matter transpired, and a company immediately went to the house of the banker, who at once gave up the money. An order was issued to the merchants of the city directing their attendance. The cavalry and infantry after a consultation amongst themselves came to the Hall of Special Audience, and complained that they did not get their allowances of pay and clothing, and stated their conviction that the physician Ahsanulla Khan and Mahbub Ali Khan were in collusion with the British. The troopers and infantry then went off to the house known as the Haveli Lal Kumu, and accused the priest Shah Nizam-ud-din of having two European ladies concealed in his residence. Shah Nizam-ud-din replied that he should be confronted with their informant, and the troopers presented some man who was a resident of Rampoor, and who said his story had been hearsay. Shah Nizam-ud-din now told the troopers that they should be at liberty to plunder his house and kill him if they should discover any European women there; but if their real object, whether or not, in this false accusation was to do so, of course they had the power. In reply to this the troopers had nothing to say. Mahbub Ali Khan made oath on the Kuran that he was not in collusion with the British. The soldiery plundered and carried away all the property from the house of Agha Muhammad Khan.

Saturday, 16th May 1857 – The King came into the Hall of Special Audience and held a Court. The Physician Ahsan Ulla Khan, the paymaster Agha Sultan, Captain Dildar Ali Khan, Rahmat Ali Khan, and other chiefs attended and paid their respects. The troopers and infantry soldiers, accompanied by their officers, attended and presented a letter bearing the seal of the physician Ahsanulla Khan and Nawab Mahbub Ali Khan, which they said they had intercepted at the Delhi gate of the city, and complained that the physician and Nawab had sent this letter to the English, inviting them to come into the city immediately and promising that, provided the English should agree to acknowledge Mirza Jawan Bakht, the son of the King by the Queen Zeenat Mahal, as heir-apparent, they would on their part engage to seize and make over all the soldiery now in Delhi. This document was shown to Ahsanulla Khan and Nawab Mahbub Ali Khan, who declared it was a forgery, got up by some person, and the impressions on it were from counterfeit seal of gypsum, and they took off their signet rings and threw before the soldiers. They further swore by the Kuran that the seal on the paper were not theirs, and that the document was a forgery. However, the soldiers would not believe their asseveration. Some persons told the troopers that a number of Europeans were concealed in one of the covered drains of the canal. Hearing this Mirza Abulbakr, accompanied by the troopers, went to the place indicated, and jumping into the drain, discharged his pistol in it; but no Europeans were discovered. After this, the men of the cavalry and infantry drew their swords and surrounded the physician Ahsan Ulla Khan, declaring their firm belief that he maintained an understanding with the English came he might make them over, and would have the soldiers killed. The matter ended in their taking the Europeans, men, women, and children, 52 in number, from the jail, where they were confined, to the reservoir near the music gallery, with the intent to kill them there. The Prince Mirza Majhli attempted to remonstrate, urging that the slaughter of women was not legal according to the Mahomedan law. The troopers on this resolved to kill the said Mirza, but he ran away and so escaped. They then made the prisoners sit down, and one of them fired his carbine at them. The bullet wounded the King's armed retainers. After this, two of the King's personal armed retainers killed the whole of the Europeans, men, women, and children, with their swords. There were about 200 Mussalmans standing at the reservoir, uttering the coarsest abuse against the prisoners. The sword of one of the King's armed retainers broke. After the slaughter the bodies were laden on two carts, and thrown into the river. This occurrence caused a great excitement amongst the Hindus throughout the city, who said that these Purbeas who had committed this heinous and atrocious cruelty could never be victorious against the English. The companies at the gates were relieved. Someone informed the troopers that some Europeans were concealed in the house of the treasurer, Mathura Das, and in the street known as the Chowdhary-ka-Kucha. They accordingly made a search, but returned without finding any. The troopers did not aggrieve any one of this occasion. An order was written to Walidad Khan, of Malagarh, noticing the anarchy prevailing on the eastern side of the Jumna, caused by the lawless conduct of the Goojurs, and directing him to go and take steps to suppress it. Two weavers in the disguise of infantry soldiers were engaged plundering in the city and were apprehended. The shopkeepers of the Lahori Gate submitted a complaint that Kashinath, police officer of their section of the town, was demanding a bribe of 1,000 rupees from them, holding out the threat that if they did not give him the money, he would send them as prisoners to the chief police station. The physician Ahsanulla Khan accordingly sent an order to Kazi Faizulla to place the said police officer under arrest.

Sunday, 17th May 1857 – The King was in his private apartment: the men of the Cavalry and Infantry, accompanied by their officers, submitted that they had fortified Salimgarh, and that they trusted His Majesty would go there and inspect what had been done. The King accordingly went in an open litter, saw how the guns had been placed in position, and then returned, assuring the soldiers that he was associated with them in common cause, desiring them to place every confidence in the physician Ahsanulla Khan, Mahbub Ali Khan, and the Queen Zeenat Mahal, and telling them he would slay with his own hands any Europeans they might seize and bring to him. On hearing this, the troops were convinced, and the physician Ahsanulla Khan was fully exculpated. A man was seized at the bridge with a letter he was bringing from some European at Meerut. The infantry soldiers tied him to a gun, and let him remain there. The mutineers had taken up their quarters in the Hall of Special Audience, whence they have been made to remove, and the hall has been done up anew with carpets, hangings, &c. Mirza Amin-ud-din Khan and Mirza Zia-ud-din Khan attended agreeably to summons, and paid their respects. Being ordered to attend Court daily, they pleaded sickness. The king then directed them to raise troops, saying that large dominions should be conferred on them, they would do so. After this, Iradat Khan and Mir Khan, brothers of Nawab Mustafa Khan of Jahangirabad, Akhbar Khan, and others attended and presented offerings of two rupees each. The disposal of the colonelcies of the infantry regiments was next considered. A trooper arrived from Garhi Harsaru, and reported that several lakhs of rupees, being revenue of the Gurgaon district, was on its way to Delhi escorted by a company of infantry and some troopers, and that near 300 Mewatis and Goojurs of that part of the country had made an attack upon this treasure, and that a fight was going on. On this intelligence, Maulavy Muhammad Bakar, of the press, was directed to go out immediately with two companies of infantry and one troop of cavalry in order to oppose the Goojurs and bring the treasure in safety. The infantry soldiers beat a sweeper in the service of Mirza Mughal very severely, on the imputation of being a spy. They, however, released him on Mirza Mughal's orders. A report was made that some of the Mewatis of Jaisinghpura who had plundered the house of the railway superintendent had been wounded; it was ascertained that these men had been in the service of the English. The landholders of the village of Nadhowli attended, and presenting a rupee each, made profession of their loyalty and allegiance. The king told them to keep up a proper management in their village, failing which they would be expatriated. Two of the King's messengers who had been sent for intelligence returned from Meerut and reported that about 1,000 Europeans soldiers, with some other English, men, women, and children, were collected there in the Suraj Kund, on which they had mounted guns drawn by elephants. They further represented that the Goojurs were committing highway robberies all along the road from Meerut to Salimpur, and had maltreated them also. The King had accordingly two companies of infantry stationed at the bridge over the Jumna. The physician Abdul Hak attended and presented five rupees. Five companies of the Sappers and Miners had come to Meerut from Roorkee. The Europeans required them to remain and perform duties there. To this the men objected, and the English attacked them in consequence. Many men were killed; and, in the end, the Sappers and Miners ran away, and have come to Delhi. Several missives were written and dispatched, by two three or four troopers each, directing early and immediate attendance to Maharaja Narendra Singh of Patiala, Raja Ramsingh, of Jaipur, the Rajah of Alwar, and the Rajahs in Jadhpur, Kotah, Budi, & c. Two children were killed by the falling of the balcony of Dewan Kishan Lal's house. It is reported that troops are coming from Ambala: otherwise everything is quiet.

Monday, 18th May 1857 – The King came from his private apartments into the Hall of Special Audience, and took his seat on the throne, in state. The bands of the five regiments attended and continued playing English music. The King bestowed arms and dresses of honour varying in grandeur, by reference to their appointments, on Mirza Mughal as Commander-in-Chief of the whole of the Forces, on Mirza Kochak Sultan, Mirza Khair Sultan, Mirza Mendu, and on others of his sons as Colonels of the infantry, and on his grandson Abulbakr as Colonels of infantry, and on his grandson Abulbakr as Colonel of the regiment of Cavalry. Mirza Mughal presented two gold mohurs, and the other princes one gold mohur and five rupees each in thankfulness for the honours conferred on them. Hasan Ali Khan attended and paid his respects. He was ordered to attend Court regularly every day, and said he would do so. The King then said that a very large portion of country would be bestowed on him, and directed him therefore to raise troops, cavalry, and infantry. Hasan Ali Khan replied that he could not undertake this, but that he would remain in attendance on His Majesty. The two sowars who had been sent with the missive to Alwar returned, and reported that thousands of Goojurs were infesting the road and committing highway robberies; that they had robbed them of their horses, clothes, and money; that they had taken the King's letter and tearing it up, had put the pieces back into their hands; and that it was after much entreaty and supplication they were prevailed on to give back the horses. A camel-rider who was sent with a missive to Nawab Ahmed Ali Khan of Farrukhnagar returned and reported that the Goojurs would not allow him to go on. The officers of the Sappers and Miners presented themselves and reported that five companies of their corps had come from Roorkee to Meerut: that all the Europeans with their wives and children were collected in their entrenchments, called the Dumduma. That the Europeans used every endeavour to tamper with the Sappers and Miners, to dissuade them from coming to Delhi, and to get them to remain at Meerut, and to join in the duties there, promising them an increase of salary; but that they declined listening to those proposals, whereupon the Europeans commenced a fire of grape on them about 3 o'clock one morning, by which 200 and upwards of their numbers were killed, and remainder ran away, and had now come to His Majesty's presence. They were ordered to take up their quarters in Salimgarh. Nawab Mahbub Ali Khan having prepared a nominal list of Ramji Das Godownwalla, Ramji Das Gurwalla, the treasurer Saligram, and the other merchants of the city, sent it to them by a confidential agent, with a message that the daily expenses of the troops amounted to 2,500 rupees, and that they were therefore collectively required to provide 5 lakhs of rupees. On this, the whole of the merchants went to Mahbub Ali Khan and reported that they were plundered of all they possessed on the outbreak of the troops, and whence now were they to raise the money? Ramji Das said that if Mahbub Ali Khan could get the other merchants to pay, he also would do so. Mirza Abulbakr went with the regiment of cavalry to the villages of Chandrawal and Wazirabad, to punish the Goojurs for robberies they were committing; but the Goojurs ran away.

Tuesday, 19th May 1857 – The King came from his private apartments into the Hall of Special Audience. Two troopers arrived from Meerut and reported that a force, consisting of infantry, cavalry, and artillery, had come to Meerut, with several lakhs of treasure from Bareilly and Muradabad. The Europeans there complained to them that the Meerut troops had revolted, and killing numbers of them, had gone off to Delhi. The Bareilly and Moradabad forces replied that the Europeans had taken their revenge by killing 300 of the Sappers and Miners, and that, no doubt, they (the Bareilly and Moradabad force) would experience similar kindness. On hearing this, the Europeans went into their entrenchments and commenced a cannonade, when the troops from

Bareilly and Moradabad erected batteries and returned the fire. Through the direction of God a shot from the latter fired the mine the Europeans had laid, and the mine the Europeans had laid, and the whole area enclosed by their entrenchments was blown up. On receiving this intelligence, the whole of the troops and the king were highly delighted, and fired five guns at Salimgarh in token of their joy. After this, information arrived that the collector of Gurgaon, on running away, had left 17,000 rupees at Harsaru Garhi. One hundred troopers and two companies of infantry went thither and brought the money away. It was ordered that it should be lodged in the treasury. A trooper sent by the Baija Bai arrived and stated that his mistress, not crediting the report of slaughter of the Europeans and their wives, had sent him for certain intelligence. The King told him that all the Europeans here had been exterminated, directing him to return to Gwalior accompanied by two troopers, and carrying a special missive, and to tell the Bai Sahib to come to the Royal presence immediately with her troops, and manifest her goodwill. After this, the King held his Court in the Hall of Special Audience. His Majesty bestowed a dress of honour of great grandeur, together with a silver inkstand, on account of his appointment to the Premiership, with the title of 'Prime Minister to the King of the conquered countries'. The said Mirza presented ten gold mohurs to show his sense of the honour conferred on him. The King conferred a similar dress a honour on his special son, Mirza Bakhtawar Shah, on his appointment to the Colonelcy of the 74th regiment Native Infantry. The said Mirza presented two gold mohurs and five rupees as his thanks-offering. His Majesty further presented each of his sons who had been appointed Colonels, with a pair of kettle-drums. The chamberlain Hasan Mirza was ordered to present Kunwar Ajit Singh of Patiala. The Kunwar accordingly attended and presented one gold mohur. The king said he well knew the Kunwar had always been residing in Delhi, and gave him a dress of honour, and the Kunwar in acknowledgement presented an offering of five rupees. Ahmad Mirza and the son of the physician Abdul Hak attended and presented five rupees each. The Risaldar sent by Muhammad Akhbar Ali Khan attended and presented an offering of two rupees on his own account, and a petition from his client, stating that after making necessary arrangements in his territory, he would speedily come to the Royal presence. There were two gentlemen, three ladies, and a child concealed in the house of Nathu tailor, the troopers hearing this made them prisoners and brought them to the palace, and burnt the tailor's house. The King placed these prisoners in the custody of the soldiery. His Majesty went to Salimgarh, where he received a general military salute from the troops. The officers of the 20th Regiment Native Infantry represented that they did not credit the story of the lowing up of the entrenchments at Meerut brought by the two troopers, and that they therefore intended to go and blow them up themselves. The King said it was not necessary; but suggested that if they went they should do so with the concurrence of their General, Mirza Mughal. An order was issued to Kazi Faiz Ulla, the principal police officer of the city, telling him that two of the boats in the bridge over the Jumna had become displaced, and directing him send 100 labourers to restore their lashings. Intelligence was received that several doctors, accompanied by a number of the Mussalman residents of the city, had erected the Mahomedan standard in the Jama Masjid as a declaration of an obligatory war of extermination against the British; and that the doctors having represented the great merit of slaying the English, who, they said, were infidels thousands of Mussalmans had joined the standard. The King hearing this sent a message, saying 'All the English have been killed, against whom have you raised this standard', and directing that it should be removed. Maulavy Sadr-ud-din Khan went to the Jama Masjid and reasoned with the doctors there, and prevailed on them to take the flag down. Several carts of grain, salt, &c., were seized outside the city, and brought it in.

Wednesday, 20th May 1857 – The King came from his private apartments into the Hall of Special Audience. The doctor Muhammad Sayad attended and exchanged greetings with him. The King remarked that he (the doctor) had erected the Mahomedan standard in the Jama Masjid against the English; but that as they had been killed, there had been no necessity for doing so. The doctor replied that it had been sent up against the Hindus. On this, the King remarked that he regarded Hindus and Mahomedans alike, and he was not disposed to acquiesce in a religious war against the Hindus; further remarking that, as for the Christians, all there had been of them, had been already killed. After this, the officers of the army attended and complained that the Mahomedans had raised the Mahomedan flag against them; but the king assured them that the object of its being erected was the slaughter of the English. The officers further represented that one of the magazine servants was seized at the bridge while in the act of taking away small brass gun he had stolen from the park of artillery. The King sentenced the man to be blown away from a gun Mirza Amin-ud-din Khan, Mirza Zia-ud-din Khan, Hasan Ali Khan, and Rahmat Ali Khan attended and paid their respects. The King bestowed a walking stick on each of them as a mark of favour, and they severally presented five rupees each. Mirza Mughal received orders to proceed to Meerut with four guns, four regiments of infantry, and the cavalry, in order to blow up the entrenchments there. The said Mirza suggested that Mirza Amin-ud-din Khan, Mirza Zia-ud-din Khan, Hasan Ali Khan, and other great chiefs holding extensive territories, might be sent with him, and promised to exterminate the English. On hearing this suggestion, the chiefs referred to remained silent. The King then directed Mirza Abulbakr to start with the force. Nawab Mahbub Ali Khan and the physician Ahsan Ulla were ordered to provide funds for the expenses of the army during its march to Meerut. The infantry soldiers searched a cart coming from Meerut and plundered some jewellery there was in it. Some troopers searched that Mubarak Bagh situated beyond the Cantonments, and killed two Europeans who had been hiding there. The officers of the army came and requested that the five European women who were prisoners might be made over to them. The King directed the doctor Mahbub Ali to present a legal opinion according to the Mahomedan law in this matter. The Maulavy presented the opinion required, ruling that the slaughter of women was not legal according to the Mahomedan code. The King now retired to his apartments, where he remained engaged in conference with the Queen and the Secretary Mukand Lal.

It being 4 o'clock the Court adjourns till 11 a.m. tomorrow.

Day seventeen: 24 February 1858

The Court reassembled this day at 11 a.m. pursuant to adjournment of yesterday, in the Hall of Special Audience in the Palace at Delhi.

The President, Members, Interpreter, and Dy. Judge Advocate-General are all present.

The Prisoner is brought into Court, attended by his attorney, Ghulam Abbas.

The following extracts from the *Authentic News* are read in Persian, and translations of them into English are then read and entered as follows:

6th July 1857 – An order attested with the Royal seal was issued to the Commander-in-Chief Bahadur, investing him with the management of the daily allowances to the army, and placing the direction of all military matters of government in his hands.

7th July 1857 – A petition from Rajah Gulab Singh, Ruler of Cashmere, reporting having established his sway throughout the country appertaining to Lahore, and a second from Dost Muhammad Khan, requesting permission to come to the Royal presence, were received under cover of one from the General Bahadur. Orders directing the dispatch of missives in answer were issued.

9th July 1857 – A report was made that General Bakht yar Khan had sent a force fully equipped and appointed to chastise the enemy, and that this force had fought with signal bravery. Couriers continued arriving every moment with reports of the progress of the fight.

11th July 1857 – From the Court, the Suraj-ul-Akhbar – It is ascertained that the King held a Court. The nobles of the realm received admittance in the order of precedence. Particulars of the operations against the accursed hostile force, of the arrangements for carrying on the war, and of the signal valour of the heroes composing His Majesty's army, were submitted for the King's information. An order was issued to Ghulam Nabi Khan to have the house belonging to the Jhajjar Nawab, situated in the section of the city known as Darya, cleared out for the accommodation of the wounded. Some funds were bestowed on the Jaihadis[84] for their expenses.

12th July 1857 – A petition was received from Syad Ali and Baker Ali, chiefs of Benares, submitting that they had made a great slaughter of the doomed infidels, and that they now desire to wait on His Majesty. A favourable answer was written immediately.

13th July 1857 – Information of the capture of Agra through the blessing of God was communicated in petition from the General Bahadur. The King had a salute of 21 guns fired, and the musicians played upon their English flutes, clarinets and drums, in token of rejoicing on the occasion. Two spies with English letters were apprehended today, and were sent to Mirza Mughal for investigation in reference to them. A petition was received from the officers from the Jhansi Regiment, reporting the slaughter of the immoral infidels, and answer was written.

15th July 1857 – A Royal missive was received to his address by Husain Bakht Khan, directing him to go out and meet the Jhansi force which was expected to come in next morning and to have them encamped outside the Ajmir Gate.

16th July 1857 – The officers of Jhansi attended and presented their swords and pistols in token of their devotion. The King with extreme munificence bestowed 2,000 rupees for their immediate expenses.

17th July 1857 – A report being made that two regiments of infantry had arrived from Ambala, orders were issued that Mirza Mughal was to assign them quarters amongst the regiments which had previously come.

18th July 1857 – Several spies of the English were apprehended at the graveyard, and were brought in as prisoners.

2th August 1857 – A petition arrived from the Governor-General Bahadur that the rebel enemy had been compelled to retreat. An order was passed on it that it should be deposited in the office.

4th August 1857 – General Sidhari Singh, of the Neemuch troops, and other illustrious officers having paid their respects, submitted their plans for driving the English away from the ridge, and the King continued conversing with them on this subject.

5th August 1857 – The King issued two orders, the one to the address of Nawab Wali Dad Khan Bahadur, in answer to his petition, intimating

84 Warriors who fought in the cause of religion.

that troops will be sent to him after the capture of the ridge occupied by the British; and the other to the Rajah of Alwar, directing him to forward his tribute with a petition.

6th August 1857 – The King was occupied listening to accounts of the bravery and valour of the troops, when intelligence suddenly arrived that the valiant army had crowned the heights of the ridge, and orders were immediately issued for the dispatch of more troops and ammunition.

7th August 1857 – It was reported that the army having gone into the batteries, was now devotedly engaged in hostile operations. Near the close of the day the awe-inspiring intelligence was submitted that the magazine in the quarter, called the Mohalla Johariwala had accidently been fired, and that the men and women who had been employed there as labourers were burnt as if they had been roasted, and that the building was destroyed by the explosion. When the infantry soldiers, always ready to take advantage of any pretext for acts of oppression, heard of this matter, instigated by some ill-disposed characters, they immediately got up a false imputation against His Excellency the Respected of the state (the court physician) of having had the place fired, and plundered and destroyed his house, and whatever came to each one's hand he carried off. Even the houses of the neighbours were plundered. The King was very much enraged on hearing this, and took the physician into his own protection. He further had a proclamation made that all those who had any of the physician's property were to restore it immediately, otherwise their bellies would be ripped open. After this, the King thought on God the avenger, and gave utterance to the following impromptu quatrain:

My enemies assembled in force on all sides.
O Ali! All powerful, for God's sake!
Thou last sent an unseen army to my aid
It is from thee I supplicate victory in my prayers.

The following paper, No …[85] is now read in the original, and the translation of it is entered as follows:

'With the approving sanction of God. The Lord of the Nation'.

All you Rajahs are famed for your virtues, noble qualities and liberality, and are moreover the protectors of your own faith and of the faith of others. Keeping your welfare in view, I humbly submit that God has given you your bodily existence to establish His different religions, and requires you severally to learn the tenets of your own different religious institutions, and you accordingly continue firm in them. God has moreover sent you into the

85 Number is not given. Ed.

world in your elevated position, and given you dominion and government that you may destroy those who harm your religion. It is incumbent therefore on such of you as have the power, to kill those who may injure your religion; and on such as have not, to engage heartily in devising means for the same end, and thus protect your faith: for it is written in your scriptures that martyrdom is preferable to adopting the religion of another. This is exactly what God has said, and what is evident to everybody. The English are people who overthrow all religions. You should understand well the object of destroying the religions of Hindustan: they have, for a long time been causing books to be written and circulated throughout the country by the hands of their priests, and exercising their authority, have brought out numbers of preachers to spread their own tenets: this has been learnt from one of their own trusted agents. Consider then what systematic contrivances they have adopted to destroy our religions. For instance, *first,* when a woman become a widow, they ordered her to make a second marriage. *Secondly,* the self-immolation of wives on the funeral pyres of their deceased husbands was an ancient religious custom; the English had it discontinued, and enacted their own regulations prohibiting it. *Thirdly,* they told the people it was their wish that they (the people) should adopt their faith, promising that if they did so, they would be respected by Government; and further required them to attend Churches, and hear the tenets preached there. Moreover, they decided and told the Rajahs that such only as were born of their wives would inherit the Government and property, and that adopted heirs would not be allowed to succeed; although according to your scriptures, ten different sorts of heirs are allowed shares in the inheritance. By this contrivance they will rob you of your governments and possessions as they have already done with Nagpur and Lucknow. Consider now and other of their designing plans. They resolved on compelling prisoners with the forcible exercise of their authority to eat their bread. Numbers died of starvation, but did not eat it; others ate it and sacrificed their faith. They now perceived that this expedient did not succeed well, and accordingly determined on having bones ground and mixed with flour and sugar so that people might unsuspectingly eat them in this way. They had, moreover, bones and flesh broken small and mixed with rice which they caused to be placed in the markets for sale; and tried besides every other possible plan to destroy our religions. At last some Bengali after due reflection said that if the troops would accede to the wishes of the English in this matter, all the Bengalis would also conform to them. The English hearing this approved of it and said, 'Certainly this is an excellent idea', never imagining they would be themselves exterminated. They accordingly now ordered the Brahmans and others of their army to bite cartridges in the making up of which fat had been used. The Mussalmans soldiers perceived that by this expedient the religion of the Brahmans and Hindus only was in danger, but nevertheless they also refused to bite them. On this, the English now resolved on ruining the faith of both, and blew away from guns all those soldiers who persisted in their refusal. Seeing this excessive tyranny, the soldiery now in self-preservation, began killing the English and slew them wherever they were found, and are now considering means for slaying the few still alive here and there. It is now my firm conviction that if these English continue in Hindustan, they will kill everyone in the country, and will utterly overthrow our religions. But there are some of my countrymen who have joined the English, and are now fighting on their side. I have reflected well on their case also, and have come to the conclusion that the English will not leave your religion to both you and them. You should understand this well. Under these circumstances, I would ask what course have you decided on to protect your lives and faith? Were your views and mine the same, we might destroy them entirely with a very little trouble, and if we do so, we shall protect our religions and save the country. And as these ideas have been cherished and considered merely from a concern for the protection of the religions and lives of all you Hindus and Mussalmans of this country, this letter is printed for your information. All you Hindus are hereby solemnly adjured by your faith in the Ganges, Tulsi, and Saligram, and all you Mussalmans, but your belief in God and the Kuran as these English are the common enemy of both, to unite in considering their slaughter extremely expedient, for by this alone will lives and faith of both be saved. It is expedient then that you should coalesce and slay them. It is slaughter of kine that is regarded by the Hindus as a great insult to their religion. To prevent this, a solemn compact or agreement has been entered into by all the Mahomedan chiefs of Hindustan, binding themselves that if the Hindus will come forward to slay the English, the Mahomedans will from that very day put a stop to the slaughter of cows, and those of them who will not do so, will be considered to have abjured the Kuran, and such of them as will eat beef will be regarded as though they had eaten pork: but will try to save them, they will be as guilty in the sight of God as though they had committed the sins of killing cows and eating flesh. Perhaps the English may, for their own ends, try to assure the Hindus that as the Mussalmans have consented to give up killing cows from respect for the Hindu religion, they will solemnly engage to do the same, and will ask the Hindus to join them against the Mussalmans; but no sensible man will be guiled by such deceit, for the solemn promises and professions of the English are always deceitful and interested. Once their ends are gained, they will infringe their engagements, for deception has ever been habitual with them, and the treachery they have always practised on the people Hindustan is known to rich and poor. Do you therefore give heed to what they may say. Be well assured you will never have such an opportunity again. We all know that writing a letter is equivalent to an advance halfway towards fellowship. I trust you will all write answers approving of what has been proposed herein. This letter has been printed under the direction of Maulavi Syad Kutb Shah Sahib, at the Bahaduri Press, in the city of Bareilly.

The following Extracts from a Native Paper called the *Suraj-ul Akhbar* are now reached in the original. Translations of them are entered as follows:

Tuesday, 25th August 1857– The time between dawn and daylight having been passed in the usual necessary religious observances, the Respected of the state (the physician) was allowed the honour of inspecting the Royal pulse. The King then took his seat on the throne in state, and the great and dignified nobles of the realm being allowed the honour of appearing in the Royal presence, discharged with extreme respect their devotions and obeisance. His Majesty inspected two orders prepared in the Royal Secretariat Office, the one addressed to Bahadur Ali Khan, Hasan Ali Khan Durgaprashad and Bhup Singh, officers of the troops at Peshawar, directing them to make all haste in coming to the Royal presence, and to bring a suitable amount of treasure with them, and the other to the Prince Royal Mirza Muhammad Kochak, ordering him to distribute the pay of the Nasirabad force. After inspection, these orders were sealed with the special seal dispatched agreeably to the Royal permission. His Majesty then proceeded to bestow consideration on the following petitions: *First* – A petition from Tanawar Ali Khan, son of Muhammad Abdul Ghafar Khan, resident of Mustafabad, otherwise called Rampur, professing fidelity and allegiance, and avowing his intention of coming to the Royal presence. *Secondly* – A petition from Rajah Nahar Singh, Chief of Ballabhgarh, through Mir Fateh Ali Khan, making processions of heartfelt fidelity, allegiance, zeal, and goodwill. *Thirdly* – A petition from Waris Muhammad Khan of Bhupal, reporting the slaughter of 56 of the accursed English, and enclosing copy of a proclamation issued to the residents of the city and country to engage in like manner in the destruction of the damnable infidels, and moreover soliciting the honour of Royal missive. *Fourthly* – A petition from Kashi Rao Holkar of Indore, expressive of his devotion and zealous activity in the service of the King; avowing his fixed purpose and determinate resolve to ruin and exterminate the English, clever in all villainy; and forwarding five of the heads of enemies killed. *Fifthly* – A petition from Muhammad Amir Khan, son of Ghulam Muhammad Khan, son of Abdul Samad Khan, resident of Dojana.

Having perused the above petitions, His Majesty decided that answer should be sent after further consideration.

The Officers of the army coming into the Royal presence, submitted that as Muhammad Bakht Khan, Governor-General Bahadur, had gone with His Majesty's victorious forces in the direction of Alipur, to fight against the infidel enemy, and was now engaged in active operations against them, it was necessary that reinforcements should be sent to his assistance. On this representation, orders were accordingly issued that a further portion of the troops should be sent in that direction.

After this, His Majesty retired to his private kingly hall: at noon, he partook of the delicacies presented for dinner, after which he enjoyed a siesta.

He then went through the prayers appointed for the first of the daily five times, continued occupied in such pastimes as those he delights in, and then read the prayers of the second time. Near the close of the day, he honoured the Respected of the state (the court physician) by allowing him to feel his pulse: after this, he condescended to visit the luxuriant garden of Salimgarh for relaxation and pleasure. Returning from Salimgarh, His Majesty retired to his private hall. The officers of the force stationed at Teliwara represented the irregularity of no force being sent to relieve them. After this, he again came into the Hall of Special Audience, and held a leave, but retired again shortly, much agitated and displeased. After sunset, those in attendance at Court were honoured with permission to leave.

Wednesday, 26th August 1857 – Having passed the time between dawn and sunrise in the observances suited to that portion of the day, His Majesty allowed the Respected of the state (the court physician) to feel his pulse, and then took his seat in state on the throne, the exalted nobles in attendance forming a circle like a halo round the moon. The officers of the army submitted that reinforcements should be sent to the aid of the forces which had gone out to combat with the enemy, and were to go. After this, the King having inspected the three following orders prepared in the Royal Secretariat Office, they were attested with the seal, and the King gave permission for their being dispatched.

1st – An order to the officers of the army, directing that the one-half of the forces should proceed to the Najafgarh Battery, and the other to the Teliwara Battery.
2nd – An order to Mirza Muhammad Zahur-ud-din Bahadur regarding his investment with power to forgive offences, and to consider the army under his orders.
3rd – An order to Thakur Chaman Singh, to bring some more of his brothers.

A petition having been received from Shahzada Muhammad Azim Bahadur, representing his difficulties in consequence of the arrival of the enemies forces, and requesting that re-enforcements including artillery might be sent to his assistance, the King gave orders that a Royal missive in reply should be written. After this, the King retired from the Court to his private apartments: at noon, His Majesty partook of the delicacies presented for dinner, and then retired to take his siesta. Having gone through the prayers of the first of the five times, he occupied himself with such amusements as he is partial to, and then read the prayers of the second time. Near the close of the day, His Majesty, accompanied by all the nobles of the state, went to the Salimgarh garden for recreation and amusement. He returned in the evening, and retired to his private apartments.

Thursday, 27th August 1857 – Rising at dawn and passing some time in the customary religious observances, the King honoured the Respected of the state, the court physician, by allowing him to feel his pulse. His Majesty then took his seat in state on the throne, when his illustrious sons, and the exalted nobles of the realm, paid their respects. Baldeo Singh Kundla Kush (?) presented his nazar, when, with excessive kindly condescension, he was honoured with the gift of a pair of shawls as treasurer of the infantry, and he accordingly presented the usual nazar to show his thankfulness for this honour, which was accepted. The king next examined the six following orders which had been prepared in the Royal Secretariat Office, and after inspection permitted their being attested with the special seal and dispatched:

1st – An order to Mirza Muhammad Khair Sultan Bahadur, assuring him that he was invested with full powers in regard to arrangements for raising money, and that no representations in this matter from any person whatsoever would be heeded.

2nd – An order to Mirza Mughal Bahadur, Mirza Khair Sultan Bahadur, the officers of the army, and the members of the court of deliberation to the effect that money having been twice received from the merchant Ramji Das Gurwalla, he was on no account to be subjected to any further demand.

3rd – An order to Mirza Abdul Hasan, otherwise Mirza Abdulla Bahadur, in answer to the petition of Amir Khan of Dojana, directing his attendance at Court.

4th – An order to Kashi Rao Holkar of Indore, directing his attendance at Court.

5th – An order to Raja Nahar Singh, Chief of Ballabhgarh, intimating that a dun horse had been received, and directing him to entertain no fears of being molested by the army.

6th – An order through Fateh Ali Khan to Tanawar Ali Khan, son of Abdulla Khan of Rampur, directing his attendance. Some troopers communicated particulars of the success, valour, and enterprise of the troops, and particularly of the Neemuch force; they also communicated the gathering of the peasantry round Najafgarh. Feeling indisposed, His Majesty issued orders for the immediate attendance of the Court physician, and retired to his private apartments. At noon, His Majesty ate of the delicacies presented for his dinner, and then took his siesta: after this, he discharged the prayers appointed for the third time of the day. The court physician being in attendance, prepared and gave His Majesty a cooling in attendance at Court were allowed to leave.

Friday, 28th August 1857 – Having discharged the usual religious observances, the King permitted the court physician to feel his pulse, and then came into the Hall of Special Audience, where the nobles and chiefs of the realm paid their respects. Khawaja Ismail Khan, a resident of Calpi, came forward and presented the offering usual on admission to the Royal presence. His Majesty feeling weak, then retired to his private apartments. At noon, he enjoyed his dinner, then took his siesta, afterwards he discharged the prayers appointed for the second and third times of the day, drank a cooling draught prepared by the court physician, and dismissed his retinue for the day.

The four following orders were then attested with the special seal, and issued agreeably to His Majesty's commands:

1st – An order to Muhammad Safi, Brigadier, &c., in answer to his petition, assuring him that His Majesty was not displeased or angry with him, nor did he entertain any suspicions against the Neemuch troops.

2nd – An order to Mirza Rahmat Bahadur to pay up the rent of the Imambara which is appropriated to the expenses of the department called the 'Nazar Nisar'.

3rd – An order to Ahmad Ali Khan, Chief of Farrukhnagar, directing him to send some matchlocks.

4th – An order to Bahadur Jang, regarding the theft in his territory of a string of 14 camels.

A petition from Abdul Latif Khan, Chief of Khanpur, promising to come to Court, and to bring some elephants with him, and representing that he had been unwell.

At 1 o'clock the Court adjourns till Saturday, the 27th of February, at 11 a.m., that Mr. Everett, a witness, may attend.

Day eighteen: 27 February 1858

The Court reassembled this morning at 11 a.m. in the Hall of Special Audience in the Palace of Delhi.

The President, Members, Interpreter, and Dy. Judge Advocate-General are all present.

The Prisoner is brought into Court, attended by his attorney, Ghulam Abbas.

Johan Everett, a Risaldar, late of the 14th Regiment of Irregular Cavalry, and now of the Constabulary Force, is called into Court and duly sworn.

Examined by the Judge Advocate

Question – Were you at Delhi on the 11th of May 1857?

Answer – I was.

Question – Relate what you then witnessed in reference to the outbreak?

Answer – About 9 o'clock in the morning, the mutineers from Meerut entered the city, and the alarm was given that they were killing the Europeans gentlemen and all the Christians. Half an hour afterwards, I heard the report of musketry near the Magazine. I remained quiet in the house till evening, being unwell, and only at Delhi on sick leave, but not thinking myself safe in the hired house in which I was living, I went, about dark, into Colonel Skinner's compound and remained there all night. Very early next morning I went to Mirza Azim Beg's house (a Sardar Bahadur and a pensioner from the 1st Irregular Cavalry), and asked him to keep me in his house during the day, and at any rate to get me out of the city. He told me to remain quiet in his house, and that he would try and do so. I remained there for a day and a night, and the second day he told me that his neighbours had got intelligence of my being hid in his house. Mr. George Skinner was also in his house. Mirza Azim Beg, with whom we were staying, went to the palace for the purpose of getting a guard from the King for our protection. He was away an hour on his errand, and then sent me word that the King's physician, *viz.* Ahsan Ulla Khan, was very angry at his protecting Christians in his house, and desired that we were to get out of his house immediately. I accordingly left his house as he desired, but Mr. George Skinner remained concealed in the apartments of the females of the establishment. I had got away about 200 yards from the Sirdar Bahadurs house, when I saw some of the mutineer sepoys. A Masjid was close to me, and I thought if I could get into it and remain quiet, the mutineers would pass on; but just as the mutineers came in line with the Masjid, someone recognized me and called out to the mutineers, that there was a Christian in the Masjid. They accordingly made me a prisoner; they then went to the house of Mirza Azim Beg, and also made a prisoner of Mr. George Skinner. Both of us were being taken to the Kotwali; but before we had reached it, about 11 troopers from the 3rd Light Cavalry came galloping up and asked the sepoys 'Who are you taking prisoners? Are they Christians?' They replied: 'Yes', when some of the troopers drew their pistols and said: 'Why take them to the Kotwali at all; why not kill them here?' The others replied: 'The Kotwali is not far off, let them go there, and you can then do as you like'. On reaching the Kotwali, the sepoys made a report to the Kotwal, saying they had brought two children, prisoners. The Kotwal gave no answer, and a trooper came up to Mr. George Skinner and caught him by the hair of his head, and pulling him away about 50 paces from the Kotwali, and placing him in front of the canal wall, shot him with his pistol: several other shots were fired at him by some other troopers, and he fell dead. I stood before the Kotwali thinking they would come and take me; but the troopers, after killing Mr. Skinner, galloped off to the fort. I was then ordered by the Havildar at the Kotwali to go and sit among the prisoners; and there I remained for 25 days with 40 others, men, women, and children, all Christians, after which we were released in consequence of a Maulavy by the name of Muhammad Ismail, giving evidence that we were all Mahomedans, and that if there were any Christians, they would become Mahomedans, and that it was not lawful to kill such as turn to Mahomedanism of their own accord. We were not, however, allowed to leave the city. I then went to live with an African of the name of Moujud.

Question – Had you had any intercourse or intimacy with this man previously?

Answer – I knew the man very well, as he had been in Colonel Skinner's service formerly, and had left it about the year 1842.

Question – At the time of the outbreak, in whose service was this African?

Answer – In the King's service; he had been so some years.

Question – Did he ever try and induce you to leave the Company's service, and go over to that of the King?

Answer – Yes, he did speak to me about it, *viz.* about three days previous to the outbreak, he came to my house while I was looking at horses to purchase for my corps, and said he wished to speak to me. I went aside with him, and he then said, 'You had better leave the Company's service and with your troops come over to that of the King'. He said this in the way of friendly advice, I asked him his reason. He said, 'This hot weather you will see the Russians all over the place'. I laughed at the fellow's ideas, and told him some other time. This conversation took place on Saturday, the 9th of May 1857, at 11 a.m. He did not come back, however, and when I was released from the Kotwali I went to him, and he said to me, 'Did I not tell you to come away?' And he then went on to tell me that there was an African of the name of Kambar, that had been sent from here, two years before the outbreak, to Constantinople: he also mentioned that this man Kambar had left Delhi on the pretence of going to Mecca, but had really been sent as an ambassador from the King of Delhi, to get some help from Russia; and that this man Kambar, on leaving Delhi, had made a promise that he would return in two years.

Question – During your stay with Moujud, did you get any further intelligence from him relative to the outbreak?

Answer – No, not exactly in reference to the outbreak; but he used to return home at night, and give me the news of the day; and on one occasion he told me that the King had assembled all his sons and his men of note at a public durbar, and remarked to them that since the battle at Ghazi-ud-din Nagar he had observed that they had been gradually sneaking away from their attendance on him, and that he imagined this must be through a fright. The King added that this was the time when they should all unite, and heartily combine to drive the British off the ridge. 'If you do not do so', said he, 'mark my words, if the British ever enter Delhi again, they will not leave one soul alive of the descendants of Taimur Shah'. This man Moujud was the Chief of 10 or 12 Africans in the service of the King; he was a private special attendant of his and was always by his side, and I think his statements to me may be perfectly relied on.

Question – Did this man Moujud offer you money or any other inducements to quit the Company's service?

Answer – No.

Question – Do you know whether his proposal to the above effect emanated from the King or any high official in the palace?

Answer – I did not take it as such; I merely thought it was the man's own foolishness.

Question – Are you aware whether any other persons in the military service of the Company were ever solicited to go over to the King?

Answer – Not to my knowledge.

Question – Did you ever hear the men of your regiment talking about the Chapatis that were circulated from village to village before the outbreak?

Answer – No, I was on leave at my own village at the time, and all that I heard in reference to the subject was that the chapatis were going about, and that nobody could make out the meaning of it.

Question – How long had you been in Delhi previous to the 11th of May?

Answer – About 13 or 14 days.

Question – During that time, had you heard the people saying and speaking among themselves to the effect that any disturbance was soon likely to occur?

Answer – No, I was sick and had little intercourse with the Delhi people.

Question – You have said that Moujud told you after the outbreak, that the Russians would soon be all over the place: do you know whether this was the general belief of the city?

Answer – Yes, I think it was: the subject was one of general conversation among the Mahomedans with whom I was able to have intercourse; they said they expected the Russians this hot season.

Question – Had you, previous to the outbreak, any conversation with the native officers and men of your regiment, on the subject of the Company's Government?

Answer – A Mahomedan officer of the 14th Irregular Cavalry, by the name of Mirza Taki Beg, said it was written in his books that a change would take place, and that the British rule would soon be overthrown. This was at Peshawar. I am not sure whether it was in the year 1855 or 1856.

Question – Have you ever heard any persons remarking on the length of time the English rule had lasted, and that in the common order of events it could not exist much longer?

Answer – No.

Question – From what you know, were the Hindus in Delhi or the Mussalmans most averse to the Company's Government?

Answer – The Mussalmans.

Question – Did you ever hear that the King of Persia was coming with an army to India: or did you ever hear the war between the English and Persians particularly alluded to by the natives?

Answer – No, I never used to talk with the natives on this subject, as I got my information from reading the English newspapers.

Question – Do you know whether the expected coming of the Russians was believed in by the natives or talked about by them before the outbreak?

Answer – No, I cannot speak to the point, as I never had any intercourse with the natives.

The Prisoner declines to cross-examine.

Examined by the Court

Question – From anything you heard whilst in Delhi, have you the least reason to suppose that the Prisoner joined the mutinous army unwillingly?

Answer – I can only declare what I have heard: that at the first commencement the King was unwilling; but when he found himself implicated, he joined afterwards, *viz.* in about a fortnight. This is mere hearsay, and I can produce no authority for it.

The witness withdraws.

Ghulam Abbas, the Prisoner's attorney, is reminded of his affirmation as a witness.

Examined by the Judge Advocate

Question – Look at these 12 papers, and say whether you think them genuine or not.

The Court at 4 p.m. adjourns till 11 a.m. on Wednesday, March 3rd, to allow the Interpreter to translate extracts from native newspapers and other documents.

Petition of Mukand Lal, Dated 2 p.m., Tuesday, 18th August 1857

To – The Nourisher of the Poor!

Respectfully Sheweth – That when the King, after holding his Court, had retired to his own apartments, Maulavy Fazl-ul-Hak, Nawab Ahmad Kuli Khan Bahadur, Budhan Sahib, and Mirza Khair Sultan Bahadur had the orders written which are detailed below: that all the officers of the army came to Nawab Ahmad Kuli Khan, demanding money for expenses; and that the King again came out at 12 o'clock. I have submitted these matters for your information. Moreover, all the order above referred to came under the King's inspection. The queen of the world[86] was asleep and the seals have therefore not been affixed. They will, however, be affixed at 3 p.m.

86 Begum Zeenat Mahal.

and though the King's Court for the day has been ended, the whole of the officers are still sitting about Nawab Ahmad Kuli Khan.

1. To the address of Rao Tula Ram.[87] To send money. Written as directed by the Shamshir-ud-dowlat.
2. To the address of Rao Tula Ram.2 Ordering the remittance of money in reference to Sadhrowli. Written as directed by the Shamshir-ud-dowlat.
3. To the address of Jiaji Scindiah. Written as directed by General Ghulam Ghaus Khan.
4. To Baijja Bai. Written as directed by General Ghulam Ghaus Khan.
5. To Rana Bhagavant Singh. Written as directed by General Ghulam Ghaus Khan.
6. To the address of Chandhari Manbedhar. Written as directed by General Ghulam Ghaus Khan.
7. To the address of Maulavy Wazir Ali. Written as directed by General Ghulam Ghaus Khan.
8. To the Officers of the Mhow and Indore troops. Written as directed by General Ghulam Ghaus Khan.
9. To the Officers of the Morar troops. Written as directed by General Ghulam Ghaus Khan.
10. To the address of Bakshish Ali. Written as directed by Hasan Bakhsh Uzbegi, directing the enlistment of 500 infantry for Malagarh.
11. Passport to Lucknow, agreeably to the request of Muhammad Baksh. Written as directed by Kuliyt Ulla Beg Khan and Hasan Baksh Khan Uzbegi.
12. To Rao Tula Ram. To remit the revenue of Sadhrowli. Written as directed by the Shamshir-ud-dowlat Bahadur.
13. To Rao Tula Ram. To send in his trusted accredited agent. Written as directed by the Shamshir-ud-dowlat Bahadur.
14. To Rao Tula Ram. To send in treasure. Written as directed by the Shamshir-ud-dowlat Bahadur.
15. To Rao Tula Ram. To send in the revenue of Tanda Malahaira. Written as directed by the Shamshir-ud-dowlat Bahadur.
16. To Hasan Baksh Uzbegi. To realize the revenue of the Aligarh district. Written in the presence of Maulavy Fazl-ul-Hak, Shamshir-ud-dowlat, Budhan Sahib, and Mirza Khair Sultan.
17. To Faiz Ahmad. Appointing him to realize the revenues of the Bulandshahr and Aligarh Districts, written as directed by Maulavy Fazl-ul-Hak.
18. To Walidad Khan. To aid the above two men in realizing the revenue – Maulavy Fazl-ul-Hak.

87 The Chief of Rewari (Haryana) who took prominent part in the Revolt.

19. To Rao Gulab Singh. To remit the revenue by the hands of Hasan Baksh and Faiz Baksh and Faiz Ahmad, 12,000 rupees.
20. To Abdul Latif Khan of Khanpoor. To remit his revenue by the hands of Hasan Baksh and Faiz Ahmad.
21. To Muhammad Ali Khan of Chatauri. To remit his revenue by the hands of Hasan Baksh and Faiz Ahmad.
22. To Zohar Ali of Dharmpur. To remit his revenue by the hands of Hasan Baksh and Faiz Ahmad.
23. To Muhammad Daud Khan of Hakimpur. To remit his revenue by the hands of Hasan Baksh and Faiz Ahmad.
24. To Rajah Damman Singh. To remit his revenue by the hands of Hasan Baksh and Faiz Ahmad.
25. To ... (illegible) of Shahabad. To preserve order in his territory. Written as directed by the Nawab Sahib.
26. To Maulavy Abdul Hak Khan. To make arrangements for realizing the revenue of the Gurgaon District. Written as directed by Maulavy Fazl-ul-Hak, whose nephew will go to Gurgaon.
27. To Narayan Das, merchant. To the effect that no demand for money will be made. Written as directed by Mirza Khair Sultan Bahadur. Petition of the slave Mukand Lal. No order or note of any kind.

Order attested with the official seal of Colonel Mirza Muhammad Khan Khair Sultan Bahadur, dated 9th June 1857

To – The Officers and Subedars of the Army.

May health and safety attend you. As the troops which have been fighting here for their religion have, through the blessing of God, been completely victorious, you are hereby directed, provided you still continue firm in your religious tenets, to come here at once, for you will be richly rewarded by the Government, and will besides preserve your religion and creed. It is confidently expected that the English will be all killed wherever they may be. As for this place, not a single Englishman has been left. The King is now established on his throne. He has done everything to keep your brethren of the army contented and satisfied, and has bestowed rewards on them.

An order from Mirza Muhammad Jawan Bakht, supposed to be in his own handwriting, dated 9th June 1857

To – The well-wisher of unsuspected Fidelity, Mir Ahmad Amir.

May you continue in health and safety. A musket, dagger, and sword have just been received through Harprasad. This is written for your satisfaction.

Note on the Reverse – This receipt for a sword and musket was received in the Police Office on 9th June 1857. Signature illegible.

Petition from the Officers of the Royal Treasury, dated 11th June 1857

To – King! Shelter of the World!

May his prosperity continue

Respectfully sheweth, That agreeably to Your Majesty's orders, Rupees 1,000 have been paid through assistant chamberlain Basant Ali Khan, as a present and on account of their daily allowances to the men of the infantry regiment come from Sirsa. Your petitioner prays he may be graciously favoured with a receipt under Your Majesty's signature. (Prayers for the prosperity of the reign.) Rupees 1,000. Petition of Your Majesty's home-born slaves, the officers of the Royal Treasury.

Autograph order by the King, in pencil

This has reached the Royal presence.

Petition from the Officer of the Royal Treasury, dated 15th June 1857

To – The King! Shelter of the World!

Respectfully seweth, That agreeably to Your Majesty's order Rupees 1,300 have been paid to the troops come from Bareily, partly as a present, and partly on account of their daily allowances. Your petitioner, therefore, prays that he may be graciously favoured with a receipt under the Royal signature.

It was necessary and is therefore submitted.

Present	...	...	Rs.1,000
Allowances	...	...	300

Total	...	...	1,300

Petition of Your Majesty's home-born slaves, the officers of the Royal Treasury.

Autograph note by the King, in pencil

This has reached the Royal presence.

Petition of Muhammad Murtaza Khan, Risaldar. No date, date of a note on the reverse, 9th July 1857.

To – The King! Shelter of the World, & c.

Respectfully seweth, That agreeably to your Royal orders your petitioner and the men of the corps of cavalry have for a month and a half had their quarters in Your Majesty's garden, generally known as that of Begam Sombre, and that, having had the bathroom under the house cleared of the accumulated filth and rubbish, at an expense of one rupee from their own funds, they have kept the cavalry appurtenances and accoutrements there. The men of the regular cavalry now come from Gwalior, have taken possession of the place, and the troopers of my corps are in consequence suffering great inconvenience from exposure to the rain, for besides this bathroom there is no other place of shelter in the garden in Question. I therefore pray that orders may be issued to the men of the regular cavalry, directing them not to disturb us in our occupancy, but to search out some other quarters for themselves, or at least to occupy one-half themselves, and to leave the other half to us. It was necessary and I have therefore submitted it. (Prayers for the prosperity of the reign.) Petition of the slave Mir Muhammad Murtaza Khan, Risaldar.

Autograph order by the King, in pencil

Mirza Mughal will explain to the Gwalior troopers that they are to occupy half of the place, and to give the other half to the petitioners.

A transcript of the King's order in ink on the reverse.

Note – Also on the Reverse – According to orders, a written order has been issued.

Dated 9th July 1857

Orders under the King's autograph cypher, in pencil

Dated 27th July 1857

To – The Officers of the Royal Treasury.

Pay 4,000 rupees from the money in your hands for the daily allowance, &c., of the army, and for the expenses connected with the magazine. Consider this imperative.

Rupees 4,000, the half of which is Rupees 2,000.

Order under the King's autograph cypher in pencil

Dated 27th July 1857

To – The Officers of the Royal Treasury.

Send 1,000 rupees to the Royal presence that it may be given as a reward to the infantry come from Neemuch! – allow no delay – consider this imperative.

Rupees 1,000, the half of which is Rupees 500.

Rough drafts of three orders from the King, without signature, seal or cypher. Note at the top to the effect that copies have been written in the books, showing that the originals had been dispatched, and that the office copies for record were subsequently made from these rough drafts – First Order, dated 21st August 1857.

Ghulam Mau'ud-ud-din Khan, subordinate Collector of land revenue and thc landholders of Baghput – With reference to your application for a military force, you are informed that Mirza Muhammad Shah and the son of Mirza Haji are with you, and you our slaves are directed to exert yourselves with heart and soul in forwarding supplies. You are directed to remain obedient to the troops and to forward your revenue and your personal pecuniary offerings in token of your allegiance under the charge of your own trustworthy agents, and the military.

Signed, dated 21st August 1857

To – The Principal Farmers, Chiefs, Landholders and Peasants of Sonepat, Panipat, Najafgarh, Bahadurgarh, &c., and to the Villagers of the Mewant.

You are hereby directed to give full Obedience and respect to the authority of Mirza Abdulla Bahadur, son of Mirza Shah-Rukh Bahadur, and our own special grandson; and to that of the army of the Lord Governor-General Muhammad Bakht Khan Bahadur, proceeding in your direction, and all you, slaves, are further directed to furnish all necessary supplies agreeably to all such orders as you may receive from the said prince and the officers of the army. You are moreover directed to send all such money as you may be forwarding on account of the revenue, or as offerings in token of your allegiance in the charge of your own trusted men, accompanied by a military guard from the prince's army, and on no account to entrust it to the care of others; observing every precaution in this matter, act according to these Royal orders. No date.

To – The Slave Siddhari Singh, and the whole of the Troops come from Neemuch and to Hira Singh.

Learn! – That you are hereby ordered to proceed in the direction of Alapur, Panipat, and Sonepat, there to join the troops come from Bareilly. In doing this, you will consult your pleasure; you are required to act with unanimity in the service of state, and to allow no delay in your departure. This order has been issued at the request of the Lord Governor Bahadur.

Petition of Muhammad Khawaja Hasan Khan, deputed to Saharanpur, &c., written from Muradnagar

Dated 9th September 1857

To – The King! Cherisher of the Poor, Lord of Mankind, &c.

Respectfully Sheweth, That your petitioner has before this, both by petition and verbal messages, sent intelligence daily of reported coming of the Europeans with six guns, for the purpose of desolating Muradnagar and Ghaziabad, and destroying the bridge over the Hindan, and requesting to be favoured with reinforcements, that he might make a slaughter of the infidels. Your Majesty has not yet been pleased to bestow any aid. Information has just been obtained from travellers coming from Meerut, that the Europeans, accompanied by Ali Khan, the former subordinate collector of revenue in the service of the infidels, and bringing four guns, have left Meerut on their march in the direction of Muradnagar, with the object of attacking your petitioner and destroying the said bridge. Before this, some Europeans went with six guns from Happar and burnt the village of Pilkhoah, killing nearly 150 of its inhabitants. The consequence of this intelligence, your petitioner has taken up a position on the road with the whole force of cavalry and infantry, the men being kept under arms. Your petitioner has no reluctance to sacrifice his life in Your Majesty's cause, but reflecting on the numerical weakness of his party, and the absence of artillery, he is to some extent afraid that the bridge may be broken. Should the bridge be in any way injured (God forbid that it should be!), the movements of the troops and the conveyance of supplies will be entirely hindered. Your petitioner trusts that a reinforcement in infantry and artillery may be speedily dispatched by Your Majesty, so that the infidels may be effectually resisted. (Prayers for the prosperity of the reign.) Petition of the slave Muhammad Khawaja Khan, deputed to Saharanpur, &c., written from Muradnagar under date the 9th September 1857.

Autograph order by the King, in pencil

Mirza Mughal will act in accordance with the requisition in the petition.

Order on the reverse: Probably by Mirza Mughal in furtherance of the King's order – The Brigade Major Sahib is directed to take such measures as may be necessary.

Order also on the reverse, by the Brigade Major apparently – Let an order be written directing the 14th Regiment of infantry to go out. Dated 10th September 1857, year of reign 21.

Order from the King, without signature, cypher, seal or date,

To – The Rajahs, Nawabs, and other influential Residents of the Province of Allahabad.

Consider yourselves receiving the Royal favour. As our special slave, the chief Ali Kasim, has been appointed to the government of the province of Allahabad and the districts subordinate thereto, it will behove you to afford him your aid and cooperation in all matters, and in no instance to act contrary to his orders, or without his consent and exterminating the accursed English. If it shall appear that you have acted with zeal, you will be graciously rewarded: if not, it will not be well for you.

Draft of an order on the reverse, without signature, cypher, seal, or date.

To – The Nawab of Banda.

As our special slave, the Chief Ali Kasim, has been appointed Governor of Allahabad, it will behove you, immediately on receipt of this Royal mandate, to join him with your artillery, cavalry, and infantry, and exterminate the English. You are, moreover, directed not in any matter to act contrary to the views and wishes of the said chief. You are to consider these orders extremely imperative, and are to act in accordance with them.

Petition of Syad Muhammad Hasan. No date.

To – The King! Shelter of the World!

Respectfully Sheweth, That your slave the petitioner has been in attendance since yesterday, but has not a place so much as to sit or stand in. I therefore pray that some quarters may be assigned to me and my companions, in all 84 Jahadis, where we may rest ourselves. It was necessary, and we have submitted it. Petition of slave Syad Muhammad Hasan Jahadi and well-wisher to His Majesty's cause.

Autograph order of the King, in pencil

You know what the state of the revenue just now is. May the Jihadis be amply commanded for all the meritorious deed they are performing.

The Court at 4 p.m. adjourns till 11 a.m. on Wednesday, the 3rd of March, to allow the interpreter to translate extracts from native newspapers and other documents.

Day nineteen: 3 March 1858

The Court reassembled this day at 11 a.m. pursuant to adjournment of yesterday, in the Hall of Special Audience in the Palace at Delhi.

The President, Members, Interpreter, and Dy. Judge Advocate-General are all present.

The Prisoner, attended by the attorney Ghulam Abbas, is brought into Court.

The following 18 papers are now read in original by the Interpreter, and the translations of them are read and entered by the Judge Advocate as follows:

No. 1

Extract from the *Authentic News*, p. 285

Local intelligence.
Persia.

It is ascertained from newspapers from Persia, that the Persian King has issued orders to all his troops not absolutely employed in the different districts, to assemble and remain at Teheran till further orders, which they have been told they will be expected to carry out with heart and soul immediately on receipt. It is currently reported here that this demonstration against the Amir Dost Muhammad Khan is only a strategic move on the part of the King of Persia, to cloak his real design of fighting against and conquering the English, because, confiding in the British power, Amir Dost Muhammad Khan has allied himself to the English, and has been the cause of all the disagreements between the English and the Persians. The King of Persia, however, has not openly thrown off amicable relations with the English, nor has he yet personally adopted a course of enmity against Amir Dost Muhammad Khan. It is nevertheless certain some change of feeling has taken place amongst the three powers.

No. 2
Extract from the *Authentic News*, No. IV, Vol. III, dated 26th of January 1857

Local News.
France.

The newspapers all agree in declaring that the King of France and the Emperor of Turkey have not as yet openly avowed themselves the allies of either the English or the Persians but the ambassadors of these two opposite parties secretly visit the courts of both the sovereigns mentioned above with gifts and presents. Some think that the King of France and the Emperor of Turkey will not mix themselves in the quarrel between the Persians and the English; but most people say, that they will both side with the Persians. Whatever is ascertained hereafter will be published without fail. As for the Russians, however, they make no secret of the readiness with which they are assisting, and will continue to assist the Persians, whether it be with funds or with forces. It may be said that virtually the Russians are the cause of this war, and that using the Persians as a cloak, they intend to consummate their own designs, regarding the conquest of Hindustan. It is to be believed that the Russians will very soon take the field in great force. If anything further is ascertained it will be published. Let the readers of the *Authentic News* be prepared to see what the veil of futurity will disclose.

No. 3
Extract from the *Authentic News,* No. II, Vol. III, dated 16th March 1857, pp. 82 and 83

Local News.
Court of Persia.

It is discovered from the late Bombay papers received at this press that the King of Persia one day summoned a number of Herat chiefs, together with his nobles, to his court, and had a conference with them regarding the war. After due deliberation, they all advised him unanimously to declare war against the English, expressing their dependence that God would will his being victorious, for, said they. 'Taking Herat you will be in a position as though you had reached the doorway into Hindustan'. They further urged that the wish of the Russians too was that the Persians should go to war with the English, and should conquer India. On this, the King declared with an oath, that he was greatly pleased with these countries, who had given advice so opposite to that of his perfidious prime minister, and solemnly promised that on reaching India, he would appoint them to the Governorships of different provinces, *viz.* one to that of Bombay, another to that of Calcutta, a third to Poona, and so on, and that they would bestow the crown on the

King of Delhi. Just at this juncture, intelligence was brought that the prime minister had clandestinely sold the King's diadem jewelled with precious stones, through a merchant named Haji Ali for a 1,25,000 francs, giving him (the merchant) a portion of the money. On this, the King sent for the wily prime minister for keeping up intrigues with people of other nations. It is reported that the duties of prime minister have been entrusted to some other statesman. It is said that the prime minister above alluded to generally counselled the King to maintain a peaceable policy. It was reported to the King that the Emperor of Russia had sent an effective and thoroughly appointed army of 400,000 men, with abundant munitions, to assist him, and that portions of these had already joined the Persians, and it was also reported that the Emperor of Russia had declared that if the force should be insufficient for the intended wars and slaughter, the constabulary army would also be sent. In answer to these communications, the King spoke in terms of the highest praise of the Emperor Alexander of Russia, and issued instructions that funds for the expenses of the Russian army should be defrayed from his treasury, and that the courier from the Russian army should not want for anything or suffer any inconveniences. After this, the French ambassador submitted as welcome news, that his sovereign, who had for some days been unwell, was now, by the blessing of god, restored to perfect health. The King hearing this, said, he thanked God for it. The Georgian ambassador now presented his master's compliments, and started that contrary to the laws of England and Turkey, the sale of slaves of both sexes still continued in his country. Throughout Persia, it is reported that the chief reason for the Persian King going to war with the English is that for five successive generations, the occupants of the Persian throne, intending to conquer India, had been accumulating all sorts of military munitions, and had been laying by treasures; but that no one of them had been able to work up his resolution to the undertaking, and that moreover Nasir-ud-din, the present sovereign, had himself long cherished the same wish, transmitted to him as it were hereditarily, when the present opportunity presented itself. On one side, Heart came easily into possession; on another, the unforeseen assistance of the Russians came to his aid; on a third, the nobles unanimously counselled an advance on India, predicting that God would bestow victory; and on a fourth the whole nation rose and assembled as for a religious war, so that the King of Persia had no alternative but a declaration of war. It is also said that the Amir Dost Muhammad Khan, the ruler of Cabul, is secretly in league with the King of Persia, while he professes to the English that he is at deadly enmity with him, urging as his reason that the sovereignty of Cabul had formerly always descended in lines of Shah Kamran and Shujah-ul-mulk, and that the King of Persia had appointed the prince Yusuf, his Vice-regent, in the government of Herat; that this Prince now counsels of the King of Persia to take the sovereignty of Cabul from the Amir and to bestow it on him, that it is in consequence of this that the

Persians are advancing towards Cabul, and that he seriously apprehends that Prince Yusuf, assisted by the Persians, will finally take Cabul from the Afghans in requital for Shah Shujah-ul-Mulk's dispossession. On leaving for Cabul the Amir wrote a letter to the King of Persia, that he was altogether a subject of the Persian Sovereignty, and that he had no relations with the British Government.

No. 4

Extract from the *Authentic News,* No. XI, Vol. II, dated 19th March 1857

Proclamation of the King of Persia.

Copies of a proclamation in the name of the King of Persia have been put up at the entrances to the streets and lanes of Delhi. One of my friends took an exact transcript of the copy which has been put up on the back of the Jama Masjid. This proclamation was seen by most people. The purport of it in a condensed form is, that people professing the true faith should, as a matter of duty, eschew assisting the Christians, and should, as being right and proper, exert themselves to the full extent of their ability to promote the welfare of the Mussalmans, that the time is at hand, when God willing, we the King of Persia, will sit on the throne of India, and will make the King and people of that country contented and happy. In the same measure as the English have done everything to make them destitute of even the means of subsistence, we will exert ourselves to make them rich and affluent. We use no interference with any man's religion. Such is the substance of the proclamation. Moreover, a person of the name of Muhammad Sadik Khan, by means of whom this proclamation has been made public, writes, that up to the 6th instant, 900 Persian soldiers, with some officers of high rank, has entered India, and 500 are staying in Delhi itself in various disguises, and as an instance, he mentions himself particularly as having reached Delhi on the 4th March, and circulated all the copies of the proclamation. He says that he receives intelligence from all parts of the country, that he sends accounts regularly of everything occurring here to the King of Persia, that they will communicate to all by means of proclamations, every; intelligence regarding the dispatch and advance of the Persian troops and whatever else may be worth making known.

People say that this proclamation has been contrived merely to get up idle speculations, and being of the same opinion, I too would ask, what is the object of Muhammad Sadiq Khan's coming to Delhi? If his object is war, his coming in this way with such purpose is absolute absurdity. He has come as a spy, then his publishing his presence by a proclamation is a senseless inconsistency, and the expenses of his mission a useless waste of money. Putting gain out of the calculation altogether, damage to his object is the likely result of such a course. Setting all this aside, however, it may be asked what cause for rejoicing would the Hindus have were the King of Persia to exercise sway over India? From the proclamation it appears that he intends himself to occupy the throne of India. The Hindus would only then have cause to be pleased if the King of Persia, acting like Abbas Shah Safi, should enthrone our own King, and where would be the wonder if he did so, for it was Taimur himself who bestowed Sovereignty on the Persians, and it was reflecting on this that induced the said Abbas Shah to assist Humayun.

No. 5

Extract from the *Authentic News,* No. XII, Vol. III, dated 23rd March 1857

Proclamation in the Name of the King of Persia.

Lately some designing and mischievous promoter of sedition of Delhi, imagining notoriety would be fame, placarded a proclamation purporting to be from the King of Persia on the back of the Jama Masjid, with the purpose of misleading the populace. The substance of this proclamation was, that the Mussalmans and Hindus should both refrain from helping the Christians, and that the King of Persia will shortly conquer Hindustan, and bestowing rewards and favours, will keep the people in peace and happiness. The man who circulated this proclamation has written his name as Muhammad Sadik Khan. It is said that the authorities of Delhi were very much annoyed by this absurd falsehood. I feel convinced that if anyone will apprehend this misguided liar, he will get some pecuniary reward; but God knows whether he will or not. However, as for our good friend Mr. Muhammad Sadik Khan, the forgerer, who issued this proclamation, we feel sure that if he falls into the hands of Government a double-soled shoe steeped in vinegar will be caused to make a precious good clatter on his crabby cranium, and his hair pretty well dishevelled. This fine gentleman with the alias will then learn, that a house of bricks may be turned into dust and how aptitude for such frolics may be expelled through the nose, much in the same way as a cold in the head finds vent, and after what fashion our fine fellows of this stamp may have the breath taken out of them.

No. 6

Extract from the Delhi *Urdu News,* No. XV, Vol. XIX, dated 12th April 1857

Local News.

Cabul.

A correspondent of the *Delhi Gazette,* writing from Cabul under date the 29th March, says, that the small force ordered by the Amir Dost Muhammad Khan to punish the people of Pesh Bolak and Surju Khail had returned to Jallalabad, after, as it appears, an engagement with Muhammad Shah Khan, in which nearly 30 of them were killed, and about the same number wounded. Although the Amir's soldiers took a great quantity of Muhammad Shah Khan's baggage, the Khan, to save his life, escaped to the forts in the country about Lumghan. The brother of Mirdad Khan had just arrived from Jallalabad, and informed the correspondent that the said Amir had marched in the direction of Tatmed, but it was not known then whether he would celebrate the festival of the new year's day at Ballabahh or at Cabul. The brother of Mirdad Khan also mentioned that some English Newspapers published in India were read to the Amir, in which the mismanagement of government was canvassed in advancing money to the Amir, who, the papers said, was keeping up relations on both sides, and that on hearing this the Amir remarked, that when the English get into any difficulty they expended millions of pounds sterling, and that now when the Persians, instigated by the Russians, were planning the invasion of Afgahanistan, with the ulterior design of disturbing the Government of India, the Governor-General had, with wisdom and judgement, considered his, the Amir's alliance, worth having. The correspondent adds, that it is much discussed at Cabul that in consequence of the instigation and mischievous designs of Sultan Muhammad Khan, Inam Haji is exciting the inhabitants of the hill country, and that it is also currently reported that Sultan Jan has, with entreat and supplication, applied to the Persian Commander-in-Chief at Herat for permission to invade Girrishk, affirming that the people of Girrishk have agreed to assist him on the condition that the games be remitted for three years.

No. 7

Extract from the newspaper in the Urdu tongue–styled *Compendium of News*, Nos. VIII, Vol. I, dated 13th April 1857

Local News.
Persia.

Some days ago a proclamation was found placarded on a wall of the Jama Masjid. A sword and shield were depicted on it, and the following as coming from the Shah of Persia was the substance of the paper, *viz.:* That it was a religious obligation on all true believing Muhammadans to gird their loins resolutely, to assist the King of Persia, and to be faithfully subject and obedient to his authority, and to fight and contend against the English, so that vanquishing and routing them in battle they may receive and enjoy the favours, rewards and titles which the King of Persia will lavishly bestow on them. The proclamation also stated that the Persian King or second Jam would very soon come to India, and annex this country as a dependency, and that great multitudes of people had already assembled, and were constantly repeating the following couplet, as if from some involuntary and irresistible impulse: 'Oh God save the very dust of Persia from the winds of misfortune, so long as even dust and wind may exist'. The news-writer states that the above is a translation from the Persian, but that it has not yet come to pass. Several petitions without names have been given into the Magistrate's Court on the same subject, and in these it was also mentioned that a month hence from this date, an overwhelming attack will be made on Cashmere, of the salubrity and beauty of which place a poet has said:

That should a parched and burnt-up soul reach Cashmere,
Though he might be a roasted fowl,
He would recover his wings and feathers.

And that this cool and heavenly country will come into the possession of the writers of the petitions. The writer of this paper considers all this as mere senseless and absurd jesting and levity, for if countries are liable thus to slip out of the hands of Governments, what is the use of armies!

No. 8

Extract from the newspaper in the Urdu tongue called the *Authentic News*, No. XIX, Vol. III, dated 11th May 1857

Proclamation of the King of Persia Regarding the Conquest of India.

The Editor of the English newspaper called *The Punjabi* in its issue No. XI writes that on the capture of Mohumra, his correspondent found the translation of a proclamation in one of the princes' tents, the substance of which communicated, to the Editor by Electric Telegraph, and which he now publishes for the perusal of his readers. The following is the purport of the proclamation:

Let it be known that the English Government first planted their victorious standard in India, and step by step subjugated all the powerful princes of the Eastern provinces. Some short time ago they conquered Afghanistan, but relinquished it in consequence of what they suffered from the restless turbulence of the Afghans. After this, they took possession of the cities of Lahore and Peshawar, and of other free and independent countries. They now wish to come through Afghanistan, and establish their sway in Persia also, and it is with this object that they are making friends of our neighbours and co-religionists, the Afghans, so that these may allow them to pass, and that they may then desolate and plunder Persia, and cause disunion among the professors of the true faith. Moreover, it has been heard that an English force, intended for the invasion of Persia by land, has already marched, and the English forces have taken a small maritime fort belonging to the Mahommedans, and have for its security placed a garrison in it, but the English do not allow their forces to advance, knowing that if they do so, they will feel the temper and sharp edge of the Mahommedan swords, and would soon be on the ground struggling in the agonies of death like fish out of water. Shah Nasir-ud-din, King of Persia, therefore, has the greatest pleasure in making the following proclamation:

Proclamation.

Let all the troops assemble at the different places on the frontiers of Persia to resist these enemies professing an antagonistic faith. It behoves the Arab tribes to act up to the precepts of the prophet (blessed for ever be he and his offspring). Slay all those who have caused you affliction in the same way that they intended to afflict you. It is now necessary that old and young, wise and foolish, peasant and soldier, should all without hesitation rise to the assistance of their co-religionists, assume arms, raise the Mahommedan standard, and inform the members of their tribes of the declaration in the name of God of a religious war of extermination, for God will bestow the fruition of their hopes on those defenders of the faith who will thus exert themselves, and we too will be much pleased with them. I have sent the Noble amongst Nobles, Mirza Jan Koshakchi Sabahi, the Champion of the nation, the Chief, Mir Ali Khan, and other Generals, Officers, and Chiefs, with 25,000 troops, to different parts of Persia. The Prince Nawab Shamshir-ud-dowlat has been sent as commanding Officers with a force of 30,000 men to Mohumra. Ghulam Hasan Khan, Duffadar, and Jafir Kuli Khan, have been sent with the cavalry regiments of Kurrachi Diggir to Kirman. Twenty thousand troops well equipped and appointed have been sent to Azibia and Karribia, and the Nawab Ahsan-Sultanant, with a force of 30,000 men, 40 guns, and other munitions, has been detached in the direction of Kutch and the Northern Provinces of Sindh. These forces have been thus distributed, that they may conquer the provinces of Afghanistan and then move onwards. The Chief Sultan Ahmad Khan, Shaha Dowlat Khan, Sultan Ali Khan, and Muhammad Alam Khan had been appointed to joining in the conquest of India in posts subordinate to the above officers. It is fully to be expected, from God's blessing, that they will be victorious. Accordingly, now is the time for all the people of that country, and all the tribes of Afghans who believe in the Kuran, and walk in the precepts of god's prophet, to join openly in the religious war of extermination, and to hold out the hand of support to their brother Mahommedans, for by doing so they will reap advantages both temporal and eternal. And as quelling disturbances along the frontiers even, is not so trifling a matter that it may be realized by a small force of the faithful, it is incumbent on all Mussalmans to assist with zeal and energy. Moreover, let it be known to all the Afghan tribes that it is no intention of the King of Persia to conquer and annex Afghanistan as a dependency; but that, on the contrary, his real desire is that Kandahar should be subject to the Chiefs Rahim Dil Khan and Kohundil Khan, and that Cabul should continue, as heretofore, under the sway and Government of the Amir Dost Muhammad Khan, and that all the Afghans may, set before, have the blessing of liberty. It is incumbent on the Amir Doss Muhammad Khan personally that he should adopt the counsel of his relations, and assist the Mahommedans, acting up to the traditional precept of the prophet that he who will assist a member of the faith will receive a good reward for doing so. Hitherto, previous to the publication of this notice, Amir Dost Muhammad Khan used always to say, that if the armies of Persia should go against a people of a different religion, he would join them with arms and money. It is manifest that now the time he used to speak of has arrived, that is, that I have declared war against the English solely in defence of the faith. Let the Amir Dost Khan now remember his promise and join me against the enemies of the Mussalmans, and let him exert every energy in his power to slay them, for no blessing, however great, can exceed the opportunity to do so. If he is killed, he will be exalted to the dignity of a martyr, if he lives he will be called a defender of the faith. In every point of view a religious war of extermination is a most meritorious undertaking. But (God forbid it should be!) if the Amir acts in different was, *first*, he will have denied his religion; *secondly*, he will be disgraced in the estimation of the world; *thirdly*, he will be called a coward; and *fourthly*, the wrath of god will be sure to visit him.

The Editor of *The Panjabi* says that the proclamation itself is a very lengthy paper, and that he has only an abstract of it, and the only good he remarks, it seems to have done, as far as he can see, is that Mohumra was taken, and this paper found, for otherwise it is very unlikely it would ever have come here. It is quite enough, however, that the sun of the British prestige still shines unobscured. It is to be confidently believed that all the endeavours of the King of Persia will be to no purpose.

Here ends the extract from *The Panjabi*. We now proceed to quote from *The Englishman*. 'It is rumoured that an effective and well-appointed force will shortly come through the Bolan Pass, but we do not credit this report, as the hot season has set in. We hear that the Chief Sultan Jan, nephew of the Amir Dost Muhammad Khan, who, taking some offence against his uncle, had joined the king of Persia, is now coming with some troops from Furrah towards Kandahar, feeling his way as he comes along. A body of Mughals devoted to their faith have proceeded in the direction of Persia. This event has caused much serious alarm to the Amir Dost Muhammad Khan, as these Mughals are reputed to be men of both strong religious principles and martial qualifications'. On 23rd April 1857, Major Lumsden, accompanied by some European officers, and Faujidar Khan, the Government agent, arrived at Narab. The Editor of the Kurrachee newspaper called *The Sindhian*, quoting *The Bombay Times*, states in his issue No. 33 that there is a report to the effect that 50,000 Persians, officered by some three or four Russians, had recaptured Bushire, but that the English had again taken the place, and that 3,000 Russians, who had part with the Persians in this fight, had suffered a very heavy loss; that a very large force is gradually assembling in the north; and that he hears the Russians are in a great strength towards the Caspian Sea and Bokhara. The Editor of *The Panjabi* writes that the Persians have fully completed their arrangements, and have established cantonments in several places, as for instance, at Awarganj, Kokan, Kursh, & c., where they have also accumulated large stores of necessaries. Ikram Khan, the Chief Muhammad Azim Khan, Haidar Khan Afzul, and Jallal-ud-din Khan, the son of the late Akbar Khan, are in league with the King of Persia, and Ghulam Haidar Khan has even been honoured with a present of 36,000 rupees from the King of Persia, and his heart and soul devoted to him, and is looking out for the time when the roads will again open. It will be nothing strange if the Persians shortly enter Kandahar, intending to advance further. From the statements of travellers coming from Peshawar, it appears that no reliance can be placed on the Amir Dost Muhammad Khan's engagements and compacts: but how observable is God's power by which he is thus openly sustained, notwithstanding, it is said, that there is a very large assemblage of the British troops just now at Peshwar. God forbid it! But should a battle occur in that direction, a great slaughter will be the consequence. Just now, the source of news from Persia is closed: let not our readers imagine, as some ignorant people assert, that the British Government has prohibited the publication of intelligence. On the contrary, it is the wish of the Government that correct intelligence from distant parts of the world should be placed before the eyes of the public generally, and that the whole country may benefit by the newspapers, and this is the reason why the authorities themselves read the papers with a trust and confidence in their faithfulness, and expend their own private funds to encourage publishers and printers. But where is the help if the news itself is not forthcoming? However, let such as are interested in news from distant countries patiently look out for an early gratification, for the next mail will certainly bring news of recent dates either of a peaceable or warlike character, and please God. I shall publish them too without prejudice or bias, for our Government is just one which does not hinder any in the free exercise of his rights, and this is the reason why its sway is daily extending, and why the arts and sciences have attained an eminence twice as great as that of former times. May the Almighty preserve this Government in the exercise of justice to the end of time.

No. 9

Extract from the newspaper in the Urdu tongue called the *Authentic News*, No. I, Vol. IV, dated 6th July 1857

Proclamation of the King of Persia.

We learn from the statements of a man come from the Punjab that the King of Persia has issued a proclamation, of which the following is the purport:

Let all the troops assemble at different places on the frontier of Persia to resist these enemies professing an antagonistic faith, *viz.* the English. It behoves the Arab tribes to act up to the precept of the prophet (blessed for ever be he and his offspring!). Slay all those who have caused you affliction in the same way that they intended to 'afflict you', if it is now necessary that old and young, high and low, wise and foolish, peasant and soldier, should all without hesitation rise to the assistance of their co-religionists, assume arms, arise the Mahommedan standard, and inform the members of their tribes of the declaration, in the name of God, of a religious war of extermination, for God will bestow the fruition of their hopes on those defenders of the faith who will thus exert themselves, and we too will be much pleased with them. I have sent the Noble amongst Nobles Mirza Muhammad Jan Koshakchi Sabhi; the Champion of the Nation, the Chief Mir Ali Khan; and other Generals Officers and Chiefs, with 25,000 troops, to different parts of Persia. The prince Nawab Shamshi-ud-dowlat has been sent as Commanding Officer with a force of 30,000 men to Buahiew, the place from which the English ran away to Bombay. Ghulam Hasan Khan, Duffadar, and Jafar Kuli Khan, Mir Panja have been sent with the cavalry regiments of Kurrachi Diggir to Kirman. Twenty thousand troops, well equipped and appointed, have been sent to Azibia and Karibia, and the Nawab Ahsan-us Sultanant, with a force of 30,000 men, 40 guns and other munitions, has been detached in the direction of Kutch and the northern provinces of Sindh. These forces have been thus distributed that they may conquer the provinces of Afghanistan and then move onwards. The Chief Sultan Ahman Khan, Shan Dowlat Khan, Sultan Ali Khan, and Muhammad Alam Khan have been appointed to join in the conquest of India in posts subordinate to the above officers. It is fully to be expected, from God's blessing, that they will be victorious, and that they will not leave the English any resting place this side of Longon. Accordingly, now is the time for all the people of that country, all the tribes of Afghanistan, and the inhabitants of India who believe in the Kuran, and walk in the precepts of god's prophet, to join openly in the religious war extermination, to stand by their faith, and to hold out the hand of support to their brother Mahommedans, for by doing so they will reap advantages both temporal and eternal. It is incumbent on all Mussalmans to assist with zeal and energy in this matter. Moreover, let it be known to all the tribes of Afghanistan and India, that it is no intention of the King of Persia to conquer and annex Afghanistan as a dependency; but that, on the contrary, his real desire is that Kandahar should be subject to the Chiefs Rahimdil Khan and Kohundil Khan; Cabul to the Amir Dost Muhammad Khan; and India to the house of Taimur. It is incumbent on the Amir personally to adopt thee counsels of his relations and assist the Mahommedans, and to expel from his heart the avarice of getting a lakh of rupees a month, according to the tradition that it is a saying of the prophet, that he who will assist a member of the faith will receive a good reward for doing so. Hitherto previous to the publication of this notice Amir Dost Muhammad Khan used always to say that if the armies of Persia should go against a people of a different religion, he would join them with armies and money. It is manifest that now the time he used to speak of has arrived, so let the Amir exert every energy in his power to kill the enemies for the Mahommedans, for no blessing can be greater than the opportunity to do so. If he is killed he will be venerated as a martyr, if he lives he will be called a defender of the faith. In every point of view a religious war of extermination is a meritorious undertaking. But (and God forbid it should be so), if the Amir acts in a different way, he will to a certainty be called a Christian, and the wrath of god will shortly fall on him. The King of Persia has sent also the following letter to the Amir Dost Muhammad Khan. 'Oh! Amir! Have you joined the English, and become a renegade from you faith! I, as a Mussalman counsel you to separate yourself from this people, and to join men and contrive means for their ruination. Know, moreover, that all the Mussalmans complain that the Amir, by joining the English, has brought disgrace on the true religion. If avarice is the cause of your conduct take twice the amount of gold from me. And have you not heard what breaches of treaties and engagements this race have practised with the princes and chiefs of Hindustan?' the Amir evinced much respect of this letter, and resolved on coming in this direction himself accompanied by the Chief of Swat. The King of Persia has entered Herat, and the troops at Kandahar have totally cut up the English, who had gone forward in advance.

No. 10

Extract from the newspaper in Urdu called the *Authentic News*, No. V, Vol. IV, dated 3rd August 1857

Arrival of the Persian Army.

A friend of mine possessing great judgement, and speaking the Persian tongue, who has recently arrived, states that the Persian forces, which had for a considerable length of time been lying at Farrah near Herat under the command of Sultan Jan Khan, son of Kohundil Khan, have now, with the permission of the king of Persia moved on to Kandahar. Hearing this, the son of Amir Dost Muhammad Khan met them with 2,000 or 3,000 effective and disciplined soldiers. The battles lasted full six days, and some hundreds were killed and wounded on both sides. Eventually the Amir's son fled from the field and took refuge in the fort, when the Persian troops completely invested Kandahar, and have almost cut off supplies of water and food. The Amir's son has therefore applied for some reinforcements from Cabul, which it is said the Amir Dost Muhammad Khan will send very shortly; it is also said that the Amir has sent a letter full of entreaty and supplication to the King of Persia, saying that he is as any other of the King's subjects or servants, that he has no desire to have anything to do with helping the English, and urging the King certainly to advance his troops towards India, promising that he will not hold back in anything he may be able to do in the way of furnishing supplies or assisting with forces. It was reported also that the Amir will send the King of Persia some money and presents of valuable rarities. The Prince Muhammad Yusuf, Chief of Herat, is in the habit of communicating to the King of Persia all matters of intelligence connected with Hindustan and the perfidious English. The King of Persia has great confidence in this prince, and occasionally adopts some of his suggestions and ideas.

No. 11

Extract from an editorial article in the newspaper in Urdu called the *Authentic News*, No. VI, IV, dated 10th August

Craftiness of the King of Persia.

With reference to the fact that the King of Persia, after several fights with the accursed unbelieving English, sent proposals for peace through Farrukh Khan, I saw through it from the first, that it was not without an object. As a poet says, 'the civilities of a censor are not disinterested' and I felt convinced that there was some concealed craftiness in the proposals. I now feel I have reason to compliment myself on my penetration, for I now learn from a trustworthy slayer of the accursed infidels that the real object of the Persians was that they might continue in occupation of Herat, and the English retire from Abushahr. Accordingly, the event has been as was expected. In observance of the treaty of peace between the two powers the English completely evacuated Abushahr; but when this was done, the King of Persia would not give up Herat. At this, the English are very much shamed and vexed, and say that they will bring the Persians to a proper understanding for this. This, however, is only an idle threat; we should reflect, when they had some power, much or little as it may have been, what were they able to do then that they would do over again now? The same person states also that the Persians, considering the present opportunity one which should not be lost, have advanced on this side of Kandahar, in force to the extent of 50,000 men; that the Amir Dost Muhammad Khan is, to all appearances still keeping up his friendship with the cursed infidels; but that secretly he is using all, means of instigation and persuasion with the Persians, and that it is in consequence; of this that the Persian army, some officers of which are from amongst the nobles of Cabul, is steadily advancing towards India. Continuing to hear such news as the above, the Christians are becoming more alarmed, and admit that the downfall of the Company has now certainly come.

No. 12

Extract from the newspaper called the Delhi *Urdu News*, No. XXXIV, Vol. XIX, dated 23rd August 1857

News of the Persian Army.

Some people coming from the direction of Peshawar and the Punjab, stated that the Persian army has reached Attock. Although I do not fully believe this myself, I have published it as hearsay gossip, for the thing is possible, and not by any means to unlikely, that it should at once be considered and pronounced false. But nevertheless it must be admitted that from the way in which people just now talk, no intelligence can be relied on or believed. Under these circumstances, when inserting news, it is right to avoid observations and speculations in reference to it.

No. 13

Extract from the newspaper in the Urdu language called the *Authentic News*, No. VIII, Vol. IV, dated 24th August 1857

Near Approach of the Persian Army.

The Editor of the *Triumphant News* says, he has heard from some people coming from the direction of Peshawar that the Persian army has fought its way up to Attock. The Editor does not believe this, but for several reasons it appears to me deserving of credence. *First*, no man says anything unless he has some little grounds. *Secondly*, there is a prophecy of the saint, the revered Shah Niamut-Ulla Maulavy, in verse, to the following effect: 'After the fire-worshippers and Christians shall have held sway over the whole of Hindustan for 100 years, and when injustice and oppression shall prevail in their government, an Arab prince will be born who will ride forth triumphantly to slay them'. *Thirdly,* When the troops mutinied at Multan, some of the men stated, that their officers had for a long time been maintaining an interchange of letters with the King of Persia. *Fourthly,* A spy sent by the King of Persia, hearing that a friend of mine in the British dominions was a staunch zealot for Mahommedanism, met and told him that the King of Persia had definitely determined on coming to India. Thus, then whether he come early or late, there is no doubt he will come. God only has prescience of the future.

No. 14

Extract from the newspaper in Urdu, called the *Urdu News,* No. XXXVII, Vol. XIX, dated 13th September 1857

Local News.

Persia.

Some people now again say that the Persian army has come through the Bolan and Bibi Narri passes, and that the Amir Dost Muhammad Khan cheerfully gave them a free passage through his dominions; but according to the common Indian adage that 'A Brahman believes in the promise of a feast only when he gets it', the people of India will believe this matter only when they have some ocular proof; but from certain signs nevertheless we cannot help allowing credence to some extent. For whether the present intelligence be correct or false, we must believe that the Persian troops will come, whether by Bolan or Bombay or Sindh it does not matter. God only is all-powerful and omniscient.

No. 15

Order under the official seal of Mirza Mughal, as Commander-in-Chief of the Army, dated 13th September 1857

To – The Emblem of Valour, the Chief Police Officer of the City of Delhi.

May you be protected. Intelligence has just been brought that the English intend making a general attack tonight, you are therefore directed to have it proclaimed by beat of drum throughout the city, that it is incumbent on all the inhabitants whether Hindu of Mahommedan, from a due regard to their faith, to assemble directly in the direction of the Cashmere Gate, bringing iron picks and shovels with them.

No. 16

Copy of an order from the King, without signature, cypher, or seal, but the order was issued under his seal

To – Our son, the illustrious and valiant Mirza Zahur-ud-Din, otherwise Mirza Mughal Bahadur. No date.

Learn! That when the troops, infantry and cavalry, first came to the Royal presence, I told them personally, by word of mouth, that I had no treasures or property with which to assist them, but that I had no reluctance to stake my life if that could help them. They all expressed themselves satisfied with this declaration on my part, and even pledged themselves to sacrifice their lives in subordination and obedience to my commands. On this, they were directed, as the first step, to make proper provisions for the magazine and treasure, so that they might afterwards be profitably used by them and me. After this, they took up their quarters in the Halls of Special and Public Audience, the Mahtab Garden, and other places, and behaved just as they pleased. In consideration of their ignorance, and from a regard to their comforts, the servants of the state were prohibited from preventing them. In the next place, although no promise had been made in the matter, money was borrowed in order that daily allowances might be paid to every man of the cavalry and infantry. Repeated injunctions have been issued prohibiting plunder and aggression in the city, but all to no purpose; for although ten days have now elapsed, the same evils are prevailing to the present time. Moreover, the regiments of infantry have certainly left the Halls of Special and Public Audience, but notwithstanding that they were imperatively ordered to encamp outside the city, and the men of the army, whether cavalry or infantry, were prohibited going about armed through the city, and oppressing the inhabitants, yet one regiment of infantry has taken up its quarter at Delhi, another at Lahore, and a third at the Ajmir Gate, within the walls of the city, and have thoroughly desolated several of the bazaars. Moreover, without reference to night or day, they enter and plunder the houses of the inhabitants on the false plea that they have concealed Europeans.

They force locks and shop-doors and openly carry away the property from the shops, and they forcibly loose the horses of the cavalry and take them off. They commit these excesses in the face of the fact that all cities taken without military operations have ever been exempted from sack and slaughter. Even Jangiz Khan and Nadir Shah, kings execrated as tyrants, gave peace and protection to such cities as surrendered without resistance. Moreover, the men of the army go about threatening and intimidating the Royal servants and the inhabitants of the city. Again, although repeated orders have been issued to the infantrymen occupying the Royal farash-khana, and the regiment of cavalry staying in the garden to vacate these places, they have not yet done so. These are places which not even Nadir Shah nor Ahmad Shah nor any of the British Governors-General of India ever entered on horseback. The troops first requested that the Princes Royal might be appointed to the different commands in the army, promising they would obey them. This was done. They next urged that it would afford them greater confidence, if dress of honour should be bestowed on the princes to give a character of stability to their appointments as commandants, and if all the (European) prisoners should be killed at once. This was also complied with and the same day a notification, under the special seal, was issued publicly, proclaiming that courts of justice had been established in the city, and prohibiting acts of violence on the part of the soldiery. This even had no effect. Setting aside all these points, it may be remarked that whenever the most distinguished officers of the highest ranks in the service of the British Government visited the place, they dismounted at the door of the Hall of Public Audience, and came from thence on foot. These soldiery, however, used, till recently, to come galloping up the Hall of Special Audience on their horses, and as a last resort, both the gates were closed a wicket only being left open; but they still ride up to the Hall of Public Audience, and the Jalwa-Khana, unsuitably dressed, and without their turbans, in utter disregard to the forms of respect due to royalty. The officers of the army too make a practice of coming into court carelessly dressed, wearing caps instead of turbans and carrying their swords. Never during the British rule did any members of their profession behaved in this way. Again, notwithstanding that they have themselves uselessly wasted the whole of the magazine stores, and the money that was in the treasury, they now clamorously demand allowances daily, and above all, daily take allowances for more men than are present. Besides this, with oppression and violence they forcibly take away the wares of shopkeepers in the city without paying for them, and commit, moreover, every variety of other excesses and aggressions imaginable. The state of things outside the city also demands notice. In consequence of no military troops going out to keep order, hundreds of people are being murdered, and the property of thousands is being plundered. As regards the civil administration of the country, in consequence of the insufficiency of the Royal troops for the management of the whole of the provinces, revenue and; police officers cannot be established, and yet none of the military troops, whether cavalry or infantry, can be prevailed on to move out beyond the palace and city. Under these circumstances, it is a matter for distressingly serious reflection how supplies are to be procured from the country, and how the revenues of the state are to be realized. Accordingly, nothing but the total desolation of the city and country can be expected as the inevitable ends of this state of matters. In addition to all that has been above noticed, the soldiery accusing the Royal servants of entertaining views and feeling s opposite to their own, subject them to indignities, and when they come to claim their daily allowances or ammunition enforce their demands with unbecoming assumption of authority, notwithstanding that the Royal servants, in consequence of orders to them to the effect, use nothing but entreaty and every other means of conciliation, and yet the soldiery will not be satisfied. Under these circumstances, how is it to be believed that these people can have the welfare of the state at heart, or that they cherish any desire to yield subjection and obedience to the Royal authority? It is further to be considered, that there is no money in the Royal Treasury, and the city merchants having been plundered and ruined have no longer the ability to provide a loan. How then are the daily allowances to be paid for any length of time? And when they shall, of necessity, have been discontinued, and the supplies from the country shall also have ceased, what will be the state of things then? The most ridiculously singular part of the proceedings of the soldiery is, that while they themselves commit these acts subversive of all rule, they lay the blame of the misrule on the Royal servants. In short, when such is the return made by the soldiery, it is evident that they have no desire to act in any way to the advantage and benefit of the Government, and it is equally evident that the utter ruin of the sovereignty must ensue. Wearied and helpless, we have now resolved on making a vow to pass the remainder of our days in services acceptable to god, and relinquishing the title of sovereign fraught with cares and troubles, and in our present griefs and sorrows, assuming the garb of a mendicant, to proceed first and stay at the shrine of the saint Khwaja Sahib, and, after making necessary arrangements for the journey, to go eventually to Mecca. It should be considered that when these troops came, the King's servants or the residents of the city did not oppose them in any way, nor did they commit any act of hostility against them, and they are accordingly not liable to the forfeiture of life and property, for if as the representative of the feelings of the people, we had considered the soldiery in the light of enemies, why should we have directly associated our offspring with them in their undertaking? The tyranny and oppression now prevailing are a disgrace to our Royal Self, as tending to the belief that we, as sovereign, are a party to them, and oppression now prevailing are a disgrace to our Royal Self, as tending to the belief that we, as sovereign, are a party to them, and that we approve of rapine and murder. It is worthy of consideration that when there is amity and good feelings between the King and populace on the one side and the army on the other, is it by acts like these that the soldiery mean to prove their goodwill – acts which even an enemy or hostile force would not commit? The more praiseworthy and prudent course for them would have been to protect and cherish the people, to study the approbation of the sovereign, and to preserve unanimity and fellowship with the servants of the state. It was the peace and quiet which would have resulted from this line of conduct that we had expected. You, our son, will now therefore send for all the officers of the cavalry and infantry, and explain to them that if they are really disposed to serve the state, they ought to execute a written agreement to that effect according to a form which will be furnished; when, for their assurance and satisfaction, we also will give them a written document; and that they should take immediate steps to suppress the evil and unbecoming acts and proceedings now prevailing; that the tents of the infantry regiments be this very day removed to the outside of the city; that every soldier of the army proved guilty of the murder and plunder of any resident of the city be adequately punished, so that others may have no hope of impunity for such acts; and that whenever Royal orders directing the movements of regiments, whether singly or in numbers, with the view of their quelling disturbances and keeping order in the country may be issued, they should march without murmur or grumbling, and should make no obstinate demands for provisions and ammunition beyond such as may be reasonable. Certainly, when authentic information of the near approach of the English army is received, both these regiments will be at liberty to return and then fight and engage in the operations of war as they may themselves arrange and deem expedient, and also determine what amount of forces should be severally kept in different places, and distribute the army accordingly. Then there will be a necessity for the troops being within the city; but there is none just now, seeing the country and city are being alike desolated, and none of the soldiery can be prevailed on to move from his quarters to make the least effort. You will further explain to them that if they are not disposed willingly and unanimously to acquiesce in the above views and wishes, desiring rest and quiet, we shall adopt the procession of a religious mendicant, and shall go to the shrine of the Khwaja Sahib. Let none of them say anything to prevent this step, but let them quietly remain masters of the palace, the city and country. For none of the kings of the old antiquity, nor of the warriors who came after them down to modern times, ever subject any one claiming shelter and quiet to oppression and hardship, but freely allowed him his own way. You will get the army to embody their answer to the two alternatives presented herein for their selection in a petition which you are directed to have attested with the seals and signatures of the officers, and to forward to the Royal presence. You are directed to consider this not as any light or trivial business, for in consequence of our advanced age and infirmity we are not able to support the burden of such excessive anxiety. The government of a nation and the control of an army are not to be treated with the same levity as child's play.

No. 17

Copy of Royal Order without signature, seal, or cypher, probably an office copy dated 17th July 1857

To – The Special Slave, Emblem of Valour, Siddhari Singh, of the Mhow Force, and Sheikh Ghous Muhammad, Hira Singh, and other Officers Commissioned and Non-Commissioned of the Force come from Neemuch.

Consider yourselves receiving the Royal favour, and know that your petition, dated 15th July 1857, reporting your arrival at Muttra, and applying for two siege guns with ammunition was perused by His Majesty.

His Majesty's written order is now sent to you, and you are directed to comply therewith and come to the Royal presence. Be assured of my kindness.

No. 18

Translation of copies of our documents as below:

1st – Copy of a petition from Muhammad Bakht Khan, purporting to enclose a missive for the ruler of Jummoo, that the King's special seal might be affixed to it.

2nd – Copy of the King's order on the above petition.

3rd – Copy of the missive to the Ruler of Jummoo which formed the enclosure to the above petition.

4th – On the reverse, copy of an order to the officers of the army.

First: A petition from Muhammad Bakht Khan, purporting to enclose a missive for the ruler of Jummu that the King's special seal might be affixed to it.

Dated 22nd August 1857

To – The King! Shelter of the World!

(May his prosperity continue!)

Your Majesty, I enclose a missive to the address of the ruler of Jummoo, and pray that it may be authenticated with an impression from the special Seal in the cypher, and returned to me. (Prayers for the prosperity of the reign.) Petition of the special slave. Copy of seal upside down thus:

Muhammad Bakht Khan,
Commander-in-Chief of the Army[88]

88 The seal on this petition has been affixed upside down. However, this autograph order is written right.

Secondly: The King's orders on the above petition.

The Special Seal engraved in the cypher has been affixed agreeably to your request to the missive which is now sent to you.

Thirdly: The missive to the ruler of Jummoo, which formed the enclosure to the petition.

Dated 22nd August 1857

To – The devotedly Faithful and Zealous Rajah Gulab Singh, Ruler of Jummoo.

Consider yourself honoured and learn. That I have been made thoroughly acquainted by your petition, with all the particulars of the slaughter throughout your territory of the accused unbelieving English. You are considered worthy of a hundred commendations. You have acted in this matter as all brave men ever acquit themselves. May you live and prosper! Of the small number of infidels, who in jeopardy of their had betaken themselves to their entrenchments on the ridge, considering them a refuge and protection, many have been killed, and the very few holding on to their precarious existence are equally doomed to extermination, and will now very soon receive the punishment due to their iniquities. The Bombay force, numerically above 60,000, has now safely reached Ajmir, having sought out and slaughtered all the accursed unbelievers about Bikanir, Jodhpur, Kotah, and Jaipur, and in the districts belonging to them, and will, it is reported, now reach the seat of government, Delhi, in a week or ten days. May god protect them from all evils! Under these circumstances, you are directed not to take into account the difficulties to be expected from the present being the wet season of the year, but giving due respect to this order, immediately on receipt to use all diligence to come to the Royal presence, bringing our tributary contributions of money with you, and to slay the accursed unbelieving English and all other enemies wherever you may find them on the way. Whatever may be your hopes and expectations, the dignity and elevation to which you will be promoted amongst your equals, will surpass all that you may be able to imagine, and you will further be rewarded and dignified with the title of Rajah. Consider yourself the object of our favour.

Fourthly: Copy of an order to the officers of the army.

To – The Officers of the Regular Cavalry, Infantry, and Artillery.

When complete victory shall have been obtained, and the revenues of the conquered countries shall again, as heretofore, be paid into the treasury, the pay of the troops will be regulated according to the following scale:

Trooper of Regular Cavalry	20 Rupees per mensem
Private in the Regular Infantry	10 Rupees per mensem
Private in Regular Artillery	---------

Other troops:

Trooper	14 Rupees per mensem
Foot soldier	8 Rupees per mensem

The monthly allowances of all others will be fixed by reference to their qualifications and exertions, and as the protection of the people is very much desired, all those who will oppress or ill-use them will receive due punishment. You are urged to trust in God's blessing, and cherish full hopes of victory, and of the realization of the revenue, and, thus animated, to exert every energy for the welfare of the State, and with full confidence of success, to fight with courage and intrepidity. You are directed to act according to these orders.

The Court at 2 p.m. adjourns till 11 a.m. tomorrow morning,[89] to enable the Prisoner to complete his defence.

Day twenty: 4 March 1858[90]

The Court reassembled this day at 11 a.m. pursuant to adjournment of yesterday.

The President, Members, Interpreter, and Deputy Judge Advocate-General are all present.

The Prisoner, attended by his attorney Ghulam Abbas, is brought into Court.

The Prisoner now delivers to the Court his defence, written in Hindustani,[91] which is now read in original by the Interpreter.

The Court, at half past 12 o'clock, adjourns till 11 a.m. on Tuesday, the 9th instant, to enable the Interpreter to translate the defence, and the Judge Advocate to reply to it, and sum up the evidence.

89 This is, seriously speaking, a problematic entry. Martin says that the Court was adjourned till 9 March. (Martin, *op. cit.*, vol. 3, p. 184) A question, however, arises here as to why the Court's entry is different? The cat will be out of the bag a little later on the 4th March.

90 As discussed seriously in the 'Introduction' above, Martin, who has candidly, meticulously, and regularly recorded, in brief, each day's important developments throughout the course of the trial so far, has not taken note of the sitting. This is the only omission. The reason was that, as indicated above (19th day proceedings, f.n. 1), the Court was actually adjourned on 3rd March 1858 for 9th March. The 4th March sitting was brought in to give credence to the conspiracy to make untruth as truth by bringing in the factor of the 'Statement of defence'. See, for details, 'Introduction'.

91 The Emperor never wrote any official or important unofficial document in Hindustani/Urdu. The official language was Persian. How could he have made an exception here? This is by all means a forged document. The Truth, wise heads say, has many strange ways of showing itself provided one is keen to see it. The present case proves the point to the hilt. For a detailed critique of the matter, see 'Introduction'.

Day twenty-one: 9 March 1858

The Court assembled in the Special Hall of audience in the Palace at Delhi, at 11 o'clock, on the morning of 9thof March 1858.

The President, Members, Interpreter, and Dy. Judge Advocate-General are all present.

The Prisoner, attended by the attorney Ghulam Abbas, is brought into Court.

The Judge Advocate now reads the translation of the Prisoner's defence,[92] which is entered as follows:

Translation of the written defence put in by Bahadur Shah, Ex-King of Delhi.

The real facts are as follows. I had had no intelligence on the subject previously to the day of the outbreak. About 8 a.m., the mutinous troopers suddenly arrived and set up a noisy clamour under the palace windows. Saying they had come from Meerut after killing all the English there; and stating, as their reason for having done so, that they had been required to bite with their teeth, cartridges greased with the fat of oxen and swine, in open violation of the caste of both Hindus and Mussalmans. When I heard this, I immediately had the gates under the palace windows closed, and sent intelligence to the Commandant of the Palace Guards. On receiving the message, he came personally, and wishing to go out where the troopers were collected, requested that the gate might be opened. I kept him from his purpose, however, and when I would not allow the gate to be opened, he walked up to the balustrade, and said something to the troopers, who then went away. After this, the Commandant of the Palace Guards left me, saying he would make arrangements immediately to put down the disturbance. Very shortly after, Mr. Fraser sent a message for two guns, and the Commandant for another two palanquins, saying that two ladies were staying with him, and requesting that I would have them taken to and concealed in my private female apartments. I sent the palanquins immediately, and gave orders at the same time that the guns should also be taken. Very

92 The whole exercise the Judge Advocate has made here on the 9th March was, when seen in the light of the facts given by Martin, a farce (Martin, *op. cit.*, vol. 3, p. 184). As a matter of fact, '*as the proceedings opened the Vakeel of the Prisoner declared in the name of his Royal Master, that he did not recognize the authority of the Tribunal* before which he had been brought, and, therefore, declined to make answer to any charge brought against him. The Public Prosecutor summed up the whole evidence ... The Court, after a short deliberation, adjudged the Prisoner guilty of all the charges alleged against him. The Court by virtue of the authority vested in it by Act XIV of 1857 sentenced him to be transported to Andaman Islands, or to such other place as should be selected by the Governor-General in Council for his place of banishment'.There is no reason not to believe Martin who has no other interest in reporting the matter except a historian's obligation not to hide facts. The matter has been discussed in detail in the 'Introduction'.

soon after this, I heard that before the palanquins could reach them, Mr. Fraser, the Commandant of the Palace Guards, and the ladies had all been killed. Not long after this, the mutinous soldiery rushed into the Hall of Special audience, crowding into the courtyard, the Hall of Special Audience itself, and the Hall of Devotion; surrounding me completely and placing sentries on all sides. I asked them what their object was, and begged of them to go away. In reply they told me to remain a quiet spectator, saying that they had risked their lives, and would now do all that might be in their power. Fearing that I should be killed, I kept quiet and went to my own private apartments. Near evening, these traitors brought as prisoners some European men and women whom they had found in the Magazine, and resolved on killing them. I had recourse to persuasion, and succeeded in getting their lives spared for the time. The mutinous soldiers, however, kept them prisoners in their own custody. Subsequently, on two occasions, they again determined on killing these Europeans, when I again restrained them from their purpose by entreaty and persuasion, and saved the lives of the prisoners. However, on the last occasion, though I again did all in my power to reason with the rebellious soldiery, they would not heed me, and carried out their purpose of slaying these poor people. I gave no orders for this slaughter. Mirza Mughal, Mirza Khair Sultan, Mirza Abu Bakr, and Basant, one of my own personal attendants, who had leagued with the soldiery, may have made use of my name; but I have no knowledge that they did; nor do I know that my own armed retainers, acting independently of my orders, joined in the slaughter. If they did so, they may have been urged into it by Mirza Mughal. Even after the massacre, no one gave me any information regarding it. In reference to what some of the witnesses have said in evidence regarding my servants having joined in killing Mr. Fraser and the Commandant of the palace Guards, I make the same answer, *viz.* that I gave them no orders. That if they did so, they did it of their own free will. I had no knowledge of it, and this matter also was not communicated to me. I swear by God, who is my witness, that I did not give orders for the death of Mr. Fraser or of any other European. Mukund Lal and other witnesses in saying that I did, have spoken falsely. That Mirza Mughal and Mirza Khair Sultan may have given orders would not be strange, for they had leagued with the revolted soldiery. After these occurrences, the rebellious troops brought Mirza Mughal, Mirza Khair Sultan, and Abu Bakr, and said they wished to have them as their officers. In the first instance, I rejected their request; but when the soldiery persisted, and Mirza Mughal in anger went off to his mother's house, from dread of the soldiers, I kept quiet in the matter, and then by mutual consent on both sides, a Mirza Mughal was appointed to be Commander-in-Chief of the army. As regards the orders under my seal, and under my signature, the Officers, had made me a prisoner, I remained in their power as such. All papers they thought fit, they caused to be prepared, and bringing them to me, compelled me to affix my seal. Sometimes they brought the rough drafts of orders, and had fair copies of them made by my secretary. At other times, they brought the original letters intended for dispatch, and left copies of them in the office. Hence several rough drafts in a diversity of hands have been filed in the proceedings. Frequently they had the seal impressed on the outside of empty unaddressed envelopes. There is no knowing what papers they sent in these or to whom they sent them. There is a petition in the proceedings without an address from Mukund Lal to some unknown party, in which a list is given of the number of orders issued on that date. In this catalogue, it is distinctly specified that so many orders were written under the direction of so and so; so many others under that of such a one; and so on; but not one is ascribed to me. Accordingly, this also proves, that whoever wished, had orders written as he chose, without my authority, not even acquainting me with their purport, while I and my secretary being in jeopardy of our lives, could not dare to say anything in the matter. It was just the same as regards the petitions bearing orders in my own writing. Whenever the soldiers or Mirza Mughal, or Mirza Khair Sultan, or Abu Bakr, brought a petition, they invariably came accompanied by the officers of the army, and brought the order they desired, written in a separate piece of paper, and compelled me to transcribe it with my own hand on the petition. Matters went on so far in this way that they used to say, so that I might hear them, that those who would not attend to their wishes would be made to repent their conduct, and for fear of them I could say nothing. Moreover, they used to accuse my servants of sending letters to and of keeping in league with the English, more particularly the physician Ahsanullah Khan, Mahbub Ali Khan, and the queen Zeenat Mahal, whom they said they would kill for doing so. Thus, one day, they did actually plunder the physician's house, and made him a prisoner, intending to kill him; but refrained from their purpose only after much entreaty and supplication, keeping him a prisoner, however, still. After this, they placed others of my servants in arrest, for instance Shamshi-ud-dowlat, the father of the queen Zeenat Mahal. They even declared they would depose me, and take Mirza Mughal king. It is a matter for patient and just consideration then, what power in any way did I possess, or what reason had I to be satisfied with them? The officers of the army went even so far as to require that I should make over the queen Zeenat Mahal to them that they might keep her a prisoner, saying she maintained friendly relations with the English. Now, if I was in the full exercise of power and authority, should I have permitted the physician Ahsanullah Khan's and Mahbub Ali Khan's imprisonment; and should I have allowed the physician's house to be plundered? The mutinous soldiery had established a court in which all matters were deliberated on, and such measures as, after deliberation, were sanctioned by this council, they adopted; but I never took any part in their conferences. Thus, without my knowledge or orders, they plundered, not only many individuals, but several entire streets, plundering, robbing, killing, and imprisoning all they chose; and forcibly extorting whatever sums of money they thought fit from the merchants and other respectable residents of the city, and appropriating such exactions to their own private purposes. All that has been done, was done by that rebellious army. I was in their power, what could I do? They came suddenly, and made me a prisoner. I was helpless, and constrained by my fears, I did whatever they required, otherwise they would immediately have killed me. This is universally known. I found myself in such a predicament that I was weary of my life, while my officials had no hopes of their being spared in this state of things, I resolved to accept poverty, and adopted the garb, coloured with red earth, or a mendicant, intending to go first to the shrine of the Kutb Sahib, thence to Ajmir, and from Ajmir eventually to Mecca; but the army would not allow me; it was the soldiery who plundered the Government magazine and treasury, and did what they pleased. I took nothing from them, nor did they bring any of the plunder to me. They, one day, went to the house of the queen Zeenat Mahal, intending to plunder it, but did not succeed in breaking open the door. It should accordingly be considered if they were subservient to my authority, or had I been in league with them, how would these things have occurred? In addition to all this, it is worthy of consideration that no person demands the wife of the poorest man, saying 'Give her to me, I will make her a prisoner'. As regards the Abyssinian, Kambar, he obtained leave from me to go on a pilgrimage to Mecca. I did not send him to Persia, nor did I send any letters by him to the Persian King. Someone has falsely circulated this story; Muhammad Durwesh's petition is no document of mine that it should be trusted; if any enemy of mine or for the Mian Hasan Askari has sent this petition, it ought not to be relied on. As regards the behaviour of that rebellious army, it may be stated that they never saluted me even, nor showed me any other mark of respect. They used to walk into the Hall of Special Audience and the Hall of Devotion with their shoes on. What confidence could I place in troops who had murdered their own masters? In the same way that they murdered them, they made me a prisoner, and tyrannized over me, keeping me in order to make use of my name as a sanction for their acts. Seeing that these troops killed their own officers, men of high authority and power, how was I, without an army, without treasure, without stores of ammunition, without artillery, to have resisted them, or make arrangements against them? But I never gave them aid in any shape. When the mutinous troopers first arrived, the gateway under the palace windows being in my power, I had it closed. I sent for the Commandant of the Palace Guards, and acquainted him with what had happened, and prevented his going amongst the mutineers. I also immediately sent two palanquins for the ladies, and two guns for the protection of the palace gate, on the several requisitions of the Commandant of the Palace Guards and the Agent to the Lieutenant-Governor. Moreover, I dispatched a letter the same night by camel express to His Honour the Lieutenant-Governor of Agra, acquainting him with the calamitous occurrences which had happened here. So long as I had power, I did all that I was able. I did not go out in procession of my own free will. I was in the power of the soldiery; and they forcibly did what they pleased. The few servants I engaged, I engaged for the protection of my own free will. I was in the power of the soldiery; and they forcibly did what they pleased. The few servants I engaged, I engaged for the protection of my own life, in consequence of my fears of the revolted and rebellious troops, when these troops prepared to abscond, finding an opportunity, go away secretly under the palace windows, and went and stayed in Humayun's Mausoleum. From this place I was summoned with a guarantee that my life should be spared, and I at once placed myself under the protection of the government. The mutinous troops wished to take me with them, but I would not go. In all the above which I have caused to be written from my own dictation, there is not the smallest falsehood nor deviation from truth. God knows, and is my witness, that I have written only what is strictly true, and the whole of what I can remember. I told you with an oath, at the commencement, that I would write only the truth, without addition or deficiency; and so I have now done.

Attested with autograph cypher.

Postscript: With reference to the copy of an order to Mirza Mughal, complaining of the acts of the soldiery and explaining my resolve, in consequence, to go to the shrine of the Khwaja Sahib and thence to Mecca, which has been field in the proceedings, I declare that I have no recollection of such an order have been issued. The order in question is in the Urdu tongue, contrary to the rule in my secretariat office, where all such papers were written in Persian, and I accordingly do not know how and where it was prepared. It appears that seeing I was thoroughly wearied by the army, and that I had in consequence resolved on discarding the world, accepting poverty and going to Mecca, Mirza Mughal must have had it written in his office, and had my seal affixed to it. At all events, my displeasure against the army as well as my perfect helplessness is proved by the order in question also, which corroborates all that I have said above. As regards the other documents, besides the one just referred to, *viz.* the copies of the missive to the address of Rajah Gulab Singh; Bakht Khan's petition; my autograph order on it attested with my seal; and other papers which have been filed in the proceedings; I affirm that I have recollection of them; but I have already stated that the officers of the army caused whatever orders they chose, to be written without my knowledge, and had them attested with my seal; and I feel convinced that there must be of the same king; and that they must have compelled me to write with my hand the order they wished on Bakht Khan's petition, in the same way that they did in the case of every other petition.

Autograph cypher.

The Judge Advocate-General then addressed the Court as follows[93]:

Gentlemen

It will be my object, in the present address, to collect the different facts which have been elicited in the course of these proceedings, and to furnish them to you as far as possible in the order in which they originally occurred. Our investigation has involved enquiry over a period of several months, when rebellion was rampant in this city; and I trust we have succeeded in tracing, with considerable minuteness, many of the different events as they evolved themselves during the time to which I have referred. Our labours indeed have not had this limit, or we should only have accomplished what might, I think, be termed the least important part of our duties. In immediate connection with the facts elicited are the charges on which the prisoner has been arraigned. Though his former rank and royalty will doubtless add somewhat of temporary importance to the verdict which you will this day be called upon to record, yet whether it be one of acquittal or conviction, it must, I imagine, prove light in the balance when weighed against those more monstrous points to which so much attention has been, and for a long time will still be, directed. I, of course, allude to the causes, either remote or immediate, which gave rise to a revolt unparalleled in the annals of history, either for the savagery which has been its distinctive feature, or for the suddenness with which elements, hitherto deemed utterly discordant on the score of religion, have united themselves in a common crusade against a faith which, as regards the inhabitants of this country, whether Mahommedan or Hindu, was certainly a most unaggressive one. I fear, however, the subject is still but imperfectly elucidate; and I may perhaps be in error in attributing to a religious influence a movement which, after all, may prove to have been merely a political one – a struggle of the natives for power and place, by the expulsion from the country of a people alien in religion, in blood, in colour, in habits, in feelings, and in everything. Whatever the final opinion on this subject may be, the questions, which as far as I am aware of have not as yet found a satisfactory solution, are, by what circumstances was this most atrocious revolt, with its series of massacres brought about, and who were its prime original instigators? I feel sure the members of this Court will join with me in deeming that our proceedings do not furnish a full and complete answer to such questions, and why do they not? I believe it is simply owing to the circumstance that any merely local investigation must be inadequate to collect evidence from the different quarters and sources, which are no doubt available elsewhere. We may still, however, hope that our efforts on

93 It has been proved in the 'Introduction' with verified and verifiable facts that the so-called 'Statement of Defence' of the Emperor was nothing but a forgery.

this point have not been fruitless or unavailing; if we cannot congratulate ourselves on an entire success, we may perhaps be allowed credit for a near approach to it. Few, I imagine, will peruse these voluminous proceedings without coming to the conclusion that intrigues and conspiracy have long been rife at this fostering Court of Delhi. Insignificant and contemptible as to an outward show of power, it would appear that this possessor of head and culminating star of its faith. In him have still been centred the hopes and aspirations of millions. They have looked up to him as the source of honour, and, more than this, he has proved the rallying point not only to Mahommedans, but to thousands of others with whom it was supposed no bond of fanatical union could possibly be established. To throw the fullest light on a subject like this, is not the work of a day, or of a month; time, the great revealer of secrets, will doubtless, sooner or later, lay bare the springs from which a stream of so much evil and misery has flowed; but, till then, we must be content with such views as our present investigation affords. That we have been able to unravel many of the secret workings of the conspirators, will, I believe, be conceded – but let me not anticipate. This is a point of our enquiry on which I purpose to offer some observations hereafter; but a concise narrative of events will perhaps best suit the commencement of this address.

I may state then, that 85 men, non-commissioned officers and troopers of the 3rd Light Cavalry, who were tried by general Court-martial at Meerut in May last, for refusing their cartridges, had their sentence read to them and were ironed on the parade ground early on the morning of the 9th of May, and that the mutiny of the three native regiments at Meerut first openly developed itself at about half past 6 o'clock in the evening of the 10th of May; during which interval of nearly 36 hours, there were, of course, plenty of opportunities for interchange of communications between the native troops who first rebelled at Meerut, and those who joined them at this station. To travel from one place to another by coach used ordinarily to take about five hours, and that the mutineers availed themselves of this facility of mutual intercourse, has, I think, been clearly established by the evidence of Captain Tytler. It appears from his statement, that a coach, full of these Meerut mutineers, came on Sunday evening to the lines of the 38th Native Infantry, doubtless to prepare the sepoys of this station for the arrival and suitable reception, on Monday morning, of their rebel comrades, and although we may not possess positive evidence to the fact, yet it may fairly be presumed that Sunday evening was not the first occasion that these plotters of evil held their secret and sinister councils together. Indeed we have it on record that, even before the Court, which tried the mutinous cavalry at Meerut, had come to any decision on their case, a compact had been entered in to the effect that if the use of greased cartridges was persisted in, the troops at Meerut and Delhi would unite, and at once unfurl the standard of revolt, and so fully had this arrangement been perfected and agreed on, that it is related that the sepoy guards at the gate of the palace on Sunday evening, made no secret of their intentions but spoke openly among themselves of what they expected to occur on the morrow. To understand the merits and demerits of the whole transaction, it must be recollected that, at the time when these resolutions were arrived at, there was not a single greased cartridge in the magazines of either of the three native regiments at Meerut, nor, as far as I have been informed, of those at Delhi either. It must be further borne in mind that the native soldiers themselves were the persons who were perhaps the best informed on these points – that the cartridges for practice had, from time immemorial, been manufactured in the regimental magazines by persons of their own colour, creed and religious persuasion – that it was absolutely impossible to palm off on them a spurious article – that the regimental khalassies, who were employed in making these cartridges, must have at once discovered their impurity, if such had really existed – that, in fact, objectionable cartridges (I mean such as would affect the religious prejudices of either Mussalman or Hindu), could not possibly have been made in their regimental magazines, as in such case the very men to be employed in their manufacture would have been refused their work – but, more than this, let it be remembered that the Mahommedan has no caste, that even the hybrid such as the Mahommedans of Central India has become, half Mussalman and half Hindu, does not pretend to loss of religion, even from touching pork. Who is there amongst us that has not and does not almost daily witness these Mahommedans, in the capacity of table servants, carrying plates and dishes which openly contain the very substance which, in reference to the cartridges, has been made the pretence and the stumbling block of their offence. Even if we were to admit that all the cartridges were thoroughly saturated with pig's and with cow's fat, still what real valid objection on the score of their religion could the Mahommedan sepoys have had in using them? Their brothers and other relatives in the private service of officers never hesitate to handle or cook the dishes which they are required to bring to our tables. The objections of the Mahommedan sepoys on this head are so transparently false, that it can hardly be a matter of wonder that not one man of sense or respectability among them appears ever to have come forward to seek information or satisfy himself as to the truth or falsity or rumours so industriously circulated about these cartridges that were to be the means of depriving them of their faith. Some few – very few – honourable exceptions have certainly held aloof from, and openly repudiated the conduct of their brethren, but such men have wanted neither guarantees nor explanations in regard to a matter which was patent to all, but have come to their own conclusions on a subject where error had any honest objection to the use of any of the cartridges at Meerut or at Delhi, is sufficiently proved by the eagerness with which they sought possession of them, and the alacrity with which they used them, when their aim and object was the murder of their European Officers, or when, united under the banners of the Prisoner at your bar, they, for months, constantly went forth to fight against the power to which they owed fealty and allegiance. Among the very numerous petitions which have been brought under your notice during these proceedings, it may have struck the Court as very strange that there is not a single one in which the slightest allusion is made to what the sepoys would have us believe to be their great and particular grievance. We have had upwards of 180 petitions before the Court, written on all possible subjects – from the tinkering of a cooking pot, to the recovery of a mule, or a crack in a horse's hoof – and each though worth of the sign of royalty, but in the free indulgence of such correspondence, when certainly not restrained by any delicacy of language or of feeling, from venting their acerbity against their quondam European masters, we can find no trace of the original sin, no grease spot staining these effusions of disloyalty. How instructive is it that, among themselves, and when applying to us such language as 'damnable hell-doomed infidels', they apparently forgo the first specific offence, which they would have us believe has led them to mutiny and rebellion, and the perpetration of crimes at which humanity shudders! When with each other, and, as they conceived, safe from the intrusion and enquiries of British officers, that insurmountable obstacle to their fidelity and allegiance, the greased cartridge is, apparently, altogether lost sight of. Not a whisper is heard of a grievance which, if a substantial one, must even have been uppermost in the memories of all – must have been continually rankling in their minds and embittering their thoughts – must have influenced them in their blood-thirstiness; and to themselves, have been their only extenuation for crimes such as may well exclude them from mercy. What a contrast this to their speeches when uttered with a prospect of reaching European ears! – Greased cartridges are then always brought forward; the use of them forms the one continuous nightmare of the sepoy's existence. Really, if we reflect seriously on this – if we remember that in reality there was not a single greased cartridge among either of the three regiments which first broke out into mutiny, murdering, not only men, but unoffending women and children, and that the sepoys were perfectly aware of this – when we call to mind that, even if greased cartridges had existed, and the use of them been required at the hands of these miscreants, not one of the Mahommedans at any rate could possibly have been injured thereby in any case prejudice, or placed even in temporary difficulty with regard to this religious tenets. When to this we add, what is well known to everyone in India, whether Hindu, Mahommedan, or European, *viz.* that the native soldier has but to ask for his discharge, and that, in time of peace, it is at once granted to him, without enquiry or difficulty of any kind – it seems beyond the bounds of reason to imagine that these men were drawn into acts of such revolting atrocity by any grievance either real or imagined. Let the chimeras, the disturbed dreams of fanaticism, of wickedness, or of folly have been what they may; let the instigations to evil have been as industrious as possible; and then allow that the sepoys to be worked upon, were as credulous as the grossest ignorance could make them – still, if the greased cartridge had been the only weapon the tampers had to work with – but the one envenomed shaft in their quiver – how easy was the remedy! It required no depth of knowledge, no philosopher to inform them, that they could at once escape from every possible perplexity by simply applying for their discharge. I know not, Gentlemen, what conclusion you may arrive at one this much vexed question, but, after pondering it in every way in which my reason has presented it to me, I am obliged to infer that something deeper and more powerful than the use of greased cartridges has been resorted to.

The machinery that has set in motion such an amount of mutiny and murder, that has made its vibrations felt almost at once and the same moment from one end of India to the other, and most successful and commanding subtlety. We must recollect, too, in considering this subject, that in many places where the native troops have risen against their European officers, there was no pretext even in reference to cartridges at all. Numbers of these mutinies, apparently, because they thought there was a favourable opportunity of doing so – because they to now against those in authority, and fancied that they might pillage, plunder and massacre, not only with impunity, but with advantage. Is it possible that such fearful results as these could have at once developed themselves, had the native army previous to the cartridge question been in a sound and well affected state? Can anyone imagine that that rancorous widespread enmity, of which we have lately had such terrible proofs, has been the result of feelings suddenly and accidentally irritated. Does it appear consistent with the natural order of events, that such intense malignity should start into existence on one single provocation? Or can it be reconciled with the instincts, the traditions, or the idiosyncrasies of the Hindus, that they should, recklessly, without enquiry, and without thought, desire to imbrue their hands in human blood, casting aside the pecuniary and other advantages that bound them to the cause of order and of the Government? Or, more than this, can it be imagined that the three regiments at Meerut, even when joined by those at Delhi, could have conceived an idea so daring as that of overthrowing, by themselves, the British Government in India?

I think, Gentlemen, even one must allow that if we had no other evidence of a plot, no testimony indicative of a previous conspiracy, the very nature of the outbreak itself must have convinced us of the existence of one. In the moral, as in the physical world, there must be cause and effect; and the horrible butcheries of the past year would remain an anomaly and a mystery for ever, could we trace them to nothing more occult and baneful than a cartridge of any kind. It will be observed, that this point of the cartridges, so openly and frequently insisted on, at Meerut and elsewhere, before the 10th of May, gradually becomes more and more indistinct as the plot gathers strength and matures itself, and after furnishing the mutineers with their first war cry at Delhi, it seems to have answered its purpose, and thenceforward was allowed to sink into disuse and neglect. With little or no vitality at starting, it soon died a natural death, and was succeeded by a reality of purpose, and a fixedness of resolve, that would have been worthy of a better cause. If we review the actions and whole conduct of these mutineers, we shall soon see that, from the very commencement, they bear the impress of cunning and of secret combination. For instance, 85 of their comrades were ironed before them and sent off to jail in their presence on the morning of the 9th of May; but this occasioned no outbreak of fury. No sound or token of dissatisfaction escaped from the men, who, then and long before, must have had rebellion in their hearts; no gesture indicative of sympathy with the culprits was exhibited by any; in fact, as far as appearances could be trusted, the infantry regiments at Meerut, and the remaining portion of the 3rd Cavalry, were as obedient and loyal as could possibly be desired; and this deception was successfully resorted to till their plans were matured, and the moment for open revolt had arrived. The night of the 9th of May, 12 hours after the imprisonment of the 3rd Cavalry mutineers had taken place, was as favourable an opportunity as the night following, for a march upon the nearest magazine; but there had not been time for preparing the Delhi sepoys for a movement which the progress of events at Meerut had doubtless precipitated sooner than their first calculations had led them to expect. Hence the necessity for communicating afresh with Delhi, and acquainting the sepoys there with the drama that was to be enacted on Monday the 11th. That such was done is established by the evidence of Captain Tytler; for it would be difficult to assign any other motive for a carriage full of sepoys coming over from Meerut on Sunday evening, and driving straight into the lines of the 38th Native Infantry.

Again, we can perceive, in the very hour chosen for the outbreak at Meerut, the same evidence of cunning and of craft. The plan, too of the Meerut cantonments gave considerable facilities for carrying out their plot. The native lines are so completely separated from that portion of the cantonments where the European troops reside, that the disturbance and uproar attendant even upon open mutiny could not be heard, or even known, from one to the other until specially communicated. Officers may naturally have been too intent on quelling the rebellion of their men to think of officially reporting it. Be this as it may, there would be some delay in turning out and supplying the Europeans with cartridges, assembling their officers, and marching down a distance of not less than 2 miles; so that taking one delay with another the mutineers might fairly calculate, considering it was an utter surprise to all, on one and a half hours of safe and uninterrupted progress; and as the outbreak commenced at half past 6, this would have secured them darkness and comparative security for their further operations. This was what in effect actually took place. On the Europeans reaching the native lines, it was already dark; no sepoys were to be seen, and no one could tell whether they had gone. Subsequent enquiry revealed that guided by the instinct of cunning, the rebels had not, at first, taken the direct or main road to Delhi, neither had they left Meerut in military formation, but as dusk set in, had gone forth in parties of 5, 6, or 10 to their fixed place of assembly. This was judicious for their departure from Meerut, but would have been highly impolitic for their entry into Delhi, where there were no European troops to avoid. Something more imposing and demonstrative was required here; and accordingly we find them crossing the bridge simultaneously, massed in columns, and in complete military array, with a portion of the cavalry sent forward as a regular advanced guard.

It is on this occasion that we first prove the mutineers in immediate connection with the Prisoner at your bar. The first point to which they turn – the first person to whom they address themselves, is the titular majesty of Delhi. This circumstance has much significance, and, at any rate, tends to show that previous concert existed between them. The Prisoner's complicity, however, was, immediately after, openly to commence. Scarcely had the very serious nature of the outbreak had time to develop itself, than his own special servants – in the very precincts of the palace – and almost, as it were, before his own eyes, rush to imbrue their hands in the blood of every European they can meet with; and, when we remember that two of these were young and delicate women who could have given no offence – whose sex and age might have tamed any hearts less pitiless than those of the human demons who destroyed them – we are able to realize some slight portion of the horribly unnatural influences that appear innate to Mahommedan treachery. How otherwise it was possible that education – the pride of Royal ancestry – a life of tranquil ease and comparative refinement – should not have exempted this old and grey-headed man from all connection with deeds which seem too barbarous for the very outcasts of humanity, or even for the untamed but less savage denizens of the jungle.

We stop to enquire whether it has been proved in this Court, and will be repeated in after years, that the last king of the imperial house of Taimur was an accomplice in this villainy. The circumstances shall now be fairly stated. These murders were committed in the broad glare of day, before dozens of witnesses, and without the slightest attempt at concealment. They were perpetrated, as has been already stated, by the Prisoner's own retainers, and within the limits of his palace, where, be it remembered even under the Company's Government, his jurisdiction was paramount. I shall not, however, attempt to infer that these murders must have been previously sanctioned by the Prisoner – mere inferences on such a point cannot be accepted in a Court of Justice. I prefer to quote from the evidence. It is Ahsanullah Khan, the physician, who is speaking, and who says, that at the time referred to, he and Ghulam Abbas the attorney in Court, were with the King, when it was told them that the troopers had killed Mr. Fraser, and had gone up to Captain Douglas to kill him, and that this was instantly confirmed by the return of the palkee bearers, who told them that they had witnessed Mr. Fraser's murder; that his body was in the gateway, and that the troopers had ascended to the upper building for the purpose of murdering those there. Why the witness suppresses all mention of the prominent part the King's own servants took in these massacres, can easily be imagined. In a subsequent part of his examination, he even asserts that he never heard that any of the King's servants joined in these murders, nay more, that it was not generally known who committed them! Such is the evasion of the King's own physician, who doubtless was aware of the importance that would necessarily attach to this point. It was not generally known who committed these murders? And yet, at this lapse of time, we have had no difficulty in tracing the individuals, and ascertaining their names. It was not generally known that the King's own servants were the murderers! And yet we find this very circumstances prominently and specifically mentioned at the time in the native newspapers of the city. I need not, after this, recapitulate the evidence of all those who have clearly and satisfactorily proved that the King's servants were the murderers; for their testimony stands unshaken and unrefuted. It will amply suffice if I quote the statement of one of them, and which is as follows: 'At this time Mr. Fraser remained below, trying to suppress the disturbance; and while thus engaged, I noticed that Haji lapidary cut him down with a Tulwar, and, almost at the same instant, some of the King's servants cut at him with swords till he was dead. One of Mr. Fraser's murderers was an Abyssinian. After this, they made a rush to the upper apartments, when I immediately ran round by another door and closed the door at the top of the stairs. I was engaged in shutting all the doors, when the crowd found entrance by the southern stair, and having forced one of the doors on that side, came and gave admission to the men who had assisted in murdering Mr. Fraser. These immediately rushed into the apartments where the gentlemen, *viz.* Captain Douglas, Mr. Hutchinson, and Mr. Jennings, had retired, and attacking them with swords, at once murdered them and the two young ladies. On this, I ran down the staircase. As I got to the bottom, I was laid hold of by one Mundoh, a bearer in the service of the King, who said, 'Tell me where Captain Douglas is; you have concealed him'. He forced me upstairs with him, I said, 'You have yourselves killed all the gentlemen already'; but on reaching the room where Captain Douglas was, I saw that he was not quite dead. Mundoh perceiving this also, hit him with a bludgeon on the forehead, and killed him immediately'. Having now established that the murderers of these ladies were the special servants of the Prisoner, it will be well to revert to the testimony of the physician, Ahsanullah Khan, and to ascertain from him the steps the Prisoner took on the murders being reported to him. The only order he gave on this occasion appears to have been to close the gates of his palace, and we naturally enquire whether this was for the purpose of preventing the escape of the murderers. The evidence distinctly proves that it was not. The physician being further interrogated, is obliged to confess that the Prisoner took no steps whatever either to discover, to secure, or to punish the guilty, and attributes it to there being much confusion at the time; but if the King's authority had actually been set aside, and by his own servants too, this would have been the most forcible of all reasons for immediately re-establishing it, by at once bringing the offenders to justice. That this was not done we have been already informed, and we can only account for it on the supposition that these acts of the prisoner's servants, if not instigated by himself, had yet actually anticipated his wishes. We are thus perfectly prepared for what is to follow, *viz.* that no servant was ever dismissed, and not the slightest investigation or enquiry was ever instituted; in fact, in the words of the question put to the witness, the King continued these murderers both in his pay and in employment, and this too, as we have seen, when the very newspapers of the day gave information against them! After this, is it necessary to question whether he adopted these deeds as his own or not? I need not quote what may be the law of the land on such a point, for there is a yet higher law which must acquit him or condemn him, the law of conscience and of sense; that law which everyone who hears me can apply, and which carries with it a verdict more terrible than that which is pronounced in mere conformity to legal codes or military legislation; it is a law that does not depend upon local constitutions, upon human institutes, or religious creeds; it is a law fixed in the heart of man by his Maker, and can it now here be set aside?

Perhaps it may now be time to turn our attention to what was doing at the magazine, and to trace the further steps of the mutineers in that direction. Captain Forrest has told us that it was about 9 o'clock in the morning when the main body of the native troops from Meerut was passing over the bridge in military formation (that is, in subdivision of companies), with fixed bayonets and sloped arms, the cavalry being in front. It was actually in less than one hour after this that a Subedar of the 38th Native Infantry, who was commanding the magazine guard outside the gate, informed them that the King of Delhi had sent a guard to take possession of the magazine, and to bring all the Europeans there up to his palace, and that if they did not consent to this, none of them were to be allowed to leave the magazine. Captain Forrest adds that he did not see the guard at this time, but that he saw the man who had brought this message, and he was a well-dressed Mussalman. Nor was this all, for shortly after the above, a native officer in the King's service arrived with a strong guard of the King's own soldiers in their uniform, and told the above-mentioned Subedar and the non-commissioned officers that he was sent down by the King to relieve them of duty.

We thus see with what alertness and dispatch this most important object, the seizure of the magazine, was attempted. Is it, however, to be believed that such was the ready, immediate, and, as it were, impulsive decision of the King, or of those who formed the Court? To attribute to them anything of this nature, would be to give them credit or a coolness of calculation, combined with a quickness of apprehension, such as pertains only to the more gifted of mankind. The scope and entire progress of the scheme speaks loudly of a plan previously arranged, and of deliberations long matured by the counsels of many. Indeed, it is difficult to conceive that any one, not previously initiated in the secret, could, on the moment, so promptly and so effectually have entered upon and adopted the details necessary for carrying it out. You will recollect the extreme importance of the decision, the magnitude of the interests at stake. You will call to mind the cogent reasons and the numerous arguments, that would naturally array themselves against adopting so headlong and precipitate a measure. It was, in fact, an invitation to a King to league himself with ruffians and with cut-throats. Any inducement or prospective advantage that they could hold out to him was faint and almost imperceptible, compared with the open risk which he was to encounter. By embarking in so forlorn a cause, he imperilled everything; his own life, and those of all belonging to him, and for what? The distant glimmer of a crown, which common reason, or the slightest consideration, would have convinced him was a mere *ignis fatuus* – a mockery of sceptre, that would evade his grasp. Are we to imagine that it was under such circumstances that this weak and tremulous old man seized and improved his occasion, and with all the rapid instinct of determination, directed his own troops upon the magazine, to establish himself there as the one point of primary and most vital importance, and this too in the first moment of a supreme? Or are we to suppose that there was a secret and a deeper knowledge of what the other portions of the army were already ripe for, and that the five or six regiments to commence with, were but the instalments of those that were to follow? Or, if such previous understanding and collusion did not exist either with the King or any of those immediately about him, are we to attribute to superstition and the pretended revelation of dreams, circumstances which scarcely admit of satisfactory solution by any more sober process? We have all heard, in this Court, of the vision of a hurricane that was to arise from the West with a great flood of water devastating the whole country, but bearing up on its surges this descendant of ancient royalty, and that this vision, as interpreted by Hasan Askari the priest, signified annihilation to the English infidels by the power of the King of Persia, who was to restore sovereignty to the heirs of the throne of Hindustan. Was it a reliance upon this, that expedited the otherwise tardy movements of these Asiatics, and gave breadth and boldness to their decisions? I am aware that under other circumstances, and in any but an Eastern land, such unmeaning flights of a bewildered imagination would be too trivial to dwell upon – too unsubstantial for the gravity of comment; but here, in seriously considering the nature and progress of an extensive military revolt, they obtrude themselves on the mind, as subjects capable of influencing for evil the destinies of thousands.

These observations have been elicited by the marked and unusual energy displayed in making the point of instant attack. It seems to me that such cannot be accounted for by conspiracy among the sepoys alone, for it was the King's own troops who were the first to seek possession, and the military and systematic way in which this was done, betrays the authority by which this was done, betrays the authority by which the orders were issued. There was no confusion here, no attempt at pillage; non-commissioned officers were appointed to the separate guards for the different gates of the magazine, while another guard superintended the labourers who were removing the instant transformation from chaos to system and to order have resulted, had not the King or some of his officials been entrusted with a sort of programmed of events? How, in fact, could the King's troops have been in readiness and preparation for such work without warning of some kind?

If I have not succeeded in tracing to the King himself, a foreknowledge of the leading events that were to take place on Monday the 11th of May, I trust it has been made obvious that the secret was in the possession of some influential inmates of the palace. The babbling garrulity of the prince Jawan Bakht sufficiently indicates this, for such is his joy at the anticipation of murdering the English, that he is unable to restrain his expression of it. My chief object, however, has been to render clear what I believe to be the truth, *viz.* that the conspiracy, from the very commencement, was not confined to the sepoys, and did not even originate with them, but had its ramifications throughout the palace and the city; and do not the murders which we have already adverted to, tend to corroborate this fact? We have evidence that the mutineers of the 11th and 20th Regiments of Native Infantry, before the Magazine was exploded, proceeded to attack and escalade it, and it is then for the first time that we find the King, through his troops, acting in open alliance with these traitors to their government. From that moment there is no further disguise, and no attempt at concealment. Fairly launched into the stream of sedition, he is hurried onward by the swollen flood which was not however to bear him, as he imagined, to the throne of Hindustan, but to leave him in its ebb a mere helpless wreck upon the sands.

I would here pause for a second, to refer to Lieutenant Willoughby, and to the brave men under him, who, for so long a time, had, held, against unnumbered odds, the magazine entrusted to them. One hardly knows which to admire most, the penetration and sagacity which, at a glance, foresaw the possible necessity for its destruction, and made arrangements accordingly; or the undaunted resolution with which the final sacrifice was accomplished. To do justice to such heroism will be the pleasing duty of the historian. I can merely give it a passing notice, having to dilate on other matters more immediately connected with the proceedings before us.

With the explosion of the magazine at Delhi, every hope of stemming the torrent of rebellion seems to have vanished; resistance had been there protracted to its utmost possible extent; the sacrifice was a final one; and thenceforward the European community if, in isolated spots, still preserving the appearance of Government authority, were left without one vestige of real power, so that it soon became a duty to the state and to themselves to save their lives by a timely retreat. Delhi was consequently abandoned to the miscreants who had in the short space of 24 hours stained themselves with crimes which can scarcely be equalled in all the catalogues of bygone iniquity. It is now that we find the King coming personally forward as the chief actor in that great drama which had more than England and Europe for its spectators; the progress of which was watched with such absorbing interest everywhere by the antagonistic powers of civilization and of barbarism. The evidence shows that on the afternoon of the 11th May, the King, having entered the Hall of Special Audience, seated himself in a chair, when the soldiery – officers and all – came forward one by one and bowed their heads before him, asking him to place his hands on them. The King did so, and each then withdrew, saying whatever came into his mind. The witness, *viz.* Ghulam Abbas, the prisoner's attorney in Court, informs us that this ceremony of the King putting his hands on the heads of the soldiery was equivalent to accepting their allegiance and services; and he further states, that though he is not aware of any regular proclamation having been made in Delhi in reference to the King assuming the reins of government, yet that such may have been done without his hearing of it, but that on the very day of the outbreak the King's authority was established, and that night a Royal salute was fired of about 21 guns.

These matters bring us to the charges against the Prisoner, and it may perhaps be as well now to consider them, not so much in regard to dates as the sequence in which they have been drawn up. The first charge against Muhammad Bahadur Shah, Ex-King of Delhi, is: 'For that he, being a pensioner of the British government in India, did, at Delhi, at various times between the 10th of May and 1st of October 1857, encourage, aid, and abet Muhammad Bakht Khan, Subedar of the Regiment of Artillery, and, diverse others, native commissioned officers and soldiers unknown, of the East India Company's Army, in the crimes of Mutiny and Rebellion against the State'. I am not going to weary the Court by repeating even a tenth part of the evidence which has been brought forward to establish these charges, but it is perhaps necessary to show that proof of them has been recorded. Mr. Saunders, Officiating Commissioner and Agent to the Lieutenant-Governor, has explained under what circumstances the prisoner became a pensioner of the British government in India, *viz.* that his grandfather, Shah Alam, after having been kept in rigorous confinement by the Mahrattas, on their defeat by the English in 1803, applied to the British government for protection. This was accorded, and from that moment the titular Kings of Delhi became pensioned subjects of the British. It will be seen, then, that, as far as this family is concerned, there was no wrong to be complained of, and nothing but benefits to be remembered. The Prisoner's grandfather Shah Alam had not only lost his throne, but had his eyes put out, and been subjected to every species of indignity, and was still kept in most rigorous confinement, when the English, under Lord Lake, appeared as his deliverers, and, with generous sympathy for his misfortunes, bestowed on him rank and pension which, continued to his successor, have maintained them in honour and in influence, till like the snake in the fable, they have turned their fangs upon those to whom they owed the very means of their existence. The evidence that connects the prisoner with Muhammed Bakht Khan, Subedar of the Artillery, and which of itself will be sufficient to establish the charge, is a document from beginning to end in the prisoner's own handwriting.

To – The especial Slave, The Lord Governor, Muhammad Bakht Khan Bahadur.

'Receive our favour, and understand that while the Neemuch Force have reached Alapur, its baggage is still here, and that you are therefore directed to take 200 troopers and 5 or 7 companies of infantry, and have all the baggage alluded to, such as tents, etc., together with commissariat supplies, conveyed by the gharis to Alapur. You are further, that if the army returns without victory, and divested of its appliances of war, the consequence must be disastrous. You have been premonished and you are to consider these orders stringent'.

It is true that there is no date to this communication, but the allusions in it leave no possible doubt as to its having been written within the period embraced by the terms of the first charge.

Perhaps this will be the best place for the few observations I have to offer on the defence. The prisoner, like every other that we have tried, has, according to his own showing, been the mere victim of circumstances; declares that he had no intelligence on the subject previous to the outbreak; that the mutinous soldiery surrounded him completely and placed sentries on all sides – and that, fearing for his life, he kept quiet, and went to his own private apartments – and that the mutinous soldiery kept the men, women and children prisoners; that he twice saved their lives by entreaty and persuasion, and that the third time he said all in his power to save them, but that the rebellious soldiery would not heed him, and eventually carried out their purpose of slaying these poor people against his orders. Now the chief objection to all this is, that it is not only unsupported by evidence, but is directly in the teeth of all the testimony, whether oral or written, and whether given by his own servants or by others. The entire defence indeed is a mere tissue of denials of guilt; assertion of his not having been a free-agent; and an endeavour to put the onus of his misconduct upon others. He cannot challenge the authenticity of the documents against him, or the evidence of his own handwriting, or his own seal; and his only expedient consists in asseverating that what he wrote was by compulsion, and that his seal was affixed in the same way. The only dilemma that he appears unable to extricate himself from, to his own satisfaction, in this way, is the going out to Humayun's Tomb, and coming in again. It was, of course, necessary to state that the last was by his own choice and free will; and this would scarcely have been possible had his going out been represented as compulsory; for if the sepoys had forcibly taken him out, they would hardly allow him voluntarily to return, so we are treated with the following curious account: 'When the revolted and rebellious troops prepared to abscond, finding an opportunity I got away secretly under the palace windows, and went and stayed in Humayun's Mausoleum'. One would have thought that if he wished to separate himself from the rebellious troops, that his best plan would have been to have stayed in Delhi, when they were preparing to abscond, instead of secretly planning to go out with them. However, I do not mean to take the defence, paragraph by paragraph, and thus refute it. My best reply to it, I believe, will be by showing how fully and completely the charges have been proved, and to this I now again address myself, and proceed to the consideration of the 2nd count, which is, if possible, still more fully established than the 1st. It runs as follows: For having, at Delhi, at various times between the 10th of May and 1st of October 1857, encouraged, aided, and abetted Mirza Mughal, his own son, a subject of the British Government in India, and diverse others unknown, inhabitants of Delhi, and of the North-West Provinces of India, also subjects of the said 'British government, no rebel and wage war was against the state'. The document and other evidence in support of this charge are so numerous that it would be tedious even to reckon them. The newspapers speak of the appointment of Mirza Mughal to the office of Commander-in-Chief; of his investiture with a dress of honour; and other matters relating thereto. The oral testimony is very strong on the same subject, while the discovered correspondence shows that Mirza Mughal, the son, was perhaps, next to his father, the leading chief of the rebels in Delhi. I shall for form's sake give a short extract from a petition of Maulavy Muhammad Zahur Ali, Police Officer of Najafgarh. It is as follows:

To – The King! Shelter of the World!

'Respectfully Sheweth, That the orders of the Royal missive have been fully explained to all the Thakurs, Kanungos, and Patwaries of this township of Najafgarh, and that the best arrangements have been established. Further, that, agreeably to Your Majesty's injunctions, steps are being taken to collect housemen and footmen, and it is explained to them, that their allowances will be paid from the revenue of this division of the district. Your slave's assurance, on this point, however, will not be believed, till some Ghazis, recently engaged, shall have arrived. As regards Nagli, Kakrowla, Dachaoo Kalla, and other adjacent villages, your slave has to represent that, unrestrained by the dread of consequences, and bent on all sorts of excesses, the inhabitants have commenced plundering travellers'.

This might, I think, be sufficiently conclusive as to the words of the charge in reference to aiding and abetting in rebellion, Mirza Mughal, his son, and diverse other 'unknown inhabitants of Delhi, and of the North-Western Provinces of India', inasmuch as the petition from which I am quoting, bears the autograph; order of the Prisoner referring it to his son, Mirza Mughal, and directing him quickly to send a regiment of infantry with its officers to Najafgarh, in accordance with the wishes, and for the purpose of aiding and abetting the petitioner's schemes of raising horsemen and footmen to fight against the English. But there is another petition, which has not yet been submitted to the Court, having only lately come to hand, and which may appropriately be introduced here. It is from Amir Ali Khan, son of the Nawab of Khurajpura, and is dated 12th of July. It runs as follows:

To – The King! Shelter of the World!

Respectfully Sheweth, That your petitioner has come to your Royal Court, at which Darius might have served as a doorkeeper, having left his house animated by the ambition to stake his life in Your Majesty's cause, and laments that he has lived to see the day when the accursed English have presumed to direct their cannon against your Royal dwelling, the guardians of which are the angels of heaven, from the first dawn of the powers of discernment, your petitioner has been trained, like the lion, to conflicts and war, and has not like the fox been concerned for his life:

> Leopards destroy their prey on the summits of mountains,
> Crocodiles devour theirs on the banks of rivers.

Your petitioner submits that if his prayer is accepted, and the plans and stratagems necessary in this war are entrusted to his judgement, aided by Your Majesty's august impress he will, in three days, exterminate these people with white skins and dark fortunes. It was necessary, and I have therefore submitted it. (Prayers for the prosperity of the reign, and curses in bitter and filthy language against those who may wish it harm.) Petition of the slave Amir Ali Khan, son of Nawab Dullaai Khan, son of Nawab Najabat Khan, Chief of Khurajpura.

Autograph order of the King in pencil

'Mirza Zahur-ud-din will make enquiries and will give the petitioner service'.

The third charge is 'For that he, being a subject of the British Government in India, and not regarding the duty of his allegiance, did, at Delhi, on the 11th May 1857, or thereabouts, as a false traitor against the State, proclaim and declare himself the reigning King and Sovereign of India, and did, then and there, traitorously seize and take unlawful possession of the city of Delhi; and did moreover, at various times between the 10th of May and

1st of October 1857, as such false traitor aforesaid, treasonably conspire, consult, and agree with Mirza Mughal, his own son, and with Muhammad Bakht Khan, Subedar of the Regiment of Artillery, and divers other false traitors unknown, to raise, levy, and make insurrection, rebellion, and war, against the State; and further to fulfil and perfect his treasonable design of overthrowing and destroying the British Government in India, did assemble armed forces at Delhi, and send them forth to fight and wage war against the said British government'.

That the prisoner was a pensioned subject of the British Government in India has already shown in treating of the first charge; and as the British government neither showed him nor any member of his family of any sovereignty whatever, but, on the contrast relieving them from misery and oppression, bestowed on them largesses and pensions aggregating many millions of pounds sterling, the duty of their allegiance will, I think, be readily admitted; yet, as we have already seen, this traitor rushes to seize the first possible opportunity of overthrowing and destroying the government of his benefactors. On the afternoon of the very first day of the outbreak, in the hall of Special Audience, he relates the obeisance of the revolted sepoys, and by laying his hands on their heads unites with them in a common brotherhood of infamy. It is perhaps difficult to realize such fame. An enfeebled tremulous old man striving with palsied hand to reach a sceptre far powerful for his puny grasp, and while bent by age and infirmity, inducing a monarch's garb to give, as it were, a benison and a blessing to the cause of the foulest treachery and murder! Dead to every feeling that falls honourably on the heart of man, this shrivelled of malignity must have formed no inept centrepiece to the group that surround him!

There are several witnesses who speak to the circumstance of the Prisoner having as proclaimed: it is variously stated as occurring on different days, and it is more than credible that such was actually the case. One or two proclamations would hardly be efficient to carry the information through all the suburbs of so large a city as Delhi. The Prisoner's attorney allows that the King's authority was established on the 11th of May and Gulab, messenger, being asked, 'Was the King proclaimed as the reigning sovereign immediately after the outbreak?' answered. 'Yes, the proclamation was made by beat of drum on the very day of the outbreak, about three in the afternoon to the effect that it was now the King's government', while Chuni, Pedlar, another witness, declares that 'On the 11th of May, about midnight, some 20 guns were fired in the palace. I heard the reports at my house, and next day, at about noon, a proclamation was made by beat of drum that the country had reverted to the possession of the King'. The next paragraph in the charge is in reference to traitorously seizing and taking unlawful possession of the city of Delhi; but this is a point that I need not quote evidence to establish. It is difficult to turn our eyes in any direction without having convincing proofs of it. The charge then goes on to assert that the prisoner 'did at various times, between the 10th of May and 1st of October 1857, treasonably conspire, consult, and agree with Mirza Mughal his son, and with Muhammad Bakht Kahn, Subedar of the Regiment of Artillery, and divers other false traitors unknown, to raise, levy, and make insurrection and war against the State'. Mirza Mughal was publicly appointed Commander-in-Chief, and a special state procession in honour of his being so, took place a few days after the outbreak. The witness who deposes to this is Chuni Lal, Pedlar; but he is unable to specify the exact date on which he witnessed it. Mirza Mughal's authority after this seems to have been uncontrolled, at any rate in all matters immediately relating to the army, until Subedar Bakht Khan, of the Artillery, arrived, and was appointed both Lord governor-General and Commander-in-Chief. The date of his arrival was the 1st of July, and after that, some jealousy and clashing of authority between the two Commanders-in-Chief is observable, for, on the 17th of July, Mirza Mughal writes and informs his father, that on that day he had formed up the army and taken it outside the city to attack the English, when General Bakht Khan interfered, and for a long time kept the whole force standing inactive, wanting to know by whose orders it had gone out, and, saying it was not to proceed without his permission, caused it to return. Mirza Mughal adds, 'that having his orders reversed cannot but cause vexation to any office high or low, and begs that definite instructions may be given as to whom the real authority over the army belongs'. There is no order on this letter, nor have we any intimation what decision was come to, but that some better arrangement was the consequence is evident, for, on the very next day, the 18th of July, we find Mirza Mughal and General Bakht Khan acting in concert, as the following letter from Mirza Mughal to his father will show. It is dated the 19th July and runs as follows: 'Since yesterday the arrangements have been completed for carrying on active offensive operation both by night and day. If aid could be afforded now from the direction of Alapur, with the divine blessing, and through the influence of Your Majesty's ever-enduring prestige, a final and decisive victory, it is to be expected, would soon be obtained. I therefore pray that positive orders may be issued from the throne to the Bareilly General to afford the aid in question, that is, that he be directed to proceed with troops to Alapur, and to make an attack on the infidels from that direction, while your slave with his division of the army makes another on this side, so that the two forces cooperating in the fight, may in one or two days consign all the damnable hell-doomed infidels to hell. Moreover, it is to be expected that the force going to Alapur will cut off the enemies' supplies. It was necessary and has therefore been submitted'. On this letter, there is an autograph order of the King to the following effect, 'that Mirza Mughal will make whatever arrangements may be proper', and also an after order apparently by Mirza Mughal – 'That an order be written to the Bareilly General'. I think this is conclusive of the three conspiring, consulting and agreeing together, but it may be as well to enter here two documents which have not as yet been submitted to the Court. One is a proclamation from General Muhammad Bakht Khan, dated 12th of July, and is to the following effect. It has, I should observe, been extracted from the *Delhi Urdu News*:

'Let it be generally known to the persons living in the city and the country, such as chiefs of free-holds, pensioners, landholders of rent-free estates, & c., that if, from anxiety for their incomes, they have hitherto continued on the side of the English, and have in any way colluded with them by conveying intelligence or furnishing them with supplies, their having done so will to be considered inexcusable. It is accordingly now proclaimed that all those who have been alluded to, are to cherish full confidence that when final and complete victory shall have been obtained, provided their title deeds, former and recent, shall on inspection be fully verified, they will leave the present provisions in their favour continued to them, and that they will also receive compensation in full for the entire period during which their incomes may have been suspended, owing to the present disturbances; but if, after receiving knowledge of these orders, any person shall, notwithstanding, forward intelligence or furnish supplies etc., to English, he will be severely punished in the way government may determine. The chief police officer of the city is, therefore, ordered to have the signatures of all chiefs of free-holds, of rent-free estates, and pensioners residing in his jurisdiction, written on the reverse of this notification to them in this matter, in acknowledgement of their having been confirmed, and then to send the notification immediately to His Excellency'.

The Government in an order from the King, dated the 6th of September 1857, and is passed to the chief police officer of the city. It runs as follows: 'You are directed to be proclaimed throughout the city by beat of drum, that this is a religious war, and is prosecuted on account of faith, and that it behoves all Hindu and Mussalman residents of the imperial city, or of the villages out in the country, as well as those residents of Hindustan who are arrayed against us on the ridge, or are anywhere employed on the side of the armies of the English, whether they be men of the eastern provinces, Sikhs, or foreigners, or natives of the Himalaya Hills, or Nepaulesse, to continue true and fair faith and creeds, and to slay the English and their servants: and you are directed to have it further proclaimed, that those who are now present with the English force of the ridge, whether they be people of Hindustan, or foreigners, or Hillmen, or Sikhs, whatever countries they may be native of, or whether they be Mahommedans, or they born in Hindustan, they are not to entertain any fears or dread of the enemy. However, if they come over to this side, kind provision will be made for them, and they will be allowed to a continue in their own creed and religion. You are directed to have it proclaimed further, that all who will join in the attacks on the enemy, whether they be or be not servants, will be allowed to keep themselves whatever property they may take to the English in plunder, and that they will beside revive additional rewards from His Majesty, and will be amply provided for'. This paper, which I have just perused, is the office copy, and was found recently among other documents in the office of the King's police station. It bears the seal of that office, and is actually attested as a true copy of the signature of Bhao Singh, assistant to the King's chief police officer. A more worthy and convincing document could hardly be laid before a Court. It seems to fully to complete the proof of the third charge, and to render further quotations of the numerous other documents unnecessary. It also tends to establish the latter portion of the fourth charge.

To this charge I will now turn my attention. It causes the Prisoner 'of having, at Delhi on the 16th of May 1857, or thereabouts, within the precincts of the palace at Delhi, feloniously caused and become accessory to the murder of 49 persons, chiefly women and children of European and mixed European descent'. As far as the murder of these poor is concerned, I have nothing to allege, the facts have been detailed before the Court for their horrid minuteness, and they are not such as to be easily forgotten. The cold-blooded hardened villainy that could reveal in leading women and young children to the shambles and this too without the miserable apology of imagined wrong, or to the mistaken zeal of religious frenzy, is something so inhuman that the mind might well refuse to accept the truth, did not all the force of concurrent ideas, of direct testimony, of circumstantial proof and elsewhere repeated reactions of the same dreadful tragedies, enforce it upon our sections. It is not then such a limited facts as the above that I am here called upon to accomplish. They are unhappily but too prominently and painfully shaped forth to require further illustration. It remains, however, to show how deeply the prisoner stands implicated on revolting butchery, and whether, as averted in the indictment, he did 'feloniously cause and become accessory to the murder of these 49 persons'. I shall not, in so doing, attempt to avail myself of that law which makes all persons joining in insurrection and sedition individually responsible for every act of violence that may be committed by those with whom they stand leagued in illicit combination, even though such acts may have been against their wishes or without their cognisance. I mean, however, separately to consider each fact connecting the Prisoner with the deaths of these women and children, I will revert to the evidence of their capture, the place of their imprisonment, the fearful privations to which they were subjected, and the more than cruel treatment which they experienced, from the commencement of their confinement, all of which were but too prophetic of the ultimate doom that awaited them. The first person whose testimony I shall have to quote is Ahsanullah Khan, the physician, when asked, 'How was it that so many English women and children were brought to the palace and placed in confinement'. He replied – 'The mutineers took them in and about the city, and having established their own quarters in the palace, they brought their prisoners in with them too'. Being further interrogated, he declares that the mutineers did not retain the custody of their prisoners, but, as each successive one was brought in, they reported the circumstances to the Prisoner, and were told to take the Europeans to the kitchen, and keep them confined there being again questioned, he asserts that the King himself appointed the kitchen as the place of their confinement, and observed, at the time, that it was a large capacious building, so that it appears that the Prisoner not only fixed upon the building himself as the place for herding indiscriminately together, men, women and children, but from its being in his own place, and from his volunteering a description of it, it is evident that he had some personal knowledge of what it was like. He terms it a large capacious building, but these are not very definite terms, and when used in reference to different objects may relatively have widely different meanings. To obviate any misconception on such a point, I have, since Ahsanullah Khan gave this evidence, visited the place myself, and taken its measurements and description. The building is 40 feet long, 12 feet broad, and about 10 feet high. It is old, dirty and dilapidated, and without the vestige of plaster; but it is worse than this, for it is dark, has no made flooring, no windows, and is entirely without the means of ventilation or of light. There is but one aperture to it, a miserable small wooden door; but I will now let Mrs. Aldwell describe it in her own words: 'We were all confined in one room, very dark, with only one door, and no other opening. It was not fit for the residence of any human being, much less for the number of us that were there. We were very much crowded together, and in consequence of the sepoys, and everyone who took a fancy to do so, coming and frightening the children, we were obliged frequently to close the one door that we had, which thus left us without light or air. The sepoys used to come with their muskets loaded, and bayonets fixed, and ask us whether we would consent to become Mahommedans and also slaves, if the King granted us our lives, but the King's special armed retainers, from whom the guard over us was always furnished, incited the sepoys to be content with nothing short of our lives, saying we should be cut up in small pieces, and given as food to the kites and crows. We were very indifferently fed, but on two occasions the King sent us better food'. Such was the return made by this traitor for the millions of pounds sterling bestowed by the English on himself and on his family. Having, as one of the witnesses has specifically stated, 'abundance of room where these English women and children would have been safe in the apartments occupied by the females of his own establishment', where, it is said, 'there are secret recesses in which 500 people might be concealed, and where, even had the rebels dared to violate the sanctity of the Zenana, all search would have been fruitless' – and there being, according to another witness, no scarcity of vacant buildings in the palace in which the ladies and children could have been kept in confinement, and in which they might have had every comfort – this minion of English generosity preferred to select for them the very den set apart for culprits and for felons, and where they even received far worse than a felon's treatment, for they were crowded into a small space, and were daily exposed to the insults and cruelty of all who chose to molest them. Such was the requital to the English for a princely pension and an imperial palace: it will be observed from the statements of Ahsanullah Khan and Mrs. Aldwell, that both agree in attributing these measures personally to the King, and when we recollect the trifling matters which were, on every occasion, referred to him, and which, as has been fully demonstrated in this Court, received not only his attention but were endorsed by his own autograph instructions, is there any room left for doubt, that the more important concerns were under his special control also? Indeed, the concurrent testimony of many witnesses, and the irrefutable evidence of his own handwriting, incontestably prove that such was the case. It is thus we find the King appointing the prison; that it is the King's special armed retainers were always on guard over the prisoners; that it is the King who supplies them with their very indifferent food, and on two occasions sends them some of better quality – and, thus too, the sepoys asked them whether they would consent to become Mahommedans and slaves, if the king granted them their lives – and who, on perusing even this much of the evidence, can doubt that he had the power of doing so? Has there been one single circumstance elicited that shows that the prisoner even wished to save them, or that he had the power of doing so? Has there been one single circumstance elicited that shows that the prisoner even wished to save them, or that he even extended to them one act of common courtesy or kindness? Very very far from it: for whilst no check was given to those who showed the prisoners every species of unmanly brutality, the ordinary charity of giving food and water to a Christian was severely punished, and a Mahommedan woman, simply on this account, was actually immured with the prisoners! Can the bitterness of rancour go further than this? Or is it possible to contemplate the place and nature of the confinement fixed for these tender women and children, without coming to the conclusion that a cruel death was from the first moment reserved for them, and that, in the words of the witness Mukund Lal, 'they were but being collected!' indeed the edge of the sword seems to have been but a merciful deliverance from the lingering death, which confinement in so loathsome a den at such a season of the year must eventually have inflicted on all exposed to it.

Might I not here stop and confidently on this point, await the decision of the Court against the Prisoner. The proof, however, swells in volume as it proceeds, and I mean to have no portion of it untraced. Gulab, a Chaprassy, or messenger, has distinctly stated that, a couple of days before the massacre took place, it was known that the Europeans would be killed in two day, and that on the day fixed for the slaughter arriving, great crowds of people were flocking to the palace. Every witness to the scene who has spoken of it in Court, has alluded to the crowds assembled, both as spectators and actors on the morning in question, and, as this was at the early hour of between 8 and 9, there seems no doubt that previous information of what was to take place must have been given. Nothing indicates that an outburst of fury either on the part of the populace or military in any way led to a catastrophe so awful. On the contrary, the witness distinctly says that without orders it could not have happened, and that there were but two sources from which such an order could have emanated, *viz.* the King and his son Mirza Mughal, adding, that he does not know which of them gave the order. He however distinctly states that he was present at the murder of these European prisoners, and that he saw them all standing together surrounded on all sides by the King's special armed retainers, or what you may term his body guard, and some of the infantry mutineers; and that though he did not observe any signal or order given, yet, on a sudden, the men just mentioned drew their swords, simultaneously attacked the prisoners, and continued cutting at them till they had killed them all. A second witness, *viz.* Chuni Lal, the news-writer, when asked by whose orders these Europeans were murdered distinctly replies that 'it was done by the King's order; who else could have given such an order? He and other witnesses concur in stating that Mirza Mughal, the King's son, from the top of his house which overlooked the courtyard, was a spectator on this occasion; this Mirza Mughal being, at that time, second only to the King himself in authority. Is it credible then, under such circumstances, that the King's own bodyguard, his special armed retainers, could have dared to perpetrate this frightful butchery without his order, and against his wishes? If a doubt could be entertained on such a subject, it would I think, be speedily dissipated on a perusal of the writings evidently approved by the Prisoner, in which blood-thirstiness and sanguine ferocity against the English are so glaringly conspicuous. In reference to the presence of Mirza Mughal, and in further proof that it was by the King's own orders that these unhappy women and children were massacred, I shall quote the testimony of the King's own secretary, Mukund Lal. The question – 'By whose order were the ladies and children that were prisoners in the palace murdered?' he replies, 'These people were being collected for three days; on the fourth day the infantry and cavalry soldiers accompanied by Mirza Mughal, came to the entrance of the King's private apartments, and requested the King's permission to kill them. The King was, at this time, in his own apartments. Mirza Mughal and Basant Ali Khan went inside while the soldiery remained without. They returned in about 20 minutes, when Basant Ali Khan publicly, and in a loud voice, proclaimed that the king had given his permission for the slaughter of the prisoners, and that they could take them away. Accordingly, the King's armed retainers, in whose custody the prisoners had been, took them from the place of confinement, and in connection with some of the mutinous soldiery killed them'. It appears, then, that Mirza Mughal had just come from the Prisoner's presence, and was armed with his authority for carrying out this most hideous deed of blood. It may seem almost superfluous to add anything to the above; but the proof furnished by the extract from the prisoner's diary is so important and convincing, that I feel bound, to quote it. The evidence of the physician, Ahsanullah Khan, regarding it, is as follows:

'Was a Court diary of occurrences at the palace kept by order of the king during the rebellion?'

Answer: 'The Court diary was kept up as usual according to the custom which had long preceded the outbreak'.

Question: Look at this leaf and see whether you can recognize the handwriting on it?'

Answer: 'Yes, it is in the handwriting of the man who kept the Court diary, and this leaf is a portion of it'.

Translation of an extract from the Court diary for the 16th of May 1857.

The King held his Court in the Hall of Special Audience, 49 English were prisoners, and the army demanded that they should be given over to them for slaughter. The king delivered them up saying, 'The army may do as they please', and the prisoners were consequently put to the sword. There was a large attendance, and all the chiefs, nobles, officers, and writers presented themselves at Court and had the honour of paying their respects.

Here then we have oral as well as most unimpeachable written testimony, all concurring on this point, and it would seem nearly impossible to make the proof clearer, had we not the Prisoner's written confession of the crime. I do not mean in his defence, which is simply a document framed for this Court, and is but a mere tissue of false denials without an effort at refuting what stands so prominently against him. I allude of course to his long letter to his son Mirza Mughal, in which he actually makes merit of the slaughter of his Christian prisoners, and urges it as a reason why the soldiery should be more attentive to his commands. After this, to prolong any argument upon the subject would be improper. There is then but the last portion of the fourth charge uncommented on; and to establish it we have copies of circulars addressed from the King to Rao Bhara, the ruler of Kutch Bhoj, to Ranjit Singh, Chief of Jaisalmir, and to Rajah Gulab Singh, of Jummoo. The following extracts will be sufficient:

To – Rao Bhara, Ruler of Cutch.

'It has been reported that you, ever-faithful one, have put the whole of the infidels to the sword, and have thoroughly cleansed and purified your dominions of their unclean presence. We have been extremely gratified to hear of such conduct on your part, and you are therefore honoured with this address, to the intent that you will institute such arrangements throughout your territory as that none of the creatures of God may in any way be aggrieved or oppressed. Further, should any number of the infidels reach your dominions by sea, you will have them slain. In doing this you will act entirely in accordance with our pleasure and wishes'.

To – Ranjit Singh, Chief of Jaisalmir.

'It is clear to our belief that throughout your dominions the name and trace of these ill-omened infidels, the English, must not have remained; if, however, by any chance or possibility some have escaped till now, by keeping hidden and concealed, first slay them, and after that having made arrangements for the administration of our territory, present yourself at our Court with our whole military following. Consideration and friendliness a thousand-fold will be bestowed on you, and you will be distinguished by elevation to dignities and places which the compass of your qualifications will not have capacity to contain'.

To – Rajah Gulab Singh, Ruler of Jummoo.

'I have been made acquainted, by your petition, with all the particulars of the slaughter throughout your territory of the accused unbelieving English. You are considered worthy of a hundred commendations. You have acted in this matter as all brave men ever acquit themselves; may you live and prosper'. Again: 'Come to the royal presence, and slay the accursed unbelieving English, and all other enemies, wherever you may find them on way. Whatever may be your hopes and expectations, the dignity and elevation to which you will be promoted amongst your equals will surpass all that you may be able to imagine, and you will further be rewarded and dignified with the title of Rajah'.

On one of the petitions to the King from a Dafadar of the 4th Irregular Cavalry, contesting of having murdered his officers at Muzuffernugur, the order for an appointment return is in the Prisoner's own handwriting.

I herewith conclude my observations on the charges, and it will now remain, gentlemen, for you by your verdict, to determine whether the prisoner at your bar, in retirement and seclusion, may yet claim the respect due to deposed majesty, or whether he must henceforth rank merely as one of the great criminals of history. It will be for you to pronounce whether this last king of the imperial house of Taimur shall this day depart from his ancestral palace, bent down by age and misfortune, but elevated perhaps by the dignity of his sufferings and the long borne calamities of his race, or whether this magnificent hall of Audience – this shrine of the higher majesty of justice – shall this day achieve its crowning triumph in a verdict which shall record to this and to all ages, that kings by crime are degraded to felons, and that the long glories of a dynasty may be for ever effaced in a day!

The consideration of the specific charges against the prisoner being now closed, I trust it may not be thought presumptuous, if I offer some observations on the evidence elicited as to the cause of the late rebellion and of the existence of previous conspiracy. I have, in a former part of his address, argued that if the native regiments, previous to the cartridge question being mooted, had been in a sound and well affected state, such a frightful, and all but universal revolt could not have occurred, that there must have been some other and more latent power at work to have thus operated on a whole army scattered in different cantonments from Calcutta to Peshawar. I think that such could not have been accomplished without some secret mutual understanding, and some previous preparation, the establishment of which may appropriately be termed conspiracy. I have stated also that it seems as if it was not owing to cartridge of any kind, that such an amount of mutiny and murder has solely to be attributed; but I should be more than blind to all that has appeared on these proceedings and elsewhere, if I failed to recognize in the cartridge question, the immediate means or instrument adopted for bringing about a much desired end. It seems to have been the spark, to accidentally shoot forth, but deliberately chosen to explode a mine previously prepared. In alluding then to the existence of a conspiracy, I do not mean to imply that we have come upon traces of a particular gang of men specially banded together for the fixed definite object of causing the late rebellion in the native army, in any manner similar to that in which we have seen developed; but such evidence as we have been able to obtain does appear to me to point out that, for a considerable time antecedent to the 10th of May, agitation and disaffection to British rule among the Mahommedans was more than ordinarily prevalent, and that such disaffection had been stimulated by active and designing men, who have most craftily taken advantage of every circumstance that could be made suitable for such a purpose. The annexation of Oudh to British rule was perhaps one of these. It seems to have been particularly displeasing to the Mahommedans, as annihilating the last throne left to them in India; and for some other reasons, it would appear to have been almost equally unpalatable to the Hindu sepoy. It may perhaps have interfered with his position there as a privileged servant of the Company; for instead of having to rely on the influence and prestige of the British government in dealings or disputes with native landholders of that province, he found himself brought at once under direct European control. One of the witnesses, Jat Mall, draws a marked distinction between the Hindu sepoy and the Hindu tradesman, in reference to their feelings for the British Government and perhaps the annexation of Oudh, with other causes, may tend to account for it. Being asked whether there was any difference between the Mahommedans and Hindus in this respect, he replies. 'Yes, certainly, the Mahommedans, as a body, were all pleased at the overthrow of the British government, while the merchants and respectable tradesmen among the Hindu regretted it'. He, however, says that the general feeling throughout the army, was the same both among the Hindus and Mahommedans, and that they were both equally bitter; and this view of the case is, I think, supported by our experiences of both. The great bulk of the infantry portion of the native army was undoubtedly Hindu; but we have not found this any check or restraint upon their revolting barbarity, and as far as army has been concerned, Hindus and Mahommedans appear to have vied with each other only in the enormity of their crimes. But apart from the army, the revolt has perhaps assumed main features of a Mussalman conspiracy, and it is, I think, probable that to Mussalman intrigue may eventually be traced those false and fabricated rumours, which, adroitly mixed up with some small portion of truth, have been so instrumental in effacing the last vestiges of fidelity in an army whose faithfulness was at one time perhaps its very chief pride and boast. It does not belong to such an occasion of this to revert to past years, and step by step to trace the causes which have combined to destroy the reliance once placed upon those who are now so notorious for their perfidy. One of these causes doubtless have been beyond government control, and were perhaps adherent to a state of continued progress on the one side, and an inveterate priestly opposition to it on the other. It will be sufficient if I here merely allude to several previous occasions, not of very distant date, when some regiments for the native army showed how little they were to be depended on. On these occasions, also it was evident that a unit of purpose and a singleness of feeling were, in a short time, organized by some process not immediately patent to their European officers; a usual correspondence either by emissaries or letters was perhaps then initiated, but the lesson thus learnt was not easily forgotten. I do not mean to argue that from that time, the native Indian Army became one large debating society. Very far from it. I believe, that, in their own fashion, most of the Sepoys were good and well meaning servants of the Government. I say, *in* their own fashion, because, it appears to me, they are always efficient in natural firmness, and have no idea of strong moral rectitude; their fidelity, as long as it exists, is more of a habit than of a principle, upheld by superstition, but wanting the sustaining power of true religion. Among such a body as this there must always be some discontented intriguers, and who that knows anything of Asiatic character will readily admit, especially with reference to Hindus, that the few are more potent for evil than the many for good? Let but three or four leaders come forth in all the open audacity of crime, or mix themselves up in the secret intrigues of sedition, and the rest, if not immediately panic struck, never think it their duty to check or oppose them. They may accuse themselves for a time, by holding aloof from what they do not approve; but active reference, even in prevention of mutiny and murder, seems to form no part of their creed, either religious or political. The most serious crimes are thus passively encouraged; and temporary immunity securing proselytes, all area eventually engulfed in the same depths of infamy. Thus the crimes of a few lead to the ruin of many. That these instances have been vigorously at work in extending the late rebellion, I think few will be inclined to deny. I am aware that no correspondence, and perhaps little direct evidence to such a point has been brought before the Court; indeed, in reference to the sepoys we have not been in a position to obtain either one or the other, still if, as has been currently, and, believe, truly reported that the number of letters passing among our native soldiers, for a month or two prior to the outbreak, was very considerably larger than usual, this circumstance, combined with such facts as leave come under our notice, would lead, almost irresistibly to the conclusion that some sinister agitation had been extensively at work, and that increased disaffection and subordination would necessarily be the result; moreover, in such a state, revolt would reduce itself to a mere calculation of time. In the above remarks, I have attributed much of what has occurred to the pernicious influence of evil intriguers, and it may naturally be enquired why these should have had greater effect at the present juncture than at any former one. Some of the causes; I have already hinted at, such as the annexation of Oudh, and the progress of European civilization outstriding, and, in its natural course, threatening to sweep away the puny barriers upraised by priestly cunning for the preservation of grossest ignorance, and these commencing the subversion of religions that are unable to bear the lights of even natural science. I believe too that the propagandists of sedition may artfully have availed themselves to future forcible interference with caste prejudices. I allude to the agitation about the remarriage of Hindu widows; the enlistment for general service; the cartridges, & c., I do not mean, in this, to offer the slightest apology for men whose conduct excites nothing but loathing and disgust. Pampered in their pride and besotted in their ignorance, they had, as a body, become too self-sufficient for military subordination and unhesitating obedience. Experienced as they were in mutual combination, they appear again easily to have entered into schemes for dictating to the Government their views in reference to imagined grievances, but that open defiant mutiny had been generally resolved upon by the army, or, at any rate, by the Hindu portion of it, prior to the trial of the 3rd Light Cavalry troopers, is more, I think, than has been established. Up to that time, there was, no doubt, a feeling of uneasiness, a restless apprehension, and an air of respectful mutiny pervading the native ranks. The sepoys, in many instances, appeared to imagine that disobedience to military command was scarcely criminal, if accompanied by a salute and a submissive demeanour. Habituated to combination, and well aware of the strength of numbers, they latterly had seldom lost an opportunity of bringing forward their grievances, not individually but in masses. On such points there was no difference between Mussalman and Hindu; they could both readily unite, and had already done so, for the purposes of insolent dictation. Indeed, if we search back into history, I believe we shall find that this has ever been, what I may term, the normal condition of Asiatic armies; and it is perhaps the necessary result of giving unity and power to large bodies of men without the checks furnished by education, loyalty and religious principle to control them. Military discipline, without these auxiliaries, is but a dangerous weapon, and one that has frequently been turned against those who have sharpened and prepared it. As a corollary to this, it may be observed that rebellion and insurrection among the unarmed and untutored people of Asia is rare indeed. Even the forcible conversion of the Hindus to Mahommedanism under former Emperors of India seems to have been insufficient to rouse them to resistance. It is then the attempt at domination by the sepoy alone that has to be guarded against. The distinctions of caste may, to a certain extent, at former periods, have proved serious obstacles to any very extensive combination of men of different sects, either for political or other purposes, but we should remember that this very circumstance of caste companionship has necessitated the existence of a number of distinct self-governing societies – has habituated the people of Hindustan to meetings among themselves where publicity is avoided – and thus giving them their primary lessons in uniting for particular objects, has endowed them with a natural facility for more extended combinations of a secret and sinister character. Under these circumstances, they wanted but the means and the occasion for carrying them out; and who does not perceive that the native army afforded the one, and a variety of incidents have favoured the other? Brahman and Mussalman here met as it were upon neutral ground; they have had, in the army, one common brotherhood of profession, the same dress, the same rewards, the same objects to be arrived at the same means. They frequently joined each other in their separate festivals, and the union encouraged by the favour of the Government was finally resorted to as a measure to subvert it. I do not, however, intend to dwell on all of the many influences which may have assisted in bringing about the recent catastrophe. Such a discussion, in this place, might not be approved of.

It seems to me, however, apparent that it was not and could not have been the greased cartridge *alone* that effected it. There was previous preparation among the sepoys; and there was also a general unsettling of men's minds throughout the country, and among the Mahommedans in particular. I believe, indeed, that the facts elicited on this point may be ranged appropriately under the head of 'Mahommedan conspiracy', the chief object of which seems to have been to spread disaffection and distrust of British rule, and, by the dissemination of false and evil reports, and by fabrications of the most insidious king, to prepare all the people for change and insurrection. As far as can be traced, the commencement of this must have originated with the Prisoner or with some of those, such as Hasan Askari and others, who were admitted to his most secret and confidential councils. Be this as it may, there cannot, I imagine, be a doubt that in sending Sidi Kambar to Persia and Constantinople as an ambassador with letters to the sovereign of that country, soliciting aid and elevation to a throne, the prisoner became the principal in a conspiracy which, indirectly, at any rate, must have been auxiliary to the recent frightful outbreak and its attendant horrors. It is worthy of particular notice, as connecting the two together, that this Sidi Kambar's departure took place, according to the most reliable account, just two years before May 1857, and that his promised return, with the aid sought for, was fixed for the time when the outbreak actually took place. Coupling this with the prophecy among the Mahommedans that English sovereignty in India was to cease 100 years after its first establishment by the Battle of Plassey in 1757, we are able to form something more than conjecture as to the causes which have given to Mahommedan fanaticism its delusive hope of recovering all its former prestige. I have already alluded to the dream of Hasan Askari the priest, and its interpretation so plausibly contrived to correspond with the wishes of the king, and of those about him. The circumstance may seem trivial to us, but it was doubtless a means well calculated to make a deep impression upon the superstitious minds of those to whom it was addressed, and to cause expectation and belief in what was predicted by one said to be possessed of miraculous powers, and accredited with holding direct communication with heaven.

We learn too from the petition of Muhammad Darwesh to Mr. Colvin, the Lieutenant-Governor, dated 27th of March 1857, that Hasan Askari had, at this time, assured the King of Delhi that he had certain information that the Prince Royal of Persia had fully taken possession of, and occupied Bushire, and that he had entirely expelled the Christians, or rather, had not one alive there, and had taken away many of them prisoners, and that, very soon, indeed, the Persian army would advance by the way of Kandahar and Cabul towards Delhi. He moreover adds, 'That in the palace, but more especially in that portion of it constituting the personal apartments of the King, the subject of the conversation night and day was the early arrival of the Persians. Hasan Askari has, moreover, impressed the King with the belief, that he has learnt, through a divine revelation, that the domination of the King of Persia will to a certainty extend to Delhi, or rather over the whole of Hindustan, and that the splendour of the sovereignty of Delhi, will again revive, as the sovereign of Persia will bestow the crown on the King'. The writer goes on to say that throughout the palace, but particularly to the King, this belief has been cause of great rejoicing, so much so that prayers offered and vows are made, while, at the same time, Hasan Askari has entered upon the daily performance, at an hour and a half before sunset, of a course of propitiatory ceremonies to expedite the arrival of the Persians and the expulsion of the Christians. It has been arranged that every Thursday, several trays of victuals, wheat-meal, oil, copper money and cloth should be sent by the King in aid of these ceremonies, and they are accordingly brought to Hasan Askari.

We thus see how early and how deeply the priesthood interested and engaged themselves in this matter, and how completely and exclusively Mahommedan in character was this conspiracy. If we could but have stepped behind the scenes, and witnessed these ceremonies at which superstition presided, and have heard these prayers and vows offered up for the arrival of the Persians and the expulsion of the Christians, we should doubtless have had depicted to us the foreshadowing of those dreadful tragedies which, to all time, will render the past year so painfully memorable. We may imagine and faintly conceive to ourselves some portion of the rancour of these Mahommedans, when we recollect not only their deeds, but the concentrated hatred which breathes through their petitions, and does not stop with this world, but rejoices in the idea of eternal torments for us hereafter. One cannot help enquiring whether there are really many millions of human beings in Hindustan imbued with these feelings for Europeans. I will leave those who hear me to form their own opinions on this subject, without venturing to proffer mine. We learn, however, from Mrs. Aldwell, that during the Muharram festival, she heard the Mahommedan women praying and teaching their children to pray for the success of their faith, and these prayers were generally accompanied by execrations against the English. Nor did even accomplishing the cruel death and sufferings of helpless women and children tend in any way to abate the ferocity of their malignity, or to waken one chord of mercy or commiseration in their breasts, for we find from the local newspapers that at the time this most hideous massacre was being perpetrated, about 200 Mussalmans were standing at the reservoir, uttering the coarsest abuse against the prisoners. Were it not too well attested, such demoniac malignity would scarcely be credible.

The next point to which I shall advert, is the circulation of the chapaties in the form of ship biscuits. Now, whether they were sent round under the fiction of a government order, signifying that in future there should be but one food and one faith, or whether, according to another interpretation, they were meant to sound a note of alarm and preparation, giving warning to the people to stand by one another on any danger menacing them, the contrivance was a most insidious one, strangers to such feelings before. That it created no stronger impression on the native mind than it did, is perhaps attributable only to the early check it received at the hands of authority, and it would doubtless be both interesting and important, if we could discover how and by whom such a proceeding was initiated. This and the false rumour about mixing ground bones with the flour had doubtless one common origin, and it is not going beyond the bounds of fair indication or reasonable inference, to attribute both one and the other to the unceasing wiles of Mahommedan conspiracy. We perceive that the Hindu sepoys under the impulse of a first reaction in their feelings, reproached the Mahommedans with misleading them, and it is a most significant fact on these proceedings, that though we come upon traces of Mussalman intrigue wherever our investigation has carried us, yet not one paper has been found to show that the Hindus, as a body, had been conspiring against us, or that their brahmans and priests had been preaching a crusade against Christians. In their case there has been no king to set up, no religion to be propagated by the sword. To attribute to them, under such circumstances, the circulation of these chapaties or the fabrications about ground bones in the flour, would be to ascribe to them acts without a meaning, and a criminal deception without any adequate motive. A very marked feature in this Mahommedan conspiracy is the activity and persistence with which it has been carried out;

the circulation of the chapaties having been early prohibited by authority, and thus rendered non-effective for the purpose of extensive sedition, some other expedient was necessary to replace it, and we at once find the tale of the 'bone dust mingled with flour' very adroitly selected as the substitute. It was, in fact, still adhering to the serial of chapaties, and continuing the symbol of 'one food, one faith'. It was indeed a chapati without its form, and without its inconveniences. The scheme had apparently learnt that the chapati was too specific and too tangible, open to European interference to be largely availed of as an agent for evil, and hence its transformation as flour, the bone dust being added to the one as the equivalent of the form of the ship biscuit to the other. To give out then that such was the nature of the flour stored at all depots of supplies along the Grand Trunk Road for, from them, during their marches, our sepoys are, in a manner, compelled to get their food, was to attain the very object the conspirators must have most desired. If true the Government had already commenced what should be deemed forcible conversion to Christianity. If they could, then, but establish a firm and general belief in this, their game was in their own hands, and that they did not succeed in doing this to a very great extent is, I imagine, undeniable. I must own that to me this apparently natural transition from the chapaties to its component parts, seems a masterstroke of cunning, and evidenced most able leadership in the cause the conspirators were embarked in.

To prove, moreover, that no mean order of talent was at work, and that all the appliances that craft and treachery could avail themselves of, were resorted to we are only to refer to the extracts from the *Authentic News,* and also to the other native applications of that period, and we shall perceive with what steadfast consistency the ulterior aim is always kept in view. The chapaties, the bone dust in the flour, the greased cartridges, were all most appropriate for the Hindus; but a different pabulum was requisite for the Mussalmans, and we shall now see with what subtlety it was administered. The first paper commences by announcing the King of Persia had ordered concentration of most of his troops to Teheran, and then declaring it to be currently supported that such a demonstration against Dost Muhammad Khan was only a strategic move to cloak the King of Persia's real design of fighting against and conquering the English, the editor makes certain that, at any rate, some change of feeling has taken place amongst the three powers. The next extract is dated the 26th of January 1857, and commences by asserting that all the newspapers agree in declaring that the King of France and the Emperor of Turkey had not as yet openly avowed themselves the allies of either the English of the Persians; but that their ambassadors were secretly visiting and presenting their gifts to both of the belligerents. 'Some people', says this editor, think that the King of France and Emperor of Turkey will not mix themselves up with the quarrels between the Persians and the English; 'but most people'. He adds, 'say that they will both side with the Persians. As for the Russians, however, they make no secret of readiness with which they are assisting, and will continue to assist, the Persians, whether it be with funds or with forces. It may be said that virtually the Russians, whether it be with funds or with forces. It may be said that virtually the Russians are the cause of the war, and that using the Persians as a cloak, they intend to consummate their own designs regarding the conquest of Hindustan. It is to be believed that the Russians will soon take the field in great force'. Here then we have not only Persia and Russia advancing immediately upon India with immense armies, but France and Turkey to assist them, while the forsaken and devoted English are represented as by no means sure even of the alliance of the Afghans under Dost Muhammad. Well might the editor, after announcing such formidable coalitions, somewhat dramatically exclaim, 'Let the readers of the *Authentic News* be prepared to see what the veil of futurity will disclose'. Accordingly, in the next extract, we perceive that 'the King of Persia had solemnly promised to his countries, the Governorships of the different presidencies and places: one is to get Bombay, another Calcutta, and a third Poonah', while the crown of Hindustan plainly spoken of as reserved for bestowed on the King of Delhi, this very Prisoner before us. You will recollect, Gentlemen, that several copies of this paper, the *Authentic News,* used to be sent to the palace, and one can imagine the joy and exultation with which such passages must have been perused, especially when, added thereto, is the assertion that the Emperor of Russia had sent an effective and thoroughly appointed army of 400,000 men with abundant munitions, to assist the King of Persia in his hostile designs upon India. But it was not in the palace, and by the princes alone, that such paragraphs were read with avidity; the whole population was intent on them. Sir Theophilus Metcalfe has told us that the subject of the advance of the Persians upon Herat was much discussed among the natives, and frequently in connection with the idea of Russian aggression upon India; every newspaper having at this time its correspondent in Cabul. Nor indeed did the discussion and interest excited by these concocted hostile movements cease here, for the same witness declares that agitation about this time prevailed among the sepoys, and that about five or six weeks before the outbreak it was currently reported in their lines, and much discussed among them, that 100,000 Russians were coming from the north, and that the Company's Government would be destroyed, and in fact that the idea of a Russian invasion was universally prevalent. The venom and virus of these false publications were then taking their intended effect, and it would seem a mere perversion of reason, long to blind ourselves with the idea that the outbreak was fortuitous, or that a greased cartridge occasioned it. In a former article of the *Authentic News,* we have seen Dost Muhammad alluded to as but a doubtful ally of the English. In this one, however as events progress, he is spoken of as being secretly in league with the King of Persia, and that superstitious aid may not be lost sight of, it is remarked how wonderfully four distinct unexpected coincidences had impelled the King of Persia to declare war against the English. The first was that Herat, in another place described as the key of India, had so easily fallen into his possession; the second the unforeseen coming of the Russians to assist him; the third, the nobles of Persia unanimously counselling an advance on India, and predicting that god would bestow victory; and the fourth, the simultaneous rising and assembling of the whole of Persia for the prosecution of a religious war. Portents and miracles were likewise brought forward still further to excite the Mahommedan mind, as the following extract from the *Authentic News* dated 15th of September 1856, will sufficiently prove. It is headed:

Local News from the Hansi District.

'A man just come from the country tells the editor, that unlike other places, the Holi is being burnt there at this season of the year, and the saturnalia attending the festival are now going on. The man who states this, ascertained on enquiry that the reason for the unreasonable observance of this festival is, that three girls were born at a birth, and the three spoke immediately. The first said: "The coming year will be one of great calamities, various calamitous visitations will affect the nation". The second said, "Those who live will see", and the third, in an impressive and forcible tone, said, "If the Hindus will burn the Holi in the present season they will escape all these evils", God alone is omniscient'.

It is too much I am afraid, the case, with persons accustomed to European habits of thinking to view such statements and articles as these merely in reference to the impression they would be likely to make on themselves. The taking of Herat, the predictions of the nobles & c., and the fabulous prophecies of these girls, would, in that case, receive hardly passing attention. But we should commit a grievous and most fatal error, if we were to gauge Asiatic thought and understandings by the same measure that would be applicable to our own. If, avoiding this mistake, we proceed to consider the above editorials in relation to the people they were written for, we shall find that they are not only most insidiously worked up to meet their particular prejudices, but are also to bear a striking affinity to the fulfilment of their prophecies; to the dreams of Askari; to the negotiations of Sidi Kambar; and the ancient traditions of Mahommedanism. Are we then to suppose that in all this there was no connection in the palace and the press? Were all these concurrences fortuitous? Can it be that dreams of the priest, the plots of the court, and the fabrications of the papers worked accidentally together? We have already seen the decoys which the Hindu sepoys were to gain: and is it not the same spirit of that we can recognize here? Are the circumstances appealing to Mahommedans into their superstitious bigotry, to their lust for religious war, and for the English dwelt upon with a less perfect knowledge of their peculiar forces? In an extract from the *Authentic News* dated the 19th of March, it is stated that Persian soldiers with some officers of high rank, had entered India, and that they were then staying in Delhi itself in various disguises. It is true that this is just on the authority of one Sadik

Khan, a person whose identity not being established, evidently in disguise even to his name; but this very circumstance was no part of the scheme. It gave an air of greater mystery to the announcement of this and seems to have been purposely contrived to let the imagination of the [unclear – Ed.] supply an exaggerated idea of his real rank and importance. How, it may be said under this cloak of a false name, could such a statement be given forth in the newspaper of the city, without some deep and ulterior object? It not only assigns conspiracy to the Persians, but, if false, as we know it to have been, is proof of conviction of the editor and those who employed him. This name of Sadik Khan, be it conferred was the one attached to the proclamation purporting to be from Persia, and from the Jama Masjid. The proclamation, them and the assertion about these 900 soldiers, were evidently parts of one and the same scheme, and seem to have been linked together that one might, in a measure, support the other. If, for many questioned the authority of the proclamation, there was the answer ready. The bringer of it was actually in the city with 500 other Persians also in disguise, *vice versa*. If the advent of the Persians was disbelieved, was not the proclamation for its reality? The same depth of artifice is apparent everywhere; and when one considers the subject, the more fully convinced we shall be of the wiles and strategy systematically resorted to. For instance, what could such a proclamation as related to the King of Persia, have been, without some demonstration, feigned or support it? The sword depicted on one side, and the shield on the other, has been equally meaningless, but for the story of the men in disguise, and is in of high rank who evidently must have been deputed to carry it through. Consummation, so evidently false, is, for that very reason, for our truest and credible expositors of conspiracy, and of Mussalman conspiracy too. It is, indeed impossible to account for it under any other hypothesis. Who then was it that wrote the proclamation? This question, I believe, could be answered in detail by the editor; of the paper, who has referred to it so frequently. It is a pet subject of his – one on which he seems to be thoroughly at home. He has exact transcript of it, is able to epitomize it, and no doubt was equally well as to the preparation of it.

I do not mean to wade through, and to quote all the extracts from the newspapers that bear out the fact of a Mahommedan conspiracy. That appears to me unnecessary, believe I shall have no difficulty in establishing it by other testimony. However, there is one other extract, which it would be wrong to leave unnoticed. It bears that date [number unclear – Ed.] of April, and must have been the origin of the report that Sir Theophilus Metcalfe alludes to, when he says that about 15 days before the outbreak, it was currently reported that an anonymous petition had been presented to the Magistrate, stating, 'that the Cashmere Gate of the city would be taken from the English. This being the chief stronghold in the city and main connection with the Cantonments of Delhi, it would naturally be the first point seized in any attempt at insurrection in the city, and being the only gate at which there was any military guard, the importance of it, in a strategical point of view, must have been obvious to all'. Sir Theophilus Metcalfe proceeds to say 'that this petition was never received; but that the current report about it is indicative of what was then occupying the thoughts of many of the natives'. So, no doubt, it was; but it was also much more than this, for it was the real exposition of an article which the editor dare not, without disguising it, put into print. With what ingenuity and craft the idea is worked out, so as to become intelligible only to those who were meant to understand it, must now be obvious to all. The editor says several petitions have been given into the Magistrate's Court, and in these it is also mentioned that a month hence from this date an overwhelming attack will be made on Cashmere, of the salubrity and beauty of which a poet has said:

> That should a parched and burnt up soul reach Cashmere, though he might be a roasted fowl he would recover his wings and feathers, and that this cool and heavenly country will come into the possession of the writers of the petition.

How, it may be asked, were the writers of the petitions given into the Magistrate's Court at Delhi to take Cashmere, and who does not now perceive that the Cashmere Gate of the city of Delhi was thus indicated by the country from which it derives its name, and that the salubrity and beauty of the former were to represent the importance and its fitness for their objects, for the latter. I shall not here pause to consider whether, under the simile of a parched and burnt-up fowl, the prisoner before us was intended. He no doubt expected to recover some of his lost plumage by seizing the gate, and with it was meditating a flight to a higher elevation. In declaring on the 13th of April, that in one month from that date, an overwhelming attack would be made on this very point – for it was here the officers were shot down – the editor of the *Authentic News* was either the confidant and accomplice of conspiracy, or had soared into the regions of actual prophecy.

The coincidence of the above cautiously worded announcement of the editor, and the indiscreet revelations of Jawan Bakht are certainly startling. The doubly foretold attack took place on the11th of May, and after what has been proved in regard to Mahommedan treachery, is there anyone who hears me that can believe that a deep planned and well concerted conspiracy had nothing to do with it?

The proofs of the intimate connection of the prisoner with it, do not, however, rest here, for Moujud, the Abyssinian, who was not merely in the service of the King, but was his private, special attendant, and was always near his person, takes. Mr. Everett aside and tells him that he had better leave the Company's service, and, with his troop, go over to the King, as this hot weather the Russians would be all over the place. Mr. Everett seems to have laughed at this, and to have thought it but the man's foolishness; but we have now direct proof that it was something far deeper than that, for at their next meeting, which occurred about a month after, the outbreak had been accomplished. Moujud says to him, 'Did I not tell you to come away?' and then as it were an explanation of the warning, proceeds to reveal to him the whole of the Sidi Kambar transaction: how, two years before, he had been sent to Constantinople as ambassador from the King of Delhi – how he had started on the pretence of going to Mecca, and how he had promised that he would return when the two years had expired. This explanation seems to me a very remarkable one. It shows clearly that it was not merely on the basis of an expected disturbance at Meerut that such a proposal was made, but that a far wider web of sedition was weaving. Who can believe that none of the Mahommedan native officers and men of the regiments at Delhi and Meerut had been tampered with? Mr. Everett, as a Christian, was surely one of the last the conspirators would apply to. It should be remembered likewise, that Mr. Everett had none of his regiments with him at Delhi, and that had there been any Mussalman officers of the corps present, they would doubtless have been preferred to a Christian. At the time too when the application was made to him, the sentence of the Meerut court-martial must have been unknown in Delhi. It was not, then, as a consequence of, but as an addition and an adjunct to, what was anticipated at Meerut, that preparation was being made there; and by whom was this being done? Could a mere private servant and personal attendant, however great and favourite he might be, offer service to a risaldar and a whole troop of cavalry, withdrawing their allegiance from the Government, without any authority for so doing from his master? Who could then have given the King's services to so large a body, but the King himself? I would beg those who hear me seriously to consider these questions, and then determine whether the answers to them do not bring home personal complicity in compassing the rebellion, to the Prisoner in Court. We have been informed too by Mukund Lal, the secretary, that it was now about three years since some Infantry soldiers stationed at Delhi became disciples of the King, and that, on that occasion, the King gave each of them a document detailing the names and order of those who had preceded him in the direct line of disciples to each other, himself included, together with a napkin dyed pink as an emblem of his blessing. Now three years ago from the present date, is about the time of Sidi Kambar's embassy to Persia, and of the apparent first commencement of Mahommedan conspiracy; and it certainly is a somewhat instructive fact to find that the occasion chosen for such an unwonted manifestation of piety on the one hand, and such an unusual display of kingly concession on the other, was, precisely that in which intimate relations between them of a more political character were beginning to be thought of. The Agent of the Lieutenant-Governor of course put a stop to these exhibitions; but, from that day, adds the witness, it may be said that a sort of understanding was established between the army and the King. I think it will be conceded, that in addition to the charges, five facts have been established, *viz.* the concerted dreams and predictions of Hasan Askari the priest; the mission to Persia and Constantinople of Sidi Kanbar the Abyssinian; a deliberate continuous plan of exciting distrust and revolt among the Hindus; a similar plan, by the fabrication of the native press, for inciting the Mussalmans to a religious war; and lastly, by these means and others, an indirect, and also a personal tampering with the fidelity of the Hindus and Mussalmans of the native army. Has or has not a guilty participation in all these five points been traced to the Prisoner? If the question (as I believe it will be), should be answered in the affirmative, there will still remain another to be responded to, of perhaps still greater importance, *viz.* has he in these transactions been the leader, or the led, has he been the original mover, the head and front of the undertaking, or has been the consenting tool, the willing instrument in the hands of others, the forward, unscrupulous, but still pliant puppet, tutored by priestly craft for the advancement of religious bigotry. Many persons, I believe, will incline to the latter. The known restless spirit of Mahommedan fanaticism has been the first aggressor, the vindictive intolerance of that peculiar faith has been struggling for mastery, seditious conspiracy has been its means, the Prisoner its active accomplice, and every possible crime the frightful result. It was however, rather as the head of the Mahommedan religion in India, than as the descendant of a line of Kings, that I believe the Prisoner's influence were desired; the one indeed is so inseparable from the other, that it is difficult to where the difference commences. It was the union of the two – the religious and the political – that gave such importance to the Prisoner as one of the abettors of conspiracy.

Thus, the bitter zeal of Mahommedanism meets us everywhere. It is conspicuous in the papers, flagrant in the petitions, and perfectly demoniac in its actions. There seems indeed scarce any exemption from its contagious touch. The Prince Mirza Abdulla robbing is confiding visitor and former friend, and then sending his uncle to compass her death, seems no exaggerated instance of it. It is again represented by the Mahommedan officer, Mirza Taki Beg at Peshawar, who, while in high employment and pay by the British Government, complacently quotes from his books that a change will take place, and that the British rule will soon be overthrown. It finds a still more unmistakeable disciple in Karm Baksh of the Delhi Magazine, who, while drawing English pay, avails himself of his scholarship and knowledge of Persian, to send circulars to the native regiments, to the effect that the cartridges prepared in the magazine had been smeared with a composition of fat, and that the sepoys were not to believe their European officers, if they said anything in contradiction of it. It will be recollected how active in his enmity, this man proved, when the King's troops were attacking the Magazine; how he kept up a secret communication with them, and how completely he identified himself, from the commencement, with the conspirators. Can there be a doubt that he was one of those who had been successfully tampered with; that, while ostensibly serving the English, he was, in reality, in the pay and confidence of those seeing destruction.

But why multiply instances of this sort? I would gladly cite some of a different tendency, and the petition of Muhammad Darwesh, in his admirable letter to Mr. Colvin, must not be passed over. It is one noble instance of faithfulness from a Mahommedan to the British. I am sorry I cannot class with it the petition purporting to be from Nabi Baksh Khan to the King, pronouncing it unlawful to slay women, and calling for a decree to that effect from the factors of the Mahommedan religion; for since I delivered the paper into Court, considerable doubt has been thrown on its having been written at the time indicated, and it seems by no means improbable that it was fabricated after the capture of Delhi, for the purpose of obtaining rewards and other advantages. Indeed, a further attentive perusal of it has convinced me that it is so; for no one in the situation of Nabi Baksh Khan would have dared to advise or propose to the King to let the soldiery first wreak their rage on his own Royal person, as Nabi Baksh Khan pretends to have done. There are certainly a few instances in which the Mahommedans have behaved with kindness to the English, and not the less pleasing on account of the humble grades in which these instances occur. We may perhaps deduce from this, that the teachings such as prescribed by their prophet, have no softening effect on the hearts of his followers, nay more, that education in such doctrines leads to ferocity and revolting crime, and is utterly incompatible with the feelings of even ordinary humanity.

In the course of this address, I have dwelt, long and frequently, upon those circumstances, which appear to demonstrate that to Mussalman intrigue and Mahommedan conspiracy we may mainly attribute the dreadful calamities of the year 1857; I have endeavoured to point out how intimately the Prisoner, as the head of the Mahommedan faith in India, has been connected with the organization of that conspiracy either as its leader or its unscrupulous accomplice; I have alluded to the part taken by the native press and Mahommedans, in general, as preparing the Hindus for insurrection, and the native army, in particular for revolt, and perhaps in further corroboration of such facts, it may be as well to advert to the share that may be assigned to the Mahommedans in getting the cartridges refused on the parade ground of the 3rd Light Cavalry. Out of these 85 troopers, the far larger majority was *Mahommedan.* These men had no caste, and to them it could not possibly have mattered whether pig's and cow's fat was smeared on the cartridges or not. Captain Martineau tells us that at the Ambala depot, as far as the cartridge question was concerned, the *Mahommedan* Sepoys laughed at it, and we thus perceive that these men initiated open mutiny without one pretext for so doing or the shadow of an excuse. They had not even the extenuation of a pretended grievance; yet they, at once, leagued themselves in rebellion against us, and induced the Hindus to join then, by speciously exciting them on that most vulnerable of points, the fear of being forcibly deprived of their caste. I say, induced the Hindus to join them, for such is the evidence before us, and this too on a pretext in which the Mahommedans could have had no possible sympathy with them, nor indeed were the Hindus long in discovering this, for as a witness, who has been frequently quoted, informs us, immediately after the battle of the Hindan, they spoke with much regret of the turn that affairs had taken, reproached the Mahommedans for having deceived them, and seemed to doubt greatly that the English Government had really had any intention of interfering with their caste. Great numbers of the Hindu sepoys at this time declared that, if they could be sure their lives would be spared, they would gladly go back to the service of the Government; but the Mahommedans, on the contrary, used to assert that the King's service was much better than that of the English; that the Nawabs and Rajahs would supply the King with large forces, and that they must eventually conquer. If we now take a retrospective view of the various circumstances which we have been able to elicit during our extended enquiries, we shall perceive how exclusively Mahommedan are all the prominent points that attach to it. *A Mahommedan* priest, with pretended visions, and assumed miraculous powers – a *Mahommedan* King, his dupe and his accomplice – a *Mahommedan* clandestine embassy to the Mahommedan powers of Persia and Turkey resulting – *Mahommedan* prophecies as to the downfall of our power – *Mahommdean* rule as the successor of our own – the most cold-blooded murders by *Mahommedan assasins* – a religious war for *Mahommedan* ascendancy – a *Mahommedan press* unscrupulously abetting – and *Mahomeddan* sepoys initiating the mutiny. Hinduism, I may say, is nowhere either reflected or represented; if it be brought forward at all, it is only in subservience to its ever-aggressive neighbour.

The arguments in reference to a Mahommedan conspiracy are now closed. I do not mean that many others might not be deduced from the proceedings before us, for I have selected only those that appeared to me the most prominent. I would wish, however, before sitting down, to quote one question and answer from Captain Martineau's evidence.

Question – 'Did you ever hear any of the sepoys speak complainingly of the efforts of English missionaries to convert natives to Christianity?'

Answer – 'No, never in my life, I don't think they cared one bit about it'. I believe there is no officer whose duties have given him much experience of the sepoy's character or any insight into his feelings and prejudices, but will readily confirm the correctness of this opinion. There is no dread of an open avowed missionary in India. It is not the rightful conversion to Christianity, that either sepoys of natives are alarmed at. If it be done by the efforts of persuasion, of teaching, or of example – the only means by which it can be done – it offends no caste prejudice, cites no fanatical opposition. A candid undisguised endeavour to gain followers to Christ, has never, that I am aware of, been viewed with the slightest sign of disapprobation by any portion of the natives, and, were it more constantly before their eyes, who can doubt that it would remove this present dark and debasing error that Christianity is itself a caste, and its only distinguishing tenet the privilege of eating everything. If this degrading idea were removed, the chief fear of the Hindus would vanish with it. Let them see that it is impossible to make converts to Christianity by force, and you deprive the seditious of their most potent weapon of mischief. Christianity, when seen in its own pure light, has no terrors for the natives. It is only when kept in the shade, that its name can be perverted to an instrument of evil. But I may, if I proceed further, be trenching on questions of state policy.

I beg then to tender my thanks to the Court for the patient hearing they have given me, and to Mr. Murphy, the Interpreter, for the able assistance he has, in that capacity, afforded me on this, and the other State trials. His very high attainments as an oriental scholar have been most conspicuous. In the fluency of the *viva voce* examinations; in the quick readiness with which all kinds of papers, in different hands, have been deciphered and read; and in the correctness and spirit of the written translations of documents of no ordinary difficulty; his complete knowledge both of Urdu and Persian has been thoroughly attested. The notes appended to many of these papers are valuable in themselves, and speak more forcibly than I can do of Mr. Murphys' very high proficiency as an Interpreter. I should be wanting both to him and myself if I did not thus record my obligations to him.

F.J. Harriott, Major,
Deputy Judge Advocate-General, and Govt. Prosecutor

Delhi
The 9th March 1858

Finding

The Court is closed to consider its finding.

The Court, on the evidence before them, are of opinion that the Prisoner Muhammad Bahadur Shah, Ex-King of Delhi, is Guilty of all and every part of the Charges preferred against him.

M. Dawes, Lieut. Col.,
President

Delhi
The 9th March 1858

F.J. Harriott, Major,
Deputy Judge Advocate-General

Approved and Confirmed.

N. Penny,
Major-General,
Commanding Meerut Division

Camp Saharun.
The 2nd April 1858.

The Court at 3 p.m. adjourns *sine die.*

3

SUPPLEMENT TO THE PROCEEDINGS OF THE TRIAL OF MUHAMMAD BAHADUR SHAH, EX-KING OF DELHI[1]

Evidence of Hakim Ahsanullah Kahn, late confidential physician to the ex-King of Delhi

Since the time when, during the administration of Lord Ellenborough, the *nazar* which used to be presented to the King of Delhi on the part of the Governor-General was discontinued, the King was always very much grieved. At first he wrote on the matter to England, and he always afterwards used to complain against the order, and to express his dissatisfaction thereat.

Subsequently, the King was very much grieved in consequence of the Government not having acceded to his wish, that his youngest son, Mirza Jawan Bakht, be recognized as heir-apparent, and having ruled that the eldest son, Mirza Fateh-ul-mulk, should be his successor. Sometime afterwards, Mirza Haidar, son of Mirza Khan Baksh, son of Mirza Sullaiman Shikoh, arrived from Lucknow with his brother Mirza Murdi. They had frequent access to the King, and, first of all, prevailed upon him to write to the Government Agent, intimating to that officer that he (the King) had appointed them (the princes) as his agents at the Government office. The Agent to the Lieutenant-Governor, however, did not consent to this arrangement, as it was contrary to usage to depute shahzadahs[2] on such duty. The shahzadahs then carried away with them several papers, after impressing upon them the seal of the King. They had free access even into the female apartments of the King.

1 This is not a part of the proceedings. It is in fact an interview of the Hakeem taken by the Secretary to the Chief Commissioner, Punjab, at his instance, for transmission to the higher authorities in India and England with the proceedings. Richard Temple was the Secretary in question. See Temple to the Secretary to the Government of India with Governor-General, no. 50, dated 29 April 1858, *vide PMR*, *Correspondence*, part 2, p. 391. Writers like Martin, etc. take no note of it. It is also not there in the hard-written copies.

2 Princes.

DOI: 10.4324/9781003320500-3

At Lucknow, Mirza Haidar offered an *alam* (standard) on the part of the King of Delhi at the shrine of Shah Abbas, and delivered to the Mujtahid (High Priest) a note written in pencil, and bearing the seal of the King of Delhi, in which the latter agreed to adopt the Shia creed, and decried the Sunni tenets. This information was obtained from communication received from one or two princes who professed the Sunni creed, and also from petitions received from several Sunnis to the address of the King. Among them I remember the names of Amin-ul-rahman Khan, a native of Delhi, but who was residing at that time at Lucknow, and Sidi Bilal, who was formerly in the service of the King of Delhi, but had subsequently taken service at Lucknow. When the circumstances became known at Delhi, a certain *Ulama*[3] waited on the King and begged to be informed of the facts. The King replied that Mirza Haider had procured the King's seal being put upon all papers which they had written, and had taken away the papers to Lucknow, and that the King had also written a *shukka* to the Mujtahid. But the King added that his shukka to the Mujtahid merely stated that he (the King) loved very much the *Ahi-i-bait* and that those who did not love them were not Mahommedans. Subsequently, at the request of the King, the Agent to the Lieutenant-Governor procured for him from Lucknow a copy of the King's shukka to the Mujtahid. The subject matter of the paper coincided with that represented in the petitions which had been received from Lucknow. It was then believed that besides the shukka to the Mujtahid, the King must have addressed the King of Oudh also, who was also a Shia, and that Mirza Haidar must have held out hopes of gain to the King of Delhi if he should unite himself with the King of Oudh.

After about a year, a report was in current which affected Mirza Haider and his nephew to the King of Delhi. This report was also published in the newspaper conducted by Maulavy Bakar, in which it was also mentioned that Mirza Najaf had been treated with consideration by the King of Persia. I enquired from Mirza Ali Bakht, who was a great friend of Mirza Najaf, whether the latter had received any letter from the King of Delhi to the Sultan of Persia. He replied in the affirmative, and described its contents to be to the effect that the King of Delhi had adopted the Shia creed, and the King of Persia should help him. Moreover, in that letter the King of Delhi described his miserable and helpless condition. Mirza Ali Bakht at the same time stated that no reply had been received from Persia. A few months afterwards, Sidi Kambar applied for leave to proceed on pilgrimage to Mecca. The leave was granted through Hasan Askari, a Pirzadah of Delhi, and some money was also given for his way expenses. After a few days, Jat Mall, who was a servant of the British Government, stationed on duty at the palace, enquired from me whether it was true that Sidi Kambar had proceeded on

3 Plural of the Arabic word *alim*, wise.

pilgrimage. He said he believed that the man had not gone on pilgrimage, but to Persia. I replied I know nothing about the matter; but having made enquiries privately, I ascertained from the eunuchs[4] that the man had really gone to Persia, and that Hasan Askari the Pirzadah, servant of the King, had delivered to him at night-time certain papers which bore the seal of the King. From this it appears to me clear that Sidi Kambar had been sent to Mirza Najaf to obtain a reply to the previous communications of the King. These matters were concealed from all the Sunnis (among whom I myself was one), because Mirza Haidar had caused the King to change his religion. But I obtained the above information from other people. It may also be mentioned that the King was always very anxious to obtain intelligence of the events which were occurring towards Persia, during the time when was going on at Bushire.

Mirza Haidar was not an insignificant man. He was a relative of the King of Delhi, i.e., his nephew, and used to receive a pension of Rs. 1,000 per mensem from Lucknow. He was a hereditary Shia; both his grandfather Sulaiman Shilkoh and his father Khan Baksh being of the persuasion. According to his faith, it was a pious and creditable act to make proselytes, and he must have seen that he would derive much personal advantage if he could succeed in converting the King of Delhi, inasmuch as he would in that case have three Kings professing the same creed as his own, viz. the Kings of Delhi, Lucknow, and Persia.

There can be no doubt that the idea of communicating with the King of Persia was first suggested by Mirza Haidar, who contemplated much advantage to himself; and it is probable that he desired that the conversion of the King should become known by means of a newspaper to the Shah of Persia previous to the arrival of his brother, Mirza Najaf, in Persia, so that the latter might be treated with consideration and honour.

The King Bahadur Shah hardly cared to observe any precautions in regard to his political plans. His common servants had much influence over him. Nothing could remain concealed from the eunuchs, because they had access to every place and at all times. This King also admitted his Begums to a share in his political policy. Accordingly, to please the Zeenat Mahal Begum, he applied for her son Jawan Bakht, though incapacitated by his younger age, to be recognized as his heir. The eunuchs were in possession of every secret, because they had free access even to the secret apartments; the eunuch Mahbub Ali was at the head of the King's affairs.

I never read the letter which was addressed by the King of Delhi to the King of Persia. I have repeated what I learnt from Prince Ali Bakht. I consider that the King of Delhi must have asked for help in the shape of money and troops, the King worshipped money; a proof of which assertion may

4 The palace guards for the *Zenana*. They had considerable influence on the King.

be seen in the fact that he changed his faith in his old age, only through covetousness.

I never heard from any person that any allusion was made in the letter to the King of Persia, to the scheme of exciting the native army to mutiny against the Government; nor do I consider that any such scheme could have been alluded to at that time, because nothing of the sort was then talked of.

I think that at the time when the King of Delhi thought of seeking an alliance with Persia, it did not occur to anyone to arrange for winning over the native army.

I learnt from the eunuchs (Basant and Kali Khanm, the persons who informed me that Sidi Kambar had been entrusted with sealed papers) that at the time when the papers were sealed and delivered to Sidi Kambar, the King directed the man to carry them to Mirza Najaf, and to obtain replies to them and the previous communications.

I think that there was nothing new mentioned in the papers which were delivered to Sidi Kambar, because, although I never read them, the eunuchs would have mentioned it to me if there had been any.

Sidi Kambar went to Persia after it had been known and published in a newspaper that Mirza Najaf had reached that country. The province of Oudh was incorporated into British territory about one year after Sidi Kambar had left India. The *emeute* at Hanuman Garhi also occurred after the departure of the Sidi.

From the conversation of the King, it appears that when war was going on in Bushire, he had strong hopes of receiving aid from Persia in the shape of money and troops, and during that period he used constantly to make enquiries regarding the events which were transpiring in that quarter.

When the King first wrote to Persia, nothing was known in regard to his expectations, because everything was concealed. But when it was known that Mirza Najaf had reached Persia, and battles were being fought at Bushire, it appeared that the King had hopes from that quarter.

Bahadur Shah was not concerned at the determination of Government to cause the palace to be evacuated by the royal family after his death, because this determination of the Government was known after the right of succession had been allotted to Mirza Fateh-ul-mulk, to whose succession the King was opposed. Indeed, the King often used to remark that the Mirza (Fateh-ul-mulk) had little reason to rejoice at his succession, for after him (the King) his successor would neither have any authority nor would he be permitted to reside in the palace. This shows that the above determination of the Government in regard to the evacuation of the palace was not the cause of the King's alienation.

During the period of the war with Persia, some of the princes used to observe that if the Emperor of Russia were to aid the Persians, the English would be defeated, and the Persians would become masters of India; and the King himself coincided in this opinion.

I never heard that Mirza Najaf conveyed an intelligence from Persia to Delhi. He might have sent news (if he did send any) to his brother Mirza Haidar at Lucknow.

When the King expected aid from Persia, no effort was made to win over any of the native princes; and the reason is that Mirza Haidar never returned from Lucknow after he proceeded to that capital. This individual was a very skilful intriguer; he first suggested the idea of communicating with the King of Persia, and it is likely that he would have also suggested the winning over of the native princes if he had been present at the court of the King.

The King was offended with Lord Ellenborough for His Lordship's having discontinued the *nazar* which used to be presented on the festival of the *Eed*, the *Bakr Eed*, the *Nau Roz*, and the King's birthday. He was also offended with the Lieutenant-Governor of Agra, for having refused to recognize Mirza Jawan Bakht as a heir-apparent, and allotting the right of succession to Mirza Fateh-ul-mulk. With the British Government generally, or any other British officer individually, he was not dissatisfied, nor was he hostile to the Christian religion.

In making '*Murids*', the King was guided more by religious than worldly motives. The sepoys of the native army were not the only men who became his Murids. Others also adopted him as their spiritual guide. This practice was in vogue before the disturbances. Bahadur Shah's father also used to make Murids, though Bahadur Shah introduced the innovation of giving a handkerchief coloured light red to his followers. This practice originated in this way. The Pirzadahs of Delhi, who were spiritual instructors to the kings of Delhi, impressed upon the minds of the people that the King was the divine viceregent in spiritual matters upon earth, and that it was a creditable act to adopt him as their spiritual guide.

After all there is much advantage in adopting the practice that the spiritual instructor is obeyed by his followers on all matters, whether secular or spiritual. The practice of making Murids first came into operation during the time of the father of Bahadur Shah; but the latter gained a larger number of followers.

Only one method existed in which Murids were made.

I never heard that the King had any idea that his making Murids of the native sepoys would alienate them from the British Government. But it is evident that a '*Pir*' expects his Murids to unite themselves to him under all circumstances.

I never heard that any sepoy out of the number who resorted to Delhi mentioned to the King that he (the sepoy) had joined in consequence of his being his (the King's) disciple. Indeed, none of the disciples came, nor did any produce the red handkerchief. Moreover, none of the sepoys adopted the King as his spiritual guide during the five months of their occupation of Delhi. I am not aware of the cause. Perhaps those sepoys who were the King's disciples were absent on leave, and so far as I could gather from the records of Mirza Mughal, which have been since taken over by Government, and which I had seen, I can say that I found no mention of any of the King's disciples therein. Nor did I observe in them any petition which contained an account of any of the Murids. No sepoy became the King's Murid during the five months following the cartridge question; I was present all along and should have known if any had become the King's disciple.

The King's *Murids* were made invariably from among Mahommedans and from no other caste.

I never heard that the King carried on correspondence with the native troops; but he used to make anxious enquiries about the native army whenever any war took place. And inasmuch as he was dissatisfied with the British Government, he took pleasure in hearing of their defeat or reverses. He expected that any other ruler who might subvert the British rule world treat him with greater respect and honour, in consideration of the King's dynasty. In short, he believed that his own prosperity would go hand in hand with the ruin of British power.

I do not remember well, but I believe information must have reached the King of the mutiny of some of the native regiments after the annexation of Punjab in consequence of the discontinuance of *bhatta*; and I doubt not that the King learnt the fact with satisfaction.

I do not remember exactly the month in which intelligence was received of the regiment near Calcutta having refused to receive the new cartridges. I only know that the information was obtained from a Calcutta newspaper; and when it was known that the discussion about the cartridges was spreading, it was remarked that, inasmuch as the matter touched the religion of the people, the excitement would spread extensively over the entire length and breadth of the country, and the native army would desert the British Government, whose rule would then be at an end. The King remarked that he would, in that case, be placed in better circumstances, inasmuch as a new dominant power would treat him with greater respect and consideration.

The princes of the royal family used to remark that the native army would go over either to Nepal or to Persia. But they had no idea that they would unite themselves with the King, because he had neither money nor troops.

Although the issue of the new cartridges was the ostensible cause of the mutiny, it was not in reality so. Some individuals of the native army had long before been adverse to and dissatisfied with the British Government. They considered that they were treated with severity, and eagerly seized the opportunity of the issue of new cartridges as affording a good pretext for their defection. The wily and intriguing among them made it the fulcrum of their designs to excite the whole army against their rulers, and, mixing therewith a religious element, alienated the minds of the troops from the Government. They believed that they alone constituted the power of Government, and that against them the British had not the means of fighting. The mass of the people were ignorant; they believed that the Government was intent upon polluting their religion; indeed, it was notorious that the Commander-in-Chief had undertaken upon himself to Christianize the whole of India in two years. Thus did the intelligent and cunning plan their designs; and the ignorant followed them.

I consider that the native army was impregnated with malevolent intentions towards the British Government; and had even the new cartridges not been issued, they would have even made some other pretext to mutiny, because they had been actuated by religious motives alone, they would have given up service; and if they wished to serve, they would not have mutinied.

It was the King's opinion that the Government really intended to change the religion of the people; but I frequently explained to him that this was only a rumour set afloat by wicked people. For, I added, the British were wise people nor could I believe that they would seek to injure an army from whom they expected good service. This argument satisfied the King, whenever I explained to him; but he relapsed into his own way of thinking as after as he listened to the representations of his eunuchs and *ranis*.[5]

No intelligence was received in my presence from Meerut. Early after sunrise on the morning of Monday, a sepoy of the volunteers, who was stationed on duty at the Lahori Gate, came and told the porters of the Dewan-i-Khas that the Government troops had mutinied at Meerut, and that the infantry and cavalry would shortly arrive at Delhi. About an hour after this, the regiment stationed in the cantonment of Delhi entered the palace, and shortly afterwards the Meerut troops also arrived in the palace. Before this no news was received.

It was never mentioned in my presence that any information had been received of a court-martial having assembled at Meerut to try those sepoys who had refused to receive the new cartridges.

It is not unlikely that news to this effect was received by means of some newspaper, five or six days afterwards.

I do not believe that anyone was sent by the King to Meerut to procure information of the proceedings at Meerut, in regard to the refusal of the sepoys to receive the cartridges, at the time when they were going to the palace.

I did not hear that Zeenat Mahal had sent anyone to Meerut for the above purpose. Yes, the King was surprised to see that the troops had come to him. I also wondered at the circumstance, because nothing had transpired immediately before their arrival, which might have led us to expect them, though when the discussion about the cartridges first became known, it was believed that it would cause some mischief.

On the evening of the same day on which the troops arrived, I represented to the King that nothing good could be expected from them, inasmuch as

5 Wrong translation; it should be *begums*.

they had mutinied against their masters. And I addressed a letter to the Lieutenant-Governor of Agra, on the part of the King, informing him of the arrival of the troops, after they had murdered their European officers, and representing the King's inability to take any measures against them, and begging for help in the form of European troops.

In the morning I had no private conversation with the King, because the palace was so much crowded with the mutinous troops, and the King's servants, that I did not find any opportunity of speaking to him.

The King was not prepared beforehand for the arrival of the mutineers, because when I and Ghulam Abbas, the King's Wakil, communicated to him (the King) the request of the officer commanding the Palace Guards and the Agent to the Lieutenant-Governor, to the effect that two of the King's guns, together with artillery men, might be sent to the Lahori Gate, and also two palanquins with bearers to Captain Douglas, the King, without making any excuse, gave orders for their being sent as requested.

Nobody can tell what was the object of the distribution of the *chapatis.* It is not known who first projected the plan. All the people in the palace wondered what it could mean. I had no conversation with the King on the subject; but others talked in his presence about it, wondering what could be the object.

I consider that the *chapatti* affair probably originated with the native troops, and the distribution first commenced in Oudh. I also wondered what it was, but considered that it implied something.

I consider that the distribution of the *chapatis* first began in Oudh.

It was the opinion of some that the native troops had designed these *chapattis* as emblematical of some particular object. Others believed that there was some charm attached to them, inasmuch as they were distributed unknown all over the country, and without it being known who first originated the idea, and whence they were first sent out. People also believed that these *chapati*s were the invention of some adept in the secret arts, in order to preserve unpolluted the religion of the country, which, it was reported, the Government had proposed to themselves to subvert in two years.

I understood from the officers of the army that they had mutinied in consequence of the Government having used fat in the preparation of cartridges, and mixed ground bones with flour, which Government wished to use as the means of converting the people. This was generally assigned as the reason of their taking up arms against Government; but I learnt from Haidar Hasan, who was very familiar with the officers of the troops, that they spoke privately as follows: 'If we continue united together, we shall not be defeated by the Government troops, but shall become masters of the country'.

I consider that the native troops mutinied in the hope of worldly gain. The admixture of religion was only intended to disguise their real object.

If they were really fighting for religion, they would not have plundered the houses and property of the people, nor would they have oppressed and injured them, but would have fought only against the British Government.

After the breaking out of the mutiny, the rebellious troops used to say they were masters of the country, and that they would take different princes to different provinces of the country.

The Volunteer Regiment of Delhi[6] said that before the breaking out of the mutiny, they had leagued with the troops at Meerut, and that the latter had corresponded with the troops in all other places, so that from every cantonment troops would arrive at Delhi.

After the defection of the native army, I understood that letters were received at Delhi, from which it was evident that they had beforehand made common cause among themselves. The mutineers at Delhi also wrote to other regiments, requesting them to come over. Indeed, at the request of some of the mutinous officers, the King addressed orders to the troops at Neemuch and Firozpur and other places, inviting them to proceed to join him. The usual drift of letters addressed by the Delhi mutineers was this, 'So many of us have come in here, do you also, according to your promise, come over here quickly'.

At the request of the mutinous officers, the King used to give orders to the munshis[7] to write as they (the officers) desired.

I cannot give any further information in regard to the preconcerted conspiracy of the native troops; I have said all I know.

Before their defection, the native troops had settled it among them to kill all Europeans, including women and children, in every cantonment.

I cannot explain, in detail, the arrangements which were made by the mutineers before their defection. I consider, however, that all their plans had not yet matured when the event took place.

I did not hear that any particular date had been fixed for the execution of the plans of the mutineers; but I am inclined to think that none was fixed time, in the letters which were addressed by the Delhi mutineers to the other troops, which was not the case. I mean some such language as the following would have been used in those letters – viz. 'You promised to rise up on such a date, but you have not arrived yet, so that you have not kept your promise'.

When I stated above, that the '*event*' took place before the plans of the mutineers had matured, I referred to the 'event' which occurred at Meerut.

Indeed, I consider that had the event at Meerut not taken place so soon, the plans of the mutineers and their union would have become more perfect with greater length of time.

6 38th N.I.
7 Clerks.

The breaking out of the mutiny at Meerut somewhat before the proper time may be ascribed to one of the two following causes: either the Meerut troops were too precipitate or the Government behaved severely towards them.

Gulab Shah, the officers of the 3rd Cavalry, who came in from Meerut, in alluding to the severity of the Government, stated that they disarmed the troops and imprisoned the troopers in irons.

In addition to the issue of the new cartridges, the sepoys numbered among their grievances and causes of their dissatisfaction with Government, the short leaves allowed to troops, the discontinuance of batta, the sending out of troops to sea on shipboard, and lastly, the little consideration (compared to previous times) shown, of late, to the sepoy army.

But they brought forward, most conspicuously, the issue of cartridges as the strongest cause to their mutiny. Their other grievances, as mentioned above, were not adduced so prominently. The reason for this is obvious. In the cartridge dispute, a religious element was involved, which served their purpose, inasmuch as the mass of the people (who are necessarily ignorant) were deceived and really believed that they were fighting for religion. The wicked were guided by motives of gain.

The mutineers spoke of the British with contempt; they called them 'Nasara' and infidels, but they did not use foul language against them. They used to say that the Government would not allow any Chief to hold territorial possessions, and would not treat the natives of India with any consideration.

In the native army, both Hindus and Mahommedans were dissatisfied with the Government, and the Hindus predominated in number, but, of the inhabitants of Delhi, the Hindus were dissatisfied to a less degree than the Mahommedans.

The reason for the great dissatisfaction of the Mahommedans was that on the occasion of the '*Bakr Eed*' when there was a quarrel in regard to the slaughter of kine [cow], the decision of the authorities was not agreeable to the Mahommedan population. In addition to this, it was reported that the Government desired to make Christians of the natives of India by causing them to eat pork.

Latterly, it was believed that the sepoys repented of their misconduct, and proof of their repentance might be found in the fact that many secretly left their regiments; some applied to their officers for promotion of rank and increase of pay, and when their request was not granted, they left openly.

The people in the palace or the princes did not know previously that the sepoys of the Volunteer Regiment at Delhi had leagued with the Meerut troops against the Government. This was only known afterwards when the officers of the mutinous groups said so at Delhi.

I consider that no correspondence passed between the sepoys and the native Chiefs before the open mutiny of the former; for if any had passed, allusion would have been made in the subsequent letters addressed to the

Chiefs, to the circumstances, which was not the case. Moreover, if any such communication had been made, some portion of the mutinous troops would have proceeded to some of the Chiefs with whom they had leagues. This also was not the case.

I consider that the native army mutinied of their own accord, and not at instigation of any Chiefs, because in the latter case the mutineers would have either themselves proceeded to join their instigator or caused him to join them.

The mutinous troops would not appear to have won over the people of the country, because if they had, they would have treated them with consideration, and would not have oppressed and plundered them as they did.

The sepoys had not before their breaking out into mutiny united to themselves the Musalman population of Delhi. If they had, they would not have oppressed and plundered the Mahommedans of Delhi in the manner they did.

The abandoned classes of the city required no instigation to rise up. The confusion and disorder of the time in itself encouraged them to unite with the sepoys.

I am of opinion that no agreement was made between the Goojurs and the mutinous troops beforehand. But, afterwards, certain mutinous officers caused the King to grant a drum and standard[8] to two Goojurs of the neighbourhood of Delhi, who were enjoined to plunder the provisions of the British Camp. In like manner, a Rao, who resided in the vicinity of Sikandrah, in the Bulandshahr District, received a drum and standard from the King for similar service.

During the period of disturbances, no complaint was made against the defects of the civil administration under the British rule. The sepoys did not complain, because they were themselves tyrannical; and the people had seen too much of the oppressive administration of the sepoys to complain against that of the British.

Among the cavalry officers, Gulab Shah; among those of the infantry regiments, the officers of the '*Runseet*' (Ranjeet)[9] and '*Alexander*'[10] regiments; and among the King's servants, Sidis Nasir Khan and Basant, eunuchs, were the principals who instigated the murder of the 50 Christians and Europeans. The reason is that Gulab Shah and his party was encamped in the Hayat Bakhsh garden, and used to be seated at the entrance of the royal apartments in the company of the eunuchs.

Among the princes, Prince Abu Bakr and Mirza Khair Sultan were the principals who caused the Europeans to be murdered. The others were only their accomplices.

8 Signs of Royal authority.
9 11 N.I.
10 74 N.I.

I spoke to the King on the subject in the presence of the eunuchs. When the latter, at the request of Gulab Shah, solicited the King's orders for killing the Europeans, I explained to the King that it was forbidden in our own religion to kill women and children. I suggested to him that it was also prudent in a worldly point of view to preserve them. I advised him to obtain a '*Fatwa*' from the factors of the Mahommedan religion, prohibiting the slaughter of the women and children, and to show the verdict to the officers of the army, and then to keep them in custody in a safe place, and to preserve them as he would his own family and children. I explained to him the immediate and also remote advantages of such conduct. I explained to him that such was the line of conduct adopted by Sirdar Muhammad Akbar Khan of Cabul towards the Europeans who became his prisoners during the Afghan war. I pointed out to the King how, consequence of such conduct, Akbar Khan succeeded in procuring the liberation of his father, the Amir Dost Muhammad Khan, from confinement in the hands of the British, and how the Amir was ultimately restored to his country and kingdom.

The effect of my suggestion was that the King at that time withheld his sanction to the murder of the Christians, and for two days their lives were preserved. But afterwards, the applicants prevailed upon the King to give his assent, and the eunuchs Basant and Sidi Nasir delivered up the Christians to Gulab Shah, who put them to death by the side of a reservoir in the palace.

If the King had kept the women and children in his own female apartments, and on their being demanded by the sepoys had explained to the latter that he would only agree to their (the Christians) being murdered, after his own women and children had been first put to death, it was very probable that the sepoys would not have dared to enter the royal seraglio to forcibly seize and kill the Christians.

The King could have safely said and done so. He frequently spoke to the sepoys as resolutely.

Had the King's consent not been given, it was not possible that a false entry would have been made in the official documents to the effect that his sanction had been given.

The officers of the Runseet and Alexander regiments were extremely hostile to Europeans and Christians, and even if Gulab Shah, and the two eunuchs Basant and Nasir, had not existed, the former would have demanded the murder of the Christians. But I do not consider that except them there were any others so extremely hostile to the Christians.

These Christians were put to death by Sidi Nasir, Allah Dad Wilayati, and the sowars of Gulab Shah, and certain Khas-bardars of the King. They were killed with swords. Allah Dad Wilayati was in the service of the King.

First of all the regular troopers came; then followed the Volunteer Regiment of Delhi and entered the palace. The troopers were accompanied by two companies of the Volunteers who were posted at the gates of the palace. The officers of the Volunteer Regiment said in a loud voice, 'Here are the sowars from Meerut, the infantry regiments will follow shortly'. I gathered from the talk of the officers of the Delhi regiments that there was perfect union of mind between the Delhi and Meerut troops. Moreover, in the letters and orders which were addressed to the native regiments in others cantonments, the sepoys never alluded to any promise of the addressees' to proceed to Delhi. It was merely stated in those letters that such and such regiments had come, 'Do you come over also'.

In my opinion, the mutineers had several inducements for throwing themselves into the city of Delhi:

First: Delhi was close to Meerut, where the mutiny commenced, and the Meerut troops were of one mind with those of Delhi.
Second: There was considerable treasure and abundance of magazine stores at Delhi.
Third: There was a wall round Delhi, and the city could be well defended.
Fourth: The King of Delhi had no army, and was defenceless.
Fifth: The King was a personage to wait upon, whom all Chiefs, Hindu or Mahommedan would have considered an honour to themselves.

The troops did not inform the King previously of their intention to go over to him, nor had the King any knowledge of the Volunteer Regiment having made common cause with the Meerut troops.

I never heard any complaints from the people of Delhi regarding the resumption of *inam* or rent-free grants, because I am not aware that any such grants had been resumed. But the sepoys used to say that the Government would gradually resume all inams and pensions, and leave note in the enjoyment thereof.

The annexation of Oudh was much talked of at Delhi. But as the majority of the Mahommedan population of Delhi are Sunnis, and a Maulavy of their sect, named Amir Ali had been blown, together with about 400 or 500 Sunnis, from the mouth of canon, on the occasion of the *emeute* at Hanuman Garhi, by order of the King of Oudh, the Mahommedans of Delhi did not regard the annexation of Oudh with dissatisfaction. On the contrary, they believed that the King of Oudh had been punished for having shed the blood of innocent Sunnis, in the loss of his kingdom. As regards the Hindus of Delhi, I never heard that they were in any manner dissatisfied at the annexation of Oudh.

The sepoys used to remark that the English would take possession of every country in the same manner as they had occupied Oudh; but I did not perceive that they were particularly grieved at the annexation of Oudh.

I heard no complaints from the sepoys regarding the revenue administration under the British rule in Oudh.

I do not consider that the annexation of Oudh was one among other causes of the revolt of the sepoys. My impression is that they had no causes to be grieved on that account. They lost nothing by it; on the contrary, they were liberated from the oppression of the Oudh Government. The sepoys who were at Delhi never complained particularly against the annexation of Oudh. But they certainly used to say that the British would take possession of every provinces as they had occupied Oudh; and that they took possession of that country even though the King did not fight against them.

I consider that the sepoys would have mutinied, even though Oudh had not been annexed, because they were ripe for revolt.

Three or four of the Lucknow mutinous regiments addressed petitions to the King, in which they stated that they would proceed to Delhi after they had made themselves masters of Oudh, and added that they had besieged the British in Bailee Guard. Kudarat-ulla-Khan, Risaldar, accompanied by a hundred sowars, also brought a petition from all the Oudh troops, and was introduced into the King's presence by Bakht Khan, he presented the coin recently struck in the name of Bahadur Shah. The impression on the coin was as follows:

'Siraj-ud-din Bahadur Shah Ghazi has struck upon gold the coin of victory'.

The petitioners stated that they had elevated a son[11] of Wajid Ali Shah on the Gaddi, on the condition that he should be the Wazir of Bahadur Shah, and acknowledge allegiance to that King. They added that they had caused the prince to write down an agreement to that effect, and had further explained to him that he had been raised to the throne subject to the sanction of the King.

The King ordered Bakht Khan to reply to the petition conveying his sanction to the arrangement.

The gold mohurs which were presented by Kudrat-ulla Khan, Risaldar, to the King, are now in the possession of the Commissioner of Delhi.

I do not consider that Wajid Ali Shah, the King of Oudh, had any share in these proceedings.

If Wajid Ali Shah or Ali Naki Khan had been in league with the sepoys, the circumstance could not have remained a secret, and moreover, the latter would have proceeded to Lucknow. Furthermore, in that case, the sepoys would not have raised to the throne the younger son of Wajid Ali Shah, to the exclusion of Wajid Ali Shah himself and his eldest son.

I am of opinion the Oudh troops would not have proceeded to Delhi after they had succeeded in taking possession of Bailee Guard (*The Residency*) because they would have betaken themselves to the management of the extensive territory of Oudh. I consider that the authority of the son of Wajid Ali Shah, whom they had raised to the throne, would have been only nominal.

I never heard that any correspondence was carried on with Wajid Ali Shah during his residence in Calcutta, and I believe that none took place.

11 Brijis Qadar who was crowned as Nawab of Oudh on 5 July 1857.

Neither was any correspondence carried on with Ali Naki Khan. Formerly some correspondence took place through the medium of Mirza Haidar; but when that individual gave out, at Lucknow, that the King of Delhi had become a convert to the Shia religion and the King denied at Delhi that he had, Mirza Haidar discontinued writing to the King, nor did he come to Delhi afterwards, and as Mirza Haidar was the medium of communication between the King of Oudh and Delhi, and that man had not accompanied the King of Oudh to Calcutta, no correspondence took place between the two kings.

I did not hear from any of the sepoys that either the King of Oudh or any of his relatives or dependents instigated the sepoys to revolt. I cannot speak of the Oudh troops, because none came from thence of Delhi.

During the disturbances I heard that Mirza Haidar was at Lucknow, but that he was detained along with other native Chiefs of influence at Bailee Guard by the British officers.

No correspondence took place between Mirza Haidar and the King of Delhi during the disturbances. Indeed, all correspondence between them had ceased, since Mirza Haidar had reported at Lucknow the conversion of the King to the Shia religion.

I shall now describe from what regiments and places petitions were received by the King.

Neemuch

The Neemuch troops addressed a petition to the King, in which they stated that they had arrived at Agra, where they had gained a victory and driven the British into the fort which they had laid siege to. But they added that they had no heavy guns, so they intended to proceed to Delhi, and return from thence to Agra, carrying along with them heavy guns from Delhi, and they would then take the Agra Fort. They mentioned in their petition that they had killed their European officers. This petition was from Muthra, and in the names of Ghaus Khan and Hira Singh, Subedars. It was brought by a shutar-sowar,[12] and was presented to the King by Bakht Khan, who spoke in very high terms of the Neemuch troops. The King directed that a reply be addressed calling them over to Delhi. A reply was sent accordingly.

Jhansi

A messenger brought a petition from the Jhansi troops, and delivered it to the eunuchs, who presented it to the King. In this petition, the writers stated

12 A camel rider.

that they had killed their European officers, and were desirous of proceeding to Delhi. The King directed a reply to the sent telling them to come over.

Danapur (Dinapore)[13]

A petition was brought from Dinapore by an officer of the Delhi troops, about two-and-a-half months after the breaking out of the mutiny, in which the writers stated that either they had started for Delhi or intended to do so. The King ordered a reply to be sent telling them to come over. I cannot say positively whether any troops came from Dinapore or not.

Allahabad

Two sepoys in the disguise of travellers brought a petition from the Allahabad troops. It was presented to the King through the officers of the Volunteer Regiment about a month-and-a-half after the mutiny. They signified their devotion to the King, and expressed their intention to proceed to Delhi. A reply was sent telling them to come over.

Aligarh

A petition was presented on the part of the Aligarh troops to the King by an officer of the Delhi mutineers about two-and-a-half months after the rebellion. I do not know whether the petition was brought by a messenger, or whether it arrived by dak. The contents were that either the petitioners had started for Delhi or intended to do so. They were told in reply that they might come over.

Muthra

Two messengers brought a petition from the Muthra troops about 20 days after the mutiny, which was presented by the officers of the Volunteer Regiment. The writers stated that they were proceeding to Delhi bringing treasure along with them. A reply was sent as usual. Shortly afterwards, these troops arrived, bringing Rs. 1 lakh of treasure.

Bulandshahr

Mirza Mughal produced before the King a sepoy belonging to the Bulandshahr troops who had brought a petition in which it was said they were marching to Delhi with all the treasure they had in their possession.

13 A town in Bihar.

Accordingly, they brought Rs. 30,000 with them. But I heard that the sepoys had appropriated a portion of the treasure to themselves, as they were marching to Delhi.

Roorki

I believe that a sepoy, in the disguise of a traveller, brought a petition from the Roorki troops, which was presented to the King about a month-and-a-half after the rebellion, by the officers of the 'Mapert' (54th N.I.) regiment. The contents were that the writers were desirous of proceeding to Delhi, and would serve the King truly. A reply was sent as usual, and about 300 men of the Sappers and Miners arrived under the command of Kadar Bakhsh. This officer became very intimate with Mirza Khair Sultan, and acquired some influence over the King. He frequently had a voice in the proceedings of the army, and, in conjunction with Bakht Khan, obtained the permission of the King to exact money from the bankers and wealthy Mahommedans of the city.

Farrukhabad

Bakht Khan had left some troops at Farrukhabad before he came to Delhi. He intimated the fact to the King a little before two months after the breaking out of the mutiny.

Hansi

Two sowars brought a petition from Hansi, in which the writers stated that they were fighting for the King and were proceeding to Delhi to fight for religion. This petition was presented to the King, I believe by Gulab Shah, the Commander of the Meerut troops, about six weeks after disturbances. Three sowars came from Hansi.

Sirsa

Three petitions were received from Sirsa. One from Gouri Shankar, officer of the 'Tukyur' Regiment, the second from a cavalry Risaldar whose name I forget, and the third from Shahzadah Muhammad Azim,[14] of the Commissariat Department. The petitioners stated that they had already performed good service to the King, and added that they were proceeding to Delhi with all the money of the Customs Department. These petitions were brought by two messengers, about six weeks after the mutiny. A reply was

14 Assistant Patrol (Customs) at Bhattu (Hissar) in Haryana, referred to earlier.

sent as usual. Shortly afterwards, the troops arrived bringing with them Rs. 30,000 treasure, about 200 bullocks, and 50 or 60 sheep.

Karnal

No petition was received from the troops at Karnal.

Nasirabad

Two sepoys brought a petition in which, as usual, the troops signified their readiness to march to Delhi. Mirza Mughal presented the petition to the King, and the usual reply was sent between 2,500 men (cavalry and infantry) who arrived with a number of guns.

Saugor and Jabbulpur

I believe petitions came from these places, and that replies were also sent.

The Punjab (Firozpur)

A sepoy, disguised as a *fakir*, brought a petition from the Firozpur troops. Mirza Mughal presented the petition to the King. The messenger was told that a reply would be given next day. The man told me he had come from Firozpur, and that the troops at the place were all ready to march to Delhi, and had mutinied against the British Government. I did not see the petition, nor did Mirza Mughal mention to me that any petition had been received from Firozpur. This petition was received about six weeks after the commencement of disturbances, before Bakht Khan had joined. Only Neemuch and Jhansi troops arrived after Bakht Khan; the greater part of other troops had already joined before him.

Ambala

A sepoy, in the disguise of a *fakir*, brought a petition from the Ambala troops, but I cannot speak positively in this matter, nor am I sure that any reply was sent.

Phillour

If I recollect right, I believe that an officer of the Baillie Regiment (the 20th N.I.) brought a petition from the Phillour troops, but none of the latter accompanied him. This was two months after the commencement of disturbances. The contents were that petitioners would march to Delhi after serving the King's cause at Phillour. The usual reply was sent. Long afterwards about 200 men came to Delhi.

Jallandhar

I believe that some sepoy, disguised as a traveller, brought a petition from the Jallandhar troops, and some officer of the 'Runsit' Regiment (the 11th N.I.) presented the petition to the King. The contents were as usual, as was also the reply.

Sealkote

No sepoy came from Sealkote with any petition, but a petition was received from that place and presented to the King by an officer of one of the Delhi mutinous regiments about two months and upwards after the mutiny. The writers expressed their desire to march to Delhi. A reply was ordered to be sent. I do not recollect whether any troops came from Sealkote or not.

Jhelum

The petition from Jhelum came very late, about three months after the commencement of the mutiny. It was received, I believe, through Kadir Bakhsh, of the Roorki Sappers and Miners. The subject was as usual, as was also the reply.

Rawulpindee

Two sepoys, disguised as Brahman travellers, brought a petition from the Rawulpindee troops, in which the writers stated that they were prepared to march to Delhi and serve the King. This petition was presented to the King by the officers of the 'Marpet' regiment. A reply was ordered to be written as usual. This petition was received about two months after the breaking out of the mutiny.

Loodhiana

I heard that a petition had been received from Loodhiana, and I believe that one was received. But I do not know through whom it came. I believe a reply was also sent. I do not remember its contents, but I heard that the troops were expected at Delhi. If any petition came, it must have arrived about two months after the breaking out of disturbances.

No petition came from the troops at *Benares*, *Azimgarh*, *Gorakhpur*, *Cawnpur*, *Meerut*, *Saharunpur*, *Bijnour*, *Mooradabad*, *Fattehgurh*, *Fattehpur*, *Bareilly*, *Budaon*, *Agra*, *Shajanpur*, and *Ghazeepur*.[15]

15 A town in UP.

None also came from the troops at *Amritsar*, *Hooshirpur*, *Kangra*, *Lahore*, *Attock*, *Peshawar*, *Mooltan*, *Googaira*, *Gujrat*, *Dehra Ismail Khan*, *Dhra Ghazi Khan*, *Shahpur*, *Khangarh*, or *Leiah*.

Likewise, no petition was received from the troops at Calcutta or Barrackpore or other cantonments in the eastern provinces.

No petition was received from the Bombay or Sindh troops; but the mutineers represented to the King that the Bombay Army had written to them to the effect that they were ready to proceed to Delhi. I heard this once or twice. I cannot speak positively whether any petition came or not.

A petition was received from the Gwalior troops from a place beyond the Chambul (of which I forget the name), in which they said that they had 50 guns and magazine stores in such abundance that 5,000 carts would be required to carry them. But they were unable to cross the Chambul which was at its height. This petition was received two months after the breaking out of disturbances. They were told in reply that they could come when the river had subsided.

No communication was addressed by the Delhi mutineers to the troops of *Bikanir*, *Jaisalmair*, *Jodhpur*, *Jaipur*, *Jhajjar*, *Alwar*, *Kotah*, or *Boondy*. Nor was any received from them at Delhi.

Petitions were received by the King from the Chiefs of *Jhajjar*, *Ballabgarh*, *Farrukhnagar*, and from Walidad Khan of *Malagarh* in the Bulandshahar district. In these petitions, they professed allegiance to the King, and excused their personal attendance on the ground that their absence would unsettle their countries. The Jhajjar Nawab sent 300 sowars under the command of his father-in-law, Abdul Samad Khan. The Ballabhgarh Chief sent 15 sowars. No troops came from Farrrukhnagar; and Walidad Khan asked for troops and guns, but none were sent until long afterwards when 200 sowars were sent. Walidad Khan was himself present at Delhi at the time of the breaking out of the mutiny. He obtained a patent conferring upon him the government of the Doab, and left Delhi.

Khan Bahadur Khan[16] sent a petition and Wakil through the medium of Bakht Khan. He also sent an elephant, a horse with silver ornaments, and 101 gold mohurs as a present. Several petitions were received from Rao Tula Ram,[17] asking for troops. He sent Rs. 40,000 treasure, which was paid into the King's treasury through the medium of Bakht Khan. 'Sukkas' were addressed to the following Chiefs at the request of the mutinous troops, calling upon them (the Chiefs) to come over with their troops and munitions of war: Jhajjar, Ballabhgarh, Farrukhnagar, Khan Bahadur Khan of Bareilly, Jaipur, Alwar, Jodhpur, Bikanir, Gwalior, and Baija Bai,

16 Of Bareilly (UP.)

17 Tula Ram (1825–1863): The Rao of Rewari (Haryana); played a significant role in the uprising; died in Kabul at the age of 38.

and Jaisalmair. Two shukkas were addressed to Baija Bai; but she replied to neither of them.

A shukka was addressed to the Patiala Rajah through Bakht Khan. It conveyed the pardon of the King for the Maharajah's faults, at the instance of Abul Islam, and called upon the Maharajah to supply cash and to fight against the English.

A shukka was also addressed to the Jummoo Chief and made over for transmission to Bakht Khan. This person had previously presented to the King a petition (which was believed to have been forged) purporting to have been written by Rahah Gulab Singh, in which the Rajah was represented to say that he would soon march to Delhi with his troops, punishing on his way the Maharajah of Patiala; also that the Amir Dost Muhammad Khan was an ally of Jummoo, and would not fail to render service to the King. The shukka to the address of the Jummoo Chief called upon him to proceed with munitions of war to Delhi.

Replies were received to the effect mentioned above from the Chiefs of Jhajjar, Ballabhgarh, Farrukhnagar, and Khan Bahadur Khan of Bareilly, but none were received from Jaipur, Alwar, Jodhpur, Bikanir, Gwalior, Jaisalmair, Patiala, or Jummoo.

These latter Chiefs sent no reply, because they had no inclination to side with the King.

The Jodhpur and Gwalior Chiefs would appear to be determined to remain staunch in their alliance to the British Government. The mutiny of their troops did not alienate those Chiefs personally from the British.

No shukka was sent to Bharatpur, because the troops at Delhi said that the Rajah was a child, and the administration was carried on there by British officers.

No communication was addressed to Indore and none was received from there.

Kunwar Singh, the rebel of Shahabad,[18] was not addressed, and no communication was received from him.

No communication was addressed to the Rajah of Benares, or the Rajah of Rewa, nor to the Nawab of Banda, and none was received from any of those Chiefs.

No correspondence took place between the King and the Chiefs in Nagpur.

Neither the Behawalpur, nor the Kaparthulla, nor the Hill Chiefs under the Simla Agency were addressed, and no communication was received from any of those Chiefs.

The Nepal Chief was not addressed and no communication was received from him.

18 One of the foremost leaders of the Revolt; the Rajput ruler was already 80 at the time of the uprising. Yet he gave a heroic fight and fell fighting after a victory on 24 April 1858.

After the accumulation of the mutinous army at Delhi, shukkas were addressed to those Chiefs who were pointed out by the troops. And as the troops signified no desire for the Nepal Chief being written to, he was not addressed.

No correspondence passed between the King and the Chief of Gujrat in the Deccan, or the Chiefs of Baluchistan, Afghanistan, or the Khyber Pass.

At first, the troops said that the King's servants had not written to the Chiefs from whom no replies had been received. But when they themselves wrote and no reply was still received, they said the Chiefs were all of them disloyal, and would be punished after the British had been vanquished.

The intelligent among the troops said that the Chiefs were watching the turn of events, and were afraid, under the existing circumstances, to act decisively. Gauri Shankar, who was the most intelligent officer, used to observe that the presence of the Government troops on the hill before Delhi was a painful thorn in their (the mutineer's) side, and that as soon as this was removed, all would be right.

The sepoys used to say that there were in the first instance only two regiments of European soldiers on the ridge, but these had diminished to 200 or 300 only. And that when these shall have been killed, the British would leave the ridge.

None of the officers of the troops expressed a wish for the Bahawalpur Nawab being addressed, and I consider that the Nawab did not address the King, because the former had an old pique against the latter, inasmuch as when Nawab Bhawal Khan, the late Chief of Bahawalpur, passed through Delhi, the King forbade his son to enter the Dewan-i-Khas, unless he agreed to lay down his arms and take off his ornaments.

No petition was received from any of the Chukladars or Governors of Oudh.

A petition was received from Maulavy Liakat Ali, the leader of the religious warriors of Allahabad, in which he intimated that he was about to proceed to Delhi, and asked for military aid in order to reduce his part of the country. No reply was sent at the time, because he was himself expected; but when he came he was introduced to the King, by Bakht Khan, and returned after obtaining a patent, appointing him Governor of Lucknow. This took place three months after the commencement of disturbances.

No petition was received from the Nana; but about two months after the breaking out of the mutiny, a confidential agent (a Maratha) of the Nana arrived at Delhi, and was introduced to the King by Mirza Mughal. At the request of the Mirza, a shukka was addressed to the Nana, inviting him over to Delhi. The agent then returned.

No petition was received from any bankers, but an order was addressed to Seth Lakshmi Chand, at the instance of the army, directing him to give a loan to the amount of a million sterling, and to send an agent of his own to be placed in charge of the treasury. The Seth was told that the revenue collections would be made over to him, and that he would be allowed interest on his loan; but no reply was received from the Seth.

So far as I am aware no petition was received from any of the servants of Government; but I heard that a Hindustani, a Mahommedan of Bulandshahar, who held a high office under the Government, had joined Walidad Khan. I do not know his name. Shukkas were addressed to Mufti Sadr-ud-din, the principal Sudder Ameen, Karam Ali Khan, Munsiff, Maulavy Abbas Ali, Sudder Ameen of Delhi, and to Mirza Muhammad Aki Beg, Tahsildar of Mahroli, inviting them to enter the service of the King in the situations held by them under the British Government. But they all declined the offer. But when Bakht Khan assembled the Moulavies and Ulamas of Delhi in the Jama Masjid, and compelled them to declare that it was incumbent to wage a religious war against the British, I am told he (Bakht Khan) compelled Mufti Sadr-ud-din to put his seal upon the verdict. Maulavy Abbas Ali left Delhi and proceeded to his home across the Jumna before the arrival of Bakht Khan.

No petition was received from Agra from any party; but Maulavy Faiz Ahmad, who was employed in the Sudder Board's office, came in person to Delhi and adopted the King's service. He was placed in charge of the Adalat.

A shukka was addressed to the Nawab of Rampur, but no reply was received from him. Bakht Khan insisted upon the Nawab of Rampur being addressed, and said that when he (Bakht Khan) went to Rampur, the Nawab promised him to remain neutral.

Shukkas were also addressed to Nawabs Amin-ud-din Khan and Zia-ud-din Khan, to Jagirdars of Luharu, to Hassan Ali Khan, brother of the Nawab of Jhajjar, to Nawab Hamid Ali Khan, all of whom were residing at Delhi, and to Ajit Singh, uncle of the Maharajah of Patiala, directing them to wait upon the King. All these Chiefs accordingly waited upon the King, but wrote no petition in reply to the shukkas addressed to them, and when, at the instance of the army, these Chiefs were called upon to pay certain sums of money according to the circumstances of each, each and all made some excuse and paid nothing. For this reason, the troops were intent upon plundering them, and in an instance carried out their intention. Mirza Abu Bakr, grandson of the King, who commanded the regular cavalry, entered and plundered the house of Hamid Ali Khan, and carried the Nawab prisoner to the palace. But Zia-ud-din Khan and Amin-ud-din Khan were prepared to resist the troops, and therefore escaped being plundered.

A shukka was addressed to the Chief of Patoudi, but he sent no reply. I do not remember whether any shukka was addressed to the Chief of Dojana, but no petition was received from him.

I will now proceed to describe from what districts petitions were received from among the general population of the country.

Gurgaon

The Zamindars of Gurgaon proper addressed a petition, bringing to the notice of the King the disordered state of the district, and begging that an officer might be deputed to assume the administration. Thereupon Maulavy Faiz-ul-hak, who had come in from Alwar, proposed that his sister's son (whose name I forget), who was formerly employed in that district under the British Government, should be appointed. This man was accordingly appointed 'Ziladar', i.e., in charge of the district. But I am not aware whether he went to Gurgaon or not. This appointment was made only about 15 or 20 days before the fall of Delhi. Faiz-ul-hak also appointed several Tahsildars under the Ziladar.

Rewari

Rao Tula Ram, the perpetual settlement holder of Rewari, sent an agent of his own through Bakht Khan with a petition in which he stated that he had been managing the territory, but that the collection of the current harvest had been expended among the army. He offered to pay a 'nazarana' to the amount of Rs. 45,000 in consideration of the territory being granted to him in jagir in perpetuity. Bakht Khan accordingly obtained a patent conferring Rewari in perpetual jagir on Tula Ram. This was done three months after the breaking out of the rebellion. Ten days before the fall of Delhi, the sum of Rs. 40,000 was paid into the King's treasury by Tula Ram.

Badshahpur

The Zamindars of Badshahpur applied for a Tahsildar. The Ziladar was ordered to arrange for the appointment of a Tahsildar.

District of Delhi

No communication was received from any party of any note out of the walls of the city.

Rohtak

The Rohtak people sent no petition to the King, but they arranged for supplying provisions to the troops.

Hissar

The guards attached to the Hissar jail, as well as the officials of the Customs Department, sent petitions to the King. I do not remember the names of the writers: they stated that they were anxious to proceed to Delhi. This communication was received two months after the breaking out of disturbances.

Karnal

No petition was received from this district.

Sirsa

I have already described the conduct of Shahzadah Muhammad Azim. No communication was received from any of the Zamindars of this district.

Meerut

No communication was received from this district.

Bulandshahar

The conduct of Walidad Khan has already been described. No communication was received from or addressed to any other party.

Saharanpur and Muzaffarnagar

No communication was either addressed to or received from any party in these districts.

Bijnur

A petition was received from the Zamindars of this district; they begged that the administration might be assumed by the King. They were informed, in reply, that the management would be assumed as soon as the troops should march to that district. This petition was received from three months after the breaking out of the mutiny.

Muradabad

No petition was received from any rebel in that district, nor was any party addressed from Delhi.

Bareilly

A petition was received from Khan Bahadur Khan, who had been elevated to the governorship by Bakht Khan. He also sent an agent with an elephant, a horse, and 100 gold mohurs as a present for the King. I forget the name of the agent; he was introduced to the King by Bakht Khan. A shukka was addressed in reply, conveying the satisfaction of the King, and directing Khan Bahadur Khan to remit to Delhi the surplus balance of his collections after defraying the expenses.

Badaon

No communication was received from any party in this district.

Pilibhiit

None from here.

Mathura

The brother of Dundi Khan, the Jagirdar of Garhi near Mathura, sent a petition by his nephew, in which he applied for the release of his jagirs which had been resumed by the British Government. Bakht Khan supported the application. This took place about three months after the commencement of the disturbances. Bakht Khan insisted upon the bearer of the petition accompanying the troops in one of their attacks upon the Government troops. The man (Umrao Bahadur) was wounded on the occasion, and died within a week. Bakht Khan had obtained a patent granting the Istimrardari rights to the applicant. But Umrao Bahadur having died at Delhi, the patent never reached the intended grantee.

Agra

No communication was received from this district; but I have already mentioned that Maulavy Faiz Ahmad came from that city in person; Wazir Khan Doctor (Sub-Assistant Surgeon) also came: he knew English well. Bakht Khan was his supporter, and caused a patent to be granted him, appointing him Governor of Agra. Wazir Khan accompanied Bakht Khan when the latter fled from Delhi.

Districts of Aligarh, Cawnpur, and Fatehgarh

No correspondence passed between Delhi and these districts.

Mainpuri

A petition was received from the Rajah of Mainpuri, asking for troops. Mirza Mughal was ordered to arrange, after consulting the officers of the army, for dispatching troops to Mainpuri. But next day the officers represented that the troops were not willing to march until they had driven off the British troops from Delhi. A reply was sent to this effect accordingly.

No communication was received from any other party in this district.

Gorakhpur and Fatehpur Haswa

I do not remember whether any communication was received from this district or from the district of Kumaon.

Allahabad

I have already mentioned that Maulavy Liakat Ali came from this district and obtained a patent appointing him Governor. No communication was received from any other party.

Rajah of Banda near Rewah

No shukka was addressed to this Chief, nor was any communication received from him.

Azimgarh, Shahjahanpur, Etawah, Ghazipur, Benaras, and Gaya

No communication passed between the King and these districts.

Bundelkhand, Jubbulpur, Saugor, Malwa, and the Deccan territories

I do not remember whether any correspondence was passed between Delhi and these districts.

The Nizam of Hyderabad (Deccan), Cutch, and Gujrat; the Eastern Provinces: Calcutta, Barrackpore, Monghyr, Dinapore, etc.

No correspondence passed between the King and the Nizam, or any of the latter's subjects, nor between the King and any parties in Cutch or Gujrat. I do not remember whether any communication was received from the eastern districts.

Patna

Neither the Nawab of Patna, nor any other party addressed the King, nor were they addressed from Delhi.

The Punjab

No communication was received from any party in the Punjab.

No communication was received from any of the Zamindars of the Bari Doab district in the Punjab, nor were any addressed from Delhi.

I did not hear the troops making mention of any hackery men from the Punjab.

No communication was received from any of the Bundelah tribes, nor were they addressed from Delhi, and no person of that tribe came to Delhi.

No correspondence passed between the King and the Akhund of Swat; but two men were introduced by Bakht Khan to the King as having been sent by the Akhund. Hasan Askari took them before the King. These men were both 'Wilayatis' (people of Afghanistan). One, who looked rather a respectable man, presented a sword on the part of the Akhund, the purport of which was that the bearer was the Akhund's 'Khalifa' (*Vicergent*). He requested that it might be proclaimed in the city as the followers of the Akhund of Swat, nor was he a follower of the Akhund, and that the man had forged the writing which he had represented as being that of the Akhund. The King gave orders to Bakht Khan to make enquiries; but I do not know what Bakht Khan did in the matter. I know, however, that the man left Delhi three days afterwards.

The King's administrative policy

An order was issued at one time, prohibiting the army and princes from interfering in the general administration of the State. It was proposed that justice should be administered by Muftis and Sadr-ul-Sadrs, and that neither the army nor revenue officers were to interfere. This order was, however, never acted upon. The princes, supported by the troops, always interfered. The King himself appointed no Tahsildars for the collection of revenue; but Bakht Khan did appoint Tahsildars at Palwal, Hodal, and Shahdarah, and a Ziladar at Gurgaon, but no revenue was collected. The princes also resolved to send their troops to collect revenue, but the measure was not carried out. The 'Adalat' was presided over by Maulavy Faiz Ahmad, who had arrived from Agra, and the princes Mirza Khair Sultan and Mirza Mughal. A Kotwal (Superintendent of City Police) and Thanedars were appointed in the city, but I do not remember the names of the Thanedars. First of all Muin-ud-din Hasan Khan, son of Nawab Kudrat-ullah Khan, inhabitant of Delhi, was appointed kotwal; but he was dismissed after a short time, in consequence of his oppressing the people. After him, the post of kotwal was given, at the recommendation of Khwaja Wajib-ud-din Khan, to Kazi Faizullah of Delhi, and next to Mir Mubarak Shahm, a Syad of Ilaka Rampur. Thanedars were also appointed at Najaf Garh, Mahroli, Shahdarah, Paharganj, and Bahadrapur; but I do not remember their names. Besides the princes, Bakht Khan also interfered in these matters. Indeed, he had caused an order to be issued to the Thanedars and kotwal enjoining them to act up to Bakht Khan's orders.

The sepoys used to say that after they had made themselves masters of the whole country, they would allot different provinces to the several princes.

I believe many men were not appointed for the purpose of conducting the administration, and those that were, were nominated either by Bakht Khan or the princes.

No governor was appointed for Meerut. The governorship of Bulandshahr was conferred on Walidad Khan. A patent was granted to Wazir Khan, doctor, appointing him Governor of Oudh; but he never left Delhi to assume charge of his office. No man was nominated for Aligarh. Khan Bahadur Khan was Governor of Rohilkhand. No more appointments were made. No man went to Rajputana, and although one was nominated to the Gurgaon district, he never went to take charge of the district.

I can give no detailed information regarding the discipline of the army. The King was never consulted in this matter; but I understand that the troops which were detached for selling out and attacking the Government forces, used to be composed of three or four sections, for instance, the Nasirabad and Neemuch sections, and so on, according to the regiments who composed the attacking column. This was arranged, the day preceding that on which the attack was to be made, by the different officers in mutual consultation at the residence of Mirza Mughal. At all other times the sepoys lodged themselves as they pleased, indiscriminately, without reference to their regiments.

Gauri Shankar had obtained permission to assemble the officers and confirm the different parties in the ranks enjoyed by them while in the service of the British Government. But no such meeting was ever convened. No vacancies which occurred were filled; each continued to hold his former rank.

My opinion is that it was not possible to preserve proper discipline in army. The troops as a body were offended at the title of Governor-General having been granted to Bakht Khan. They actually addressed a petition on to the King in which they signified their unwillingness to be commanded by Bakht Khan. They represented that Bakht Khan was only an artillery officer unfit for the office of governor; that he had neither brought in any treasure, nor did he show proper deference to the King. And they added that Mirza Mughal, the King's son, who had been already entrusted with full powers in military matters, was fit for the post of Governor-General, and that the troops as a body were willing to be commanded by him. The King forwarded this petition to Bakht Khan, with a request that he would suggest a proper reply. He suggested that the army might be divided into three divisions: the first to be composed of the infantry regiments of Delhi and Meerut; the second, of the troops who accompanied Bakht Khan, the Neemuch brigade and the Sirsa men; and the third division to comprise the rest of the troops. The King sent for Mirza Mughal, and explained to him accordingly.

The reason of the ascendancy of Bakht Khan was this. When he first arrived, he advised the King not to entrust too much power in the hands of his sons, and suggested that all orders be communicated to him (Bakht Khan), in which case everything would go on as should be desired by the King. The King was already dissatisfied with the insubordinate conduct of his sons, so this advice of Bakht Khan suited his own wishes, and Bakht Khan rose daily in the estimation of the King.

The Wahabis

During the disturbances, a number of Wahabis arrived from Tonk. They complained that the Nawab had neither given them money nor any help. Wahabis also came from other directions.

Bakht Khan was himself a Wahabi, as were also Muhammad Ghafi, a Risaldar, and Maulavy Imam Khan, a Risaldar. Maulavy Abdul Ghaffur and Maulavy Sarfaraz Ali were also Wahabis. Sarfaraz Ali was constituted by Bakht Khan the leader of the religious warriors, and Bakht Khan supported these men.

A larger number of Wahabis joined after the arrival of Bakht Khan.

These Wahabis printed and published a proclamation inviting all Mahommedans to arm and fight for their religion. A fatwa was also published, declaring that it was the duty of all Mahommedans to make religious war, and that otherwise their families and children would be destroyed and ruined.

This proclamation was distinct from that of Bahadur Khan.

Wahabis came from several parts of the country; from Jaipur, Bhupal, Hansi, Hissar, and some Wilayatis; but I do not remember the names of the particular places from which they came. The details were contained in the records of Mirza Mughal's office.

Out of Delhi, the Hindus were as much hostile to the British Government as the Mahommedans at first, and the same was the case within the city itself. But when Bakht Khan came in and assembled the Mahommdeans, and compelled the Moulavis to give in 'fatwa' enjoining upon the Mahommedans the duty of making religious war upon the British, their fanaticism was aroused, and rose up in a body against the Government.

At Bulandshahar, Aligarh, Meerut, etc., the Hindus were as much hostile to Government as the Mahommedans.

Bakht Khan once represented to the King that a man had arrived from the Akhund of Swat. The next day two men were introduced to the King by Pirzadah Hasan Askari; one of them presented a sword on the part of the Akhund.

APPENDIX

APPENDIX 1

Act No. XIV of 1857[1]

Passed by the Legislative Council of India

The Act received the assent of the Governor-General on 6 June 1857[2]

Whereas it is necessary to make further provision for the trial and punishment of person who endeavour to excite mutiny and sedition among the Forces of the East India Company, and also for the trial of offences against the State: It is enacted as follows:

Whoever intentionally seduces or endeavours to seduce any Officer or Soldier in the service or pay of the East India Company from his allegiance to the British Government or his duty to the East India Company, or intentionally excites or stirs up, or endeavours to excite or stir up, any such Officer or Soldier, or any Officer or Soldier serving in any part of the British Territories in India in aid of the Troops of the British Government, to commit any act of mutiny or sedition; and whoever intentionally causes, or endeavours to cause, any other person to commit any such offence shall be liable upon conviction to the punishment of death, or to the punishment of transportation for life, or of imprisonment with hard labour for any term not exceeding 14 years; and shall forfeit all his property and effects of every description.

ii. Whoever shall knowingly harbour or conceal any person who shall have been guilty of any offence mentioned in the proceeding section,

1 Taken from Kaye, *op. cit.*, vol. 3, pp. 661–64.

2 An Act to make further provision for the trial and punishment of certain offences relating to Army/State.

shall be liable to imprisonment, with or without hard labour, for any term not exceeding seven years, and shall also be liable to fine.

iii. It shall be lawful for the Governor-General of India in Council, from time to time, by Order in Council, to empower every General or other Officer having the command of Troops in the Service of Her Majesty or of the East India Company, or any of such General or other Officers, to appoint General Courts-Martial for the trial of any person or persons charged with having committed an offence punishable by this Act or by Section I or Section II of Act XI of 1857, and also to confirm and carry into effect any sentence of such Court-Martial.

iv. Any General Court-Martial, which may be appointed under the authority of this Act, shall be appointed by the Senior Officer or the spot, and shall consist of not less than five Commissioned Officers, the number to be fixed by the General or other Officer appointing the Court-Martial. The Order in Council may direct that a General Court-Martial to be appointed under the provisions of this Act shall consist wholly of European Commissioned Officers or wholly or Native Commissioned Officers, or partly of European Commissioned Officers and partly of Native Commissioned Officers; and in such case the Officer appointing the Court-Martial shall determine whether the same shall consist wholly of European Officers or wholly of Native Officers, or partly of European Officers and partly of Native Officers.

v. Sentence of death or other punishment to which the offender is liable by law, may be given by such Court-Martial, if a majority of the members present concur in the sentence; and any such sentence may be confirmed by, and carried into effect immediately or otherwise by order of the Officer by whom the Court-Martial shall have been appointed, or, in case of his absence, by the Senior Officer on the spot.

vi. It shall be lawful for the Governor-General in Council to countermand or alter any Order in Council which may be issued under the authority of this Act.

vii. It shall be lawful for the Governor-General in Council, or for the Executive Government of any Presidency or place, or for any person or persons whom the Governor-General in Council may authorize so to do, from time to time to issue a Commission for the trial of all or any persons or person charged with having committed within any district described in the Commission, whether such district shall or shall not have been proclaimed to be in a state of rebellion, any office punishable by Sections I and II of Act XI of 1857, or by this Act, or any other crime against the State, or murder, arson, robbery, or other heinous crime against person or property.

viii. The Commissioner or Commissioners authorized by any such Commission, may hold a Court in any part of the district mentioned in the Commission, and may there try any person for any of the said crimes committed within any part thereof, it being the intention of this Act that the district mentioned in the Commission shall, for the purpose of trial and punishment of any of the said offences, be deemed one district.

ix. Any Court held under the Commission shall have power, without the attendance of a Law Officer, or the assistance of Assessors, to pass upon every person convicted before the Court of any of the aforesaid crime any sentence warranted by law for such crime; and the judgement of such Court shall be final and conclusive; and the said Court shall not be subordinate to the Sudder or other Court.

x. If a Commission be issued under the authority of this Act, any Magistrate or other Officer having power to commit for trial within the district described in the Commission may commit persons charged with any of the aforesaid crimes within such district for trial before a Court to be held under this Act.

xi. Nothing in this Act shall extend to the trial or punishment of any of Her Majesty's natural born subjects born in Europe, or of the children of such subjects.

xii. This Act shall not extend to the trial or punishment of any person for any offence for which he is liable to be tried by the Articles of War.

xiii. The word 'Soldier' shall include every person subject to any Articles of War.

xiv. This Act shall continue in force for one year.

APPENDIX 2

Police stations (*Thanas)* in 'Independent' Delhi, and the officers in charge of them[3]

There were 13 police stations in Delhi and its suburbs during the British days. But their strength went up to 23 after the new order replaced the old in 1857.

	*Police station (*Thana*)*	*Officer-in-Charge (*Thanedar*)*
1.	Kotwali	*Kotwals*: Faizullah Khan, SayedMubarak Shah *Naib Kotwals :* Khuda Bakhsh Khan, Bhao Singh, Bhan Singh
2.	Delhi Fort	*Kotwal*: Muhammad Yar Khan *Thanedars*
3.	Chandni Chowk	Hafiz Aminuddin (up to 3 July) Sayed Nazar Ali (after 3 July)
4.	Mehrauli	Not known
5.	Bhojlapahari	Mohd. Mirza Amani
6.	Gujar Allahabad (Hauj Qazi)	Mir Amanat Ali
7.	Gujar Dariba	Kunwar Lal (up to June) later, Bishambar Das, Faiz Talab Khan
8.	Karawali	Ishaq Khan
9.	Begumpura	Mohd. Amir Ali
10.	Nazafgarh	Mohd. Zahur Allah
11.	Paharganj	Saiyed Hussain Ali Khan, soon replaced by Habib Ali
12.	Gujar Qasim Khan	Mirza Mohd. Khan Beg
13.	Lahori Gate	Sheikh Mohd. Siddiq
14.	Shahdara	Not known
15.	Chandni Chowk	Mir Nazar Ali
16.	Faiz Bazar	Mohd. Nizamuddin
17.	Kashmiri Gate	Ikramula Khan
18.	Badarpur	Nasiruddin Khan
19.	Turkoman Gate	Mohd. Ehsanulla Khan
20.	Alipore	Jangbaz Khan
21.	Gujar Itiqad Khan	Ghulam Husain
22.	Hauz Khazi	Mir Amanat Ali Khan
23.	Rajghat	Ghulam Husain Khan
24.	Basant	Zabita Khan

3 See NAI, Mutiny Papers, 1857–58; also K.C. Yadav, ed., Delhi in 1857: A Documentary Study of Policing during the Rebellion (forthcoming).

APPENDIX 3

British spies in Delhi, 1857–1858[4]

There was a widespread spy network throughout Delhi – in the Palace, in the Army (Royal), in the streets, *mohallas*, bazaars, and public places. Capt. Hodson organized them with the help of one-eyed Maulavi, Rajab Ali. It is difficult to count their actual numbers, because many of them worked indirectly (through somebody) in secrecy. The prominent ones whose reports are available in print and in hand were as follows:

1. Kulru
2. Pirbhu
3. Meghraj
4. Gopal
5. Souki Ram
6. Mouhin-ud-din
7. Rajab Ali
8. Rujja Gujar
9. Kalu
10. Turub Ali
11. Salauddin
12. Ganga Ram
13. Dhanna Jat
14. Harbhajan Gujar
15. Data Ram
16. Sadhu
17. Rustam Ali
18. Jawahar Singh
19. Inayatullah
20. Amir Chand
21. Meer Muhmmad Ali
22. Mehbub Khan
23. Hari Chand Gosain
24. Fateh Muhammad
25. Mohan
26. Bihari Lal
27. Gauri Shankar Shukla (Subedar Haryana Light Infantry)

Note: The List is not exhaustive.

4 Based on information contained in *The Punjab Mutiny Records, Correspondence*, Part 2. Delhi Archives has the original English translation (in hand) of most of these reports.

GLOSSARY

Alighol the Army of Ali, son-in-law of Prophet Muhammad (contextually, Special Army)
baggi horse cart
bakar-ied an important Muslim festival
bargir irregular cavalryman
bazaar market
bhattaa allowance
bywastha *vyavastha* (Hindi) religious code of conduct
chapatti flour flat bread
chaprasy *chaprasi* (peon)
chaudhari headman of traders, etc.
deen (din) *deen-deen* was a popular war cry not only of Muslims but also of many Hindus in 1857
Diwan-i-khas Hall of Special Audience (Red Fort, Delhi)
diwani the privilege of collecting revenue and governing on behalf of the master (here Emperor)
Dum Duma Artillery School (Meerut)
durbar official assemblage of a king/chief
fatwa religious decree (Muslims)
fidwi servant
firman royal decree or grant
hookah smoking water pipe/hubble-bubble
kafila caravan
Kanungo revenue official keeping land records
ketany corrupt form of word Christian (Kristan/Kerany)
khilat robe of honour bestowed upon a subordinate by a superior authority, especially king
lakh 100,000
mafidar a tenant enjoying a free grant of land
mujawor sweeper in the mosque

murid disciple
nazar customary token of tribute (here presented to the Emperor)
parwanah royal order decree or letter (special)
patwari village accountant for land rights and revenue records
peshkash present or tribute to a superior authority (here the Emperor)
sais caretaker of horse
shukka mandate
thakur principal land proprietor
zer-i-jharokha the place in the palace where kings used to show up to the public in the morning (literally 'under the lattice')

BIBLIOGRAPHY

Unpublished Records

National Archives of India, New Delhi

(i) Proceedings of the following Departments of the Government of India for the years 1857-59.
- (a) Foreign: Political, Secret and Miscellaneous.
- (b) Home.
- (c) Legislative.
- (d) Military.

(ii) Letters to and from the Court of Directors, 1857-1859.

(iii) Mutiny Papers.

Delhi Archives, New Delhi

(i) Delhi Residency Records, 1857-1859.
- (a) The Trial of Bahadur Shah (complete).
- (b) The Mutiny Series, Files.
- (c) Bahadur Shah Trial Series, Files.
- (d) Mutiny Papers.
- (e) Spies' letters (original English Translation.

Printed Records

District Gazetteer of Delhi, Delhi, 1883–84, reprint 1972.

Forrest, G.W. *Selections from the Letters, Despatches and Other State Papers, Preserved in the Military Department of the Government of India, 1857–58*, vol. 1, Calcutta, 1893–1912.

Further Papers Relative to the Mutinies in the East Indies, Presented to both House of Parliament by Command of Her Majesty, 9 vols.

Muir, Sir William, *Records of the Intelligence Department of the Government of the North-West Provinces of India during the Mutiny, 1857*, 2 vols. Edited by Cold Stream, Edinburgh, 1902.

Narrative of Events Regarding the Mutiny in India of 1857–58, and the Restoration of Authority, 2 vols. Calcutta, 1901.
Parliamentary papers, (British) 1857–1863.
Press List of Mutiny Papers (Urdu, Persian) 1857, Calcutta, 1921.
Proceedings of the Trial of Bahadur Shah, Calcutta, 1895.
Selections from the Punjab Government Records:
(i). Delhi Residency and Agency Records, vol. 1, 1806–1857.
(ii). *Mutiny Records, Correspondence*, in 2 parts, Lahore, 1911.
(iii). *Mutiny Records, Reports*, in 2 parts, Lahore, 1911.
(iv). *Trial of Bahadur Shah*, ed. H.L.O.Garret, Lahore, 1932.
Sivestre, A.A. A *Short Compilation from the Calcutta Gazette about the fall of Delhi*, Calcutta, 1858.

English Books, Primary

Anson, Maj. O.H.S.G., *With HM 9th Lancers during the Indian Mutiny*, London, 1896.
Atkinson, Capt. G.F. *The Campaign in India, 1857–58*, London, 1859(?).
Ball, Charles, *History of Indian Mutiny*, 2 vols. London, 1858–59.
Barter, Richard, *The Siege of Delhi, MutinyMemoirs of an Old Officer*, London, 1984.
Bourchier, Col.G., *Eight Months' Campaign against the Bengal Sepoy Army during the Mutiny of 1857*, London, 1858.
Buckler, F.W. 'The Political Theory of the Indian Mutiny, 1922', in *Pearson, Legitimacy and Symbols, The South Asian Writings of F.W. Buckler*, London, 1985.
Campbell, Sir George, *Memories of My Indian Career*, 2 vols., London, 1893.
Cave Browne, J., *The Punjab and Delhi in 1857*, 2 vols., Patiala, rep.1970.
Chick, N.A., *Annals of the Indian Rebellion, 1857–58*, Calcutta, 1859–60.
Coopland, R.M., *A Lady's Escape from Gwalior and Life in the Fort of Agra during the Mutinies of 1857*, London, 1859.
Copper, F., *The Crisis in the Punjab, from the 10th of May Until the Fall of Delhi*, London, 1858.
Cunningham, J.D. *History of the Sikhs*, ed. Peter Cunningham, Kensington, 1853.
Dodwell, H., *The Cambridge History of India*, vol. 6, Delhi, rep. 1963.
Duff, A., *The Indian Rebellion: Its Causes and Results in a Series of Letters*, London, 1858.
Edwards, W., *Facts and Reflections Connected with Indian Rebellion*, Liverpool, 1859.
Forbes Mitchell, W., *Reminiscences of the Great Mutiny 1857–59*, London, 1897.
Forrest, G. W., *A History of the Indian Mutiny*, 2 vols, London, 1904.
Ghalib, *Life and Letters*, Eng. tr. Ralph Russell and Khurshidul Islam, London, 1969.
Greathed, H.H., *Letters Written, During Siege of Delhi*, London, 1858.
Griffiths, C.J., *Siege of Delhi*, London, 1910.
Hancock, A.G., *A Short Account of the Siege of Delhi in 1857*, Shimla, 1892.
Hasrat, Bikramjit, ed., *The Punjab Papers*, Hoshiarpur, 1978.

Hedayet Ali, *A Few Words Relative to the Late Mutiny of the Bengal Army and Rebellion in the Bengal Presidency*, Calcutta, 1858.
Hewitt, James, ed. *Eye-witness to the Indian Mutiny*, London 1972.
Hilton, Richard, *The Indian Mutiny*, London, 1857.
History of the Delhi Massacre, by a Lady, London, 1858.
History of the Siege of Delhi, by an Officer Who Served There, 1861.
Hodson, G.H., *Hodson of Hodson's Horse*, London, 1889.
Hodson, W.S.R., *Twelve Years of a Soldier's Life in India*, London, 1858.
Holmes, T.R., *A History of the Indian Mutiny*, London, 1857.
Innes, Lt. Gen J. J. Mcleod, *The Sepoy Revolt: A Critical Narrative*, London, 1877.
Jwala Sahai, *The Loyal Rajputana*, Allahabad, 1902.
Kaye, Sir J. W., *A Historyof the Sepoy War in India, 857-1863*, 3 vols., London, n.d.
———, and Col. G. B. Malleson, *History of the Indian Mutiny of 1857–58*, 6 vols., London, n.d.
Keene, H. G., *The Fall of the Mughal Empire*, London, 1876.
Keith, Young, ed., *Delhi 1857*, London, 1902.
Lang, John, *Wanderings in India*, London, 1859.
Lecky Edwards, *Fictions Connected With the Indian Outbreak of 1857 Exposed*, Bombay, 1859.
Mackenzie, Col. A.R.R., *Mutiny Memories*, Allahabad, 1892.
Majumdar, J. K., ed., *Raja Ram Mohan Roy and the Last Mughals*, Calcutta, 1939.
Malleson, Lt. Col. G.B., *The Red Pamphlet (The Mutiny of the Bengal Army)*, London, 1858.
———, *History of the Indian Mutiny*, 3 vols., London, 1880.
Martin Montgomery, R., *The Indian Empire*, 3 vols., London, 1859(?).
Marx, Karl and Engels, F., *The First Indian War of Independence, 1857–59*, Moscow, n.d.
Mead, H., *The Sepoy Revolt: Its Causes and Its Consequences*, London, 1857.
Meldley, J.G., *A Year's Campaigning in India from March 1857 to March 1858*, London, 1858.
Metcalfe, C.T., ed., *Two Native Narratives of the Mutiny at Delhi*, Westminster, 1898.
Moin-ul-Haq, ed., *Memoirs of Hakim Ahsanullah Khan*, Karachi, 158.
Norman, H.W., *A Narrative of the Campaign of Delhi Army*, London, 1858.
Nortron, J.B., *The Rebellion in India: How to Prevent Another*, London 1857.
Owen, M., *Memorials of Christian Martyrs*, London, 1859.
Proceedings: Proceedings of the Trial of Muhammad Bahadur Shah Titular King of Delhi Before a Military Commission up on a Charge of Rebellion, Treason and Murder, Calcutta, 1895.
Proceedings of the Trial of Muhamman Bahadur Shah II, Titular King of Delhi, before Military Commissioner for trial of Rebellion, 1858, London, 1858, 1895.
Raikes, Charles, *Notes on the Revolt in the North-Western Provinces of India*, London, 1858.
Roberts, FM Fred, *Forty One Years in India*, 2 vols. London, 1897.
———, *Letters Written During the Siege of Delhi, Indian Mutiny*, London, 1924.
Rotton, J.E.W., *Chaplain's Narrative of the Siege of Delhi, from the Outbreak at Meerut to the Capture of Delhi*, London, 1858.
Russel, Sir W.H., *My Diary in India in the Years 1857–59*, 2 vols., London, 1860.

Sedgwick, Lt. Col. F. R., *Indian Mutiny of 1857*, London, 1908.
Smith, R.B., *Life of Lord Lawrence*, 2 vols., London, 1883.
Temple, Sir Richard, *Men and Events of My Time*, London, 1882.
Wood, Sir E., *The Revolt in Hindustan, 1857-1859*, London, 1908.
Yadav, K. C. ed., Delhi in 1857: A documentary study of policing during Rebellion (forthcoming).

Secondary Works

Andrews, C.F., *Zakaullah of Dehi*, Cambridge, 1929.
Bell, L.D., *The 1858 Trial of Mughal Emperor Bahadur Shah 'Zafar' for 'Crimes against the State,'* Ph.D. Thesis, Faculty of Law, Melbourne University, 2004.
Burke, S.M. and Salamuddin Quraishi, *Bahadur Shah, the Last Mughal Emperor of India*, Lahore, 1995.
Cardev, Maj. F.G., *Hodson's Horse, 1857–1922*, Edinburgh, 1922.
Chatopadhyaya, H.P., *The Sepoy Mutiny, 1857*, Calcutta, 1957.
Chaudhari, S.B., *Civil Rebellions in India*, Calcutta, 1955.
———, *Theories of Indian Mutinies*, Calcutta, 1965.
Chopra, P. (Ed.), *Delhi: History and Places of Interest*, Delhi, 1970.
Collier, Richard, *The Great Indian Mutiny*, London, 1964.
Dalwymple, William, *The Last Mughal: The Fall of a Dynasty, Delhi, 1857*, Delhi, 2006.
David, Saul, *The Indian Mutiny*, London, 2002.
Domin, Dolores, *India in 1857*, Berlin, 1979.
Embree, Ainslie T. (ed.), *1857 in India*, Laxington, 1963.
Farooqui, Amar, *Zafar and the Raj: Anglo-Mughal Delhi, 1800–50*, Delhi, n.d.
Griffin, Sir, Lepel, *Rajas of Punjab*, New Delhi, rep. 1977.
———, et al., *The Punjab Chiefs and Families of Note*, Lahore, n.d.
Hasima, Shakila Tabassum, The Trial of Bahadur Shah Zafar, Representation and Reality in Mughal – British relations, B.A. (Hons.) thesis, Department of History, National University of Singapore, 1999.
Husain, Mahadi, *Bahadurshah II and the War of 1857 in Delhi*, Delhi, 1958.
Irwin, W., *The later Mughals*, 2 vols., Delhi, rep. 2006.
Joshi, P.C. (Ed.), *Rebellion 1857*, A Symposium, Delhi, rep. 2007.
Khadgawat, N.R., *Rajasthan's Role in the Struggle of 1857*, Jaipur, 1957.
Leason, James, *The Red Fort, an Account of siege of Delhi in 1857*, London, 1956.
Macmunn, Sir, G.F., *The Indian Mutiny in Perspective*, London, 1931.
Majumdar, R.C., *The Sepoy Mutiny and the Revolt of 1857*, Calcutta, 1957.
———, *History of the Freedom Movement in India*, vol. I, Calcutta, 1962.
Mehta, Ashoka, *1857: The Rebellion*, Bombay, 1946.
Moti Ram, ed., *Two Historic Trials of Red Fort; An Authentic Account of . . . The Trial of a European Military Commission of Emperor Bahadur Shah*, Delhi, 1946 (?).
Nayar, P.K., ed., *The Trial of Bahadur Shah Zafar*, Hyderabad, 2007.
Nigam, N.K., *Delhi in 1857*, Delhi, 1957.
Noorani, A.G., *Indian Political Trials*, Delhi, 2005.
Palmer, J.B., *Outbreak of Mutiny at Meerut in 1857*, Cambridge, 1966.
Panigrahi, D.N., *Charles Metcalfe in India*, Delhi, 1970.

Panikkar, K.N., *British Diplomacy in North India*, Delhi, 1968.
Qureshi, I. H., ed. *Trial of Muhammad Bahadur Shah*, Karachi, 1972.
Robin, Nick, *The Corporation that Changed the World*, Bangalore, 2006.
Rough, H.E., *The Rough Bibliography of Indian Mutiny, 1857–1859*, Solihul, 2015.
Savarkar, Sir Jadunath, *The Fall of the Mughal Empire*, 4 vols., Delhi, rep. 1991–97.
Sen, S.N., *Eighteen Fifty-Seven*, Delhi, 1957.
Spear, Sir Percival, *Twilight of the Mughals*, Delhi, rep. 1991.
Taylor, P.J.O., *Chronicle of the Mutiny*, Delhi, 1992.
———, *What Happened during the Mutiny*, Delhi, 1997.
Thompson, Edward, *The Other Side of the Medal*, London, 1930.
Wilson, Jone, *Britain's Rajand the Chaos of the Empire, India Conquered*, London, 2006.
Yadav, K.C., *The Revolt of 1857 in Haryana*, Delhi, 1977.
———, *Rao Tula Ram*, Delhi, 2007.
———, ed., *Delhi in 1857: The Trial of Bahadurshah*, Delhi, 1980.
———, ed., *1857: Muhammad Ali Khan*, Gurgaon, 2008.
———, ed., Delhi in 1857: A documentary study of Policing during the Rebellion (forthcoming).

Urdu Books

Ahmed Khan Syed, *Risala Asabab-i-Baghawat-i-Hind*, 1858.
Aslam Parvej, *Bahadur Shah Zafar*, Delhi, n.d.
Ghulam Nabi, *Tarikh-i-Jhajjar*, Lahore, n.d.
Kanhaiya Lal, *Tarikh-i-Hind, Muharba-i-azim*, Lucknow, 1916.
Maharaj Kishan, *Tarikh-i-Zila Hisar*, Lahore, 1886.
Man Singh, *Abhirkuldipika*, Rewari, 1900.
Moin-ud-din Hasan Khan, *Khadang-i-Ghadar*, ed. K. A. Faruqui, Delhi, 1972.
Nazir Ahmed, *Masaib-i-Ghadar*, Luchnow, 1893.
Zakaullah Khan, *Tarikh-i-uruj-i-saltanant-i-Englishia*, Delhi, 1904.

Hindi Books

Dwivedi, Shivnarain, *San 1857 ke Ghadarka Itihas, 4 Parts*, Allahabad, 1922.
Mahaur, Bhagwan Das, *1857 ke Swadhinta Sangram ka Hindi Sahitya par prabhav*, Delhi, 2008.
Nagar, Amrit Lal, *Ghadar ke phool*, Delhi, 2003.
Pandey, Ram, *Rajasthan mein 1857: Eik jana andolan*, Jaipur, 2008.
Rizvi, S.A.A., *Swantantra Dilli*, Lucknow, 1957.
Sharma, Ram Vilash, *1857 ki rajyakranti*, Allahabad, 1957.
Yadav, K.C., *Begum Hazrat Mahal*, Delhi, 2008.
Yadav, K.C., *Haryana ka Itihas*, Gurgaon, 2016.

Newspapers/Journals

Bengal: Past and Present, Calcutta.
Calcutta Review, Calcutta.

Delhi Urdu Akhbar, Delhi.
Haryana Research Journal, Rewari.
Illustrated London News, London.
Indian Antiquary, Calcutta.
Indian Historical Records Commission Proceedings, Delhi.
Islamic Culture, Hyderabad.
Journal of Haryana Studies, Kurukshetra.
Journal of Indian History, Trivandrum.
Journal of the United Service Institutionof India (USI), Shimla, New Delhi.
Modern Review, Calcutta.
Quarterly Review of Historical Studies, Calcutta.
Royal Historical Society, Transactions, London.
South Asian Studies, New York.
Soviet Features, Delhi.

INDEX

Note: Page numbers in italics refer to figures. Page numbers followed by "n" refer to notes.

For Product Safety Concerns and Information please contact our EU representative GPSR@taylorandfrancis.com Taylor & Francis Verlag GmbH, Kaufingerstraße 24, 80331 München, Germany